TEACHING THE INTEGRATED LANGUAGE ARTS

TEACHING THE INTEGRATED LANGUAGE ARTS

SECOND EDITION

SHANE TEMPLETON

UNIVERSITY OF NEVADA, RENO

HOUGHTON MIFFLIN COMPANY

BOSTON   NEW YORK

Senior Sponsoring Editor: Loretta Wolozin
Associate Editor: Lisa Mafrici
Senior Project Editor: Charline Lake
Senior Production/Design Coordinator: Sarah Ambrose
Manufacturing Manager: Florence Cadran
Marketing Manager: Pamela J. Laskey

Cover design: Darci Mehall, Aureo Design
Cover art: Fae Kontje

Printed in the U.S.A.

Library of Congress Catalog Card Number: 96-76967

Student Text ISBN: 0-395-79656-3
Examination Copy ISBN: 0-395-84399-5

6789-DH-07 06 05 04 03

To my students:
The finest teachers I've ever had.

Contents

CHAPTER 4

Diversity and Multiculturalism in the Integrated Classroom Community 89

CHAPTER 6   **Constructing Meaning Through Reading**   183

CHAPTER 7

Constructing Meaning Through Writing   229

CHAPTER 8

Exploring Words: Vocabulary and Spelling in Context   285

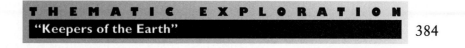

Preface

The preface to the first edition of *Teaching the Integrated Language Arts* observed that these were "monumentally exciting times" for language arts education. A few years later the times are still as exciting and the challenges to schools are—if possible—even more pronounced. We realize the critical necessity of preparing teachers to reflect, to problem solve, and to empower students within the broader contexts of diversity and cultural plurality.

While it is important to hold out a vision for novice teachers of what their classrooms can be, it is equally important to show them how to get there. That is what this text strives to accomplish. Novice teachers must have a solid foundation in the language arts, the development of language and literacy, and ways of thinking about integration. The second edition of *Teaching the Integrated Language Arts* provides this foundation. It attempts to make accessible and immediately applicable the best of what we have learned about kids, their development in the language arts, and their use of all the language arts as *tools* throughout the curriculum and their lifelong learning.

Audience and Purpose

Teaching the Integrated Language Arts has been written for preservice elementary school teachers. It is intended for a first course in language arts as well as for courses in which reading and language arts theory and methods are combined. The book can also serve as a foundations text for professional teachers returning to pursue further graduate work; in this capacity it can familiarize teachers with the new thinking and developments in writing, reading, language, and integrated instruction. For both of these groups of students, the book is intended to serve as a practical classroom resource. The text can also provide a solid grounding in the language arts—the core of the elementary curriculum—for students in educational leadership and administration who are doing coursework in curriculum and instruction.

The book's fundamental premise is that elementary students must be engaged in frequent reading, writing, and speaking throughout all areas of an integrated curriculum. Furthermore, this integrated curriculum should reflect real school and community contexts—the diversity that surrounds all of us as it enriches all of us—and include authentic literature.

Knowledgeable teachers play a critical role in orchestrating this involvement and in helping students to think critically. Always considering the needs of the novice teacher, *Teaching the Integrated Language Arts* establishes a supportive and reassuring tone, directly addressing the concerns of novice teachers and providing considerable practical information about the what, when, and how of teaching the integrated language arts.

Basic Organization of the Second Edition

Novice teachers must know about reading, writing, listening and speaking. That's why there are chapters addressing each of these language arts. Novice teachers must also know how to integrate—both within the language arts and between the language arts and the rest of the curriculum. That is why the concept of *integration* is addressed in every chapter of the book as well as explored in depth in Chapter 10 and in the two new Thematic Explorations.

The second edition of *Teaching the Integrated Language Arts* is divided into three sections:

Part One establishes the *Background* for teaching the integrated language arts. Chapter 1, Integrating the Language Arts in All Contexts, maintains and updates the nature and roles of the language arts and how they can be effectively integrated throughout the elementary curriculum, as well as presenting the nature and influence of different *contexts* on learning. Chapter 2, Understanding Thought and Language as Meaning-Construction, updates the continuing research in these areas from a *constructivist* perspective as well as the implications for learning.

Part Two develops the *Learning Environment* for the integrated language arts. Establishing and maintaining effective contexts for learning are addressed in Chapter 3, Organizing and Managing the Integrated Classroom Community. Because this community of learners increasingly reflects a wide range of diversity, Chapter 4 addresses Diversity and Multiculturalism in the Integrated Classroom Community. These issues are integral to the learning environment and should be explored early as a foundation for culturally responsive instruction.

Part Three, *Integrated Teaching and Learning*, applies in seven chapters the knowledge base established in Parts One and Two. As in the first edition, Chapter 5 presents the *developmental* bases of reading and writing, a central aspect of effective teaching and learning. The order of Chapter 6, Constructing Meaning Through Reading, and Chapter 7, Constructing Meaning Through Writing, is reversed from the first edition to reflect better the reciprocal relationship between these two processes in learning and teaching. Chapter 8, Exploring Words: Vocabulary and Spelling in Context, maintains the important role of word knowledge in all aspects of the language arts. The chapter on Listening, Speaking, and Creative Dramatics in the first edition is significantly revised and positioned more appropriately now as Chapter 9, Integrating Oral Communication and the Performance Arts. While "listening and speaking" are still central, you will find that they have been covered throughout the text and that performance aspects are highlighted here more. Chapter 10, Pulling It All Together: Integration, Inquiry, and Theme Exploration, effectively integrates the content of the previous chapters through demonstrating how integration and inquiry can best be accomplished through thematic teaching. Chapter 11, Assessing Student Learning in the Integrated Language Arts, is placed at the end of the text — in spite of the reality that classroom assessment begins early on and continues throughout the year. Understanding assessment builds on a necessary understanding of development and of instruction.

Critical concepts on language history now appear in the new *Teacher's Sourcebook* at the end of the text.

Revisions in the Second Edition

New and expanded coverage include the following:

Chapter 1

The nature of "integration" is clearly developed within the language arts and between the language arts and the rest of the elementary curriculum. The nature of thematic units is introduced here and brief examples provided. *Constructivism*, the guiding theoretical framework of learning and teaching, is highlighted, explained, and applied through Cambourne's model of instruction and learning. There is increased coverage of technology, a feature of almost every chapter in the text.

Chapter 2

Updated coverage of cognitive, linguistic, and social factors in the development of thought and language is provided. This coverage includes the perspective of cognitive science and its implications for learning. There is expanded coverage of *conceptual* development, the development and role of *symbolic* thinking, and the role of *culture* in the development of language and how it is used. Implications for teaching are presented here, setting the stage for the focus on culture and diversity throughout the rest of the text.

Chapter 3

This chapter provides more concise, clear examples of what a truly "integrated" classroom is like. There is stronger emphasis on the *collaborative* nature of establishing and maintaining the classroom environment. The important concepts of a *composite classroom culture* and *culturally responsive* instruction are introduced, and there is continued strong emphasis on involving the home and community more directly in the classroom culture. Reading Workshop and Writing Workshop are introduced as contexts for authentic exploration and growth.

Chapter 4

With its broader and practical coverage of issues of diversity and multiculturalism, this chapter offers new coverage of different interaction patterns and styles, and expanded discussion of second language acquisition and appropriate instruction, including "sheltered English." Matters of "playground" vs. "academic" English are explored, as well as dialect. Students who have special needs are addressed with expanded coverage of aspects of *inclusion* and instructional strategies.

Chapter 5

Chapter 5 maintains the strong developmental foundation that characterized the first edition, though some material has been condensed, allowing for more teaching examples along the way.

Chapter 6

Foundations for response-based reading experiences are established and updated. There is an expanded discussion of Literature Circles, Literature Discussion Groups, Grand Conversations, and Student Book Clubs. This discussion occurred in Chapter 9 of the first edition, but is more appropriately addressed here. The response-based activities included in the first edition have also been moved to this chapter and expanded. The concept of the Reading Workshop is elaborated here. The second edition retains the strong coverage of language-experience activities, with new coverage of how to adapt the approach for students who are learning English as a second language in the early and extended speech production stages.

This chapter also features expanded coverage of foundational skills such as phonics, sight word vocabulary, and spelling in a way that supports effective teaching of these elements while never losing sight of the larger context in which they fit. This includes more on word sorts and upper-level word identification strategies. Other expanded topics include book selection, conferencing, and informational reading. The discussion of informational reading includes an expanded K-W-L strategy and the addition of reciprocal teaching. The issue of accommodating less-able readers in the classroom is also addressed.

Chapter 7

Texts that students read provide models of the types of writing they may do. Thus, placing this chapter on writing after the chapter on reading allows us to build on concepts already established in Chapter 6. Chapter 7 includes charts and other graphic arrays that directly present aspects of the writing process. All phases of the writing process are explored and modeled in depth. *Application* of the process in the different genre is an expanded section on writing stories, then writing poetry, and next an expanded treatment of expository writing. There is expanded coverage of technology and writing as well.

Chapter 8

The new chapter title highlights the *contexts* in which vocabulary and spelling knowledge best develop and sets the tone—*exploring* words. This does not mean words are never looked at outside of context; they are. What is important is *how* they are taken out of context, examined, and put back into authentic contexts. A new feature included in the second edition is the sequence for presenting word elements. There is expanded coverage of how to apply word knowledge in determining the meaning of unknown words in reading. There are new examples from students' writing of their application of different types of word knowledge, and a perspective on educational technology and word study. The discussion of etymology has been moved to the Teacher's Sourcebook and abbreviated.

Chapter 9

In its new placement, this chapter on oral communication and performance arts now pulls this information together more appropriately and addresses it in more depth—for example, reading aloud to students. In addition, new concepts are addressed, such as critical listening and viewing. There is expanded treatment of students' oral reading—choral reading, reader's theatre, and author's chair, as well as expanded treatment of *storytelling*.

There is new coverage of how students can use new multimedia and hypermedia technology to integrate listening and speaking with writing, reading, art, and so forth.

Chapter 10

In as concise yet thorough a presentation as possible, Chapter 10 offers guidelines and examples of how to go about planning and implementing themes. It is considerably broader in scope than its counterpart in the first edition (Chapter 9), allowing for more thorough, in-depth coverage of *literature-based* themes and across-the-curriculum *integrated* themes. The conceptual foundations for theme explorations are presented, including the important distinction between themes that are truly *conceptual* and those that are merely topical. Theme teaching is, at heart, a theory of curriculum and instruction; this chapter guides novice teachers towards determining how to help students establish ownership of their learning while still honoring the curriculum established by the district in which they teach.

There is explicit step-by-step guidance in developing thematic units. This process includes establishing goals and objectives, selecting culturally authentic texts, and determining and embedding skills instruction meaningfully within the unit. In the context of thematic units, activities are included that integrate reading, discussion, and writing with genuine inquiry. There is thorough discussion of response journals, learning logs, and the Writer's Notebook. There is expanded coverage of an exciting new area—responding and exploring through art.

Chapter 11

This chapter offers expanded coverage of classroom-based assessment, including portfolios and other authentic assessment measures. The discussion of "formal" testing is shortened, though the essential concepts are still covered.

Special Teaching Features

◆ *New Thematic Explorations*   Whether referred to as themes, thematic units, theme studies, or theme cycles, the basic concept of organizing learning and instruction around a central focus is a powerful idea that is enjoying a renaissance. *How* to go about this process is a challenge, however, particularly for novice teachers. The two extended thematic explorations are intended to illustrate the development and the implementation of the two major theme categories. The first, found after Chapter 4, is a literature-based theme conducted earlier in the year in a primary class; the second, following Chapter 9, is an integrated theme conducted later in the year in an intermediate class.

◆ *New Teacher Sourcebook*   Intended as a ready-reference guide for information and teaching strategies, this Sourcebook presents an overview of language history and its relation to students' learning and our teaching; children's literature resource lists; multimedia resources; grammar as a tool for writing; lists of words representing different spelling patterns, developmentally arranged; key study skills for intermediate students; and information on teaching handwriting.

◆ Concise *focus questions* highlight the major concepts in each chapter, *key terms* highlighted in the text are listed at the end of every chapter, and a *concluding perspective and summary* for each chapter summarizes the major concepts in the chapter.

◆ *Classroom Examples* are virtually minicases and help situate new teachers in action. They are an integral part of the chapter and provide real modeling of effective teaching strategies.

◆ *Build Your Teaching Resources* are annotated bibliographies that appear directly within the chapters and that list *both* children's literature and professional resources.

◆ *Expand Your Teaching Repertoire* provide in-depth walk-throughs of instructional strategies and activities intended for use in the elementary classroom.

◆ *At the Teacher's Desk*, set-off "advice and tips boxes" that run throughout the chapters, offer observations about a wide range of teaching and learning issues.

Acknowledgments

The role of reviewers in the development of a book is critical. I wish to express my sincerest appreciation and heartfelt thanks to the following colleagues for their considerable time spent reading over drafts, their thoughtfulness, their excellent advice and criticism: William Anderson, Shippensburg University; Robert Gaskins, University of Kentucky; Marjorie Hancock, Kansas State University; George Labercane, The University of Calgary; Sabrina Mims, California State University, Los Angeles; and Eileen Walter, Indiana East University.

There are so many others that I would thank by name if space permitted, but I do wish to single out the following individuals because of their direct involvement in this book:

Sandra Madura, once again—for her exemplary teaching, continuing advice and counsel, and the marvelous ideas that coalesced into the first Thematic Exploration; Tamara Baren, as exemplary a guide to intermediate students' inquiry as ever there was, for her exciting ideas and for the second Thematic Exploration; Brenda Sabey and Lynn Terry, for their support directly and indirectly of this project, of me, and for their contributions to the Instructor's Manual and the text itself.

At the University of Nevada: Diane Barone—so much a presence in the first edition and still a significant presence this time around; Donald Bear and Meggin McIntosh—for their perspectives and all the good talk. And to the students of CI 469, spring semester '96—you endured, you supported, you gave wonderful feedback to my minilessons involving the revision phase of this work — thanks once again.

At Houghton Mifflin, two very special people I cannot thank enough: Lisa Mafrici, for her unflagging support and understanding, gentle prodding, and impressive orchestration of all that went into putting this second edition together; and Loretta Wolozin, once again — for believing, and for helping me sustain the vision.

—Shane Templeton

TEACHING THE INTEGRATED LANGUAGE ARTS

PART

BACKGROUND

CHAPTER 1

Integrating the Language Arts in All Contexts

- ◆ What *are* the "language arts"?
- ◆ What does it mean to say that children *construct* their own knowledge and understanding?
- ◆ How do we integrate instruction *within* the language arts?
- ◆ How do we integrate language arts instruction with the rest of the curriculum?
- ◆ What are the types of *contexts* that influence children's learning?

INTRODUCTION

Listening, speaking, reading, and writing: these are the **language arts**. Their fundamental purpose is to *communicate*—to convey or to share beliefs and feelings and ideas both old and new. As human beings, we communicate with others and with ourselves through the language arts. The sense we make of others, of ourselves, and of our world will be profoundly influenced by the ways in which we can use the language arts as *tools* for communication and thought.

In an integrated language arts classroom, teachers and students are actively and meaningfully engaged in learning—in exploring ideas, topics, and the whole elementary curriculum—and often that exploring is organized around a common theme. While learning together, teachers and students have a genuine sense of *ownership* of how, what, and why they learn (Pappas, Kiefer, & Levstik, 1995).

You are now embarked on a course of study, exploration, and practice that will lead toward helping your future students use the language arts effectively and powerfully. Part of your journey will involve this book. Together, we'll explore the teaching and learning of these most critical elements of the elementary curriculum, and in the process, we will be exploring the critical relationship between the language arts and *thinking*.

This chapter lays the groundwork for our knowledge and understanding:

◆ We begin by defining the *integrated* language arts.

◆ Next, we take a brief look at how children learn; this process establishes the theory of *constructivism* on which all our instruction is based.

◆ We look more closely at *how* the language arts are integrated within themselves and with the rest of the elementary curriculum.

◆ We examine the *contexts* in which the language arts are applied, focusing primarily on the broader cultural contexts in which the language arts are taught—the contexts of our multicultural and information-rich society.

◆ On the basis of this overview, we see implications for the classroom and for *our* roles as teachers of the language arts.

How Children Learn: The Bases of the Language Arts

As we will be seeing in Chapter 2, children are "meaning makers" (Wells & Chang-Wells, 1992). They cannot help but be, for this is the way human brains are constructed and have evolved. Through their thought and language processes, children organize and try to make sense of their environment (Gardner, 1991; Piaget, 1975; Vygotsky, 1934/1986). They "make meaning," and in the process they *learn*. This learning process is based on what children bring to their world and on what the world presents to them: Jean Piaget emphasized how their minds are biologically set up to organize and make sense of their world as the children grow and develop. Lev Vygotsky investigated how the outside world influences this development. He described the instructional zone of a child in terms of a "zone of proximal development"; that is, the zone within which the child is guided in applying what he or she already knows to the construction of new knowledge and understanding.

Constructivism is the name given to the fundamental theory that underlies this concept of learning and defines our approach to language arts in this text (Eisner, 1991; Katz & Chard, 1989; Spivey, 1987). Constructivism holds that learners are actively "constructing" their knowledge of the world and of language, rather than passively "absorbing" knowledge from their environment. They relate *new* information to *known* information. We can be reassured that we will be effective teachers of the integrated language arts if we always keep this "construction process" in mind.

Integrating within the Language Arts

Integrating the language arts means that speaking, listening, writing, and reading influence one another and are used together in a real or *authentic* context. Think for a moment: when you pair any two of the language arts, do you see the many possible ways in which each can affect the other?

◆ *Reading/Writing*
What we read influences what and how we write. For example, after reading about George and Martha (two hippopotami who are the best of friends) in several books of James Marshall's *George and Martha* series, primary students write their own books modeled on the George and Martha format. A common theme in their books—just as with George and Martha—is likely to be best friends who sometimes do things that *really* bother each other.

◆ *Listening/Speaking*
As children listen to each other explain the important points in different parts of a chapter in a social studies text, they also become aware of why

there are "gaps" in their own understanding—aware of how the information might be presented orally in a better way.

◆ *Listening/Reading*

When children are actively *listening* as someone reads to them and they anticipate what will be happening in a story and why, they will apply these same strategies when they read on their own. The *voice* children hear when they listen is important as well; for example, after listening to an audiotape of James Earl Jones reading the South African folktale "Abiyoyo," children will, from that time on, "hear" that voice when they read this or similar tales.

◆ *Reading/Speaking*

The form and nature of text can help organize information students present orally. For example, as part of his class's thematic unit "Technology and Us," an intermediate student has chosen to find out about and make a presentation on how compact discs work. He has already read part of David Macaulay's *The Way Things Work* and enjoyed the way a sense of humor infuses both Macaulay's art and his prose. The student decides to develop props for his oral presentation with diagrams modeled after Macaulay's, and he models his spoken presentation on Macaulay's tight, clever descriptions.

◆ *Writing/Listening*

Writing can focus, clarify, and deepen our thoughts for later discussion. For example, after reading Angela Johnson's *Tell Me a Story, Mama* (1992), eight-year-old Chandra describes in her response log how she and her mom enjoy telling and retelling stories about when Chandra's mom was little—just like the boy and his mom do in the book. Chandra later shares responses with her partner, Deshawn. As Chandra listens, she realizes that having written about the story helps her understand better Deshawn's response about his sadness when his grandma passed away—an event only hinted at in *Tell Me a Story*. Writing, in other words, helps Chandra reflect on the story and process it more deeply, preparing her for grasping the meaning that another student will make.

◆ *Speaking/Writing*

Talking can help organize and focus writing. For example, before Writing Workshop (see Chapter 7), students talk briefly about how they are going to use their time that day: will they be starting a new story, revising an existing one, conferencing with someone else to give feedback on that student's story, illustrating the cover for the final, published version of a book they've written? Thinking and discussing *beforehand* brings more efficiency and better quality to students' writing efforts.

The history of language arts instruction, however, has in large part ignored this integration. More often than not, language arts instruction was a story of isolation rather than of integration, a story in which focus was on discrete "skills" within each of the language arts. The theory was that by sequencing skills and having students learn these skills one at a time, eventually a language art would be mastered. Most often "instruction" meant using worksheets, workbooks, exercises out of textbooks, copying from the chalkboard. Students were seldom shown the relationship between knowing the skill and how the skill might help them—much less how reading, for example, could help their writing, and vice versa.

When we truly integrate the language arts in our classrooms, we are involving our students in *meaningful* reading, writing, talking, listening, and learning. We are able to teach concepts, strategies, and skills when children need them; therefore, the children understand their purpose. They see how learning about the "parts" fits into the bigger picture.

In general, what do children learn as they construct their knowledge and understanding of the language arts?

◆ They learn about the different *functions* and *forms* of written and spoken language: stories, informational texts, discussion, poetry. . . . As we'll see later on, stories, informational texts, and discussion have identifiable forms that present content in particular ways. Learning about these forms helps students comprehend better in their reading and compose more effectively in their writing.

◆ Students also learn about different *strategies* and *skills* for reading, writing, listening, and speaking. Language arts *strategies* are procedures for approaching and engaging in particular tasks.

The strategy children will use depends on what they are reading, writing, or talking about, and on their purpose for engaging in the task. Here are just two examples:

◆ Because of their different purposes, students learn to use one type of strategy for reading about African Americans in the South of the 1930s in Milton Meltzer's *The Black Americans: A History in Their Own Words* (1984), and a different strategy for reading Mildred Taylor's trilogy about the African-American Logan family in the South during the 1930s (*Roll of Thunder, Hear My Cry* (1991a); *Let the Circle Be Unbroken* (1991b); *The Road to Memphis* [1992]).

◆ After reading Graham Salisbury's *Under the Blood-Red Sun* (1994), a story of how the attack on Pearl Harbor affected the lives of Japanese-American and Anglo-American boys living in Honolulu in 1941,

Reading	Writing	Listening and Speaking
Literature Discussion Groups	• Interview three different people to find out what *they* think a friend is; make a list and combine it with those of other students to create a "What Is a Friend?" class book.	**Teacher Reads Following "Core" Texts to Whole Class, with Discussion Afterward**
Amigo Means Friend, by Louise Everett ("Easier" Selection)		*Amos and Boris*, written and illustrated by William Steig
Three at Sea, written and illustrated by Timothy Bush ("Average" Selection)		*Ira Sleeps Over*, written and illustrated by Bernard Waber
Best Friends for Francis, by Russell and Lillian Hoban, illustrated by Lillian Hoban ("Average" Selection)	• As different stories are read, add to a comparison chart listing the characters, problems, and solutions for each of the stories (for example, *Amos and Boris, Frog and Toad, George and Martha*).	*Make a Wish Molly*, by Barbara Cohen, illustrated by Jan Naimo Jones
Frog and Toad Are Friends, written and illustrated by Arnold Lobel ("Challenging" Selection)		
Independent Reading		**Other Listening/Speaking Activities**
My Best Friend, written and illustrated by Pat Hutchins (Easier)		• Dramatize one of the episodes from one of the "core" texts.
Overnight at Mary Bloom's, written and illustrated by Aliki (Easier)	• Respond in your journal to one of the following: Which *Frog and Toad* (or *George and Martha*) episode is your favorite, and why? Which was the funniest? Which are like ones you've had with a friend of yours?	
Two Good Friends, written and illustrated by Judy Delton (Easier)		• Using any one of the books we've read, rehearse the story so that you can retell it as an oral "storytelling" activity.
Chester's Way, written and illustrated by Kevin Henkes (Average)		
Little Bear's Friend, by Else Minarik, illustrated by Maurice Sendak (Average)		
George and Martha, written and illustrated by James Marshall (Average)	• Create your own "friendship" story (if you wish, yours may be modeled on any of the readings).	• Readers Theatre performance based on different poems in *Bein' with You This Way* by W. Nikola-Lisa, illustrated by Michael W. Bryant.
Fox and His Friends, by Edward Marshall, illustrated by James Marshall (Challenging)		
Fast Friends: A Tail and Tongue Tale, by Lisa Horstman (Challenging)		

Figure 1.1   Selected Activities from "Friendship" Theme: Second Grade

intermediate-grade students write their own stories of close friendships. While the students *type* their final drafts on the word processor, to be printed out and displayed, they *handwrite* their final drafts of letters to Graham Salisbury in which they share the reasons why they enjoyed his book. They have learned about the audience for their writing: the "audience" for a personal letter deserves and appreciates the "personal" nature and thoughtfulness of handwriting as opposed to word processing.

A *skill* involves the application of specific knowledge as part of a strategy. Appropriate use of skills, for example, occurs when students are reading or writing and use their knowledge about grammar and word structure to identify or spell an unknown word. Grammar, punctuation, spelling, word identification, understanding cause and effect in reading—these are all examples of skills we might teach students. I say *might* teach, because some students may not need to be taught a particular skill or may not be ready for our explicit instruction. If we are in fact going to be effective teachers of the integrated language arts, sensitive to children's processes of meaning construction, how do we know *when* to teach *what* strategies and skills to *which* kids? The rest of this book is an answer to that question. We will learn about the *developmental* nature of children's growth in the language arts, and we will find out what children will need to learn along the way as a function of this development. We will be combining our knowledge of children with our knowledge of the content of the language arts. There is no firmer foundation than this for effective and rewarding teaching.

Figure 1.1 should give you a sense of how we integrate primarily *within* the language arts; this thematic unit is focused on "friendship," an appropriate and effective theme at this level.

Integrating the Language Arts Across the Elementary Curriculum

In a very real sense, language provides *access* to the curriculum. The language arts are *tools* that enable students to communicate better and to explore content areas with interest, motivation, and genuine learning. In every content area of the elementary school curriculum—science, math, social studies, music, art, physical education, and so forth—speaking, listening, writing, and reading occur.

Let's take *science* as an example. Children can learn about interrelationships among plants, soil, temperature, and atmosphere by *discussing* the reasons why more droplets form on the inside of a terrarium in the morning than in the afternoon. Children can sharpen their observations and focus their thinking by *writing* about their observations in a journal or a learning log. *Reading* about the phenomenon on a large-scale basis—as it applies to a region of the country—helps the students stretch their current understanding of weather patterns.

Figure 1.2 presents an integrated thematic unit on Japan, appropriate

Social Studies

Small-Group Research Topics

- Review strategies for reading informational texts: K-W-L/Guided Reading-Thinking Activities.
- Review note-taking strategies in informational texts.
- Peer conferencing on first drafts and revisions.
- Correspond on the Internet with keypals in Kobe, Japan.

Language Arts

Read-Aloud to Whole Class

Born in the Year of Courage, by Emily Crofford

Literature Discussion Groups (Reading and Writing)

The Warrior and the Wise Man, by David Wisniewski (Easier)

In this story, what do you think it means to be twins? Why is it sometimes best *not* to be strong? How do the differences in the brothers affect the plot of the story?

The Two Foolish Cats, by Yoshiko Uchida, illustrated by Margot Zemach (Average)

What kind of cat is Big Daizo? How do we know this? What do the cats have to teach us? What other circumstances parallel those of the two foolish cats?

The Funny Little Woman, by Arlene Mosel, illustrated by Blair Lent (Average)

Describe the "oni" character. What other characters have we seen that are much like the oni? How is the "trickster" motif played out in this story?

The Master Puppeteer, by Katherine Paterson (Challenging)

Do you feel that your life is often shaped by events that are beyond your control? What events were beyond the control of Jiro and Kinshi? How did they deal with them?

"Japan: Blend of Traditional and Modern"

Math

- Obtain the exchange rate for the *yen.*
- Brainstorm: How to convert dollars to yen? Then, *demonstrate* the procedure and match it to brainstormed suggestions.
- In pairs, make conversions for purchasing the following: house, car, groceries, clothing; *write* the process in math *learning logs.*

Science

- Why are there so many earthquakes in Japan?
- How is construction affected by these natural occurrences?
- Compare and contrast the geography and geology of the west coast along the entire Western Hemisphere with that of Japan.
- Using *Sadako and the Thousand Paper Cranes* by Eleanor Coerr as a starting point, investigate the short- and long-term effects of the atomic bomb.

Figure 1.2   **Selected Activities from Integrated Thematic Unit: Intermediate Grades**

for the intermediate grade levels, a unit in which all content areas are integrated.

Integrating the language arts ensures that students will learn about them best by applying them in all areas of their learning. In a very real sense, students' understanding of the nature and application of these tools will lead to deeper understanding in the different subject areas of the elementary curriculum. As Kenneth Goodman effectively defines our role: ". . . helping students to achieve a sense of control and ownership over their own use of language and learning in school, over their own reading, writing, speaking, listening, and thinking, will help to give them a sense of their potential power" (1986, p. 10). By teaching language arts through an integrated perspective, we can help students develop this important sense of control and ownership as they grow and develop.

The Contexts for the Language Arts

We are influenced at any given moment by *context*; actually, by several contexts:

◆ *Physical*—*where* we are;

◆ *Social*—other individuals who may be around us;

◆ *Psychological*—our knowledge, emotions, and attitudes in a particular situation;

◆ *Cultural*—the "culture" of the school, of the home, of the ethnic/racial/socioeconomic groups from which children come.

What goes on in a classroom cannot help but be affected by all of these contexts. The way we teach writing, reading, listening, speaking, and how they are applied in order to get things done and to think critically will be determined in part by the contexts we are functioning in. As we'll explore in Chapter 3, we establish a culture of the classroom that represents norms for how we use resources, space, and time and for how we behave and interact with one another (Pappas, Kiefer, & Levstik, 1995). We are all, students *and* teacher, a "community" of learners in the culture of the classroom.

The Context of Our Multicultural Society

Let's spend a moment considering the implications of *cultural* contexts. Broadly defined, **culture** refers to the beliefs, values, language, literature,

The environment and tone you establish in your classroom should allow for and respect the diversity of your students.

music, dance, art, artifacts, and institutions of a group of people. The United States and Canada include a diverse range of cultures representing various socioeconomic, ethnic, and racial groups. Most classrooms reflect this diversity, and it affords a strong foundation for learning. It is important to realize that ours has *always* been a *multi*cultural nation and society (Takaki, 1993).

A culture is a framework for making meaning. The meanings children construct—how they perceive themselves, others, and the world beyond their homes—are affected by the culture in which they are raised. The language spoken within a culture is a framework for expressing and for shaping meanings. In the culture of their home and neighborhood, children learn how to interact with other children and with adults, and they bring these interaction patterns and expectations with them to school. Because of this, our instruction will be *culturally responsive* (Au, 1993). As we'll see in Chapter 4, **culturally responsive instruction** emphasizes the backgrounds, needs, interests, and abilities of *all* students, not just those from the mainstream culture.

For many years, the influx of immigrants into the United States led to the concept of American society as a huge "melting pot," a common culture, primarily European American in nature, which different peoples would simply blend into, keeping few if any vestiges of their own culture. In recent years, sociologists and social historians have challenged the notion of a true "melting pot" (e.g., Banks, 1993; Garcia, 1994). Rarely does such a complete assimilation occur. Although most cultural groups do adjust over time to the mainstream of American culture, their language, values, art, religion, and so forth rarely are forever shed. For example, not only do African Americans, Native Americans, and Hispanic Americans value and retain aspects of their cultures, but elements of these cultures influence and enrich the broader "mainstream" American culture.

Although it is quite difficult to speak of an "American" culture in specific terms, there is a more "general" culture in the United States. Most often referred to as the "mainstream" culture, it is described in terms of traditional values such as thrift, hard work, honesty, and patriotism. Our form of government and our institutions, literature, language, and so forth all are expressions of the general culture. Of course, the more closely we look, the more variety we see—the effects, in turn, of the many different cultures that make up the United States.

Many writers and educators have emphasized that in order to be productive and informed citizens of the predominant society, it is necessary for people to be at least familiar with many of the names and terms associated with this cultural tradition (Hirsch, 1987). Although this is an important point, some controversy surrounds the content of this tradition because the contributions of women and of groups that lie outside the traditional European sphere of influence—such groups as African Americans, Hispanic Americans, Native Americans, and Asian Americans—are not widely represented.

AT THE TEACHER'S DESK

MOVING BEYOND STEREOTYPES

There are many ways we can help students become aware of the value of diversity among people, even as they are noticing commonalities that unite all of us. We wish to help students move beyond stereotypical thinking (a way of thinking that most of *us* fall into from time to time). One of the best ways to address issues of diversity in a positive way is through literature. For example:

- Many primary children and most intermediate children will be engaged by Mary Hoffman's *Amazing Grace*. They can share and discuss their responses to Grace's dilemma when she is told she cannot play Peter Pan in the school play because she is black, and they can predict what she will do in the face of this situation.

- Young children can begin to explore gender stereotyping after reading and discussing Bill Martin's *White Dynamite and Curly Kidd*, a story about a bronco rider and his daughter, who wants to ride in the rodeo too—though we don't find out until the end of the book that Curly Kidd is, in fact, a girl.

As teachers, we are the primary transmitters of the nation's cultural heritage. Our position should be realistic and well grounded. Undeniably, there is an orientation toward and a respect for much of the traditional American heritage, and as elementary teachers of the language arts, we will prepare our students for more in-depth study of this heritage in later years. Much of this heritage is important simply because it represents the values and ideals of the nation over the years. On the other hand, many of the nation's values and ideals are shared by cultures more recently represented in the society at large, and much of the literature and arts of these cultures will become part of the more general cultural heritage of the nation. Our cultural heritage is not fixed; it is living and organic. It should represent both the ideals of our society and what the society is continually in the process of becoming.

The Context of Our Information Society

Ours is an **information society,** and our students will need to learn how to navigate through the sheer volume of information that will be surrounding them. If they learn how to use the language arts effectively to evaluate information and ideas, they will be much better prepared for the decisions they must make as adults and as responsible citizens. Because ours is an information-based society, our students need to become knowledgeable consumers of information, so that they are not overwhelmed by or excluded from the economic, political, and educational mainstream.

Children's access to information now is so much greater than in years past. Our students need to learn how to access, select, and receive information, as well as how to organize it and evaluate it—in other words, how to think *critically* about it. Our classrooms may be the one place where students can learn how to make more sense out of more information and to respond appropriately.

Content and Context: Interactions with Information

Sources of information are both the *content* of language arts and the *context* within which we are formed. We *are* what we read and hear; what we write and speak reflects who and what we are. Information of course comes to us through direct, face-to-face contact with other individuals as well as through print and electronic media. This section will discuss the impact of each of these sources of information and the nature of individuals' interaction with them.

Print

Print serves a variety of purposes in our society (Purves, 1990). We take it for granted that print can illuminate us, extend our knowledge and our perspectives, and instruct and assist us in any number of undertakings. In our society, we have come to believe in the power of being literate and the knowledge and wisdom that this ability conveys (Scribner, 1983). The language arts are *tools*, and the ability to read is a powerful tool indeed.

As we'll see in Chapter 6, in addition to helping us get things done, print can allow us to interact in significant, and at times life-changing, ways with situations, information, and individuals. Because of these interactions we become wiser, more understanding, and better able to deal with our world in a more meaningful sense. Reading and responding to books such as *Roll of Thunder, Hear My Cry* (Mildred Taylor), *A Bridge to Terabithia* (Katherine Paterson), or *Tuck Everlasting* (Natalie Babbitt) can help students understand and perhaps deal with some very powerful ideas and emotions for the first time: the real meaning of friendship, for example, and the meaning of life and the acceptance of death.

The act of reading is similar to the other language arts in important ways, but it is also quite different. Notably, the reader is in control of the rate and the type of "information intake." Regardless of the type of material being read, readers are free to vary the rate, to pause and reflect, to skip forward quickly, to go back. An engaging scene in a story, for example, can be read more slowly, thought about, and reread. Print gives instructions to readers on how to construct images, but the images are unique to each reader; they are not already provided, as would be the case with a movie or a television program.

Unlike other sources of information, print freezes the writer's language and the writer's ideas as expressed in language; the language is always there. Spoken language, in contrast, flows along in real time and is gone. The speaker's words can be taped for replay, of course, but spoken language remains more difficult than printed language to reflect upon and analyze. Because of the permanence of print, several scholars (Havelock, 1982; Olson, 1977) have observed that in significant ways, print can affect *how* we think. These researchers have noted that one of the most profound influences of print has to do with logical, analytic thinking. Exposure to the more explicit representation of ideas and relationships among ideas in print will have an effect on how readers organize ideas, and more generally on how readers organize and apply their thinking skills.

In addition to providing and capturing information in a permanent form, print serves a variety of purposes in our society. The way in which printed information is read should vary, depending upon the purposes for which it is being read. Consider for a moment the different kinds and contexts of print: books (modern romance novels versus *War and Peace*), newspapers (the *National Enquirer* versus the *New York Times*), magazines (*Pro Wrestling Review* versus *Time* or *Newsweek*), "environmental" print such as signs or labels, and advertisements; the list goes on. Each of these examples may be read for a variety of purposes.

Most students, however, do not adjust their reading strategies and their attention according to the nature of what they are going to read and to what they expect to bring away from that reading. Our students should read their social studies textbook, for example, differently from the way they read a story. There are differences in the strategies for approaching these different types of reading material, just as there are differences in the way we analyze, evaluate, and respond to them. One of our responsibilities will be to guide our students carefully toward both determining the purposes for reading different types of material and learning how to adjust their reading strategies accordingly.

As we'll explore in Chapter 7, when students *write*, they become better at critical reading and thinking as well. Through writing, students come to understand how writers go about their craft, and they come to think of themselves as authors. In presenting ideas, a writer must provide much more explicit information than in communicating face to face. Not only must the writer's ideas be clearly expressed; how these ideas go together must be made clear. In other words, a writer must do a better job of creating the "context" for the information than if he or she were talking directly with another person.

In a classroom context in which lots of reading and writing is going on, students gradually gain control over the conventions of writing—grammar, punctuation, spelling—as they better understand the perspective of their audience. They become readers of their own writing and discover the power of writing to extend and elaborate their own thinking. And as they discover their own "voice" in writing, students develop a truer sense of themselves.

Computers and Telecommunications

During Writing Workshop in one fifth-grade classroom, students pair up at the computer to edit the first draft of their coauthored story. A few minutes later, two other students use the *Children's Writing Workshop* software to make final adjustments to the appearance of their short book on puffins, which they will then print and bind for the classroom library. Still later, three students who are working on a project addressing pollution will gather to check their e-mail messages from "keypals" in Surrey, England, who are engaged in a similar project. Then they will compose replies to the messages and send them.

This type of scene, occurring more and more every day in classrooms, is of course the result of advances in hardware design—of the physical "body" of the computer—that have made desktop and laptop computers widely available. It is also the result of similar advances in software design—of programs and applications that run on computers. Notably, the explosion of the Internet, the World Wide Web, and the resulting information and communication possibilities are revolutionizing our work and our learning. We have a whole new vocabulary with which to talk about such phenomena, and we may even have created a new world or dimension, **cyberspace**, a term that includes both the infinite number of communicative links that can be established through the Internet and the information that "lives" through that network.

At the elementary-school level, computers are being used to address everything from reinforcing skills, teaching reading comprehension strategies, doing word processing, and accessing sources of information on the Internet to using a spreadsheet format to organize information for specific subject areas. Computers can interface with compact discs and videodiscs to help make a novel, a scientific phenomenon, a tour of a museum, or a historical period come alive.

While computers will not replace all the other information sources we have, they will be increasingly present and increasingly valuable in our lives.

Build Your Teaching Resources

SITES ON THE INTERNET

Here are just a few sites to illustrate the potential of the Internet for extending the language arts for us and for our students.

- "The Children's Literature Web Guide" (http://www.ucalgary.ca/~dkbrown/index.html). This is an excellent up-to-the-minute resource for teachers. (Doucette Library of Teaching Resources, University of Calgary)

- *Electronic Elementary* (grades K–5) (http://www.inform.umd.edu:8080/EdRes/Topic/Education/k-12/MDK12_stuff/homepers/emag) and *Midlink Magazine* (ages 10–15) (http://longwood.cs.ucf.edu:80/~Midlink/). Both publications are by and for students and engage them in cooperative projects as well as in publishing on the Web. Each issue of *Midlink Magazine* is organized around a theme and includes students' electronic artwork. (University of Central Florida)

- *ISN KidNews* (http://www.usa.cape.com/~powens/kidnews.htm) is an international student newswire that publishes all types of pieces from students all over the world; for example, news, reviews, sports, fiction, poetry. (University of Massachusetts, Dartmouth)

- KidPub (http://en-garde.com/kidpub) is an open forum in which students of all ages can publish their writing. There is also an ongoing collaborative writing project. (En-Garde Technical Communication)

As we will continue to observe throughout this text, students will use computers more and more to access information, do problem-solving, write, and communicate with others hundreds or thousands of miles away. As teachers, we will be able to keep records, make notes, and use computers on-line with students for all types of purposes—as well as communicate more often with many other teachers. If we're looking for a particular resource, have a particular problem, or wish to connect with other teachers anywhere in the world who may be involved with the same theme-study we are, we can post an e-mail message on any number of listserves and newsgroups for educators.

Social Interaction

Much of the information that individuals attempt to make sense of comes from their environment, particularly when they are talking with others. Talking is a way of finding out about what we know (Galda, 1984). In a world that increasingly involves a constant flow of information electronically conveyed in bits and pieces, students will need to learn how to work together. These collaborative efforts will often depend on face-to-face communication. Children start out learning much about their world this way, of course, and we can continue this exchange through meaningful social interaction in our classrooms. The noted British educator Douglas Barnes observed, "Speech makes available to reflection the processes by which [children] relate new knowledge to old. *But this possibility depends on the social relationships, the communication system, which the teacher sets up*" (Barnes, 1976, emphasis added). Barnes also stated, "Through your interaction with children you will be helping them [put] old familiar experience into words in order to see new patterns in it" and to "make sense of new experience by finding a way of relating it to the old" (Barnes, p. 83). Other researchers have noted that children come to understand the conventions and the meaning of written language better through social interaction (Dyson, 1989, 1993).

Social relationships always occur in a context that is governed by certain conventions, even though these conventions often are known only tacitly or subconsciously (see Chapter 2). In addition to the context of the family and other adults, there is the context of the student's peers, and there is the context of the classroom.

Smith (1983) pointed out that in this classroom context, children are "learning all the time": important information is being conveyed regardless of what the teacher is doing and how he or she is doing it. Researchers have examined carefully the nature of the interaction among students in classrooms, as well as the impact of this interaction on the nature and extent of children's learning (Cazden, 1988; Cohen, 1994; Guthrie et al., 1995). This

One of your challenges as a teacher will be to create a positive learning environment in which students feel free to take risks and to stretch themselves in language and in thought.

research underscores the observation that the more humans communicate face to face, the more they learn. People have more opportunities in this context to express themselves and gauge the effect on others, as well as to interpret the ideas that others express. The exciting challenge of the classroom is to set up an environment that encourages productive interaction. This way, each child's natural propensity for communicating is directed toward both the content and the processes of learning. Speaking about and listening to what one knows are bridges to writing and reading and eventually to conversing with oneself, and thereby learning, through writing and reading.

The Language Arts: Implications for a Framework of Teaching and Learning

Now that we have a sense of what the language arts are, how they may be integrated, and the cultures within which learning them will occur, I'd like to present a framework for teaching and learning the language arts. Based on the work of Brian Cambourne (1984, 1988), this framework brings our theory of *constructivism* into the heart of the classroom and will underlie our learning throughout this book.

◆ **Immersion:** We will *immerse* our students in a reading, writing, and oral communication classroom, surrounding them with the potential for communication.

◆ **Employment:** Students will be "employed" in meaningful, purposeful, and authentic language activities that make sense to them.

◆ **Demonstration:** Through *our* modeling and "thinking aloud," we will demonstrate for students how to engage in and apply appropriate strategies and skills, and we will follow up by monitoring their application of each strategy or skill.

◆ **Responsibility:** When students are meaningfully and purposefully engaged in our culturally responsive classroom culture, they are quite able to assume *responsibility* for much of their own learning, including making decisions about what and how they will be learning. They are committed to their own learning and have a stake in it.

◆ **Approximation**: As students develop knowledge *about* the language arts and *through* the language arts, they will inevitably make mistakes. They will also fall short of correctly applying all of the conventions of oral and written language. This, of course, is precisely what "learning" is all about: throughout the elementary years, students will be *approximating* the forms, content, and conventions of oral and written language; in other words, "taking risks" with their learning.

◆ **Expectation:** Because we understand our students—how they learn and who they are—we *expect* them to be successful. They know we expect this, and they know we believe in them. Our expectations for them are defined within our "instructional" zone—*their* **zone of proximal development**.

We are learners right along with our students. In fact, one of the greatest joys of teaching is the opportunity to be lifelong learners ourselves (Calkins, 1994; Graves, 1983). When we think of ourselves as learners, we are recognizing that our students have something to teach *us*. Throughout the year, as we demonstrate for our students how to be sensitive and effective learners, we are often delightfully surprised at how much we really can learn about our students' worlds and about them as individuals—which in turn makes us more effective and sensitive teachers.

For years in our profession, there has been an ongoing debate involving "student-centered" versus "curriculum-centered" instruction. This debate revolves around the role of the teacher: how much control should the teacher exercise over what the students do, and how much of a role should the students have? A related issue is the role of published instructional materials in the classroom. A teacher who uses these materials is often described as "curriculum-centered" rather than "student-centered."

These types of issues are never either/or, and it is important that we realize this from the outset. Throughout this book, I will try to give you a balanced perspective on these issues — a *realistic* approach that will allow you and your students the opportunity to realize a maximum learning and teaching potential. Building upon our framework for teaching and learning, I will be advocating the type of teacher who, above all else, is tuned in to the students, allowing and supporting their active involvement in their own learning. This type of teacher invites students to take risks with their learning, to question, to wonder, to actively explore and experience the thrill of discovery. I will be advocating the type of teacher who will combine his or her developing creativity with a full understanding of when and how to select activities to address specific instructional ends. Often such a teacher creates these activities and instructional units; often he or she pulls them from published materials. Such a teacher knows that many published materials offer little more than "busy

work" but that many other such materials can offer important and productive tasks. Good teachers know the difference and choose accordingly.

You will find ongoing support for your teaching and learning by joining one or more professional organizations. See your professor about joining as a student member. Organizations most directly related to your interests as an elementary-school teacher of the language arts are the following:

- *National Council of Teachers of English (NCTE)*
  1111 Kenyon Road
  Urbana, IL 61801
  (Publisher of the journals *Language Arts* and *Primary Voices K–6*)

- *International Reading Association (IRA)*
  800 Barksdale Road
  PO Box 8139
  Newark, DE 19714–8139
  (Publisher of *Reading Teacher*)

- *American Library Association*
  50 E. Huron Street
  Chicago, IL 60611
  (Publisher of *Book Links*)

As a member of one or more of these organizations, you will be exposed to the most up-to-date journals and professional books that will enable you to keep up with cutting-edge developments in theory and practice. In addition, you should attend local NCTE and IRA meetings and conferences. These are affiliations you will want to continue when you become a professional teacher.

We are also readers and writers with our students. They will see us using these abilities every day in a meaningful way. We share with the students our excitement about a particular book or story we are reading. Much of our reading will be books appropriate for our students—good children's literature—and we will rarely fail to be excited, moved, and motivated by these books. Because such experiences demonstrably make a difference in our lives, our students will come to appreciate how such experiences can make a difference in their lives.

CONCLUDING PERSPECTIVE AND SUMMARY

Teaching is an enterprise no less complex than human beings themselves. Our challenge as teachers is to create a fertile classroom environment where students can develop communication skills and strategies to comprehend their world better and thus enrich their lives. We can create a supportive classroom environment where students can take responsibility for their own learning and become independent thinkers as well as work collaboratively and learn from others. When students are free to explore and experiment through communication, they gain self-esteem and self-awareness. They also develop a sense of control and purpose which is essential for a productive learning process.

In this chapter we've addressed the following main points:

◆ The fundamental purpose of the language arts—listening, speaking, reading, and writing—is to communicate.

◆ Students learn by constructing their own knowledge. Their brains are biologically programmed to organize and make sense of their world through their thought and language processes.

◆ We integrate instruction within the language arts by creating experiences where speaking, listening, reading, and writing influence one another and are used in real contexts—such as having students discuss a book they have read.

◆ Language arts *strategies* are procedures for approaching and engaging in learning tasks. A *skill* involves applying specific knowledge as part of a strategy.

◆ We integrate language arts instruction with the rest of the elementary curriculum by having students use the arts as tools for exploring and analyzing other subject areas—such as writing about observations in a science experiment.

◆ Physical, social, and psychological contexts affect learning. Our multicultural and information societies are the most important contexts influencing *how* we teach the integrated language arts. We must create a classroom culture within these contexts that is a positive learning environment.

Key Terms		
constructivism (p. 5)		information society (p. 14)
culturally responsive instruction (p. 12)		language arts (p. 4)
culture (p. 11)		zone of proximal development (p. 20)
cyberspace (p. 17)		

CHAPTER 2

Understanding Thought and Language as Meaning-Construction

- Why do we say that children are "hypothesis-testers"?

- How do children develop concepts and awareness of the relationships among concepts? What is the role of spoken language in this development?

- What are the four "systems" of language and how does context influence their use?

- What can adults do to support language development in the preschool years? In the elementary-school years?

◆ ◆ ◆   **INTRODUCTION**

In Chapter 1, children were described as "meaning makers" who are "learning all the time." The following excerpts from young children's speech help us see how they are making meaning as they construct their language:

◆ Cindy, a seventeen-month-old in a stroller at the grocery store checkout counter, points to the male checker and squeals, "Daddy!"

◆ Thirty-two-month-old Brian proudly announces to a visitor, "I *wented* to poddy by myse'f!"

◆ Five-year-old Kirstin confidently tells her older brothers that "Tyrannosaurus rex got his name because he goes around and *wrecks* things!"

◆ Michelle, age six, informs her mother that "once you know someone, you can never *un*know them."

In this chapter, to examine how this meaning and language are made, we'll take a brief excursion through the nature and the development of thought, or **cognition**, and **language**. This foundation for thought and language is the one we will continually build on as we guide our students toward understanding and using the language arts.

In order to be effective teachers, we must understand the nature of children. Children's thinking and language are critical aspects of what we are to understand. In this chapter, I will be presenting the essential information about thought and language and their development in the following order:

◆ The development of thought and language occurring throughout phases of childhood, revealing processes that will continue throughout the school years

◆ Common principles of children's development

◆ Types and nature of the various **systems of language**.

Foundations for the Development of Thought and Language

In recent years we have learned much about cognitive development from *developmental psychology* (Bruner, 1983; Gardner, 1983) and from the field of *cognitive science* (Bruer, 1994)—a newer field that addresses "the study of human intelligence in all of its forms, from perception and action to language and reasoning" (Lasnik, 1995, p. xi). We understand better how children's development is determined by both *biology* and *environment. Biology* ensures that the mind of a child has a tremendous potential for learning. The *environment* helps determine the degree to which this potential is realized. Environment includes parents (and other caretakers), siblings, other children, and teachers; all of these individuals reflect one or more cultures (see Chapter 1).

Our brains are already programmed at birth to follow certain paths of development. This programming is part of our biological heritage (Karmiloff-Smith, 1992). It allows for a marvelous flexibility, so that each individual can incorporate and adapt to a wide range of experiences. Our brains are set up from the start to make sense of the world in the following ways (Bussis, Chittenden, Amarel, & Klausner, 1985, p. 12):

◆ The brain constructs perceptions and thought, as opposed to behaving like a sponge.

◆ The brain's central function is to create meaning.

◆ Meaning arises through the perception and interpretation of patterns, or relationships, in events.

◆ Anticipation and intention exert a directing influence on perception and interpretation.

Our brains are *not* passive; they are always active—perceiving, interpreting, and making meaning of what's "out there." They are built to organize and use information in exquisitely effective ways. They allow us to build a "theory" of what is going on in the world and our relationship to it: "Human beings are theory builders; from the beginning we construct explanatory structures that help us find the deeper reality underlying surface chaos" (Carey, 1985, p. 195).

Once we begin school, the nature, quality, anticipation, and intention of the meaning we make—the theories we build—depend critically on the type of information we receive. Much of this information and the way in which it is presented comes from teachers—and can affect both the nature of the knowledge that each one of us constructs *and* how we feel about that knowledge.

Learning has a very real basis in the neurobiology of our brains. After birth, a child's brain does most of its developing by the time the child is five years old. In fact, between the ages of two and five, the child's brain will increase from 75 percent to 90 percent of its adult weight. This increase is not primarily in number of brain cells but in the *interconnections* among these cells. These interconnections are established as a result of *learning*—by actively interacting with the physical and social environment. (This process, by the way, is not limited to children. As *we* acquire new information and construct new knowledge, we are also establishing new connections among our brain cells.)

There appear to be some **universal features** in the development of cognition and language in the preschool years. Just as most children learn to crawl, walk, and run at certain ages — or at least in a fairly typical order — children around the world usually begin to talk at a certain age and to follow a similar pattern of cognitive development, regardless of their language or culture. Much of this development is biologically determined; young children's initial language and cognitive development "just happens" as the children interact with their physical and social environment.

An engaging way of thinking about how children go about their early learning or "theory building" is to see them as **hypothesis-testers**. They construct hypotheses, try them out, and receive feedback about how language and the world around them work. This process of knowledge construction begins early, with the visual, auditory, tactile, and affective interaction between parent and child. At first, of course, children are not consciously "testing hypotheses," but at a subconscious or *tacit* level, their brains certainly are. At a later point in development, this hypothesis-testing will come under the child's conscious or *explicit* control.

The Components of Thought: What Is to Be Learned, and How?

It is difficult to talk about "thought" separately from language. Most of us have the impression, in fact, that our thoughts *are* language: we might say we "hear" a little voice inside our heads most of the time — and that voice is the sound of thinking going on. While that little voice may indeed seem to be there for most of us, it is not *all* that is doing the "thinking." Perhaps the best test of the fact that thinking and language are separate is the familiar example of saying something and then realizing that *what* we said was not what we had actually *meant* to say. The developmental psychologist Steven Pinker reminds us that in order for us to have that feeling, "there has to be a 'what we meant to say' that is different from what we said" (1994, p. 57). The "what we meant to say" is the *meaning*.

Thought or cognition, therefore, includes not only language-related activities such as conversing with a friend or reading a novel, but also activities such as walking across a narrow log that spans a creek, whistling a tune, or making our way home after work or class. When we come right down to it, most of our cognitive activity does not have to do with language. Does this mean that language is unimportant? Of course not. It *does* mean that language has very rich and deep cognitive resources to draw from and that language can be used as a very powerful tool to help us become aware of and explore our thinking and our world.

The Development of Thought

As teachers, it's important for us to think about two very significant aspects of cognitive development. The first is **concept development**. The second is the influence of symbolic thought on conceptual development.

Concepts may be defined as "the basic constituents of thought and belief" (Smith, 1995, p. 501). Human beings construct concepts, and over time these concepts *differentiate* as well as *integrate*. As preschool and school-age children grow and mature, this **differentiation and integration** is affected by the development of *symbolic* thought. Put simply, symbolic thinking involves using one thing to stand for another: a broom symbolizes a horse as the child "rides" it; the stick figures drawn by the five-year-old symbolize her family; the spoken word *cat* symbolizes the family pet. As children develop, symbolic thinking leads to a *restructuring* or *reorganization* of their conceptual networks. Let's examine more closely both concept development and how it is influenced by symbolic thinking.

Concept Development

The knowledge that young preschool children develop is based primarily on the interaction between

◆ their naturally maturing brains, and

◆ their own actions upon their environment (Bruner, 1983; Piaget, 1977).

Children learn about objects and other people in their world — what they are and how they behave — through observation and action. In the process, they learn about the causes and consequences of their actions and the actions of others. Learning about objects, actions, and other people is the foundation of conceptual development.

For young children, *words* play an important part in this process. Words of course are part of *language*, but I am making reference to them here because of their important role in concept development. At a tacit or

Through experiences with their environment, preschool children develop knowledge, begin to establish concepts, and come to understand the actions and consequences of things happening in the world around them.

subconscious level, young children seem to understand that words refer to something in their environment that they need to pay attention to — and for which, therefore, they need to set up a concept.

Each concept in the mind is represented by a "core example" that typifies the concept best. Something encountered in the environment is compared to the "core example" in order to check whether it is an instance of that concept (Smith, 1995). As you might expect, young children's concepts are quite different from ours. To the sixteen-month-old toddler, for example, the verbal labels "doggie" or "bow-wow" stand for the concept *four-legged animals*. A horse shares enough attributes with "doggie" that when the child compares the horse he or she sees in the field with his *core concept* for "doggie," there is a match. With continued experience and interaction with others, however, the toddler's conceptual domain will become more *differentiated*: four-legged animals will become sorted into "dogs," "horses," "cows," "squirrels," "cats," and so on. These concepts in turn will *integrate* with other concepts that represent, for instance, "forest creatures," "things that are pets," and "animals that help humans." *This process of differentiation and integration continues throughout life.*

The processes of differentiation and integration often involve over- or undergeneralizing the range of things to which a particular concept or word refers (Anglin, 1977; Clark, 1993). An example of overgeneralization is fifteen-month-old Gavin's use of his word *moont* to refer to the full moon — but also to refer to lamps and streetlights. These objects share common features with the moon — brightness, shape (somewhat), and being important at nighttime; they matched his core concept of "moont." With time, this large category of things became differentiated so that Gavin used *moont* to refer only to the moon and used other verbal labels to refer to lamps and streetlights. An example of underextension is Gavin's use of *fork* to refer only to small forks — not to large ones.

As preschool children establish and develop their concepts and conceptual network through interacting with their environment and the people in it, they build up an understanding of various relationships among people and things in that environment; for example, cause/effect and who (the *agent*) is doing what (the *action*) to what or whom (the *object*). All of this information — concepts and the relationships among them — helps children understand and anticipate what goes on. They are constructing a "theory" of how the world works.

In addition to constructing, differentiating, and integrating concepts, children — indeed, *all* of us — need to mentally represent recurring events and situations. We need to *organize* the concepts that are involved in frequently occurring situations, arrange them in a way that helps us make sense of our world, and interpret new situations that we encounter. Researchers have termed these recurring events and situations **schemas** or *scripts*; the two terms are used interchangeably (Nelson, 1986). Some examples of schemas that young children experience and organize are what happens at bathtime, what they do at daycare, and what usually happens when they go to McDonald's or Burger King.

How *Symbols* Affect Concept Development

In addition to concept development, I mentioned at the beginning of this section the influence of **symbolic thought** on conceptual development. Human beings are symbol-makers and symbol-users. The development of cognition is in many ways a story of the development of symbolic functions — how one thing comes to stand for something else.

Over the years, several prominent theorists have researched this development, the most influential being Jean Piaget in Switzerland, Lev Vygotsky in Russia, and Jerome Bruner and Howard Gardner in the United States. I will not undertake a comprehensive comparison and contrast of their theories here, but I will emphasize what is *most* important for teachers to be aware of. While these theorists differ with respect to the emphasis they place on the *causes* of cognitive development, they appear to agree on the developmental sequence of symbolic thinking presented in Table 2.1; children's conceptual representations — their knowledge of the world — follows a concrete-to-more-abstract trend.

Now, let's step back and reflect on this sequence. Do you see how the child's internal, conceptual representation of the external world moves from concrete to increasingly abstract? from concrete actions related to the here-and-now to abstract, arbitrary relations that apply not only to the present

TABLE 2.1

Development of Symbolic Thought	
18 Months Through 2 Years of Age	Young children's conceptualization of their world is based on their *actions* upon their world; *movement* is the primary symbolic mode.
3 Years of Age	Children's conceptualization comes to include *spatial* relationships — size, shape, and orientation — and *visual imagery* becomes a dominant symbolic mode. Whereas younger children's drawings of themselves, for example, are a mass of scribbles, now, at age three, they are likely to draw two circles; they'll call the top one the "head" and the bottom one the "body" (Gardner, 1991).
4 Years of Age	Children's conceptualizations are powerfully influenced by the emergence of *number*. This influence helps them attend more specifically to features and characteristics of their world and the correspondence between these characteristics. They will, for example, make *very* sure that each stuffed animal at "lunch" has the *same* number of dishes and cups.
5 Through 7 Years of Age	Most children are attracted toward *notational* symbolization (Gardner & Wolfe, 1983): they can encode one type of information in another form. It is important to note that the relationship between the notational system and what is "noted" or encoded is *arbitrary*. There is no obvious relationship between the symbol and what is symbolized. For example, the symbol 4 represents four objects; the letter *m* represents a sound in speech.

but to the past and the future as well? Significantly, all the theorists referred to earlier appear to agree on this sequence and on its nature, for children the world over, regardless of culture.

Thinking about Thinking: Metacognitive Development

For most of the elementary-school years, children have a broader cognitive perspective and possess the potential for moving beyond the things, people, or events in their immediate environment. Conceptual development and the accompanying construction of schemas provide every child with a complex and impressive network of knowledge about the world and about language. This network is in turn influenced by the evolution of symbolic thinking. We have noted that in the preschool years, most of this knowledge is at a subconscious or "tacit" level (Tirosh, 1992), which means that children are not aware that they possess it. As children grow and develop, they do become aware of this knowledge—they can think about their own thinking and about *how* they think—on a conscious or "explicit" level. They are moving beyond the immediate present in time and space and beyond their own personal perspective. For example, a child comes to understand another child's ideas about whether the Big Bad Wolf really was all that bad. This ability is broadly termed **metacognition**.

Simply put, metacognition is the ability to think about thinking. One of our goals as teachers is to help our students develop their metacognitive abilities. *Self*-knowledge and *procedural* knowledge are dependent upon metacognition. Students have to reflect on their thinking in order to be aware of what they need to know (*self*-knowledge) and of how they can go about acquiring that information (*procedural* knowledge).

This expanding awareness will continue throughout the school years. Throughout the remainder of this text, we will examine how teachers can present, model, and *guide* the process of inquiry—helping students become aware of what they know and what they need to know, then helping them with the procedure for finding things out. With time, our students should internalize the nature and application of these strategic tools. As Vygotsky noted, "What the child can do today in co-operation, tomorrow [he or she] will be able to do on his [or her] own."

The Components of Language: What Is to Be Learned, and How?

Language is a spoken or written symbol system in which sounds or marks are associated with meaning. Language is not meaning, and its association or relationship with meaning is marvelously complex. A well-known linguist, Leonard Bloomfield, once wrote that language learning is "doubtless the greatest intellectual feat any one of us is ever required to perform" (Bloomfield, 1933, p. 29). Another well-known and influential linguist, Noam Chomsky, attempted to explain how learners can in fact produce and understand so many utterances that they have never heard before (Chomsky, 1965). Chomsky's explanation revolutionized the way scholars think about language development. For many years, language development and use had been considered fairly simple, following a small set of learning principles (Skinner, 1957). We now realize that even learning a first language is "a complex interaction between the child's innate capacities and the social, cognitive, and linguistic supports provided in the environment" (Gleitman & Newport, 1995, p. 21).

Consider for a moment what young children accomplish. In acquiring a language, they must learn words and how these words are pronounced, as well as how to construct sentences with these words, and this learning in turn depends upon learning about the complex correspondence between language and the underlying meaning it is meant to express. In addition, children must learn about the many ways language is *used*, as the following description makes clear:

> Language varies according to the topic, the persons involved, and whether it is written or spoken. The language used in church is different from the language used when talking with one's playmates; the language we find in books is different from the language we find on street signs. Language which sounds right at home may sound funny in church. Children learn naturally to make adjustments in their language by having many opportunities to be present in different kinds of settings where language is being used. Successful language users adjust their language to meet the demands of the setting in which they find themselves. (Harste, Woodward, & Burke, 1984, p. xvi)

When we produce and comprehend language in natural settings, we are attuned primarily to the *meaning* that underlies speech or print. We are seldom aware of other aspects of language, even though different types of language *systems* — purposes, pronunciation, arranging words into phrases and sentences — interact to create and support meaning. These systems do not really function independently in normally developing language-users, but by discussing the systems separately, we can gain a better understanding of language as a whole and can better understand its development.

Language, as Harste, Woodward, and Burke (1984) point out, is largely a social event. It usually occurs between at least two individuals, and it is learned in a social context. Of course, we can use language on our own when we think, write, or read, but its ultimate purpose is usually social: to communicate with others. Even when we read, we are in effect communicating with another person, since that person's ideas are expressed through written rather than spoken language (you and I are at this moment engaged in communication).

Figure 2.1 represents the relationships among the different knowledge systems underlying language use: *semantics*, *syntax*, *phonology*, and *pragmatics*. Let's consider each system, then examine how these systems interact between two language-users during the process of communication.

1. **Semantics:** How we come to establish relationships between particular words and the underlying concepts those words represent.

2. **Syntax:** How we structure our sentences by putting words and phrases together. Syntax also plays a significant role in representing meaning; compare for instance, the sentences *Dog bites man* and *Man bites dog*.

3. **Phonology:** How we *pronounce* the sounds, words, and phrases in our language. This includes the intonation patterns—the "ups" and "downs"—that flow across the words and phrases.

4. **Pragmatics:** The larger system that encompasses the above systems.

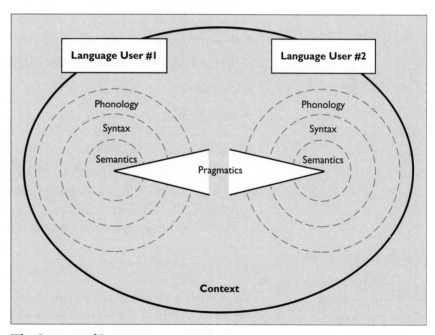

Figure 2.1   **The Systems of Language**

SOURCE: Adapted from Fig. 16.5, "Reading and Writing in a System of Language," Jerome C. Harste, Virginia A. Woodward, and Carolyn L. Burke, *Language Stories & Literacy Lessons*. Adapted and reproduced by permission of Heinemann Educational Books, Inc., Portsmouth, NH.

Semantics

As we saw in the case of children first learning about their world, the initial concepts children develop reflect their actions upon things in their real world. A child's initial definition of an object—perhaps a toy truck—is based very much on the physical attributes of that truck and on what the child can do to it. As the child gains experience with language and with the world, the concepts underlying words become refined and the child's definitions approximate "conventional" definitions more closely. This does *not* mean that the child's initial definitions are "wrong"—just that we should be sensitive to how those definitions vary from ours.

An important point to make about our semantic knowledge is that it is never fixed; it is always developing. As Moskowitz noted, "The meanings of words continue to expand and contract through adulthood, long after other types of language acquisition have ceased" (1978, p. 106). As we'll see later on, in a classroom context this awareness should guide our introduction of new concepts and new vocabulary words.

Syntax

There are many ways in which words and phrases can be combined to form sentences, and language-users already know *tacitly* just about all of the ways. A language-user knows, for example,

◆ that articles always precede nouns in English,

◆ that adverbs can precede or follow the verbs they modify,

◆ how to turn one sentence form into another (for example, "Carrie squished the mango" becomes "The mango was squished by Carrie," and declarative sentences become questions: "John broke the spatula" becomes "Did John break the spatula?"), and

◆ how to embed a clause within a sentence ("I borrowed a magazine from Warren. The magazine is no longer published" becomes "The magazine *that I borrowed from Warren* is no longer published").

Phonology

When we talk about the *phonological knowledge* of a speaker, we are talking about how he or she knows how to pronounce sounds and places stress or emphasis on syllables, words, and phrases. As with semantics and syntax, most of this knowledge is tacit.

Knowledge about accent or stress placement within *words* helps the speaker pronounce appropriately the italicized words in the following sentences: "The guitarist plans to *record* a new CD" and "His *record-keeping* is really disorganized." In the first *record*, the stress is placed on the second syllable (re-CORD); in the second *record*, the first syllable is the one stressed (REC-ord). In fact, with most words of more than one syllable, speakers must place stress appropriately within the word: re-DUC-tion, POP-ulate, em-PLOY.

Knowledge of stress placement within *phrases and sentences*, often referred to as *prosody*, allows speakers to control the meaning depending on where the stress is placed:

"She bought a *coat?*" (rather than a sweater)

"She *bought* a coat?" (rather than borrowing one)

"*She* bought a coat?" (rather than her mother's buying one for her)

Obviously, where speakers place strongest emphasis, or stress, reflects what they want highlighted, which in turn depends on the meaning they wish to express in particular contexts.

Pragmatics

From Chapter 1, we know the importance and the role of *context*. Depending on our intentions, the context in which we are speaking determines how we *use* the systems of language. The socially acceptable use of language in a particular situation is termed *pragmatics*—the appropriate selection of words, sentence structure, and emphasis. Here are two examples:

◆ When speaking with a child who knows little English, we are likely to use active rather than passive voice in our sentences.

◆ If we are conducting a minilesson during Writing Workshop, we'll be guiding students whose sentences are short and rather flat toward including more information while making their sentences come alive: "I have three cousins" becomes, for example, "Ever since I can remember, I have had three weird cousins who act like a bad dream."

Learning the tacit "rules" of pragmatics takes quite some time. The beginnings of this learning, however, lie in the very first year of life and are a critical part of "learning how to mean" (Halliday, 1975). A young child will learn about the **functions of language**—how to use language to express what she wants for herself and what she wishes others to do, to express how she feels, to pretend, to share intimate moments with others. Context and pragmatics help link the language systems together in a common purpose; they determine the ways in which each speaker puts the three language systems to use. Table 2.2 presents the seven functions of language that are

TABLE 2.2

Young Children's Use of the Functions of Language	
Instrumental	"I want"—Using language to get something *right now*
Regulatory	"Do as I tell you"—Using language to control the present situation in reference to an action the child wishes the adult to perform
Interactional	"Me and you"—Using language in intimate, special moments shared between the child and the adult
Personal	"Here I come"—Using language to "announce" that the child will be "controlling" in a particular situation
Heuristic	"Tell me why"—Using language to seek information
Imaginative	"Let's pretend"—Using language to create and talk about imaginative situations
Informative	"I've got something to tell you"—Using language to provide information that others do not have

acquired by very young children; these functions—as we will discuss in later chapters—will continue to be used in more developed fashion as children grow.

Let's summarize the relationships among the systems of language: one's intent within a particular context determines the appropriate social rules of language (*pragmatics*), which then influence the selection of words (*semantics*) and the types of sentence structure (*syntax*) and oral expression (*phonology*) used to convey meaning.

The Development of Language

The Preschool Years

As with thought, the development of language is a marvelously complex phenomenon. Although we cannot delve into it here in any great depth, we can get a feel for the complexity and the general trends of language development. We can chart a child's language development by noting the "errors" the child makes—by seeing how a young child's language varies from that spoken by older individuals. By studying the way a child's spoken language varies from a model, we can gain insights into the development of *written* language in young children as well. We will look at this more closely in Chapter 6.

Children learn their first words through active explorations in a social context.

Language development in young children seems to have a lot of the magical about it. As some of the examples at the beginning of the chapter illustrate, children continually amaze and delight us with the ways they express their ideas. In fact, young children have been characterized as "poets," and for many reasons (Egan, 1987):

◆ First, children's language often strikes us as poetic as they test their hypotheses about words and experiences. This testing helps children sort out the defining characteristics of concepts and the words that represent those concepts. For example, while riding in an old Volkswagen, Jason (age three) pointed to the round speedometer and its needle and exclaimed, "That's a toothpick clock!" Kirstin (age five) described a dancer's back-and-forth movements as being "*back*wards and *this*wards."

◆ A second poetic characteristic of young children's language is their sensitivity to *rhythm* and *rhyme* in oral language (Goswami & Bryant, 1992). Children enjoy repeating rhymes, often as an accompaniment to play (jump-rope jingles, for example), and making up spontaneous rhymes. Often, to adults' dismay, these rhymes have to do with taboo words concerning subjects such as bodily functions.

A young child's oral language world can be a powerful springboard into writing and reading. Throughout the elementary years, this world can provide a stimulating foundation for imagination, humor, metaphorical thinking, and sense of narrative. My primary focus in this section will be on oral language and communication—emphasizing the complex interaction among pragmatics, semantics, syntax, and phonology. The first two years of life "provide the basis for breaking into language but, once acquired, language becomes a means of extending the range and complexity of thought" (Wells, 1981, p. 87). For this reason, I have divided the preschool period into birth to approximately two years, and approximately two years to five years. Why end at five years? As Moskowitz has noted, "although many subtle refinements are added between the ages of five and ten, most children have completed the greater part of the basic language-acquisition process by the age of five" (Moskowitz, 1978, p. 92).

Birth to Two Years

Very early in the first year of life, babies babble—and they do it a lot, trying out lots of different sounds and intonation patterns. This is critically important language play. It leads to the first recognizable words of the native language by the age of about twelve months. These first words represent things and people that are important and interesting to babies: a particular child's use of the words *keys, doggie,* and *juice* are more likely to appear before words for *table, diaper,* or *chair,* the latter being things that are simply there and that are not particularly exciting objects in the young child's life.

How do children pick out words from the ongoing stream of speech? *Stressed syllables* are probably the cues (Wanner & Gleitman, 1982). The child tacitly picks up on these cues. Segments of speech that are given more emphasis usually correspond to the important *words*—and therefore the important *objects*—in the environment. In addition, parents also play the "name game," which involves asking "What's that?" and then providing the label (Bruner, 1983). The name game usually occurs in the context of playing some other game with the child or as an accompaniment to some other activity, such as taking a bath. Eventually the child understands at a tacit level that *things* have labels—*names*—and then the name game, along with language development more generally, really takes off.

While it may seem fairly easy to pair up a word with what the word refers to, it is actually a remarkable feat for the young child. Think about it: A parent says "Doggie" when the family dog comes up and licks the twelve-month-old's face. There are a *lot* of things this young child can link *doggie* to: the word could refer to the dog's tongue, to the act of being licked in the face, to the smell of the dog's breath, or to the act of being approached by a large thing, as well as to the dog itself. And yet, very young children seem to focus on the "right" connection between the word and what it refers to, and this is remarkable.

As children grasp, kick, suck, crawl, and eventually toddle about, their actions and the consequences of their actions represent *relationships*—location, causality, recurrence—and these various relationships come to define the early language structure of the child (Brown, 1973). Jerome Bruner (1975) suggested that it is this close correspondence between actions in the world and the language relationships that represent those events that help the child construct this early syntax. Lindfors gives a succinct example of this process: the "differentiation of actor and action is one that comes about through the child's increasingly varied physical interactions with an increasing range of objects and people" (1987, p. 167).

Note the role of other *people*. The child's active explorations occur in a *social context*. Early in the child's development, the adult caretaker and the child jointly focus on the same object, and the young child is tacitly picking up on the following idea: "*You* [the adult] and *I* [the baby] are talking about *it* [whatever the adult and baby are jointly focusing their attention on]." This is an important communication "triangle" that lays the foundation for language development within a social context.

At around eighteen months, children begin to put words together. They say things such as "Hat on. . . . Wear hat. . . . All gone." This phase (for obvious reasons) has been labeled the "two-word utterance" phase. It is an exciting time, and it lays the groundwork for an "explosion" in language growth.

Two Years to Five Years

During the third year of life, language begins to extend the range and complexity of thought. *What* children notice, *how* they notice it, and *why* and *when* they pay attention to it will usually depend on the conversations the children have with other children and with adult caretakers.

At around two years of age, children begin to put three or more words together. Over the course of their third year, their utterances will grow dramatically in length and in complexity. At first, they're simply stringing more **content words** together ("Give doggie paper. Big doggie.") and leaving out **function words** and **grammatical markers**. Function words "glue" the content words together and express relationships among the words (for example, *the*, *and*, and *of*). Grammatical markers include inflectional endings such as *-ed*, *-ing*, and the plural *s*.

Before long, however, children's utterances expand and change in dramatic ways. They *do* include function words and grammatical markers.

Expressions of relations that would have stood by themselves earlier, such as "I play" and "My game," are now *combined*: "I play my game." One statement becomes *embedded* within another: "Give doggie paper" and "Big doggie" become "Give big doggie paper."

Children learn how to phrase questions and express negative relationships. Instead of asking questions by uttering sentences with a rising intonation, they construct the appropriate **syntactic transformations**: "The man is here?" becomes "Is the man here?" (Pinker, 1994). Asking and answering questions can be fairly complex, because questions serve different functions, and children must tacitly learn the distinctions among these functions. For example, questions can elicit information or yes/no responses, or they can express "polar" relationships ("Did Herbie sleep over last night or the night before?"). Moreover, questions can be identical syntactically but represent more complex underlying relationships. As an example, Lindfors (1987) lists the questions "Where did you go?", "Why did you go?", and "When did you go?"

As children during these early years are testing their hypotheses about how their language works, they make errors. Such errors are evidence of growth. Far from being a "regression," they show that children have moved beyond a single memorized item to a level at which they are applying a rule—testing a hypothesis—that covers a number of situations: "I *goed* to the doctor" and even "I *wented* to the doctor." Just as they do when they're learning what *words* represent, children very often overextend the application of a "rule"; one week they correctly say "I *watched* TV today," but the next week they pronounce the verb as *watchded*.

Language development continues at a phenomenal pace during the fourth and fifth years of life. Children's sentences grow in length and in syntactic complexity. By four and a half to five years of age, children have acquired most of the sentence structures and sound patterns of their language. By the time they begin first grade, they have learned approximately 5,000 to 6,000 words. While many of these words are learned through the "name game," most are learned in the business of day-to-day interaction with the environment and with others.

Language from this point on will allow children a means by which they can *act* upon their world and *reflect* upon those actions. This is also when most children begin their formal schooling. Enter the teacher, who will play a pivotal role in facilitating this action and reflection. "As teachers we can organize the social environment of the classroom to support the language user's perception, organization, and presentation of texts in reading and writing" (Harste, Woodward, & Burke, 1984, p. 206). Such a social environment will guarantee that *meaningful* language use is going on—and that children are free to communicate.

AT THE TEACHER'S DESK

OBSERVING LANGUAGE GROW: A LESSON FOR THE CLASSROOM (AND FOR A FIRST-TIME PARENT)

I'd like to share a "home movie" with you. I think it illustrates how children go about establishing *semantic* and *syntactic* distinctions—and contains a lesson on the role of a teacher.

About eight months after my first child, Jason, was born, I went back to graduate school. It seemed a wonderful opportunity to observe the development of thought and language firsthand as I studied about it in my classes. Young children, I was learning, test hypotheses about how language works. Usually this process takes some time, but with the pride and conceit of a first-time parent, I thought that maybe I could move things along more rapidly. . . .

I well recall one such attempt. Jason, age 23 months, had just stated, "My go outside," and I figured I could get him at least to say, "*I* go outside." The interchange went something like this:

DAD: "Oh, *you* go outside?"
JASON: "Uh-huh. *My* go outside."

DAD: "No, Jason: *I* go outside." (I suddenly realized this was going to be harder than I'd thought. . . .)
JASON (excitedly): "*Daddy* go outside?"
DAD: "No, Jason. You should say '*I* go outside.'"
JASON (impatiently, starting for the door): "*My* go outside!"

Now I'll put this episode in a broader context: oral language development among preschoolers holds many implications for learning in the elementary-school years. What this example illustrates is that (1) children first organize information according to *their* theory of how the world works and (2) their process of hypothesis-testing often takes a while. As teachers, therefore, we need to be patient. We should indeed provide good examples, effective demonstrations, and appropriate feedback, but it may take more time and more exposure before a child's hypothesis is truly modified.

Early Language Learning: Cultural Differences and Implications for Teaching

Learning to talk should be thought of "as the result of a partnership between parents and other members of the community" and the child (Wells, 1986). Let's turn our attention more specifically to contexts or situations in which this partnership occurs—where young language-learners interact with more knowledgeable language-users. These contexts—which usually include aspects of diversity—and how we respond within them have definite implications for the elementary classroom as well.

A number of researchers have studied the characteristics of language use in homes reflecting different racial and socioeconomic groups (for example, Au, 1993; Taylor & Dorsey-Gaines, 1988; Heath, 1983). They have found that the ways parents and other adults interact with children *do* differ. The social appropriateness of certain types of interactions—the *pragmatics*—differs from group to group. The *types* of interaction also vary. For example, in asking children to retell an event, some parents expect simply a literal account of what happened. On the other hand, other parents may ask about the reasons why it happened. Still others, by their responses to the child, may encourage him or her to embellish the story by adding events and actions that were not part of the original event.

It is important to note that these differences in contexts do not lead to "better" language in some groups than in others. On the other hand, as teachers, we should be aware of these differences because we will be interacting with children from cultural backgrounds different from our own. Different cultural groups have different rules and patterns for communicating and interacting, and the children will bring these expectations with them to school. If we are not aware of these different expectations and are not prepared to respond appropriately, confusion and frustration may result—for us as well as for the children. We may assume that children are less able than they really are, while in fact they simply have different skills and different ways of showing us what they can do. So part of our job will be to facilitate children's learning the cultural patterns expected in school (and in the mainstream culture), while at the same time we are honoring the cultural patterns of their homes (Delpit, 1988; Reyes, 1992). This is an extremely important issue, one that we'll explore further in Chapter 4.

Many studies have been conducted into the types of language that caretakers and teachers *should* use with young children; should we restate what the child has said, for example, or expand and elaborate upon it? First and foremost, we should follow this advice: "There is no set of rules of how to talk to a child that can even approach what you unconsciously know. If you concentrate on communicating, everything else will follow" (Brown, 1977).

So what, in general, can parents, teachers, and other caregivers of preschool children do to facilitate language growth? Reviews of the research yield the following recommendations (Fromkin & Rodman, 1993):

◆ The *amount or quantity of interaction* between the child and adults is important.

◆ Interaction should be *one-to-one* as much as possible, and it should concern *things that are important* to the child.

◆ *Clarity of expression* should be attempted. Adults should rephrase and adjust the length of their utterances, when necessary, to ensure that they understand what the child is trying to say and respond appropriately and effectively to the child.

◆ Assume that *the child has something important to say* when she or he appears to be trying to communicate, and treat the attempt accordingly.

◆ *Be sure you have understood the intended meaning* before responding; children's utterances are often unclear or ambiguous.

◆ *Take the child's meaning as the basis of what you say next*—confirming the intention and extending the topic or inviting the child to do so.

◆ In order to accomplish the previous suggestions, adults absolutely *must be good listeners.*

As we'll see later on, these recommendations are relevant for elementary-age children as well.

CONCLUDING PERSPECTIVE AND SUMMARY

A common misconception is that "learning" is a linear process of accumulation—that we simply add more information to what we already know. In reality, learning is far more complex. While we do take in information from our environment, our minds organize and process it in particular ways in order to understand it. As we grow from childhood to adulthood, our minds evolve and continually restructure the ways we perceive, comprehend, and relate to the world.

As elementary-school teachers, we need to know how preschool children's systems of thought and language initially develop if we are to comprehend and affect how they learn when they reach our classrooms. Though children's potential is partially determined by biology, it is realized in a social context. As they learn language and develop thought, children become "meaning makers," assimilating, processing, and testing new data gleaned from interactions with their environment and other people. To teach them effectively, we must apply our knowledge of thought, language, and their intricate relationship within the developing child.

In this chapter we've addressed the following main points:

◆ In their early stages of learning, children are "hypothesis-testers." Through contact with their physical and social environment, they receive information which their brains process and organize. They subconsciously devise theories about external reality and their relationship to it. They then test these hypotheses on other people and receive feedback that enables them to construct knowledge. As children grow older, they *consciously* engage in hypothesis testing.

◆ Children develop concepts—the basic components of thought—by observing objects and people in their world and fixating on "core examples" that to them best represent the particular components. Each "core example" becomes a concept that the child labels through word use, then tests and refines as he or she interacts with others. As the child experiences more of the world, he or she formulates more concepts and "differentiates" or distinguishes among them. The child also "integrates" similar concepts to represent broader categories. In addition, the child comes to understand relationships among elements of his or her world by constructing *schemas*, mental representations of recurring events.

◆ Use of the four "systems" of language—semantics, syntax, phonology, and pragmatics—is influenced by context. The application of semantics, the selection of words to represent concepts, varies with the subject discussed and the audience addressed. Syntax, the way we combine words and phrases to form phrases, is determined by *what* we are conveying—questions, demands, or statements—to whom. Phonology, oral expression and emphasis, also varies with the content and purpose of communication. These three systems are employed within the larger system of pragmatics (determining the socially acceptable use of language in particular contexts).

◆ Adults can support language development in the preschool years by talking with their children one-on-one as often as possible about matters the children consider important. Adults should respect children's attempts to communicate and listen carefully to ensure that they've understood the children's meanings correctly. Adults should then confirm the children's intent and respond clearly to encourage further conversation.

Key Terms

cognition (p. 26)

concept development (p. 29)

content words (p. 41)

differentiation and integration (p. 30)

function words (p. 41)

functions of language (p. 37)

grammatical markers (p. 41)

hypothesis-testers (p. 28)

language (p. 26)

metacognition (p. 33)

schemas (p. 31)

symbolic thought (p. 31)

syntactic transformations (p. 42)

systems of language (p. 26)

universal features (p. 28)

PART 2

LEARNING ENVIRONMENT

CHAPTER 3

Organzing and Managing the Integrated Classroom Community

- ◆ How and why are the characteristics of integrated instruction, risk taking, and talking important in your classroom management?
- ◆ What are the central issues for establishing the physical environment of the classroom?
- ◆ How can we involve parents in their children's schooling?
- ◆ How should we determine goals for the academic environment?
- ◆ What are the different group configurations possible in the classroom, and what are the reasons for each particular organization?

INTRODUCTION

In *Ramona the Pest*, Beverly Cleary writes about Ramona's first encounter with a substitute teacher. Ramona and her friend Howie arrive at the kindergarten door one morning and discover a stranger. Howie, obviously aware of who this stranger might be, says, "I bet the substitute won't even know the rules of our kindergarten." Ramona, responding to Howie with concern about this stranger's expertise, replies, "Miss Binney said following the rules of their kindergarten was important. How could this stranger know what the rules are? A stranger would not even know the names of the boys and girls. She might get mixed up."

Faced with the dilemma of the substitute teacher, Ramona abandons kindergarten and hides behind the trash cans. Eventually, she is discovered and returned to her classroom. This scenario ends with Ramona's remarks about the substitute's ineptness. Ramona grumbles, "Here it was seatwork time, and Mrs. Wilcox was not even having the class do real seatwork, but was letting them draw pictures as if this were the first day of kindergarten. . . . Things were not supposed to be this way."

Ramona, like other elementary-school children, clearly understands her classroom's management and organization. How did she develop this understanding? Certainly Miss Binney considered the classroom environment and her kindergarten students when she planned her classroom organization. And during the first weeks of school, expectations for behavior and procedures for classroom routines were established.

Kids expect structure. But "structure" doesn't mean a strict, quiet, boring, and lifeless classroom. In this chapter, we'll look ahead to the classrooms we'll teach in and discuss the elements necessary to establish a structured and well-tuned classroom environment that supports integrated language arts instruction. We'll look at the planning needed to organize and manage our classrooms. Because the language arts flow into and out of other subjects—social studies, math, science, art, music, physical education—this chapter will provide the foundation for establishing a classroom that runs smoothly throughout the day and over the months.

Special Characteristics of Integrated Language Arts Classrooms that Support Learning

Three characteristics distinguish the type of classrooms we will be establishing:

◆ *Authentic* integration of the language arts

◆ Different types of social interaction

◆ Children and teachers who "take risks" with their learning.

The classroom is a complex teaching and learning environment: if it is structured appropriately, students will be sharing and discussing as they work *together*. They will be busy reading, writing, drawing, and talking with other students and the teacher. Quite often, a variety of activities will occur simultaneously.

Note how these three characteristics of true integration, different types of social interaction, and risk taking are evident in Kay Webb's first-grade classroom.

CLASSROOM EXAMPLE

Kay Webb's First-Grade Community of Learners

Each child enters the class, puts away personal belongings, and quickly moves to his or her desk. Before school, Kay placed each child's journal on his or her desk so that the journals would be ready when the children arrived. Jim opens his journal and reads Kay's response to the entry he made yesterday: "I remember getting a sunburn too. It was hard to sleep. I hated being all red and having my skin peel."

Jim leans over to Mary and asks her to help him read some of the words in Kay's message. Meanwhile, children throughout the class are helping each other read. After reading their messages, the children write another entry in their journals. As the children are reading and writing, Kay moves around the room offering support if children need it. Heather asks her how to spell *balloon*. She replies, "Well, how do you *think* it is spelled, Heather?" Kay then guides Heather through a "sounding out" process in which Heather creates the spelling "*BLUN.*"

The children continue writing for about fifteen minutes. Then a few share their journals with the whole class. At this point a transition from the journal-writing activity occurs, and Kay takes a few minutes to give the children directions before they begin a new activity. First, she reminds them to turn in their journals before lunch.

After this brief reminder, she gives several groups of children specific directions:

"Those of you who have just read *Rosie's Walk* [Hutchins,

C L A S S R O O M
E X A M P L E

**Kay Webb's
First-Grade
Community of
Learners**

(Continued)

1968] need to continue working on your mural. All the materials are under the back table where they were left yesterday.

"If you read *The Jigaree* [Cowley, 1983] yesterday, please go to the listening center and listen to the story one time, then join in and read the story [as you listen to] the tape. After you have listened and read, take a piece of paper from the listening center and draw a picture of the Jigaree and write about [it].

"Mary and Jeff, please go to Mrs. Hamilton's table [Mrs. Hamilton is a parent volunteer]. She will be listening to you read, and you will write a new story with her. I will be working with Pat, Jill, John, Chris, Anne, and Sam.

"Don't forget to check the chart on the board so that you know when it is time to switch activities. Those of you working on the mural will not work with me until last today, so you have a large block of time to paint. Does anyone have any questions? Okay, Jigaree and mural people, please get started. Those people working with Mrs. Hamilton or me, let's move."

Clearly, all the language arts are being engaged and integrated in this "community." Journal-writing, creating a mural after reading, listening to a story, and participating in follow-up drawing and writing activities illustrate the way Kay Webb *integrates* all the language arts components—reading, writing, speaking, and listening—in her teaching. The journal-writing has everyone involved in the same activity at the same time. The children share their writing with their neighbors, and talking is certainly going on, but it doesn't interfere with the children's journal-writing. This interaction enhances the activity and provides a real audience for the children's reading and writing. Though not so obvious, Heather's attempt at spelling *balloon* illustrates her willingness to take risks while learning to write. After Kay gives directions, the children take part in a variety of activities.

Teaching in the Integrated Language Arts Classroom

Let's look more carefully at these three critical characteristics—integrated language arts, social interaction, and risk taking—that were present in Kay's classroom. As we saw in Chapter 1, the language arts are integrated both within themselves and with other subject areas; they are *tools* for exploring, thinking, and learning. When language arts are truly integrated, the curriculum components often flow together or overlap. While we may designate certain times of day as *reading and writing block*, *science*, or *social studies*, there is more going on during these times than the labels suggest.

Let's consider how the language arts are integrated within other areas: Kay Webb used the "Jigaree" activity to integrate *art* with her language arts. Art activities in fact often correlate with reading and writing lessons (Madura, 1995). Likewise, *music* can enrich children's experiences with books and writing. For example, traditional Chinese music would complement the Chinese "Little Red Riding Hood" story *Lon Po Po* (Young, 1989). We will help students apply different reading strategies when they use their science and social studies textbooks or explore informational trade books for research project materials. We can incorporate *writing* in a science lesson to help children learn how to observe, as when they learn to record daily observations of the seed growth.

Pappas, Kiefer, and Levstik (1995) describe integrated classrooms as places where teachers do not consider reading, writing, listening, and talking as separate subjects: "They are used together for learning worthwhile and interesting content, ideas, and information. Activities and projects span the curriculum so that there is enough time for children to engage in systematic and reflective inquiry on a range of topics. As children use language to learn, teachers collaborate, respond, facilitate, and support their efforts" (p. 1).

Social Interaction in the Diverse Classroom

We know that learning is a *social* phenomenon. Children need to talk with one another, *collaborating* in their activities and learning. Most of the activities described in this book require the students and the teacher to engage in thoughtful and meaningful discussion focused on important issues related to a topic or project. We can use the content of students' conversations as a gauge to determine whether a discussion is appropriate.

This social interaction occurs within a *composite classroom culture* (Au, 1993). In this type of classroom culture, our instruction is *culturally responsive*, and our students view themselves as competent and successful learners. Our instruction must respond appropriately and effectively within this composite classroom culture. As noted in Chapter 1, we will strive to be sensitive to *all* students' needs and all aspects of diversity. We'll explore this issue in much greater depth in Chapter 4.

"Risk Taking" in Learning

Children and teachers must be free to take risks, inevitably making mistakes while learning and teaching. This risk taking is part of how they test their hypotheses about the world and how it works. As teachers, we are learning right along with our students and taking risks in our own learning. We are also taking risks when we give the children in our class the freedom to make decisions about their learning. By giving them choices, we are showing them that we will not always be making decisions *for* them, directing and controlling their activities. We won't jump into this new orientation overnight; we will gradually move into it.

If students are allowed to keep turning in safe, correct, neat work, are they really growing as learners? Conversely, what happens if students — as they test hypotheses while attempting to solve a problem — are scorned and ridiculed by their peers? Neither of these situations will provide an environment where children will work to reach new levels of understanding. Likewise, neither of these situations will give us opportunities to examine carefully the children's "mistakes." When children take risks and make mistakes, then we teachers have the information necessary for providing appropriate and timely instruction.

Organizing the Physical Environment of the Integrated Classroom

Classroom organization and management go together. Because we need to accommodate a wide variety of activities, we'll need stable areas within the room where students know certain activities occur and materials are available. These centers should be distant from areas where most of our small-group lessons will be conducted and away from places in the room with a lot of traffic, like the space near the drinking fountain or pencil sharpener. The following are areas we definitely should have available:

◆ *Reading Corner*
The **Reading Corner** should have a comfortable "tucked away" feeling about it; an old sofa or pillows work wonderfully. For young children, using a bookcase where the covers of books are displayed is a good idea; young students often choose books for their cover illustrations. We'll discuss criteria for selecting your classroom books later on, but meanwhile keep in mind that a good rule of thumb is to have at least four times as many books as students.

◆ *Writing Center*
The **Writing Center** is a centralized location for writing materials and should include pencils and pens, white-out fluid, magic markers, crayons, scissors, a stapler and a staple remover, and plenty of paper of all sizes — both rough-draft quality and good quality. Many teachers have discovered the value and popularity of another writing center implement: the *DRAFT* or *WORK IN PROGRESS!* stamp. When stamped at the

Different grouping arrangements allow you and your students to make best use of teacher-guided learning and independent learning.

top of a composition, this message clearly indicates to students (and parents!) that a particular composition is not a finished product.

The Writing Center should also be a place where students' **writing folders**—an important feature of your writing program—are kept. Writing folders provide a means for you and your students to keep track of all those drafts and completed manuscripts they'll be generating. You may keep one or two folders for each student; I prefer to keep two folders, one for completed drafts (published and unpublished, filed oldest to newest) and one with current ongoing work. In the latter folder students can also keep lists of possible ideas or topics. You may also wish to include your assessment of the student's progress in this folder. For example, when you see a student correctly using quotation marks, you can write this observation on a small gummed label and later attach the label to the folder's inside cover or to an evaluation sheet for the student to see. Journals and learning logs may also be stored at this location.

◆ *Listening Center*
One or more audio cassette recorders should be available at the **Listening Center**. For young students, the stories we share as read-alouds may be recorded and listened to repeatedly with the book in hand. Older students also enjoy listening to well-recorded versions of stories—for

pleasure as well as for perhaps creating a performance model of a Readers Theatre script. For older students who are struggling readers, the Listening Center provides a place where they can listen to books being discussed in literature groups as well as informational trade books and textbooks that would be too challenging to read on their own.

◆ *Computer Center*

The **Computer Center** includes at least one computer and a printer. It supports all the language arts and the content areas. For example, in addition to playing a role in all aspects of the writing process, the computer can be used by *us* to take "dictations" from students (see Chapter 6).

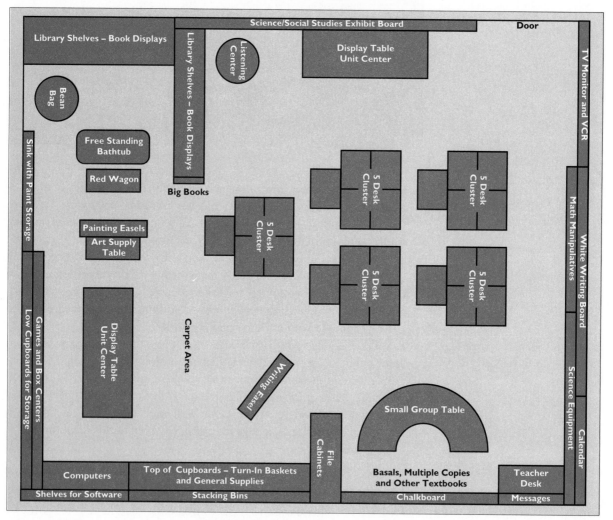

Figure 3.1   Two Classroom Diagrams

◆ *The Art Center*

Located close to the sink (if available), the Art Center includes construction paper, yarn, paint, collage materials, colored pencils, chalk, glue, and rulers.

Many different physical arrangements of classrooms are possible. Figure 3.1 shows two examples. In both of these rooms, the teacher can view

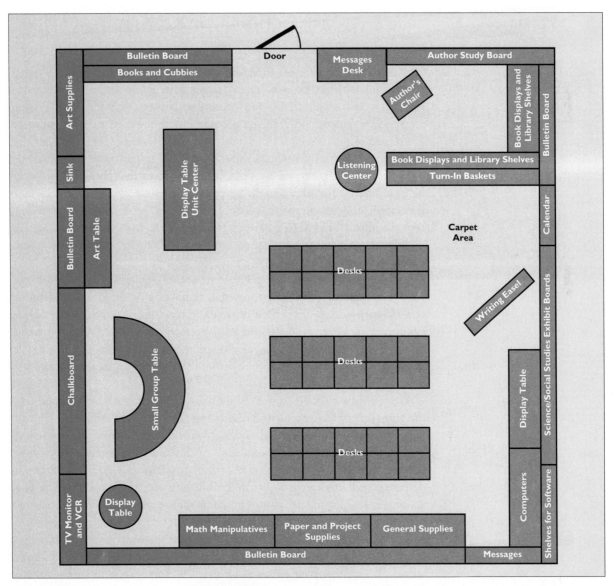

Figure 3.1 (*continued*)

the entire class during small-group or whole-class instruction. The high-traffic areas in the room are not near teaching-learning centers. The supplies are accessible, and students should have no difficulty observing the teacher during a lesson. Storage for long-term projects is solved by using the space under the tables.

Organizing and Managing the Social Environment

It is not the teacher's job to initiate all activities in a classroom. Rather, he or she has the responsibility to "create a structure and an environment conducive to learning, provide resources, present options, and demonstrate strategies to help children become independent learners" (Hubbard, 1986, p. 185).

While teachers and students should definitely collaborate on setting rules at the beginning of the school year, it is important that some rules already be established. Teachers should keep these rules to a minimum and share them with students on the first school day. For example, teachers should determine ahead of time regulations for bathroom use, sharpening pencils, and dismissal from the classroom. Students and teachers can then cooperatively create other rules.

In her multi-age primary classroom, for example, Sandy Madura presents very general guidelines phrased in terms of a "safe, kind, and productive" classroom. Students then discuss the specifics of establishing such an environment. When students are involved in formulating rules and provide input about the consequences for violating them, they have a genuine stake in constructing a collaborative environment that supports a community of learners.

We can solicit serious input from our students through either open class meetings or private writing and discussion. Teachers *and* students—not the teacher alone—should be responsible for managing classroom behavior. As the year moves along, discussions about rules and regulations may focus on revising rules that were established earlier. Teachers and students could participate in a discussion group to determine how the whole class will manage waiting in line for lunch, or how students will decide who plays on the soccer field. Teachers and students can also meet to make specific decisions about the interior classroom space. When problems arise in the classroom or in the school, classroom meetings should be called so that the class as a whole can jointly arrive at a resolution. The key is to have a few rules in place to begin and then to add or revise rules with all students participating fully.

Managing the Integrated Classroom Environment

Effective teachers display **continuity** and **momentum** in their teaching. They have devised and prepared engagements with students that are paced appropriately and for which they give clear directions. Because of these efforts, students realize that the classroom is truly a learning community.

The best way to keep our classrooms creative is to establish consistent and predictable routines—routines that children can internalize so that they can sustain their focus and feel secure with choices they make. Although a class may enjoy breaks from the routine, continual disruptions interfere with purposeful learning. For example, an unexpected learning opportunity such as a hot air balloon's landing in the playground should definitely not be missed. On the other hand, if we always appear "spontaneous" and never have an underlying and predictable structure for what we do, our students will frequently be left to wonder, what next? When we provide the necessary structure, we "open choices to [our] students limited only by the students' experiences and imagination, which they constantly work to expand" (Hubbard, 1986, p. 180).

Home and Community Involvement

Another way to keep a complex classroom running smoothly is to bring in other adults. Many teachers have solicited help from parents, either through direct participation in the classroom or indirectly through involvement at home. Whether or not they volunteer in the classroom, parents need to be involved with the classroom's academic concerns from the first day of school. One way to facilitate this involvement is to develop a short booklet that addresses the parents' immediate concerns. This booklet may include a letter to parents describing a typical day, a school calendar, a list of necessary supplies, a sample report card, or an invitation to the first parents' meeting.

Parents' Meeting

It is important to have this **parents' meeting** early in the year. During this meeting, we discuss our expectations, both academic and behavioral. We discuss the type of reading and writing that will be going on in the classroom—perhaps sharing examples of children's writing from the previous year (or from this book if it's your first year) so that parents can see how writing will develop over the year.

An excellent strategy at this first meeting is to have parents perform many of the activities that their children accomplish during a school day. For instance, give each parent a schedule of activities and a starting place for rotation among activities. Here are some possibilities:

◆ Read a Big Book (see Chapter 6).

◆ Read a child's published story.

◆ Write a letter to his or her child and place it in the child's writing folder.

◆ Look at books about frogs and toads and write down two facts or questions to leave in the child's folder.

◆ Participate in a word-study activity (see Chapter 8). Sort picture cards according to two categories: *school things* and *home things*. Then write ten words related to school on word cards and sort them. (Provide an example.)

◆ Calculate some math on the computer.

◆ Add and subtract with the Unifix cubes.

◆ Make a pattern with the pattern blocks.

◆ Make a prediction and graph that prediction. For example, how long will it take a candle to burn out?

◆ Enjoy a treat.

After participating in these activities, the parents will better understand their child's learning. Many of them will now have had their first experience in learning without completing a worksheet or workbook page. Figure 3.2 illustrates a form that was distributed to parents during a back-to-school parents' night. Parents want to participate in their children's education but often are not sure what they should do. Together with other information we've shared at this parents' night, a form similar to the one in Figure 3.2 communicates clearly that parents definitely are a welcome part of their children's education.

Keeping Parents Informed and Involved

Once the school year is underway, another way of involving parents is to send them student gifts periodically as well as booklets that include samples of all the students' work. Often, a thematic unit will provide direction for the form of a booklet.

For example, during a thematic unit on "vehicles," students might interview their parents about when they learned to drive. These interviews can be used as the basis for stories about learning to drive. When these stories

```
Our classroom needs your support. If you are interested in volunteering
extra time for our class, please complete and return this form.


NAME_____

CHILD'S NAME_____


I am interested in the following:

_____ one hour per week working with children in the classroom

_____ room parent (help with parties and special events)

_____ baking for parties

_____ special projects (art, cooking)

_____ field trip chaperone

_____ working at home making and compiling books

_____ I need more information before I volunteer. Please call

             me at this number _____.


Thank you,
```

Figure 3.2   **Parent Volunteer Sheet**

SOURCE: Diane Barone. Used with permission.

reach the publishing stage, each story is photocopied. These photocopies can then be collated so that every parent receives a booklet that includes one story from each child in the class. The same procedure can be used for other stories or poems written about a particular theme. The children can create a newspaper that reports what is happening in their class or compile a calendar with several child-created stories for each month as a holiday gift for parents.

Another way to include parents in the academic curriculum is to foster their participation in literature-response journals (see Chapter 6). When parents read the same book that their child is reading, they can 1) respond to their own reading; 2) respond to their child's responses; 3) use their responses to write comments to the teacher or to ask questions about the book.

Parents can be involved in *word-study* activities (see Chapter 8). If you're exploring words related to "vehicles" in your thematic unit, for homework the students might ask their parents to help them jot down five words that correspond to the topic. The following day the children could work with you or in small groups to categorize the words that they brought from home. Parents and children have fun with this activity. Searching for words is an easy way for parents to help with homework.

A final suggestion for keeping parents involved comes from Kathy Perrone. Kathy teaches the academically talented students in her school. She asks one child from each student group to write a note to parents about what the group has done in class that week. These notes are then photocopied and distributed to the parents. A sample from Perrone's class is displayed in Figure 3.3.

These methods, along with others that you can create, will keep parents aware of exactly what is happening in class.

Working with Parent Volunteers

Although including **parents as volunteers** *in* the classroom requires some additional planning on our part, this planning need not be very complex. Initially, we can schedule a meeting for all our class-parent volunteers. The meeting agenda should include

1. greeting (express appreciation for their volunteering),

2. discussing what parents will be doing with students,

3. establishing a place where parents will be working with students,

4. discussing the rules and routines of the classroom (these parent volunteers will be managing a child or a small group of students, so they will need to know your behavior expectations), and

5. establishing a schedule so parents know when to arrive at school (provide a list of other volunteers and their phone numbers so that when a parent can't come, he or she can call a substitute).

At the beginning of the year, your parent helpers could listen to the students read or read to the children. Eventually, the activities conducted by parents can be expanded. For example, parent volunteers can take individual dictations from students and participate in word-study activities. The parents are particularly helpful in providing additional small-group time for individual students. Parent volunteers also make overall classroom management easier because they are directing the teaching and learning of several students. Additional benefits of having parent volunteers are the support you will gain as a teacher and the clearer understanding parents will gain of the complex requirements for teaching and managing many children.

Some parents won't be able to volunteer in school, perhaps because of young children at home or job commitments. These parents might still be willing to prepare materials at home for the classroom. Perhaps these

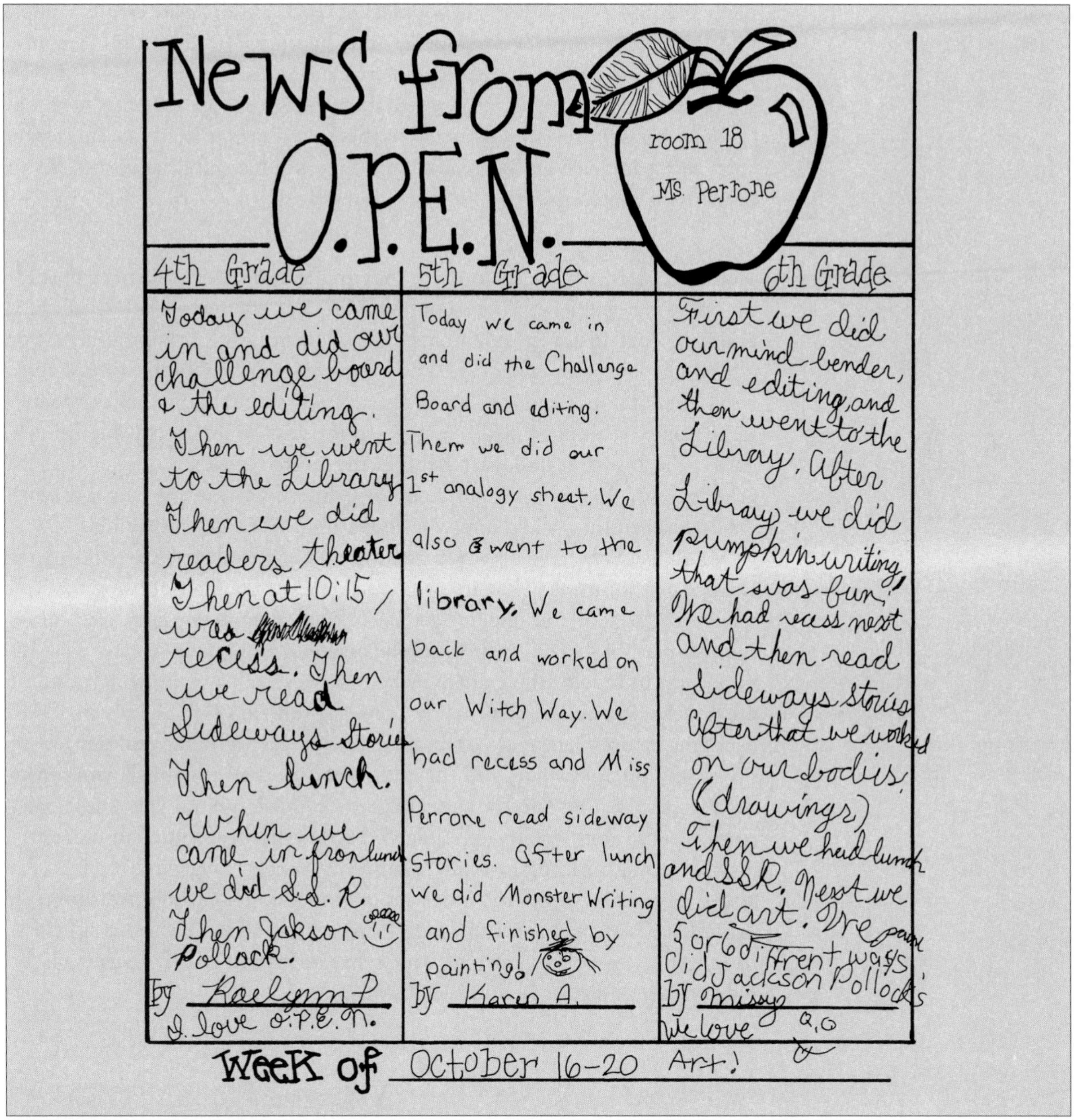

News from O.P.E.N.

room 18
Ms. Perrone

4th Grade

Today we came in and did our challenge board & the editing. Then we went to the Library. Then we did readers theater. Then at 10:15 / was ~~recess~~ recess. Then we read Sideways Stories. Then lunch. When we came in from lunch we did S.S.R. Then Jackson Pollock.

by Raelynn P.
I love O.P.E.N.

5th Grade

Today we came in and did the Challenge Board and editing. Them we did our 1st analogy sheet. We also went to the library. We came back and worked on our Witch Way. We had recess and Miss Perrone read sideway stories. After lunch we did Monster Writing and finished by painting!

by Karen A.

6th Grade

First we did our mind bender, and editing, and then went to the Library. After Library we did pumpkin writing that was fun. We had recess next and then read Sideways Stories. After that we worked on our bodies. (drawings) Then we had lunch and SSR. Next we did art. We painted 5 or 6 different ways. Did Jackson Pollocks

by Missy
We love A.O.

Week of October 16–20

Art!

Figure 3.3   **News to Parents about Class Activities**

SOURCE: Kathy Perrone, Bakersfield, CA. Used with permission.

parents could assemble small booklets so each child could create a book after hearing a story. For example, after hearing *The Bus Ride* (Wagner, 1976), a group of first-graders could create their own individual bus books if a parent could first cut and prepare thirty bus-shaped booklets. On an occasional basis, parents enjoy creating these materials, but if you enlist parents' help with such an idea, make sure they will have at least two weeks to prepare the materials.

Other Helpers

Not only parents but also foster grandparents and older students can serve as classroom helpers. Many communities already have established programs so that foster grandparents can volunteer in the classroom. Senior citizen centers often coordinate these programs. The senior citizens' roles would be similar to those of the parents. These more mature helpers particularly enjoy reading and discussing stories with children. In one kindergarten the foster grandfather became the primary resource for a unit on grandparents. It was a delight to observe his very serious discussions with children when they asked him what it was like when he was a child.

Many teachers have also had great success with using older students as classroom volunteers. The older students' teacher could establish a rotating schedule so that all the students get a chance to help in a primary classroom. A small pool of student helpers can be created from several classrooms. It's important to involve the students who always seem to be in trouble and/or are not the best academic achievers; these "problem" kids usually turn into excellent tutors. These older students know exactly what children do to drive other people crazy, and they don't put up with these behaviors from children they tutor. The younger children establish a bond with these older students, and both groups of students become friends. Often an older student is seen protecting a younger student on the playground or bus. An added advantage is that the older child, who so often is close to trouble in his or her own classroom, becomes a surrogate teacher in the second classroom. This sense of responsibility often has long-term positive effects on the older student's academic and social skills.

Integrating Language Arts: How to Organize and Manage the Academic Environment

Goal Setting

How do teachers know what to teach, how to teach, and when to teach a particular lesson? These are the questions that shape our classroom curriculum and organization.

School districts develop **curriculum guides** in all subject areas and for all grade levels. These guides reflect the state's requirements, the community's concerns, and the teachers' and principals' interests. These curriculum guides specify what the district expects students to learn and what attitudes and habits the students are expected to acquire within each grade level or levels. The curriculum guides are a starting point for establishing what we will be teaching. Next, we can check the **teacher's editions** of the subject matter programs that will be used at our grade level. Note the scope and sequence charts that are presented there. These charts indicate which concepts and skills are to be addressed. We should compare the goals, skills, and concepts in these charts to our district's guidelines. If the school district expects more teaching of skills or of specific concepts, then we may need to supplement our materials.

During the first year of teaching, many teachers rely more heavily on the material and order of presentation in the programs and textbooks. That's okay. Even experienced teachers who rely very little on these resources often plan around the curriculum guides and the scope and sequence charts.

At the beginning of the year, after our classroom has been arranged, we will want to spend several days looking over programs, textbooks, and guides and making a very brief yearly plan; an outline often works best. We will establish what content will be taught in each subject area and a possible teaching sequence. Naturally, this plan will be modified because of the children we teach and unanticipated scheduling changes. We should consider the length of the school year:

◆ Will we be able to fit in all the topics we want to address?

◆ If not, which content areas are most important and must be scheduled?

◆ Which content areas can be integrated with others, and when?

As we'll see, this type of thinking will also guide us in our planning of thematic interludes. Figure 3.4 shows how a third-grade teacher organized her year around monthly themes and author studies.

Once we've made a tentative yearly plan, we'll want to take a narrower focus, perhaps on the first month of school. What do we hope to accomplish academically during this month? What concepts, skills, and content will we introduce to students during this month? Remember, we can check the curriculum guidelines and teacher's editions when we make these decisions.

Scheduling

After working out our yearly and monthly plans, we'll want to focus on one week at a time, then on the days within that week. What do we want to accomplish by Friday afternoon? What materials need to be prepared? How

	Sept.	Oct.	Nov./Dec.	Jan.	Feb.	March	April	May/June
Writing	Beginning Journals Selected Topics (Prewriting)	Lead Sentences Capitals, Periods Giving Positive Response	Word Choices Capitals Other than Beginning of Sentence Plurals	Using Feedback to Improve Story Subj./Predicate Revising	How Stories Begin Sources of Story Collecting Back to Response Groups	Oral Story Telling Mapping a Story for Sharing	Use of Punctuation Dialogue Subj./Verb Agreement Editing	Pulling All Together Lead Sentences Paragraphing etc.
Reading	Beginning/Middle/End Family Stories & Nonfiction Family Books—Cultural	Setting/Repetition Native American Stories	Plot—Biography Journey Stories Map Books Streets Atlas	Charac-terization European Folktales Fact Books on Castles	Point of View Asian Folktales Body/Health Books	Info Text vs. Story African Folktales Zoo Books	Theme Environ-mental Awareness Stories Dino Books	Style Space Stories Space-Fact Books
Author Study	Vera Williams Cynthia Rylant	Paul Goble Jane Yolen	Eric Carle Ezra Jack Keats	Paul Galdone James Marshall	Ed Young Allen Say	Verna Aardema Leo & Diane Dillon	Bill Peet Brian Wildsmith	Joanna Cole Seymour Simon
Art	Watercolor Pencil-Drawing Still Life	Watercolor Landscape	Collage Mixed Media	Crayon Black Line Drawing	Watercolor Oil Pastels	Mosaic Pottery	Mural Tempra	Cartoon vs. Photography
Science	Animal Families	Living with Animals	Seasonal Changes	Cells Germs Disease	Body Systems	Soils Habitat Regions	Rocks and Minerals Fossils	Solar System Solid/Liquid/Gas Space Travel
Social Studies	Family	Community North American Continent	Mapping	Europe Shelters Different Kinds of Homes	Asia Healthy Eating First Aid	Africa Animal—Pop-up Books Reports Human Interaction	Man's Use of Rocks & Minerals Dinosaur Posters	Transpor-tation
Math	Addition Sorting Classifying	Subtraction Place Value	Measuring Advanced Add. and Sub.	Geometry Multiplication	Volume Area Perimeter Graphing	Basic Functions $+/-/\times$ Mixed Applications Word Problems	Data Collection Multistep Word Problems Division	Symmetry Congruency Fractions

Figure 3.4   Overview Plan for the Year

will we schedule the day? This is the planning that is most often recorded in the teacher's plan book. As we begin to work in the plan book, the schedule for each day should be considered. List the times when school begins and ends. Block out recess and lunchtime. Check each day so that special classes are included. For instance, our class might be scheduled to use the library only on Thursday at 2:00. Here is an example of this type of schedule for a second-grade class:

Regular	
9:00–9:20	Children arrive
	Journal writing
	Record keeping
	Group discussion
9:25–10:15	Writing Workshop
10:15–10:30	Recess
10:35–12:00	Reading Workshop/Literature discussion groups/Guided reading
12:00–12:45	Lunch and recess
12:50–1:15	Teacher Read-Aloud/Sustained silent reading
1:15–2:15	Math
2:15–3:00	Science, social studies, and physical education
Special	
Monday	2:30–3:00 Library
Tuesday	9:45–10:15 Music
Friday	10:35–11:15 Art
	1:15–1:45 Music

This type of schedule can accommodate our theme explorations (see below). Time blocks for reading, writing, and the subject areas allow for our activities and projects. Moreover, areas such as art and creative dramatics can be part of the morning times as they support the reading and writing in which students are engaged.

The Lesson Plan Book

This general schedule should be recorded in the **lesson plan book**. Any special classes which students will attend should also be marked, and certainly any assemblies or unusual programs should be indicated. During the first year, the number of boxes in the plan book will probably not be sufficient. We often need to attach extra sheets with more carefully structured plans.

Another strategy is to have two books: one for reading and writing activities, and a second to include plans for other subject areas. Likewise, a teacher could use one book for morning plans and another for afternoon plans.

Figure 3.5 shows the first week of school in a first-grade teacher's plan

	9:00	9:20	10:35	12:50	1:15	2:15
MONDAY	journal record keeping calendar sharing	WRITING draw pictures of themselves illustrate whole-page dictated stories about themselves	READING teach Sam, Sam poem DLTA Hairy Bear create Big Book	SSR Bear book poem-share after SSR	MATH graph shoes explain tubs unifix cubes pattern blocks cubes kids at these tubs	kids do cover of booklet with pictures & stories about themselves 2:30 library
TUESDAY	journal record keeping calendar sharing	Share some of published stories from previous year brainstorm possible topics for writing 9:45 - 10:15	review Sam, Sam reread Hairy Bear concept sort toys, clothing music	SSR Bear book poem	people pattern explain tubs jewels geoboards junk boxes kids at any one of 6 tubs	science curly hair straight hair microscopes (get at media center)
WEDNESDAY	journal record keeping calendar sharing	Discuss writing folders - how kids will store folders begin writing	1) evaluate concept of word 2) tape of Hairy Bear 3) drawings of Hairy Bear	SSR Bear book poem	graph clothing explain tubs stamps macaroni 2/3 at tubs 1 group patterning	social studies Who are the people in our school? list & discuss roles
THURSDAY	journal record keeping calendar sharing	have students share some of their writing - continue writing	1) spelling inventory 2) cut pictures from magazines school things home things 3) listening center letter center	SSR Bear book poem	graph birthdays 2/3 at tubs 1 group patterning rotate	p e working with partner mirrors - kids take turns being mirror
FRIDAY	journal record keeping calendar sharing	have students share some of their writing - continue writing close with discussion	1) Brown Bear 2) find brown things in magazines cut - paste 3) listen to Brown Bear - draw pictures	SSR Bear book poem	graph bedtime 2/3 at tubs 1 group patterning rotate 1:15 - 1:45 music	art children with partners They draw their partner.

Figure 3.5   Plan Book

SOURCE: Diane Barone. Used with permission.

book. These plans are relatively abbreviated. The teacher who used them had more extensive lesson details on supplementary sheets. When planning, we should budget "transition time"—time lost between subjects and before and after recess. The children will make these transitions more slowly during the first month of school, and we will often need to remind them how to accomplish these transitions more quickly. If we take time at the beginning of the year to establish carefully the routines associated with transition times, the children will become more efficient, and fewer problems should occur as the year progresses.

A brief aside is in order here. During the first few weeks of school, we may feel we aren't really "teaching" very much. Don't worry. This first month is a time to establish the procedures; if we do a good job at this point, the children will be able to focus on teaching and learning for the remaining months of school.

Now let's think about "fine tuning" our scheduling. Because we are *integrating* the language arts throughout most of our instruction, we will need large blocks of time. For instance, our students might spend five minutes getting settled into writing. Then, they will reread what they wrote the previous day. After this reading, they might start writing, stop, reread, and write. This process will most likely be repeated several times. Midway through this process, a student might need to confer with a friend about a specific part of his or her composition. Such activities take time. If only thirty minutes had been allocated, some children might not have even started writing.

The plan book illustrated in Figure 3.5 demonstrates the larger blocks of time that have been allocated for more integrated instruction in a first-grade class. Separate blocks of time are earmarked for writing and reading during this first week of school, but it is easy to visualize how these time blocks will eventually merge or overlap. For the first week of school, the teacher has planned a small integrated unit that focuses on getting acquainted and building a classroom community:

- On *Monday* each student will dictate a story about himself or herself and draw a picture to accompany it. Later in the day, during math, the children will build a bar graph detailing the shoes that they are wearing. Finally, the children will design a cover for their own books about themselves. The first entries in these books will be their individual dictations and self-portraits.

- On *Tuesday* the children will investigate the differences between curly and straight hair. As part of the science lesson, the children will study their own hair and add these discoveries to their books.

- On *Wednesday*, *Thursday*, and *Friday*, other discoveries about self occur during math lessons. The children will be graphing clothing, birthdays, and bedtimes. Physical education is brought into the unit by having the children take turns being a mirror for each other. As one child moves, a second child tries to mirror the movement of the first. Art is included as a parallel to the mirror activity. Each child observes a partner and then draws his or her portrait. While the teacher has begun to integrate instruction of different subject areas, other blocks of time are reserved for more discrete activities. Instructional blocks in math and reading include assessment and procedural issues. That is, the teacher uses many of the initial subject-related instructional sessions to assess literacy (see Chapter 11) and math development informally and to establish procedures for selecting and cleaning up materials.

This blend of integrated and more discrete subject matter instruction often occurs in classrooms, particularly at the beginning and end of the school year.

Let's consider this weekly plan a second time with a new perspective, focusing now on the *time allocation* for reading. An hour and a half has been allocated for reading. The teacher has divided her class into three groups during this block. Sometimes these groups will bring together students of the same ability level, and other times students of varying abilities. In this case, the students are grouped according to varying abilities in math and similar abilities in reading. During reading, one group will be doing a Guided Listening-Thinking Activity (GLTA) for the book *Hairy Bear* (Cowley, 1980), another group will be learning the poem "Sam, Sam, the Baker Man," to grasp the concept of word assessment (see Chapter 8); and a third group will be creating a Big Book based on *Hairy Bear*. At the end of a designated period, the students will rotate so that they can participate in all of the activities:

	Group 1	Group 2	Group 3
10:35–11:00	Teacher: Guided Listening-Thinking Activity	Learn "Sam, Sam, the Baker Man" poem	Create "Hairy Bear" Big Book
11:00–11:25	Create "Hairy Bear" Big Book	Teacher: Guided Listening-Thinking Activity	Learn "Sam, Sam, the Baker Man" poem
11:25–11:50	Learn "Sam, Sam, the Baker Man" poem	Create "Hairy Bear" Big Book	Teacher: Guided Listening-Thinking Activity

However we choose to organize the day, children need extended periods of time to work on projects that are a part of integrated instruction and the themes that we will be exploring throughout the year. In addition, they need to know that writing or reading time, for instance, will recur on a regular basis so that they can plan their activities. That means that these time blocks should be predictable in their time slots within the day and their frequency during the week.

Grouping

In each classroom there will generally be a variety of groups to facilitate teaching: **whole-group**, **small-group**, and **individual instruction**. For some guided instruction, children of similar abilities should be brought together. Before organizing students into groups, we should review each learning situation to determine which type of organization is most appropriate. With regard to *guided* instruction, students of similar needs should work together part of the day for two major reasons. First, we will be better able to offer developmentally appropriate instruction. Second, we can interact more effectively with a smaller number of students than with a whole class.

The first-grade teacher described above organized her students into several grouping patterns. Her plan book shows that she has considered a number of grouping configurations for her students. For example, during physical education the children are paired off, and during silent sustained reading and Writing Workshops the whole class is working together. How were these groupings determined by the teacher? What rationales were used to form groups?

Purposes of Grouping

As teachers, we will want to consider each learning episode and determine the optimal form of organization. Contemplating the learning needs of the approximately twenty to thirty students in our class, we will realize that it's not reasonable to teach exclusively to the whole class all the time. In particular, after assessing the children for competencies in reading and math, we will see the need for meeting with smaller groups of children who have similar needs.

Certainly, teachers do not want to have *all* of their groupings organized on the basis of ability—as was often done in the past—but as the following example demonstrates, this type of grouping makes sense for certain instruction.

After assessing her students' word knowledge through an informal inventory (see Chapter 11), the teacher realized that some children were representing words with only initial consonants (*b* for the word *bed*), others were including short vowels ("*bad*" for *bed*), and a few children were using silent

Throughout the school day, you will make use of a variety of groups— for example, to give students an opportunity to pursue special interests in greater depth.

letters to spell long vowels (*"trane"* for *train*). (See Chapters 6 and 8 for an explanation of these spellings.) Based on this information, the teacher formed *word-study* groups. One group investigated initial consonants, one group studied short-vowel patterns, and a third group considered long-vowel patterns. *Had* the teacher attempted to conduct long-vowel word-study lessons with the whole class, however, the group using initial consonants to represent words would not have been able to participate, since this material would have been at a frustrational level for those children, therefore beyond their understanding.

Besides grouping students on the basis of similar needs, teachers often use smaller groups when teaching material that requires direct student involvement. When children are conducting a science experiment, the teacher can organize groups of three or four students to work together. These smaller groups allow each child an opportunity to participate in the investigation and discuss the process and results. Often informal small groups naturally evolve during reading and writing time. Children seek out other children who are willing to listen as they read a passage from a book or who will provide a critical ear to a portion of a story they have just written.

During certain instructional portions of the day, the teacher uses different types of groupings. The "Writing Workshop" is an example of such arranging. The beginning minilesson in the Writing Workshop usually includes *all of the students*. When students write, they are usually working individually but may also—depending on the activity—work with a *partner* or a *small group*. The teacher may also assemble a group of students who need help with a specific skill such as the use of quotation marks. In addition, individual students may request the teacher's assistance through *conferences* on topics like the content of a story.

Forming Groups

Teachers generally form groups based on a teaching or learning objective. So far I've focused primarily on groups resulting from assessment of students' abilities in certain subject areas. However, there are many situations in the classroom that lend themselves to other grouping arrangements.

Special Interest Groups   Many groups are formed on the basis of special interests. For example:

◆ Raphael (1995) and Eeds and Wells (1989) describe *literature study groups* or *book clubs* in which students read the same book independently and come together on a daily basis for discussions (see Chapter 6). Each literature study group stays together until members finish reading and discussing the book.

◆ Several students decide that they want to write a classroom newspaper. The students write together until this project is complete and ready to distribute to the class.

◆ Another group of students plan a bulletin board display of information that they discover about dinosaurs.

As is apparent, the types of **special interest groups** that might be formed are endless.

Cooperative Groups   Another way of looking at groups is to focus on the interaction or *discourse* patterns—the social dynamics—that occur within the groups. **Cooperative groups** are characterized by positive goal interdependence as well as individual accountability. *Positive goal interdependence* requires children to work together to achieve a goal. In cooperative groups *every* child must participate in order for the group to be rewarded, and each child is *held accountable* for his or her unique contribution.

For example, teams can be formed to explore and study material, and each student can have a specific topic to research and report back to the group. When groups form, each student has a responsibility for facilitating the process of working together. One student might be a reader, another the discussion leader, a third the recorder, and a fourth the checker to ensure that all participants are fulfilling their roles. All group members would be assigned the same grade for the completed task.

In cooperative groups, students gain a more thorough understanding of the subject matter through their attempts at teaching or explaining material to other students. In addition, students are more positive about school, curriculum, and teachers. Most important, students are supportive of each other regardless of differences in abilities, challenging physical conditions, or ethnic backgrounds (Stevens, 1994).

Reading and Writing Workshops in the Integrated Language Arts Classroom

Because Reading and Writing Workshops are such integral parts of our daily routines, we'll take a brief look at them here.

The Reading Workshop

Nancie Atwell (1986) selected the term **Reading Workshop** to describe the environment for *authentic* reading—a time when each student reads and responds in some fashion to a book of his or her own choosing. Reading Workshop often begins with a short mini-lesson on a reading strategy or an element of literature. The students then read, and afterward there is a sharing time when students talk about their responses to their reading.

The Writing Workshop

Writing Workshop follows a similar procedure. We begin with a mini-lesson which can focus on the process of writing or a specific piece of writing. Our minilessons are based on needs that have emerged in the students' writing. For example, we can model a strategy for brainstorming ideas, making a cluster or list, and keeping the ideas in a writing folder. We can demonstrate how to get started with our writing and how to apply different conventions of writing. Students then write. During this writing time, we can help specific students as well as have individual and group conferences (more on this later). Toward the end of the workshop time, students can come together to share their writing and ideas.

Exploring Themes in the Integrated Classroom

Much of our teaching of concepts, skills, and strategies can occur within the context of **thematic units**. As we'll explore in depth, themes are powerful ways to integrate students' learning. While authorities have different labels for different types of themes (Walmsley, 1994), I think it's helpful to think in general of two broad categories of theme explorations: those that are *literature-based* and those that are *integrated* with other areas of the elementary curriculum (Lipson, Valencia, Wixson, & Peters, 1993; Templeton, 1995). The *literature-based themes* have a narrower focus while *integrated themes* are broader in focus. In the context of exploring literature, literature-based thematic units engage students in applying their developing language arts knowledge and strategies; other curricular areas are not directly included. Cross-curricular thematic units *do* include most or all of the curricular areas, and the theme often runs throughout the day.

The two thematic explorations in this text illustrate the development and structure of two thematic units. The first is an example of a *literature-based* theme (p. 129) and the second of an *integrated* theme (p. 384). We'll explore the planning and implementation of thematic units quite extensively in Chapter 10.

At the beginning of the school year, we can have a simple theme such as "Who Are We?" that helps students become comfortable with our learning environment and with each other. One of the bulletin boards might have all of the students' names on it. On another board, the children could list facts about themselves, such as number of brothers and sisters, color of eyes, distance from home to school, or bringing hot or cold lunch. Throughout the year, our *themes* help us plan art, music, and physical education activities. This first week, for example, in art we can group our students in pairs and have them create portraits of each other.

Earlier in this chapter, I discussed using the district guides and teacher's editions to plan a curriculum. I also suggested selecting a *theme* that incorporated art and music. As novice teachers gain confidence and experience, they experiment with more involved thematic units or theme studies (see also Chapter 10).

Children's literature is usually a central element in the development of a theme unit. Moss (1984, 1990) has described several units of study that can be developed from children's literature. Her units center on topics like toy animals, pig tales, or the night. She recommends books and related writing activities for large groups and small-group story sessions. A number of other authorities have developed resources that are excellent guides for planning and implementing thematic units, and we will draw upon their expertise in Chapter 10 (for example, Pappas, Kiefer, & Levstik, 1995; Walmsley, 1994; Weaver, Chaston, & Peterson, 1993).

Literature can provide a beginning place for teachers to organize subject matter within a thematic unit. For example, Peter Spier's book *People* (1980) provides the impetus for a second-grade teacher to create a large theme study of the similarities and differences among people. The curriculum that had been mandated by the school district required second-graders to study graphing in math and health in science, as well as to consider character analysis in literature and develop respect for different cultures in social studies. This teacher decided to combine all of these requirements under the large theme of "People—How Are We Alike and Different?"

As the "core" text, therefore, *People* was selected. This book looks at all of the world's people. Spier carefully represents the similarities and differences among people. Each page of his book is filled with comparisons and contrasts of physical and social characteristics. On one page, he illustrates how fashions differ from country to country; on another, he shows people's need to write and all the different methods of representing words.

◆ The teacher began this unit by having children build bar graphs based on many of the characteristics described in the book.

◆ Then the teacher asked parents and students to supply lists of their favorite foods, vacation spots, countries of origin, and so on. This information was used to form additional graphs.

◆ The children then began to investigate themselves. They studied the foods that they usually ate and compared these to the foods eaten by children living in other places. The students studied their own and their classmates' hair type, eye color, and skin color.

◆ During reading and writing, the children investigated the characters in stories that they were reading. The children then developed charts that compared the physical and personality traits of the characters in various stories.

◆ The teacher and the students invited guests to school to share some of the unique aspects of their particular cultures.

◆ The students then researched their own families to discover personal traditions.

This unit could also be shifted slightly to consider family members and include a generational theme. For instance, students could investigate the roles of babies and grandparents in stories. Clearly, with a little brainstorming, a theme unit can be created that provides more in-depth coverage of a topic while it simultaneously fulfills the curricular requirements of a district.

Once we've decided which curriculum elements can be combined into one unit, we should visit the library in order to check out a large quantity and variety of books related to the topic. These books should be at various reading levels, so that all of the children in our class can enjoy them. After selecting the books and referring to various teacher's resource books, we can plan the activities that will occur during the unit. A teacher planning sheet for a fairy-tale unit is provided in Figure 3.6. The teacher used this sheet to ensure that all areas of the curriculum were included.

Many teachers find the integration of diverse subject matter a complex task. They can be overwhelmed by the planning. However, this task can be simplified if we rely on curriculum guides and grade-level textbooks and develop a form similar to the one presented. Doing these things will assure us

The Jolly Postman - Ahlbergs
  letters to characters
Dialogue journals
  children will write in notebooks
  as they read fairy tales
Write a fairy tale
Word Study
  collect size words (giant,huge)
  collect "wee" words (sweet,sweep)
  collect character words (elf,goblin)
	Fairy-tale museum
	  collections of real objects that
	  accompany fairy tales
	Fairy-tale homes
	Murals of fairy tales
	Fairy-tale quilt
	  quilt blocks representing
	  original fairy tales
	Bread-dough figures
	ABC book of fairy tales

WRITING	**ART**

Storyteller
  shares tradition of fairy tale
Grandparents, parents, teachers,
  principal share favorite fairy tale
Fairy-tale party
  dress as character
  food from stories
  dramatize stories
Mark on world map where fairy tales
  originate
	Cooking
	  foods from fairy tales
	Cooking transformations
	  (bread, Jello)
	Use magnifying glass (small to big)
	Plant bean seeds

SOCIAL STUDIES	**SCIENCE**

Surveys to discover
  favorite fairy-tale character
  scariest fairy-tale character
  most disliked fairy-tale character
Measurement--capacity
  fairy cupfuls to giant-sized
  container
Working with threes
	Tape-recorded noises made by big and
	  small creatures
	Listen to
	  The Witch's Sabbath - Berlioz
	  The Peer Gynt Suite - Grieg
	Creative movement to music
	  selections and to an entire fairy
	  tale

MATH	**PE & MUSIC**

Figure 3.6   Teacher Planning Sheet

SOURCE: Diane Barone. Used with permission. Some of the ideas adapted from *The WEB: Wonderfully Exciting Books.* The Ohio State University, Columbus, OH.

Developing thematic units is simpler if teachers plan together. The brainstorming activities centered on books and activities are richer when several people are participating. Same-grade-level teachers often work in teams to develop these units and then share them. In this way the amount of background research is shared by all of the teachers. When a group of teachers gathers to participate in this brainstorming activity, they should be free to include any idea. Sometimes the best thematic units develop around ideas that seemed very strange at first. For example, the idea of exploring "size" words from fairy tales and comparing stories with magic items began this way. There are many resource books that can help with planning and implementing theme units. Use them! Here are some titles:

Gamberg, R., Kwak, W., Hutchings, R., & Altheim, J. (1988). *Learning and loving it.* Portsmouth, NH: Heinemann.

Roser, N., & Martinez, B. (Eds.). (1995). *Book talk and beyond: Children and teachers respond to literature.* Newark, DE: International Reading Association.

Moss, J. (1984). *Focus units in literature.* Urbana, IL: National Council of Teachers of English.

Pappas, C., Kiefer, B., & Levstik, L. (1995). *An integrated language perspective in the elementary school* (2nd ed.). New York: Longman.

Templeton, S. (1995). *Children's Literacy: Contexts for meaningful learning.* Boston: Houghton Mifflin.

Walmsley, S. (1994). *Children exploring their world: theme teaching in elementary school.* Portsmouth, NH: Heinemann.

that we'll be teaching the important aspects of the curriculum. These organizing strategies will help us focus and plan a thematic unit more easily.

The Role of Assessment

Assessment is an *ongoing* process that helps teachers determine their students' specific abilities and characteristics. Teachers use information from these informal assessments at the beginning of the year to group children for some kinds of instruction. The plan book in Figure 3.5, for example, shows that this teacher would be evaluating her students for *concept of word in print* (see Chapter 5) by using a simple poem and for *word knowledge* as demonstrated through each child's performance on a spelling inventory.

Teachers can also supplement their initial observations and assessments of students with information included in the students' cumulative folders. These folders follow children as they move through a school. Many teachers are reluctant to read these folders before students arrive at school because they don't want to be biased about children before meeting them. Teachers know that students act differently in various environments. A child who was disruptive in a third-grade setting might never exhibit this behavior in the fourth grade. Although we may not want to read every folder diligently before school begins, we should scan the folders to determine if a child has a health problem. For example, we'll want to know if a child is allergic to a particular food or insect or is asthmatic.

Remember that groups are flexible and many of our students will be rusty after that long summer vacation, so we shouldn't worry about not placing them accurately. Children can easily be moved from one group to another, and these movements should happen routinely during the year. These initial groupings help us establish the organization that we'll maintain during the school year. The advantage of screening so early is that children can quickly be brought into the organizational patterns that the teacher has set up for the class, such as a rotation schedule during reading and math.

Teachers use informal observation to determine characteristics of children beyond academic ability. When we form heterogeneous groups, we need to consider characteristics such as shyness, impulsiveness, and the ability to complete tasks. These groups should include a variety of students so that children will derive maximum benefits from working together.

Periodically throughout the year, we will revise our assessments and include other informal measures so that our evaluations of students are current. In conjunction with these evaluations, we will update information about children through routine daily observation.

It's time to pull together the ideas that create a true community of learners and see them applied in the classroom. We'll visit David Young's class — a fifth grade class — on the first day of school, in the middle of the year, and toward the end of the year. As you read about this class, consider David's planning for both *management* and *academic* concerns and notice how the students internalize the structure of the classroom as the year progresses.

CLASSROOM EXAMPLE

David Young's Fifth-Grade Community of Learners

First Day

The room is ready. Several of the boards are waiting for projects that the students will complete on the first day. David has used little notes to indicate which desk belongs to which student. Each desk has construction paper on it, so that each child can create his or her own name tag.

◆ David welcomes the students and gives directions about designing their name tags. As they are making the tags, he calls roll and asks about lunch. He tells the class, "Tomorrow, I will assign a student to call roll and take lunch count. Don't worry; I'll show you what to do." In about fifteen minutes, he asks the students to stop working on their name tags. "We'll have time to finish the name tags later. When you are finished, I want you to put the tags in the file on the bookcase near my desk. After school, I will laminate them and we'll put them on our desks tomorrow."

◆ Next, David begins a discussion about rules and goals. He tells his new students about a few rules he has developed and asks for their thoughts. They agree with the rules and suggest a few others. David adds these to the classroom rules chart. He then talks about *goals*. His goals for this year are to set up the room so that students work together and to teach math, writing, science, reading, and social studies. He also talks about his goals as a university student: "I want to learn to speak Spanish. I'm taking a class twice a week. I might even practice with you."

◆ David next passes out writing paper and drawing paper. He tells the class, "We're going to draw ourselves. After your picture is the way you want it, write *your* goals for this year. Try to come up with four or five." (Periodically throughout the year the children will look back at these goals and write about how well they are doing in achieving them.) When the children finish, a few are willing to share. (Paul wants to read and spell better. Denise wants to stay out of trouble.)

◆ David talks about the daily schedule with his students as he writes it on the board: "We'll begin the day with SSR—Sustained Silent Reading. Please find a book in our class library or bring one from home. You will need one every day. Next we'll have math, and after math, writing and reading. Remember, we don't have morning recess anymore. If you need to visit the restroom, sign out on the chalkboard. When you return, erase your name. Only two people may be out of the room at one time. You may leave for the restroom, sharpen your pencil, turn in work, and get supplies when I'm not working with you directly. In the afternoon, we'll have science, social studies, p.e., and music. We'll be doing art in our projects, so we usually won't have a special art time. Most of our projects will be part of our theme explorations. That's the way most days will be."

◆ David moves to the front of the room and asks the students to tell him all the math words that they know. He quickly builds a

(Continued)

list of many words. He and the students begin to sort them: multiplication words, subtraction words, measurement words, and so on. He then asks his students to create their own worksheets that have examples of all the problems they know how to do. He adds that they also need to solve the problems. He'll use this information as he plans for grouping in math.

It's the fifth-graders' first full morning without a recess break. David is pleased with how well they have worked through this first morning. Now it's time for lunch and recess. He hasn't squeezed in everything he had planned, but the children seem to be developing an understanding of the classroom environment.

◆ After lunch David begins the afternoon by reading a chapter from *Dear Mr. Henshaw* (Cleary, 1984). Then he explains that for the first two weeks of school, the class will be exploring a theme relating to the "Environment of the School."

◆ Following this overview, he begins the social studies lesson: "We're going to start by studying our school. Let's list the people in our school." When the list is quite large, David points to the word *principal*. He asks, "What do you think the principal does?" The children come up with several ideas. David then says, "We are going to create a book that tells about all of the people in our school. We'll discuss their jobs here, then we'll interview them. We'll practice with each other before we really do the interview. Today we'll each work with a neighbor and brainstorm about what this person might do." David assigns people to each pair. The pairs work for fifteen minutes deciding what the people in the school do. Then the pairs work for another twenty minutes developing questions that they might ask each individual. David ends the lesson here. Tomorrow the students will share questions and role-play to see which questions result in the best answers. Then it will be time to revise the questions, making sure that each question is very open-ended.

Middle of the Year
◆ The children are reading at their desks. SSR usually lasts for thirty minutes. David indicates that the children should finish the paragraph they are reading, put their books away, and get ready for math.

C L A S S R O O M
E X A M P L E

**Kay Webb's
Fifth-Grade
Community of
Learners**

(*Continued*)

◆ Today David has planned for two math groups. One group will work on double-digit multiplication with regrouping, and the other will work on two-step word problems. David teaches a lesson to one group while the other students work in their math books. The students rotate after half an hour.

◆ When the math lesson is completed, David directs the students to move into Reading-Writing Workshop. The students are divided into three groups, even though each group is basically performing the same activity. David wants every student to be able to participate in the discussion that will accompany his lesson, so small groups are needed. All the students are reading biographies and writing in their literature logs. They read independently and freely write their thoughts in the logs. To connect their reading of biographies and writing, the students are all working on their interviews of community people. These interviews will eventually be published in a class book, and copies will be sent to the parents. Using part of Russell Freedman's biography of Eleanor Roosevelt, David is conducting minilessons with three small groups of students on types of questions and how to determine answers. Reading-Writing Workshop lasts for two hours, and the students rotate among these three activities. At the end of the workshop, the children leave for lunch and recess.

◆ When the students return from lunch, they write in their journals. David gives them about fifteen minutes for this writing. He then reads to them from *Mary McLeod Bethune: Voice of Black Hope* by Milton Meltzer (1987).

◆ The next hour is spent on science. The students are studying the ocean. Today several small groups of students are performing an experiment about wave action with a ball and a tray of water. After participating in and observing the experiment, the children write in their science logs about their observations and why they think the waves formed as they did. David finishes the science block of time by conducting a Guided Reading-Thinking Activity (GRTA) using the section on ocean waves in their textbook. Many of the children understand their experiment better after reading this portion of text.

◆ The day ends with the music teacher's visit.

(Continued)

End of the School Year

◆ Jeremy is calling roll, and Mark is taking the lunch count. Most of the children are reading silently at their desks, but every so often a giggle breaks the silence. David ends SSR after thirty minutes. The children, without any directions from him, prepare for math.

◆ David is teaching a lesson about long division to the whole class today. He begins the lesson with a quick mental math review. Each student writes his or her answer on a scrap of paper after completing the mental calculations. David moves from this activity to using overhead examples of many of the long-division problems that the class had worked on yesterday. He has the calculations accompanying the problem so that the students can see them. He then tells the students, "Now I want you to be the teacher. One of your students has just turned in this paper with many problems done incorrectly. We'll go through each problem and discover what the student did wrong. That way we'll know what to do to help this student correct his errors." David and his students work through five problems in this manner. He then writes a new problem on the overhead and says, "I'd like each of you to solve this problem with a partner. One person will work the problem and say everything that he or she is doing out loud. The other person will listen carefully and offer help if it is needed. " When the students have solved the first problem, David puts a new problem up, and the other half of the pair solves this one using the think-aloud procedure. The students repeat this procedure one more time. Then David passes out one worksheet with long-division problems for each pair to complete by using the think-aloud procedure. Both students in each pair will receive one grade for their combined efforts.

◆ As the students finish, they turn in their worksheets and either work on their stories or continue reading Katherine Paterson's *A Bridge to Terabithia* (1979). Each day, after reading, they write about what has happened in the book or how they feel about the actions. While the students are reading or writing either responses or stories, David confers with individual students about their revised drafts of friendship stories. The students continue with these projects for the remainder of the morning. Some students read and then work on their stories. Other students choose the opposite sequence. Several students hold conferences with each other about their friendship stories. There is a busy, calm pace throughout the morning workshop.

◆ The theme being explored for science, math, and social studies is "Machines." The afternoon begins with the students writing in their journals. Once most of the journals are closed, David reads *Charlie and the Chocolate Factory* by Roald Dahl (1964). This book contains descriptions of some very unusual candy machines. These machines are fanciful and an extension of the more realistic machines that the children are studying.

The unit on machines began when a student brought in David Macaulay's *The Way Things Work* (1988). The students were glued to the book, so David decided to take advantage of this enthusiasm.

◆ He quickly went to several libraries and collected as many books as he could about machines.

◆ He next called several repair shops to see if they had any small appliances that were beyond repair. These, without their cords, were brought into the classroom. He also located tools that the students could use to take the appliances apart.

◆ Each day David would lead a minilesson and small-group experiments on several topics such as levers, gears, and pulleys described in the book. The students kept logs of all the experiments.

◆ About a week into the unit, each student chose one particular topic mentioned in Macaulay's book to investigate and share. The students researched their topics during the second half of the afternoon. Each student negotiated a contract with David for a project that included a report—either oral or written—about the topic and some sort of visual presentation to accompany the report.

◆ David contacted many businesses in the area that were willing to send speakers to help students understand specific machines. The students particularly enjoyed the speaker who talked about repairing computers.

(Continued)

♦ A field trip was also arranged so that students could see an assembly line in action. David was really pleased that he had followed the students' direction with this unit. In a few cases, he is learning about several machines right along with the students.

The students work right until the dismissal bell. Then they quickly clean up and are heard talking about computers and microchips all the way to the bus.

David will be staying late this afternoon as he has scheduled conferences with the parents of several students. He will be sharing assessment information he has collected throughout the school year. Each parent will take a final look at his or her child's portfolio and note the child's academic growth.

David has carefully involved the parents and the community in his teaching. Many of the speakers who have been included in the "Machines" unit are parents of students in his class. These adults feel very important about sharing information that so interests the students and are very excited about being invited to the final machine presentations. David has also made sure that each parent will be coming to an end-of-the-year conference. He wants the parents to be aware of their children's academic growth.

CONCLUDING PERSPECTIVE AND SUMMARY

Chapter 3 presented an overview of an integrated language arts classroom's organization and management. We began by planning the classroom's physical, social, and academic environments. Remember that these elements are interrelated; each helps or hinders the functioning of the others. We then "visited" a sample fifth-grade classroom at the beginning, middle, and end of the school year to observe the teacher's practical applications of the methods we've been examining.

When you structure your own classroom environments, keep this chapter's theoretical frameworks in mind and be open and adaptable. Take time to get to know your students. Begin with more structure rather than less, and move gradually toward more student responsibility and decision-making. Be patient with yourself. These changes will take time, require determination, and demand lots of outright physical energy.

In this chapter we've addressed the following main points:

◆ Successful classroom management promotes integrated instruction, social interaction, and risk taking. Since the language arts are tools for learning, the classroom environment should accommodate simultaneous or combined applications of these arts with other curriculum instruction. This integrated teaching approach involves social discourse. Varieties of small- and large-group discussions and activities should be encouraged. The atmosphere must also be flexible enough to let students experiment with their own learning and "test hypotheses."

◆ The classroom's physical environment should 1) foster a wide variety of activities by 2) featuring stable areas where students *know* certain activities take place and supplies are available. These centers shouldn't be near noisier areas where small-group projects occur. The teacher should be able to move freely around the room to view and interact with the various groups.

◆ Teachers should establish basic guidelines for classroom behavior but should also collaborate with students to create and revise other rules for managing their environment. If problems arise, the group as a whole can resolve them. In addition, teachers should devise consistent, predictable routines so students can feel secure enough to experiment with other aspects of their learning.

◆ We teachers can involve parents in their children's schooling by letting them know what their children are studying and what our expectations are. We can invite them into the classroom to replicate their children's activities, involve them in homework assignments, and send them copies of class projects. Parents can also be classroom volunteers who help with small-group activities.

◆ Teachers should determine goals for their academic environment by considering state and district course content requirements, teacher's guides, and their students' abilities. School district curriculum guides outline subject matter and behavioral expectations, while scope and sequence charts in teacher's editions of texts and programs cite concepts and skills which should be addressed. By tailoring these expectations and methods for their particular students, teachers can first create a yearly planning guide, then devise flexible monthly and daily lesson plans.

◆ Teachers organize students for whole-group, small-group, or individual instruction based on teaching or learning objectives. Such grouping allows *guided* instruction; the teacher can employ appropriate techniques to teach students with similar abilities. *Special interest* groups encourage children to take their studies in focused new directions. Members of *cooperative groups* participate in activities requiring lively discourse and cooperation and "teach each other" as they collaborate on projects.

Key Terms	

assessment (p. 78)

Computer Center (p. 56)

continuity (p. 59)

cooperative groups (p. 73)

curriculum guides (p. 65)

individual instruction (p. 71)

lesson plan book (p. 67)

Listening Center (p. 55)

momentum (p. 59)

parents as volunteers (p. 62)

parents' meeting (p. 59)

Reading Corner (p. 54)

Reading Workshop (p. 74)

small-group instruction (p. 71)

special interest groups (p. 73)

teacher's editions (p. 65)

thematic units (p. 75)

whole-group instruction (p. 71)

Writing Center (p. 54)

writing folders (p. 55)

Writing Workshop (p. 74)

CHAPTER 4

Diversity and Multiculturalism in the Integrated Classroom Community

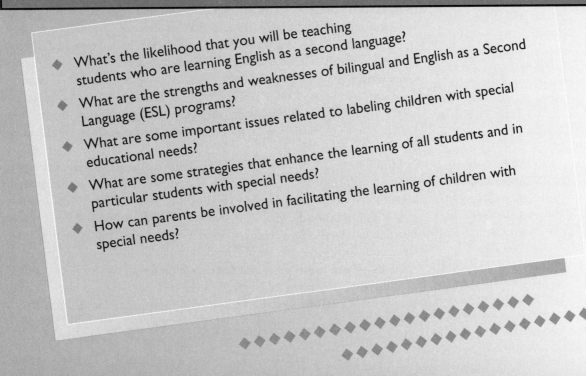

◆ What's the likelihood that you will be teaching students who are learning English as a second language?

◆ What are the strengths and weaknesses of bilingual and English as a Second Language (ESL) programs?

◆ What are some important issues related to labeling children with special educational needs?

◆ What are some strategies that enhance the learning of all students and in particular students with special needs?

◆ How can parents be involved in facilitating the learning of children with special needs?

INTRODUCTION

We first noted in Chapter 1 that, as the twentieth century draws to a close, we are realizing more than ever that ours is a diverse, *multicultural* society — and has *always* been so (Takaki, 1993). Sleeter and Grant (1994) point out that a **multicultural perspective in education** is broad; it recognizes and accepts differences and similarities among individuals related to gender, race, class, and disability. In this chapter, we will lay the foundation for responding appropriately to this diversity within the regular classroom. We will begin with an overview of the various perspectives on culturally and linguistically diverse children. Next, we will consider students with special education needs. Finally, building upon the foundation we established in Chapter 3, we will discuss classroom strategies for language arts instruction that will enable *all* our students to view themselves as competent and successful earners. These strategies are part of instruction that is **culturally responsive** and of a classroom environment that reflects this **composite culture**.

Instructional Overview

In order to teach well, we must build on each child's unique strengths rather than focus on perceived individual deficiencies. All of us as teachers need to broaden our classroom instruction so that all children can succeed at developing language and literacy abilities. Researchers who have studied children who are culturally different and speak variant dialects of English — dialects often spoken in nonmainstream cultures — emphasize the importance of our *sensitivity* (Cazden, 1988; Heath, 1983; Michaels, 1986). This sensitivity to the children in our classrooms will be even more critical for teaching second-language learners since they often represent greater cultural and linguistic differences.

I must stress a fundamental point here: instructional strategies and practices for culturally and/or linguistically diverse students and for students with special needs are, in most instances, the same quality teaching strategies — with minor adjustments — that we will normally use in our regular instruction (Boyle & Peregoy, 1990; Goldenberg, 1990; Spangenberg-Urschat & Pritchard, 1994). We should keep in mind this observation: "All students — both exceptional and nonexceptional — are more alike than they are different" (Ysseldyke & Algozzine, 1994, p. 35). In most of your teaching, you will be using strategies considered appropriate for all students.

Culturally and Linguistically Diverse Students

Certain areas of the United States contain greater numbers of culturally and linguistically diverse students than do other areas. California, Florida, New York, and Texas have the majority of these students at present (Olsen, 1989). Enright and McCloskey (1988) write that "the trend is toward the creation of linguistically different households in a growing number of communities across all regions of North America"—including Canada as well (p. 4). And while we may feel that this trend is in the distant future, by the year 2000 one of every three students will be a member of a minority group.

All new teachers will not, of course, begin their teaching careers in an area of the country like California that has a large number of children learning English as a second language. However, statistics and predicted trends guarantee that sometime during our careers, we will be teaching culturally and linguistically diverse children, even in Middle America. As teachers, *our* own cultural and linguistic heritage—African-American, Anglo-American, Asian-American, European-American, Hispanic-American, or Native American—underlies how we respond to our students. Therefore, understanding our own heritage and realizing that it is not "first" among all cultural and linguistic heritages will be our first step towards understanding and responding to our students.

Doubtlessly children are and will continue to start school either without or with very minimal abilities in speaking, reading, and writing English. Remember, however, the great variety among these students. For example, some children arrive in the United States having had considerable school experience in their native country. If these children are already reading and writing in their native language, their skills will readily transfer as they learn to read and write in English (Barnitz, 1985). Other children, such as the sons and daughters of migrant workers and refugees, will have had few experiences with formal schooling; their adjustment to American schools is usually more difficult. They not only have to learn to speak English but also need to learn how to read and write for the first time in this second language, a much harder task than the one facing the first group of children.

When determining how best to respond to culturally and/or linguistically diverse students, educators are often influenced by prevailing political notions. Early in this century, the metaphor of the "melting pot" (now considered inappropriate) was the guiding principle in schools. Children were expected to disregard or forget their native language and quickly learn English. As noted in Chapter 1, people can retain the qualities of their ethnic backgrounds and still be considered part of the American culture. Children are no longer expected to abandon their first language as they learn

All students benefit from culturally responsive instruction.

English. Most individuals believe it is important for immigrants to retain some sense of an original culture. The writer Bette Bao Lord beautifully describes our belief that students who are acquiring aspects of a second culture should not be expected to abandon or ignore characteristics of their first culture. Shirley Temple Wong, the main character in Lord's *In the Year of the Boar and Jackie Robinson* (1984), leaves mainland China with her family in the mid-1940s for a life in America. Shirley's character is based on Lord's real-life experiences. The author makes a compelling observation: "Many feel that loss of one's native culture is the price one must pay for becoming an American. I do not feel this way. I think we hyphenated Americans are doubly blessed. We can choose the best of both."

One of the fundamental issues for developing effective instruction with any group of students is understanding the students' home cultures. Indeed, the classroom culture should be adjusted to be responsive to these cultures: "When teachers act to broaden the rules for what is acceptable in the classroom, in terms of how students speak and write about their lives and how they answer questions, they are moving toward creating a composite classroom culture" (Au, 1993, p. 103). Teachers are then in a position to respond to the needs, interests, and abilities of students. Au reminds us that this environment "allows students both to affirm their cultural identities and to strive for high levels of literacy and academic achievement . . . . [This] puts both teachers and students in a win-win situation" (1993, p. 105).

Research by Au and Kawakami (1985), Garcia (1994), and Heath (1983, 1986) reveals what happens when the culture of the classroom is *not* adjusted. There is a mismatch of teaching and learning expectations between the teacher and the culturally and linguistically different child which results in academic failure. In these situations, teachers are not building from the language strengths culturally and linguistically diverse children exhibit at home. They are not being considerate of — or even *aware* of — the language competencies that children bring to school and focus instead on what they perceive as the children's language *deficiencies* in accomplishing school tasks. When this situation occurs, students from minority cultures may eventually appear "lazy" or act out and misbehave, thus "confirming" the stereotype held by the dominant culture (Au, 1993; Garcia, 1994).

AT THE TEACHER'S DESK

AN OPPORTUNITY, NOT A PROBLEM

Although, as we're pointing out here, the reasons for the success or failure of culturally and linguistically different children in our classrooms are quite complex, it is important for us as teachers to remember that each child in our class comes to school with unique literacy strengths. As teachers, we have two choices when adopting an attitude that we will share with our students about their differences:

- We can see the cultural and linguistic differences that children bring to school as a problem. Our jobs then become the eradication of these differences.

- We can see these cultural and linguistic differences that children bring to school as wonderful contributions to everyone's social, academic, and personal growth. We can all serve as resources to understand each other and the world in richer ways. As we all develop a broader world view, our classes will become places where our students investigate and come to understand the similarities shared by all the world's people. *This is* **culturally responsive instruction**. As Au (1993) concisely explains, such instruction "is responsive to the values and standards for behavior of students' home culture and also directed toward the goal of academic achievement. . . . [T]eachers help students affirm their cultural identities while expanding their knowledge through school literacy experiences" (p. 92).

Effects of Varied Language and Literacy Experiences: Home vs. School

The culture in which children learn their native language powerfully determines how they interact with adults and other children and how they think about and use literacy. Quite often these children are caught in a bind. What is expected at school directly contrasts with what is expected at home, and this conflict contributes to school behaviors that create stereotypes about different cultural groups. For example, in many cultures whose family structures strongly emphasize respect and deference to elders — such as Mexican-American, Appalachian, and Native American cultures — "conversations with adults are usually brief and abrupt" (Garcia, 1994). Such responses are contrary to expected interaction patterns in the mainstream school culture of the United States. Furthermore, while collaboration and cooperation are stressed in many cultures at home, emphasizing the *group* rather than the *individual*, school often sets up a competitive environment where children are discouraged from helping each other and where the individual is accountable for acquiring and demonstrating knowledge (Phillips, 1983). Again, such an environment may very well establish values that contradict those found in the students' home cultures. Garcia (1994) points out that it's important for teachers from other cultures to be aware of this situation lest they misinterpret these children's responses as shyness or delayed language development and, as a result, lower their expectations for these students.

Michaels (1986) highlights a final example of different expectations due to culture. She has provided engaging and important information about children's oral discourse styles based on her studies of "sharing" or "show and tell" time among children. Michaels concluded that while school encourages students to "stick to the point" when relating information or telling a story — a **topic-specific style** — in many African-American communities children acquire a **topic-associating style**. This style brings in information and events as they occur to the speaker "along the way," but ultimately the story or information reaches a logical end. Similarly, Heath (1983) described oral discourse styles and literacy events in two poorer communities, "Roadville" and "Trackton" (not the real names of the communities). Roadville residents, predominantly Anglo-American, expected their children to tell stories that were accurate, exact renditions of actual events. Most often these stories were retellings of events that were combined into good stories that contained morals. Heath reported that "children in Roadville are not allowed to tell stories, unless an adult announces that something which happened to a child makes a good story and invites a retelling. When children are asked to retell such events, they are expected to tell non-fictive stories which 'stick to the truth'" (1983, p. 158). In contrast,

Our teaching helps students affirm their cultural identities as their knowledge grows through experiences with language and literacy.

Trackton children, who are predominantly African-American, told stories that exaggerated the real events. Heath describes the stories told by Trackton residents as being based "on an actual event, but they creatively fictionalize the details surrounding the real event, and the outcome of the story may not even resemble what indeed happened" (1983, p. 166). When these children arrive together at school, among their other unique qualities will be these very different concepts of a story: "For Roadville, Trackton's stories would be lies; for Trackton, Roadville's stories would not even count as stories" (1983, p. 189).

Heath noted that the success or failure of particular children in school very much depended on how well the child's literacy behavior matched the teacher's expectations. Even activities as simple as storytelling and sharing-time routines, therefore, can support or interfere with school success.

A Perspective on Second Language Education

Second-language acquisition has been an issue in American education since the early 1900s. As we first noted in Chapter 1, during the second half of this century a change occurred in U.S. immigration patterns. One pattern was first noticed in Florida as an influx of Cuban immigrants arrived in the early 1960s. The children of these immigrants, Spanish-speaking young-sters, were quickly enrolled in the public schools. As a result of the influx of Spanish speakers into the school population, Dade County began a *bilingual* program in 1963 which provided instruction in Spanish for Cuban children.

Over the next several years, more and more second-language students entered schools throughout the nation; while the majority spoke Spanish, an increasing number came from Southeast and East Asia. In 1974, the Supreme Court decided in *Lau v. Nichols* that schools must provide edu-cation to students in languages that they can comprehend. To comply with this decision, schools attempted to provide instruction for students in their native languages. This Supreme Court decision significantly reinforced the importance of multicultural perspectives on the part of teachers and schools.

The bilingual emphasis that was predominant in the 1960s and 1970s is currently being challenged. Calls for "English only" laws at the national and state levels have increased. As in the past, the matter of instruction for second-language learners is still molded by political and philosophical be-liefs. The issues of which language to use in instruction and how best to teach second-language learners continue to be debated, often on the front pages of our nation's newspapers, as political leaders argue the merits for or against "English only" curricula.

Let's consider the nature of both language minority students and of the developmental sequence they follow in acquiring English as a second lan-guage. First of all, let's define **language minority students** — students whose native language is not English. They participate primarily in a non-English-speaking environment and have developed the "normal communicative abilities" of that environment. Their regular exposure to English occurs only in the school environment. By the year 2000, the population of lan-guage minority students in the elementary grades is projected to be 76 per-cent Spanish, 8 percent Southeast Asian (Vietnamese, Cambodian, Hmong), 5 percent East Asian (Chinese, Korean), 5 percent "other" European (East-ern European, Baltic, Russian), and 5 percent "other" (e.g., Arabic, Native American) (Garcia, 1994).

In the United States there are currently three general orientations for ed-ucating children whose native language is not English:

◆ **bilingual education** — where emphasis is placed on instruction in both a child's native language and in English. Usually instruction in academic subjects is conducted in the child's native language.

◆ **English as a Second Language** (ESL) — programs where the emphasis is on learning English with no instruction conducted in the child's native language.

♦ sheltered English—which refers to accommodating second-language learners in a regular classroom (Garcia, 1994). While no systematic instruction in English is provided, the teacher *is* sensitive to students' needs and tries to adjust his or her use of English appropriately for them—as we'll see later in this chapter. Most of us will be teaching in this "sheltered English" situation.

Which of these approaches provides the best instructional and learning environments for this acquisition? The research on this issue is varied and controversial, but studies that have followed students over a period of many years suggest that *bilingual education* is most effective (e.g., Collier, 1992). For a number of reasons, however, presently this option is becoming increasingly less available.

Three Stages of Second-Language Acquisition

Researchers have identified three stages through which learners move when acquiring a second language (Krashen & Terrell, 1983). Table 4.1 summarizes these stages.

Hakuta and Gould indicate that the primary goal of instruction for language minority students is "the development of the students' English to the level of participation in all-English classrooms" (1987, p. 39). This goal implies that students, in addition to learning to speak English, are developing the ability to learn academic concepts through English. As teachers, we will

TABLE 4.1

Stages of Acquiring a Second Language: Summary of Characteristics	
Stage	**Characteristics**
Comprehension	• "Silent" period • Comprehend through carefully observing what is going on • Learn simple words and phrases • Responses to simple questions are short, usually one word • At first, expand utterances by stringing words together
Early Speech-Production	• Later, try out more complex syntactic expressions
Extended Speech-Production	• Use oral English extensively • Fewer noticeable "errors" • Sentence structure quite close to standard conversational speech • Occasional subject/verb disagreement

want to focus on this primary goal for second-language learners and facilitate their use of their first languages and their new language when it is appropriate to do so. For instance, children need to be able to converse in school talk, home talk, friend talk, and store talk (Gee, 1987). All students need to have enough flexibility in their language use so they can adapt their level of discourse as the situation demands. They should also have enough facility with English so they can consider abstract and concrete issues related to instruction.

Whereas fluent **playground English** can for most students develop in a reasonably short period of time, **academic English** requires anywhere from four to seven years (Gibbons, 1993; Wong-Fillmore, 1982). In other words, even when students have moved into the third stage of acquiring English, the "extended speech-production" period, there is still considerable development needed if *academic* English is to be acquired.

Whether or not the school where you eventually teach offers a bilingual or an ESL program, the chances are great that you will have students who are in the process of acquiring English. As many as 90 percent of the total student population just beginning to speak English is taught in "English only" classrooms. The strategies we use with these children are often the same quality teaching strategies that we'll already be using with the other students in our class. We'll consider these strategies after discussing the other students with special needs in our classrooms.

A Perspective on Dialects

Every language has several "versions," referred to as **dialects**. Dialects of a language vary according to sound, syntax, and vocabulary. American English comprises many different dialects. Nevertheless, even if we're from

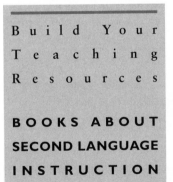

B u i l d   Y o u r

T e a c h i n g

R e s o u r c e s

BOOKS ABOUT

SECOND LANGUAGE

INSTRUCTION

Garcia, E. (1994). *Understanding and meeting the challenge of student cultural diversity*. Boston: Houghton Mifflin.

Gibbons, P. (1993). *Learning to learn in a second language*. Portsmouth, NH: Heinemann.

Peregoy, S., & Boyle, O. (1993). *Reading, writing, and learning in ESL: A resource book for K–8 teachers*. New York: Longman.

New England and talk to someone from Appalachia, it is still possible for us to understand one another; we know we're speaking the same *language*. Regardless of where we live, however, we may or may not speak in a way that others recognize as **standard English**. This is the version of American English that is spoken by those who have assumed educational, social, political, and economic control in the society. This is also the dialect that children are expected to learn and use in school. Every language has a preferred or "standard" version, and this version is inherently no better or worse than any other version. The way we speak in particular situations, however—just as the way we dress—projects who we are and gives listeners some basis from which to make judgments, fair or not, about us. It's important to help elementary students develop an awareness of this social, *pragmatic* aspect of speech. For students who speak a **nonstandard dialect**, acquiring and learning when to use the standard dialect will empower them to pursue all opportunities available to them.

As teachers, we can address the dialect issue by placing an emphasis on the appropriateness of our speech in the different contexts in which we find ourselves. As we saw in Chapter 2, we all adjust our speech depending on the situation and the *pragmatics*, but some of us will have to work on this adjustment more than others, particularly if the dialect of American English that we speak varies significantly from the standard dialect. When we're talking to friends informally, our speech is informal. The degree of informality can change, too, often depending often on whether we are talking to friends of the same gender. When we are presenting information in a class, our speech is more formal—although the degree of formality depends on factors like the professor or the course—and on our ability to "read" the contextual cues appropriately. Linguists term these different levels of formality and informality **registers**.

We all know adults who have never seemed to master the knack of reading contextual cues—the pragmatics—appropriately and who thus respond in an inappropriate "register." Therefore, we must be understanding of our pupils and yet be dedicated to helping them become aware of different situations and the appropriate response to each one. For most children this process begins in the preschool years with parents' constant prods to say "please" and "thank you." As Elizabeth comments in Elaine Konigsberg's *Jennifer, Hecate, Macbeth, William McKinley, and Me, Elizabeth* (1967), "All my life my mother had taught me a politeness vocabulary. I didn't mind. I thought 'please' and 'thank you' made conversation prettier . . ." Whether you agree or disagree, it's valid to suggest that there's an important "politeness vocabulary" that accompanies the "rules" of social interaction.

As teachers, we provide examples of standard English and model appropriate language use in different situations. As we help students in this process of language awareness and acquisition, it's important to remember that we will not be trying to *replace* their native dialects but will be giving them an additional language skill—in effect, helping them become *bidialectal*.

Students with Special Education Needs

Up until the late 1800s, children and adults with special education needs were generally set apart from the rest of society. In keeping with this practice of separation, residential schools for hearing- and visually-impaired individuals as well as for the mentally retarded were established during the mid-1800s. Children who exhibited relatively minor learning difficulties generally were not provided with special academic support. Warner (1994) observed that "[p]rior to the 1960s, the education and treatment of disabled children . . . was for the most part segregated; it was often quite underfunded; and it was sometimes abusive" (p. 53). Most of the laws and initiatives related to special education have been enacted during the last 25 years. Notably, in 1975, Public Law 94–142 was passed, requiring states to provide a free education to all children with physical disabilities between the ages of three and eighteen. PL 94–142 is responsible for many of the special education programs that we consider routine today.

PL 94–142 defined several key principles related to special education services. Children should be placed in the least restrictive environment, spending as much time in a regular classroom setting as possible. In most schools students with special education needs routinely move between a regular classroom and a resource room (a designated classroom and a teacher who provides special services). Efforts to include these children in the regular classroom as much as possible are examples of **inclusion**, which is an offshoot of the term *mainstreaming*. Hunt and Marshall (1994) define *inclusion* as "the practice of providing children with disabilities as 'normalized' an education as possible, ideally in classrooms with their nondisabled peers in their neighborhood schools" (p. 17).

In recent years special education theorists have emphasized a *constructivist* orientation toward instruction (Campione et al., 1994; Englert, Rozendal, & Mariage, 1994). Simply because a child may be classified as a "special ed" student does not mean he or she has a significantly different way of making sense of the world or learning than other children do. Our response to these students—what we do and the environment in which we do it—is much the same as it is for all our students (Skrtic, 1991; Warner, 1994).

A Perspective on Special Education

Children who qualify for special education services in the public schools fit many different categories. At the beginning of the 1990s, over four million children and youth aged from birth to 21 years were receiving special education services. Almost 94 percent of these individuals fell into four categories: **specific learning disabilities** (49 percent), **speech or language impairments** (almost 23 percent), **mental retardation** (almost 13 percent), and **serious emotional disturbance** (9 percent) (U.S. Office of Special Education and Rehabilitative Services, 1992). As elementary-school teachers, we can expect that most of the special education needs students who are placed in our classes will come from these four groups. The remaining 7 percent of special education students are children with *orthopedic disabilities and other health impairments*; children with *severe or multiple disabilities*; children who are *hearing impaired*; and children who are *visually impaired*. Most of the children in these **low-prevalence categories** are identified by the medical profession long before they are ready for formal schooling (Ysseldyke & Algozzine, 1994).

◆ *Learning disabilities*
Children labeled as *learning disabled* represent the fastest-growing category of special education for several reasons. One is that parents accept this term more easily than they do other labels; another is that in the past federal money has more often been allocated for learning disabled programs than for remedial programs. Children qualify as learning disabled when there is a significant discrepancy between their potential and their academic performance. The definition of *learning disabled* excludes children who are below grade level in performance due to physical disabilities, mental retardation, emotional disorders, or economic or cultural environments. The ways in which these criteria are applied, however, vary from state to state.

◆ *Speech and language impairments*
Children who have difficulty communicating because of speaking or listening impairments also have problems in reading and other subject areas in the curriculum. Most of these children do not exhibit any physical symptoms; children with cleft palate, cerebral palsy, or a facial birth defect are among the exceptions (Orlich et al., 1994).

◆ *Mental retardation*

Several factors cause retardation, such as the diet of pregnant mothers, premature birth, lead poisoning, neglect, fetal alcohol syndrome, and heredity. Often children who are identified as mentally retarded come from families living in poverty. In the following passage, Ysseldyke and Algozzine (1994) support these earlier observations and extend them to all children living in poverty:

> Children who grow up in environments where resources and experiences are limited can develop intellectually at a very slow rate. Poor children as a group tend to earn lower scores on intelligence tests, one criterion for placement in classes for students who are mentally retarded. The end product is classes comprised heavily of youngsters from poor families. As we've come to recognize the relationship between test scores and economic status (and that has taken a very long time—longer in some communities than in others), our thinking about mental retardation has changed, as has our thinking about the factors that cause retardation. (p. 165)

Boyer (1987) elaborates on the relationship between hunger and brain development. A developing fetus requires a diet that contains proteins, vitamins, and minerals, but many poor pregnant mothers have diets that do not include these elements. He goes on to say that the human brain develops very rapidly during a child's first year. Poor children, who constitute 40 percent of all persons living in poverty, have inadequate diets and often suffer from malnutrition.

◆ *Emotional disturbance*

Children who are emotionally disturbed exhibit unusual behavior over an extended period of time. These children might misbehave, refuse to interact with other children, or perform other behaviors not thought to be typical of their peers. The persistent behavior problems exhibited by these children interfere with their academic performance. Ysseldyke and Algozzine (1994) indicate that the majority of children (80 percent) referred for testing for this category are boys in the intermediate grades.

◆ *Low-prevalence categories*

At some time in your teaching career, you may have children from a low-prevalence category in your classroom. Some school districts bus children with similar disabilities to one or more district schools, so you may, for example, have a child who is hearing-impaired "mainstreamed" into your classroom for part of the day. This child would also spend part of his or her day in a special class that focuses specifically on learning strategies for the hearing impaired. Similarly, we can adjust the classroom to accommodate children who are visually impaired, and a visiting teacher

B u i l d   Y o u r
T e a c h i n g
R e s o u r c e s

**BOOKS ABOUT
SPECIAL EDUCATION
INSTRUCTION**

The following recommended texts include very good information on both high- and low-prevalence types of special education conditions:

Bos, C., & Vaughn, S. (1994). *Strategies for teaching students with learning and behavior problems* (3rd ed.). Boston: Allyn & Bacon.

Ford, A., Schnorr, R., Meyer, L., Davern, L., Black, J., & Dempsey, P. (Eds.). (1989). *The Syracuse community-referenced curriculum guide for students with moderate and severe disabilities.* Baltimore: Paul H. Brookes.

Hunt, N., & Marshall, K. (1994). *Exceptional children and youth: An introduction to special education.* Boston: Houghton Mifflin.

Orelove, F., & Sobsey, D. (1991). *Educating children with multiple disabilities* (2nd ed.). Baltimore: Paul H. Brookes.

Snell, M. E. (1987). *Systematic instruction of persons with severe handicaps.* Columbus, OH: Merrill.

Yesseldyke, J., & Algozzine, B. (1994). *Introduction to special education.* Boston: Houghton Mifflin.

can help them with Braille (Viadero, 1989). These situations may seem unusual, but they demonstrate the flexibility educators exhibit while attempting to solve the problem of how best to educate youngsters with physical disabilities.

Overall, individuals receiving special education services represent about 10 percent of the total school enrollment. Category labels for students with special education needs abound, and these may facilitate discussion about a child or group of children. We always need to remember, however, that often a child becomes buried beneath the label, and we consequently don't see the characteristics that make him or her a unique individual.

Strategies for Instruction of the Integrated Language Arts

Now that we've had an overview of the types of student diversity possible within a classroom, let's look at what we can do in the regular classroom to support the language arts learning of all the children. We may have students who are at different levels of acquiring English, who speak a variant dialect, or who may be classified as "special ed." As we learned earlier, the majority of students with special education needs will come from the categories of learning disability or speech/language impairment. This means that most of the language arts activities and strategies that we share with our regular-education children will also be appropriate for students with special needs. Our activities will be structured so that all children can successfully participate in the teaching and learning experience. In those few instances where students from low-prevalence categories are included for part of the school day, teaching usually will be trained and supported in their endeavors to help these particular children.

We will first consider some general strategies for classroom organization, reading, writing, and thematic unit implementation, then discuss specific activities directly related to language arts instruction. Remember, effective teaching strategies are appropriate for *all* of the learners in your classroom.

Social Interaction in the Diverse Classroom: Involving All Learners

As I've recommended for all our students, a predictable and organized routine for what gets done and how it gets done in the classroom is fundamental to effective learning and teaching. I'd like to reiterate this point particularly for students who may be acquiring English as a second language or who may be classified as "special ed." In addition to this classroom predictability, there are *groupings* or "participant structures" (Campione et al., 1994) that become automated—such as discussion groups and jigsaw activities—and which serve as supportive structures for students' further interaction and learning. Moreover, as Campione and his colleagues conclude, in such an instructional environment, "[e]ach child can find a niche in which to develop independent talents" (1994, p. 272).

Cooperative Groups

Barnes (1975) tells us that "pupils' talk is important, in that it is a major means by which learners explore the relationship between what they know, and new observations or interpretations which they meet" (p. 81). We can routinely incorporate small-group instruction, which often includes cooperative learning strategies and, as a result, more student talk. The use of cooperative learning in small groups is strongly recommended for all students, especially students of diverse backgrounds (Campione et al., 1994; Cazden, 1988; Pinnell & Matlin, 1989).

Cooperative groups make a lot of sense when we are educating children who are very diverse. (See Chapter 3 for a full description of cooperative groups.) The small group provides a more intimate and safe forum for expressing ideas. Each child has a greater opportunity to talk than during whole-class instruction and thus has a greater chance to practice English and refine or clarify understandings. The use of small groups facilitates the acceptance of students from diverse backgrounds into the regular classroom because it helps other students realize, perhaps tacitly, that these individuals have important ideas to contribute (Johnson & Johnson, 1975; Slavin,

1986). In cooperative situations, students have more opportunities to "find their own niche" (Campione et al., 1994), "owning" and becoming experts in some aspect of the classroom routine and focus.

Recall Vygotsky's concept of a "zone of proximal development" presented in Chapter 1. Vygotsky observed that students can accomplish problem-solving tasks beyond their individual competence when working in heterogeneous groups. Even in groups, however, no child will be able to acquire knowledge very far beyond his or her current level of understanding. The following two examples illustrate this point:

◆ One child in Matthew's writing response group did not understand the part in Matthew's story when the villains drilled a hole through the ground and escaped to China. Matthew had to use a globe to explain what he meant. The child who questioned the story then began to acquire this new understanding.

◆ Craig, a member of a group of students convened to work on long-division problems, is still trying to learn simple multiplication. Certainly Craig's membership in this group will not result in his mastery of the process of long division.

Cooperative groups are a vital forum where children can formulate ideas about issues. As each child listens to the others, the group comes to a consensus about a topic, and the youngsters build trust that encourages them to risk sharing personal thoughts and ideas. It is important to integrate your learners with special needs into many groups so that each student can learn from a variety of perspectives. For example, an activity as simple and concrete as brainstorming about "all of the different ways to cure hiccups" can allow students to discover the similarities and differences in behavior across cultures. In one case, four first-graders—Ryan, Ann, Carlos, and Anita— engaged in just such a brainstorm about curing hiccups. Anita said that her father scared her by jumping up and down. Ryan asked if that technique really worked; he thought that a drink of water would be better. Anita stubbornly responded that being scared worked more quickly than drinking water. Carlos said that his sister pinched him when he had hiccups. At that point, all of the students agreed that pinching might work—but that they would rather try another remedy! The discussion continued in this manner for another ten minutes until the teacher brought all the groups together to share their information.

The discussion that occurs during these small-group experiences should be at a level that enables all the children to participate. If the topic is quite abstract, perhaps one group activity could be to have each child share a concrete example of the idea. Say, for instance, that the children are each given the job of acting out a specific emotion displayed by a character in a book they are reading. Following this simple drama activity, the children create drawings of this emotion. This activity can help the below-level reader or second-language learner understand the more abstract elements in a story, and all the children will realize the wide range of ideas elicited from a single emotion.

Peer Tutoring

Peer tutoring, particularly during reading and math, is another highly recommended small-group strategy that can help all children—especially diverse students—learn. You can form pairs in many ways, but it's wise to avoid pairing the student most proficient in reading or math with the student least proficient. Such pairs often have difficulty working together. A better strategy is to rank the students by math and reading abilities. Then divide the class into two halves. Now you can match the most proficient reader with a child who is at the top of the lower half of students, a pairing that functions much better.

In these paired sessions, the tutee could read a story to the tutor, with the tutor supplying help when necessary. These partners could also write reports and stories together. Another strategy might be to form partnerships between students from different classes or grades and have the older student read or write with the younger student. Both members of the partnership benefit from this activity, since the more able partner receives additional practice and the chance to be the expert, and the less able partner has a willing helper for practice (Topping, 1989). If you form partnerships in both of these ways, each of the students in your class will feel responsible for another student's learning and have the additional confidence-building benefit of being the expert.

For example, in one school the kindergarten students were linked with third-grade writing partners. One afternoon a week, each third-grader visited his or her kindergarten partner and read aloud a story that had been practiced especially for the child. Following the reading, the two students would talk about the story, and the third-grader would record the kindergartner's thoughts. Another partnership, a first-grade and fifth-grade pairing, was established in that same school for a short-term research project. Each first-grader chose an animal that he or she wanted to know more about. The first-grade teacher then enlisted the fifth-graders to help the first-graders locate and read pertinent material about the animal. The fifth-graders were rewarded when they watched their first-grade partners share the animal information at a special gathering.

It's important to meet with potential "tutors" before they work with other students to talk about *how* they can best help and ways they can most effectively interact with their "tutees."

Teaching in the Zone of Proximal Development: Learning English and the Standard Dialect

Recall that "sheltered English" is the term used to refer to the type of language environment you will be establishing for your second-language learners. While "sheltering" the learner from a "total immersion" in English which would likely overwhelm him or her, we present information to the student that is just a little beyond his or her current competence in any subject area. In order to determine exactly where this level is, we consider our own use of English, the child's background knowledge, our method of presenting information (concrete or abstract), and other important elements, since information or language far beyond a child's competence can appear to be nonsense if the child can't make sense of it. Let's look at two examples that suggest how you might apply the concept of *comprehensible input* to the language you use in the classroom.

First, Heath (1978) illustrates the difficulty that second-language learners in particular can have understanding some "simple" directions given by the teacher. Heath portrays the following typical classroom episode:

[The teacher and students are working at a table with boxes and objects of different shapes.]

Hold the red box *up*.

Put the blue circle *in* the red box.

Hold the sheet of brown paper *over* the red box.

In this reading setting, the students are learning to deal with a paradigm: they learn to display, to be exact, and—most important—to pay attention to the examiner's actions. They learn [how] to learn by following directions; they probably learn little about the meaning of prepositions—the explicit focus of the lesson.

Contrast the use of prepositions in the following routine expressions as the teacher attempts to maintain classroom control throughout the day:

We've got to get *over* this habit of everyone stopping at the water fountain on the way to lunch.

Let's put the scissors *up* now.

Are we all *in* line?

Hold your work at your desk until the reading circle is *over.* (1987, p. 17)

Heath's example vividly demonstrates just how confusing it is for a child to learn a second language. The other learners in the class may have an equally difficult time with these "simple" directions. No wonder children periodically give their teacher looks that suggest they are totally lost. If you are sensitive to the nuances of language, you will realize the difficulties a child may be having trying to sort out exactly what a word *means* and exactly when it really has that meaning.

Enright (1986) provides another example of the importance of thinking about language when working with diverse students. During a summer practicum, Enright observed an ESL intern, Molly, as she changed her language and instruction to aid the learning of her students. Molly's class had 16 primary students who spoke six different languages and four students who were native English speakers. Molly made some major adaptations:

First, Molly began to see classroom language as performing both a language teaching as well as a subject-matter teaching function. Seeing this, Molly then began to use more and more small-group and individualized activities in place of full-group activities. Finally, Molly adapted her view of her own role in the classroom from viewing herself as a language *giver* to viewing herself as a language *facilitator* and *user* with her students. (p. 122, emphasis added)

The adaptations Molly made were strategies that we already consider essential for quality instruction. These types of adaptations will certainly enhance the learning of all your diverse students.

Role-Playing

Have students **role-play** different situations: meeting parents' friends, meeting the school principal for the first time, buying a movie ticket, telling a friend about a particularly bothersome habit or attending a formal banquet. If you are working with children who have not been exposed directly to formal social situations, remember that they nevertheless will have some background information to draw upon. You may have to remind them of this background knowledge, but the images will be there. You can role-play the situations both ways—as students believe they should be played and, for contrast and fun, as they shouldn't be played. These activities can also be excellent stimuli for writing.

Table 4.2 presents a number of effective techniques for providing an appropriate "sheltered English" learning environment for second-language learners.

TABLE 4.2

Sheltered English Techniques in the Mainstream Class

1. **Increase wait time.**

   Give your students time to think and process the information before you rush in with answers. A student may know the answers, but need a little more processing time in order to say it in English.

2. **Respond to the message.**

   If a student has the answer correct and you can understand it, don't correct his or her grammar. The exact word and correct grammatical response will develop with time, especially with young children. Instead, repeat his or her answer, putting it into standard English, and let the student know that you are pleased with his or her response.

3. **Simplify your language.**

   Speak directly to the student, emphasizing important nouns and verbs, and using as few extra words as possible. Repetition and speaking louder doesn't help; rephrasing, accompanied by body language does.

4. **Don't force reticent students to speak.**

   Instead, give the students an opportunity to demonstrate his or her comprehension and knowledge through body actions, drawing pictures, manipulating objects, or pointing.

5. **Demonstrate; use manipulatives.**

   Whenever possible, accompany your message with gestures, pictures, and objects that help get the meaning across. Use a variety of different pictures or objects for the same idea. Give an immediate context for new words.

6. **Make use of all senses.**

   Give students a chance to touch things, to listen to sounds, even to smell and taste when possible. Talk about the words that describe these senses as the student physically experiences something. Write new words as well as say them.

7. **Pair or group students with native speakers.**

   Much of a child's language learning comes from interacting with his/her peers. Give your students tasks to complete that require interaction of each member of the group, but arrange it so that the student has lingisti-

(Continued)

TABLE 4.2 (*Continued*)

Sheltered English Techniques in the Mainstream Class

cally easier tasks. Utilize cooperative learning techniques in a student-centered classroom.

8. **Adapt the materials.**

Don't "water down" the content. Rather, make the concepts more accessible and comprehensible by adding pictures, charts, maps, time-lines, and diagrams, in addition to simplifying the language.

9. **Increase your knowledge.**

Learn as much as you can about the language and culture of your students. Go to movies, read books, look at pictures of the countries. Keep the similarities and differences in mind and then check your knowledge by asking your students whether they agree with your impressions. Learn as much of the student's language as you can; even a few words help. Widen your own world view; think of alternative ways to reach the goals you have for your class.

10. **Build on the student's prior knowledge.**

Find out as much as you can about how and what a student learned in his or her country. Then try to make a connection between the ideas and concepts you are teaching and the student's previous knowledge or previous way of being taught. Encourage the students to point out differences and connect similarities.

11. **Support the student's home language and culture; bring it into the classroom.**

Your goal should be to encourage the students to keep their home languages as they also acquire English. Many children in this world grow up speaking more than one language; it's an advantage. Let students help bring about a multicultural perspective to the subjects you are teaching. Students might be able to bring in pictures, poems, dances, proverbs, or games. They might be able to demonstrate a new way to do a math problem or bring in a map that shows a different perspective than that given in your history or geography book. Encourage students to bring these items in as a part of the subject you are teaching, not just as a separate activity. Do whatever you can to help your fluent English-speaking students see all students as knowledgeable persons from a respected culture.

SOURCE: P. Sullivan, *ESL in Context*. Copyright © 1992 by Corwin Press. Reprinted by permission of Corwin Press, Inc.

Discussion

With intermediate students you may directly address the social issue of variant dialects and standard English. This explicit treatment often works well with role playing. Rare are the parents who will challenge you on this matter, but you may encounter some degree of "*I* don't need that" from some students. If you have been raised speaking primarily standard English, the students may, with some justification, challenge your credibility on this issue. For this reason, you will find it extremely helpful to invite to your classroom an adult who has acquired standard English—someone who is "bidialectal." The credibility of *these* adults is unquestionable, and they can be a powerful motivating force.

Identify and work on changing specific variant-dialect constructions. Once intermediate students understand the importance of using standard English in certain situations, you can survey their writing for nonstandard constructions.

Once again, it is important to mention that this process of targeting variant constructions must be kept in perspective; many of these constructions are common and accepted in literature, film, and contemporary music. Even for budding adolescents who come from a standard English background (as many of your fifth- and sixth-graders probably will), these forms are usually a harmless expression of independence from parents, schools, and adult authority. Indeed, these constructions are common among such students because their purpose is to challenge and, in some instances, to outrage. We are not denying students the right to these forms, but we are helping them understand when and where they are acceptable.

Facilitating Reading and Writing in the Diverse Classroom

Teachers often feel that reading instruction is difficult to provide to children who are culturally and linguistically diverse or who have special education needs. They are concerned that the cultural backgrounds of the students will interfere with their comprehension of American children's stories. They also wonder how to teach a child who speaks very little English to read. We will address these concerns as we look at some strategies that are particularly appropriate for teaching our diverse students to read.

I'd like to emphasize the need for involvement in our students' home cultures so we can make adaptations in the classroom. These two examples help illustrate this process:

◆ Teachers in Hawaii incorporated into their reading curriculum the "**talk story**" **format** so familiar to the children (Au, 1980). In the "talk story," children produced narratives developed by more than one student at the beginning of the reading lesson. The children came to understand that the focus of their reading engagements was comprehension and understanding, rather than simply "decoding"—figuring out words and sounds. With these simple additions to the curriculum, the children's reading competency increased.

◆ Heath (1982) describes a similar adaptation made by teachers in North Carolina. When the classroom work included some of the story structures the children experienced at home, the academic performance of the children improved.

In each of these examples, teachers discovered the home literacy strengths of the children, and added these factors to the classroom curriculum. Without requiring an immense amount of time and energy, these simple additions resulted in the increased academic performance of children who are not often successful in school.

The Language Experience Approach (LEA)

We'll address the "how to's" of the **Language Experience Approach** in depth in Chapter 6. I'd like to emphasize here, though, the appropriateness of the Language Experience Approach for learners with special needs (Dixon and Nessel, 1983; Sutton, 1989). In this approach, students share their personal experiences as they "dictate" what they want to say to the teacher, then the teacher writes the narrative. This focus on self is particularly important for children experiencing emotional difficulties and children with physical disabilities. The Language Experience Approach allows them to share stories from home, another way of informally helping children make the transition from home to school.

◆ The process of taking an LEA dictation involves the children in extended talk about topics. Working in small groups helps students with special needs build confidence by reinforcing the importance of their ideas and understand topics that they might not risk talking about with the whole class. Perhaps most important, LEA provides time for a small group of students and the teacher to work together closely and develop mutual understanding.

◆ Finding appropriate reading materials for older beginning readers is often more difficult than it is for younger students. LEA allows older students to participate fully in thinking with the rest of the class as their reading proficiency develops. (For a detailed account of using LEA with second-language learners, see Dixon and Nessel, 1983.)

One of the dilemmas in working with special needs students is providing activities that tap their cognitive capabilities. Many picture books lend themselves to work assignments for these students (see, for example, Benedict and Carlisle, 1992). Aside from using such books, we can adapt the Language Experience Approach for older students who want to explore, discuss, and read about topics. We will want to keep our below-level readers involved in the higher-level thinking and discussing that is occurring in class and to assure them that their ideas are worthwhile.

One strategy is to have the special needs student create his or her own text about the topic being studied. The teacher, a parent, or another student reads the pertinent chapter or chapter section into a tape recorder. The student then listens to this tape and dictates to a partner the ideas he or she considers important. This dictation now becomes the student's "text." Through such minor adjustments, our students with special needs will fully participate in regular class activities, and their knowledge of subject matter will not lag behind as they build power in reading.

Carlsen (1985) further suggests that students who are hearing impaired should participate in an activity or a field trip before dictating an LEA. The combination of real experience and the written record helps these students understand vocabulary and sentence structure and aids reading development.

Reading Aloud, "Narrow Reading," and Repeated Readings

Read-alouds One of the ways to help special needs students become readers and writers is to share a variety of literature with them through a "read-aloud" format (see Chapter 6, p. 196). For young beginning readers and writers, we read aloud predictable books and books that are well illustrated. These books, based so often on rhymes and songs, help acquaint children with storybooks. *Older* students also enjoy and benefit from listening to the teacher's oral reading. Often, once we have read a story to the class, our less proficient readers will attempt to read the book themselves, feeling more confident about their abilities.

Wordless books (see Chapter 6) take on a new importance for learners with special needs. Dixon and Nessel (1983) specifically recommend wordless books for students who are learning English as a second language. These authors suggest that students supply their own oral texts for a picture story, which then can be written down using LEA or can be tape-recorded for other listening experiences. Wordless books can enable parents who do not speak or read and write English to "read" aloud with their children, using the students' first language to share the story. Parents who do speak English but can't read it can also share stories this way. It's important to note that wordless books have been published for older as well as younger students.

Narrow Reading   In **narrow reading**, a student experiences several works of one author or several books on a single topic. A student who reads several works by Beverly Cleary, for instance, would find the first book the most difficult to read but would find subsequent books easier. While reading the first book, the student becomes familiar with the author's writing style and vocabulary. Since many authors employ the same characters and settings in book sequels, the student has only to focus on the new plot while reading a second or third book in the series. To each new book the student brings more background knowledge about the characters and the author's style.

To employ "narrow reading" on a single topic, share with students books that vary in complexity from very simple introductory texts to works with more complete discussions. The students will build background knowledge from each book and can bring it to bear on their reading of subsequent books. This strategy helps below-grade-level readers develop a fuller understanding of the topics being studied in class.

Repeated Reading   **Repeated reading** of the same dictated text, story, or poem allows the student to come to the text focused only on meaning. On second and subsequent readings, the student recognizes a story's sequence and vocabulary and doesn't need to give as much attention to these details. Second-language learners and below-level readers have a better chance of forming predictions after a second or third reading of a story (Sutton, 1989; Wong-Fillmore, 1982). We should try to choose books that are particularly interesting or that easily provide for a second focus. For example, during the first reading of *The Doorbell Rang* (Hutchins, 1971), the children could listen to discover what happens to the cookies and who appears at the door. During the second reading, we could ask students to focus on the mother to discover the difficulties she has keeping the floor clean.

Another way to encourage repeated reading is through "paired reading." In this approach, students practice a story with a partner so that they can then read it to a third child. Many times teachers have older students choose a picture book to read to a kindergarten or first-grade child. The practice reading sessions that occur before the sharing let the older student experience truly fluent reading. Readers Theatre (Chapter 9) is another excellent forum that involves students in repeatedly rereading a story for an informal performance.

An important advantage of repeated readings is that students' comprehension becomes deeper on successive readings. They talk more about familiar stories and develop a greater understanding of the story. Morrow

(1987) pointed out that after reading a story once, students often talk about the illustrations. After subsequent readings, they comment on and question the plot and characters. These extra readings let all of the children in the class—even the least proficient reader—understand the importance of discovering the meaning of a story.

Reading aloud and repeated readings are critical components of early intervention programs—programs targeted at young children who are "at risk" as learners (Hiebert & Taylor, 1994; Pikulski, 1994). Each time we meet with these children, we should introduce a new reading selection to them *as well as* rereading a favorite story or a dictation. These "shared-reading" experiences are seen as critical elements in helping at-risk first-graders develop literacy skills (Pinnell, Fried, & Estice, 1990).

In all of these activities, we can develop students' thinking skills by having them make predictions before and while they read, an assignment which keeps them involved in achieving meaning. Students can compare and contrast the similarities and differences among several stories they have read. For example, we can use very specific vocabulary when we ask our students to make comparisons. Simply saying, "Let's look at these stories" is too general. Specific terms such as *compare* and *contrast* help focus a student's thinking and allow him or her to concentrate on the problem-solving requirements of a task.

Writing

Second-language learners can certainly write in English before they have mastered the oral and written systems of English. Reading and writing develop as children participate in the process of *composing* text. Not surprisingly, writing is also recommended for students with special education needs. Rhodes and Dudley-Marling (1988) indicate that many of these students "have plenty to say if they would only leave behind their nearly paralyzing concern about conventions, spelling in particular" (p. 114). We'll work toward developing these students' writing fluency before emphasizing correct usage (see Chapter 7).

Children who are *writing* in English as they *learn* English often include elements of their first language in their stories. Figure 4.1 includes two responses to the story *Buenos Noches* (Oxenbury, 1987), written by two first-graders in a predominantly Hispanic classroom. The teacher read the story to the children in Spanish, and then they wrote about it in Spanish using invented spelling and illustrations. (The teacher provided a Spanish and an English translation for us.) These children are still predominantly using Spanish when they write; the relationship between their invented spelling and the conventional Spanish provided by the teacher is clear.

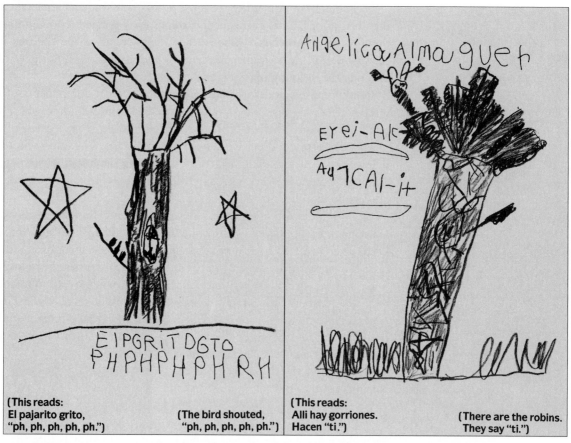

(This reads:
El pajarito grito,
"ph, ph, ph, ph, ph.")

(The bird shouted,
"ph, ph, ph, ph, ph.")

(This reads:
Alli hay gorriones.
Hacen "ti.")

(There are the robins.
They say "ti.")

Figure 4.1   *Story Responses Written by Two Hispanic First-graders*

Figure 4.2 comes from a second-grade class studying a unit on insects. The teacher asked the children to write about what insect they might like to be and what they would do as that insect. As the figure shows, a second-grader wrote a story about being a bug and flying over people, schools, trees, parks, and stores. She thought it would be okay to be a bug during the day, but at night she would turn back into a person. Notice that her story is relatively easy to read and that the carryover from her first language is the use of "de" for *the*.

We needn't worry when students mix their home language and English (Edelsky, 1986; Nathenson-Majia, 1989). Those who have studied the writing of second-language learners emphasize that students

◆ use what they know about their first language when learning a second language, and

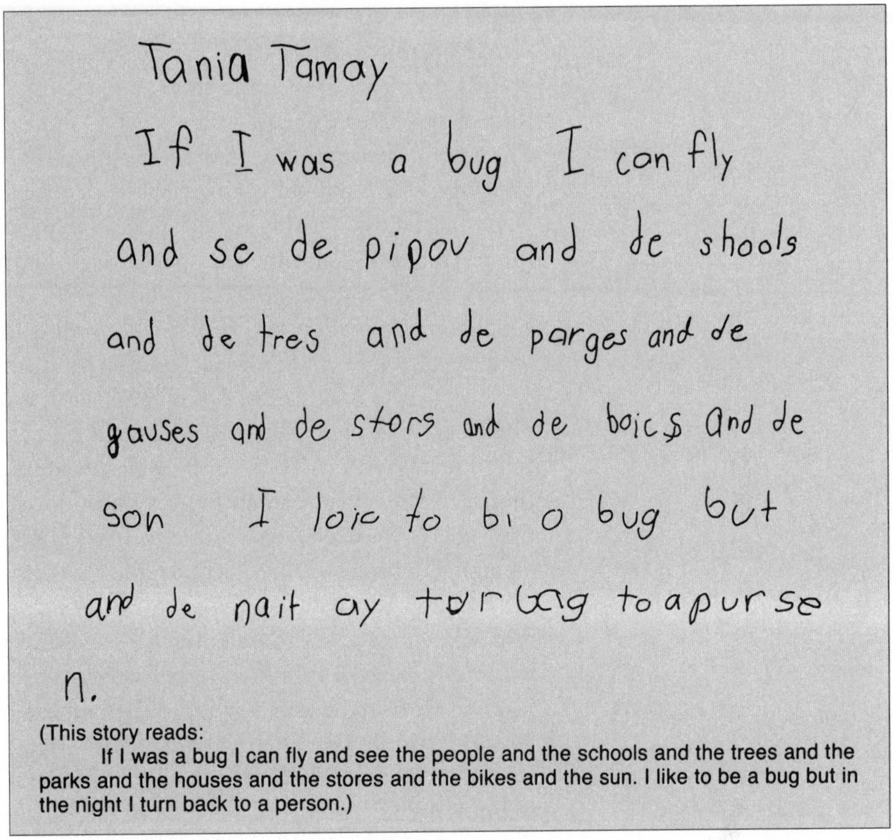

> Tania Tamay
>
> If I was a bug I con fly
>
> and se de pipov and de shools
>
> and de tres and de parges and de
>
> gauses and de stors and de boics and de
>
> son I loic to bi o bug but
>
> and de nait ay tur bag to a purse
>
> n.
>
> (This story reads:
>   If I was a bug I can fly and see the people and the schools and the trees and the
> parks and the houses and the stores and the bikes and the sun. I like to be a bug but in
> the night I turn back to a person.)

Figure 4.2   **Story Written by a Second-grader Whose First Language is Spanish**

◆ they follow the developmental spelling strategies described in Chapter 8 when writing English.

Their invented spellings may have characteristics unique to their first language—for example, "de" for *the*, "es" for *s* ("estop"), or "ch" for *sh* ("wach") for Hispanic children—but these features will disappear as the children become more proficient readers and writers of English. Hayes and Bayruth (1985) caution that these errors will not disappear overnight but that "the errors are not a cause for alarm, and teachers should not correct them. Children learning English as a second language will make errors, but as they become more proficient, as their production increases, as they read and write more, the number of errors will decrease" (p. 102).

Strong support for the reading and writing strategies previously described comes from a demonstration school in California (Bird, 1989). The Fair Oaks School, which has a student population that is 85 percent Hispanic-American, 10 percent other minorities (Filipino-American, African-American, Asian-American), and 5 percent Anglo-American, began a program a number of years ago to change its grim statistics: the students were three to four years below grade level as measured by an achievement test. The core ingredient of the new program was to have students read and write each day, and today the majority of students test at grade level.

As interactive writing experiences, **dialogue journals** are recommended for all students—and they are particularly effective for the diverse students in our classes (Staton, 1988; Sutton, 1989). These journals allow for personal communication between teacher and students. Many times, students with special education needs feel distant from classmates and from the teacher; this distance is especially noticeable with older students who have experienced several years of academic failure. By having students communicate directly with us about interesting ideas that they find in books, for instance, we teachers can show through our responses that we truly value their ideas. We may even be able to share similar personal experiences that let students know we are "real people" in addition to being their teachers.

Dialogue journals combine many of the practices I have mentioned that support literacy development (see Chapter 10, p. 425)— working within the zone of proximal development, writing experience, and the intimacy of working in small groups. The student initiates the writing, and the responder builds on the content of the original entry, taking the student slightly beyond his or her original understandings. In addition, dialogue journals stress the communicative nature of the writing task. The student develops his or her writing abilities so that another student or the teacher can read the communication. The following example, from a student who is learning English as a second language, provides an apt illustration (Staton, 1988):

STUDENT'S ENTRY: Ms. Reed, I like dis room and I like you Bekes you are a good teshir and teach my English. I like evryBety.
TEACHER'S RESPONSE: Everybody likes you, too, Laura. Did you read the book? We will read every day. (p. 1)

The teacher welcomes Laura and gives her a nudge to read a book. She helps Laura understand the class routine by telling her that they will be reading each day.

Interactive writing can also occur between students in the class or students from other classrooms. The students might converse about their classes in general and about books they are reading or stories they are writing. These informal opportunities for communicating through writing will spark reading and writing development in all of your students.

Throughout all the work in which we engage our students, we should allow for a *variety* of responses. Though the children's responses may differ, every student should be able to support his or her viewpoint through concrete examples. This ability to cite examples will probably be part of your criteria for assessing students. Smith (1989) observes that since "modern attitudes tend to accept events, without judgment about their value, students and adults may drift along quite nicely as mere observers, not as critical thinkers. When those same people read, they will continue to be passive—unless their teachers or friends jolt them into changing" (p. 424). You and all of the children in your class will be responsible for "jolting" one another into more active, charged kinds of thinking.

Technology Use in the Diverse Classroom

We'll be visiting the following applications, activities, and types of software again, but they should be mentioned here because of their applicability to teaching so many students from diverse backgrounds.

The classroom environment reflects and supports a composite classroom culture.

Educational software developers are designing programs that let students interact with a story on the screen—for example, to use problem-solving skills to extricate a character from some predicament. In order for the program to incorporate the suggested remedy, the children must type their directions into the computer—*an effective way to integrate reading, writing, and thinking.* Students also can interact with electronic books that offer stories with engaging audio and graphics.

Particularly for students with special education needs, computers can provide motivation for learning that is quite compelling. In addition, computers can offer support for aspects of literacy that are especially challenging for some kids. For example, children who have considerable difficulty writing by hand can use the keyboard and gain instant legibility on the monitor screen. For some older students, this accomplishment alone can be a breakthrough.

Word processing is an important frontier in writing, and many applications are available for students. For example, children of varying abilities can write stories on a computer (Hummel & Balcom, 1984). We can pair up students who each have different strengths and weaknesses, then each child can contribute sentences to a story. Sam and Amanda, for instance, might decide on a setting for their story and perhaps write the first sentence together. Then Sam writes a sentence. Amanda next uses Sam's sentence as a starting point and continues the story. Then it's Sam's turn again. This process continues until the story is completed. One benefit of using the computer in this way is that it eliminates the difficulty children may have reading each other's handwriting. Just using a computer can itself be rewarding; children enjoy seeing their writing take shape on a screen and are less inhibited about engaging in and revising this writing.

Many of these word-processing applications are complete desktop publishing programs such as the Student Writing Center (The Learning Corporation/Houghton Mifflin).

Using Thematic Units to Teach Special Needs Students

Integrated, thematic organization of curriculum is recommended for all learners in our classrooms, *particularly* those with special needs. Based on variations from a specific topic, **thematic units** give children many opportunities to explore a concept and more actively participate in their own learning. Thematic units allow students to explore a topic in depth rather than merely being exposed to it; more conceptual "handles" are provided for kids. Children are encouraged to read many books on a topic as they discover other ideas related to the theme.

◆ An intermediate-grade unit on weather (California State Department of Education, 1987) is introduced by reading Steven Kellogg's *Paul Bunyan* (1984) and a Chinese tale called *The First Snow* (Coutant, 1974). The children then research weather using various books and newspapers. The unit includes many reading and writing activities and (what is particularly interesting) literature from many different countries.

◆ Another unit focuses on the feelings of being physically challenged; it includes books such as Helen Keller's *The Story of My Life* (1903) and Elizabeth Speare's *The Witch of Blackbird Pond* (1958). The children participate in many activities that sensitize them to the difficulties of such conditions. For example, they try to block out sight and sound for one hour before reading about Helen Keller. Rather than focusing on each situation and creating a list of related conditions, the students experience feelings that are common to many conditions. In this unit the students spend time considering prejudice and how it affects people who are physically challenged and others considered "different."

We will explore thematic units in considerable depth in Chapter 10; refer to both of the thematic explorations for examples of how activities and materials have been incorporated to facilitate teaching students with diverse needs.

Involving Parents in Special Needs Instruction

Schools that have large populations of learners with special needs and are considered successful at meeting the needs of these students all have close ties with parents. These connections often involve teachers in learning more about the students' home cultures so they can make adaptations in the classroom. For example, a program in New Haven (Comer, 1987) was developed to enhance the academic and social success of at-risk students and was grounded in "the understanding that suggestions and interests of parents, teachers, and other participants must be taken seriously, and that representatives of these groups must have meaningful roles in the school program" (p. 16). Recent efforts to involve the home environment in learning are very encouraging (Morrow, 1995).

Specific activities can welcome students and involve parents in the curriculum. On a September bulletin board, for example, the teachers and students write "Welcome" in many different languages. Later each of the students develops a "Me" collage for the display. In the collage each child includes his or her birthplace, baby pictures, favorite things, names of siblings, and so on. Building on this activity, students investigate their names.

The study can expand to discovering the origin of surnames and to naming customs, including the transformation their names undergo in different languages (for example—John, Jan, Johan, Juan, Jean, Giovanni). These activities often require expert advice from home. Students need to check with parents to learn how they were named, why the family moved to the United States, and other important facts. These activities allow parents to participate informally and indirectly in the school curriculum. They also foster important discussion between the student and his or her parents and may motivate parents to become more active participants in the school.

It's important to realize the value of language interactions that occur at home with parents who do not speak English. Heath (1986) recommended that parents use the language with which they're most comfortable and capable so that children become aware of the multiple opportunities to use language. She observed that "those students who have the most diverse, well-developed, and extensive language use (even in a language other than English) will be best prepared to learn a rich and powerful English in schools" (p. 26).

How do we involve and communicate with parents who do not speak English?

◆ We can have a bilingual student or adult translate notes we send home.

◆ The students can create tapes in the parents' native languages explaining some of the events happening in school. (Students may need to borrow the tape recorder to play the message at home.)

◆ For parent conferences, arrange for an older student or a bilingual member of the community to help communicate. Remember that having samples of the student's work on hand is not only a very good idea but should also make the conference go more smoothly.

Homework is another aspect to consider. First and foremost, we should also make sure that our assignments address the specific needs of the students. Enright and McCloskey (1988) suggest that we give children more than one night—preferably a week—to complete homework assignments. The children in our classrooms come from all types of homes and may return from school to discover that their parents won't be available to help with homework. Sometimes, too, special family events compete with homework time. Flexibility in allowing assignments to be completed over two or three days should result in a better rate of homework completion.

Expand Your Teaching Repertoire

Following are some specific activities that can be assimilated into the classroom. These are ideas and assignments that should help as we begin to plan instruction for our students from diverse backgrounds.

1 Children can participate in a search for environmental print in and around the school. They will notice that writing is everywhere (Enright & McCloskey, 1988) and that they can read it. Garcia (1994) has pointed out that children learning English as a second language will rely longer on environmental print than children whose first language is English. We can also ask students to look for international signs so that they realize there are common ways of communicating across languages. A driver's education booklet would be a likely resource for some of these signs.

2 Include books in the classroom library that are written in different languages or different dialects. There are many books available in Spanish, for example. All children will enjoy comparing the words written in different languages, and they might even discover that many of the words are similar. We can also include books from the children's homes. Often children select these because they are familiar and provide connections to home reading.

3 Students can perform a research study that involves interviewing parents, friends, and other children in the school. They might try to discover what the first day of school was like for individuals of all ages and then create a time line that shows how "going to school" has changed. Another question children might ask the adults they interview is how people learned to drive and what the rules for getting a license were. The students could investigate the changes in United States driving laws. They might also compare the driving laws of various countries. The list of possible questions is endless; to narrow the possibilities, we can develop questions that relate to a thematic unit.

4 Parents and children might share a special night. Sets of parents and children could cook and share dishes that have significance in their families. A child might bring a special object from home and explain its personal significance or meaning for the family. This type of evening would help reduce the anxiety that usually accompanies family trips to school (Ramsey, 1987), and everyone certainly would get to know each other better.

(Continued)

Expand Your Teaching Repertoire

5 We can incorporate special holidays and important events from other cultures into the classroom. Teachers and students might celebrate Chinese New Year and Mexican Independence Day, for example. Inclusion of special cultural events could occur monthly throughout the school year.

6 When children create class books, they can include a Braille script or a translation to another language on each page. They might tape their stories so that other students could read along in English or some other language. Tapes and books can be shared with parents through a checkout system. Parents or other community members might even respond to the stories on cards provided in the books.

Children's Literature Related to Diversity

Our **classroom literature collections** will include books that describe cultural, linguistic, academic, and physical diversity. In addition, it is important to add that this range of literature should be discussed and celebrated throughout the year. Celebrating African-American literature only during Black History Month or Mexican-American literature only around Mexican Independence Day is problematic and suggests to students that these rich collections of works are separate sets of literature that are simply being tacked onto the main curriculum at various times. Instead, these bodies of literature should be an inextricable part of a culturally diverse curriculum that acknowledges the writings and accomplishments of a diverse range of individuals who have contributed to our world.

Once again, *thematic units* provide opportunities to share books that represent all cultures:

◆ A unit on "Economics: Hard Times or Good Times?" could include Cleary's *Ramona and Her Father* (1977), Hazen's *Tight Times* (1979), and Greenfield's *Grandmama's Joy* (1980). Ramona is an Anglo-American child growing up in a middle-class family, the male character in *Tight Times* is Hispanic and has an urban background, and Greenfield's Rhondy is an African-American child living in the city.

◆ A unit on grandparents or senior citizens would include Miles's *Annie and the Old One* (1971), Mathis's *The Hundred Penny Box* (1978), and dePaola's *Nana Upstairs and Nana Downstairs* (1973).

Build Your
Teaching
Resources

**RESOURCES FOR
CHILDREN'S
LITERATURE
RELATED TO
DIVERSITY**

Part III in the Sourcebook includes a wide array of multicultural literature for children. For further exploration, the following is a selection of the best available resources:

Bishop, R. (1994). *Kaleidoscope: A multicultural booklist for grades K–8.* Urbana, IL: National Council of Teachers of English. [Annotations of 400 multicultural titles published from 1990–1992]

Day, F. (1994). *Multicultural voices in contemporary literature: A resource for teachers.* Portsmouth, NH: Heinemann. [Author and illustrator studies of over 39 individuals from 20 cultures]

Harris, V. (1993). *Teaching multicultural literature in grades K–8.* Norwood, MA: Christopher-Gordon.

Wong, S. (1993). Promises, pitfalls, and principles of text selection in curriculum diversification: The Asian-American case. In T. Perry and J. Fraser (Eds.), *Freedom's plow: Teaching in the multicultural classroom* (pp. 109–120). New York: Routledge Kegan-Paul.

These books represent three very different cultures, but children can discuss these stories thoroughly without explicitly realizing this fact. Students do not need to be made aware of these cultural differences in any formal way. What *is* important is for them to realize that common emotions are shared by all humans, regardless of their particular cultural backgrounds. By sharing literature that deals with themes common to humanity, children will focus on the similarities among members of various cultures rather than on the differences.

The following criteria will help you effectively evaluate literature in terms of **cultural authenticity**, avoiding stereotypes that support racism and sexism (Harris, 1993; Ramsey, 1987). Here is a checklist for evaluating children's books with particular emphasis on recognizing racism and sexism. As you prepare to read any book to your students, you might consider these elements:

1. Check the illustrations. Look for stereotypes and observe what people are doing.

2. Check the storyline. What are the standards for success? Do minorities have to exhibit extraordinary skills to be successful? Who is responsible for resolving the problems?

3. Look at lifestyles. Who is living where? Are all the minority children living in a ghetto or barrio?

4. Weigh the relationships between people. Who is subservient?

5. Who are the heroes and heroines?

6. Provide different perspectives on American history events such as the Chinese-American view of the Exclusionary Acts of the latter nineteenth century or the Seminole or Navajo interpretation of "resettlement."

7. Consider the author's and illustrator's backgrounds.

8. Check out the author's perspective. What cultural, social, and economic perspectives does the book portray?

9. Watch for "loaded" words.

10. Consider the effects on a child's self-esteem.

CONCLUDING PERSPECTIVE AND SUMMARY

The multicultural nature of today's language arts classrooms offers a myriad of learning opportunities for both teachers and students. However, teachers must also meet the daily challenge of educating culturally and linguistically diverse students and children with special needs within the context of regular classroom instruction. Chapter 4 presented strategies and activities for teaching diverse students but particularly focused on ways to develop their language and thinking skills while building their reading and writing abilities. As we incorporate aspects of our diverse students' backgrounds and cultures into our teaching strategies, we will enable the multicultural and special needs students to gain self-esteem and also provide all our students with a better understanding and appreciation of the world's peoples.

In this chapter we've addressed the following main points:

◆ Although currently California, Florida, New York, and Texas have the greatest numbers of children learning English as a second language, statistics and trends indicate that teachers in all parts of the country will soon be instructing such students in their regular classrooms. By the year 2000, one of every three students will be a minority group member.

◆ Comprehending the home cultures of diverse students is essential for teaching them effectively. Teachers must use such knowledge to adjust their classroom cultures and broaden their instruction to be responsive to these students.

◆ The primary goal when teaching language minority students is to develop their English to a level where they can participate and learn in a classroom where only English is spoken. Beyond learning to speak English adequately, the students must be able to grasp abstract concepts necessary for academic learning.

◆ The strength of English as a Second Language (ESL) programs, which emphasize learning English and do not provide instruction in students' first languages, is that they work toward achieving this goal. However, the weaknesses of such programs are that 1) they may not encourage flexibility in students' use of two languages to adapt their discourse as situations demand; and 2) they do not support students' academic learning in their native language.

◆ Supreme Court–mandated bilingual programs provide instruction of academic subjects in students' native languages as well as some instruction in English. As strengths, these programs don't devalue the students' first languages and encourage using either English or the first language as conditions warrant.

◆ Because school districts cannot always provide bilingual or ESL programs, most teachers will rely more on "sheltered" English methods to teach the growing numbers of language minority students. In this approach the teacher accommodates the second-language learners by being sensitive to their needs and adjusting instructional techniques to include these students in regular class activities.

◆ Most students who have special needs should spend as much time as possible in a regular classroom setting participating in its normal activities.

◆ Teachers should employ small-group and individual strategies to enhance the learning of all students, particularly those with special needs. Students can interact in predictable, organized environments such as cooperative group activities or peer tutoring sessions. In addition, we will read aloud to them and encourage interactive writing, as for example through dialogue journals. We can also take "dictations" to encourage communication and bolster self-esteem.

◆ We should involve parents of special needs students and second-language learners in their children's education. They can serve as resources of information about students' families or cultures that can be shared with the class for special projects. We can enlist in our instruction the help of a bilingual adult or older student to include parents who don't speak English. The person could translate notes about class activities or participate in a parent conference. The class could also create tapes in their first languages to send home to these parents.

Key Terms

academic English (p. 98)

bilingual education (p. 96)

classroom literature collections (p. 124)

composite culture (p. 90)

cultural authenticity (p. 125)

culturally responsive (p. 90)

culturally responsive instruction (p. 93)

dialects (p. 98)

dialogue journals (p. 118)

English as a Second Language (ESL) (p. 96)

inclusion (p. 100)

Language Experience Approach (p. 112)

language impairments (p. 101)

language minority students (p. 96)

low-prevalence categories (p. 101)

mental retardation (p. 101)

multicultural perspective in education (p. 90)

narrow reading (p. 114)

nonstandard dialect (p. 99)

peer tutoring (p. 106)

playground English (p. 98)

registers (p. 99)

repeated reading (p. 114)

role-play (p. 108)

serious emotional disturbance (p. 101)

sheltered English (p. 97)

specific learning disabilities (p. 101)

speech impairments (p. 101)

standard English (p. 99)

"talk story" format (p. 111)

thematic units (p. 120)

topic-associating style (p. 94)

topic-specific style (p. 94)

THEMATIC EXPLORATION

Cynthia Rylant: An Author Study

Sandra Madura: Primary Classroom

Through this thematic exploration, I'd like to give you a sense of the planning, organization, and cumulative learning that develop over the course of such an inquiry. This thematic unit is one that I conducted for seven- and eight-year-olds beginning in mid-October. Our school services working-class and professional neighborhoods, and my class comprised twenty-four children — including two of Philippine heritage, two from mainland China, one from El Salvador, and one from Thailand.

I had already shared some of Cynthia Rylant's books with the class, and she had proven to be a favorite of the students. They really wanted to read more of her work and learn more about her as an author. I have found that most primary students love her humorous books such as the *Henry & Mudge* and *Mr. Putter and Tabby* series. These books deal with some of the same themes as Rylant's more reflective works, so she was a natural for our "author" theme study. I realized that many of the instructional goals I had for the children could be addressed through a thematic unit focusing on an author.

For my brainstorming phase I worked with Ann, a third-grade teacher I've worked closely with during the last few years. We often share themes, and she knew Rylant would be a theme she could eventually use. She had also read a number of Rylant's books with her students over the years. With a large piece of butcher paper in front of us, we brainstormed connections. We realized that many topics or subthemes have struck us as we've read Rylant's work and many of them overlap:

- Commonalities of experience and life across generations — what *all* of us share (for example, the childhood recollections of grandparents or other senior citizens, of parents, and of the students themselves)

- Where a writer's ideas come from — first and foremost, his or her own life and experiences

- Family and friendship

- The passage of time and aging, city/country, attachment to a place and land

THEMATIC EXPLORATION

Goals

My goals emerged from this initial brainstorm:

◆ Develop a "deep" understanding of a particular author.

◆ Develop an understanding of the *source* of narratives—where a writer's stories come from.

◆ Develop an awareness of the *elements* of narrative that are guides to deeper insight and understanding: *plot*, *setting*, *characterization*, and *theme*.

◆ Explore how to get writing going.

◆ Write personal stories/histories.

◆ Gain awareness of different themes presented in Cynthia Rylant's stories—family, friendship, aging, the passage of time, attachment to place/land.

◆ Understand ways that character and setting are developed (including illustrations).

◆ Develop an awareness of word choice and select phrases.

Selecting and Reading the Books

As I pulled from my own collection and from the school media center, I realized it would be important to include the light-hearted as well as the more reflective of Rylant's work; all would potentially lend themselves to inquiry. It looked like my *core* and *extended* texts would all be Rylant's, and many *recreational* texts were also hers—though here was where other authors would fit well. Representing a range of ethnic and social cultures, they addressed similar themes such as friendship and family. I realized that there were many possibilities for meeting the range of my children's reading abilities and for addressing the second-language development of three of my students.

As I do before we explore any author, I read up on my choices. I'm always on the lookout for write-ups about authors in journals; my favorites are *BookLinks* and the vignettes about children's authors provided on the *Children's Literature Web Guide* (http://www.ucalgary.ca/~dkbrown). I also

THEMATIC EXPLORATION

turn to *Something About the Author* (see Resource list on p. 408). In reading the latest entry about Cynthia Rylant in this resource, I was struck by the following:

> Critics laud Rylant for her straightforward approach, economic yet lyrical language, lifelike characterizations, and ability to express powerful emotions with restraint . . . Rylant's poignant tales, well-crafted, rhythmic texts, and evocative poetry have provided young readers with memorable examples of sincere and elegant writing.

That captured it for me. I wanted this unit to give my students a sense of that writing—the voice and the words—and to build multiple perspectives on story, language, and the transaction between illustration and text in well-crafted picture books.

In addition to the books listed in *Something About the Author*, I checked *Books in Print* on the library's computer to see what else Rylant had done as well as to check for titles that have been published since the *Author* review. I've read most of Rylant's picture books, though not all—and I haven't read all of her *Henry & Mudge* and *Mr. Putter & Tabby* series books, so I snuggled down one evening and read through many of my and my former students' personal favorites again. Reading through these, I saw how her different themes fit with the categories Ann and I had brainstormed and the goals that had developed from these. Once again I was struck by how often her characters are elderly, living alone, and dealing with the hardships of living in the country or the city. However, my students were all beginning to move in significant ways beyond their own focused perspectives and to see those of others—and I've found that grandparents and the elderly fit meaningfully and comfortably into children's world views at this time. I was also struck, when reading *Miss Maggie* (1983), by the emotional wrenching that can accompany the loss of a pet; several children had experienced a loss already that year, and this book helped place such losses in perspective. We had read Judith Viorst's *The Tenth Good Thing About Barney* (1971) at these times, but *Miss Maggie* took this reflection to a deeper yet appropriated level.

In reading Rylant's first-person account of her life and her writing in *Best Wishes* (1992), I was struck by the sense of her strong roots in Appalachia, even though she no longer lives there. She returns regularly, however, as if to renew those roots and the sources of inspiration for her writing. For me, this comes through powerfully in *Appalachia: The Voices of Sleeping Birds* (1991). While there is subtlety in this beautiful book that will elude most

THEMATIC EXPLORATION

eight-year-olds, the words are magical and work as poetry on the children. With successive rereadings, I suspect they'll notice more about the words and the images.

I thought about those books all of us should experience, live with, and respond to. I then choose the following for our *core texts*:

When I Was Young in the Mountains (1982)

The Relatives Came (1985)

Night in the Country (1986)

Birthday Presents (1987)

All I See (1994)

Henry & Mudge: The First Book of Their Adventures (1987)

Miss Maggie (1983)

Mr. Grigg's Work (1989)

An Angel for Soloman Singer (1992)

Appalachia: The Voices of Sleeping Birds (1991)

These books represent Rylant's major themes and would help us address the goals I had established for the unit.

Among the *extended texts* I included Rylant's *Everyday Garden* (1993) book for students who need guided reading in easier texts. I also included other *Everyday* books as *recreational texts*; these are "boardbooks" that are types of simple concept books for younger children. I wanted to use these as examples of how illustration works with text to engage a particular audience. Those students who choose to do so can create their own "Everyday" books to be shared with kindergarten students. Some of the extended texts address themes similar to Rylant's, and because they also fit with the instructional reading levels of my students, I included them—for example, Judy Delton's *Two Good Friends* (1985) (Easier) and Marjorie Sharmat's *I'm Not Oscar's Friend Anymore* (1975) (Challenging). In addition to having lots of copies of Rylant's *Henry & Mudge*, *Mr. Putter & Tabby*, and the *Everyday* books on hand for recreational texts, I included other books that address our themes as well as books by several of the illustrators of Rylant's works.

THEMATIC EXPLORATION

Objectives

◆ Identify how writers create different points of view in a story.

◆ Identify how writers represent the passage of time in stories.

◆ In response to reading and through discussion and writing, demonstrate understanding of the different themes in Rylant's writing.

◆ Use writing for different purposes.

◆ Discuss Rylant's experiences and students' own experiences as possible sources for writing—what *inspires* us to write?

◆ Compose personal "autobiographies" modeled on Rylant's *Best Wishes* (1992).

◆ Through discussion and in writing, show how *characterization*, *setting*, and *plot* are developed.

Activities/Projects

I like to think of our activities and projects in terms of *introducing, developing*, and *culminating* the unit. For an author theme study, I've found one of the best *introductory* activities is, quite simply, a read-aloud. Rylant's *When I Was Young in the Mountains* is excellent for this; we talk about how this was her first book and how she relied so closely on her own childhood as a source of ideas. We then tie the discussion with the students' own experiences and reflections about "when *they* were young . . ."

There is quite a range of *developing* activities in this unit; in fact, most of our writing and other creative work such as producing visual art and storytelling stretch throughout the unit. These will result in *culminating* activities when these efforts are shared, published, and celebrated.

The following activities and projects will help us realize our objectives:

◆ Story Maps

◆ Comparison Charts

◆ Writing a story about growing up

◆ Writing a "friendship" story

◆ Music—Beethoven's 5th Symphony (featured in *All I See*)

THEMATIC EXPLORATION

◆ Art—Perspective: Drawing near and far away (based on the *Everyday* books); Drawing what is *there* vs. what is "in our heads" (featured in *All I See*)

◆ Writing: Leaving notes/messages (based on messages the boy and the artist leave each other in *All I See*)

◆ Writing and illustrating an original *Everyday* book

◆ Acting out figurative language

◆ Storytelling

◆ K-W-L Chart

Skills Instruction

For all my students' reading levels, there are different types of skills I'd like to work on. Meaning construction in narratives is important; many students still need support with establishing and maintaining *sequence* as they read. Others need help understanding how "time" changes in narratives—how authors tell us how much time has elapsed, whether "flashbacks" are used, and so forth. Rylant's books offer plenty of examples; I can conduct minilessons and engage the students in discussion as well as see which ones try out certain "patterns" of time change in their own compositions.

For our word study, students will continue to work on the spelling patterns that are developmentally appropriate for them (see Chapter 11 and the Sourcebook). Rylant's books provide excellent terrain for "word hunts" (see Chapter 8) to locate other words that illustrate these patterns. We will also work on applying our word knowledge in identifying unfamiliar words in reading. The books I've chosen for extended reading—much of which is conducted in a guided-reading format—lend themselves to this application of developing word-identification skills.

Sequence and Schedule

I've thought in terms of four weeks for this unit. You'll see my final schedule with representative activities/projects in this thematic exploration. To give you a sense of the day-to-day flow, I've also included a schedule for the first week of the unit (it fits within the basic daily schedule presented in Chapter 3). There is always room for adjustments, of course, and when I first share our theme with my students, there may be some changes. I've always felt

Cynthia Rylant

Week 1

Core Selection: *When I Was Young in the Mountains*
Repetitive Text-Pattern in Students' Writing — "When I was young in the mountains . . ."
Personal Memory Writing: "When I was young in . . ."
Heritage Search: What was life like for your parents?
Group Chart: Compare parents' second-grade experience to your experiences now
Core Selection: *The Relatives Came*
What's it like when your relatives come to visit?
How is the passage of time marked within the story?
Core Selection: *Night in the Country*
Discuss "sound words": descriptive and action words
Core Selection: *Birthday Presents*
Autobiography: Ties in to "When I was young" theme . . .
Core Selection: *Appalachia: The Sounds of Sleeping Birds*

Week 2

Explore concept of "Friendship" in the core and extended texts
Core Selection: *All I See*
Writing: Leaving notes/messages
Outdoor Painting
Beethoven's 5th Symphony: Play
Perspective: Drawing near and far away
Core Selection: *Henry & Mudge: The First Book of Their Adventures* — Characterization
How do we get to know about Henry and Mudge as characters? (Rereading to find examples)
What type of family is represented? How like or different from your family?
What feelings grow between Henry and Mudge?
What patterns in the H&M stories do we see?
Core Selection (Reread): *Birthday Presents*
Writing modeled on *Birthday Presents*: "On your first one . . . on your second one . . . on your third one . . ."
Mr. Putter and Tabby books
What patterns in the Mr. Putter and Tabby stories do we see?
Everyday "Boardbooks": Write and construct

Week 3

Concept of "Friendship" flows into this week
"Aging/Living Alone" emerges as a theme
Characteristics of the people in Rylant's stories
    Tied to a place
    How to connect to a different place when we need to
Core Selection: *Miss Maggie* — Plot/Characterization/Setting
Story Map for some students
Stories of people we're unsure of but we discover their qualities through an encounter with them; people we've been afraid of.
On what do we base these decisions?
"Good dog" — How pets are incorporated into Cynthia Rylant's stories — How pets often help in healing
Core Selection: *Mr. Grigg's Work* — Characterization/Setting
Having a job you love — why is that important?
What job in the classroom you really like and why
Get to know your own postman/woman; write a letter to him/her and leave it with a drawing
Core Selection: *An Angel for Soloman Singer* — Characterization/Setting
Compare city to country — how illustrations show comparison
Stories of moving or change in lifestyle (why do these things happen?)
Guided imagery of a different environment from where classroom is located
Discussion — Is it important to love where you live?

How are these three books alike? Characters? How are the characters alike/different?
Construct a character cluster for one of these characters

Week 4

(A week of sharing, rereading, and reflecting)
Storytelling and Sharing our compositions: Classmates, kindergartners, field trip to Senior Citizens Center to share
Figurative Language: Students act out

THEMATIC EXPLORATION

better thinking through my thematic units to this level of organization, however. Some years the students seem to move towards independence in work and planning more quickly than others. Because this unit is being studied earlier in the school year, I'm more structured than I may be later in the year.

BOOK SELECTIONS:

Core Texts

When I was young in the mountains. (1982). New York: Dutton Children's Books. [Illustrated by D. Goode.]

The relatives came. (1985). New York: Bradbury Press. [Illustrated by S. Gammell.]

Night in the country. (1986). New York: Bradbury Press. [Illustrated by M. Szilagyi.]

Birthday presents. (1987). New York: Orchard Books. [Illustrated by S. Stevenson.]

All I see. (1994). New York: Orchard Books. [Illustrated by P. Catalanotto.]

Henry & Mudge: The first book of their adventures. (1987). New York: Bradbury Press. [Illustrated by J. Stevenson.]

Miss Maggie. (1983). New York: Dutton. [Illustrated by T. Di Grazia.]

Mr. Grigg's work. (1989). New York: Orchard Books. [Illustrated by J. Downing.]

An angel for Soloman Singer. (1992). New York: Orchard Books. [Illustrated by P. Catalanotto.]

Appalachia: The voices of sleeping birds. (1991). Orlando, FL: Harcourt. [Illustrated by B. Moser.]

Extended Texts

Henry & Mudge under the yellow moon. (1992). New York: Simon & Schuster. (Average)

Henry & Mudge in the sparkle days. (1988). New York: Simon & Schuster. (Average)

Mr. Putter & Tabby walk the dog. (1994). Orlando, FL: Harcourt. [Illustrated by A. Howard.] (Average)

Everyday garden. (1993). New York: Macmillan Children's Book Group. (Easier)

Two good friends (by J. Delton 1985). New York: Crown. [Illustrated by J. Delton.] (Easier)

Fox and his friends (by E. Marshall 1994). New York: Puffin Books. [Illustrated by J. Marshall.] (Challenging)

I'm not Oscar's friend anymore (by M. Sharmat 1975). New York: Dutton. (Challenging)

Harlequin and the gift of many colors (1973), by R. Charlip. Chicago: Parents Magazine Press.

What kind of baby-sitter is this? (1991), by D. Johnson. New York: Simon & Schuster. (Average)

THEMATIC EXPLORATION

Recreational Texts

Henry & Mudge Books:

Henry & Mudge under the yellow moon (1992). New York: Simon & Schuster. [Illustrated by S. Stevenson.]

Henry & Mudge in the sparkle days. (1993). New York: Macmillan. [Illustrated by S. Stevenson.]

Henry & Mudge in puddle trouble. (1987). New York: Bradbury Press. [Illustrated by J. Stevenson.]

Henry & Mudge in the green time. (1987). New York: Bradbury Press. [Illustrated by S. Stevenson.]

Henry & Mudge & the forever sea. (1989). New York: Bradbury Press. [Illustrated by S. Stevenson.]

Henry & Mudge get the cold shivers. (1989). New York: Bradbury Press. [Illustrated by S. Stevenson.]

Henry & Mudge & the happy cat. (1990). New York: Bradbury Press. [Illustrated by S. Stevenson.]

Henry & Mudge take the big test. (1991). New York: Bradbury Press. [Illustrated by S. Stevenson.]

Mr. Putter & Tabby Books:

Mr. Putter & Tabby pour the tea. (1994). Orlando, FL: Harcourt.

Mr. Putter & Tabby fly the plane. (1996). Orlando, FL: Harcourt.

Mr. Putter & Tabby pick the pears. (1995). Orlando, FL: Harcourt.

Mr. Putter & Tabby bake the cake. (1994). Orlando, FL: Harcourt.

Mr. Putter & Tabby row the boat. (1996). Orlando, FL: Harcourt.

Everyday books series. (1993). New York: Macmillan Children's Book Group:

Everyday House

Everyday Pets

Everyday Children

Everyday Garden

Everyday Town

THEMATIC EXPLORATION

MONDAY	TUESDAY	WEDNESDAY

MONDAY

9:00–9:30
 Children arrive
 Journal-writing:
 What was it like when you were four years old . . .
 Record-keeping:
  Hot lunch
  Calendar and Weather
 Read-Aloud: **Core Selection**
 Introduce Rylant as the focus author
 When I Was Young in the Mountains
 Discussion: Where and when does the story take place? How do you know? How was Rylant's life different from yours? like yours?
9:35–10:15
 Writing Workshop:
 Minilesson: Prewriting and Begin Drafting
 •Do a web with "When I was young in . . ." as the focus—jot down two of my own recollections, then elicit some from the students
 •On large chart paper, model how to take a couple of recollections from the students and begin writing
 Students Write:
 Personal Memory Writing: "When I was young in . . ."
 •Prewrite: Cluster, then share with partner
 •Begin Draft
10:15–10:30
 Recess
10:35–12:00
 Reading Workshop
 Minilesson: Brief "Booktalk" about the different types of books and topics Cynthia Rylant addresses—
 How do we decide which books we think we'd like to read?

Select from Rylant's "Recreational" titles which we'd like to read during Reading Workshop. After reading individually, share some of our responses and reactions

Small Groups
 Guided Reading of *Everyday House*—students in beginning literacy phase
 Guided Reading of *Mr. Putter & Tabby Walk the Dog*—students in early transitional literacy phase
 Listening Center: *When I Was Young in the Mountains*

Word Study
 Working individually, students categorize words
 K-W-L Chart before lunch: What do we know or want to know about Cynthia Rylant?
12:00–12:45
 Lunch and Recess
12:50–1:20
 Read-Aloud: Reread *When I Was Young in the Mountains*; afterwards discuss when and why Cynthia Rylant keeps repeating the phrase "When I was young in the mountains . . ."
1:25–2:15
 Math
2:15–2:30
 Physical Education
2:30–2:55
 Library

TUESDAY

9:00–9:40
 Children arrive
 Journal-writing
 Record-keeping:
  Hot lunch
  Calendar and Weather
 Read-Aloud: **Core Selection**—*Best Wishes*, Rylant's "autobiography"—
 Discuss where writers get their ideas
 Reread *When I Was Young in the Mountains*—Discuss: What more do you notice or think about this time around?
9:45–10:15
 Music
10:15–10:30
 Recess
10:35–10:50
 Writing Workshop:
 Discuss "Heritage Search":
 •What do you think life was like for your parents?
 •Brainstorm questions you'd like to ask your parents (or grandparents)
10:50–12:00
 Literature Discussion Groups/Guided Reading
 Read-Aloud: **Core Selection** *The Relatives Came*
 After reading, discuss: When relatives come—compare/contrast with book
 Reading Workshop:
 Plot and *Sequence*
 How is the passage of time marked within the story?

Small Groups:
 Literature Discussion Groups—Choral-reread *When I Was Young in the Mountains*; Find favorite line, reread to yourself, then share with group—why your favorite?

Guided Reading: *Amos and Boris*—Students in later transitional literacy phase. How is Amos and Boris's friendship like friendships *people* have sometimes?

(When students not reading individually or meeting with teacher, *write* questions they'd like to ask their parents)

Word Study
 In small groups, students categorize words—compare and contrast, discuss with teacher and other students
12:00–12:45
 Lunch and Recess
12:50–1:20
 Teacher Read-Aloud
 Sustained Silent Reading
1:20–2:15
 Math
2:15–3:00
 Social Studies and Physical Education

WEDNESDAY

9:00–9:30
 Children arrive
 Journal-writing: Record two of your favorite lines from *When I Was Young*. Why are they your favorites?
 Record-keeping:
  Hot lunch
  Calendar and Weather
9:35–10:15
 Writing Workshop:
 •Minilesson:
 Group Chart: Compare parents' childhood to second-graders' now (Venn diagram). Add information to your "When I was young in . . ." piece
10:15–10:30
 Recess
10:35–12:00
 Read-Aloud: **Core Selection**, *Night in the Country*
 Reading Workshop
 Minilesson: How Rylant uses words to create sound and visual images for us—"Sound" words: Description and Action

THEMATIC EXPLORATION

WEDNESDAY	THURSDAY	FRIDAY

WEDNESDAY

Small Groups
Guided Reading of *Everyday Garden*: students in beginning literacy phase
Guided Reading: Dolores Johnson's *What Kind of Baby-Sitter Is This?* Simon & Schuster. (Average)

Word Study
Students work in buddy pairs to sort and write words — word games such as "Go Fish" and board games (using word cards), "Boggle"

Listening Center: *The Relatives Came*

12:00–12:45
Lunch and Recess
12:50–1:20
Teacher Read-Aloud:
First part of *Appalachia: Voices of Sleeping Birds*

Sustained Silent Reading
1:20–2:15
Math
2:15–3:00
Science and Physical Education

THURSDAY

9:00–9:30
Children arrive
Journal-writing
Record-keeping:
  Hot lunch
  Calendar and Weather
Read-Aloud: **Core Selection**—Reread
9:35–10:15
Writing Workshop
Close eyes—listen.
Identify sounds.
Describe them.
Class Chart: What sounds do *you* hear at night? Describe them. Discuss.

Individual Writing: Describe your "night sounds"

10:15–10:30
Recess
10:35—Noon
Reading Workshop/Literature Discussion Groups/Guided Reading

Read-Aloud: **Core Selection**, *Birthday Presents* Autobiography—each year of second-grader's life bring in pictures; share

Small Groups
Guided Reading:
The City Mouse and the Country Mouse (1996) (A Play) (retold by Hal Ober). (Average) In Cooper & Pikulski, *Invitations to Literacy*, Boston: Houghton Mifflin.—Students in later transitional literacy phase

Echo-Read: *Everyday Garden*—students in beginning literacy phase

Word Study
"Word Hunts"—Working in buddy pairs, students hunt for words that follow the pattern(s) they are learning about

12:00–12:45
Lunch and Recess
12:50–1:20
Teacher Read-Aloud:
Second part of *Appalachia: Voices of Sleeping Birds*

Sustained Silent Reading
1:20–2:15
Math
2:15–3:00
Social Studies and Physical Education

FRIDAY

9:00–9:30
Children arrive
Journal-writing
Record-keeping:
  Hot lunch
  Calendar and Weather
Read-Aloud: **Favorite Core Texts**
9:35–10:15
Writing Workshop:
Those who wish to do so, share "When I was Young in . . ." compositions—these will be bound in a class book

Using her *Everyday* books as examples, discuss how Rylant has composed her illustrations; how do they work together with her words?

10:15–10:30
Recess
10:35–11:15
Art: Paper collage—Rylant's *Everyday* books as examples

11:20—Noon
Reading Workshop/Literature Discussion Groups/Guided Reading
Whole Class: What do we think and feel about Cynthia Rylant as a writer? Which Cynthia Rylant book was your favorite, and why?

12:00–12:45
Lunch and Recess
12:50–1:20
Teacher Read-Aloud:
Core Selection—More from *Appalachia: The Voices of Sleeping Birds*
Discuss: Repeated mentioning of "good dogs"—Why does Rylant keep this phrase throughout the book? Why are dogs so important to the people of Appalachia? Do we feel the same about our dogs? Our other pets? Why? *[this discussion will set the stage for next week's focus on "Friendship"—specifically, between human and a pet]*

1:20–1:45
Music
1:50–2:20
Math
2:20–3:00
Science

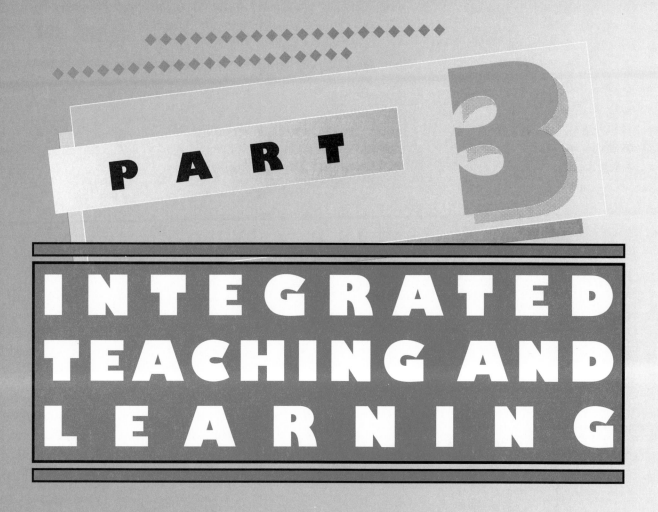

PART 3

INTEGRATED TEACHING AND LEARNING

5

Development of Reading and Writing as Reciprocal Processes

◆ Why are writing and reading "two sides of the same literacy coin"?

◆ What types of knowledge about written language do children acquire throughout the elementary grades?

◆ Why is the application of knowledge about reading and writing such a complex process? Why is it necessary for much of this knowledge to become "automatic"?

◆ What are the characteristics of most children's writing and reading knowledge during each of these periods: the preschool years, the primary school years, and the intermediate school years?

◆◆◆ INTRODUCTION

Our teaching will focus on reading and writing as being two sides of the same literacy coin. Both processes call upon many of the same skills and strategies, and children can apply the understandings they develop in one area to the other. As children write, they learn how authors think; as children read, they learn how authors write (Hansen, 1987). In other words, as children come to think of themselves as *authors*, their insights into the purposes, form, and content of print develop in critical and exciting ways.

This chapter lays an important cornerstone in the foundation we will build to successfully provide integrated reading and writing in our classroom. The first section outlines and describes briefly the nature of written language. The second section looks at the *processes* of writing and reading. The third section presents an overview of the developmental stages through which children proceed as they understand the nature and processes of reading and writing.

What Is to Be Learned: The Functions, Forms, and Content of Written Language

The Functions of Written Language

Written language has many functions. It can entertain, instruct, inform, label, remind, persuade, or warn, as well as perform any combination of these functions simultaneously. In this chapter and the next, we will refer to these purposes or functions using the traditional terms more common in professional literature and in the classroom: **narrative, description, direction, persuasion,** and **expression.**

The Content and Form of Written Language

Because it represents much more information than we usually realize, the nature of written language invites a good deal of analysis. For now, however, we'll keep to fundamentals and consider the information in written language in terms of **content** and **form.** From here on, you should refer to Figure 5.1 as a good "organizer" of the terms and concepts we will be addressing in this section.

The *content* of written language represents the purposes and the in-

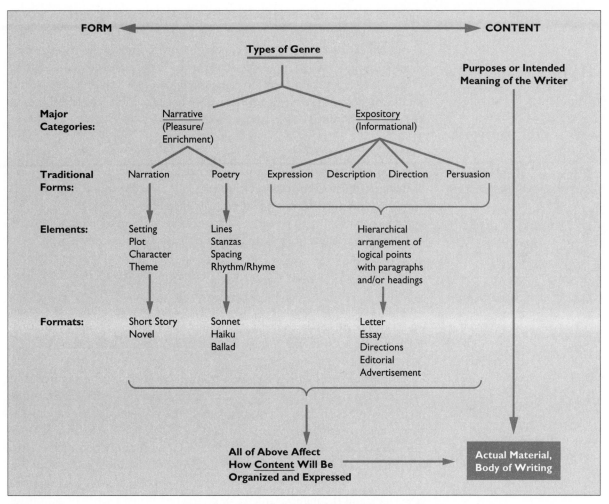

Figure 5.1   The Structure of Written Expression

tended meaning of the writer. What the writer wants to say and his or her purposes for saying it determine whether the writing will be more formal or informal and whether it will be "removed" from the present time and situation. Content, in other words, influences the writer's choice of **genre,** which organizes the form of writing in certain important ways.

   The *form* of written language represents information about spoken language: phrases, words, and sounds. This information is arranged linearly on the page—in English, left to right, and top to bottom. Sentences organize ideas and relate to each other to form a coherent whole. Separate paragraphs signal main ideas, major or minor topical changes, and turn-taking in conversation. Also, the particular genre writers select will affect decisions they make about how to organize and express the content. There is a *reciprocal* relationship, then, between content and form. The two major categories of genre are **narrative** and **expository** or informational. As Figure 5.1 illustrates, these two major categories can be further partitioned according to specific purpose and form (for example, poetry, description, persuasion) and format (sonnet, essay, editorial). Let's begin our analysis at the level of the two major categories: narrative and expository.

Narrative Structure

The roots of narrative—of stories—reach beyond the medium of written language almost to the dawn of humankind. Seated around the fire of the clan, for example, elders told stories that helped unite the clan and protect it from the unknown. The earliest narrative forms may have been more poetic or lyric because they would then be easier to remember, recall, and retell.

Stories are "metaphors" for our existence and our experiences (Bruner, 1988; Coles, 1989). They give us frameworks for imposing order on what could otherwise be random events. Stories also help us rediscover or reinvent our reality so we can understand it more deeply and meaningfully. In addition, there is always a sense of the familiar, even when the story presents quite new experiences.

In most cultures stories follow a predictable format or structure. Story writers follow this format, and readers set up their expectations according to it. Several researchers have investigated the structure of stories and the effect it has on readers' recall of stories (Gee, 1985, 1991; McCabe & Peterson, 1991). Stories have beginnings, middles, and endings, and each of these parts has its own characteristics. For example, the beginning of a story usually states a problem or a goal (say, a magical good-luck stone is stolen from a village), and the main character or characters begin a series of actions directed toward achieving the goal (a boy and girl set out to find the stone). The middle of the story usually includes one or more attempts to achieve the goal (the boy and girl have to pass through three trials, each of which tests their cunning and their resolve, but each trial successfully moves them further toward their major goal of finding the stone), and the ending provides the resolution (face to face with the villain who stole the stone, the boy and girl outwit him, seize the stone, and return to their village, where they receive a tumultuous welcome—and through their quest, they have grown and matured). When readers undertake the reading of a story, they subconsciously or tacitly expect to find these basic components, and this expectation helps guide their comprehension.

Nested within this story structure are the traditional elements of stories that breathe life into the structure: **setting**, **plot**, **characterization**, and theme. Other elements we often consider important aspects of stories are **style** and **point of view**. In a good narrative, these elements will be interwoven in a richly textured tapestry, complementing each other. During the elementary years, students gain a foundation for understanding these elements through the literature they read and the writing they produce while using that literature as a model. One of our major responsibilities will be to build on that foundation — facilitating students' awareness and understanding of these elements through guided instruction and exploration — because most students do not discover these elements on their own (Sloan, 1993).

◆ **Plot**   Plot is the means whereby action is developed in a story. It consists of an ordering of events and some type of *conflict* or tension. Conflicts can be (1) between the main character and nature, (2) between the character and society, (3) between the character and another character, or (4) internal, within the character. Students can develop an understanding of plot by thinking about the types of conflict described in a story and talking about them. Discussing the conflicts in this way will reinforce their recall of the story's events.

◆ **Characterization**   Writers best develop their characters by showing us how they behave, what others say and think about them, and what they themselves say and think. The definition of this element — how an author develops characters — is straightforward enough, but exploring the ways in which various authors develop their characters will provide some instructive and delightful insights for our students. The shift from focusing on plot to focusing on characterization is fairly natural. Once the students identify the conflict or obstacles the character or characters must face, they can then go about discussing how the characters respond to the conflict. In so doing, they learn something about the characters themselves — their personalities, their beliefs, and so forth.

◆ **Setting**   This is the *context* within which the story occurs, including its place in time. How an author develops the setting will depend on how important a role it will play. The setting can establish the mood, provide much of the symbolism, and contribute to the conflict in a story. We can explore setting with students by discussing why the author spends as little or as much time establishing it. With students of any age we can discuss the mental pictures, the *imagery*, that the author helps us construct through the setting.

◆ **Theme**   Theme is what the story is *really* about, what it says most directly to each individual. Theme underlies the elements of plot, characterization, and setting. For example, the main characters in several different stories may go on a long journey that takes many years. The underlying theme in each of the stories, however, may be different. In one story the theme may be individuality—how the main character comes to understand himself or herself in relation to the world and to others. In another story the theme may involve life versus death and the inevitable necessity of accepting death. Themes may be stated explicitly, as in many fables, or may be implicit.

◆ **Style**   Style is how the author uses language—words and sentences—to develop the story. We can talk generally or more specifically about how style underlies the development of the other elements. For example, an author may be more direct, using shorter sentences and few modifying words or phrases, or more elaborate, employing sentences that are more complex.

◆ **Point of View**   Point of view is the stance the narrator or writer takes in the story. Is it "omniscient," in which the narrator sees, knows, and is able to describe everything? Is it first person ("I"), second person ("you"), or third person ("she," "he," "they")? Authors assume a particular point of view to create a certain effect or establish a certain perspective.

Poetry is classified as a part of narrative structure, and we will explore it in depth in Chapter 7.

Expository Structure

The structure of expository text is usually quite different from that of narrative text. Rather than telling a story, it explains facts and ideas by organizing them in terms of their logical relationship to each other. This organization is usually presented hierarchically:

◆ At the highest level in the hierarchy are major ideas or topics, often signaled by headings; important supporting topics are indicated by subheadings.

◆ Nested within each major idea are paragraphs, each with a topic sentence that is in turn supported by other sentences that clarify, elaborate, and extend it.

◆ At the most basic levels are the *logical relationships* among these sentences, referred to as **coherence** (Halliday & Hasan, 1976). Are the sentences clearly related, flowing one into another, with the referents for pronouns definitely understood and the sequence and cause/effect relations explicitly expressed?

◆ The format of expository texts often includes diagrams, pictures, or maps that support and elaborate on the text and may emphasize important terms by printing them in boldface or italics.

Traditional expository forms are defined as follows:

Description conveys the observations of a detached observer. It relates aspects of some present situation by detailing the attributes of a person, object, or event.

Direction (traditionally termed *exposition*) usually explains how to do something, explaining the steps involved in a particular task or procedure.

Persuasion attempts to convince the reader to hold a certain opinion or attitude.

Expression focuses on the writer's own attitudes and beliefs.

Because expressive writing comes naturally for most children, it does not usually need the instructional attention that the other types require. For this reason, we will focus later on the other three types of expository writing and how they may be taught.

We can also look at expository texts in terms of their underlying structures or patterns (Armbruster, Anderson, & Ostertag, 1989; Richgels, McGee, Lomax, & Sheard, 1987). Students' ability to construct meaning as they read informational texts may be improved if we help them become aware of these underlying structures (see Chapter 7).

The four most common structures are presented in Table 5.1.

TABLE 5.1

Underlying Patterns in Expository Texts	
Type of Underlying Structure	Example
Problem-Solution	Settlers moving west traveled on rough, narrow trails that had been packed down by animals or carved through the woods by Native Americans. These paths were often too narrow for the settlers' wagons. In addition, the trails were terribly dusty in dry weather. In rainy weather, they became thick with mud. As more and more settlers made their way west, the government decided to help them. Construction of a road west, called the National Road, was begun in Cleveland, Maryland, in 1811. Seven years later, the National Road reached Wheeling, West Virginia. By the time it was finished, the crushed-stone road stretched all the way to St. Louis, Missouri.

(Continued)

TABLE 5.1 *(Continued)*

Underlying Patterns in Expository Texts

Type of Underlying Structure	Example
Comparison/ Contrast	Marsupials are either meat eaters or plant eaters. Generally speaking, one can tell what type of food a marsupial eats by looking at its teeth. Meat-eating marsupials have a great many small, sharp teeth designed to tear flesh. In contrast, the front teeth of the plant-eating marsupials are large and designed for nipping and cutting. The feet of meat-eating marsupials also differ from those of plant-eating marsupials. The meat eaters have feet that look rather like a dog's or cat's feet. The plant eaters' feet are quite different. The second and third toes on the hind feet are joined together and the big toe is opposed to the other toes, just as a person's thumb is to his or her fingers.
Sequence	Many settlers on the vast American plains in the mid to late 1800s used sod, or earth, as a building material for their houses. Sod houses were usually built on a slight rise of hillside to escape flooding. First, a floor space was leveled out with spades. Then the bricks were laid to make the walls. When the walls were about three feet high, wooden frames for the doors and windows were put in place. Finally, the roof, made with cedar beams and sod bricks, was put on.
Cause/Effect	In cold or mountainous regions, rocks are often subjected to the action of freezing water because of daily changes in the temperature. During the day, when the temperature is above the freezing point of water ($0°$ C), rainwater or melted snow or ice trickles into cracks in the rocks. During the night, if the temperature falls below freezing, the trapped water changes into ice. The trapped water expands as it changes into ice. Because the expanding ice pushes against the sides of the cracks with tremendous force, the rocks are split apart. In this way, large masses of rock, especially the exposed rocks on the tops of mountains, are broken into smaller pieces.

These forms and underlying structures of writing often occur in many different formats of expository writing. They can also occur in narrative formats, but they are traditionally addressed in the context of informational writing because they play such an important role there. From an *instructional* standpoint, exploring these forms with students helps them understand that their structure of a composition will vary depending on whether their primary purpose is to describe, direct, or persuade.

The Processes of Reading and Writing

Elementary students come to understand, appreciate, and appropriately use narrative and expository forms and their various formats through much reading and writing. The following list, adapted from Bussis et al. (1985), gives the types of knowledge upon which individuals draw when they read and write:

◆ Background knowledge—the concepts and schemas about the content of the book to be read or the topic for writing, as well as information about the author

◆ Knowledge of grammatical structure, or *syntax*

◆ Knowledge of *genres*, including literary styles and rhythms of writing

◆ Knowledge of the information encoded in writing itself (This knowledge has two aspects: *word knowledge*—which includes letter/sound relationships, spelling patterns, prefixes/suffixes/word roots, and vocabulary knowledge; and *punctuation*.)

◆ Prerequisite understandings about the nature of writing and reading and the conventions of writing and print.

Let's examine how these types of knowledge are applied during the processes of reading and writing.

The Process of Reading

The process of reading occurs when the present understandings that a *reader* brings to the text come together with a *writer's* intended meaning in a text (Iser, 1976; Rosenblatt, 1978). Texts, which we define as *any* written material, are "blueprints" for the construction of meaning. Readers use this "blueprint" to construct meaning based on their own background knowledge and understanding.

The process of reading is efficient when readers do the following: (1) maintain *satisfactory comprehension or understanding* while (2) moving through a selection *at a reasonable rate* while (3) *maintaining accuracy to the text*—to the words that the writer used. It's important to remember that most of this process must be "automatic" if the process is to work efficiently (Rayner & Pollatsek, 1994).

The Interactive Nature of the Reading Process

Let's examine the reader and the text more closely before discussing how they come together to create a "model" of the text—the meaning that results from their interaction. The *text* presents readers with words arranged according to the conventions of print in an overall format that suggests how the words, sentences, and paragraphs should contribute to the construction of meaning. The writer has arranged these elements in such a way to help readers construct his or her intended meaning. Readers draw upon their knowledge of language—syntax and phonology—as well as background knowledge and knowledge of different contexts, to interpret what is on the page. Readers draw upon these types of knowledge depending on what they are reading, where they are reading, why they are reading, and how they feel about their reading (Rosenblatt, 1978). The same is true for children *learning* to read, although, of course, the information upon which they draw is not as extensive as is the mature reader's.

We will adapt the model of communication that was presented in Chapter 2 to illustrate the transaction between the text—which represents an absent communication partner—and the knowledge in the reader's head that he or she will use. For a diagram of this interaction, see Figure 5.2.

The context is the "what, where, and why" of reading and determines in part the "pragmatics"—the rules—that govern how the reader, in this particular situation, will apply the rest of his or her knowledge. For example, we are likely to interact with a certain text differently depending on whether we're reading it during a coffee break on the job or skimming it in class to find a particular paragraph that supports a point we just made.

Let's use ourselves to think about the process of reading:

◆ As we move through a text, we must identify the words appropriately (*print information*).

◆ We must understand the meaning of the words in the particular context in which they occur (interplay among *print information*, *syntax*, and *semantics*).

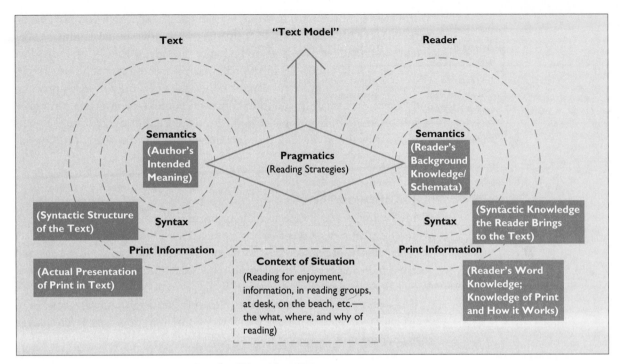

Figure 5.2 Reader/Text/Context

♦ We must construct the underlying relationships among the concepts that the words represent, both within and between sentences (*syntax* and *semantics*).

♦ We must also form an overall understanding or "text model" in our heads. This model represents the constructed meaning we have created as a result of reading this text; it did not exist prior to our reading. As we go along in our reading, this overall understanding becomes more elaborate while at the same time it helps guide further meaning construction.

This process of reading depends on the efficient—and therefore effective—use of the types of knowledge listed earlier—background knowledge, knowledge about words, and so forth. The activity also includes the information-processing capacity of the brain itself—the type and amount of information that the brain uses at any given instant. Readers make effective and efficient use of these types of knowledge and their cognitive resources if understanding is occurring with good fluency and is true to the text.

There are a number of things that can inhibit this process, however, in which case the quality of the reading suffers. For example, a large amount of processing "space" in the brain may be occupied with trying to identify words. When this situation happens, sentence-to-sentence comprehension gets bogged down and, consequently, the overall text model cannot be adequately constructed. On the other hand, the identification of individual words may be fine, but the appropriate overall meaning that the words represent in a particular context cannot be accessed because too much processing "space" is taken up trying to construct context-appropriate meanings. Appropriate comprehension at both the sentence and the text level breaks down (as would be the case if *I* were attempting to read a text on, say, nuclear physics!).

Types of Comprehension

Traditionally, readers' construction of meaning has been discussed in terms of three categories or types of comprehension. These types are still widely used in education and referred to most often in professional literature and instructional materials: **literal comprehension, inferential comprehension,** and **critical comprehension** (Irwin, 1991).

The best way to think about the differences among these categories is to consider the degree to which the reader must rely upon *prior knowledge* when constructing meaning.

◆ *Literal* comprehension [perceiving facts or details] involves understanding what is *explicitly* stated in the text—what is "right there." Prior knowledge is important in order to understand what is "right there" because [we] must know the meaning of the actual words on the page.

◆ *Inferential* comprehension involves understanding what is *implied* by the text. [It] is often referred to as "reading between the lines." Prior knowledge helps [us] relate or pull together ideas in the text which have not been explicitly linked [there].

◆ *Critical* comprehension involves understanding how to go beyond the information on the page, either to connect the information with what [we] already know or to realize that [we] don't have enough information in [our heads] to make a connection—in which case [we] will need to go elsewhere to get that information ("beyond the lines") (Raphael, 1986).

Let's summarize. The more we know about a topic (*background knowledge/schemas*) and the genre of the text we are reading, the more efficient our reading will be because we will be able to construct a text model that is clearly organized. We cannot effectively use these types of knowledge, however, unless we understand how information is encoded in writing (*word structure*) and how print "works." We must understand the "blueprint" so that we can construct a solid text in our heads.

<table>
<tr><td>

Build Your Teaching Resources

BOOKS ABOUT COMPREHENSION IN READING

</td><td>

The following book offers a complete treatment of the nature of comprehension from the perspective of cognitive science and information-processing theory, yet because it is written by reading educators, it is directly applicable to classroom instruction:

Pearson, P. D., & Johnson, D. (1978). *Teaching comprehension*. New York: Holt. (See particularly Chapters 4–8.)

Another text that explores specific theoretical and teaching issues and techniques within the domain of reading comprehension is

Irwin, J. (1991). *Teaching reading comprehension processes* (2nd ed.). Englewood Cliffs, NJ: Prentice Hall.

Two texts that emphasize practical teaching strategies, especially for transacting with literature, are

Cooper, J. D. (1997). *Literacy: Helping children construct meaning* (3rd ed.). Boston: Houghton Mifflin.

Templeton, S. (1995). *Children's literacy: Contexts for meaningful learning*. Boston: Houghton Mifflin.

</td></tr>
</table>

The Process of Writing

There is no mystique about writing—it requires effort and is usually a very deliberate process. There are few writers who can sit down and have ideas, words, syntax, sentences, and organization all flow from their minds through their hands and onto the page in "final form." For most of us, writing is a *process* that involves a continual interplay among these components. Though this process is often challenging, it can also be exhilarating, liberating, and sometimes life changing.

What is going on when we engage in writing? We must coordinate the planning of the form and content of our written work with the actual mechanics of composing. These factors in turn depend on our intentions and our expected audience. Scardamalia (1981) describes this process well:

> [T]he number of things that must be dealt with simultaneously in writing is stupendous: handwriting, spelling, punctuation, word choice, syntax, textual connections, purpose, organization, clarity, rhythm, euphony [the quality of the sounds within words], the possible reactions of various possible readers, and so on. *To pay conscious attention to all of these would overload the information-processing capacity of the most towering intellects* (p. 81, emphasis added).

Writers avoid "overload" by automating many of these aspects so they can direct conscious attention to their most important concerns. To write well, individuals must learn how to balance automated functions and con-

Writing requires effort but can be exhilarating, liberating, and sometimes life-changing.

scious functions. For example, sometimes using good handwriting will be the foremost concern in the writer's mind. At other times he or she may focus on spelling or content and form, as when writers concentrate on concepts or characters to be developed or points to be made.

By considering writing in terms of the efficient processing of different types of information, we are able to think about how long it takes to perform certain aspects of writing as well as how much "room" these aspects occupy in cognitive "space" as we write. What writers are able to focus on depends on development and purpose. From a developmental perspective, younger children often need to spend a significant amount of time figuring out how to spell words they want to use, how to form the words' letters, and so forth. Performing these tasks doesn't leave much cognitive space for thinking about the topic or another reader's point of view. As these "lower-order" skills become more automatic, however, then more processing time, cognitive space, and downright energy become available for attending to other types of important information.

The process of writing can occur in a comparatively short burst of time,

AT THE TEACHER'S DESK

TECHNOLOGY, READING, AND WRITING

With all the current emphasis on computers and technology, we need to keep in perspective *how* we plan to use them. Preferably, we can employ them in our classrooms to support the *processes* of reading and writing, as when students coauthor a story on the word processor (see Figure 5.11, p. 177) or interact with electronic books. There is, in other words, a meaningful *context* for applying technology to the language arts.

On the other hand, Willis, Stephens, and Matthew (1996) discuss the role of "out of context" software—programs that focus on specific skills outside of authentic reading and writing. These programs have predominated in schools over the years, and they may have a *small* place in our instruction—but only to reinforce skills we have introduced and discussed (for example, a vocabulary program that focuses on combining and recombining prefixes, suffixes, and base words).

as in writing a shopping list. For more significant efforts, though, the process will extend over a longer period of time and may involve more deliberate planning during the prewriting phase. Then come writing the actual initial draft, revising that draft, and editing the final draft. Throughout the remainder of this text, we'll discuss the process of writing using these more convenient and common terms: *prewriting*, *drafting*, *revising*, and *editing*. We'll further explore the nature and teaching of these aspects of the writing process in Chapter 7.

The Development of Reading and Writing

In order to be effective teachers, it's important that we know the general outline of literacy development. Children's evolving understandings about reading influence their evolving understandings about writing, and vice versa. Also, in the real world reading and writing occur together much of the time. Just as we saw with the development of oral language, the development of print literacy—in reading and writing—occurs in a *social* context. Children learn about written language—its features, forms, and functions—in an environment filled with examples of written language and people using and talking about written language.

Recent research in the development of literacy has mapped part of the terrain that children must explore while becoming literate (Juel, 1991; Langer, 1986; Templeton & Bear, 1992). Bussis and her colleagues (1985) have observed that children in first, second, and third grade "displayed much greater uniformity in what they knew about reading and print than in how they brought their knowledge to bear on text. . . . Many differences . . . turned out to be more a matter of how they *used* knowledge than of knowledge acquisition or knowing per se" (p. 65, emphasis added). In other words, the nature of this knowledge and how it develops will be quite similar from one child to the next.

As we survey the course of literacy development, you may find it helpful to refer to Table 5.2 which provides at-a-glance developmental milestones.

The Preschool Years: Birth Through Kindergarten

Much of the wonder and complexity of early literacy development has been explored by researchers investigating what is called **emergent literacy** (Strickland & Morrow, 1989; Sulzby & Teale, 1991). For preschool children, written language is everywhere. How often their attention is directed toward it and how this attention is directed will influence young children's emerging concepts about literacy. With support from literate adults and/or siblings, preschool children can build upon their general language and cognitive development as well as their background knowledge about their world to learn the following about written language:

◆ *The beginning development of schemas for different "genres"*
   The basic understandings developed here are the concepts of "story" and often of "nursery rhyme."

◆ *Knowledge of grammatical structure, or syntax*
   Related to the development of genre schemas, the nature and structure of the language of books, or "book talk," differs from normal conversational talk because it is often expressed through a fuller, more complete syntax.

◆ *Prerequisite understandings about the functions of reading and writing and the conventions of writing and print*
   It stands for speech.
   It reads left to right and top to bottom.
   It labels things in the world and gives information about them.
   It often exists within the concept of "book"—and this concept includes front and back, beginning, middle, end, and so forth.

◆ *Knowledge of the information encoded in writing*
   The minimal units of writing are *letters*, and there is a limited number of letters that are used over and over.

In this section we will examine the development of these different types of knowledge through reading and writing.

TABLE 5.2	Developmental Milestones of Literacy Development			
	Emergent Literacy (Birth to 6 Years of Age)	**Beginning Literacy (5–8 Years of Age)**	**Transitional Literacy (7–11 Years of Age)**	**Proficient Literacy (10 Years of Age and Up)**
Text Knowledge	• A beginning concept of what a "story" is, and in some cultures, beginning concepts about simple rhymes and nursery rhymes • Aspects of the sound and content of "book talk"—the language of books (primarily narratives) is different from that of everyday speech	• A more elaborate concept of "story" as well as a beginning awareness of expository or "informational" texts; children will begin consciously to differentiate between these two types of texts • Responding to what is read: able to recall "what happened"	• Better able to adjust prior knowledge to expository material • Responding to what is read: Summarizing, analyzing, generalizing	• In-depth knowledge of organization of expository material • Critical analysis of and generalization from what is read; includes in-depth knowledge of elements of stories and poems
Reading Behaviors	• "Pretend" reading at first; picture somehow "contains" the story • Later, print "tells" the story and children point to it as they "read" a memorized text	• Characteristics of oral reading; word-by-word, "out loud"	• Toward fluency/expression—read with more expression, more "naturally," rate increases • Silent reading begins to take over	• Flexible, strategic reading based on purpose • Silent, fluent reading
Writing Behaviors	• Pretend writing/drawing	• Word-by-word writing • Personal, descriptive, "retelling" types of writing • Amount of writing increases from a few words to a half page or more of writing	• Approaching fluency • Greater planning time • Growth in different *forms* of writing	• Fluent writing • Building expression and voice • Broad development in form, content, and style

(Continued)

TABLE 5.2   **Developmental Milestones of Literacy Development**

	Emergent Literacy (Birth to 6 Years of Age)	Beginning Literacy (5–8 Years of Age)	Transitional Literacy (7–11 Years of Age)	Proficient Literacy (10 Years of Age and Up)
Reading Words	• Prerequisite under-standings about the nature of reading, including many important conven-tions of print such as the fact that it stands for speech	• A "concept of word in print" (voice-to-print match) • Phonemic aware-ness: sensitive to phonemic structure of words • "Alphabetic" con-cept of how print works (sounds are matched to letters, left to right)	• "Pattern" concept of how groups of letters form units within words to represent sound • Very rapid growth of sight words	• Knowledge of word structure includes awareness and un-derstanding of word bases/roots and prefixes/ suffixes as well as the ways in which these elements combine to form the meaning of words • Vocabulary of con-tent-related words develops rapidly
Writing Words	• *Semiphonemic* PNK (pink) BD (bed) DF (drive)	• *Letter Name (Phonemic)* FES (fish) CHRAN (train) BUP (bump)	• *Within-Word Pattern* TRANE (train) DRIEV (drive) PACKD (packed) • *Syllable Juncture* STOPED (stopped) SUDEN (sudden) CARRYS (carries) CATOL (cattle)	• *Derivational Relationships* COMPASITION (composition) BENIFIT (benefit) ATRACT (attract) ACCOMODATE (accommodate)

Reading

It is almost impossible for a child to be cut off completely from print. It is evident on signs, doors, shelves, cereal boxes, and automobiles. Print is also used and is noticed in many contexts in the home: storybooks, news-papers, magazines, TV guides, grocery lists, phone messages, checks, rec-ipes, and microwave cooking directions. During children's early years, their experience with *books* begins to teach them about visual, two-dimensional representations that differ from images they usually experience in the three-dimensional world. They learn that the real world can be graphically portrayed and that this portrayal can be organized in a format we call "books."

Adult caretakers (usually parents) play an extremely important role in helping children learn to mediate between print and speech and to negotiate the different contexts within which written language occurs. This role is also critical for eventually preparing children for the culture of the school (Morrow, 1995). Although some children can learn to read from the "environmental print" that surrounds them, most do not. For example, many preschool children who can recognize the word *McDonald's* in the context of the actual fast-food restaurant cannot recognize it out of context on a plain sheet of paper. Most of the print we interact with in our society — that is, print in books and booklike materials — does not have as much contextual support as environmental print does. Environmental print certainly plays a crucial role by providing the foundation for children's early awareness of the form and function of print literacy.

Of all the ways in which young children are exposed to print, the context of the *storybook* is one of the most important. The experience that adult and child share while reading together contributes to the development of literacy *and* oral language in general (Yaden, Smolkin, & Conlon, 1989). Children will learn much about "reading" itself and will also develop concepts and vocabulary as adults point to and discuss objects, characters, and actions represented in the storybook's pictures.

Reading to Children During the Preschool Years   Most preschool children enjoy being read to by adults. The most effective approach is to sit the child in your lap or right next to you so that he or she can see the pages. This simple, comfortable context of shared storybook reading will allow the child to develop many of the understandings about print literacy listed earlier as well as to associate a feeling of love and closeness with reading. Before we investigate these more specifically, let's consider some of the ways young children respond when they are read to.

Little children love to latch on to a favorite book, and they will want you to read the same book over and over. For a parent of a first-born who wishes to oblige the child, this situation can *literally* go on for weeks. Such was the case with my first child. He requested the same book repeatedly, and his mother and I grew extremely weary obliging him. Finally, in exasperation, I told him I couldn't find the book anywhere! Then it was "miraculously" discovered several months later, at a time when he had become interested in other books.

The desire to hear the same story or book repeatedly is a natural phenomenon with young children. *This repetition is critical.* It allows children to memorize, almost effortlessly, a number of texts. With time, as the child recites the story while turning the pages, he or she will read it exactly as the adult did, turning the pages precisely at the right point. Furthermore, the child is also developing a simple concept of story. During the preschool years, this understanding is quite basic and will include the narrative elements we discussed earlier: setting, plot, characterization, and theme.

By being read stories, these children have had the "language of books" revealed to them. Although in one sense writing is "speech written down," in many others it is not. As we have seen, speech is usually less formal and more context-dependent, allowing for back-and-forth communication. The storybook is different. It tries to create its own world, and much of this world is suggested by the way the story is read to young children. Imagine for a moment how an adult's voice changes the instant he or she begins to read aloud the words "Once upon a time." There is a different kind of sound in the voice.

Parents who read to their children at some point usually include nursery rhymes, and children definitely enjoy and delight in these rhythms and rhymes. Several scholars have suggested that such rhymes lay the earliest foundations for children's sensitivity to the sounds of language, a sensitivity that will be extremely important later on during the beginning of conventional literacy learning (Bradley & Bryant, 1985; Chukovsky, 1925/1971).

Children who have been exposed to storybooks have begun to develop knowledge of the *conventions* of print. At first young children do not pay much attention to the print on the page as a book is being read aloud; they are busy examining the pictures. Gradually, however, they begin to attend to the print, and adults are probably the cause of this activity. As adults read to children, they occasionally point to the lines of print, sliding a finger from left to right, with a return sweep to the beginning of the next line. In this way adults model the **directionality of print** for the child: left to right and top to bottom. Because adults point to the print and say the same thing every time they read the book, children come to understand that these marks somehow "contain" the story—that each time around the marks represent the same things. Gradually children will come to understand that these marks represent spoken language.

Writing

Preschool children also form ideas about the function, conventions, and characteristics of writing. They can learn much at a general level about how print "works" before they focus in on its specific features.

Scribbles and Drawing   At anywhere from 15 to 24 months of age, young children begin scribbling. They seem to enjoy making marks—and just about *anything* can be a writing surface. In the early stages, the marks appear to be random. Later on, however, the scribbles are identifiable as pictures. Later still, drawings and scribblelike writing will coexist in the same picture.

Young children are excellent observers. They watch how adults interact with written language as well as what adults read and take their cues accordingly. They imitate the act of writing and the appearance of the writing as best as they are able. Figure 5.3 illustrates the contrast between the same child's writing in a grocery list, for example, and a "story": the general appearance of the writing represents the child's global perceptions of the print. The "list" does not go all across the page, whereas the "story" does. The child does not draw pictures of items to be bought, but writes them in a list format.

Approaching Alphabetic Writing   Young children's foundation of experience and experimentation with written language helps them understand how information is visually represented in two-dimensional space. Their writing grows out of their drawing and early scribbling (Ferreiro & Teber-

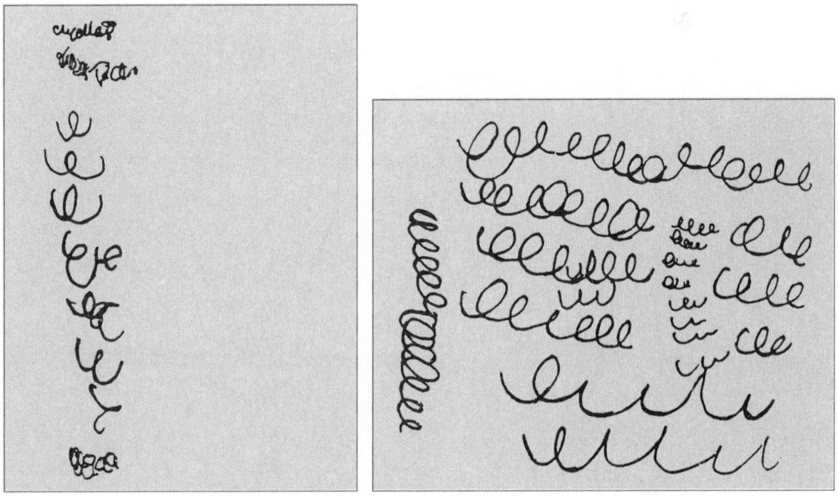

Figure 5.3   **A Child's Uninterrupted Writing—Grocery List and Story**

SOURCE: Fig. 12.2, "Uninterrupted Writing: Shopping List & Story (Hannah, Age 3)," Jerome C. Harste, Virginia A. Woodward, and Carolyn L. Burke, *Language Stories & Literacy Lessons*, p. 157. Reproduced by permission of Heinemann Educational Books, Inc., Portsmouth, NH.

osky, 1985). It seems that for most young children, letters and letterlike characters first begin to appear as parts of a picture; the child includes them in a drawing mainly because they are features of what he or she has seen elsewhere on paper (see Figure 5.4). Somewhat later, letters come to stand for the picture's *name* because children understand that the picture itself cannot be a "name." They recognize that "name" is a feature of writing, not of pictures. At about this point, children apparently begin to establish a type of relationship between the letters they write and the objects to which the letters refer. Writing appears more often by itself, not merely as an embellishment of a picture. Eventually, when children begin to relate letters to speech, they do not match letters with individual sounds, but rather with *syllables.*

Children will now begin to include letters in their writing that, while still corresponding to syllables, more closely relate the *sounds* of syllables to the *names* of letters. An excellent example of this is the message written by my son Gavin when he was five years old: "BBCUS." When asked to read this, Gavin pointed to each letter as he read, "Bye-bye, see you soon." The next

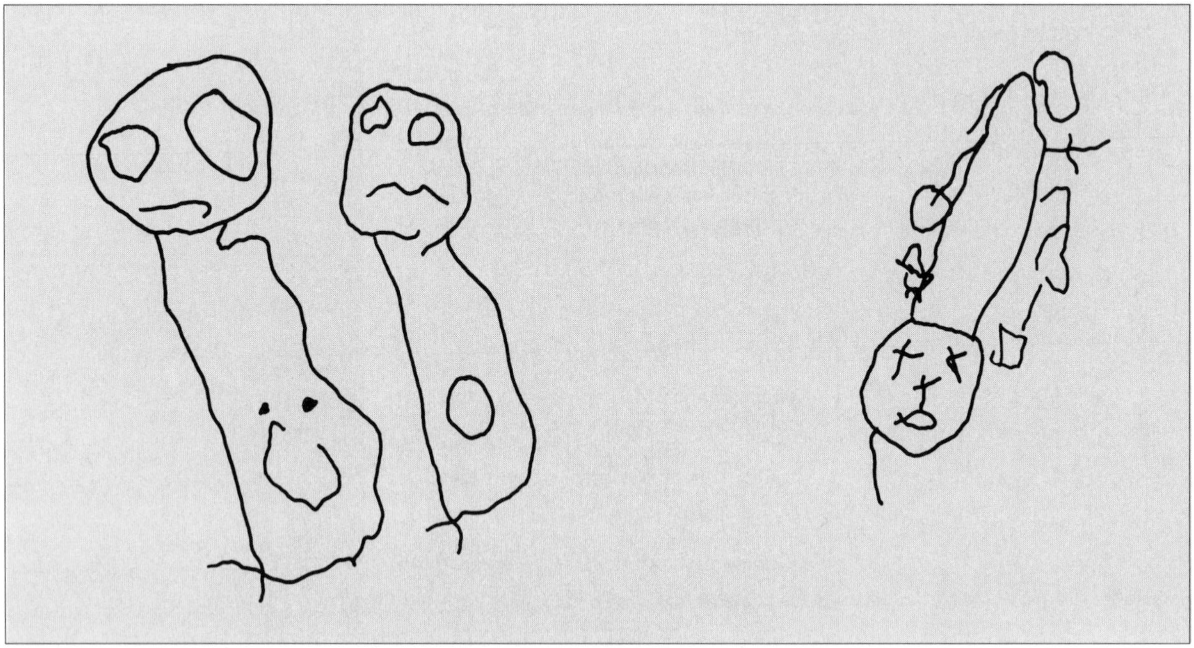

Figure 5.4   **Young Child's Drawings Incorporating Letterlike Characters**

SOURCE: Reproduced by permission of Victoria University from E. Ferreiro, "The Underlying Logic of Literacy Development," *Awakening to Literacy*, eds. Hillel Goelman, Antoinette Oberg, and Frank Smith (Portsmouth, NH: Heinemann Educational Books, Inc., 1984), p. 159.

You can assess the degree to which children have a concept of word in print by asking them to point at the words as they recite a short poem, nursery rhyme, or story that they have already memorized (Morris, 1993). If they do not know such a text, however, you may orally teach them a short rhyme—such as "One, two, button my shoe/Three, four, out the door"—and then ask them to point to each word as they recite the two-line poem. Most preschool and many beginning first-grade children have little or no concept of word in print. They may slide their finger across a whole line as they are saying one or two words; they may jab randomly at the text as they recite; they may point to individual letters, right to left, matching each letter up with each syllable they pronounce. Eventually, children will reach a point where they exhibit the following "pointing" behavior: They will point to words of one syllable as they are pronouncing these words; it will appear as if they are "really reading." For example, pointing to and reciting the "one, two" rhyme, the child may first point to "one, two" as he or she says each word, next point to *button* as he or she says "buh," and then to *my* as he or she says "ton." What is this child doing? She or he is matching the words in print with *syllables* in speech. It should not be long before she or he is pointing to *button* and saying "button."

major step in understanding the relationship between oral language and print is the development of what Morris (1992) termed a **concept of word in print.** Children understand that a printed word is *a group of letters with spaces at both ends.* Why is this such an important concept? Because knowing what a word in print actually *is* enables children to focus more directly on the important units in print, to remember many of them, and to examine more closely *all* the letters and the corresponding sounds in a word.

Let's take stock of what children have learned up to this point. First, they have developed a concept of *directionality*—they write from left to right and from top to bottom. Second, they clearly understand that writing is separate from pictures and is meant to convey information. Third, they have developed a foundation for understanding how alphabetic characters are used and combined, even though there is not a correct correspondence between the characters and sounds. Fourth, toward the end of this emergent phase, they have grasped a *concept of word in print.*

We can appreciate the distance these young children have come in their development. Although "BBCUS" may appear somewhat primitive and simple to a naive adult, it represents a long process that has been nurtured by immersion in a print-rich environment *and* by encouragement to explore that environment. Children engage in a complex interplay between the information that print represents in their environment and their own evolving concepts about how print works.

The Primary School Years: First Through Third Grade

Primary school students will develop and draw upon the following types of knowledge when they read and write:

◆ *Background knowledge*

Simply by virtue of living, children will be developing concepts and schemas about their immediate environment and the world beyond them. They will begin to bring this knowledge to what they read and write about and in turn be better able to use information they read to expand and elaborate upon their own world.

◆ *Knowledge of grammatical structure, or syntax*

While children are increasing their syntactic knowledge—learning to "fine-tune" their syntactic competence by handling more sophisticated and lengthy constructions—they will learn how to read the longer sentences they are already able to use orally. In the first grade, much of this ability will develop if these longer sentences occur in attractive "predictable" books (see p. 189) and in texts based on their own oral language, written down exactly as they have said it (see p. 193).

◆ *Knowledge of genres*

At first, these children's concept of a story is primarily sequential. Problems in the story are addressed and resolved—but only in a straightforward, linear sequence. A little later, children will expand their understanding of the concept of a story. Episodes will become more involved and time sequences may be switched around (the story may begin at one point, for example, then shift to an earlier point in time). The children begin to understand how "chapter books" work—as longer stories broken into parts. They also begin to explore simple informational books and poetry.

Throughout the primary years, children grow in their ability (1) to identify relevant information in texts and understand how this information is related and (2) to respond to this information—that is, to evaluate or to make judgments about it.

The genres that children experience in reading will subtly begin to influence their writing. The language of narration, for example, and the organization of informational writing will emerge.

◆ *Knowledge of the information encoded in writing itself*

Children's understanding of the nature of written *words* follows an identifiable sequence. They move beyond their earlier "syllabic" spelling of words and begin to spell the beginning and ending sounds they hear in words. This is the start of "alphabetic" spelling, in which they attempt to match letters with sounds. When reading, they also apply this beginning/ending-sound strategy when they do not know a word. A little later, they fully grasp this alphabetic principle when they can spell both the consonant and vowel sounds they hear in words. For example, *bat* is spelled "B-A-T," and so is *bait*. When reading, they also apply this left-to-right strategy.

Later still, children come to understand that sounds within words are not always represented in such a straight left-to-right fashion. There may be "silent" letters that influence how other letters are pronounced: *bike* has a "long *i*" because there is a silent *e* at the end of the word that "makes" the *i* have a long sound; *bait* has a "long *a*" because there is a silent vowel letter that follows the letter *a*. Children come to understand how groups of letters work in *patterns* to represent sound. Most of the printed words children will learn to read during the primary years will be those that they already use in oral language.

Children will also acquire a basic knowledge of simple *punctuation* conventions—employing periods, capital letters at the beginning of sentences, and some comma usage.

Our overview of developing literacy in first, second, and third grades will look at the reading and writing behaviors that characterize the two developmental literacy phases which children move through during these years: *beginning literacy* and *transitional literacy*.

Beginning Literacy

Reading　As you observe children's reading at this point, you will usually notice most of the following behaviors:

1. They may mark their place with their finger as they read.

2. They will read out loud—usually loud enough for you to hear—or softly, under their breath.

3. They will read quite slowly and choppily, in more or less a monotone, a phenomenon often described as "word-by-word" reading or **voice pointing** (Clay, 1991).

4. If they are reading material in which they know most of the words by sight, their literal comprehension will be good, and they will be able to reflect on what they have read and draw inferences.

Children's oral, choppy reading at this stage is natural because they examine almost every word they encounter carefully, letter by letter. As they gain more experience reading, they are able to identify more and more words immediately by sight without having to sound them out or guess. Words that are immediately identified are termed **sight words.**

Writing From a developmental perspective, writing now moves beyond egocentric to audience-considerate writing. Dyson (1989) has described the complexity of the beginning writing process in the school setting: "[T]he gist—the challenge— . . . is not simply to create a unified text world but to resolve tensions between the real and the imaginary, between self and others, and among images, sounds, and written words" (p. 331). Dyson refers to "multiple worlds" consisting of (a) the child's imaginary world—one that is based on talk, pictures, and text; (b) the child's ongoing social world—involving others in one's own task and involving oneself in others' tasks; and (c) the child's wider experienced world of people, places, objects, and events. Let's look at Jesse's story in Figure 5.5. The story's focus is not as extensive or its language as elaborate as it would be if Jesse had told us orally about the accident, but again this is because of the time that must be given over to "lower-level" processes.

At this early stage children's writing is usually egocentric. They assume the reader or listener has the necessary background knowledge about their lives and worlds to comprehend what they are writing about. This egocentric writing will often reflect features of both narrative and expository texts.

Development of Word Knowledge in Reading and Writing We need to look more closely at children's word knowledge at this point because all the rest of the information children use in reading and writing depends on this knowledge. We need to begin at the point where children develop a *concept of word in print*. Their "invented spellings" in this phase will appear much like the writing in Figure 5.6. They use single consonant letters to

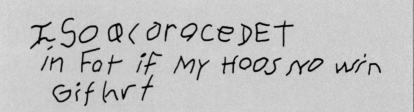

(This story reads: I saw a car accident in front of my house. No one got hurt.)

Figure 5.5   A First-Grader's Story

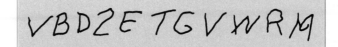

(This sentence reads: A bird is eating the worm.)

Figure 5.6 Semiphonemic Spelling

stand for consonants and vowels: "bird" is spelled *BD*; "worm" is spelled *WM*. Note also that there are few if any vowels and no spaces between "words." This type of spelling is also termed *semiphonemic*.

Beginning writers make an important jump in their invented spelling; they are now spelling *every* sound they hear and feel with a letter—including vowels. Jason's story in Figure 5.7 provides an excellent example of this: "was" is spelled *WIS*; "picked" is spelled *PICT*; "next" is spelled *NACST*. If you had observed Jason while he was writing—when he was actually encoding his oral language—you would have seen how slowly the operation proceeded. He is a "word-by-word" *writer* just as he is a word-by-word

At all phases of development, literacy growth is a social phenomenon.

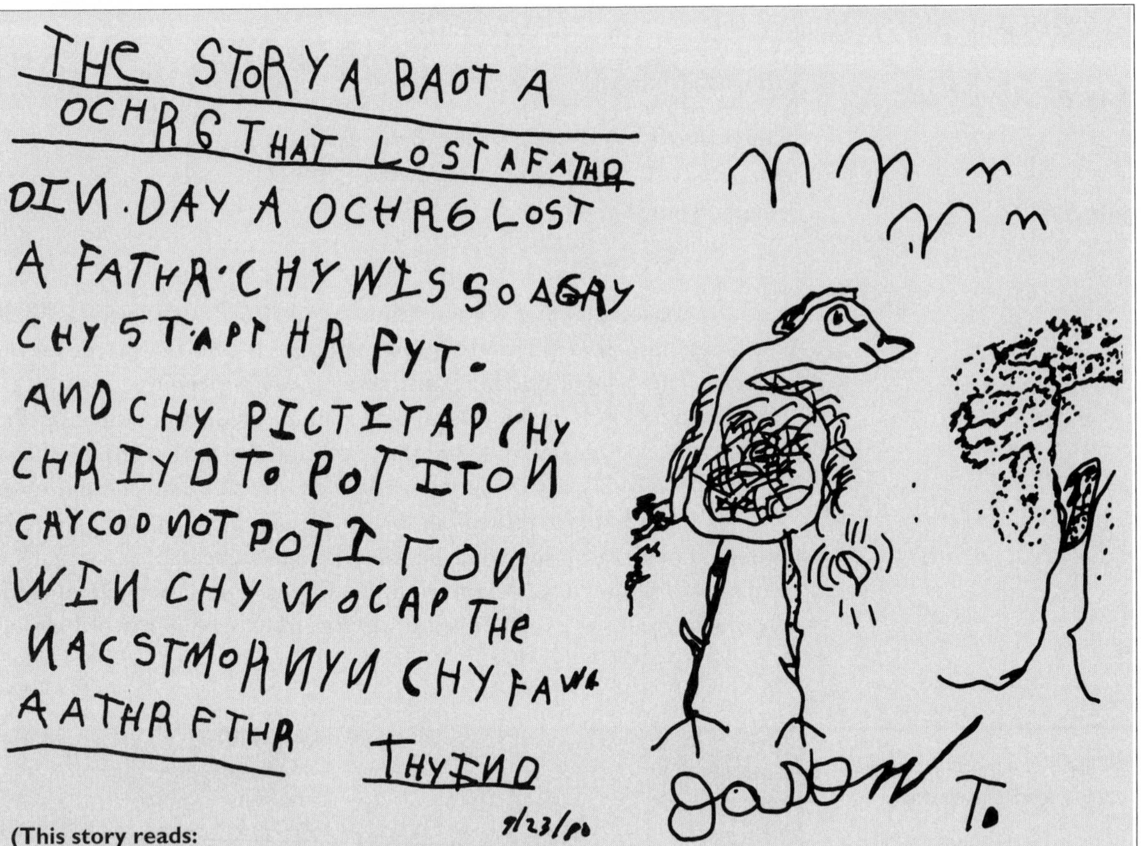

THE STORY A BAOT A
OCHRG THAT LOST A FATHR
DIN. DAY A OCHRG LOST
A FATHR. CHY WLS SO AGRY
CHY STAPT HR FYT.
AND CHY PICTITAP CHY
CHR IY D TO POT IT ON
CHY COD NOT POT I TON
WIN CHY WOCAP THE
NAC STMOR NYN CHY FAWD
A ATHR FTHR   THY END
                  9/23/90

(This story reads:
The Story About An Ostrich That Lost a Feather
   One day an ostrich lost a feather. She was so angry she stamped her feet. And she picked it up.
She tried to put it on. She could not put it on. When she woke up the next morning she found an-
other feather. The End)

Figure 5.7   Story by a Child Well into the Letter-Name (Phonemic) Stage

reader. Much of his processing time and space must be allotted to figuring out how to represent the sounds within the words he wants to write. It is also common to see children at this phase begin to spell correctly many of the words they are encountering in their reading. Notice Jason's spellings of *story*, *day*, *and*, and *lost*.

In summary: there is a reciprocal relationship between children's learning about words in their reading and their "exercising" this knowledge in their writing, and vice versa. Inventing the spelling of words in their writing helps children to read words and understand letter-sound relationships (Ehri, 1993).

Transitional Reading and Writing

Beginning in second grade and continuing through third grade, most children are in the **transitional phase of literacy**. The term "transitional" is appropriate because this is the time when children are making a *transition* from beginning to more fluent and proficient reading and writing. This is a time of *consolidating* much of the different types of knowledge that children draw upon when they read and write. It is also a time when *lots* of reading, rereading, writing, and exploring the meaning and structure of words occur.

At this phase children are moving beyond themselves to consider at a more conscious level the viewpoints and needs of others (see Chapter 2). This developing awareness combines their experiences with 1) the structure, language, phrasing, and nuances of narrative texts; and 2) the structure, language, and means of addressing and presenting material in informational texts. This combination of experience and potential helps children negotiate the "multiple worlds" within which their story writing and informational writing take place.

Reading   Most children now read silently. They rarely point to keep their place while reading, and when they do read orally, it is with more natural expression. Their *rate* or speed of reading increases as does their *fluency*, which is the expression with which they read orally. Their comprehension during *reading* is more aligned with their comprehension during *listening*. All of these developments occur because many of the lower-level word-identification processes are now becoming automated, leaving more cognitive "space" for constructing ideas suggested by the text—for *thinking* while reading. Children are now analyzing, summarizing, and generalizing from their reading. These characteristics usually correspond to the children's advancing cognitive and linguistic development.

Children's Writing and Spelling   Just as with reading fluency, *writing* fluency depends on "automatic" functioning. Writing is now more rapid because the encoding of words is more rapid—more automatic, with only occasional conscious reflection on spelling. As fluency grows, children can allocate more attention to how and what they want to express and begin understanding and incorporating conventions of style and mechanics in their writing. Children are also now much more aware of the audience for their writing and of that audience's expectations in terms of writing content and mechanics.

In the early transitional phase (second grade for most children), compositions are often characterized by a complete rendering of "what happened." There is little differentiation in the attention children give to varied bits of information; they weight them all equally. An example of this feature is Kirstin's story, "Let's Go on a Walk, Buster," from which selected pages are shown in Figure 5.8.

For second-graders longer stories that seem to cover an exhausting list of information may result from the simple desire to "write more," to have one's own composition go on for pages—just as in "real" books. If the children wish to revise a composition, however, they are certainly capable of doing so, as we will see in Chapter 7. Kirstin's final draft, shown in Figure 5.8 in its final "published" version—produced on a word processor (with invented spellings corrected), illustrated, and laminated—differs from the first because she realized her story would be more enjoyable if she substituted different words for "*said* Buster."

In the later transitional phase (third grade for most children), students may be persuaded to trim their lengthy accounts. They experiment more with form, as Gavin's "pigons" poem attests (Figure 5.9). In these cases, the form is "in control"; note the forced rhyme. Children's increasing cognitive sophistication allows for this interest in differing forms, although they may also decide to "play it safe" with writing and stick with predictable formats, using words they know how to spell. Exposure to a variety of appropriate texts at this level can "stretch" children's writing to the challenges that new literacy experiences can offer. Notice the spellings in Gavin's poem. In contrast to the previous developmental phase, a greater proportion of total words in the composition is spelled correctly. And the spellings that *are* created reflect conventional spelling patterns; notably, silent letters are usually included to indicate long vowels. (We'll look at the logic underlying these invented spellings in Chapter 8.)

The Intermediate School Years: Fourth Through Sixth Grade

The knowledge and experiential bases that underlie children's reading and writing are more developed and interrelated now than during the primary school years. This is the time when most students move into the *proficient* phase of literacy. Lower-level tasks involved in processing print are becoming even more efficient and automated than they were during the transitional phase. Readers have more cognitive "space" available not only to follow the "blueprint" in the text but also to draw from their own knowledge of the world. During these years children demonstrate a striking advance in their powers of reasoning. This advance allows them to interact in important and critical ways with what they read, be it published material or peers' compositions. These are also the years when students can explore their interests through reading and writing, truly becoming "experts"—often to the extent that they will know more about a particular area than the teacher!

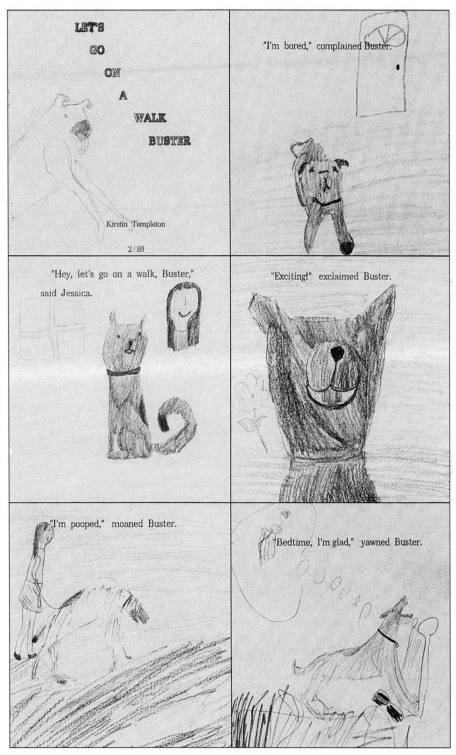

Figure 5.8 Excerpts from a Second-Grader's "Published" Story

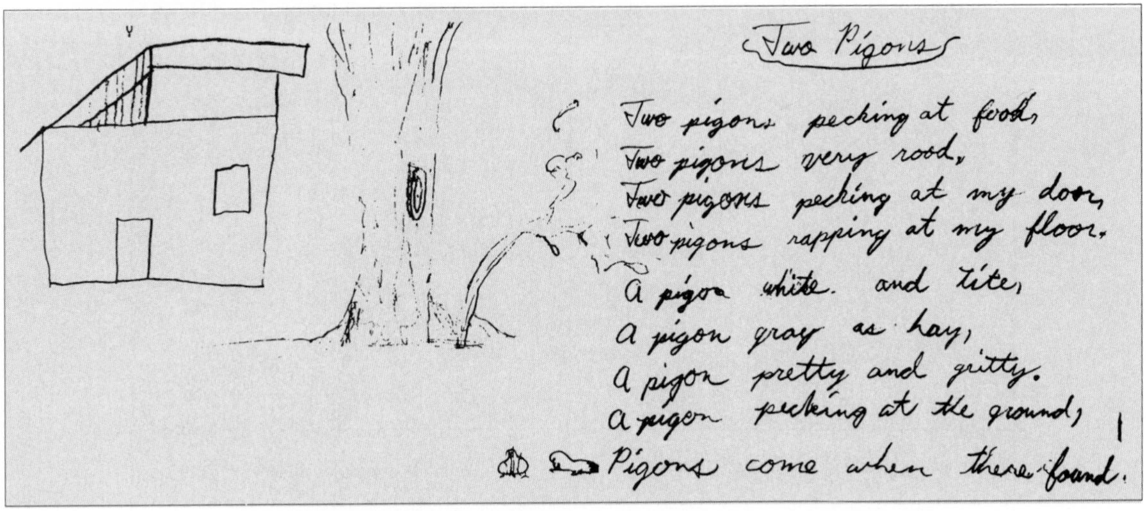

Figure 5.9   Child's Poem Showing Experimentation with Form

By the time most students are in the intermediate grades, they will primarily draw upon three types of knowledge in their reading and writing: background knowledge, knowledge of genres, and knowledge of the information encoded in writing itself. Let's look at each.

Background Knowledge or Content Schemata

In the intermediate grades children's expanding cognitive sophistication has the potential for an informational and conceptual explosion. They are capable of bringing much more background knowledge to bear on their encounters with new texts and material. In fact, quite often the major instructional challenge for teachers at this level is reassuring students that it is okay, even desirable, to bring so much of *themselves* to the learning process. But there are also limits to their knowledge acquisition in many areas; there may not be much background knowledge to support much of their reading about specific topics. Therefore, students at this phase need to learn how to adjust to this situation.

"Strategic" reading is an important focus here. This is the point where *metacognition*—thinking about thinking—is applied more broadly than at earlier levels. Students will learn

◆ what to do (*procedural knowledge*) and

◆ when and why to do it (*self-knowledge*).

Many skills and strategies that will develop in the intermediate years rely on the reader's conscious awareness of what he or she is attempting and the ability to ask the following kinds of questions:

◆ How should I approach this next bit of reading I have to do? What if I don't know much about the topic?

◆ When I'm reading, what do I do when I don't know a word or am having trouble locating a specific answer?

◆ How do I *know* when I *don't know*, and what should I *do* when I don't know?

◆ When I'm finished with the reading, how do I deal with the information I've obtained from it?

We have two main objectives in bringing together intermediate students and expository texts, whether these texts be trade books or textbooks. First, students must learn how these texts are structured and organized and how to read them. Second, students must learn *how to learn* from these texts; although books will certainly not be their sole source of information, they will be a very important source, now and throughout their school lives.

Knowledge of Genres

Because of their increasing cognitive sophistication, students have the potential to follow and to understand more elaborate text structures in their reading. They can consciously explore more complex characterization, plot structure, and themes. Their life experiences provide the raw data of understanding.

As we will explore in Chapter 6, *expository* texts play a much bigger role in instruction in the intermediate grades, and most students will need to be taught explicitly about their structure and organization. Otherwise, many if not most of your students will apply the same strategies for reading narratives to reading informational material. Part of their new knowledge will involve learning how major and supporting ideas are linked together. As we saw earlier, these patterns of organization in most expository texts are *sequence, cause and effect, problem and solution,* and *comparison/contrast* (McGee & Richgels, 1985).

The National Assessment of Educational Progress has shown over the years that there are definite gains in the quality of students' writing throughout the intermediate grades. Notably, toward the end of this period, the length and quality of many students' written expression can surpass the length and quality of their spoken expression (Loban, 1976). This also is a time for experimenting with different forms and types of elaboration. Writing in the intermediate grades will reflect students' real-world experiences and their literary experiences and knowledge.

As an example of the type of writing students at this level are capable of creating, consider fifth-grader Danielle's poem (Figure 5.10) written in response to Richard Garcia's "The City Is So Big." Garcia's poem describes trains rushing by and house demolitions and concludes with an image of ". . . [e]levator doors opening and closing" and people disappearing within. Danielle has certainly grasped a "sense" of **poetry**, going beyond mere form, and has engagingly incorporated her reaction to particular ideas expressed in Garcia's poetry within her own poem.

Figure 5.11 is the first draft of a composition coauthored by two fifth-graders on a word processor. They have been reading Alfred Hitchcock's *Three Investigator* books. The first page of three pages is reproduced here. Already, though, we can see inclusion both of real-world experiences (in the

Figure 5.10   A Fifth-Grader's Poem Written as a Response to Garcia's "The City Is So Big"

interchange with the mother) and of literary knowledge about establishing a setting and foreshadowing an exciting event.

It is in the intermediate grades that many students acquire flexibility with their writing. They have passed through the stage where entire compositions, for example, are written as dialogues, and they are now able to use dialogue more appropriately. What they before had to write out in full to see if it worked can now be examined first in their heads.

At the intermediate levels many students have the potential to become aware in a much more sophisticated sense of their audience (Calkins, 1995), reading their own compositions as others would read them. Students' *reading* and discussion about what they read contribute to this development because they are able to incorporate this knowledge into the composing process (Langer, 1986). In addition, as students write, they develop a deeper sense of what they know and what they are learning. For example, while

```
                 THE MYSTERY OF MR. GUNMAN'S DEATH

        One day, Jimmy Gordon was sitting on the front porch steps
   with his sister, Katie Gordon. "I'm bord," said Jimmy. "Me too!"
   said Katie. "Nothing exiting happens around here any more."
   Jimmy agreed. "That is unless your counting the time when Mrs.
   Waterman had the minnows coming out of the kitchen faucet!"
   Jimmy said. "No" said Katie "I mean like a safe cracking or
   something." Jimmy said "We haven't had one of those since 1924!
   And I don't think we"ll have one of those for a long time.
   Because the guy, I think his name was Jonathan Henry or
   something like that, served a 20 year sentence in prison!"
        "Well, I still think there's going to be some kind of a
   crime around here soon, I can feel it in my bones," said Katie.
        "Don't get your hopes up," said Jimmy. "And besides,
   Christmas is coming so we'll have something to play with," Jimmy
   said.
        Just at that moment their mom came out. "Jimmy and Katie,
   it's almost dinner time."
        Jimmy and Katie both said together "Oh, mom." Jimmy said
   "By the way, what is for dinner?" His mom answered "We're having
   pizza..." "Goodie!" Jimmy and Katie interupted.
        "Wait,let me finish" said their mom "Your father and I are
   having pizza, and you're having liver." "Yuck!" said Jimmy and
   Katie. "Can't we skip dinner tonight?" said Jimmy.
        "No, but I suppose you could have a couple of pieces of
   pizza," said there mom. Jimmy and Katie looked relieved. And
   right at that point they heard a cry of pain from next door, Mr.
   Gunman's house. Jimmy and Katie rushed over to help him. "Wait!"
   cried
```

Figure 5.11   **A Mystery Story by Two Fifth-Graders**

writing in his journal about a stepparent he doesn't like, a student may suddenly realize *why* he has had these feelings and move toward a resolution. The writing in Figure 5.12 hints at this type of writing. Taken from a sixth-grader's response journal (see Chapter 7), this piece was the student's spontaneous reaction written just after finishing reading Katherine Paterson's *A Bridge to Terabithia* (1996). In a very simple, straightforward way, this student has voiced the realization and the wisdom that many students reach after reading this book: after the loss of a very close friend, life must go on. In addition to its more obvious role in putting thought "out there" to be examined over time, writing at this level allows writers to have intensive and extended conversations with themselves. As writers read more examples of texts that reflect this type of writing, their "conversations" increasingly resemble the form of these models. This interactive process involving writing and reading leads to growth as well in critical thinking.

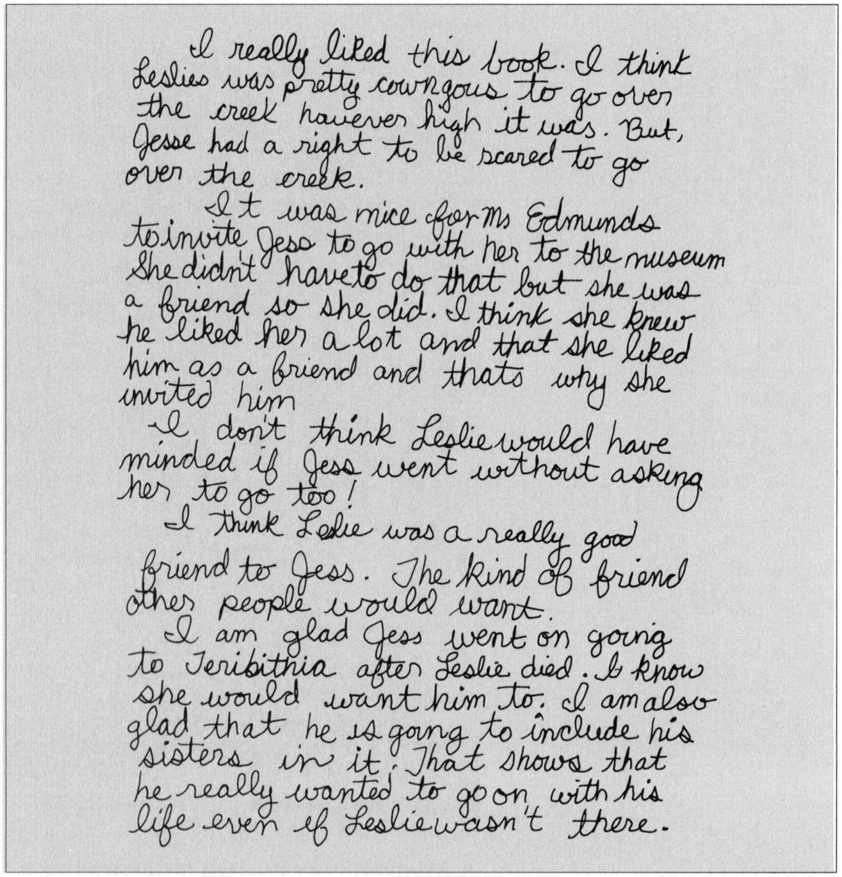

I really liked this book. I think Leslies was pretty cowrgous to go over the creek however high it was. But, Jesse had a right to be scared to go over the creek.

It was nice for Ms Edmunds to invite Jess to go with her to the museum. She didn't have to do that but she was a friend so she did. I think she knew he liked her a lot and that she liked him as a friend and thats why she invited him

I don't think Leslie would have minded if Jess went without asking her to go too!

I think Leslie was a really good friend to Jess. The kind of friend other people would want.

I am glad Jess went on going to Teribithia after Leslie died. I know she would want him to. I am also glad that he is going to include his sisters in it. That shows that he really wanted to go on with his life even if Leslie wasn't there.

Figure 5.12   A Sixth-Grader's Response to a Story (Journal Entry)

Knowledge about Word Structure

We will begin considering students' word knowledge, an issue we will explore further in Chapter 8. For the moment, however, know that students at this level will be learning much about the *structure* of words—their syllabic structure, and even more important, their *morphemic* structure. Structural or "morphemic" analysis is the study of how *morphemes*—the smallest units of meaning in words—combine to represent the primary meaning of words. Far and away the most important aspect of structural analysis is the systematic exploration of the ways in which prefixes, suffixes, base words, and word roots combine to create meaning. The elements of structural analysis include

- **Concept of "base word"**   After removing any prefixes and/or suffixes, if the element that remains can stand by itself as a word, then it is referred to as a *base word*.

- **Common prefixes and suffixes**   These elements, collectively referred to as "affixes," amplify or change the meaning of the base words or word roots to which they are attached. Examples are *un-*, *re-*, and *-er/ -or*, *-ment*.

- **Concept of "word root" and common word roots**   After removing any prefixes and/or suffixes, if the element that remains *cannot* stand by itself as a word, then it is referred to as a *word root* (in + *spect* + ion = in-*spect*ion; in + *cis* + ion = in*cis*ion). Word roots usually are of Latin or Greek origin.

When students at this level understand how words "work," they are empowered to

- determine the meaning of unknown words they encounter in their reading

- expand and elaborate their vocabulary

- spell more effectively and knowledgeably.

The bottom line is this: *the more students know about words and word structure, the better readers and writers they will be.*

CONCLUDING PERSPECTIVE AND SUMMARY

Chapter 5 has presented a synthesis of the most significant current work in developmental literacy. It should provide you with a general framework for understanding children's literacy development and a firm foundation for creating teaching strategies. By applying this knowledge, you will better know how to "stretch" your students while you simultaneously help them consolidate their new and existing knowledge.

We first looked at *what* will be learned: the form and content of written language—the nature of narrative and expository structures. We then examined the processes of reading and writing, particularly how students' understanding of and experiences with them will be built upon background knowledge (concepts and schemas), knowledge of syntax, types of genre, word knowledge, and punctuation. Finally, we considered *how* this information will be learned—the characteristics of literacy development in the preschool, primary school, and intermediate school years. The next three chapters will explore how you as a teacher can facilitate this literacy development—focusing on reading, writing, and combining the two processes in a learning environment rich in children's fiction, nonfiction, and inquiry throughout the curriculum.

In this chapter we've addressed the following main points:

◆ Reading and writing are "two sides of the same literacy coin" because much of the knowledge and many of the same skills and strategies are used in both processes. Also, children can apply knowledge they learn in one language art to the other.

◆ In the elementary grades students gain knowledge of written language— its functions/purposes, how content represents an author's meaning, and how content determines form—as well as the writer's choices of genre and methods of organization to express the content. Children particularly learn about the elements of narrative—setting, plot, characterization, theme, style, and point of view—through the literature they read and the writing they produce using it as a model. They also learn that expository writing explains facts and ideas by organizing them in terms of their logical relationships.

◆ The application of knowledge in reading and writing is a complex process because it involves the interplay of so many kinds of knowledge—background information, grammatical structure, genres and their components, information encoded in writing (word knowledge, punctuation), the very nature of reading and writing, and the conventions of writing and print. Moreover, the application of most of this knowledge must be automatic so that the information-processing capacity of the child's brain isn't overloaded by being simultaneously engaged in too many lower-level tasks. The processing and application of this knowledge must be efficient to be effective.

◆ Readers apply three types of comprehension to grasp a text's meaning: 1) literal — understanding what is explicitly stated; 2) inferential — understanding what is implied; 3) critical — relating the text to information beyond it. These categories differ in the degree to which the reader relies on prior knowledge to construct meaning.

◆ Children learn most about written language in an environment where people are using and discussing it and where many examples of it are available.

◆ Most children's reading and writing knowledge during the preschool years — emergent literacy — includes understanding that writing differs from pictures and conveys information, grasping the concept of directionality of writing, a rudimentary sense of how alphabetic characters are used, and grasping the concept of word in print.

◆ During the primary school years, most children's reading and writing knowledge evolves from beginning to transitional literacy. In beginning "conventional" literacy children's knowledge is egocentric, gradually becoming more aware of and responsive to other people and the external environment. Their development of word knowledge is experimental as they invent spellings and otherwise interact with texts. In the second and third grades (transitional literacy), children consolidate more of the kinds of knowledge they utilize when reading and writing. These language arts now reflect children's increasing awareness of others and their willingness to practice and experiment. Also, their processing of knowledge about reading and writing is now more automatic.

◆ During the intermediate school years, the bases of knowledge and experience for most children's reading and writing are more developed and interrelated. Lower-level cognitive processing tasks are more efficient and automatic. In addition, children's rapidly increasing reasoning abilities enable them to develop more sophisticated reading and writing skills.

Key Terms

characterization (p. 146)	direction (p. 144)
coherence (p. 148)	directionality of print (p. 162)
concept of word in print (p. 165)	emergent literacy (p. 158)
content (p. 144)	expository (p. 146)
critical comprehension (p. 154)	expression (p. 144)
description (p. 144)	form (p. 144)

CHAPTER 6

Constructing Meaning Through Reading

- ◆ How has reading traditionally been taught?
- ◆ What is the role of the Reading Workshop?
- ◆ How can we best facilitate Beginning Reading?
- ◆ How can we facilitate reading comprehension? What strategies can we teach so that students will have successful engagements with different types of texts?

◆◆◆ INTRODUCTION

Our knowledge of the process of reading and how we might go about teaching it have advanced dramatically over the last two decades. We now understand that

◆ Children need to read *a lot* in real, *authentic* texts. Such texts are meant to inform, to entertain, or to help us do something. They are trade books, newspapers, flyers, CD-ROMs, and the Internet. Our **authentic literacy contexts** emphasize enjoyment, strategic reading, and using reading as a tool that can be applied to all areas of learning.

◆ Skills, while an important part of proficient reading, are best learned in this more authentic context.

Reading Instruction within an Integrated Language Arts Program

Children learn to read by reading. We can facilitate this process by providing time for students to read often and widely—much of the time letting them *choose* the texts they wish to read—and by reading *to* them, thereby enticing them to try new authors and titles. Embedding reading and reading instruction in meaningful contexts is vital (Templeton, 1995). Students must come to understand that both the *content* of the reading and the reading *strategies* we are helping them develop are meaningful and applicable in a broader context, including all areas of the curriculum. Knowledge of the skills and strategies is not an end in itself, as many children have believed of reading instruction in the past.

Studies that have addressed the effectiveness of literature-based instructional programs seem to underscore one central and obvious finding: students who read more are better readers (Taylor et al., 1990). That conclusion is hardly a surprise, but more important are the students' *attitudes* about reading and the degree to which they value it. Their attitudes are more positive than those of students who are not systematically exposed to real literature (Tunnell & Jacobs, 1989). Not surprisingly, students in classrooms where literature is readily available—and whose teachers place a high value on reading that literature—do on the whole tend to read more. For beginning readers in particular, intense involvement with books, supplemented by word-analysis instruction, yields better achievement than do other instructional emphases. Not only are test scores and attitudes better,

Immersion in authentic texts builds reading ability and positive attitudes toward reading.

but the quality of students' language (Chomsky, 1972) and in many instances their reasoning (Stanovich, 1992) are more advanced than that of students who have not been systematically exposed to real literature.

It certainly makes sense that if children read more *authentic* texts, they will be better readers and writers and will enjoy these undertakings more. Even publishers of basal reading programs have been encouraging teachers not to rely solely on a program for students' reading experiences but to supplement and extend such instruction (Anderson, Osborn, & Wilson, 1984). The belief in the "discrete subskills" approach has held powerful sway in teachers' perceptions (Ridley, 1990). Most educators hope this belief will gradually be transformed during the next few years. We will not abandon attention to skills and strategies, however, because it is our responsibility to guide students toward learning "specific strategies to use while reading . . . instruction related to language conventions, comprehension, literary elements, and response to literature" (Raphael, 1995, p. 76).

A Perspective on Reading Instruction and Published "Reading" Programs

In years past most reading instruction was heavily "skills based." Discrete skills such as learning letter/sound correspondences and factual recall were presented and reinforced in **basal reading programs** that built stories around the presentation of these skills. Authentic literature was rarely used in these basal programs.

Elementary school reading instruction in the United States and in many other countries has traditionally depended upon basal reading series. Historically, there are many reasons for this reliance (Shannon & Goodman, 1994). When basals first took hold earlier in this century, they reflected a "behavioristic" model of learning that was prevalent at the time and that still holds sway in much of education. Basals also reflected the "product" orientation of the American marketplace; if Henry Ford could train workers to produce a better automobile more rapidly, couldn't the same model be incorporated into an instructional program? School administrators have traditionally believed that basals better "control" and systematize the teaching of reading so that it is uniform throughout a school district, thus making testing more uniform and "accountability" easier.

Published reading programs are used in most elementary schools in the United States. This does not mean that these programs are used *exclusively* (without supplemental books) in every school, but they probably do define the curriculum in at least 90 percent of the nation's schools (Winograd, Wixson, & Lipson, 1989).

Traditionally, basal reading programs have primarily reflected a **skills approach to teaching reading**. In a nutshell, the approach's underlying philosophy is "teach specific skills in a specific order and students will become readers." The ironic consequence of this orientation was that very little *real* reading was going on during the school day. Students spent much more time filling out worksheets and workbook pages than they did reading—up to 70 percent of "reading time." Only seven to eight minutes were spent actually *reading* (Anderson et al., 1985). Couple these findings with the fact that most students don't spend much time reading independently (Campbell et al., 1995), and the limitations of the traditional "skills approach" become clear.

In recent years several major publishers of reading programs have attempted to incorporate the implications of reading research more directly as they develop their programs. More authentic literature is now included, strategies are emphasized, and in many instances additional links are made to the other language arts. Despite these efforts, some educators argue that basal programs still fall far short of the mark (Shannon & Goodman, 1994).

The schools where we will teach will most likely have a strong published reading series component underlying their reading curriculum. What should be our position on using this material? First, this component's inclusion does *not* mean that we should base our own reading instruction entirely on the program. Rather, we should feel that we have the *flexibility* to use whatever we choose from it. We should have the latitude to use only certain selections and certain lessons we have found to be particularly useful. Winograd expressed the situation aptly when he observed that "basal readers are most effective when they are used flexibly and as part of a comprehensive, balanced program of reading instruction" (Winograd et al., 1989, p. 1).

When used *flexibly*, a well-constructed basal program can play an important role in at least the following four areas:

◆ Most series include good lesson formats for guiding students toward learning important strategies and skills. When we wish to teach about *characterization*, for example, we will often find a focused lesson in the teacher's edition and a corresponding selection in the student text that highlight the understanding of characterization particularly well.

◆ Most series provide good types and sequences of *questions* that facilitate meaning construction and critical thinking.

◆ Most series now include extensive lists of suggested related readings to accompany selections that appear in the series. Some series now include multiple copies of books, excerpts of which have appeared in the basal.

◆ Most published reading series provide a developmentally based progression for engaging children with texts and with phonics and structural analysis.

The Reading Workshop

In the **Reading Workshop** students apply skills and strategies to enjoy and learn from their reading. As we first noted in Chapter 4, the Reading Workshop is an environment where

◆ we discuss and demonstrate through minilessons the skills, strategies, and concepts for reading texts, and

◆ students read independently and discuss their reading.

◆ After we are settled in for a new year or term, we can expand what goes on to include **conferencing** with individual students about their reading and meeting with small **literature discussion groups**. We can post a schedule of the groups we'll be meeting with each day.

In our Cynthia Rylant Thematic Exploration (see p. 129), Sandy Madura

Part of "Reading Workshop" involves independent reading and discussion.

began one Reading Workshop during Week 3 by discussing how the illustrator can work with the writer's text to create an overall "feeling" for the reader. First, she talked about Barry Moser's illustrations in *An Angel for Solomon Singer* (Rylant, 1992): How do they help us *visually* understand what Rylant is showing us through her words about how Solomon thinks and feels—his loneliness, his memories of his home in the country, how he feels about living in the city? After paging through the book and discussing this topic for a few minutes, Sandy tells the children to look carefully as they read their books today to explore how the illustrations work with the words.

In our "Keepers of the Earth" Thematic Exploration (see p. 384), Tamara Baren conducts a minilesson in which she responds to some students' questions about why certain characters appear, seem to be important, and then are gone—and we never see them again. She first uses examples from the core text *The Listening Silence* (Root, 1992) as she talks about how authors employ "minor" characters to help readers understand the *main* characters in more depth. Then she asks the students to think of other examples from books they are reading; these are discussed briefly. She next summarizes what they have discovered: Those minor characters assist in "fleshing out" the main characters, usually by helping the main characters grow in awareness, maturity, and wisdom.

While Reading Workshop is similar to Sustained Silent Reading or "DEAR" ("Drop Everything and Read") in that students usually read books they select themselves, it is different because students may chat about their reading—just like we adults do when we're reading something interesting and want to share it with someone else in the room. Students also respond to the reading they are doing through writing (see Chapter 10), and they may conduct dialogues with one another through their journals.

Beginning Reading in the Integrated Classroom

As we saw in Chapter 5, preschool children's emerging literacy concepts grow out of experiences with print in a variety of contexts. Children remember what is written in favorite texts; together with their explorations in writing and drawing, this knowledge supports development of a number of important literacy concepts. For kindergarten and first-grade children who have developed these concepts, we can begin with these strategies: **Shared Reading** with **predictable books** and the **Language Experience Approach**.

Shared-Book Experiences with "Predictable Books"

Used with either a small group or a whole class, "shared-book" reading involves children in a situation similar to the one-to-one experience they have when an adult reads to them. While we cannot plop every child in our laps as we read to them, we *can* involve them with a book in every other way. The shared-book experience centers around a *predictable* book. Beginning readers need *support*, and predictable texts provide a good deal of it.

"Predictability" in language and in story—in syntax and semantics— plays a seminal role in beginning conventional reading (Yaden, 1988). Heald-Taylor (1987) pointed out that good predictable books for young children provide "strong rhythm and rhyme, repeated patterns, refrains, logical sequences, supportive illustrations, and traditional story structures" (p. 6). The predictability of texts also reinforces children's *memory* of a particular text, and as we saw in Chapter 5, remembering specific texts underlies the development of much of the rest of a child's knowledge about print.

Shared-book experiences with either small groups or a whole class use a

"Big Book" so that children can view the text and the pictures. Publishers now offer many predictable texts in a Big Book format (Slaughter, 1993). Their fundamental feature is their size. **Big Books** have large illustrations and print so that all children can see them. They are designed for reading activities with either large or small groups. The large print allows the teacher to model many conventions of print, such as left-to-right and top-to-bottom directionality, and the correspondence between spoken and written language, including the concept of word in print. During the shared-book experience, the teacher discusses the text, reads it, asks questions, and engages the children in discussion. The book is reread on a number of occasions, thus reinforcing memory for the text and also allowing the teacher to point out features and conventions of books—the author and illustrator, the title page and publication date, and so forth.

Most publishers of Big Books add an accompanying set of "little books" that includes multiple copies of the big book so that several children can have access to the story independently. One of the most famous predictable texts is *Brown Bear, Brown Bear* (Martin, 1983; illustrated by Eric Carle). It is an excellent book to use on the first day of first grade and is also appropriate for kindergarten. The recurring word pattern is highly predictable, and the pictures support both content and language. Here are the first few lines:

> "Brown bear,
> brown bear,
> what do you see?"
> "I see a red bird
> looking at me."
> "Red bird,
> red bird,
> what do you see?"
> "I see a yellow duck
> looking at me . . ."

This is the suggested sequence for guiding children in a shared-book experience:

◆ Read the book to the children. As they grasp the pattern, encourage them to join in. You may wish to pause before a word that seems to be heavily cued by the picture and text to allow the children the chance to supply the word. In the case of a book such as *Brown Bear, Brown Bear*, the text is so predictable that the children will most likely be joining in during the very first reading.

◆ Go back and *model* the reading, using a pointer to identify each word briefly as it is read. Often teachers also make comments about the print and its placement on the page. Avoid doing too much the first time around, however; keep the experience fun and appropriate.

◆ Reread the story several times over the next few days. Each time have the children focus on a different aspect of the story content or text features. Through these rereadings children will learn to read particular words, and you will be able to model the application of phonics knowledge. Most predictable texts will have repetitive rhymes and/or alliteration that will facilitate young children's *phonemic awareness* (see the *Build Your Teaching Resources* feature below).

◆ After they have read and reread several predictable, enlarged texts in class, children love to create their own "big" texts. These will usually be based on the original; the text can be dictated and/or written by the children who can also create illustrations for each page. The teacher prints the text on each page for the children, and the book is then laminated and placed in the classroom library.

B u i l d   Y o u r   T e a c h i n g   R e s o u r c e s

PREDICTABLE TEXTS

The following are excellent, highly predictable books that will get your predictable literature resource list under way. They can be modeled for the children, and eventually they will be able to read many of the books for the first time on their own.

RHYMING AND "WORDPLAY" BOOKS

Ahlberg, J., & Ahlberg, A. (1978). *Each peach pear plum*. New York: Viking.

Aylesworth, J. (1994). *My son John*. New York: Henry Holt. [Illustrated by D. Frampton.]

Barchas, S.E. (1975). *I was walking down the road*. New York: Scholastic. [Illustrated by Jack Kent.]

Benjamin, A. (1987). *Rat-a-tat, pitter-pat*. New York: Crowell. [Photographs by Margaret Miller.]

Brown, M. (1947). *Goodnight moon*. New York: Harper.

Brown, M. (1993). *Four fur feet*. New York: Doubleday.

Carle, E. (1971). *The very hungry caterpillar*. New York: Crowell.

Carter, D. (1990). *More bugs in boxes*. New York: Simon & Schuster.

Charlip, R. (1964). *Fortunately*. New York: Parents.

Cherry, L. (1988). *Who is sick today?* New York: Dutton.

Crews, D. (1995). *Ten black dots*. New York: Morrow.

Dabcovich, L. (1982). *Sleepy bear*. New York: Dutton.

Deming, A. (1994). *Who is tapping at my window?* New York: Penguin Books.

Emberley, B. (1967). *Drummer Hoff*. Englewood Cliffs, NJ: Prentice Hall.

Emberley, B. (1992). *One wide river to cross*. Boston: Little, Brown.

Build Your Teaching Resources

PREDICTABLE TEXTS

(*Continued*)

Florian, D. (1987). *A winter day*. New York: Greenwillow Books.

Florian, D. (1989). *Nature walk*. New York: Greenwillow Books.

Florian, D. (1990a). *A beach day*. New York: Greenwillow Books.

Florian, D. (1990b). *City street*. New York: Greenwillow Books.

Gag, W. (1929). *Millions of cats*. New York: Coward-McCann.

Galdone, P. (1961). *The house that Jack built*. New York: McGraw-Hill.

Galdone, P. (1968). *Henny penny*. New York: Scholastic.

Geraghty, P. (1992). *Stop that noise!* New York: Crown Publishers.

Gordon, J. (1991). *Six sleepy sheep*. New York: Puffin Books.

Hoberman, M. A. (1978). *A house is a house for me*. New York: Viking.

Hoffman, P. (1990). *We play*. New York: Scholastic. [Illustrated by Sara Wilson.]

Hutchins, P. (1968). *Rosie's walk*. New York: Macmillan.

Krause, R. (1970). *Whose mouse are you?* New York: Macmillan.

Kuskin, K. (1990). *Roar and more*. New York: Harper.

Langstaff, J. (1974). *Oh, a-hunting we will go*. New York: Simon & Schuster. [Illustrated by N. Parker.]

Lewison, W. (1992). *Buzz said the bee*. New York: Scholastic.

Lyon, G. (1989). *Together*. Richard Jackson. [Illustrated by V. Rosenberry.]

Macmillan, B. (1990). *One sun: A book of terse verse*. New York: Holiday House.

McLenighan, V. (1982). *Stop-go, fast-slow*. Chicago: Children's Press.

Numeroff, L. (1995). *Chimps don't wear glasses*. New York: Simon & Schuster. [Illustrated by J. Mathieu.]

Ochs, C. (1991). *Moose on the loose*. Minneapolis, MN: Carolrhoda Books.

O'Connor, J. (1986). *The teeny tiny woman*. New York: Random House.

Pomerantz, C. (1993). *If I had a Paka*. New York: Mulberry Books.

Prelutsky, J. (1982). *The baby Uggs are hatching*. New York: Mulberry Books.

Provenson, A., & Provenson, M. (1977). *Old Mother Hubbard*. New York: Random House.

Sendak, M. (1962). *Chicken soup with rice*. New York: Harper.

Sheppard, J. (1994). *Splash, splash*. New York: Macmillan. [Illustrated by D. Panek.]

Slepian, J., & Seidler, A. (1967). *The hungry thing*. New York: Follet. [Illustrated by Richard Martin.]

West, C. (1986). *"Pardon?" said the giraffe*. New York: Harper.

Yektai, N. (1987). *Bears in pairs*. New York: Macmillan.

Zemach, M. (1972). *The teeny tiny woman: A folktale illustrated by Margot Zemach*. New York: Scholastic.

The Language Experience Approach in the Integrated Classroom

Using the *Language Experience Approach* (LEA) is an excellent way to integrate children's language and background knowledge with beginning reading and writing. LEA draws upon the language and experiences of children, tailoring written material to where *they* are coming from (Stauffer, 1970; Hall, 1981).

Because the students have produced the text, the Language Experience Approach (LEA) provides an effective way for them to understand the features and functions of written language. As with predictable texts, LEA affords teachers the opportunity to model "how print works" for children. The following are the basic steps of the Language Experience Approach:

◆ Build on an experience the children have had (one they have talked about a lot) through sharing, responses to read-alouds, discussion, and examination of firsthand and secondhand experiences. Any and all of these activities can serve as the experience from which the dictation will stem.

◆ As different children volunteer contributions, write down *exactly* what each child says about the experience.

◆ After writing down several contributions, read the dictated account to the children, as naturally as possible, while pointing to each word. Repeat this process one or more times, and then read the account with all of the children in chorus, leading them gently with your voice, fading in and out as necessary. Individual children may then "read" the sentence they contributed.

In addition to its use with a small group, the Language Experience Approach may be used with individual students (Templeton, 1995). It is particularly effective for use with students who are having difficulty acquiring a sight vocabulary and for older students who are struggling as beginning readers and writers. For these students, following the steps outlined in Figure 6.1 is recommended.

Language Experience for Second-Language Learners

The Language Experience Approach is very effective for ESL students at stages two and three of second-language acquisition (see Chapter 4). LEA incoporates the students' level of language acquisition with the experiences in which they've been engaged—thereby concretely linking object, action, and word. Figure 6.1 shows the steps for using LEA one to one with students learning English as a second language. These steps can also be used with a small group.

CLASSROOM
EXAMPLE

Group
Dictated-
Experience
Chart

Here is an illustration of the language experience approach being used with a group or a whole class:

Getting Underway: Writing the Dictated-Experience Chart

The "stimulus" is a basket of newborn kittens. Conversation focuses on how they look, smell, and behave, and how cute and cuddly they are. After about ten minutes of discussion, the teacher, Rhonda McGuinness, sits next to an easel on which several sheets of chart paper are tacked. She begins the "dictation" phase of the experience:

RHONDA: "Boys and girls, we've been *talking* about the kittens, and now we're going to *write* and *read* about them. Tell me what you'd like me to write down, and I'll write exactly what you say. Let's think about the things we said about the kittens. Who would like to say something and then have me write it down? [Several hands shoot up.] Yes, Cory?"

CORY: "I think the kittens are cute."

RHONDA: "Okay! I'll write that down, and everyone watch and listen as I do it."

Using a broad-tipped felt marker, Rhonda begins printing. Starting at the left margin, she first writes "Cory said" and then puts down exactly what he said. (She writes the child's name because she knows that most children in the beginning of first grade are able to read their own names; the students can use this word as a "locator" for finding their sentence later on.) Rhonda pronounces each word naturally as she writes it, trying to read with as much expression as she can.

RHONDA: "All right! What else can we say about the kittens? Yes, Bernadette?"

BERNADETTE: "They're furry."

RHONDA: "Okay!" [She then writes *Bernadette said, "They're furry."*] Yes, Adrianna?"

ADRIANNA: "Their eyes are closed."

RHONDA: "Okay! Let's write that down . . ."

Rhonda continues in this fashion, stopping after seven children have contributed; she doesn't want a text that goes on and on.

(Continued)

Thus far, Rhonda has

- Modeled *how print "works"*—It reads left to right, top to bottom.

- *Pronounced* each word as she has written it—helping to develop children's *concept of word in print*.

- Modeled the *formation of letters*—Over time this type of demonstration will promote children's developing knowledge about spelling and letter formation.

Reading the Dictated-Experience Chart

Rhonda continues:

"Boys and girls, now that we've *written* about the kittens, we're going to *read* what we've written. First, watch and listen as I read this back to you because we're soon going to read it all together."

As in shared-book reading, Rhonda uses a pointer so that she does not block the chart with her arm or body. She then reads the composition aloud as naturally as possible, pointing to each word as she reads it. If she feels it is necessary, she reads the chart a second time for the children.

Next, Rhonda says, "Boys and girls, let's read what we've written *all together*." She then reads as she did the first time, as naturally as possible, letting her voice lead the children if necessary as they choral-read, dropping her voice slightly if the children seem to be recalling the lines fairly well on their own. If she feels it's necessary, she leads a second and perhaps a third choral reading.

Follow-Up

Follow-up activities for LEA are very similar to those for the shared-book experience. For example, Rhonda will invite children to do any or all of the following: locate their names, read what they said, read what someone else said, or locate specific words—depending on how much they know about print and how comfortable they seem to be. Children who have not dictated a sentence are, of course, free to locate another child's sentence and "read" it. For most first-graders a 15- to 20-minute session is possible; this includes the "stimulus" and the accompanying discussion as well as the dictation writing and reading. Children can draw a picture of the kittens; as they are drawing, the teacher can walk about and label the drawing for them or encourage them to write their own labels (see Chapter 7).

On subsequent days Rhonda will use the dictated story to probe further to discover the children's knowledge of print and facilitate their learning of sight words:

- Many teachers reproduce the dictated-experience chart in a format suitable for placing in a sturdy composition book. The story may be photocopied or typed on a computer and then printed.

- Every so often during the actual dictation phase, you may wish to type what the children are dictating into the word processor while the computer is hooked up to an overhead display. Most classrooms will have easier access to television monitors than to overhead display screens, and these can be easily viewed by the children. I suggest you alternate this technique with printing by hand on chart paper. Even though you're not talking explicitly about how you're forming the letters, it's important that children see this formation in the context of meaningful composition.

- Even at this stage, we can model how we change the text once we have written something down (see Chapter 7). For example, if a child decides to change a word, we can draw a line through what we initially wrote and write the new word above it. If we need to insert a word or phrase, we can put in a caret sign ("^") and write the addition above the line. If we're typing on the word processor, of course, this process will be "cleaner" because our changes can be made without crossing out and inserting. Again, however, it's important that we model both hand-written and computer-written ways of making changes.

Read-Alouds with Primary Children

Before Reading

As we read through the picture book or poem we plan to share with children in the primary grades, we should think about how *we* are responding to it. What thoughts, emotions, or associations come to *us*? We might share some of these with the children after we've read to them. What *questions* might we ask of them? Our questions should help the children find "per-

Language Experience for ESL: Early Speech-Production Stage	Language Experience for ESL: Extended Speech-Production Stage
DAY 1:	**DAY 1:**
• Discuss experience; dictate story.	• Take the dictation. Assess the types of oral-language grammatical and vocabulary miscues.
• Read *to* student, then reread with student several times.	**DAY 2:**
DAY 2:	• Read the story to the student exactly as it was dictated.
• Student reads dictation to him/herself, underlining *known* words.	• Student reads the dictation—with your support, if necessary.
• Student reads dictation to you; support the reading by immediately supplying unknown words.	• With the student watching and listening, *rewrite* the dictation, using conventional English syntactic patterns and vocabulary. As you rewrite, state *what* your correction is, then have the student read the corrected sentence.
• Present all the words to the student *sequentially*—in a list—and note those that are identified correctly.	• Student reads your rewrite of the *whole* dictation [keep a record of this rereading].
DAY 3:	**DAY 3:**
• Student reads dictation to him/herself, underlining in a different color known words.	• Student rereads the corrected version and underlines only those words he or she does *not* know.
• Student reads dictation to you.	• With your support, student rereads the dictation several times.
• Present known words from previous day's word list in *random* order and note those that are identified correctly.	**DAY 4:**
DAY 4:	• Student rereads corrected version; again, he or she underlines only those words that are *not* known.
• Present known words from previous day's list in random order.	• Reread corrected version with student.
• Write words correctly identified on cards.	• Show student copy of the *first* version of his or her dictation; ask the student to make the types of revisions, orally or in writing, that he or she has been reading in your corrected version.
DAY 5:	
• Present word cards from previous day; words that are correctly identified are placed in word bank.	

Figure 6.1   Language Experience Approach for Second-Language Learners

sonal significance" in the selection, "as revealed through the relationships among the characters, setting, dialogue, events, images, language, or other literary elements" (McGee, 1995, p. 111).

Reading to Children and Guiding Discussion

At important points in the reading, we should pause and talk with the children; it's important to allow spontaneous observations and comments. We should encourage them to make predictions about what might be happening next in the selection. We shouldn't take too much time at each stopping place, however; we will want to stay "on track" with the selection. And there will be some selections that we simply read straight through, not wishing to break the "magic" that it might be weaving for the children. Just as with other beginning reading texts, many texts can be reread, and there will be many opportunities to think about all aspects of the selection.

Learning about Words: Developing a Sight Vocabulary

Developing a **sight vocabulary**—words that are recognized *immediately*—is critically important as children learn to read:

◆ *First*, many of these words are "high frequency" words, which means they occur often in texts students will be reading. Because children will know many of these words, they will have the all-important experience of feeling they are "really reading," without having to stop and try to figure out most of the words.

◆ *Second*, these words will be a starting point for learning more about how words "work"—their structure and their meaning. Sight words are the foundation for **phonics instruction**—learning how letters correspond to sounds, enabling children to analyze unfamiliar words in their reading.

While children can pick up sight words from just about any source, they can acquire most of their initial sight words from environmental print, predictable texts, and LEA dictations. The key to acquisition is familiarity with the text and the context in which words appear. As predictable texts and dictations are read several times, important words begin to "stand out" for children—particularly if we help direct their attention to the words.

Word banks are excellent "depositories" or collections of children's sight words. Each child can have one, can see her sight vocabulary grow, and can examine the words for a number of purposes. The word bank can be a large envelope, margarine tub, or file box—any means of storage that is sturdy and easy to manipulate. Words that the child knows automatically are "deposited" in the bank and reviewed on a regular basis—about once a day, either individually or with a buddy.

Here is an example of how we can begin the process of acquiring a sight vocabulary:

◆ The teacher meets with a group of children who have read the predictable text *Poor Old Polly* the previous day in a shared-book experience format. The teacher has prepared for the meeting by writing on separate cards several words which she believes the children should be able to identify when presented with them in isolation.

◆ Displaying the word card for *shark*, for example, the teacher asks a child, "Marcie, can you tell me what this word is?" If Marcie responds correctly (as the teacher is almost certain she will), the teacher hands the card to her as she says, "Wonderful! Marcie, this is *your* word." The teacher makes a "big deal" about this answer to emphasize the importance of Marcie's knowing the word; it really does *belong* to her now.

In addition to important content-bearing words, high-frequency *function words* such as *of*, *the*, *was*, *of*, and so forth—potential "toughies" when encountered in isolation—are usually acquired through repeated meaningful exposure through LEA dictations and predictable books. These words are, of course, important—they are the "glue" words that hold the content-bearing words together.

Learning about Words: The Role of Phonics

Phonics refers to the study of letter/sound (or *grapheme/phoneme*) relationships. These relationships are studied as they apply within *single-syllable* words. Sounds are classified as either *consonants* or *vowels*. Research has consistently demonstrated that knowledge of letter/sound correspondences facilitates conventional literacy learning at the primary grade levels (Adams, 1990; Ehri & Wilce, 1987). We encourage this learning, along with teaching the use of contextual clues, but it's important to keep in mind that phonics instruction can be *over*emphasized at the beginning reading phase to the exclusion of other word-recognition clues and strategies.

Phonemic awareness is an important aspect of a child's coming to understand how letters and sounds correspond. Children's ability to become aware of individual sounds within words—to be phonemically aware—develops over a long period of time. This ability develops from

◆ the many experiences with reading and print in which adults involve children

◆ learning of the names of the letters of the alphabet

◆ children's writing and their use of invented spelling.

Much that we read to young children includes *rhyme* and *alliteration*, as illustrated in these lines from Wong Herbert Yee's *Big Black Bear* (1993). At the beginning of the book, Big Black Bear caught a scent and

> Followed that scent from tree to tree,
> Down to the city, where he shouldn't be.
> Shuffling along on four furry feet
> To a Brown Brick House on Sycamore Street.

The rhyme, of course, is obvious—and the alliteration with *four furry feet*. *Rhyme* highlights what is common and constant *across* words (f*eet*, str*eet*). Rhyme also makes what is *different* stand out: the beginning of the word.

Because of these experiences, when a child nears the end of the *emergent* phase of literacy, we can begin phonics instruction (see Figure 6.2). Here is the general sequence of our instruction:

◆ *Beginning single-consonant letter/sound correspondences* — At some point during their learning about beginning sounds, children will develop a *concept of word in print.* This important milestone strongly supports the development of phonics knowledge.

◆ *Short vowel correspondences*

◆ *Consonant digraphs and blends*

◆ *Long vowel patterns*

Figure 6.2 shows the general sequence of phonics instruction. Notice that

---

Learning about Consonants
- *Letter names*
- *Beginning single consonants*

b	m	r	s
t	g	p	n
h	f	d	c
l	j	k	w
y	z	v	q

Learning about Short Vowels
Teach concept of short vowel phonograms, or "patterns" (the term we use with the children) following this sequence: short *a*, short *i*, short *o*, short *u*, short *e*. The fundamental pattern is the "VC" phonogram. For example:

VC:	-at	-ad	-ack
	-it	-ig	-ick
	-op	-ot	
	-ut	-un	

- *Beginning consonant digraphs*

ch	sh	th	wh

- *Beginning consonant blends*

bl	cl	fl			
br	cr	dr	fr	gr	tr
sm	sp	st	sn		

Learning about Long Vowels
Teach concept of long vowel phonograms, or "patterns":

CV:	go, me, my					
VCe:	-ake	-ame	VV:	-ee	-ay	-ai-
	-ike	-ide				
	-oke	-ope				

Figure 6.2   Suggested Sequence of Phonic Elements

CLASSROOM EXAMPLE

Minilesson in Applying Contextual Clues and Phonics Knowledge

The teacher has written the following:

Bryan did not know what he tripped on in the dark. It made a scary sound. He turned the light on and looked at the room. He was happy when he saw it was only a bucket.

"Okay, we don't know what this word is [pointing to *bucket*] but we still know something about it. We know how it begins and ends, and together with the rest of the information we may be able to figure it out. Let's read this and find out." [Rereads the paragraph.] At *bucket*, the teacher reads the word this way:

". . . when he saw it was only a *buh* . . ."

The teacher pauses on this sound, and this action is usually enough to cue the word. At least one if not more students will call out, "Bucket!"

"Excellent! Let's reread to see if it fits." [Teacher rereads.] "Does it make sense? Does this *look* like the word 'bucket'? Why were you able to figure that out?" [Here the teacher is probing to get the students to restate, in their own words, her description of the word's beginning and ending and the rest of the information.]

The teacher can also point out words that are similar to parts of *bucket*. For example, she could write the word *duck* on the board—a word the students know—and ask them if they see how it could help them with part of *bucket*. She next reminds them that they can use this strategy with any unfamiliar word: look at the parts and try to think of other words that look similar.

The teacher summarizes: "Kids, sometimes when you're reading and you come to a word you don't know right away, you can use what you know about other words together with the meaning of what you're reading to try to figure the word out."

vowels are not taught in isolation but rather as *patterns* or **word families** such as *-at* and *-ig* ("VC" or vowel/consonant) and *-ake* and *-ide* ("VCe" or vowel/consonant/silent "e").

By emphasizing *patterns* we will also help children learn the following strategy: when you're trying to figure out an unknown word in your reading, think of *other* words that are similar; they often provide a clue.

Expand Your Teaching Repertoire

Activities to Reinforce Sight Vocabulary and Facilitate Knowledge about Phonics

1 Sentence Construction   Words from predictable texts or language experience dictations may be used to reconstruct sentences from the original texts as well as to create new sentences.

a. At first copy sentences from the book or the dictation on tagboard strips. Then cut them up word by word and keep the words from each sentence in a separate baggie. Students can then dump out the words, reconstruct the sentence, and check it against the original.

b. Later, as students are acquiring more words in their sight vocabularies, they can *create* new sentences. It's challenging for them to see how many different sentences they can construct using a set number of words. To keep track, write each sentence down after it is constructed.

2 **Consonant/Phonogram Substitution**   Manipulating elements within words is a powerful support for learning about words and for generalizing phonics correspondences. We begin by talking with students about "word families"—the term we use to refer to words that share the same *phonogram*.

a. Keeping the phonogram constant, substitute different beginning consonants and blend each consonant with the phonogram to form new words. Example: beginning with the known word *bag*, use the consonants *g*, *n*, *r*, *s*, *t*, and *w* to form new words. Once children have the hang of this, they can take any phonogram and run through the alphabet trying out different consonants. Words they will create will often not be *real* words, but that is part of the fun; they are often humorous and pronounceable.

b. Keeping the beginning consonant constant, substitute different phonograms and blend the elements together. Example: beginning with the known word *bag*, use the phonograms *-am*, *-at*, and so on to form new words. Then move to another set of short vowel phonograms such as *-ig* and *-it*.

3 Word Sorts   In these activities students search for and examine features of words through comparison and contrast as they categorize the words (Bear, Invernizzi, & Templeton, 1996). By their nature word sorts lead to deeper processing and learning about words because students are *actively* involved in exploration, as opposed to simply being told about the way words work.

(*Continued*) ## Expand Your Teaching Repertoire

Word sorts utilize *known* words. Students categorize these words in different ways and may compare their categories with those of other students. In this way the students are involved in elaborating the concepts underlying the words they already know. They then become aware of word features and distinctions that had not previously occurred to them.

For kindergartners and first-graders, sorting activities usually should not begin with words but with concrete objects and then move to pictures so that children can understand the task and learn from the sorting process (Henderson, 1990). Here are some examples:

- Small colored blocks, Cuisenaire rods, or pasta of different shapes and sizes are good objects.

- Pictures can be sorted according to different concepts: large objects versus small objects, "live" things versus those that are not, or tools versus toys.

When children have acquired two to three dozen sight words, they can begin word sorts. The elements are simple: students categorize words written or printed on separate chips of tagboard or cardboard according to specific criteria—sounds, spelling, and concepts. Word sorts may be performed in a group or individually. Initially, word sorts should be introduced in a group to make sure that each child understands the fundamentals of how to sort. The words can come from the children's word banks, or the teacher can prepare small word cards for the students. In this activity word-bank words can be sorted or categorized according to

- sound and/or structure (words that rhyme with *flat*; words that begin with *m*)

- meaning (for example, words that stand for things you can play with).

Figure 6.3 illustrates two different word sorts:

- The first is appropriate for a child in the late emergent or early beginning literacy phase. It illustrates an activity in which the child sorted picture cards according to beginning sounds and then searched her word bank for words that began with these sounds.

- The second sort is appropriate for a child in the late beginning literacy phase. Notice that the first sort is done according to *sound* ("short a" vs. "long a") and the second is by *spelling pattern* ("short a" words are sorted into VCC vs. VC patterns and "long a" words are sorted into VC*e* vs. VV patterns).

(Continued)

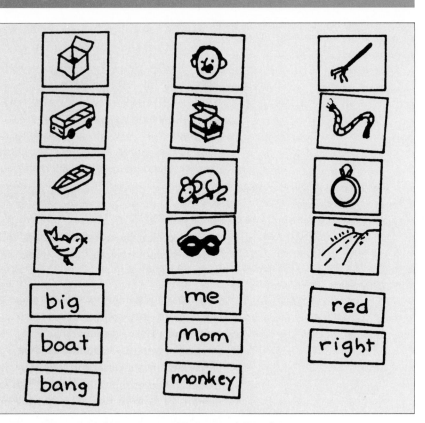

Figure 6.3a Initial Consonant Picture and Word Sort

SOURCE: From Bear, D., Invernizzi, M., and Templeton, S. (1996). *Words their way: Word study for phonics, vocabulary, and spelling instruction*, reprinted with permission from Merrill/Prentice Hall.

4 **Spelling** Talk about the *spelling* of a few words that illustrate a pattern you are examining. For example, when children begin examining a particular short vowel pattern in words, present a handful of words that illustrate the pattern—such as the consonant/vowel/consonant (*CVC*) pattern in *cat*, *rag*, and *ran*. Children may write these words throughout the week in the context of different activities (see Chapter 8). At the beginning literacy phase, writing of these simple conventional spelling patterns reinforces the application of developing word knowledge in both reading and writing.

5 **Alphabetizing** The activity of alphabetizing words will play a necessary role in word-bank activities. For first-graders who are regularly maintaining word banks, alphabetization should probably not exceed the first

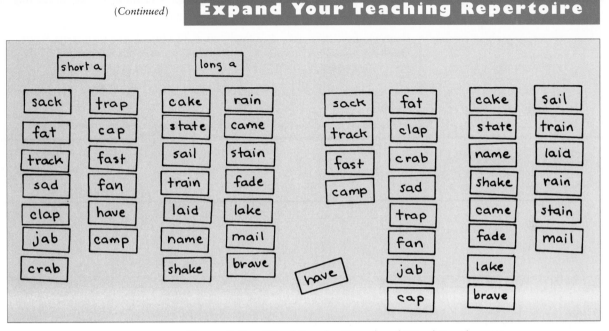

Figure 6.3b Word Sort by Sound and Word Sort by Pattern

SOURCE: From Bear, D., Invernizzi, M., and Templeton, S. (1996). *Words their way: Word study for phonics, vocabulary, and spelling instruction,* reprinted with permission from Merrill/Prentice Hall.

two letters of words. As word banks grow, students can put envelopes for different beginning letters in the banks. When they study consonant digraphs (e.g., *ch, th*) and blends (e.g., *st, pl*), they can add separate labeled envelopes for each digraph or blend to the word bank.

6 **Card Games** Students can play any number of card games with words. One of the most popular is "Go Fish," a variation on the popular game. You can ask, "Do you have a word that begins like *boat,* . . . that has the same vowel sound as *tape,* . . . that rhymes with *row?*"

7 **Board Games** Different types of word features can be reinforced within the basic board-game format. A board with a winding path that students can follow from start to finish can be used for consonant and vowel elements. Laminate the board, then write a different word on each square; the words will represent whatever phonic element or elements you want to highlight. Each student throws the dice, lands on a particular word, and looks to see if he or she has a word-bank word that fits the pattern (such as a word that begins the same way or has the same vowel pattern) in order to advance. Later on, this task can be made more challenging by requiring students to *recall* a word that fits the target pattern.

Build Your
Teaching
Resources

**BOOKS ABOUT
WORD
IDENTIFICATION**

Phonics and word identification instruction for the beginning phase of reading are comprehensively addressed in the following two texts:

• Bear, D., Invernizzi, M., & Templeton, S. (1996). *Words their way: Word study for phonics, vocabulary, and spelling instruction.* Englewood Cliffs, NJ: Prentice Hall.

• Cunningham, P. (1995). *Phonics they use* (2nd ed.). New York: Harper-Collins.

Selecting Books for the Authentic Reading/Integrated Literacy Classroom

There should be lots of *real* literature—authentic texts—in our classrooms. Textbooks and published instructional programs can play a role, but most of the available texts should be **trade books**. Trade books are so named because they are published by the *trade* division of a publishing company, not by the *school* division, which publishes textbooks. Trade books cover the whole range of genres. An extensive listing of Children's Literature is found in the *Teacher's Sourcebook* at the end of the text. It presents the different genre and representative titles for each category.

We also should collect *multiple copies* of good books (see Chapter 10). (A positive feature of "literature-based" instructional programs is their inclusion of real, authentic selections. This provides a built-in "multiple copy" aspect.) Here are additional criteria to keep in mind when selecting authentic literature for our classrooms:

◆ "Readability"—Because there is usually a range of different developmental levels of literacy in our classrooms, we need to make sure that every student will find books that he or she can read.

◆ Since there will be topics and themes that students will be investigating, there should be plenty of books and resource materials at all levels of readability that address them (see Chapter 10).

◆ Select books from across all the genres.

AT THE TEACHER'S DESK

LITERATURE, CONTROVERSIAL ISSUES, AND CENSORSHIP

When we emphasize *literature* strongly in teaching and learning in the language arts, we are directly addressing and encouraging critical thinking. Authentic literature is going to encourage thinking and questioning by children in all grades. As the writers, publishers, and educators who support the annual Banned Book Week (a week during which the perils of censorship are underscored) have stated, "We believe . . . that what people read is deeply important, that ideas can be dangerous, but that the suppression of ideas is fatal to a democratic society. Freedom is a dangerous way of life, but it is ours."

Anything that adult literature deals with is now reflected in children's literature as well. As Cullinan (1981) sagely observed, it may perhaps be better for children to experience occasionally the "unpleasantries" of reality once removed—through literature—than to experience them directly. I would add that for those children who tragically may experience severe and distressing situations, dealing with them in part through literature—or escaping them from time to time through literature—is far better than feeling powerless and confused in the face of such situations.

We can never know for certain when or why objections might be raised about books we are using with our students. At the start of the school year or well before beginning a thematic unit which will use potentially controversial books, it's a good idea to send a letter home listing the books. If parents do object to a particular text, then their children will not read it but will, of course, have access to many other books.

The issues of controversial topics, of censorship, and of the accuracy of information provided in books students read will always be a part of education. Objections to the books children encounter come not only from "radical" or "reactionary" fringes but also from within our midst. Sebesta (1989) cites the example of the art teacher who objected to the way great artists were portrayed through cartoons in *Rembrandt Takes a Walk* (Strand, 1987).

Sebesta suggests we adopt the following policy statement. It can reflect our own beliefs as well as, we would hope, those of our school and our school district:

Trade books for this class are selected for quality, many of them for pertinence to the curriculum. They do not ignore controversy but attempt, instead, to handle controversy with fairness and accuracy. We discuss books openly, and we attempt to evaluate them with students. We teach an open, inquiring attitude, and we do not teach that authors' messages are irrefutable. Authors are fallible, like the rest of us, but we attempt to select those who are thoughtful and knowledgeable. (Sebesta, 1989, p. 120)

◆ Choose books that reflect many different cultures and cultural perspectives.

◆ As we come to know our students better and learn about their interests, we should include books that address these interests.

◆ Children's magazines should also be available (Stoll, 1994).

The Transitional and Proficient Literacy Phases

Much of our next discussion pertains to the beginning literacy phase as well as to the transitional and proficient phases. Its main focus, however, is on students who have moved beyond the beginning phase.

In Chapter 5 we referred to *context* as the "what, where, and why" of reading. In the following sections we will examine different reading strategies students can use, depending on the context—which includes the text they are going to read and their purposes for reading it. However, the major reason students should apply different strategies depends on the type of text to be read—*narrative* or *expository*.

Constructing Meaning in Narrative Texts

Literature Discussion Groups in the Integrated Classroom

In recent years educators have emphasized the importance and value of bringing students together in small groups where they talk about the book they are all reading. Realizing that *adults* enjoy talking informally about the books they read, educators have pointed out that, if allowed to do the same, *children* really aren't any different in this regard. There are many different labels for this type of informal, enjoyable engagement with books—such as literature circles, literature discussion groups, grand conversations, and student book clubs (Eeds & Wells, 1989; Roser & Martinez, 1995). These groups can function independently with the teacher as a participant or as a guide. They are not usually based on *ability*; rather, students of varying reading levels may be in the same group. Here are some advantages of these groupings:

◆ "High quality literature" is explored, usually in the form of trade books.

◆ All students have opportunities to participate, including those whose reading abilities may not be as developed as those of other students.

◆ "Personal" responses are accepted and valued.

◆ Conversations and the selection of discussion topics are more "naturally" determined. (Raphael et al., 1992)

This "free response/talk time" is termed "meaning space" (Corcoran, 1987); "it is a time for free expression of thoughts and ideas" (McGee, 1995, p. 108). This talk creates an interpretive community (Fish, 1980)—readers who share their own interpretations as well as construct a *group* interpretation of the selection.

When we function as "guides," we often pose questions that will help students explore particular issues. At times our questions can focus on particular issues or elements of narratives; at other times we can pose questions in response to the direction the students' discussion is taking.

If it's necessary to work as a guide with a group, this procedure is suggested (Templeton, 1995):

◆ Read a story or chapter in the book.

◆ Determine how much of the book students will read at a time. In the beginning, this will usually be a single chapter.

◆ In each chapter write down three or four key events you can refer to later to assess the whole group's understanding.

◆ Prepare questions that you believe will facilitate productive discussion.

◆ Have the students read the material.

◆ When they'll be comfortable doing so, have the students write in their response journals before gathering to discuss the reading with the group.

◆ Engage the students in discussing the reading and allow a range of individual responses.

◆ Create other opportunities for responding to the reading in many different ways.

◆ Teach the following *process* of engaging in these discussions (Sloan, 1992):

  • Encourage participation. ("Has everyone given an opinion so far?")

  • Encourage qualification. ("Your idea was interesting. What was your reason for thinking that?")

  • Probe the thinking behind comments. (Ask "why?")

  • Be tactful yet firm when dealing with those who have a tendency to monopolize discussions. ("Wait a minute, Aaron. Sarah isn't finished yet.")

  • The group leader and/or participants can summarize ideas.

As students become used to participating in literature circles, we often find that sticking to one chapter at a time may be too limiting. Many students may want to keep going. Our questions can then be based more broadly on the book as a whole, and the groups will really not need to meet on a daily basis.

Questions to Guide Critical Thinking and Reflection

When students are comfortable reading narratives—first stories and later "chapter" books—they can focus on particular elements in order to explore and understand how writers develop characters, plot, resolution, and so forth (see Chapter 10)—components that encourage students' critical thinking and reflection. Many of the following questions guide students towards this focus (Sloan, 1992; Templeton, 1995). As we'll see in Chapter 7, students will be applying their understanding of these elements in their own *writing* of narratives.

Setting and Plot

How do you know where and when the story takes place?

If the story had taken place in a different setting, how would that change affect the plot?

What incident, problem, or situation gets the story started?

How does the author make us want to keep reading?

What is the problem [character name] faces?

What kinds of people and events were working against the main character?

Trace the main events/episodes in the story. Could we change their order or leave any of them out? Why or why not?

Characterization

Did you feel you were really "right inside" the main character—feeling, thinking, and seeing as he or she did?

Do any characters change during the story? How are they different in the end?

Do you recognize any character types from other stories you've read? Why?

Theme

What is the moral of this story? What do you think it's *really* about?

Why did the author write this story? What is he or she trying to tell us?

What does the title tell you about the story? Does it tell the truth?

Style

Does the style fit the subject?

Is the language comfortable and understandable?

How did you feel? Happy? Sad? (Did the author make you laugh or cry?)

(Continued)

Point of View
Why did the author have [_____] tell the story?
Did the point of view switch back and forth? Why?

Guided Reading-Thinking Activity: Narratives

In contrast to the more informal literature discussions in which we will engage our students, the **Guided Reading-Thinking Activity (GRTA) for narratives** is a teacher-facilitated process where we play a more direct role by organizing and guiding students' narrative reading. In the GRTA students consciously combine their prior knowledge with information in the text to predict, confirm, or revise their expectations. It allows us and our students the focused opportunity to think about and apply a number of strategies and skills we have been developing.

Originally devised by Russell Stauffer (1969, 1975) and termed a *Directed* Reading-Thinking Activity, the GRTA is a teacher-facilitated process in which students combine their prior knowledge with information in the text to predict, confirm, or revise predictions. As Haggard (1988) noted, this activity "is frequently identified as an exemplary instructional activity for developing comprehension and critical thinking" (p. 527). From the beginning of reading instruction, the GRTA reinforces the *active*, as opposed to passive, role that readers must play.

The following are guidelines for conducting a Guided Reading-Thinking Activity with narratives:

◆ *Students establish purposes for reading a story.*
   After students read the title of a book and look at any accompanying pictures, we should ask, "What do you think this story might be about?" To encourage responses, we might tell them, "Just as detectives use clues to figure out how to solve a crime, when we read, we also use clues to help us figure out what might happen in the story. If we can guess what might occur in a story before we read, we will enjoy it more and be better able to notice the clues. In other words, we can be 'reading detectives.'"

   Write the students' predictions on the chalkboard or on chart paper. Take down several ideas; a half dozen are good for starters. In guiding children to anticipate what will happen in a story, notice that we focus the children's attention on the story *in relation to* their prior knowledge ("What do you think a story titled *Willie Mae and the Day the Martians Landed* might be about?") rather than *on* their prior knowledge ("Have any of you ever seen a movie version of a martian?"). This is a subtle but important difference between GRTAs and the way stories are often introduced. Unless we focus on the story, we are likely to get a lot of stories about Martians (often with one child trying to outdo another) and wind up with the whole class thinking about their own experiences rather than about the story.

◆ *Tell the children to read to a predetermined stopping place.*
At first this place should probably be at the end of the first paragraph or the first page. When students reach this stopping point, they should mark their place in the reading with a thumb or forefinger and close the book. This action prevents reading ahead.

It's helpful to say, "If you come to a word that you don't know, try to figure it out as best you can. If you cannot, just read ahead and we'll figure it out later." After the students have read the story, we can turn their attention to unknown words.

Stopping early in the reading provides quick feedback for the children, and they can revise or maintain their predictions as necessary. We can ask, "*Now* what do you think?" and "Why do you think so?" We then cross out rejected predictions and place a question mark by those we cannot yet verify or reject. The students then read to the next predetermined stopping place. We tell them where it is or write it on the board—and remind them to close their books when they reach it.

◆ *Subsequent stopping places should occur at points in the story where the plot and/or action has been raised to a high level of suspense and excitement.*
At each point we should ask, "*Now* what do you think is going to happen?" and "Why?"

◆ *After the reading ask a few questions that will help refine the students' reading and thinking.*
Questions that elicit a "deeper" response should usually come *after* the story or chapter has been read rather than interrupt the reading. For example, you could ask, "How did you know that Timothy would probably tell his brother about the plan?" Such questions require students to recall, integrate, and apply information from the story and from their own backgrounds. We have the opportunity to reinforce students' application of reading skills by asking them to "find the place in the story where it says Teresa wasn't afraid, and read that for us." We remind the students that—just like the detective—they were using clues from their reading to stick to, change, or discard their predictions.

◆ *Discuss unknown words.*
Finally, after dealing with questions and students' reactions to the reading, we should ask: "Were there any words in the story you didn't know?

Students read at different rates or speeds. What about those who reach a stopping point before others?

Usually several seconds will separate the students' finishing times. You can take advantage of this time by leaning over and, in a whisper, asking a student who has finished for a prediction. Ask if there were any words the student did not know and whether or how he or she figured them out. Just a few seconds spent with a student this way will accomplish much. In addition, you may hand out a card to each student as he or she finishes. Each card can have a different discussion question written on it so that students can then use their ideas productively by thinking of responses.

Students who are placed appropriately but still read more slowly than necessary (and whose finishing times may be quite a bit behind those of others) have probably just fallen into a "habit" of slow reading.

Why aren't new words taught before the students read a story?

Once children have learned a few word analysis skills, they should have the opportunity to *apply* these skills in actual reading. When we preteach words, we deny them that opportunity. Occasionally there *is* a word that must be pretaught. For example, explain a word crucial to understanding the story if you believe the students do not know enough about words and how to use contextual clues to figure it out on their own.

Don't the students "peek" ahead to see what's going to happen so their predictions will be "right"?

This peeking is a possibility. We can best prevent it by setting a tone that stresses *our* purpose is not always to be right but to think divergently and creatively about possibilities.

How did you try to figure them out?" By getting students to talk through their strategies, we are reinforcing what we have been teaching about analyzing unknown words—letter/sound knowledge and/or structural knowledge and how to use contextual clues. The discussion may also give us the opportunity to model the application of word knowledge in context.

Story Maps

A number of researchers (Beck, 1984) have noted the usefulness of **story maps** for both teacher and students. These graphic aids serve two purposes:

◆ For the *teacher*, constructing the story map helps identify the important elements in a story that the children will be reading, thereby delineating aspects on which he or she can focus questions.

◆ For the *students*, viewing the story map helps them focus on the significant elements of narratives—setting, characterization, plot, problem and resolution—and on the relationships among these elements.

As with any visual or graphic aid, story maps should not become ends in themselves; students should not spend a lot of time constructing them and then be graded on them. Rather, the story maps should be a means to an end. You should introduce them after students have been reading and enjoying stories for some time and are ready to deal with them analytically.

In their simplest form story maps include only the essential information in a story. As such, they help students distinguish the most important information and elements from other information. This "other" information is still relevant insofar as it affects the reader, but story maps will help identify the "skeleton" of the story.

Once students understand the concept of a story map, they can construct their own versions. For example, this could be one story response option. Importantly, you would have them do this if they are puzzled about the sequence of events in a story or seem to be having difficulty with longer stories.

Constructing Meaning in Expository Texts

The beginning of strategic reading is realizing that expository texts differ from narrative texts. Therefore, each text—the narrative and the textbook—should be read differently and for different purposes. Moreover, students should start learning about these differences in the ele-

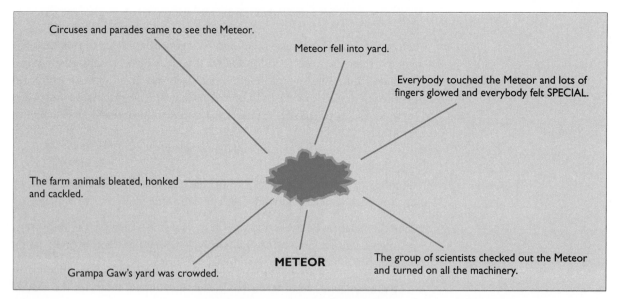

Figure 6.4   Student-Generated Story Map Based on *Meteor* by Patricia Polacco

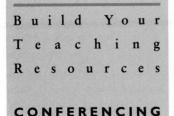

Build Your
Teaching
Resources

CONFERENCING

It's important to have one-to-one conferences with our students from time to time. We can get a sense of where students are in their reading of a particular text, what they think about it, and what help they may need. The conference is also an opportunity to conduct a "minilesson" with a student. There are several ways of conducting teacher/student reading conferences. The following steps are common to all variations (see, for example, Hancock & Hill, 1987; Hornsby, Sukarna, & Parry, 1986; Routman, 1991):

- **Sharing** Each student knows ahead of time that he or she is to share a response or reaction to a particular element of the book. We may request focusing on a particular element or leave the choice up to the student. When we meet with the student, this response is what he or she will share with us first.

- **Questioning** Ask a question or two about the book—for example its theme, what the characters are like, from whose point of view the story is being told.

- **Oral Reading** The student reads aloud a passage from the book that he or she would enjoy sharing with you. The passage should be longer than those children read in groups to answer questions and support ideas.

- **Discuss** Where will the student go from here with the reading? If the student will continue to read the same book for a while, what will be his or her primary interests and why? If the student has finished the book, what is he or she planning to read next? If the student is going to base some extension activity or project on the book, discuss what this plan will entail. We can demonstrate that we are genuinely interested in the student's project and will be available to respond and offer support.

- **Records** Immediately after meeting with the student or not long afterwards, we should jot down relevant information. What book is the child reading? What does the student need help with? (We'll talk about other observations and record-keeping in Chapter 11.)

mentary grades. They can then learn how to use various strategies in their reading.

The Guided Reading-Thinking Activity with Informational Texts
In the past we too often assumed that simply because upper elementary students could read narratives, for example, and identify words, they could make the transition to reading expository texts. This progression is not necessarily so. Most students need to be taught *how* to read expository texts, and this teaching should continue until they almost automatically apply an effective strategy to such texts. Using the informational GRTA is a critical step in this process.

Together with providing instruction about the *structure* of informational texts, we should help students learn an overall *strategy* for approaching this type of reading. The **Guided Reading-Thinking Activity for expository texts** is such a strategy. Initially, we focus on the *process*, so it is important that the selections we use are well organized and logically constructed. Later, we can help students deal with selections that are less well constructed. Follow these steps:

1. Read through a chapter or part of a chapter in a content-area textbook or an informational trade book. Next, determine the major concepts. If these concepts are presented in terms that will be unfamiliar to students, and if the context does not offer sufficient support for determining the meanings of these terms, we should introduce these terms in advance (see Chapter 8).

2. When conducting an informational GRTA for the first time, we should tell the students *why* we're doing this. Just as with a reading story, they will be making predictions about the information they are likely to encounter in the reading. Making such predictions and thinking about what they *do* know about the topic will help them read and retain new information much better than if they simply read through the book from the first to the last page.

3. *Preview* the selection. After reading the title, go through the selection, reading each heading as well as the captions for any pictures or diagrams.

4. After the preview, use the chapter title, headings, and subheadings to make *predictions* about the content of each section. This is the "purpose setting" phase. For example, we could ask students, "What information do you think we'll find in a section with the heading 'The Great Basin'?" As with the narrative GRTA, we will write the predictions down so that students can see *and* refer back to them. (For some students you may need to be even more concrete. This strategy works particularly well with an informational trade book: Draw a box each for the categories "who, what, when, and where" and then get students to predict elements for each category.)

5. Go back and *read* the first section under the first heading. Then stop and review the predictions, confirming or rejecting any. At this point ask the students if there is any important new information they could add to their predictions.

6. Continue in this format: read each heading, make predictions, read the section, check the predictions, and add new information.

7. When you have finished reading the selection or an appropriate part, review the major points that were covered.

Most textbooks usually include a list of objectives and/or prereading questions that may help students focus on important concepts. These lists can supplement and even provide a foundation for the predictions that students will make — and we need to point this out to them — but always allow for students' own questions and predictions along with the text's.

Students who are introduced to the informational GRTA after they have been reading informational texts for a while may complain that it takes much longer to read a *textbook* this new way. Initially, it *does*. Eventually, though, they will find they actually *save* time by reading this way; for the same amount of time or less, they will understand more and remember information longer.

As Pearson and Johnson (1978) so aptly expressed it several years ago, comprehension in reading is a process of building bridges between the "new" and the "known." While students are engaged in learning activities in different areas of the curriculum, there are ways that we can facilitate and help them become *aware* of their learning — by acquiring and applying strategies before, during, and after their reading.

The Prereading Plan (PReP)

When we undertake more extensive study of a new topic with our students, we want to help them make connections between the new topic and what they already know. We also need to find out *how much* they know about the topic. Also, we need to activate students' prior knowledge and draw them in. For this process we'll need to determine the degree to which the instructional materials we are organizing for a study unit are appropriate and how we may need to adapt or adjust them for particular students. With all of these concerns in mind, Judith Langer (1981) developed the **prereading plan (PReP)**, a "common sense" approach to these objectives. The plan is actually an umbrella for many types of prereading activities. Here's how it works, using the topic of the solar system in a fifth-grade classroom:

1. We begin by asking the students, "Tell me whatever comes into your mind when you think of Earth and the other planets." This is a *free association* time, so we take down the students' suggestions in either a list format or a cluster. During these initial associations, we ask other questions to keep the information coming — for example, "Why do you suppose most of the outer planets are made of gas?" and "Why are the inner planets so small?"

2. Ask students *why* they thought of the things they did. This question allows students to examine *what* they thought as well as to hear what other students have to offer.

3. *Categorize* the responses. This activity will help students organize all the information that has been contributed. Initially, we may have to suggest some categories, such as "smaller planets," "larger planets," "moons," "asteroids," and "sun."

4. Beginning with the first category, ask if there is anything else that the students can add to each category. Because this exercise is "evolutionary" in the sense that new ideas are being built upon one another, by this step we usually find that several of the students' responses are more sophisticated than they first were.

The K-W-L Procedure: What Do I *Know?* What Do I *Want* to Know? What Have I *Learned?*

The **"K-W-L" procedure** (Ogle, 1986) is very effective when used as part of reading an informational selection as well as for accompanying a unit of study. Begin by brainstorming what students know about the topic. Next, students generate *purposes* for reading by listing what they want to find out about the topic. After the reading, discuss and/or write down what new information and ideas students have learned. At this point students may also list what they *still* want to find out; the selection may not have addressed all of their "want to know" questions. This is a good place to discuss other possible sources of information.

Figure 6.5 shows a K-W-L generated by a group of sixth-grade students before and after reading Russell Freedman's *Eleanor Roosevelt: A Life of Discovery* (1995). The book was an "extended" text for a two-month the-

What Do We **K**now?	What Do We **W**ant to Know?	What Have We **L**earned?
Wife of President Roosevelt (FDR)	Was she important for women's rights?	She was very important for African Americans and for the United Nations.
Depression	Was she like Hillary Clinton?	Her childhood wasn't that happy.
She was famous.	Why is she famous?	Women couldn't vote until 1920.
		A lot of people didn't like ER.
		There have always been people who have opposed immigration.
		FDR had polio and was paralyzed.

Figure 6.5   **Using the K-W-L Procedure to Learn about Eleanor Roosevelt**

matic unit on "The United States in the Twentieth Century." This particular student group was investigating the period between the end of World War I and the end of World War II.

Question-Answer Relationships (QARs)

A procedure developed by Raphael (1986) is extremely effective for teaching about questioning and also helps students understand the differences among the three major categories of comprehension: literal, inferential, and critical (see p. 154). The effectiveness of the procedure, termed "**Question/Answer Relationships**" (**QARs**), "lies in the way it clarifies how students can approach the task of reading texts and answering questions" (Raphael, 1986, p. 517). There is a distinction between "In the Book" and "In My Head" sources of information for answering questions. "In the Book" information comes primarily from the text itself; "In My Head" information comes from students' own prior knowledge. If students understand this distinction, they are on their way to becoming efficient strategic readers.

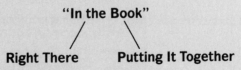

CLASSROOM EXAMPLE

Minilesson for the QAR Strategy

The following script illustrates how a fourth-grade teacher presents and teaches the "QAR" strategy:

TEACHER: "It's important to know *how* and *where* to look for the answers to questions. The key is to think about the wording of the question itself because *this* is what will determine how and where you will look for the answer.

"Sometimes the answer to a question may be right there in your reading; other times you may have to come up with it by putting other information together. At still other times, the answer really isn't in your reading at all, and you have to rely on information in your own head to come up with the answer. We're going to use the labels you see here to talk about answers we can get in the book." [Displays the following diagram:]

"In the Book"

Right There   **Putting It Together**

TEACHER: "Answers that are 'In the Book' are of two types—they are either right there, where you can see them easily, or you may have to combine the 'Right There' information to get the answer.

"Now let's look at the labels we will use to talk about answers we *can't* get in the book." [Displays the following diagram:]

"In My Head"

Author and Me   **On My Own**

TEACHER: "Answers that are not in the book but come from your head are of two types. In the 'Author and Me' type, you need to think about what you already know and what the author tells you in order to come up with the answer. 'On My Own' answers, the second kind, come entirely from what you know or need to find somewhere else; you can often answer this type of question without even reading the text."

Modeling

TEACHER: "Let's read this paragraph [Displays it on a transparency] and then consider the questions that follow."

Voyager II, which was launched in 1977, flew by Neptune in 1989. Scientists estimated that it should be able to continue to send messages back to Earth for another twenty-five years. Built to last for just five years, Voyager II was intended to send back information about only two planets. It lasted for twelve years and sent back information on four planets. The computer on board Voyager II is its only means of communication with Earth and is *far* less powerful than the simplest microcomputer we use today!

Then below this passage the teacher places a transparency with the following questions written on it:

TEACHER: "Okay, here's our first question based on this passage. [Displays "When did Voyager II fly by Neptune?"] Okay, what's the answer to this one? Dianne?"

DIANNE: "1989."

TEACHER: "How do you know?"

DIANNE: "It says so right there!"

TEACHER: "Right you are! So we would say that the answer to this first question is 'In the Book'—in this case, on this page—and is 'Right There.' You can tell because the wording of the question and the wording of the information in the book are the same.

"How about this question? [Displays "Has Voyager II lasted longer than scientists expected?"] Dreanne?"

(Continued)

DREANNE: "Yes!"

TEACHER: "Okay—how do you know?"

DREANNE: " 'Cause it says it was 'built to last for just five years' and that it lasted for twelve years instead."

TEACHER: "Good! Dreanne, although the answer was 'In the Book,' in order to answer it, you had to *put together* those two pieces of information. When we look at the passage, *nowhere* do we find where it says 'Voyager II has lasted longer than scientists expected.' So we have to *put together* information that is supplied for us to answer the question.

"Here's another one. [Displays "Did Voyager II visit all the planets in our solar system?"] Okay, Lisa?"

LISA: "No, it didn't."

TEACHER: "Okay! But how do you *know* that it didn't?"

LISA: " 'Cause there are nine planets in the solar system, and it says Voyager II only visited four."

TEACHER: "Did it say there are nine planets in our solar system?"

LISA: "No . . ."

TEACHER: "Then how'd you know that?"

LISA: "I just *knew* it already!"

TEACHER: "Good for you! In order to answer this question, you needed to combine the information in your own head—there are nine planets—with the information that the author gave you about Voyager II visiting four planets.

"Lisa's answer is what we call an 'Author and Me' answer because there is no way she could have come up with it unless she called on information she already has in her head and related it to the information in the reading.

"Let's do one last question, just for fun." [Displays "If it were possible, would you like to be a traveler on Voyager II?"]

[At this point, several voices are heard at once, some saying "Yeah!" and others "No way!"]

TEACHER: "Okay, okay! We obviously have a difference of opinion on this one! But let's think for a moment about where our answers come from. Did you need any help from the author of this passage to answer the question or were you 'on your own'?" [Several students say "On our own."] "Right! You were on your own because you could answer such a question without really even reading the passage. Either you would enjoy long space flights or you wouldn't!"

Reciprocal Teaching

Reciprocal teaching is a strategy for assisting students who are uncertain about or don't know how to use the "blueprint" for meaning construction offered by a particular text (Palincsar & Brown, 1989). **Reciprocal teaching** involves the modeling of *questioning*, *summarizing*, *clarifying*, and *predicting*. These are the steps:

◆ Work with a small group. Students read a portion of a chapter silently. Afterward, we ask two or three *questions* based on this passage. If necessary, we *model* how to determine the answer.

◆ We next "think aloud" as we provide a brief oral *summary*.

◆ We then check our progress thus far. Does something need to be made *clearer*? Is there anything the students are uncertain of or do not understand about this passage?

◆ Once this passage is comprehended, students can make *predictions* about information and ideas that they may encounter in the next reading section.

Accommodating Less-Able Readers in the Integrated Language Arts Classroom

We have already seen that students who are not as advanced in literacy development as their peers need to meet with us for guided instruction. *However*, they also need to meet with other students at other times for literacy experiences. For example, they can be involved in literature discussion groups about books that they may not be able to read on their own. They can, however, still experience them via partner or "buddy" reading or when parents or siblings read the books to them at home. Here are guidelines for accommodating these students in the intermediate grades:

◆ Balance *homogeneous* literature-discussion sessions and Guided Reading-Thinking Activities with *heterogeneous* discussion groups.

◆ Perform word-study activities based on the less-developed readers' level of word knowledge.

◆ Provide successful opportunities for reading grade-level material:

• Listen to a content selection (for example, from a textbook).

- Retell what was recalled. (This "retelling" should be written down like an LEA dictation and will become the student's own "text" for the content material.)

◆ Combine dictations and writing activities; alternate between the student's dictating a sentence and his or her writing a sentence.

◆ The student can dictate a "book" about a topic; a sentence or two can be on each page.

- The student then can illustrate each page.

- This book can be reread many times; sight words can be harvested from it.

- The book also can be "published" and shared with younger students in the school.

◆ Take smaller steps!

Using Technology in the Diverse Classroom

We know that students need to learn how informational books are structured and how that structure provides clues for locating information. The same holds true for computers. CD-ROMs, laser disks, and the Internet provide information, but students need to learn something about their organization and how to navigate them in order to access the information they need.

For example, an intermediate class is exploring "immigration." Two students are investigating the topic in a CD-ROM encyclopedia. While there is much text information in the article on "immigration," there is also an engaging visual display and part of a recorded interview with Helen Rosenthal, an immigrant who came through Ellis Island and who—in her own words that are displayed on the screen and played through the speakers—describes her initial experience in and feelings about America (see Figure 6.6). One student tells the other how the different screen icons work. Almost every one is a pull-down menu of options for different features on the screen—different places students can go to get further information and/or to mark and print aspects of the display. The less-experienced student quickly learns how to print some of the main entry as well as parts of the media display.

There are hundreds of programs now available on floppy discs, CD-ROM, and the Internet that involve students in engaging ways with subject matter. For example, students can listen to some of Mozart's music as the screen displays information about the composer. A native speaker can work

Interviewer: So can you remember, first of all, coming into the New York Harbor?

Rosenthal: Yes, I remember.

Interviewer: What was that like?

Rosenthal: It was beautiful. We were so elated. We were so happy. We stood all by the rail, and we were blessing America that we could get there. It wasn't an easy trip, and it wasn't a light trip, but we got here. And the first, when they landed, they said, "What do you want? You want something to eat?" I said, "I want a good glass of milk." That's all I wanted. And the milk tasted like cream. It was delicious.

Excerpted from an oral history provided by the Ellis Island Immigration Museum.
Immigrant: Helen Rosenthal.

Ellis Island InterActivity

First Sight of America

Most immigrants were exhausted by the end of their journey. But when word spread that land was in sight, passengers rushed to the ship's deck to catch their first glimpse of America—the New York Harbor skyline and then the Statue of Liberty.

Figure 6.6   **Computer Literacy Allows Many Students to Learn from Multimedia Presentations**

SOURCE: "First Sight of America," Microsoft® Encarta® 96 Encyclopedia. © 1993–1995 Microsoft Corporation. All rights reserved.

with a student who is learning English as a second language to load a pro-gram for English vocabulary and syntax in which pictures are paired with their spoken and/or written counterparts and used in short conversations by animated characters. In the process the native speaker is learning the corre-sponding words in the other student's language.

◆ ◆ ◆ CONCLUDING PERSPECTIVE AND SUMMARY

Chapter 6 has covered a broad terrain: the nature of meaning construction, word knowledge as it is applied in reading, and the role of the reader. We have addressed the learning progression from beginning conventional read-ing to experiencing different kinds of texts to analyzing those texts both to understand them better and to think more critically about their content and its relation to readers' lives. In keeping with our integrated approach for teaching the language arts, we have examined various methods for students to improve their reading comprehension through writing exercises, compar-ing reading matter and visuals, and participating in different types of group discussions. We have also considered the importance of oral, silent, and in-teractive group reading for different levels of readers.

Many people attribute a monumental change in their lives — in their out-look or beliefs — to reading a particular book. In an age where so much im-mediate stimulation competes with the extended, though often more com-pelling, world within a book, it would be wonderful if we could facilitate similar significant reading experiences for our students. In this chapter we have built a foundation for such experiences.

In this chapter we've addressed the following main points:

◆ Students become better readers by reading, by being read to, and by be-ing encouraged to read as much and as often as possible. Literature-based reading programs taught by supportive instructors can improve students' language use and reasoning abilities and promote their enjoy-ment of reading.

◆ Although beginning readers should encounter a variety of texts as often as possible, their skills are best honed by reading favorite "predictable" books. Repetitive reading of such books reinforces children's memory of the texts, fostering their understanding of logical sequences, traditional story structures, and the conventions of books. Such repeated reading also increases students' sensitivity to language, particularly since their familiarity with the word patterns and rhymes can serve as a base for learning vocabulary-building strategies.

◆ The role of word knowledge is crucial to reading instruction. Repeated reading enables children to recognize word patterns and to develop sight vocabularies—words that they encounter frequently in texts and immediately recognize. Their knowledge of sight words is the foundation we use for teaching word sounds, structure, and meaning and for modeling strategies to decipher new words and build vocabulary.

◆ The classroom library should contain a wide range of good quality trade books from all genres and for all reading levels that reflect many cultures and cultural perspectives. These books and children's magazines should address topics that interest the students and can be utilized for class projects.

◆ We should teach students strategies for reading narrative and expository texts, and use different discussion group and writing strategies to help them analyze and learn from their reading.

◆ We can facilitate students' reading comprehension, reflection, and critical thinking by asking pertinent, broad-based questions that draw on both prior knowledge and the text at hand after they have completed an assigned reading.

◆ One-on-one teacher-student conferences play a critical role in helping teachers develop, direct, and evaluate students' reading. They enable the teacher to assess an individual student's progress and determine what strategies or kinds of activities will best develop his or her reading ability.

Key Terms

authentic literacy contexts (p. 184)

basal reading programs (p. 186)

Big Books (p. 190)

conferencing (p. 187)

Guided Reading-Thinking Activity (GRTA) for narratives (p. 211)

Guided Reading-Thinking Activity for expository texts (p. 216)

K-W-L Procedure (p. 218)

Language Experience Approach (p. 189)

literature discussion groups (p. 187)

phonemic awareness (p. 199)

phonics instruction (p. 198)

predictable books (p. 189)

Prereading Plan (PReP) (p. 217)

Question-Answer Relationships (QARs) (p. 219)

CHAPTER 7

Constructing Meaning Through Writing

◆ What are the best environments in which students can learn to write?

◆ How can we use Writing Workshop and minilessons to teach strategies and skills?

◆ What are the components of the writing process? How can we develop students' understanding of each in narrative writing? in expository writing? How does a teacher's modeling of the writing process help students learn to write?

◆ Why is peer feedback important?

◆ What is unique about poetry? Why do we teach students to write poetry?

◆◆◆ ## INTRODUCTION

Through writing we can become aware of what we believe, why we believe as we do, and the degree to which we can soundly justify our views. For most students many of the ideas that nurture creativity and beliefs come not only from their own life experiences but from their reading and discussions based on reading. In their classic book on the teaching of writing *They All Want to Write* (1939/1952), Alvina Truet Burrows and her colleagues describe the role of written composition:

> We believe that writing can play a significant part in a child's development. For that reason we have sought a way to release freer, more genuine self-expression and at the same time to cultivate the skill necessary for writing with correctness and ease. . . . We have become clearly certain that this concept of writing brings children deep personal satisfaction as well as effective control of its essential mechanics . . . (p. 1)

This affirmation of the *value* of writing is real. Beginning in the mid-1930s, Burrows and her colleagues' classroom studies—and the many investigations since that time—have demonstrated that it is indeed possible to have the best of both writing worlds: a richness and fluency of creativity and expression *as well as* a command of correctness or *conventions*—spelling, punctuation, and grammar or "usage" (Graves, 1983; Calkins, 1995; Dyson, 1991). Not until recently, however, has consistent documentation surveying a wide range of children demonstrated the potential for writing both to address deep personal needs and to meet standards of correct usage. Most of the significant research on writing has been conducted within the past two decades, but as the previous excerpt shows, significant insights into the teaching of writing have existed for years.

In this chapter, we will be exploring **the writing process** and the many ways we will be able to facilitate students' learning this process as well as other aspects of writing.

Contexts for Constructing Meaning Through Writing

The research on writing instruction is clear on one important point: children do not learn to write by working exclusively on exercises in grammar texts; they primarily learn to write by writing. When children write, we then have the contexts for facilitating their writing and thinking. These contexts include (1) *opportunities for students* to write about what most interests and concerns them, to get feedback from their peers, and to revise their writing after peer interaction; and (2) *opportunities for teachers* to present and model aspects of writing.

These contexts are part of an environment where effective writing instruction can occur; "it is our job as teachers of writing to create a context that is as appropriate for writing as the gym is for basketball" (Murray, in Atwell, 1987, p. 54). Students will be able to write frequently and for different purposes, and we will be able to present and model each of the steps of the writing process: **prewriting**, **drafting**, **revising**, **editing**, and **sharing** or **publishing**. Here's a good rule of thumb: "[t]he child's purposes come first, but the teacher deliberately creates a setting in which writing in different forms can be perceived as useful" (Nathan et al., 1989, p. 93).

The Writing Workshop in the Integrated Language Arts Classroom

Designated writing periods or **Writing Workshop** time may be combined with reading instruction, alternated with it, or held just before or just after reading time (see Chapter 3). A common framework for Writing Workshop is (1) "minilesson"; (2) sustained writing; (3) **conferences**, both formal and informal; and (4) sharing of writing.

The time allotted for each activity will vary. Our organizational plan should be clear to students so that they understand our expectations and their own responsibilities. Students should also know that they may work on a writing project at other times of the day, during free time, or when other work has been completed.

Many specific strategies and skills are addressed in the minilesson phase of Writing Workshop:

◆ Writing Workshop *procedures*

◆ steps in the writing process

◆ exploring how to develop elements of stories such as plot, characterization, and setting

◆ features of expository compositions

◆ word choice, grammar, punctuation, format, and spelling.

Minilessons can be taught as the need for them arises as well as when we intentionally schedule them because we anticipate the students' need to learn a particular strategy or skill. In minilessons we provide the knowledge of a specific strategy or skill and the vocabulary for discussing that skill.

Children's purposes come first in writing — but we also create environments where children will want to explore different forms.

(For example, we can explain, "When we want to show when somebody is talking in our stories, we put these marks called *quotation marks* at the beginning and the end of the person's words.") How detailed each minilesson is depends on our purpose and our students' needs. In the Classroom Example minilesson on p. 233, the teacher models the procedure for writing conferences.

Modeling

We must write *ourselves*. **Modeling** the writing process simply means that we show the students how writing is performed. As we walk through the process for them, we "think aloud" and describe each step.

It's important that we try not to allow our own misgivings about writing — if we have them — to become an obstacle. By learning, applying, and then modeling, teaching, and facilitating the writing process, we usually

The setting is a third-grade classroom. The teacher, Stacey Drum, has already asked one pupil, Mike, if he would share his story with the class. The teacher asks the students to come up and sit in a semicircle around the Author's Chair. Seated beside the chair, the teacher begins:

MS. DRUM: "Boys and girls, we will be sharing a lot of the writing we will be doing this year—my writing as well as yours. Whether we share in a group or with a partner, we will usually respond to one another's writing in a similar way. Mike is going to share his story with us, and together we're going to learn how we will be responding to each others' writing. Okay, Mike, as an author you are going to sit in the Author's Chair." [Mike then reads his composition to the group; it's about a snake that turned up in his yard and how he and his dad captured it and took it to a safer location.]

MS. DRUM: "Thank you, Mike! Kids, who listened really well and can tell Mike what you heard in his story? Mike, you may call on whomever you want."

MIKE: "Okay. Dreanne?"

DREANNE: "I heard that you and your brother were shooting baskets, and then your brother saw the snake behind the ball bucket. You called your dad, and he came with a bucket and asked you to hold the bucket while he tried to catch the snake to put it into the bucket. I liked that part—where your dad was chasing the snake!"

MS. DRUM: "Okay! Let's tell Mike what else we liked about his story . . . [The teacher waits several seconds. It may take a little while this first time around, but eventually students will respond. After a few students answer, the teacher continues.]

MS. DRUM: "Is there anything you'd like to *ask* Mike about his story?"

YOLANDA: "Weren't you scared when your dad told you to hold the bucket down on the ground?"

MIKE: "Kind of, but I wanted to show my dad how brave I was!"

LEWIS: "I got kind of confused at the end when you said you put the snake in the trunk of the car while you went looking for a place to dump him. You mean you let him loose in the trunk or was he in something?"

MIKE: "No, no, we put him in a *box* before we put him in the trunk."

LEWIS: "Oh, *that* makes sense!"

MS. DRUM: "Mike, if you were to change your story, can you think of a way that would make that last part clearer?"

The teacher wraps up the session by pointing out, "Kids, when we share our writing with each other, we'll usually do it just like Mike did. Someone will read his or her piece to us, we'll listen, and then we'll tell the person what we heard him or her say. Next, we'll tell what we liked, and then we'll ask questions about any more information we might need. That will help all of us with our writing."

That's it for the first time around. Like Stacey, we should keep it simple—letting the "author" call on and interact with the other students as we gently guide the process. We can close out the sharing by reiterating what the group just did and why.

find that we can overcome our own doubts, particularly as we see the process transforming the way our students think and respond. Many teachers have, in fact, first "liberated" themselves as writers when they began modeling the process of writing for their students (Calkins, 1983).

How does modeling bring about this liberating effect—and why is it so important for our students? By modeling the process of writing, we not only are showing our students that *they* can write—that, in fact, *anyone* can write—but we are also taking the "mystery and mystique" out of writing. Most students believe that published writing somehow springs full blown from authors' pens. By modeling the full process, we will be showing them that most writing requires time and effort to evolve. Modeling shows the process behind the product.

The Writing Process: Putting Understanding into Practice

Much of our knowledge of teaching and guiding students' growth in writing is based on the work of researchers and educators such as Nancie Atwell, Lucy Calkins, Donald Graves, and Donald Murray. During what Harste, Short, and Burke (1989) have termed the "authoring cycle," each experience before, during, and after the writing process provides students with new information and perspectives which further growth and writing are based on. Reading and discussion are critical variables that fuel the cycle, helping to develop students' knowledge and experiential bases for further writing.

Components of the Writing Process

We define the *writing process* as the "before, during, and after" of writing. The writing process comprises five main components: *prewriting*, *drafting* or *composing*, *revising*, *editing*, and *sharing/publishing*. As students learn and "fine-tune" this process, not only do they grow and mature as writers, but they also develop their critical thinking and problem-solving skills.

Prewriting

Prewriting is the first stage in the writing process. It refers to whatever students need to do to get thoughts out of their heads and down on paper. Since the purpose of prewriting is to record ideas for later use and elaboration, students needn't use complete sentences but can express these thoughts in as simple a form as possible. During prewriting students also consider what they will want their audience to gain from reading their compositions.

A number of strategies and practices exist for demonstrating prewriting. Teachers should model and facilitate each one so that students will not get bogged down with the age-old questions "What do I write about?" and "How do I get started?" It is important for students to understand that a composition usually begins not with sustained writing but with ideas. An effective prewriting activity will result in the writer's feeling ready to write, that tell-tale moment when he or she knows it's time to move on to the drafting or composing stage.

Drafting

During the drafting—or "composing"—stage, the expression of *meaning* and *intent* are foremost. Although punctuation and spelling certainly play a part, they should not be the primary focus at this stage; addressing them later allows students to allot more cognitive space to the expression of meaning.

Most of the writing is usually created during the drafting stage. This is the point when mature writers have a "conversation" with themselves. For students, interactions with the teacher and with peers will develop this ability to carry on an internal conversation and will also help them learn to write on their own. As with the development of thought, *internalization* of such social interactions contributes to the content and the nature of these conversations with oneself. The language, emotions, and content the student experiences through reading also add to the conversation. Obviously, there won't always be an external "ear"—an audience or editor—during this drafting stage. One of the important transitions to mature writing is developing one's own ear rather than continuing to rely on conferences and teacher input.

Students must understand something important about the drafting stage: drafts are usually *first* drafts. By definition, therefore, they are incomplete and tentative—a time to try things out and take risks. All too often, students get the message that what is valued in writing is good handwriting, proper spacing between words, correct spelling, correct margins, thorough erasure of mistakes, and so forth. This emphasis leads to compositions that are usually wooden and dull. "Older children often want to know what topics you expect," Donald Graves pointed out, "correct spelling, how to line off the page. It is only right that they ask. This has been the pattern in previous years. They don't want to be censured for their mistakes. Many will need weeks or months to be convinced you seriously wish to know what they have to offer" (1983, p. 19). As we'll see, however, with appropriate and sensitive guidance, such students can be turned around. You can sometimes convince them by showing them how *you* write a first draft. For example, you can demonstrate how you use "placeholders" when you don't know how to spell a word—simply getting an approximation down or drawing a line to come back later.

Revising

Once the writer has a first draft in hand, the process of revision may begin. A little bit of revision goes on during the actual drafting of a composition, but significant revision is a reworking of the first draft. This "re-vision" (literally, "seeing again") involves making whatever changes are necessary in the first draft so that the purposes and intentions of the writing will be more precisely met. Substitutions, additions, reordering, and deletions of ideas can be made at any level—word, phrase, sentence, or paragraph. Sometimes the student revises under the teacher's direction; at other times revising is done after sharing the writing with other students.

First drafts rarely achieve the level of precision and comprehensibility their authors intend, so the process of revision allows authors the opportunity to determine not only the strengths of their first drafts but also what can be elaborated, clarified, omitted, or reordered. While revising, students will come to think critically about writing and the eloquence and precision with which they are communicating to their audience. Revision depends upon a clear understanding of the writing's purpose because only then will the writer be able to judge the effect the writing will have on the intended audience.

Editing

At this stage the writer gives explicit attention to the **mechanics**—spelling, punctuation, and grammar or usage—for final "fine-tuning" of the composition. Although the mechanics remained pretty much in the background during the previous stages, these aspects are nevertheless important. Peter Elbow aptly describes their relevance this way: "When you meet strangers, you can hardly keep from noticing their clothing before you notice their personality. The only way to keep someone from noticing a surface is to make it 'disappear,' as when someone wears the clothes you most expect her to wear. The only way to make grammar disappear—to keep the surface of your writing from distracting readers away from your message—is to make it right" (1981, p. 168).

In the editing stage, the writer has reached a point where he or she is at least satisfied, if not outright pleased, with the composition and probably will make no further changes to its content. The writing is then ready to be prepared for publication. The major task of readying a composition for publication is a careful reading—editing—of the manuscript.

Editing becomes something other than a dull, routinized, and mildly irritating duty when students see a clear and worthwhile purpose for it. The primary purpose is usually publication: their writing is going to be published—publicly shared—in a meaningful way. There will be an interested and appreciative audience for their writing. Very often it is easier at first for students to edit other students' writing; this activity in turn helps them notice mechanical errors in their own writing. The *Sourcebook* at the end of this text provides a general scope and sequence for elements of grammar and punctuation.

It's also important to keep in mind that students shouldn't be expected to edit their work for *everything*; it's the *process* of editing we want them to learn. If a piece needs to be "perfect" for some reason, then the teacher can be the final editor.

Sharing and Publishing

By now it is obvious that students' writing has a much broader readership than the traditional "audience of one" that was the teacher. Writing may be shared as it is being developed—as in "response" sessions—or when it is finished, through the "Author's Chair" concept. In this manner students will come to think as writers when they read, and think as readers when they write. Our students will begin to consider *themselves* authors, kindred spirits with the absent authors who have written their trade books.

Often students' writing will be published to be shared with the whole class and occasionally with even a wider audience. The publication of writing simply means that the writing will be prepared so that it will be available for reading by this wider audience. Publishing can take many forms, as we will see later in this chapter.

In summary, the process of writing comprises five stages: prewriting, drafting or composing, revising, editing, and sharing or publishing. These stages certainly do not represent discrete, exclusive tasks but rather overlap. Neither does all writing follow these steps, nor do students complete all the steps for every piece. What distinguishes one stage from another is the degree of focus placed on particular tasks at different points in the evolution of a composition. Discussing each stage with students as their need for understanding and guidance arises is the teacher's challenge.

How do we introduce these stages to our students? The illustrative dialogues that follow demonstrate how our initial discussions might proceed. Later in the chapter we will explore what will happen as we build on these beginnings and our students learn, with our help, how to take more control of their writing.

Helping Young Children Become Comfortable with Writing

Our primary concern with children in kindergarten and first grade is to make them fairly comfortable with the act of writing. When children are not hesitant about writing and are no longer awkward in their handling of pencils, crayons, and paper, we can move on to revising and editing. But let's look at the very beginnings: how can we get young children to start writing?

First of all, most young children entering first grade seem to believe they *can* write, although they will admit that they may not know how to read (Graves, 1983). Early on we can let them draw, and if they choose to include letters or letterlike characters, so much the better. As we saw in Chapter 5, many children will spontaneously sound out whatever they want to say, using their knowledge of the names of the letters in the alphabet. However, many other children, for any number of reasons, do not spontaneously make these attempts and will deny that they know anything about how to write or print.

When you do need to offer encouragement—let's say to a reluctant six-year-old, Camille—your wording may go something like the dialogue in the Classroom Example on p. 239.

Children such as Camille will probably need continuing support of this sort; an excellent way to reach several such children at once is to work with a group. Sounding out a word in a group is a particularly effective means of showing even the most reluctant child "how it's done."

What if a child asks, "Is it right?" The most effective and satisfying response is something like "You know, you'll see it spelled differently in

CLASSROOM EXAMPLE

Minilesson: Encouraging Young Children to Invent Their Spelling

TEACHER: "Camille, tell me about your drawing here."

CAMILLE: "It's a elephant."

TEACHER: "What's the elephant doing?"

CAMILLE: "Nothin' much—he's just standing there."

TEACHER: "Well, you've done a good job of drawing him. Why don't you label your drawing by printing *elephant* underneath the picture?"

CAMILLE: "I don't know *how* to write!"

TEACHER: "I bet you know a *lot* about how to write; in fact, you might surprise yourself! You know the names of a lot of the letters, and they will help you write down what you want to say. Let's try it with *elephant*. What's the first sound you hear in *elephant?*"

CAMILLE: "*L?*"

TEACHER: "Good! Write down the letter that makes that sound." [Teacher points to the place on the drawing where Camille can begin to write.] "What's the next sound you hear?" [Teacher pronounces the word carefully and slowly by syllables: "el-e-phant."]

CAMILLE: "*A?*"

TEACHER: "Okay! Write that down . . . What's the next sound?" [Teacher again pronounces *elephant*, slightly emphasizing the *f* sound.]

CAMILLE: "*F?*"

TEACHER: "Good! Write that down . . . What else do you hear?" [Usually by this point children have caught on. Camille finishes her writing: *LAFNT*. Teacher continues: "Good, Camille! How about that! You've written *elephant*!"]

books, but I really like the way *you* listened for the sounds and spelled this word the way it sounds." This response sends two important messages: (1) Yes, words are often spelled differently in books, and (2) you appreciate and support the child's spelling, even if it *is* different. This support encourages children to keep up their attempts.

Journal writing is an excellent means of keeping young children writing in a nonthreatening context. With continued development, they will write more and in time will be ready to apply some phases of the writing process. We can adjust it for young children only to include the prewriting, drafting, and publishing phases, omitting the revising and editing phases. One of the best ways to begin is to put some ideas or topics into "little books." These books are just a few half-pages stapled together. Children write one fact or observation on each page and illustrate each page. We then type up the little book, using conventional spelling and punctuation. Children can illustrate these and reread them as often as they wish.

Teaching, Modeling, and Applying the Writing Process

At any level when we *first begin* the writing process, we should set students up for success. We can talk about the phases in the process, make charts for each phase (students' input is important here), and make sure we model and demonstrate the process. In addition, the first few writings should probably be short; we want students to get a feel for writing by experimenting with several different pieces.

Prewriting

The classic response from students when you announce, "Let's write!" is "I don't know what to write about." In time, your students won't respond this way; their purposes will easily dictate the form and content of their writing.

The overriding aim of **prewriting activities** is to free up the students' thoughts and feelings—the cognitive and affective realms—and to generate ideas they can elaborate upon in their subsequent writing. At first the prewriting phase will address the basic issue of identifying a writing topic. With time, this phase can help writers identify concepts they may use in their writing and knowledge they may want the audience to gain from it. The techniques you introduce and how much you encourage students to use them will depend upon the students' age, developmental levels, and purposes for writing.

We must remember and remind our students that they have much to draw upon for writing topics, but in the beginning we must encourage them to tap this wellspring. With time, the prewriting phase will come to include any type of activity that precedes and helps focus a written composition. These types of activities, presented throughout this book, can range from show-and-tell to reading different types of literature, journal writing, field trips, interviews, films, class discussions, clustering, brainstorming, and story maps. More prewriting techniques are discussed next.

Objects   We can bring in objects that generate interesting associations—a stuffed animal, a dog collar, a box of cracker jacks, a book—and ask students to write a word or phrase describing a memory the object calls to mind. Later, students can select which object they'd most like to write about. They can also bring in things that "mean a lot" to them, such as a favorite stuffed animal, a special memento of a trip or of a friend or relative. Any of these may be writing prompts.

Drawing For many children drawing is the most natural type of prewriting activity and is most effective in the primary grades (Dyson, 1993). In first grade writing is usually merely a "comment" on the drawing; with time the two processes will better complement each other, and soon the writing will usually surpass the drawing in complexity and effort. You can follow up on a child's drawing by asking questions to elicit more information; for example, ask what the child is illustrating and why. You may encourage the child to add to the drawing (if appropriate) and/or identify one element in it to write about.

Clustering *Clustering* refers to a technique that has variously been called "webbing" and "mapping." Interestingly, it closely mimics the ways information-processing theorists have described information being organized in our brains (see Chapter 2). The technique of clustering allows us to access associations to a particular idea in a free flowing, nonlinear manner. Clustering helps writers identify specific topics or twists on topics to explore and realize when the "moment to write" has struck—when they have shifted from "randomness to a sense of direction" (Rico, 1983, p. 10). Eventually, students will use clustering individually. At first, however, it is done with a group or the whole class as shown in the Classroom Example on p. 242.

Brainstorming Like clustering, brainstorming usually involves a group of students and taps the thoughts associated with a particular idea. The idea may be represented by a word, phrase, or picture. Originally intended as a group problem-solving technique, brainstorming can be adapted for prewriting by having students call out ideas that a "scribe" writes on a chalkboard or chart paper. The scribe (initially the teacher) accepts all suggestions without evaluation. That will come later in the problem-solving process. As a prewriting activity, brainstorming usually stops after many ideas have been recorded; these may or may not be part of the subsequent writing.

After compiling a list of the ideas, you can extend brainstorming by asking the students if any item in this list catches their interest. If so, that idea can be pulled to the side and a list of "specifics" brainstormed for it, or the idea can be used as the focus for clustering. You can also ask students if they sense any connections among the items in the list. If they do, these can be circled and connected with a line or arrow. This connection can be the starting point for a piece of writing, especially if you encourage more brainstorming or clustering around it.

CLASSROOM
EXAMPLE

Minilesson:
Clustering as
a Prewriting
Technique

The teacher first writes a word or phrase in the middle of the chalkboard or on a piece of chart paper. He then circles it and asks the students what it brings to mind. As students offer suggestions, he writes them around the central "idea" and draws a circle around each. In the course of offering ideas, at least one and usually more specific areas will develop as spin-offs of the general idea.

Figure 7.1 shows a cluster generated by a class of second-graders. The main idea here is "gerbils." The class first contributed the words connected by lines to the main idea. Notice, though, that after "cages," the teacher has drawn arrows to connect the circles; they show how other ideas were spun off from "cages," eventually winding up with a child's comment about "noises I hear from the gerbil cage at night." At this point the children are ready to write, having had their schemas and perhaps their imaginations stimulated. They may use the words on the cluster if they wish, but they certainly should not be required to do so. And if some students are stimulated to write about something other than gerbils, that's okay!

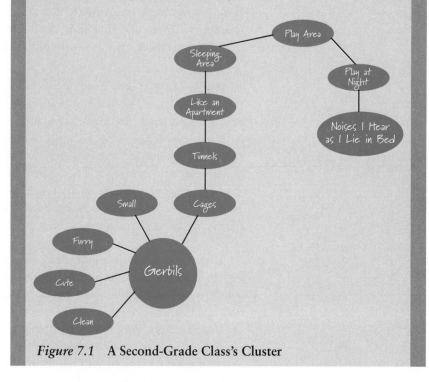

Figure 7.1 **A Second-Grade Class's Cluster**

(Continued)

Figure 7.2 shows a cluster generated by fifth-graders. Notice that it is not only more elaborate than the previous one but that, given its complexity, the teacher has numbered major concepts to illustrate how to order the cluster, a first pass at organizing the main ideas.

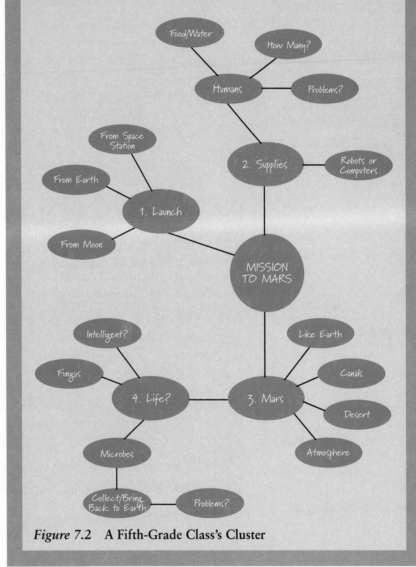

Figure 7.2 **A Fifth-Grade Class's Cluster**

CLASSROOM EXAMPLE

Minilesson: Brainstorming as a Prewriting Activity

The teacher begins the lesson standing in front of the class at an overhead projector. A clear transparency is placed on the projector. She is going to be "thinking aloud" for the students, modeling how she generates information about her topic.

TEACHER: "When I have a topic that I want to write about—in this case, the upcoming balloon races this weekend—I simply write down anything that comes to me that has to do with my topic. This gets me in the mood to write about my topic, and it also gets many of the ideas that I will use when I'm writing down on the page for ready reference. The important thing about this list—and something that you will need to keep in mind when you do this on your own—is to write down whatever comes to your mind, no matter how silly or unimportant it may seem to you.

"Okay, when I think about the balloon races, I think about blue skies [writes *blue skies* on the transparency], the dragonlike sounds of the balloons when their burners are turned on [writes "dragonlike sounds" on the transparency] . . ."

[The teacher continues in this fashion for approximately one minute. When she is finished, the transparency contains eight ideas. Figure 7.3 shows the completed transparency.]

"You know, I've just gotten a feeling that I'm ready to get started with my actual writing. You will usually get this feeling too; sometimes it comes almost right away, and sometimes it takes a while, but it usually comes . . . To me, it's simply a feeling that I want to get going with my writing—I want to say more about these first few ideas that have come to me."

blue skies   huge wicker baskets
dragonlike sounds   early morning
a party   wet grass
excitement   balloons blocking
                      out the sun

Figure 7.3 **Brainstorming about Balloon Races**

Stream-of-Consciousness Writing   Also referred to as "quickwrite," this activity is most effective for the intermediate grades and above. Stream-of-consciousness writing can identify ideas for writing as well as ease students into the flow of writing. Your instructions to students are simple: "When I say 'begin,' start writing down whatever comes into your head. You do not have to write in complete sentences or be concerned with spelling or punctuation. Just *keep writing*! If you find that there are no new thoughts in your head, just keep writing the last word you wrote until a new thought does come along."

Stream-of-consciousness writing is an activity that many published authors have found useful. The technique helps curb the self-editing to which even professional writers succumb at the prewriting stage. When a thought pops into our heads, we may often say to ourselves, "That idea is unimportant" (or silly, dumb, or weird) and not write it down, thereby editing out ideas that could be developed. Stream-of-consciousness writing helps to break the self-editing habit and save all the ideas. It should most definitely be kept personal, so that students do not avoid writing down certain thoughts for fear others will read them.

The Classroom Example minilesson on p. 244 illustrates the prewriting phase in action as a teacher uses a variant of brainstorming and frees herself to write by homing in on her topic.

Using Journals for Prewriting   Journals can be a rich source of ideas for writing stories. A journal—usually a spiral-bound notebook—provides students with a nonstructured and usually ungraded opportunity to write just about anything. Journals can become an effective and enlightening type of diary, providing students with a means of seeing themselves and how their thoughts unfold over time. When any of us read what we wrote two months ago, we confront what was really going on for us at the time. The impressions and ideas have not been recast in light of subsequent experience; this information is critical to seeing ourselves more objectively and maturely. (Journals can also function as a useful "learning log" where students write summaries of their observations in science, social studies, and mathematics; see pp. 432–433).

Many teachers now realize that some guidelines for journal writing are usually necessary since many children who simply are told every day to "write in your journals" will run out of stimulating ideas. There are a number of variations we may employ, but we shouldn't change emphases too frequently. For starters, we may need to model in a "think-aloud" format the type of writing one can do in a journal. In addition, we should write regularly in our own journals because students will value what they see us valuing. Our writing may be simply a general listing of the day's anticipated highlights, something more retrospective about ourselves, or analytical notes about a student or two.

Occasionally, we can ask students to respond to something we put on the board: a "puzzler," an open question, a poem, or an interesting trivia fact. In addition to responding to what they are reading (see below and Chapter 10), they can brainstorm possible topics for writing. Start a list that can be posted and expanded throughout the year. For starters, we might consider the following possibilities (Atwell, 1987; Tchudi & Tchudi, 1983; Tompkins, 1995):

◆ Write about dreams you've had.

◆ Write as though you're a character in a book you're reading.

◆ Record observations about new places or people you've met.

◆ Write about something that may be worrying or bothering you.

◆ Write about how you thought about things when you were younger.

◆ Write to another student in class about whatever you've been reading.

◆ Write down favorite quotations.

◆ React to TV programs, movies, or articles you've read.

◆ Write down conversations you've overheard.

◆ Make lists and categorize interesting words (see Chapter 8).

◆ Keep dialogue journals (see Chapter 10).

In summary, assigning journals can be an extremely effective way of getting students to write, to generate ideas for writing, and to keep writing. They can connect students and teachers through important and meaningful dialogue. A good many "story ideas" may first surface in journals.

Drafting

Because it is difficult (for obvious reasons) to model the entire composing of a first draft, teachers usually model both the beginning—the "getting-started" phase—and how to keep the writing going. A primary objective at the getting-started stage is to help children realize that they don't have to sit and wait for just the right sentence or words to pop into their heads. When they feel they're ready to write, they can begin by working with the ideas they jotted down during the prewriting phase.

Once again the teacher is at the front of the classroom standing next to the overhead projector. She places the list of ideas based on the balloon races shown in Figure 7.3 on the projector.

TEACHER: "Kids, yesterday when we were thinking about what to do before starting our writing, I told you I felt I was ready to write after jotting down these ideas about the balloon races." [She turns on the overhead projector.] "Today I'd like to show you what I do when I get started writing, when I am actually ready to write what we call the *first draft*.

"Well, now. Okay . . . I'll start with this idea." [She writes, "I always look forward to the balloon races each year." Then she pauses, looking down at the transparency.] "That's an okay start, but where do I go from here? What should I say next? Hmm . . . Okay, I've got another idea . . . [While pronouncing each word softly but loudly enough to be heard, she writes: "The first time I went to the races, I wasn't sure if I would really enjoy them. I had never seen balloons like that up close before." She pauses, still looking down at the transparency, then continues writing, still pronouncing words softly as she writes them: "But when I saw them being inflated and heard the hissing sound of the burners when flame came out, I was reminded of dragons. I was amazed! I had never seen anything like them before." She pauses again.]

"I'm not sure exactly where I want to go now, so I'm going to look back at my list of ideas." [She places the list quickly on the transparency and exclaims, "Oh! I've got it!" She then returns to writing: "All around me, it felt like one large party. People were shouting as the balloons went up. One minute the sun was shining brightly. The next minute it was blocked by one of the balloons."]

"Well, class, now I feel as though I'm really rolling with this particular piece of writing. I feel most comfortable right now describing what my first experience at a balloon race was like, and I'm going to continue to develop this main idea when I go back to my writing.

"What you've seen me doing is exactly what I do when I write by myself; I may not talk out loud while I write, but I'm *thinking* the kinds of things I've been saying out loud to you.

"A lot of your first drafts will begin this way. With other first drafts you will have a pretty good idea about what your main focus is going to be. Often, though, you may want to write and feel like you're ready, but you're not sure exactly where your piece is going. When that happens, then just begin writing with the first ideas in your list as a guide. The focus will usually come along, just as the feeling that you were ready to write came along."

After students understand the nature of getting the writing going, we can facilitate their transition from prewriting to drafting in a whole-class or small-group context.

- After doing a cluster, for example, have students work in pairs and choose what they feel are the three most important ideas.

- Next, get back together to begin a collaborative composition. Ask, "How can we start our composition?" and take two or three suggestions. Then turn to chart paper or a transparency and ask, "How can we say that?" [Ask a student to help you remember exactly what a particular student said.] Then begin writing.

Revising

Teachers play an extremely important role helping students to "see their writing again" in light of their audience. Often a student can be his or her own most demanding and severe audience, particularly in the intermediate grades. When a child has invested much energy in a piece, the compulsion to "get it *right*" —wording, structure, focus, or whatever—may take over.

Another significant process comes into play during the revision stage. Teachers model response strategies for their students and show them how they in turn can help each other revise by responding to their first drafts as the teacher would. This response process can become an effective type of *collaborative learning*—sharing with peers. It can facilitate critical thinking arising from questions that will be asked both during the initial drafting and during the follow-up reactions to that first draft.

After students have decided to revise a draft, they don't have to worry about copying it over as they make changes. Rather, they can use editing marks to indicate the changes they want. Figure 7.4 shows the common marks that elementary students will find helpful. Students may also do a bit of "cutting and pasting," moving sentences or perhaps paragraphs around.

When the teacher first models the revision stage, she is also able to model *how to respond* to a piece of writing. This modeling reinforces the feedback students are giving and getting in writing conferences. Based on the paragraph in Figure 7.5, let's examine how a teacher might model the process of revision for students. Notice how the teacher addresses different aspects of the elements of writing, all within the context of revision.

Mark	Explanation	Example
¶	Begin a new paragraph. Indent the paragraph.	¶ We went to an air show last Saturday. Eight jets flew across the sky in the shape of V's, X's, and diamonds.
∧	Add letters, words, or sentences.	The leaves were red ∧ orange. *(and inserted)*
ℓ	Take out words, sentences, and punctuation marks. Correct spelling.	The rain passed ∕ quickly. The sky is bright blew now. *(blue)*
/	Change a capital letter to a small letter.	The /Fireflies blinked in the dark.
≡	Change a small letter to a capital letter.	New York ≡city is exciting.

Figure 7.4   **Proofreading Marks**

SOURCE: From *Teaching the Writing Process: A Guide for Teachers and Supervisors* by Nancy Carolyn Millett. Copyright © 1990 by Houghton Mifflin Company. Reprinted by permission of Houghton Mifflin Company.

CLASSROOM EXAMPLE

Minilesson: Revision

TEACHER: "What we are going to be doing, class — thinking about what we like and what we would change in this piece of writing — is called *revision*." [She writes *revision* on a clear transparency.] "If we want to continue working with a piece of writing in order eventually to publish it, there are almost always some changes that can be made to make it more effective — to say what we want to say more precisely and to affect our reader more powerfully. When we think about our writing in these ways, we are talking about *revision*. Revision usually leads to second drafts and sometimes to third and fourth drafts, depending on how important we feel a particular piece of writing is. In order to learn about revision, we're going to continue sharing our drafts with one another.

"I've put the first paragraph of a composition on this transparency. It is from a story written by a sixth-grade student last year. Listen as I read it aloud to you." [Teacher reads out loud to the class.] (See Figure 7.5 on page 251.)

"Okay, kids, the first thing we do when we work with another's writing in the revision stage is to tell what the writer has done *well*. As I read over this piece, I especially like the way the author talks about the flat surface and its curling up at the end; she shows how she feels that's pretty unusual or strange. We usually take for granted how the tides work, but she's showing us that she's really *thinking* about it. It's complicated, and it really does seem like magic when you think of the ocean that way.

"Something else that I like is how she grabs our attention when she writes, 'Suddenly, she saw a dark object just above the water.' She doesn't tell us what she thinks it is yet, and that's good; she really creates a sense of excitement and anticipation. She's also able to create this feeling because she mentions the object right after a really quiet, thoughtful part where she's wondering about the waves. It has more of an effect on you than if she simply began with something like 'Pam thought she saw a dark object above the water.' She has set us up in kind of a thoughtful mood, and then . . . pow! She hits us with the exciting, suspenseful part . . . The writer has done some things well, some things that get our attention as readers.

"Now let's change our focus on this piece. Our next step in revision is to think about anything that might need to be changed. It's important that we concentrate on the *meaning* of the piece—on anything that is unclear or confusing to you.

"Look at the beginning of the piece where she's talking about the end of the ocean and says, 'The end was where it reached the shore.' That kind of seems stuck out there by itself, really cut off from the first part. We could make a change by connecting it to the sentence before it and seeing how that would sound. Here's how I would make that change: I would put a 'delete' mark through the period after *end*. [She does this on the transparency.] Then I would put a comma after *end* at the end of the first sentence, and then, so it won't sound odd, I would cross out 'The end was.' Now the sentence reads, 'When Pam looked out at the ocean, she wondered how that kind of flat surface could wind up curling into waves at the end, where it reached the shore.'

"That's an effective change, isn't it? It pulls the thought, the *flow*, together more tightly. I've noticed something else. It seems she left a *the* out before *sun*. This is how I would insert it." [She makes the caret mark, then writes *the* above it.]

"There's one last revision I would make to this fine first draft.

(*Continued*)

Remember how we've been talking about paragraphs lately? It seems like there should be two paragraphs here because the author is talking about two different things. She's gone from just sort of looking at the ocean—sort of peaceful and calm—then there's this pretty dramatic change. I would start the second paragraph where she writes, 'Suddenly, she saw a dark object just above the water,' but since I don't want to have to rewrite this over again, down at the bottom in a separate paragraph, I'm simply going to put this mark [she draws a ¶ in front of the word *Suddenly*], which means "begin a new paragraph here."

"Okay! That does it for now. In this revision stage, then, I've done two important things. I've shown what I like about what the writer has done—she has written her beginning in a way that really draws us into the piece and interests us right away—and I've pointed out how some unclear places can be made clearer."

When Pam looked out at the ocean, she wondered how that kind of flat serface could wind up cureling into waves at the end of ~~The end was~~ where it reached the shore. She had read about the sun and the moon and how they were important in making the waves but she didn't really understand it. It seemed like magic, she thought. ¶ Suddenly, she saw a dark object just above the water. She looked closer but it was gone.

Figure 7.5 Paragraph from a Sixth-Grader's Story—Showing Revision

Editing

Editing refers to the proofreading and preparation of the final manuscript. Whatever skills students have learned about "fine-tuning" a composition may now be brought into play. Handwriting now assumes a more important role because students know that its quality—its legibility—is what readers will first notice (see Chapter 11). Students can use the editing symbols presented in Figure 7.4, but they now focus more on *mechanics* than on content.

Students best appreciate how editing works if they set aside their compositions for a few days. Then, when they come back to them, two important things happen. First, they are better able to focus on specific errors. Second, because they have "taken a break" from the sustained work on a piece, they feel renewed motivation to make it as good as they can.

A general rule for editing is to have students read for one or two aspects at a time. For example, the first feature of punctuation they can check is whether each sentence ends with a period. At the same time we can ask them to make sure each new sentence begins with a capital letter. We help them understand that editing involves several readings, each time looking for one or two specific things. Many of our minilessons will focus on the fine points of editing. With time, of course, students' awareness of these points should become automatic.

Editing is modeled in much the same fashion as revision is. Students will come to understand, however, that the difference between the revision and editing stages is that revision still deals with *content* while editing deals with *mechanics*.

The teacher in the Classroom Example on p. 254 has previously modeled how to read through a piece with an "editing" eye. This time she is engaging the students in the process before turning them loose on their own writing. She uses the story shown in Figure 7.6.

Publishing and Sharing the Finished Work

The excitement students feel when their work truly reaches and is appreciated by a larger audience is perhaps the best *motivator* for writing and inevitably for further *growth* in writing. The value of sharing work with other students in the classroom is considerable, but the audience beyond the classroom will come to play a larger role as the writing program develops over the course of the year.

Earlier in this chapter we mentioned the "Author's Chair." This is the valued place in your classroom where in-progress as well as published works may first be shared with the class as a whole or with a group. The Author's Chair will continue to be a prominent place in the publishing and

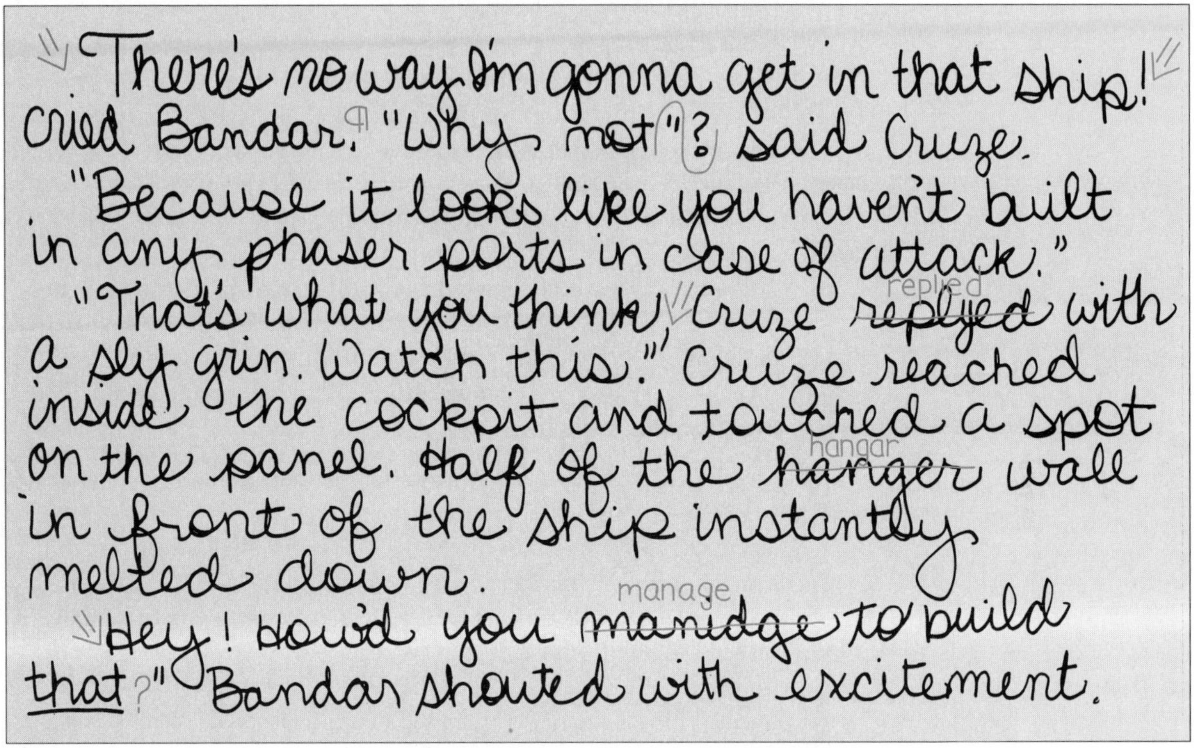

> "There's no way I'm gonna get in that ship!" cried Bandar. "Why not?" said Cruze.
> "Because it looks like you haven't built in any phaser ports in case of attack."
> "That's what you think," Cruze replied with a sly grin. Watch this." Cruze reached inside the cockpit and touched a spot on the panel. Half of the hanger wall in front of the ship instantly melted down.
> "Hey! How'd you manage to build that?" Bandar shouted with excitement.

Figure 7.6   **Sixth-Grader's Story—Showing Editing**

sharing phase of our writing program. The following list provides other possibilities:

◆ Bulletin boards (featuring several students or an "author of the week").

◆ Books written by individual students or a group of students, which may be assigned reference numbers (e.g., Dewey Decimal System) by the librarian or media specialist (including books for primary students written and illustrated by intermediate students).

◆ Radio scripts, plays for actual performance, and puppet shows.

◆ Books written on specific topics that can be placed in waiting rooms in the community (Nathan et al., 1989).

◆ Compositions read aloud by students in homes for the elderly and other institutions, then left for residents to read.

◆ Classroom and/or school newspaper.

CLASSROOM EXAMPLE

Minilesson: Editing

TEACHER: "We've been discussing quotation marks a bit lately. When we edit our finished drafts this week, let's pay particular attention to these marks. I suspect most of you will need to be on the lookout for when and how you've used them because most of you have been writing stories in which there's a fair amount of dialogue.

"One of your classmates has kindly given me permission to make a transparency of part of his story. Let's look at this part and edit it, looking just for how he has used quotation marks." [The teacher and students silently read the story shown on the transparency, then discuss it.]

After discussing quotation marks, the teacher then guides the students through the composition again, this time looking for spelling errors. She then makes the appropriate changes on the transparency. A third pass can look for another feature. It's important to remind students that if a piece is truly going to be published—shared with a wider audience—they will need to read through their pieces each time they are editing for a particular element. This balancing of older and newer aspects of mechanics is a crucial part of teaching editing.

◆ Book with pictures and illustrations of class field trips.

◆ Writing contests sponsored by children's magazines, local newspapers, or television and radio stations.

◆ Several short-term publication possibilities exist as well, such as sending notes home, putting up schoolwide bulletin board displays, writing lyrics for original songs, and making greeting cards.

An excellent way to celebrate the best of a semester's or a whole year's publications (class, school, or districtwide) is through a *Young Authors Conference*. Students share their best published work in different categories through exhibits in a fairlike setting with booths and entertainment. The categories include fiction, informational, poetry, and drama (including puppetry). Readings and panel discussions are held. Awards may be given, but it is often best to award certificates of participation rather than first-, second-, and third-place ribbons.

Predictably, *books* remain one of the most popular formats for publica-

A highlight of your students' engagement in the writing process will be the students' sharing their writing with an audience.

tion, in part because of their permanency. This is particularly true if the students' books are to be coded just like all the trade books in the media center and placed with them on the shelves. There are many ways to bind books, and students may wish to experiment with different styles. Figure 7.7 illustrates a simple way of binding students' books that will stand the test of time — and many readers — quite well.

Process Writing and the Computer in the Integrated Classroom

In the third edition of his classic work *On Writing Well*, William Zinsser (1985) begins his chapter on writing with a word processor by making the following observation:

> There's nobody more filled with anxiety than a writer who has been told that he should start writing with a word processor . . . And there's nobody more evangelistic than a writer who has made the leap. (p. 205)

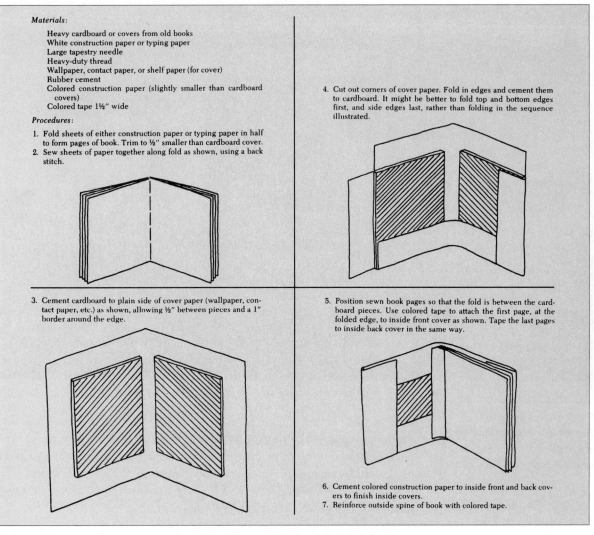

Materials:

    Heavy cardboard or covers from old books
    White construction paper or typing paper
    Large tapestry needle
    Heavy-duty thread
    Wallpaper, contact paper, or shelf paper (for cover)
    Rubber cement
    Colored construction paper (slightly smaller than cardboard covers)
    Colored tape 1½″ wide

Procedures:

1. Fold sheets of either construction paper or typing paper in half to form pages of book. Trim to ½″ smaller than cardboard cover.
2. Sew sheets of paper together along fold as shown, using a back stitch.
3. Cement cardboard to plain side of cover paper (wallpaper, contact paper, etc.) as shown, allowing ½″ between pieces and a 1″ border around the edge.
4. Cut out corners of cover paper. Fold in edges and cement them to cardboard. It might be better to fold top and bottom edges first, and side edges last, rather than folding in the sequence illustrated.
5. Position sewn book pages so that the fold is between the cardboard pieces. Use colored tape to attach the first page, at the folded edge, to inside front cover as shown. Tape the last pages to inside back cover in the same way.
6. Cement colored construction paper to inside front and back covers to finish inside covers.
7. Reinforce outside spine of book with colored tape.

Figure 7.7   **An Easy Way to Bind Student's Books**

SOURCE: Reproduced by permission of the publishers from Nessel, Denise D. and Jones, Margaret B., *The Language Experience Approach to Reading: A Handbook for Teachers*. (New York: Teachers College Press, © 1981 by Teachers College, Columbia University. All rights reserved.), pp. 157–159.

What do we know about elementary students, computers, and writing? While the research in this area is still quite new, three fundamental observations consistently seem to emerge.

1. The social context in which computer use occurs may significantly affect children's awareness of their writing and how it communicates with an audience.

Computers can be an important aid to students with their writing—especially as they revise and edit.

2. In the early stages of computer use, students' motivation to write can be enhanced.

3. Revising and editing can become easier and perhaps more effective on the computer than on paper.

At present many elementary schools locate their computers in labs, and individual classes come in to use them at scheduled times during the week. However, we need to remember that there will often at best be *one* computer per classroom in other schools. Therefore, scheduling time for students to use computers in the writing process may be a factor for the next few years. Our recommendations for the following activities will depend on computer availability.

Prewriting

For *prewriting* activities the teacher can use the **word processor** during brainstorming, typing a list or cluster of students' ideas and then printing out copies for the students. Older students can create their own clusters and modify or categorize them (Willis et al., 1996).

Drafting and Revising

At first it's more practical to have students prepare handwritten drafts before going to the computer. This will save considerable time for beginning writers, who are more fluent on paper.

When the draft is displayed on the screen or printed, its different appearance often leads students to notice parts to revise. Quite often students will want to make changes as they are typing the draft into the computer.

Editing

Although we do not yet know how the ability to delete, add, and move blocks of text around may facilitate writing among elementary students, we at least know that word processing makes the simple aspects of editing easier for children. And research does suggest that it isn't that important to spend time on keyboarding in the elementary grades. Rather than separately learning the layout of the keyboard and practicing the keystrokes for different letters, students are better off becoming keyboard literate through the "hunt and peck" method. Spending valuable computer time on keyboarding is the equivalent of trying to teach excellent penmanship before allowing children to compose their own written texts.

An almost unavoidable aspect of word processing in schools is its public nature. It's nearly impossible for children not to notice one another's writing on the screen. Most of the time this is not a problem, just another example of the social nature of writing in the classroom. As students become more familiar with conferencing and questioning, you will notice these activities going on around the computer.

Publishing and Sharing

Many word processing programs for students make the "publishing" phase of writing more engaging and motivating (*Student Writing Center*; *Children's Writing and Publishing Center*). This is because students have the opportunity to experiment with print size, different fonts, spacing, placement on the page, and so forth. Programs offer the versatility of allowing experimentation; they also have set "templates" or formats already set up. "Clip art," graphics, and "paintbrush" packages are now included in most word processing programs. Students can paste ready-made art into their compositions as well as create their own art with the paintbrush utilities.

An additional word about the evolving role of computers in writing: they will continue to be extremely helpful, but at least for the near future they will not replace pen and paper. For some time to come, and for many reasons, handwritten communication will continue. A widespread "etiquette" in our written communication somehow demands this. For example, thank-you notes, sympathy cards, and the like should not be produced on a printer; they should be handwritten as neatly as the writer can manage.

Applying the Process: Different Purposes, Different Forms

Teaching Narrative Writing: Composing Stories in the Integrated Language Arts Classroom

Imitation plays a seminal role in students' learning to write. All writers, either by accident or design, begin by imitating the style and structure of other writers. As you share literature with your students, you will similarly find your students engaged in imitation. Take advantage of this and encourage it. You will see students creating, usually spontaneously (or after one student does it), one after another story based on a published book or story, such as "George and Martha" (James Marshall), "The Stupids" (Harry Allard), "Encyclopedia Brown" (Donald Sobol), and so on. You will also see imitation strictly of form, apart from content. For example, when students are studying *Aesop's Fables*, they may want to create their own fables; you can list two or three morals on the board and have each student select one and write a fable that goes with it.

Beginning in the primary years, the groundwork is laid for children's understanding of at least three important story elements: *plot* (what happened?), *setting* (where did it happen?), and *characterization* (what were the characters like?). *Plot* includes the main problem or goal the characters have, attempts to solve the problem or reach the goal, and solution to the problem, or *resolution*. We can make a chart of an element as it is developed in a story. We can provide a list of the element's features, then the students can add their features (see Figure 7.8). Some students need an additional support for generating their stories and/or understanding how certain narrative elements can be developed—such as understanding of characters, the overall sequence of events, the problem to be addressed, and the possible resolution. After modeling how to brainstorm and list these aspects, we can provide individual "thinksheets" for students to use in planning the following:

◆ Where will the story take place?

◆ Who will the characters be?

◆ What will the *goal* be?

◆ What problems will the main character encounter?

◆ How will the story end?

While these "thinksheets" can be very helpful in focusing students' thinking and planning, we also need to be realistic about their application: Our plans

---

Plot

Plot is the sequence of events in a story. It has four parts:

1. A Problem: The problem introduces conflict at the beginning of the story.
2. Roadblocks: Characters face roadblocks as they try to solve the problem in the middle of the story.
3. The High Point: The high point in the action occurs when the problem is about to be solved. It separates the middle and the end.
4. The Solution: The problem is solved and the roadblocks are overcome at the end of the story.

Setting

The setting is where and when the story takes place.

1. Location: Stories can take place anywhere.
2. Weather: Stories take place in different kinds of weather.
3. Time of Day: Stories take place during the day or at night.
4. Time Period: Stories take place in the past, at the current time, or in the future.

Conflict

Conflict is the problem that characters face in the story. There are four kinds of conflict:

1. Conflict between a character and nature
2. Conflict between a character and society
3. Conflict between characters
4. Conflict within a character

Characters

Writers develop characters in four ways:

1. Appearance: How characters look
2. Action: What characters do
3. Dialogue: What characters say
4. Monologue: What characters think

Figure 7.8　　　　　**Important Features of Story Elements**

will almost certainly change *as* we write—this is natural—so students shouldn't feel absolutely tied to their initial ideas.

More specifically, we can nurture students' development in writing stories in the following ways:

◆ *Develop a "sense of story"*
As students listen to stories in kindergarten and first grade—often in the Guided Listening-Thinking Activity (GLTA) format—they will be developing a "sense of story." Although their command of the writing basics has not yet developed to the point that they can write a lengthy narrative on their own, they *are* capable of dictating such a story. After listening to fairy tales or folktales, for example, the students can compose their own tale together by dictating it to the teacher. This dictated composition can entail more than one sitting and can undergo revision each time the children hear it reread.

◆ *Focus on a specific story element*
Develop a literature-based thematic unit (see Chapter 10) around a *particular* story element, reading aloud stories with excellent examples of it. Discuss how the author develops the element; this reinforces the issues we are examining in writing and reading minilessons and conferences. We can then help students increase their understanding as they develop the elements in their *own* stories. *Clustering* works very well here; for example, Figure 7.9 shows a cluster for *characterization*.

Another example is *point of view*. As students consider point of view in stories that they themselves write, you may wish to suggest they begin with the *omniscient* or "all-knowing, all-seeing" view, simply because it is easier. Later they can move on to the other types. As students experiment with other points of view—first-person point of view, character point of view, and so forth—and share these efforts with others, they will come to understand much better what you are able to do with a story depending on the point of view you take.

◆ *Important minilessons*
After students have been composing narratives for a while, experimenting with elements, and in some cases sticking with the same subject for an inordinate amount of time (for example, a particular cartoon character), stretch them by emphasizing and teaching minilessons on the following aspects of good story writing:

◆ They should write what they know—what they have themselves experienced. As Atwell (1987) reminded her middle grade students,

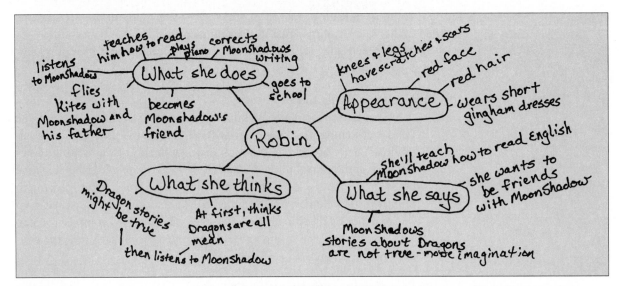

Figure 7.9   "Characterization" Cluster for Robin in Laurence Yep's *Dragonwings*

most authors' first published novels are autobiographical (see Kelsey's story excerpt in Figure 7.10). This was the underlying theme in the Thematic Exploration following Chapter 4 that focused on the author Cynthia Rylant.

◆ They should create one main character and develop him or her.

◆ They should maintain the same point of view to develop a consistent "voice": for example, third person or first person.

◆ They should experiment with different *leads* (Atwell, 1987). Stories can begin with action (a character doing something), dialogue, or reaction (a character thinking about something). Kelsey's teacher pointed this out to the class in a minilesson where she shared examples from the students' writing; eight-year-old Kelsey had begun a story with her mother's reaction to a stray cat and wound up developing it into a longer story in her journal (see Figure 7.10).

You'll find additional activities that develop students' understanding of stories and the ability to compare stories in Chapter 10.

Teaching Narrative Writing: Composing Poetry in the Integrated Language Arts Classroom

Children naturally play with and enjoy sounds and words during the preschool years. In the elementary grades we can sustain this delight and

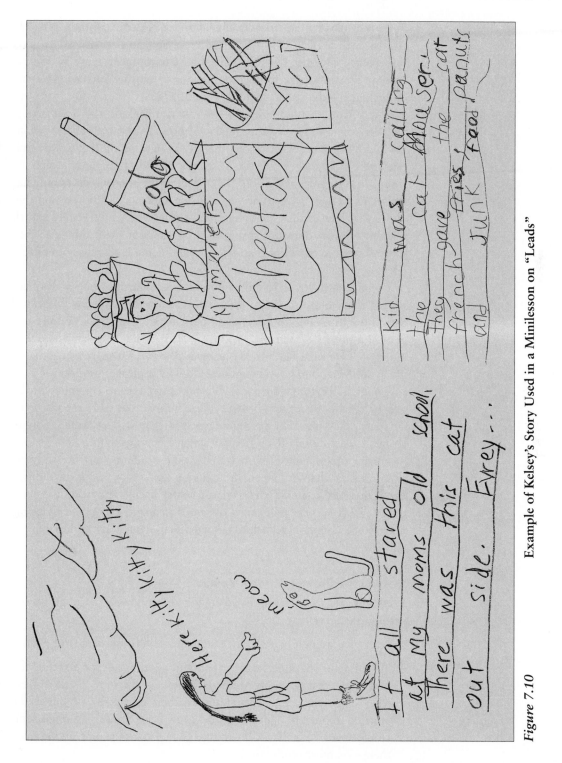

Figure 7.10

Example of Kelsey's Story Used in a Minilesson on "Leads"

interest by developing an environment where children continue playing with words. Such a context nurtures the reflection and sensitivity to language that poetry can tap. We'll explore this environment more in Chapter 8; here we'll examine the motivation for poetry writing and the manipulation of *language*—the "poet's paint" (Heard, 1989).

Poetry turns a unique lens on the world, making the ordinary special and, oftentimes, the special ordinary. Appropriately presented, it can inspire in children special reflections on the way things are, on themselves and others, and on language. "Poems," Georgia Heard (1989) points out, "come from something deeply felt" (p. 14). Specifically, poetry focuses on whatever causes us to feel "something *move* inside" (Heard, 1989) and on the language that best creates the images and expresses them precisely and rhythmically. "Poetry does not spring from satisfaction with things as they are but rather from our doubts and desires and fears. It searches out new possibilities; it would change things" (Rouse, 1983, p. 713).

It's important for us to model how students can *read* poetry. Rather than having them blaze through the poem when reading silently, we can show them how to pause, go back, and "play around" with the sounds and images of a poem. We can do this in a "think-aloud" format where we read aloud as if we were reading to ourselves. We can pause, repeat some particularly pleasing phrase, and comment on why it pleases us (because of repetitive sounds, rhythm, or rhyme). We can also pause to comment on the image or idea a word or phrase evokes for us. We can emphasize to the students that when *they* are reading poetry, they will have the leisure to examine it more closely than they can when listening to it.

Poetry integrates well with whatever our students may be studying: for example, sea chanteys when we focus on the sea or *haiku* for natural science. In such contexts children can most easily and readily appreciate poetry. This section will focus on ways to begin poetry writing and explore some common yet effective forms that elementary children can learn and use.

Getting the Poetry Writing Going

Poets who teach poetry writing suggest the following basic guidelines for getting started (Heard, 1989):

1. Start by reading poetry to the students and having them read poetry.

2. Tell students that poets can write about anything—not just the "flowers and love" that so many students believe is the only "stuff" of poetry. They can write about their families, their memories, or things they've worried about, thought about, or know a lot about. We often find that emphasizing "big issues"—things of real consequence and concern to them—is most productive.

3. To get students to write, first have them close their eyes for a minute or two and focus on the mental image that their topic suggests—then have them begin.

We shouldn't feel that we must know a lot about poetry or be a poet to motivate our students and keep them writing poetry. We can tell them that we're learning right along with them and think aloud for them as we model how we generate ideas, begin writing, and revise.

"Structured" Formats

Many children actually write poetry more freely if they are given a structure or format. Poetry teachers often differ sharply on this issue, but we may find it easier to move some children into poetry writing by trying out different structures. Let's consider some of the more effective formats.

Collaborative Poetry **Collaborative composition of poetry** is an effective way to begin developing an appreciation of and interest in poetry. The students together—as a whole class or within smaller groups—compose a poem. Two such possibilities are offered here.

1. **Transforming prose into poetry** The very form of poetry does things to language. Ordinary prose recast in poetic form can acquire an extraordinary or singular sense. Jennifer's following descriptive piece on "Change" was recast in poem form after discussion by a group of third-grade children.

People can change
in many ways.
Children change their size
as they grow older.
When the seasons change,
the temperature changes.
Green grass changes
to brown
in very hot or cold weather.
Pumpkins change
to happy, mean, monstrous,
and funny jack-o-lanterns.
Snow changes
to water,
And lava changes
to rock.

We can see many changes
All around us.

Jennifer's original composition was certainly a thoughtful piece as it stood. However, as the students talked about changing the structure — breaking up the *linearity* of the sentences — they realized that the images and ideas were somehow highlighted even more. As readers, they now focused on the individual images because these now stood out, and the final sentence — Jennifer agreed — became much *more* final and forceful when set apart in the poem.

2. **"Original" collaboration**   Students agree on what content they want in each line of a poem, then each individually composes a line. For example, they may decide to include a sports figure, a food, and a type of clothing in each line and that each line should begin with "I would never . . ." After the students have had time to compose their lines on separate slips of paper, the slips are collected and selected at random to assemble as a poem. A class of fifth-graders composed the following poem this way:

I would never be Deion Saunders eating broccoli wearing Spandex
shorts.
I would never wear sweaters with cheese and a picture of
Michael Jordan on them.
I would never try always to play Steffi Graf after eating
burritos in my pajamas.

And so it goes. Silliness, perhaps, but once the lines are assembled, students are often impressed by the structural and thematic patterns that emerge. For students it is a short step from the excitement of group composition to the motivation for writing their own poems. Philip Lopate (1975) suggested a variation on this format with more structure in terms of content. Children can assume someone else's personality; for example, "becoming" an elderly woman after reading *Miss Maggie* (see the Thematic Exploration following Chapter 4) and Patricia Polacco's *Mrs. Katz and Tush*. Each child could offer a line that the character may speak.

Repetitive Beginnings   An extremely popular strategy for helping students generate original poetry was first explored by Kenneth Koch and described in a book that has since become a classic: *Wishes, Lies, and Dreams: Teaching Children to Write Poetry* (1970). Koch encouraged children to create their own poems, using the same "stem" for each line in the poem. For example, he originated the now well-known "I wish" poem format. This superficially simple beginning proved to be quite powerful in eliciting poetry from children. Why? Koch suggests that "I wish" is a simple phrase that all children frequently and easily use; it is not "unusual," as the language of poetry often appears to elementary children. In addition, the simple repetition is engaging, providing its own structure without insisting on rhythm and rhyme, which children also too often believe is characteristic of all "good" poetry. Note how the following poem by a fifth-grader establishes its own "feel" through repetition:

I wish I were someone with money and happy.
I wish that all people were bluish and fun.
I wish I could do math without any thinking.
I wish I could fly and leave math far behind.

Other similar formats that release children's thinking and motivate them are *I used to . . . / But now . . .* and *I used to think . . . / But now I know . . .*

Incidentally, an interesting but important twist to Koch's experiments with poetry was his use of Spanish words and the way he encouraged children to think about them. He chose Spanish because so many of the students in the New York school where he worked spoke Spanish, although they all did know English. He realized two objectives: (1) the Spanish-speaking students were thrilled to have their language included and valued; (2) the native English-speaking students were intrigued by the sounds and images of the unfamiliar words. With the latter students, Koch probed for what colors and moods the words suggested and encouraged them to use the words in their own poems, even though they might not be sure about their meanings.

Word-Count/Syllable-Count Poems

These types of poems integrate with and extend our exploration in both content-area and literature-based thematic units. A delightful benefit is how they help students focus on and learn the labels for certain parts of speech (see *Sourcebook*, pp. 510–512). Following are three popular types of word/syllable-count poems.

Cinquains   A *cinquain* (pronounced "SIN kane") is a five-lined poem (from the French word for five, *cinq*, pronounced "SANK"). The formula for a cinquain not only produces an engaging poem, but perhaps more important, it directly channels children's attention and observation and helps them more precisely choose the words that best evoke the images they are striving to represent. Here's the formula for a cinquain:

Noun	The title
adjective, adjective	Describing the title
three words expressing action	
four words expressing feeling	

Noun	Repeating the title or giving another word related to it

Here's the formula put into action by a sixth-grader:

Worry
scary, tight
writing, guessing, erasing,
hoping, fearing, risking, uncertain
Test!

Diamantes   *Diamantes* (pronounced "DEE uh MAHN tays") are a variation on cinquains. Named after their "diamond" shape, they can tell a story or contrast two concepts and may be introduced when children have a good sense of and enjoy working with cinquains. Here is the format:

Noun	The subject of the poem
adjective, adjective	Describe the subject
three participles	Words ending in *-ing* having to do with the subject
four nouns having to do with the subject	First two have to do with the subject: second two have to do with the opposite
three participles	Have to do with the opposite
adjective, adjective	Describe the opposite
Noun	Opposite of the subject

Danielle wrote the following diamante as part of a thematic unit on deserts:

Desert
sandy, windy
baking, hardening, drying
coyotes, cacti, grizzlies, pines
rising, cooling, changing
fresh, crisp
Mountains

Haiku   *Haiku* is a fascinating form not only because of what it accomplishes but because of its application to English. Its rather rigid structure, adhering to certain numbers of syllables in each of the three lines, springs from the nature of the Japanese language, in which syllables correspond more straightforwardly to morphemes than they do in English. Nonetheless, applying the form to English brings striking results. *Haiku* is not meant to be abstract or necessarily symbolic but should be as concrete as possible, focusing awareness on only one thing or action—thus attempting to capture its essence.

The traditional structure of *haiku* is as follows:

first line = five syllables

second line = seven syllables

third line = five syllables

It is also fine not to focus on the number of syllables in each line but simply to capture an impression in three lines while keeping the effective visual form of *haiku*. Two examples of *haiku* by fifth-graders as part of a "Literature and the Seasons" thematic unit appear below; the first follows the syllable format and the second does not.

Baseball won't be hit
comes too fast you'll swing and miss
Strike out sit and watch.

The cat hunches
Scrunches and twitches
Grasshopper gone.

Now that we've observed a few ways that students can begin generating poetry, let's consider a concern that some educators share. The strict format of word/syllable-count poems—not to mention the rhythm and meter of other verse forms—have the potential of stifling children's attempts at poetry or at best lead to "poetry by formula." This worry can be avoided, however, if we do *not* insist on adherence to a format or discourage experimentation. On the other hand, many children appreciate this type of guideline at first; it gives them a starting place. As in all such matters, if we're sensitive to our students' different approaches, we can provide appropriate options for them.

Revising Poetry

When poets revise, the following strategies work well (Heard, 1989):

◆ Have someone else read your poem to you.

◆ Put the poem away for a while until it feels new when you read it again.

◆ "Try memorizing your poem, then reciting it. Places that are unclear, or that you can't remember, usually need attention" (Heard, 1989, p. 51).

◆ Reorganize by switching lines around and experiment with line breaks.

◆ Write "tired" words in the margin and brainstorm other words and/or use the thesaurus.

Teaching Expository Writing: Composing Informational Texts in the Integrated Classroom

After students have gotten into the swing of writing during the first weeks of the school year, we can move on to simple expository writing. We can do this by tapping into their existing interests and providing them with clear-cut purposes.

Expository writing requires students to determine how ideas are ordered and related. We can facilitate this process by helping them learn (1) how to balance the requirements of expository writing effectively; and (2) how to plan for, identify, and organize their information.

Just as with narratives, students should be *reading* and analyzing expository texts—primarily *trade books*. Informational trade books' format and design present content in many ways. When we discuss all of these features with students, we are providing them with *many* options for composing, designing, and presenting their work. Figure 7.11 is one such example, part of a short book coauthored one afternoon by Sarah and Terese, both nine years old. The book that inspired their "opposite" theme was Bruce McMillan's *Puffins Climb, Penguins Rhyme* (1995).

Build Your Teaching Resources

TEACHING POETRY TO CHILDREN

The following list contains titles that are excellent resources for expanding our background in teaching poetry:

Carpenter, J. (1986). *Creating the world: Poetry, art and children*. Seattle: University of Washington Press.

Collom, J. (1985). *Moving windows: Evaluating the poetry that children write*. New York: Teachers and Writers Collaborative.

Graves, D. (1994). *A fresh look at poetry*. Portsmouth, NH: Heinemann.

Hopkins, L. (1987). *Pass the poetry, please*. New York: Harper and Row Junior Books.

Koch, K. (1970). *Wishes, lies, and dreams: Teaching children to write poetry*. New York: Harper.

Koch, K. (1974). *Rose, where did you get that red? Teaching great poetry to children*. New York: Random House. For an interesting and dissenting critique of Koch's approach, see Myra Cohn Livingston's "But is it poetry?" in two issues of *The Horn Book*: December 1975, 571–580, and February 1976, 24–31.

Mathews, D. (Ed.). (1981). *Producing award-winning student poets: Tips from successful teachers*. Urbana, IL: National Council of Teachers of English.

Figure 7.11

Excerpts from Nine-Year-Olds' Co-authored Book Modeled on *Puffins Climb, Penguins Rhyme*

Guidelines for Generating Major Types of Expository Writing

Students will be exploring the three major types of expository writing: **description, exposition,** and **persuasion.** The process of composing (not surprisingly) does not significantly differ among these forms, but what the writer focuses on and how he or she organizes and presents the information does change.

Description Description is such a basic component of writing that it's often taken for granted, but its purpose is quite important—it helps the reader construct the appropriate picture or idea. The words must be as precise as the writer can make them. To initiate descriptive writing, have students generate lists of objects, events, or people to describe. Usually these ideas come from assignments students are already writing. Then tap into their senses: vision, hearing, touch, taste, smell. Anything can be described well, regardless of how important or trivial it may seem.

1. Give students these directions: "Brainstorm/cluster whatever words and phrases come to mind as you think about what you wish to describe. Be as free and crazy as you want because by exaggerating you are more likely to capture the real sense of what you're describing. Remember to call upon all your senses; if you are describing how something looks, think also about how it feels to the touch. If you are describing a place, think about the smells in the air when you were there, how the air felt on your skin, and so forth."

2. Then tell them: "You're ready to write!"

When students are comfortable with informational writing, *description* can be extended to include the classic journalists' format—the "5 *W*'s plus 1": *Who, what, when, where, why,* and *how* (Tompkins, 1995).

Exposition Give students these directions:

1. What do you want to explain—how to do something or how a situation has evolved or an event has happened? (For example, what are the steps to follow in making and launching a model rocket? Why does your mother never believe you when you really *are* telling the truth? How did the jam get all over your sister's new shoes?)

2. When you have decided what you want to explain, brainstorm or cluster whatever comes to mind about the "how" or "why." Don't worry about the order of things yet—that will come in the next step.

3. Now decide the order in which you will explain your idea.

4. You're ready to write! Remember that your reader may not have much background information about your topic, so you will want to avoid gaps in your explanation. When you finish your draft, make sure your sentences and paragraphs clearly relate to each other.

Persuasion   Give students these directions:

1. What do you want to have happen that will require agreement and perhaps participation from other people? For example, do you want to get more money for an allowance? Be allowed to ride your bike on busy streets? Raise money for a family whose apartment was destroyed in a fire?

2. Brainstorm or cluster reasons for supporting your request.

3. Now put your reasons in order from strongest to weakest or vice versa.

4. Select one or two reasons and try them out with a partner. In the process write down any additional evidence—details and examples—that you could use to support your argument.

5. You're ready to write.

Keep your audience in mind because this focus will help you select the appropriate words to convince them. For example, is formal, polite language or informal and chatty language more appropriate?

Begin with a paragraph that states your position, follow with a paragraph for each of your major reasons that support the position, and end with a paragraph that summarizes it.

Most of students' expository writing will grow out of our thematic units. In the Thematic Exploration following Chapter 4, for example, primary students developed descriptive pieces about their parents and grandparents. In the Thematic Exploration following Chapter 9, intermediate students investigated questions they themselves had generated at the beginning of the unit. Their decisions about which expository forms to use emerged as they explored resources for information.

We can effectively integrate writing with oral language as well. Keep in mind that *oral* presentations of reports may precede written presentations. The steps for preparing each are quite similar. In each of the progressively more "abstract" steps that follow—from the self, to others, to print resources—the writing process is at work.

A Three-Step Process

1. The student as "expert"   At both primary and intermediate levels, when students first begin writing a composition meant to inform the reader,

AT THE TEACHER'S DESK

IDEAS FOR
EXPOSITORY WRITING

Imitation plays a critical role in learning how to read, write, and respond to informational selections. As students are immersed in reading the following types of expository forms, we can suggest they try some of them in their own expository writing (list adapted from Tchudi & Tchudi, 1983):

Thumbnail sketches:

- famous people

- places

- content ideas

- historical events

"Guess who or what" descriptions

Letters to the editor

Letters to imaginary individuals

Applications

Case studies:

- school problems

- local issues

- national concerns

- historical problems

- scientific issues

Reviews of television programs

Historical "you are there" scenes

Utopian proposals

Practical proposals

Dictionaries and lexicons

Notes of options for the future:

- careers

- employment

- school

- training for the military or public service

Slide-show scripts

Captions for photographs

Memos, dialogues, and conversations

Telegrams

Fact books or fact sheets

writing authorities suggest starting with the students' domain of expertise (Graves, 1983). The use of reference materials can come later. Here's how we can approach the process (adapted from Harste, Short, & Burke, 1989):

◆ Distribute several slips of paper or tagboard slips to each student.

◆ Tell your students that they are all "experts" in something. Ask them each to think of one area where he or she is an expert and to write it on a slip of paper.

◆ Next, tell them to think of other things or ideas that relate to their areas of *expertise* (this may be a good time to teach this word because it's related to *expert*; see Chapter 8). They then write each related idea on a separate piece of paper; each will be a "heading" or "main idea" for the area of expertise.

◆ Ask the students to write ideas and information that will elaborate on their headings on the other cards—one piece of information per card.

◆ The students then arrange the cards sequentially. This ordering may change, and you may actually wish to encourage them to try different orderings until they feel secure with one.

◆ Using the cards as organizational "handles," the students can then write about their area of expertise. The "reports" need not be long; one or two pages will do nicely at first. The development of these compositions can follow the drafting/revision/editing phases of the writing process.

Figure 7.12 shows one "expert's" arrangement of her cards.

2. **Using other resources: Interviews**   An excellent way to help students focus on collecting and gathering information without having to use print resources yet is to rely on *interviews* as a source (see the Thematic Exploration following Chapter 4). The following is a suggested plan for such prewriting and drafting:

◆ Tell students they will be writing an informational composition, but instead of using themselves as experts, they are going to be interviewing other experts on a particular topic. These interviews will be conducted outside of school, so practice in conducting the interview and taking notes is probably advisable first!

◆ Have students brainstorm different topics that they could write about after interviewing someone. Just as with the "self-as-expert" prewriting, they will write topics and related ideas on separate pieces of paper. However, they will use paper of regular size and put the idea at the top.

◆ On each separate sheet of paper, students will list what they already know about the particular idea. Later they will list questions for each idea that represent what they do not know but would like to know. These questions will then be pared down to become the interview questions.

◆ Students then conduct their interviews, taping them if possible, and then transpose the information from them onto their separate sheets. They next organize the sheets sequentially and compose the report, again following the writing process for drafting, revising, and editing.

3. **Using other resources: Print material**   The next step in this progression is using *print material* as resources, so we should have plenty of books on

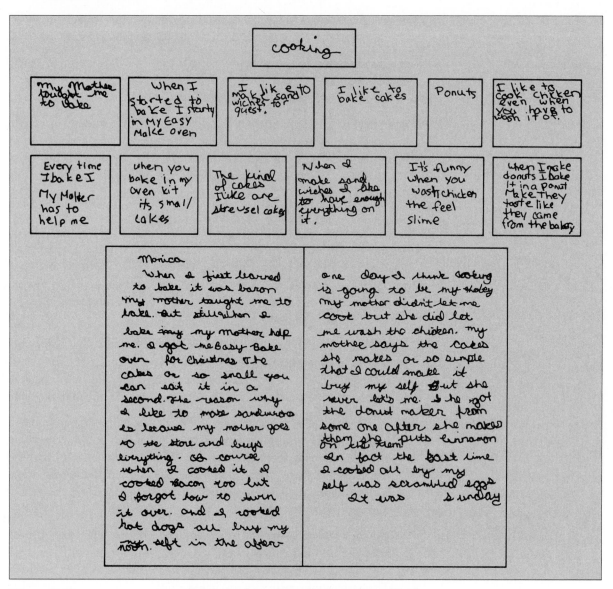

Figure 7.12   **Using Cards to Organize Expository Writing**

SOURCE: Fig. CC12.1, "Notes and Article Using Generating Written Discourse," Jerome C. Harste and Kathy G. Short, *Creating Classrooms for Authors*, p. 271. Reproduced by permission of Heinemann Educational Books, Inc., Portsmouth, NH.

hand in the classroom. The interview strategy will then be modified as follows:

◆ After the students write ideas on separate pieces of paper, the questions they ask will represent what they don't know but want to find out. They now have a purpose for delving into the books for information.

◆ At this stage students will often think that every bit of information that might answer their questions is important and should be written down; here copying could be a problem. Students may copy specific data and facts — for example, the average rainfall in their state — and note the book and page where they found them, but no such direct copying is advised for other information. Instead, students should only write down the source and page number next to their question so they know where to go to find the material again. They will not only save time but will also learn how to paraphrase because they'll remember the information but not the exact wording.

Once again they will organize the information and draft the writing. The use of print resources will be taught and reinforced throughout the intermediate grades, so students will become increasingly knowledgeable about where to go for specific types of information. How to read these books effectively is addressed in Chapter 6.

As students develop as writers of expository pieces and learn to use the basics of word processing programs, they can begin composing multimedia presentations on the computer. These reports will incorporate the students' written texts and their art as well as recorded images and sounds (Grabe & Grabe, 1996). Arranged in a "HyperStacks" program, students' reports can be presented individually or as a group project (see Figure 7.13).

Using Conferences for Writing Instruction in the Integrated Classroom

In conferences the writing of individual students is received, valued, and responded to in a supportive and effective context. Conferencing employs a type of question-response format where the teacher helps the writer identify aspects of his or her writing that could be clarified, expanded, or elaborated. Through this process we are helping students develop and refine their thinking as well. Also, as we'll explore, conferencing is often an excellent context for minilessons. The questions and feedback that make up a large part of student-teacher interaction are instructional in their own right. In turn, conferencing skills can be modeled through a direct teaching format.

Having students conference with each other is also very effective. To help students learn conferencing skills, the teacher models questions that stu-

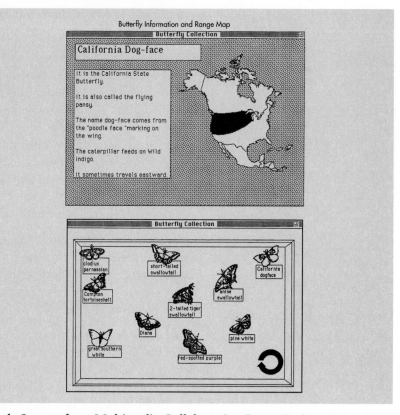

Figure 7.13

Sample Screens from Multimedia Collaborative Group Project

SOURCE: Grabe, M., & Grabe, C. (1996). *Integrating Technology for Meaningful Learning.* Boston: Houghton Mifflin Company.

dents can ask about their own writing and that of their peers. Through sharing one's writing with peers and responding to their questions, a student develops writing competence and a sense of audience. Therefore, many of the "basic skills" of writing—spelling, grammar, and punctuation—are addressed in a context where their use has real meaning and significance.

Conferences or small response groups where individual students' writing is read, appreciated, and commented upon provide important learning experiences. In conferencing the focus is notably not only on developing a more polished piece of writing but also on elaborating and refining students' thinking. A conference is yet another means for facilitating critical thinking.

Vivid understandings and appreciation of the craft of writing most often result after students closely examine their own writing or that of their peers. Conferences, which may be used at any stage in the writing process, are a forum for such close work. This section will present general guidelines for conferencing along with questions that will facilitate students' thinking and revision throughout a composition.

Teachers can model the format of conferencing through the following sequence:

1. Listen as the student reads his or her draft.

2. Focusing on content and then (if necessary) on order, ask questions to probe what the student means, feels, likes best, and finds difficult. Also ask where he or she will go next with the composition. Calkins suggests that the best way to begin is with these simple questions: "How's it going?", "Where are you with this?" or "How can I help you?" (1995).

3. Respond to the students' questions, but do not take over the process.

4. Emphasize only one or two aspects in a single conference.

Our conferences with students may be informal—a word or two here and there to keep things moving along as they write—or formal, when we set aside several minutes to discuss a student's writing individually.

Students' conferences with each other adapt the teacher's basic format (Calkins, 1995; Nathan, Temple, Juntunen, & Temple, 1989). The following student conferencing guidelines are appropriate, beginning with the first draft of a composition:

1. The writer reads his or her composition aloud.

2. The listener(s) respond to the piece. If there are parts that are confusing, listeners may ask questions for clarification.

3. The focus is on the *content* of the writing; responding to questions, the writer elaborates on the content and "teaches" the listener(s) about the topic.

4. Finally, the emphasis returns to the composition itself: "what will the writer do next and how will he or she do it?"

As students conference more with each other and us, their questions seeking feedback and help will become more precise; they will become more aware of what their audience may want or need.

The specific questions that you ask in individual conferences will vary, depending on the student's progress with the composition and its nature and purpose.

Questioning in Teacher-Student Conferences

Most students reach a point in their development as writers where they have a "feel" for whether an idea or topic is worth pursuing. If they decide it isn't, they can put it in their writing folder for possible future use. When

Teacher Questions to Guide Students' Writing

- *Getting the writing "off the ground"*

  How's it going?

  Where are you with this?

  How can I help you?

- *Identifying the central focus of the writing*

  What part is most interesting to you?

  What is the most important thing in this piece?

  How do you feel about this?

  Which idea matters most to you?

  What made you decide to write about this topic?

- *Expanding and elaborating on the writing*

  Tell me more about . . .

  Is that important to add?

  Do you think others might have more questions about this?

  How did you get to this part in your draft?

- *Establishing the sequence of information*

  Did this happen before or after?

  Where could this new idea go?

  Which parts talk about the same thing?

  How might you put these parts together?

  Are there parts you could save for another piece of writing?

  Why did you put these things in this order?

  How about your beginning and/or ending? Are you happy with them? Does your beginning really "grab" your reader?

- *Refining sentences, word choice, and phrasing*

  Could you break this longer sentence into shorter ones?

  How could you combine two or three of these short sentences?

  How would changing this statement into a question work?

(Continued)

Which sentences do the best job of *showing*, not just telling?

How could you *show* instead of *tell* about this?

Could you be more specific here?

What "action" words have you used? Could you use others?

How does this draft sound when you read it out loud?

Show me where I can really tell it's *you* writing this piece.

- *Helping students see their own development as writers*

What did you learn from this piece of writing?

How does this piece compare to others you have written?

What did you try that was new in this draft that you haven't tried before?

students first begin the writing process, however, they need guidance in sustaining a topic or idea long enough to expand, elaborate, and develop it. The questions you ask them in individual conferences, both formal and informal, will provide this guidance. During the first few days or weeks of school, our students will realize that writing is not completed once the first draft is finished. In this sense, we are teaching not only *writing* but also *thinking* through writing.

To compile the list of questions for teacher/student conferences, I have drawn upon those questions suggested by several specialists in the teaching of writing (Calkins, 1995; Graves, 1983; Murray, 1982; Nathan et al., 1989). I've categorized these questions according to six ways in which they direct students' thinking about their writing; because children respond differently to questions, the varied phrasings cited offer different ways of reaching the main objective for each category.

Questioning in Peer Writing Conferences

As students internalize both the procedure for responding in groups and the types of questions we ask in teacher/student conferences, they can better respond to one another's compositions while working in pairs. At this point we can provide guidelines for both authors and responders. At first these should be kept simple, but in time—particularly with older students—they can be expanded. The following are basic guidelines for peer conferences:

Guidelines for Peer Responses

1. Read your draft to your partner.
2. Ask your partner what he or she likes or thinks is interesting about your draft.
3. Read your draft again to your partner.
4. Ask your partner if he or she has any questions about your draft. Your partner may also write down any questions for you.

When our students are more comfortable with the writing process, we can provide additional, more specific questions that they can ask each other. These will reflect the questions we ask in teacher/student conferences as well as whatever particular skill or strategy we may be working on at the time. Some examples follow:

1. Read your draft to your partner.
2. Ask your partner what he or she likes or thinks is interesting about your draft.
3. Ask your partner any one or more of these questions:
   a. Is my lead interesting?
   b. Am I too wordy?
   c. Do you have trouble following me?
   d. What is unclear in my draft?
   e. Do I get off my topic anywhere?
   f. How's my ending?
4. You may discuss these questions with your partner, and/or he or she may write down responses you can use for your revisions.

◆ ◆ ◆

CONCLUDING PERSPECTIVE AND SUMMARY

Writing is a developmental phenomenon. As they grow older, children move beyond understanding the basic differences between spoken and written language; they appreciate and utilize writing as a means of self-expression and self-knowledge as well as a way to comprehend their world better. Through application of the integrated language arts, students master the basic conventions of writing and develop an awareness of audience. They also come to respect the tremendous communicative value of writing.

We teachers must be sensitive to the ramifications of children's developing writing competence. By understanding how children's perceptions of self and the world change as they learn the purposes and conventions of writing, we will be better able to assess what they can accomplish through their writing rather than focus on their shortcomings. We will then be good teachers of writing—and our students will grow as writers, learners, and thinkers.

In this chapter we've addressed the following main points:

◆ Students primarily learn to write by writing rather than by working on discrete skills exercises isolated from a context that is relevant to them.

◆ To develop their writing effectively, students need a supportive learning environment where they can write about what interests and concerns them and can get oral and written feedback from the teacher and their peers at all stages of the writing process.

◆ The components of the writing process are prewriting, drafting, revising, editing, and publishing or sharing.

◆ Writing Workshop is a designated writing period where we can address particular strategies or skills, direct focused activities, discuss students' writing formally and informally, or relate their writing to reading activities or instruction.

◆ Minilessons enable us to model a specific writing strategy or skill or explain the terminology needed to discuss a skill. They can be planned and scheduled or taught as the need for them arises.

◆ We must teach writing by writing ourselves. We can "model" the writing process—show students how we compose—by describing our activities and thoughts during each step of the process. This demonstration will illustrate the time and effort any writer must apply to produce a polished piece of writing.

◆ Journal writing is an effective way to get students to generate writing topics that interest them. It is also a nonthreatening activity that keeps young students writing freely, thus bolstering their confidence in their writing abilities.

◆ Having students study and write poetry can encourage reflection and sensitivity to language. Poetry is also easily incorporated into our teaching of other parts of the curriculum.

◆ Teacher-student and peer conferences help students develop a sense of audience, refine their writing, use their critical thinking skills, and appreciate the craft of writing.

Key Terms

collaborative composition of poetry (p. 265)

conferences (p. 231)

description (p. 272)

drafting (p. 231)

editing (p. 231)

exposition (p. 272)

journal writing (p. 239)

mechanics (p. 237)

modeling (p. 232)

persuasion (p. 272)

prewriting (p. 231)

prewriting activities (p. 240)

publishing (p. 231)

revising (p. 231)

sharing (p. 231)

word processor (p. 257)

the writing process (p. 230)

Writing Workshop (p. 231)

CHAPTER 8

Exploring Words: Vocabulary and Spelling in Context

- What principles should guide our vocabulary instruction?

- Why are "word sorts" so effective for developing word knowledge?

- What are some important categories of language use, and how can they support the development of vocabulary?

- How should we teach students about prefixes, suffixes, base words, and word roots?

- What are the characteristics of the stages of spelling knowledge? What features of words should students examine at each of these stages?

- How can spelling knowledge support the learning of vocabulary? How can vocabulary knowledge support the learning of spelling?

◆ ◆ ◆ **INTRODUCTION**

"A word," the Russian psychologist Lev Vygotsky once wrote, "is a microcosm of human consciousness." The poet and teacher Georgia Heard observed that "a word is like a geode: rough and ordinary on the outside, hiding a whole world of sparkling beauty inside" (1989, p. 74). Words — what they suggest to us, how they sound and feel, and how they look — offer much to children. In this chapter we'll learn how to engage students in interesting and meaningful word exploration.

Just about all young children delight in playing with language and words. In previous chapters we have discussed ways teachers can help channel this natural interest by encouraging children to think about and reflect on the language they read and write. This chapter will address this exploration in terms of words themselves and of the underlying concepts they represent. We will examine vocabulary and spelling together because knowledge about *word meaning*, *word structure*, and the relationships between the meaning of words and their structure share common roots. As we consider how children become familiar with vocabulary and spelling, we will see how these common roots can be extended and elaborated. There are two important points to keep in mind as we explore instruction and learning at the primary (grades K–3) and intermediate (grades 4–6) levels:

◆ Knowledge of vocabulary and spelling underlies the efficiency with which students read and write.

◆ Vocabulary and spelling are two sides of the same knowledge coin: knowledge about vocabulary helps spelling development, and knowledge of spelling will help expand vocabulary.

Principles for Learning and Teaching Vocabulary in the Integrated Classroom

In referring to vocabulary development, Nagy (1988) suggested that learning occurs both *incidentally* and *directly*; this observation applies to *spelling* development as well. That is, much of students' knowledge about words will occur through wide and frequent reading as well as through informal wordplay and word exploration. "Increasing the volume of students' reading is the single most important thing teachers can do to promote large-

If we establish an environment that facilitates students' exploration of words, they will develop a lifelong interest and curiosity about words and how they're used.

scale vocabulary growth" (Nagy, 1988, p. 32). The next most important aspect is the teacher's direct role in facilitating and encouraging students' explorations.

Fundamentally, vocabulary development can be considered in terms of **elaboration**, the growth of existing concepts associated with particular words, and **expansion**, the development of new concepts and the new vocabulary that represents them. Several researchers have outlined principles for teaching vocabulary (Baumann & Kameenui, 1991; Beck & McKeown, 1991; Stahl, 1986). Essentially these principles embody the following fundamentals:

◆ Word study should be integrated with prior knowledge and with learning in the content areas.

◆ Word study should involve intensive, "deep" study of *some* words, involving many exposures to the words in *meaningful* contexts, both in and out of texts.

◆ Teachers should engage in direct teaching or modeling, talking explicitly about word meaning and structure.

◆ Students should be actively involved in instruction; an important side effect of this involvement is the development of favorable attitudes toward words and word learning.

◆ Students should be taught strategies for learning new words independently.

◆ Teachers should introduce words in meaning "families" so that semantic and structural relationships among the words are made explicit.

These principles are clearly more applicable at the intermediate-grade levels and beyond, when students' cognitive development has advanced to the point where they can explicitly deal with increasing conceptual abstraction. Nonetheless, you will see aspects of these principles at work in much word study at the primary level as well. When most children first come to school, they know lots of concepts and the spoken words for them, but they don't know the printed forms that represent these words. Therefore, at the primary-grade level a strong emphasis is placed on developing students' *sight vocabularies*—words they can identify immediately in print (Chapter 6). This emphasis in instruction begins to shift as children move to the intermediate grades (4–6), when their reading vocabularies typically become larger than their oral vocabularies and when their reading becomes increasingly more fluent. At that point, although sight vocabulary will continue to develop, the emphasis in vocabulary instruction will be on elaborating and expanding *meaning* vocabulary.

Vocabulary Development in the Primary Grades

Beginning at the primary-grade levels, children become consciously able to step back from language. They are becoming more **metalinguistically aware**—and can think about the *form* of language as well as its *meaning*. These grade levels can be a marvelous time for language play (Geller, 1985). Such play increases children's sensitivity to and understanding of words and word structure. This growing sensitivity in turn provides an important part of the background knowledge so critically important for developing literacy (see Chapter 6). As we now know, this knowledge includes the information encoded in writing itself—letter/sound relationships and vocabulary knowledge—as well as knowledge of grammatical structure, or *syntax*.

This section will focus on how primary-grade students develop meanings for new words and suggest some teaching applications. Primary students should develop a vocabulary that is conceptually solid and rich based on

◆ the oral language that surrounds them

◆ the written language brought to life through read-alouds

◆ the concrete examination of the here-and-now world of six-, seven-, and eight-year-olds.

Reading, writing, and examining words and word structure will help develop essential sight vocabulary, which in turn helps make reading and writing more fluent and rewarding.

Elaborating and Expanding Conceptual Development in the Integrated Classroom

Chapter 2 noted that the best way to elaborate and expand conceptual development is through meaningful experiences that are examined through purposeful and relevant discussion. For primary students everyday surroundings offer the best potential for concept development. Once children examine existing, familiar concepts and begin to elaborate them, they will be better able to grasp firmly new information, concepts, and the words that represent them. Vygotsky (1987) noted how "everyday" concepts can be learned rather informally, but more "abstract" concepts require a teacher who can facilitate their acquisition. Once children understand additional abstract concepts, they are able to reorganize their conceptual foundations underlying everyday concepts. *Dogs, cows,* and *people* come to be understood as "mammals," and once children realize this, they quite literally think differently about dogs and cows!

As they move from the familiar to the new, children rely on pictures, films, and—as much as possible—on reading and writing. They also rely on the teacher's modeling of language in general and vocabulary in particular. For example, when children are examining familiar objects in a first-grade classroom, our language will direct them to consider features that they perhaps noted only tacitly before; now they have a conceptual frame that we label with a new word and reinforce over the succeeding days. A common goldfish, for example, becomes a vehicle for talking about how different creatures breathe; once the children learn that those undulating flaps on its side are called "gills," they can use the term several times during their discussion of the fish.

Teachers should also combine **hands-on experiences** with observation. In exploring new areas with primary students, we should rely on concrete experiences whenever possible. For example:

◆ In *math* we can use real objects to illustrate the processes of combining and separating and discuss familiar terms before introducing new terms and old terms used in different ways—such as *addition*, *subtraction*, or even *sets*, *borrowing*, or *trading*.

◆ In *science* we can begin with autumn leaves or the idea of cooler temperatures before we describe how the Earth's annual trip around the sun and its tilt along its axis cause our seasons.

◆ In *geography* we can construct maps of the classroom (complete with a "scale of measurement") before we ask students to map their houses, neighborhoods, and other parts of their world, incorporating all along the way the new map-related concepts and vocabulary that become essential for representing each new domain.

In the primary grades we should also talk about words "for their own sake," showing our students that we enjoy words and find them interesting and often humorous. Looking puzzled, we might wonder aloud, "Have you ever really thought about an *eggplant*? Surely it can't be made of eggs, and yet . . ." Many of our read-alouds can be from the rhyming, songlike verses that illustrate the type of wordplay—often nonsensical—that young children enjoy (see list on pp. 191–192 in Chapter 6).

Developing Vocabulary and Concepts Through "Word Sorts"

Playing with words and ideas in the classroom context just described lays the groundwork for children to explore and learn about *written* words. Specific exploration of sight vocabulary, corresponding concepts, and knowledge about word structure can most effectively occur through **word sorts** (Bear et al., 1996; Henderson, 1990). In this section we will see how this word-categorization technique can elaborate concepts while incidentally reinforcing the learning of sight words.

Word-sort activities were briefly mentioned in Chapter 6 as a type of word-bank activity. The format for word sorts is fairly standard throughout the grades; what will change is *how* the words are sorted. There are two types of word sorts: *closed* and *open*. In **closed word sorts** the teacher determines the category labels. In **open word sorts** the students decide what the categories will be, determine the criteria, and sort accordingly. When we first introduce word sorts, we begin with *closed* sorts because students learn the fundamentals of the sorting process more easily when we provide the labels for them.

Build   Your
T e a c h i n g
R e s o u r c e s

BOOKS ABOUT
WORDS FOR
PRIMARY STUDENTS

Barrett, J. (1983). *A snake is totally tail*. New York: Atheneum.

Burns, M. (1981). *The hink pink book*. Boston: Little, Brown.

Degen, B. (1983). *Jamberry*. New York: Harper.

Houget, S. (1983). *I unpacked my grandmother's trunk: A picture book game*. New York: Dutton.

Juster, N. (1982). *Otter nonsense*. New York: Philomel Books.

Maestro, G. (1984). *What's a frank Frank? Tasty homograph riddles*. New York: Clarion.

Merriam, E. (1993). *Quiet, please*. New York: Simon & Schuster. [Illustrated by S. Hamanaka.]

Most, B. (1980). *There's an ant in Anthony*. New York: Clarion.

Most, B. (1991). *A dinosaur named after me*. San Diego: Harcourt.

The Classroom Example on the following page is an example of a closed word sort with first-graders.

After your students understand the format for sorting according to a single category, you may suggest that they include another column or category for words that don't seem to fit—a "leftover" or "miscellaneous" category. This allows a "safety valve" for uncertainty. For example, on another occasion when the first-graders were sorting according to the categories "big" and "little," Michael put one of his word-bank words, *hyena*, in the leftover column. Although he knew that a hyena was an animal and had seen a picture of it, he was uncertain about its size.

Critical thinking is going on during these sorts—about the words and concepts they represent. The students must keep the criteria for one or more categories in mind and must justify their sorts in discussion afterwards. They also see that other students may have sorted the same words differently and will learn why. For example, Jeremy's explanation for categorizing *tank* as something "small" was that he had several small toy tanks at home.

When students do *open* word sorts, the categories and criteria are up to the students. In such instances, students can play "Guess My Category," which is much like the game "Twenty Questions": once students have sorted their words individually, they can pair up and question each other, attempting to guess the category label. Primary students familiar with word-sort techniques can become quite good at this game! Once again, the value is in the discussion generated and in the type of thinking that is going on. Short of actually handling or experiencing the objects represented by words, in word sorts students are engaged in the active manipulation of concepts. This is why word-sort activities are such powerful learning experiences.

The teacher has the children dump out 10 to 15 word cards from their word banks, arrange them in one or two columns for easy reading, and then search them with specific criteria in mind. For example, the teacher says, "Kids, let's look for words that have to do with *big* things. The words can either stand for big things themselves or have to do with something that is big."

The words that Nathan is working with are *tank, wastebasket, bear, kangaroo, broom, mouse, book, speck, hat, zoo, green, messy, the,* and *happy.* He selects the following as words he associates with "big":

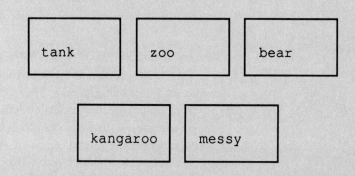

After Nathan and the other students have selected words they believe fit in the category, the teacher asks each student why he or she chose particular words. Curious about Nathan's inclusion of *messy,* she first asks him about *tank* and then about *messy.* He explains that his mother always tells him he makes the biggest messes of anyone she's ever seen, "and *messy* has to do with messes!"

Vocabulary Development in the Intermediate Grades

Learning How the Structure of Words Represents Meaning

Vocabulary and spelling become even more closely connected in the intermediate grades and beyond. By learning about word elements (*morphemes*) and the ways in which they combine to create the meaning of a word, students build a foundation for independent word learning. This knowledge is termed **morphemic** or **structural analysis**. **Morphemes** are the smallest units of meaning in a word: prefixes, suffixes, bases, and word roots. Let's look more closely at the overall processes by which morphemes or word elements combine to form words.

◆ First, we will examine how the meanings of individual words combine to create the meaning of a new, compound word.

◆ Next, we will explore the basic processes in which prefixes and suffixes attach to **base words**. Once your students know how **prefixes** and **suffixes** work with base words, they will have a strong foundation for learning how these processes work with word roots.

◆ Finally, we explore **word roots**—word parts that usually cannot stand alone as words.

Morphemic Elements

Prefixes   Many students are ready to begin studying simple prefixes in the latter part of third grade. These prefixes include *re-* ("again"), *un-* ("not"), and *im-* or *in-* ("not"). These prefixes represent *opposites* or the *repeating* or *undoing* of an action. Although *re-* and *im-* or *in-* do not always have a single meaning, they occur so frequently with these meanings that it is wise to begin with them. The meanings of other prefixes that are invariant are usually too abstract to use when first presenting prefixes.

Suffixes   Once they understand a few simple prefixes, students can examine simple suffixes. Although their effect does not usually seem as dramatic as that of prefixes, suffixes serve heavy duty in the English language. Often students can appreciate the study of them more if we point out that it otherwise takes several words to express an idea that a suffix can represent:

> Instead of having to say "an individual who is skilled in geology," we can express the same idea by simply adding a suffix to *geology* and referring to a *geologist*.

> Instead of having to say "a smaller set of dining furniture," we can use *dinette*.

> Instead of having to describe "the state of being puzzled," we can use *puzzlement*.

As we will explore, we can reinforce this appreciation by having students categorize words that share the same suffix and infer its probable meaning. As with simple prefixes, it's good to begin with suffixes that mean "the opposite." For primary students, *-less* ("without") fills the bill quite well. By noting the effect *-less* has when affixed to base words such as *aim*, *child*, *hope*, and *dream*, students can usually come up with the meaning of *-less* on their own. They can also examine the effects of the suffixes *-ly* ("like" as in awkward*ly* and bad*ly*) and *-ness* ("condition" as in sick*ness* and kind*ness*).

Meaning families form an important aspect of learning vocabulary. A meaning family is a group of words that is derived from the same base word—for example, *handed*, *handing*, *handful*, *handle*, and *handmade*. We can begin exploring them when we show students how several words can be derived from base words. The *Teacher's Sourcebook* presents the most frequently occurring prefixes and several of the most frequently occurring suffixes, in addition to affixes that occur less frequently but whose meanings are stable enough to allow productive exploration.

Word Roots   Word roots are important meaning-bearing word elements that come from Latin or Greek; they usually cannot stand alone as words.

Exploration of roots is based on students' understanding of how simple affixes combine with base words. When we begin word-root study, we select

---

CLASSROOM EXAMPLE

Minilesson: Developing an Awareness of Word Roots

We've chosen the word root *-spect-* ("to look") and the example words *spectator*, *inspect*, and *spectacles*. After we list the words on the board, here's how our discussion might go with fourth- and fifth-graders.

TEACHER: "Kids, let's talk about these words for a minute. The first thing we're going to do is discuss what each of them means. Okay, what's a *spectator*? Lianne?"

LIANNE: "That's someone who watches something, like a game."

TEACHER: "Okay! Thank you—now how about *inspect*? Garrett?"

GARRETT: "It's like when you check something real close for a problem, or maybe you're a detective and you're inspecting something."

TEACHER: "All right. Now for our last one, *spectacles*. You don't hear this one much anymore, but you run across it in your reading sometimes. Yes, Danny?"

DANNY: "Spectacles are like glasses you wear; it's an old word for glasses."

TEACHER: "Good! Now these words all have something in common—does it have anything to do with their meaning?" [She lets several seconds pass.]

(Continued)

LIANNE: "Well, they all talk about seeing something or how you see . . . and they've got letters that are the same."

TEACHER: "Okay! Do you think that these letters — *spect* — could have anything to do with *seeing*?"

A few more seconds pass, then murmurs of "Yeah, they could!" are audible. Looking around the group of students and nodding, the teacher confirms this: "Absolutely! These letters, *spect*, all stand for the same meaning, actually 'to look.' This part that is the same in all of these words is called a word *root*, and it is a part of our language that came from Latin. So *spect* means 'to look,' and when you see it in a word, it will usually have this same meaning.

"Let's look at a couple of our words to see how the root *spect* works with the rest of the word. In *spectator*, the suffix *-ator* actually means 'one who does something,' so the word literally means 'one who looks.' *Inspect* has the prefix *in-* — in this case meaning 'into' — so this word literally means 'to look into.'"

Students could also experiment with additional possibly unknown words: *retrospect, spectacular, respect, circumspect, spectrum*. Since these words are not so concrete, the students may have to check their hypotheses about their meanings by referring to the dictionary.

It's critical that students understand how roots and affixes work together to create the meaning of words. After studying *-tract-* ("to pull"), for example, we can ask students, "If you *retract* something that you've said, what do you do?" Then we can explore the longer word, *retraction*, on the board:

"Let's cover the prefix *re-*, and what do we have left? Right, *traction*. Now let's cover the suffix *-ion*, and what is our word root? Right again — *tract*. We've learned it means 'to pull,' so when we add *-ion* again, we've got 'the process of pulling.' Now put *re-* back on, and we've got 'the process of pulling back.' The word appears in this sentence: 'The paper promised to publish a retraction.' This means they've printed erroneous information, so they have to 'pull back' what they said."

Usually a few "walk-throughs" of this sort will cue most intermediate students to the way words work. It pays, as we've noted, to begin by analyzing common words and then to move to unfamiliar words that contain the same element.

a frequently occurring root to focus on and list several words the students know that share this root (see *Teacher's Sourcebook*). The meaning of the root should be clear as it functions in each of the words. As with base words, we can see how "meaning families" grow from word roots as well.

Talking about word roots, as in the preceding Classroom Example, helps set the stage for students to figure out the meanings of word roots on their own. Our underlying purpose in learning about word roots is to establish a "feel" for word roots as significant elements of words. This understanding will support the learning of many roots and help students recognize new words as they read. As they explore roots, students develop an appreciation for the origin and use of words. (The *Teacher's Sourcebook*, pp. 473–532, can serve as a resource when you prepare activities involving word roots.) The following are two strategies for facilitating students' exploration of how affixes and word roots combine:

◆ Use a *visual schematic*. Such a schematic is the beginning "word-root web" illustrated in Figure 8.1. Based on the root *-spect-*, the word root web demonstrates at a glance the "generative" power of applying knowledge of word combinations, in this case a root and several different affixes.

◆ *Word building* with word roots and affixes can be reinforced easily yet enjoyably through combining word parts and discovering how many

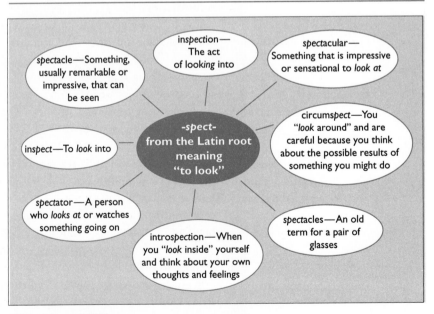

Figure 8.1   "Word-Root" Web

real words can be created. This can be done in a two- or three-column format:

Prefix	Word Root	Suffix
re	dict	ic
pre	tract	ion
sub	gress	able/ible
contra	port	er/or
im	phon	ably
in	spect	ful
un	press	ation
trans	ject	

As students get caught up in playing with these important structural elements, they will discover that it is possible to generate words that do not exist in English but that *could* exist; for example, "transpectable" and "intractation." Also, if we have the word *respectful*, why can't we have "predictful" or "suspectful" — or, for that matter, "constructment," "observement," or "puzzleation"? While these "words" may cause chuckles, they also provide excellent practice in combining word elements.

Table 8.1 presents a sequence for introducing and exploring the most common structural or morphemic elements. A more comprehensive list of morphemic elements is presented in the *Sourcebook*.

Applying Word Knowledge in Context

In the intermediate years students will encounter unfamiliar words as they read. These words will be one of two types: 1) words with which the students *are* familiar if they hear them; and 2) words with which the students are unfamiliar in *both* reading and speech. These words will need to be examined through *syllabication*, *morphemic analysis*, and some *context clues*.

Syllabication refers to dividing a word into syllables, pronouncing each syllable, then blending the syllables back together to see if an unfamiliar word sounds like one the reader already knows. Because so many unfamiliar words have not been previously encountered, however, *morphemic analysis* plays a critical role. It involves examining a word in order to locate the *morphemes*, which are the smallest units of meaning in a word (*prefix*, *suffix*, *base word* or a *word root*), and then determining the word's meaning based on the combination of the meanings of the morphemes.

TABLE 8.1	Morphemic Elements That May Be Examined in the Intermediate Grades		

Fourth-Grade Level	*Simple Prefixes + Base*		
	un-	*not*	*un*lock
	dis-	*not*	*dis*pleased
	non-	*not*	*non*fiction
	in-	*not*	*in*active
	re-	*again, back*	*re*apply
	mis-	*bad, wrong, incorrect*	*mis*lead, *mis*inform

	Base + Simple Suffixes		
	-ion/-tion/ -ation/ition	*state of, characterized by action*	perfec*tion*, examin*ation*, compe*tition*
	-able/-ible	*capable of, like*	lik*able*, incred*ible*
	-ous	*having*	courage*ous*

Fifth-Grade Level and Beyond	*More Simple Prefixes + Base*		
	uni-	*one*	*uni*cycle
	bi-	*two*	*bi*cycle
	tri-	*three*	*tri*angle
	en-, em-	*make*	*en*able, *em*power
	pre-	*before*	*pre*view
	de-	*opposite of*	*de*salt
	inter-	*between, among*	*inter*national
	con-, com-	*with*	*con*struct ("build *with*"), *com*press ("force *with*")
	trans-	*across, over*	*trans*port ("carry *across*")
	anti-	*against*	*anti*pollution, *anti*freeze
	dis-	*opposite*	*dis*union

	Base + Simple Suffixes		
	-al	*having to do with*	coast*al*
	-ness	*condition*	prompt*ness*
	-ity	*condition*	prosper*ity*
	-ment	*action, process of*	govern*ment*
	-ful	*full of, like*	grace*ful*
	-less	*without*	shame*less*
	-logy	*study of*	bio*logy*

TABLE 8.1 (continued)	**Morphemic Elements That May Be Examined in the Intermediate Grades**					
Fifth-Grade Level and Beyond	*Greek Roots*			*Latin Roots*		
	graph	*write*	tele*graph*	spec	*look*	ins*pec*t
	micro	*small*	*micro*scope	vid/vis	*see*	*video/vision*
	photo	*light*	*photo*graph	aud	*hear*	*aud*itory
	bio	*life*	*bio*logy	tract	*pull*	*tract*or
	tele	*distant*	*tele*graph	rupt	*break*	inter*rupt*
	hydro	*water*	*hydro*electric	struct	*build*	con*struct*
	phon	*sound*	tele*phon*e	port	*carry*	trans*port*
	scop	*watch*	peri*scop*e	dict	*say*	*dict*ation
	auto	*self*	*auto*graph	fract	*break*	*fract*ure

SOURCE: Adapted from Templeton, S. (1995) *Children's Literacy: Contexts for Meaningful Learning.* Boston: Houghton Mifflin. Reproduced by permission.

Following is the *strategy* for analyzing an unfamiliar word during reading.

Expand Your Teaching Repertoire

Analyzing Unfamiliar Words

1 *If the word is an important word*, go back and think about the overall *context* as well as looking for meaningful parts and applying *syllabication*.

2 Look for known base words, prefixes, suffixes, and roots—Does the base or root look like any other words you know?

3 Sound the word out: divide it into syllables, pronounce them, then blend them together.

If the word is still unknown:

4 Ask someone or check the dictionary.

5 Try the meaning you've found back in the context of your reading.

(Continued)

Expand Your Teaching Repertoire

When we help students learn how to analyze a word to determine its meaningful parts, we should teach this strategy:

◆ First, take away any prefixes.

◆ Next, take away any suffixes.

◆ Finally, see what's left. Is it a base word or word root? Do you know its meaning? Does it look like any other words that you know? Put the word back together, paying attention primarily to the combination of the meaning of the base or root together with the meaning of the prefix.

Here's how it looks with specific words:

unfailing	reinvestment
failing	investment
fail	invest
failing	investment
unfailing	reinvestment

Changing Word Meanings

Even in the primary grades, students can get a sense of how the meanings of particular words in English have changed over the centuries. Explore with students the effects of language change as a result of migration, war, and technological advance (Dale, O'Rourke, & Bamman, 1971). Tompkins and Yaden (1986) suggest that you give students a list of words and have them research what they once meant; intermediate students can classify the changes as language scholars would.

Over time, the change of meaning for specific words can occur through the following four processes:

1. **Specialization**   **Specialization** narrows the meaning of a word. For example, *cattle* once referred to any group of four-legged animals. Similarly, *deer* originally referred to any four-legged animal. *Corpse* once referred to any body, alive or dead.

2. **Generalization**   The opposite of specialization, **generalization** extends the meaning of words. For example, *lady* once referred only to the wife of a lord. *Ghetto* was originally the part of a city where Jews lived; it now means an area of a city, usually economically depressed, where any group

may be restricted. Brand names quite often become generalized: *kleenex* now is used to refer to all tissues of a similar form and purpose, regardless of the manufacturer.

3. **Elevation**   Words that at one time had quite ordinary meanings have often come to mean something more exalted or **elevated** with the passing of the years. *Knight* once meant a boy, but later came to refer to one who served—often in a military capacity—a lord or king. *Mansion* once referred to a farmhouse; *angels* were simply messengers. *Nice* once meant stupid or foolish.

4. **Degeneration**   The opposite of elevation is **degeneration**. Many words that once had a more positive meaning now have a negative meaning or connotation. *Silly* once had a positive connotation, meaning "happy, prosperous, and blessed"; a *villain* was once merely a servant on a farm. *Stink* originally meant simply "to rise up"! *Temper* could at one time refer to any state of mind, but now it has a negative connotation, specifically of anger.

Diversity in Speech and Vocabulary: Regional and Social Variation

I began my teaching career in rural Virginia. I taught first grade, and it wasn't long before the children told me I "talked funny." They were right, of course. I had grown up in suburban Southern California; they were growing up in the rural South. As we saw in Chapters 2 and 4, *dialects* account for this type of speech difference. But dialects also have different words for different things—and even speakers of so-called "standard" American English in different regions of the country often use different words and expressions. For example:

Is that large sandwich you eat called a *hoagie, submarine*, or *grinder*?

Do you *look like* or *take after* your mother?

Do you shop for food at a *grocery, super market*, or *store*?

Do you get a drink of water at a *cooler, bubbler*, or *drinking fountain*?

It is both instructive and interesting for students to explore the different words for familiar objects and actions. Much of the literature for children uses regional and social dialects.

Presenting and Reinforcing Content-Related Vocabulary

It is essential that we teach some words *intensively*. In the Thematic Exploration following Chapter 9, Tamara chose words that would likely need to

Build Your
Teaching
Resources

**BOOKS ABOUT
WORD ORIGINS
AND WORDPLAY**

BOOKS FOR TEACHERS

Ayers, D. (1986). *English words from Latin and Greek elements* (2nd ed.). Tucson: University of Arizona Press.

Bear, D., Invernizzi, M., & Templeton, S. (1996). *Words their way: Word study for phonics, vocabulary, and spelling instruction.* Englewood Cliffs, NJ: Merrill/Prentice-Hall. (see especially Chapter 8)

Clairborne, R. (1988). *The roots of English.* New York: Time-Life Books.

Dale, E., O'Rourke, J., & Bamman, H. (1971). *Techniques of teaching vocabulary.* Palo Alto, CA: Field Educational Enterprises.

Davies, P. (1981). *Roots: Family histories of familiar words.* New York: McGraw-Hill.

Funk, W. (1954). *Word origins and their romantic stories.* New York: Grosset and Dunlap.

Laird, H., & Laird, C. (1957). *The tree of language.* Cleveland, OH: World.

Partridge, E. (1991). *Origins: A short etymological dictionary of modern English.* New York: Random House.

Robinson, S. (1989). *Origins.* (2 vols). New York: Teachers and Writers Collaborative. (Vol. 1: Bringing words to life; Vol. 2: The word families)

Schliefer, R. (1995). *Grow your vocabulary by learning the roots of English words.* New York: Random House.

Tompkins, G., & Yaden, D., Jr. (1986). *Answering students' questions about words.* Urbana, IL: National Council of Teachers of English.

Watkins, C. (1987). *American heritage dictionary of Indo-European roots.* Boston: Houghton Mifflin.

BOOKS FOR INTERMEDIATE STUDENTS

Asimov, I. (1961). *Words from the myths.* Boston: Houghton Mifflin.

Asimov, I. (1968). *Words from history.* Boston: Houghton Mifflin.

Burningham, J. (1984). *Skip trip.* New York: Viking. (See also several other titles by Burningham, all published by Viking.)

Cox, J. (1980). *Put your foot in your mouth and other silly sayings.* New York: Random House.

Davidson, J. (1972). *Is that Mother in the bottle? Where language came from and where it is going.* New York: Franklin Watts.

Hall, R. (1984). *Sniglets.* New York: Macmillan.

Hazen, B. (1979). *Last, first, middle and nick: All about names.* Englewood Cliffs, NJ: Prentice Hall.

Juster, N. (1961). *The phantom tollbooth.* New York: Random House.

Lambert, E., & Pei, M. (1959). *The book of place names.* New York: Lothrop, Lee and Shepard.

(*Continued*)　**Pickles, C., & Meynell, L.** (1971). *The beginning of words: How English grew.* New York: G. P. Putnam's Sons.

Sarnoff, J., & Ruffins, R. (1981). *Words.* New York: Scribner's.

Spier, P. (1971). *Gobble, growl, grunt.* Garden City, NY: Doubleday.

Terban, M. (1983). *In a pickle and other funny idioms.* New York: Clarion.

Terban, M. (1987). *Mad as a wet hen! and other funny idioms.* New York: Clarion.

Terban, M. (1988). *Guppies in tuxedos: Funny eponyms.* New York: Clarion.

Wolk, A. (1980). *Everyday words from names of people and places.* New York: Elsevier/Nelson Books.

be taught directly and intensively. She followed these steps when selecting the words:

◆ First, look for words that are central to the major concepts and understandings in the reading selection or the unit.

◆ Next, consider these words in relation to several factors — particular students' background and pre-existing word knowledge and the text's presentation of the words. The meanings of some centrally important and unknown words often are sufficiently addressed in the text. Even for these words, however, follow up *after* the reading to make sure students really understand them.

◆ Finally, focus the preteaching on the remaining important and unknown words — those for which context alone is not full or rich enough.

In order to help students learn these new words, which are really new *concepts* for the students, we can link our preteaching to a number of other activities (Nagy, 1988; Nelson-Herber, 1986). The following Expand Your Teaching Repertoire considers the most effective of these activities.

Expand Your Teaching Repertoire

Structured overview　Words may be presented in a "hierarchical" format; a linear format may also be appropriate if the terms reflect a causal relationship, as in a science or history unit (Marzano & Marzano, 1988; Nagy, 1988). The following is an example for a unit dealing with the *flora* and *fauna* of Australia. The overview shown in Figure 8.2 presents the fauna; the teacher has added terms the students already know in order to provide clear organization.

(*Continued*)

Expand Your Teaching Repertoire

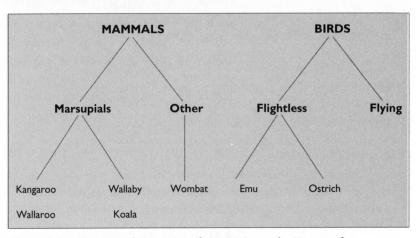

Figure 8.2   Structured Overview for a Unit on the Fauna of
Australia—New Words Intermingled with Familiar Ones

Based on this structured overview and the students' existing word knowledge, we can engage the students in general or small-group discussion.
Usually the discussion will focus on how the words are alike or different,
structurally as well as semantically. In this case the new terms are *marsupials* and probably almost all of the animal names except *kangaroo* and
ostrich. We can begin by discussing the kangaroo, describing its characteristics and suggesting that these might provide clues to the characteristics of the other marsupials. Students may notice the spelling features
shared by *wallaroo* and *wallaby*, and perhaps *wallaroo* and *kangaroo*.
This similarity can lead to a discussion about the *spellings* as clues to the
relationships among these three animals—probably accompanied by
pictures of the animals.

2   **Word map**   This type of graphic array combines definition, features,
and examples in a manner that supports students' understanding. As the
example in Figure 8.3 shows, we put the term and its definition at the
center. To the right, we list the most important features or attributes of
the word, and underneath we list examples.

   The next two activities are beneficial when students are partially familiar with most of the terms and may also be used for follow-up in later
instruction.

(*Continued*) ## Expand Your Teaching Repertoire

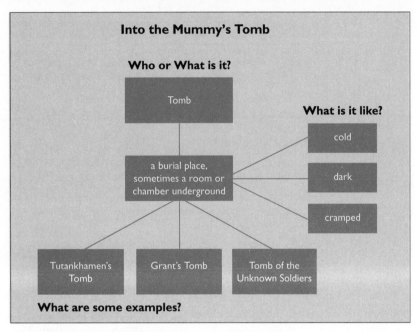

Figure 8.3 Word Map

3 **Semantic maps** Constructing a *semantic map* (Heimlich & Pittelman, 1986) is quite similar to the process involved in developing the Prereading Plan (PReP) we discussed in Chapter 6. The major differences are that with semantic mapping you use a specific visual representation (cluster or "map") and introduce new terms. To illustrate this activity, let's take a look at how it might be used by a sixth-grade teacher exploring a unit based on William Pène du Bois' *The Twenty-One Balloons* (1947).

a. *Brainstorming* Using the term *volcanoes*, students suggest words that come to mind, and the teacher writes these on the board.

b. *Categorization* After drawing an oval and writing *volcanoes* in it, the teacher involves the students in a discussion about how their suggested words can be categorized; each category represents one branch on the map (see Figure 8.4).

c. *Teacher-added terms* These are words that will be important in the upcoming study but that were not suggested by the students. The teacher places them in the appropriate category. This categorization orients students' understanding of the new terms (for example, *tidal wave* goes under characteristics of eruptions). In Figure 8.4 these new terms are indicated in parentheses.

Expand Your Teaching Repertoire

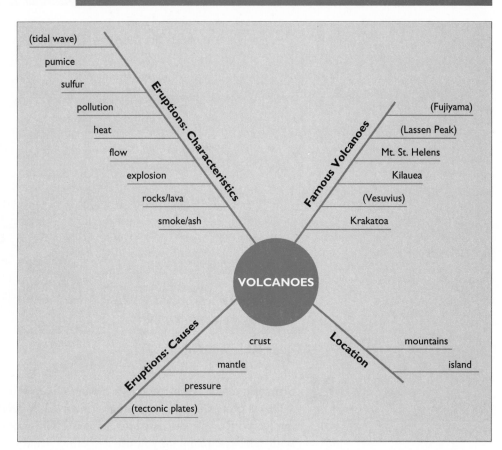

Figure 8.4 A Semantic Map Combining Familiar Terms Brainstormed by Sixth-Grade Students with New Terms (in Parentheses) Added by the Teacher

As with several other activities we have discussed, semantic mapping stimulates students' prior knowledge about the concepts or topic/theme to be explored. It also affords us the opportunity to determine how much the students already know.

4 **Semantic feature analysis** This analysis (Anders & Bos, 1986; Johnson & Pearson, 1984) allows students to examine how concepts relate to each other—whether in a semantic map, structured overview, or PReP (see Chapter 6). As with any categorization activity, this involves noting comparisons and contrasts among the words/concepts. Figure 8.5 illus-

(*Continued*) **Expand Your Teaching Repertoire**

trates a semantic feature analysis for specific volcanoes. Develop the analysis in this manner:

- Write the specific features of volcanoes across the top of the grid and the target words (in this case, names of volcanoes) down the left-hand margin. When we first introduce this activity, we should list these features ourselves so that students can concentrate on the analysis. Later we can involve them in generating the features.

- Discuss the matrix with the whole class or in small groups. The students will use the following symbols to complete each cell: a plus sign (+) indicates a definite relationship between the specific volcano and a feature; a minus sign (−) indicates the absence of the feature for

	On a Continent	On an Island	Explosive	Active	Extinct	Dormant
Fujiyama	−	−	?	?	?	?
Lassen Peak	+	−	?	−	−	+
Mt. St. Helens	+	−	+	+	−	−
Kilauea	−	+	−	+	−	−
Vesuvius	−	+	+	?	−	?
Krakatoa	−	+	+	+	−	−

Figure 8.5 Semantic Feature Analysis

(Continued)

that volcano; a question mark (?) indicates that more information is needed before responding.

◆ After the students complete the matrix as best they can, we point out that (1) they now realize how much they already knew about these volcanoes, and (2) they also know what they still need to find out.

If most of the analysis is complete, we can point out that the matrix now provides them with a quick means for differentiating the volcanoes: all they have to do is look down any column to see how one volcano differs from the next. To quickly summarize the features of each volcano, they can simply read across each row.

The words we select for direct teaching must be reinforced in ways that require the students to *use* the words rather than simply to identify their meanings. After we have introduced these words in a meaningful context, as we have just discussed, the next two activities will reinforce new words in productive ways.

5 **Word association** Given a group of new words, students decide which one belongs with a target word they already know. For example, you could ask, "Which of our new words goes with the word *movement*?" (The words are *dormant*, *tectonic plates*, *inactive*, and *Vesuvius*.) Another question could be "Is a *wombat*, a *wallaby*, an *emu*, or a *wallaroo* most like a bear?"

Students should defend and discuss their answers. Although simple and straightforward, this exercise is nevertheless qualitatively better than those that require selecting a definition or writing a sentence. This is because students must see the new words/concepts *in relation to other concepts* rather than simply remember them as discrete items.

Here is a good variation on the word-association technique:

◆ Could an *eruption* be an *explosion*?

◆ Could a *cliché* be an *idiomatic expression*?

◆ Could a *prestidigitator* be a *magician*?

6 **Sentence completion** Students are more likely to retain the meanings of new terms if they complete a sentence with a word or phrase than they are if they make up their own sentences. For example:

(Continued)

Expand Your Teaching Repertoire

"You are most likely to find a *wombat* in _____." versus "I saw a wombat."

"A *dormant* volcano is one that is _____." versus "I like dormant volcanoes."

Dictionary Use

We should model exhibiting a favorable attitude toward the dictionary and call upon it for timely information. The dictionary should be used to supply information for words students encounter in their independent reading that they either cannot figure out on their own or, after making an educated guess, wish to check. Information about *word histories* is now included in most dictionaries intended for the intermediate grades, and additional features help provide the tools students need to think about and analyze their language.

For example, dictionaries provide a major pronouncing key (see Figure 8.6) and a briefer key on every other page. The dictionary will provide information about pronunciation for each entry, occasionally indicating whether a word has varied regional pronunciations. All dictionaries intended for elementary students include additional types of reference material, such as information specific to language itself: a history of the language, explanations about homographs and homophones, discussion of synonyms, an overview of how etymological information is presented, and a thesaurus. Figure 8.7 presents a page from an intermediate dictionary. Note the etymological information and the synonyms box.

In recent years publishers have assembled dictionaries for the primary grades that are usually well done and attractive. For children who can benefit from them and who understand alphabetical order, they are most appropriate. Their rich illustrations and informative photographs are a strong plus. The object or action that is pictured provides appropriate visual support for the word while at the same time not obscuring the concept. Careful use of these dictionaries in second and third grade can develop students' positive attitudes toward the more complex dictionaries they will encounter later on. In addition, dictionaries are now available on CD-ROM for students. They are colorful, quick, and easy to use—and if a computer has audio capabilities, a simple click of the mouse yields the word's pronunciation.

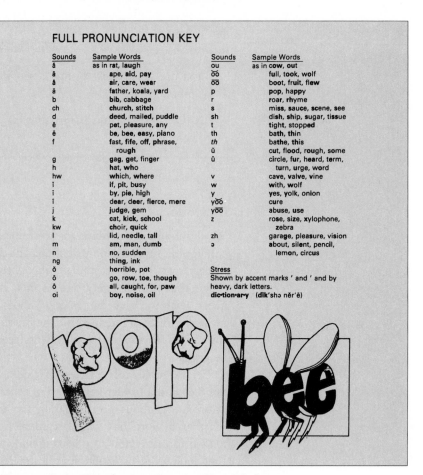

FULL PRONUNCIATION KEY

Sounds	Sample Words	Sounds	Sample Words
ă	as in rat, laugh	ou	as in cow, out
ā	ape, aid, pay	ŏŏ	full, took, wolf
â	air, care, wear	ōō	boot, fruit, flew
ä	father, koala, yard	p	pop, happy
b	bib, cabbage	r	roar, rhyme
ch	church, stitch	s	miss, sauce, scene, see
d	deed, mailed, puddle	sh	dish, ship, sugar, tissue
ĕ	pet, pleasure, any	t	tight, stopped
ē	be, bee, easy, piano	th	bath, thin
f	fast, fife, off, phrase,	*th*	bathe, this
	rough	ŭ	cut, flood, rough, some
g	gag, get, finger	û	circle, fur, heard, term,
h	hat, who		turn, urge, word
hw	which, where	v	cave, valve, vine
ĭ	if, pit, busy	w	with, wolf
ī	by, pie, high	y	yes, yolk, onion
î	dear, deer, fierce, mere	yŏŏ	cure
j	judge, gem	yōō	abuse, use
k	cat, kick, school	z	rose, size, xylophone,
kw	choir, quick		zebra
l	lid, needle, tall	zh	garage, pleasure, vision
m	am, man, dumb	ə	about, silent, pencil,
n	no, sudden		lemon, circus
ng	thing, ink		
ŏ	horrible, pot	**Stress**	
ō	go, row, toe, though	Shown by accent marks ′ and ′ and by	
ô	all, caught, for, paw	heavy, dark letters.	
oi	boy, noise, oil	dic•tion•ar•y (dĭk′shə nĕr′ē)	

Figure 8.6   **A Pronunciation Key from an Intermediate Dictionary**

SOURCE: Copyright © 1986 by Houghton Mifflin Company. Reproduced by permission from *The Houghton Mifflin Intermediate Dictionary*.

Working with Categories of Language Use in the Integrated Language Arts Classroom

Sometimes we talk about language for its own sake—language can be fun—but most of the time we discuss the way we use language to under-stand something more clearly, to make a finer distinction, or to focus on something we haven't thought about before. In the elementary grades students can benefit from learning about categories of language use such as

◆ homophones/homographs/homonyms

◆ antonyms

◆ synonyms

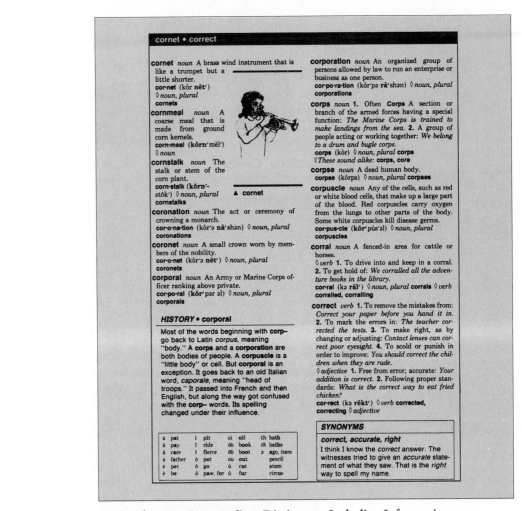

cornet • correct

cornet *noun* A brass wind instrument that is like a trumpet but a little shorter.
cor·net (kôr nĕt´) ◊ *noun, plural* **cornets**

cornmeal *noun* A coarse meal that is made from ground corn kernels.
corn·meal (kôrn´mēl´) ◊ *noun*

cornstalk *noun* The stalk or stem of the corn plant.
corn·stalk (kôrn´stôk´) ◊ *noun, plural* **cornstalks**

coronation *noun* The act or ceremony of crowning a monarch.
cor·o·na·tion (kôr´ə nā´shən) ◊ *noun, plural* **coronations**

coronet *noun* A small crown worn by members of the nobility.
cor·o·net (kôr´ə nĕt´) ◊ *noun, plural* **coronets**

corporal *noun* An Army or Marine Corps officer ranking above private.
cor·po·ral (kôr´pər əl) ◊ *noun, plural* **corporals**

HISTORY • corporal

Most of the words beginning with **corp–** go back to Latin *corpus*, meaning "body." A **corps** and a **corporation** are both bodies of people. A **corpuscle** is a "little body" or cell. But **corporal** is an exception. It goes back to an old Italian word, *caporale*, meaning "head of troops." It passed into French and then English, but along the way got confused with the **corp–** words. Its spelling changed under their influence.

▲ cornet

à	pat	i	pit	oi	oil	th	bath
â	pay	ī	ride	ōō	book	th	bathe
â	care	î	fierce	ōō	boot	ə	ago, item
ä	father	ŏ	pot	ou	out		pencil
ĕ	pet	ō	go	ŭ	cut		atom
ē	be	ô	paw, for	û	fur		circus

corporation *noun* An organized group of persons allowed by law to run an enterprise or business as one person.
cor·po·ra·tion (kôr´pə rā´shən) ◊ *noun, plural* **corporations**

corps *noun* **1.** Often **Corps** A section or branch of the armed forces having a special function: *The Marine Corps is trained to make landings from the sea.* **2.** A group of people acting or working together: *We belong to a drum and bugle corps.*
corps (kôr) ◊ *noun, plural* **corps**
‖ *These sound alike:* **corps, core**

corpse *noun* A dead human body.
corpse (kôrps) ◊ *noun, plural* **corpses**

corpuscle *noun* Any of the cells, such as red or white blood cells, that make up a large part of the blood. Red corpuscles carry oxygen from the lungs to other parts of the body. Some white corpuscles kill disease germs.
cor·pus·cle (kôr´pŭs´əl) ◊ *noun, plural* **corpuscles**

corral *noun* A fenced-in area for cattle or horses.
◊ *verb* **1.** To drive into and keep in a corral. **2.** To get hold of: *We corralled all the adventure books in the library.*
cor·ral (kə răl´) ◊ *noun, plural* **corrals** ◊ *verb* **corralled, corralling**

correct *verb* **1.** To remove the mistakes from: *Correct your paper before you hand it in.* **2.** To mark the errors in: *The teacher corrected the tests.* **3.** To make right, as by changing or adjusting: *Contact lenses can correct poor eyesight.* **4.** To scold or punish in order to improve: *You should correct the children when they are rude.*
◊ *adjective* **1.** Free from error; accurate: *Your addition is correct.* **2.** Following proper standards: *What is the correct way to eat fried chicken?*
cor·rect (kə rĕkt´) ◊ *verb* **corrected, correcting** ◊ *adjective*

SYNONYMS

correct, accurate, right

I think I know the *correct* answer. The witnesses tried to give an *accurate* statement of what they saw. That is the *right* way to spell my name.

Figure 8.7

A Page from an Intermediate Dictionary, Including Information on Synonyms and Etymology

SOURCE: Copyright © 1986 by Houghton Mifflin Company. Reproduced by permission from *The Houghton Mifflin Intermediate Dictionary.*

◆ **denotative** versus **connotative meaning**

◆ **similes and metaphors**

◆ **analogies**

Most intermediate students can learn the labels for these different relationships and understand the underlying processes they represent, but they should also continually apply this knowledge in their acquisition of vocabulary. As we will explore in the second half of this chapter, a playful and sensitive curiosity about words can easily be incorporated within spelling instruction as well.

Antonyms and Synonyms

Basically, *antonyms* refer to words that are opposite in meaning, though there are different types of opposite relationships. Antonyms can be words with no middle ground such as *right* and *wrong* or *yes* and *no*, or they can be relative terms, such as *happy* and *sad*, which have degrees of emotion between them. Combined with synonym study, working with antonyms gives students the opportunity to make finer distinctions among relationships and to improve their critical thinking.

Synonyms are words that are *very* close—though not identical—in meaning. When students study the fine gradations of meaning that separate synonyms, they learn progressively finer *conceptual* distinctions. During recess, for example, are the students simply *loud*, or are they *garrulous, boisterous, raucous, shrill,* or *noisy*? Even terms that appear identical convey different feelings or senses in a sentence. For example, do we live *below* a particular form of government, *beneath* it, or *under* it?

The best way to begin synonym study is to categorize words that are in the same conceptual domain. The next step is to discriminate among the synonyms in actual use in the students' writing and reading. Finally, students should analyze and discuss the distinctions among lists of synonyms. For example:

◆ To categorize words according to a concept, the students first brainstorm words that have to do with a particular idea. For example, the word *fear* elicits the following responses from a group of third-graders: "afraid," "worried," "scared," "terrified," "frightened."

◆ The teacher then discusses with students what they think each word means and how they might use these words in their writing. This is as far as the initial discussion goes.

◆ Later, as students are writing Halloween stories, for example, they can use these and other words to represent the concept of fear.

◆ In reading and writing response groups, students discuss the writer's intentions in choosing one synonym over another.

◆ Finally, the teacher discusses the concept of synonyms and helps students develop an abstract understanding of it. This activity should at first be done in a group. The teacher can begin by steering the students' discussion toward those words that are farthest apart in meaning, then moving to finer and finer distinctions: why is *terrified* scarier than *worried*? why is *terrified* scarier than *afraid* or *frightened*? This type of discrimination is challenging at first, but the teacher and students can draw upon their previous discussions in reading and writing for examples and clarification.

We can further develop students' ability to make these distinctions by having them first work individually and then in pairs to rank synonymous words (Johnson & Pearson, 1984). For example, given the following format, the students will rank these words according to the scale of 1 = most intense, 4 = least intense:

tiny

small

microscopic

puny

Two students ranked the words this way:

Student 1		**Student 2**	
2	tiny	2	tiny
3	small	4	small
1	microscopic	1	microscopic
4	puny	3	puny

Although the students agreed that *microscopic* was the most intense synonym, they differed at the other end of the scale—whether *small* or *puny* was least intense. In this case is *puny* "smaller" than *small*? In their discussion the two students offered different examples as support for their decisions; usually one student will wind up persuading the other. If there is a deadlock, however, the time to resolve it is back with the whole group. To check the majority opinion or to resolve a problem that perhaps the whole group experienced, have your students refer to the dictionary as the final judge.

Students should explore synonyms and use their knowledge of them in reading and writing throughout the elementary grades and beyond. This knowledge provides the foundation for learning and examining other types of word relationships.

Denotation and Connotation

As students think and talk about synonyms, their discussions will naturally lead them into distinctions involving the denotative and connotative meanings of words. These distinctions are important because they help students understand how and why writers use words—and how they can apply this knowledge in their *own* writing.

Denotation refers to the literal meaning of a word; *connotation* refers to the feelings and emotions associated with the word, often its *implied* meaning. For example, the denotative meaning of *weak* is "lacking in strength," but its implied meaning may connote lack of character and resolve. Dictionaries often make this type of distinction by presenting literal meanings first, followed by connotative meanings. Explain to students that we can think of words in terms of both what they literally mean and how they affect our emotions and feelings.

In this context present word pairs for discussion and ask students to determine which word has a negative or bad connotation. Here are some sample word pairs:

leave/abandon	thrifty/stingy
retreat/withdraw	eat/devour
bold/reckless	debate/argue
clever/sly	

To further develop comprehension of these distinctions, present students with sentences in which one word is omitted. Then ask them to substitute given words and note how each word affects the meaning differently. Here is an example:

Jeremy _____ down the street.

walked	sauntered	loped
strutted	ran	stumbled
lumbered		

As students move through the grades, their understanding of how denotative and connotative meanings are used will become more refined. The students can analyze propaganda techniques, sarcasm, and irony as examples of connotation and denotation at work.

Similes and Metaphors

As you read the following passage, listen for the bark of Sounder, the faithful and competent coon dog in the book of the same name by William Armstrong (1969):

The trail barks seemed to be spaced with the precision of a juggler. Each bark bounced from slope to slope in the foothills like a rubber ball. But it was not an ordinary bark. It filled up the night and made music as though the branches of all the trees were being pulled across silver strings.

Armstrong crafts his description of Sounder's bark through figurative language, primarily *simile* and *metaphor*. Students can understand these aspects of figurative language as they explore the ways that words are used in reading and in writing. Similes and metaphors are the two aspects of figurative language covered most thoroughly in the upper elementary grades. As with the previous language categories, these are effective labels that represent a convenient shorthand for talking about language.

The term *simile* comes from the Latin root *similis,* meaning "like." It is the logical place to begin considering figurative language because it is the most explicitly "signaled" figure of speech. Used as a means of comparison, similes are introduced by the words *like, than, as . . . as,* or *so . . . as.* Introducing similes to our students through *clichés* is effective. Clichés are overused, overworked similes. Students can complete such clichés as

as easy as p_____. (pie)

as dead as a d_____. (doornail)

as quick as a w_____. (wink)

as slow as m_____. (molasses)

quick like a b_____. (bunny)

as happy as a cl_____. (clam)

Students quite often are amazed to discover how frequently similes are used in literature. After a read-aloud, for example, we can note some of the similes that the author has used and ask the students if they can recall any. We can then reread a passage that has used some particularly effective similes. Consider the first sentence of *Tuck Everlasting* (Babbit, 1975):

The first week of August hangs at the very top of summer, the top of the live-long year, like the highest seat of a Ferris wheel when it pauses in its turning.

A popular activity for students is to keep a list of similes in their journals for a day or so and then to discuss and reflect on the effect of this use of language. Being aware of similes helps students learn how language can more precisely tap and express the feelings, senses, and ideas they experience and wish to convey. After listening to several teacher read-alouds in which she pointed out and discussed these comparisons, for example, nine-year-old RaySean generated several similes in his journal. We get a sense of his dawning awareness in these sentences: *"The atom is like darkness to me . . . the dark stormy night is like dreams are coming to me . . ."*

At first tacitly and later consciously, elementary students are quite capable of appreciating and manipulating similes and metaphors (Winner, 1988). The degree to which they will do so depends on how they develop an awareness and then an appreciation of metaphor.

Metaphors are comparisons or contrasts in language that are *not* explicitly signaled. Coming from the Greek (*meta*, over + *phor*, carry), metaphors "carry over" a comparison or contrast with one object, event, or person to another object, event, or person. They are powerful language devices that enable writers to express ideas in new ways. Once again, teachers should point out effective metaphors, such as this one from Norman Juster's *The Phantom Tollbooth*: "Symphonies are the large beautiful carpets with all the rhythms and melodies woven in" (1961, p. 157). Eve Merriam's *Quiet, Please* (1993) provides a feast of metaphor: "invisible writing of butterflies" and "milkweed pods, their silky threads sprinkling the air." We should focus at first on identifying instances where metaphor is used to express a thought in a fresh, new way. Fairly quickly, then, we should turn students' attention to applying this awareness of metaphor in their writing and reading. Figure 8.8 shows nine-year-old Sarah's dawning awareness of the power of metaphor as she stretches her concept of "circle."

Homophones, Homographs, and Homonyms

Homophones (literally, "same sound") are words that *sound* the same but are spelled differently—for example, *pail* and *pale*. *Homographs* (literally, "same writing") are words that are *spelled* the same but are usually pronounced differently, such as *dove* (the bird or the past tense of "to dive") and *lead* (the chemical element or "to guide something along"). *Homonyms* (literally, "same name") include words that are spelled and pronounced the same but differ in meaning, such as *bat* (the mammal) and *bat* (a club used to hit baseballs).

At the second- and third-grade level, the category of homophones especially allows for great wordplay—at the same time as *spelling* is reinforced (see p. 498 in the *Sourcebook* for a list of homophones). Books by Fred

Figure 8.8 Nine-year-old Sarah's Dawning Awareness of Metaphor

Gwynne such as *The King Who Rained* (1979) highlight the silliness of confusing homophones in print. You can talk with students about what it means to write "I saw a *bare* in the woods" (oops!) or "That squirrel sure has a long *tale*" (quite a storyteller!). Combining the meanings of homophone pairs through art, as in Figure 8.9, entertains at the same time as it reinforces meaning *and* spelling.

Analogies

After discussing the previous types of language categories and conceptual relationships, students are ready to examine *analogies*. Basically, analogical

Figure 8.9   **Art Reinforces Meaning and Spelling for Homophones**

SOURCE: Bolton, F., & Snowball, D. (1993). *Teaching spelling: A practical resource.* Portsmouth, NH: Heinemann.

thinking expresses relationships among pairs of words or concepts. An understanding of analogies and how they work helps students comprehend complex relationships and logical reasoning in various subject matter areas such as science, math, and history. Learning to apply analogical thinking, in other words, is a powerful tool that extends far beyond the simple format in which students first encounter analogies. The following is a sequence of instruction for directly addressing analogies:

◆ Begin with simple analogies such as *love* is to *hate* as *strong* is to *weak*; *father* is to *son* as *mother* is to *daughter*.

◆ Present analogies where one word is omitted, and several possibilities for completing the analogy are offered. For example, *ice* is to *cold* as *fire* is to _____. (fireplace, hot, water)

◆ Next, present analogies without possible choices. For example, *football* is to *field* as *hockey* is to _____. (ice rink)

◆ Finally, present analogies where the missing word occurs in places other than the final slot. For example, *table* is to _____ as *book* is to *page*. (leg)

The Foundations of Learning and Teaching Spelling

Spelling plays an important role in the language arts:

◆ First, spelling knowledge facilitates reading and writing performance (Perfetti, 1985; Templeton & Bear, 1992). Effective spelling instruction beneficially affects the quality of students' *reading* experiences and significantly influences the quality of their *writing* experiences as well.

◆ Second, because spelling knowledge reflects structural and vocabulary information about words, it can reinforce word-analysis strategies and expand vocabulary.

◆ Third, spelling makes writing easier and is a courtesy to the reader.

Research has demonstrated that learning to spell—indeed, learning about words at all—involves making *generalizations* from specific words rather than simply memorizing every word as an individual unit (Read & Hodges, 1982). What children are able to learn and generalize about words changes throughout the elementary school years. Remember the developmental picture we painted in Chapter 5? Children's developmental word or

**PUBLISHED AND
TEACHER-DEVELOPED
SPELLING PROGRAMS IN
PERSPECTIVE**

"**S**pelling instruction" is a perennially controversial issue in education (Templeton, 1992a). Much of this controversy stems rightfully enough from the poorly organized spelling programs of the past, which often depended upon low-level, boring exercises. In recent years, however, some publishers have attempted to develop spelling programs that represent the recent theory and practice of word learning (Zutell, 1994). Although research suggests that students themselves should explore words in word lists, comparing and contrasting them in ways we will address, teachers will play a seminal role in this exploration. We need to determine the levels for placing our students for such study (see Chapter 11) as well as to assist the students as they develop their own personalized word lists — words whose spelling they wish to learn.

A well-constructed published spelling program can help in the following ways:

- Provide a scope and sequence of spelling patterns that will be a good guide for your word-study program over the elementary years.

- Provide appropriate list words that students know from their reading and need to use in their writing; at the intermediate-grade levels, include some new words that are related in spelling and meaning to these familiar words.

- Offer instructionally sound activities that do not emphasize rote memorization but that involve students in examining words from a variety of perspectives. These activities lead to generalizations about spelling patterns that apply to many other words, not just to those in the list.

- Reinforce the messages that spelling

is logical, is rarely haphazard, and at the intermediate levels can be tied directly to vocabulary through the "spelling-meaning connection" (Templeton, 1991).

For those teachers who choose to develop and maintain an ongoing spelling program in their classrooms without using a published program — usually within the context of a thematic unit — their programs should have these two critical components:

- Students should be exploring and learning words that have spelling patterns that are developmentally appropriate.

- These words should be grouped so that students can discover common spelling patterns in them.

Many teachers have learned to avoid the pitfall of selecting spelling words from the reading that students are doing as part of a thematic unit — and then realizing that the words are not developmentally appropriate and/or do not share any apparent spelling patterns. For example, it would *not* be appropriate for most students in a second-grade thematic unit on "Our Natural Environment" to have as spelling words *chlorophyll*, *ecosystem*, and *topography*. While it might indeed be possible for some second-graders to memorize these words for a Friday quiz, it is unlikely that they would know these spellings automatically at a later time. Nor would they be able to generalize any spelling patterns in these words to other words.

In addition to pulling *developmentally appropriate* words from students' reading and writing, you will find lists of words arranged according to spelling pattern in the *Sourcebook*. Another resource for words as well as for extensive activities is the book *Words Their*

AT THE TEACHER'S DESK

PUBLISHED AND
TEACHER-DEVELOPED
SPELLING PROGRAMS IN
PERSPECTIVE

(Continued)

Way: Word Study for Phonics, Vocabulary, and Spelling Instruction (1996) by Bear, Invernizzi, & Templeton.

Should students select words they wish to learn to spell? Of course — this activity can be highly motivating. However, these should not be the *only* spelling words the students have. A few student-selected words can be added to the "core group" of words we present each week. These "self-selected" words can be those that particularly interest the students (dinosaur names, for example, are popular during a unit focusing on the earth's history) or that they find continually troublesome.

spelling knowledge determines how they will *spell* words and how they will *read* words. This knowledge becomes increasingly more complex and abstract as children develop, and our understanding of this knowledge gives us a clearer sense of when and how to introduce spelling or orthographic patterns to children at different levels.

Encouraging young children to invent their spelling: "What sounds do you hear and feel?"

English Spelling: Three Layers of Information

There are three layers of information in the English spelling system (Henderson, 1990; Templeton, 1991)—**alphabet**, **pattern**, and **meaning**. Our understanding of these layers will help us teach more effectively.

◆ The *alphabetic* layer represents letter/sound information in a more or less left-to-right sequence. For example, in the word *bat*, the letter-sound correspondence is obvious: *b* = /b/, *a* = /ă/, *t* = /t/. In the word *grab*, the correspondence is again straightforward: *g* = /g/, *r* = /r/, *a* = /ă/, *b* = /b/. Of course, spelling is not always so straightforward; letters and combinations of letters can represent more than one sound, and one sound can be represented by more than one letter. The second two layers explain this variability.

◆ The *pattern* layer provides information about the sounds that *groups* of letters represent. For example, the long vowel sound in words is often indicated by the presence of silent letters, as in the *vowel-consonant-silent e* pattern in words like p*ine* and m*ake*. Another common long vowel pattern is a vowel *digraph*, in which the second, silent vowel often "marks" the first letter as long, as in r*ai*n.

◆ The *meaning* layer reflects the fact that *meaning elements* within words are usually spelled consistently, despite sound change. For example, note the consistent spelling of the base words in the word pairs *legal/legal*ity and *sign/sign*al.

The key to understanding these three layers of information is to examine words that share common spelling features. When we organize words this way, we can better understand and appreciate the logic of the spelling system and realize that it is far more regular than it is often thought to be. As the within-word pattern principle and the meaning principle illustrate, this regularity exists at levels beyond a simple left-to-right, letter-to-sound alphabetic match-up.

The Development of Spelling Knowledge

Students' understanding of spelling structure follows a developmental sequence (Henderson, 1990; Templeton & Bear, 1992). Consistent with the sequence of developmental phases of reading and writing discussed in Chapter 5, this sequence represents the ways that students organize their knowledge about words. As their word knowledge becomes more advanced, children reorganize the ways that they conceptualize words and their spelling. Understanding this sequence enables us to provide appropriate, enjoyable, and systematic instruction.

The Semiphonemic Phase

Toward the end of the *emergent literacy* phase, children are writing with recognizable letters. They have moved beyond the "scribbling and drawing" phase discussed in Chapter 5, and their spelling is characterized as primarily **semiphonemic**: They spell some but not all of the sounds within syllables. For example, they use *BD* for *bird*, and *WM* for *worm*. Few vowel letters occur.

The Phonemic or "Alphabetic" Phase

This level of word knowledge corresponds to the *beginning literacy* phase. As children are exposed to print more often and are read to, their *concept of word in print* develops, and their spelling becomes primarily **phonemic** or **alphabetic**. They are able to pick out most sounds or phonemes and to represent them with a corresponding letter: FETHR for *feather*; BECIM for *become*; CHRANCHRAK for *train track*. As several researchers have demonstrated (Henderson & Beers, 1980; Read, 1975), these invented spellings are logical and in fact quite impressive. They are based on phonetic and physical properties of the sounds the children are attempting to spell as well as on a visual memory for some spellings.

Here are some common spelling correspondences that children establish at this stage:

Long Vowels	Short Vowels	Consonant Blends
ā: TAK (take)	ă: SAD (sad)	/dr/: JRIV (drive)
ē: SET (seat)	ĕ: BAD (bed)	/tr/: CHREP (trip)
ī: BIK (bike)	ĭ: SET (sit)	
ō: BON (bone)	ŏ: GIT (got)	
ū: SUT (suit)	ŭ: BOPY (bumpy)	

Children will also spell some of their sight words correctly. Jeffrey's writing in Figure 8.10 provides an example of "alphabetic" spelling. During this phase as children learn—through reading instruction and examining words—how certain sounds are represented in simple words, their invented spellings in single-syllable words begin to look more conventional. At this point they are moving into the next developmental phase of word knowledge.

The Within-Word Pattern Phase

This level of word knowledge is characteristic of the *transitional phase* of literacy development. As the label implies, the **within-word pattern phase**

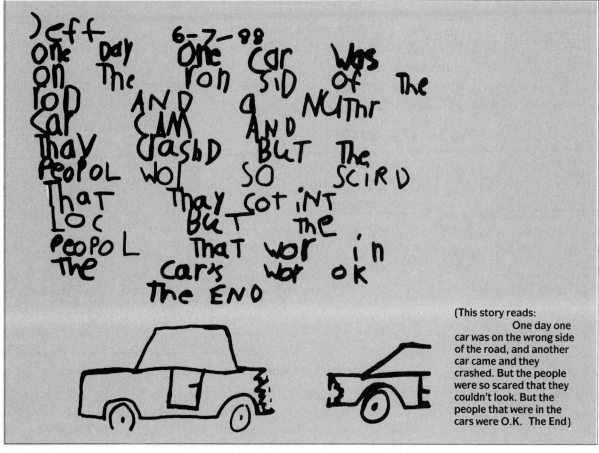

(This story reads:
One day one car was on the wrong side of the road, and another car came and they crashed. But the people were so scared that they couldn't look. But the people that were in the cars were O.K. The End)

Figure 8.10   Jeffrey's Letter-Name Writing

involves an understanding of the *patterns* to which letters and sounds correspond within single-syllable words. *Sight words* provide the foundation for this understanding.

The following spellings come from children's compositions: MAIK, MAEK, and MEAK, for the word *make*; RAUWND for *round*, and TUREN for *turn*. Jason's "79 Dungeons" story (see Figure 8.11) demonstrates within-word pattern word knowledge. Children's spellings of *make* illustrate how they attempt to represent the silent letter — or as it's often called, the "marker" — that indicates that the word contains a long vowel. The children may misplace this marker or, as the first word (MAIK) illustrates, include a logical marker that is correctly placed but not appropriate in this particular word. Other invented spellings reflect students' attempts

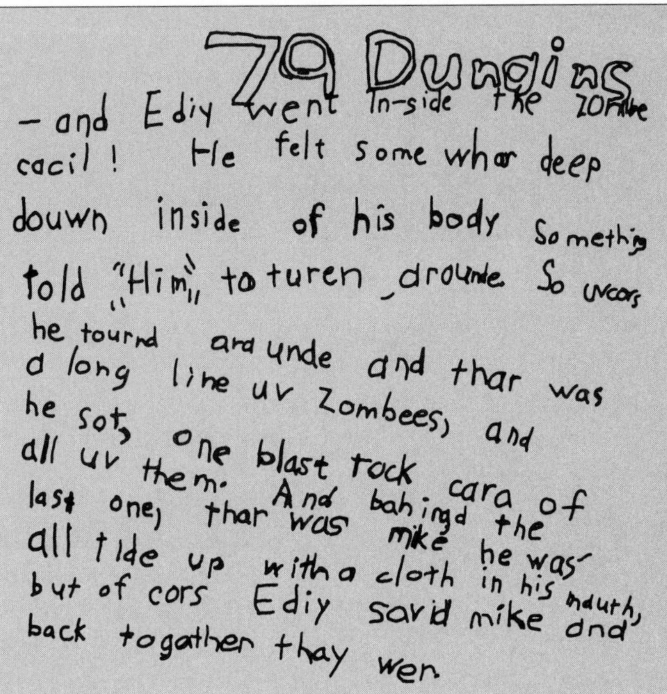

79 Dungins

— and Ediy went In-side the zomve cacil ! He felt some whor deep douwn inside of his body Something told "Him", to turen droune. So uvcors he tourn araunde and thar was a long line uv Zombees, and he sot, one blast rock cara of all uv the m. And bahind the last one, thar was mike he was all tide up with a cloth in his mauth, but of cors Ediy savd mike and back togather thay wen.

(This story reads:
And Eddie went inside the zombie castle. Something told him to turn around. So of course he turned around. There was a long line of zombees. And he shot, one blast took care of all of them. And there was Mike. He was all tied up with a cloth in his mouth. But of course Eddie saved Mike and back together they were.)

Figure 8.11   Jason's "79 Dungeons" Story, Demonstrating Within-Word-Pattern Spellings

to handle vowels that are not clearly long or short, as in RAUWND and TUREN. As students read and examine words that evidence these letter/sound, within-word relationships, and as they exercise this knowledge in their writing attempts, they gradually come to sort out and correctly use the various spelling patterns within single syllables.

The Syllable Juncture Phase

This level of word knowledge is characteristic of the *Late Transitional and Early Proficient* phase of literacy development. Once students understand most of the basic within-word single-syllable patterns, they are conceptually ready to examine words of more than one syllable and to examine what happens at the *juncture* of syllables within words—the place where the syllables come together. At these junctures letters may be

◆ doubled, as in bas*k*et, si*tt*ing, and begi*nn*ing

◆ dropped (mak*e* + ing = making)

◆ changed (gloom*y* + er = gloom*i*er).

The following types of invented spellings signal that students are ready for systematic study of syllable patterns and affixes:

BAKEING	(baking)	PALICE	(palace)
STOPED	(stopped)	DAFEND	(defend)
SUDEN	(sudden)		
NEDDLE	(needle)		
CARRYS	(carries)		

In the first column, note the uncertainty about when and where to double consonants or to drop final letters. In *palace* and *defend*, notice that the errors occur in the least-stressed syllables.

Understanding **syllable juncture** depends on a firm grasp of the alphabetic and within-word pattern principles. This is because the basic clue to doubling, dropping, or changing letters depends on the structure within the joined syllables. For example, *sit* has a short vowel pattern, and when you add a suffix that begins with a vowel, you must double the final consonant in *sit*. Otherwise, you have a different word — *siting* (site + ing).

Children explore the conventions that govern the joining of syllables, prefixes, and suffixes first in common two-syllable words, and later in common polysyllabic words. Students will also notice where the stress or accent is placed within words, as well as the role that an accent can play in focusing attention on what needs to be studied in these words. Some fine-tuning of this knowledge will occur at the next stage, but most of these conventions will be learned now.

The Derivational Patterns Stage

This level of word knowledge is characteristic of the *mature/proficient phase* of literacy development. Many students at the fifth- and sixth-grade levels are moving into this phase. They now are fully able to understand and apply the fundamental *meaning* principle in our spelling system: words that are related in meaning are often also related in spelling, despite changes in sound. The following misspellings are characteristic of the **derivational patterns stage**:

INTERUPT (interrupt)	ATRACT (attract)
COMPASITION (composition)	CONDEM (condemn)
BENIFIT (benefit)	ACCOMODATE (accommodate)

SPELLING FOR STRUGGLING READERS AND WRITERS

Students who are struggling with reading and writing are usually struggling with their spelling as well. It is rare that a student *only* has difficulty with spelling. When this does happen, however, we usually find that the students have not developed ways of looking at words closely. We then engage them in the types of activities presented earlier in this chapter that involve exploring and examining words. Over time we will see their spelling ability become more aligned with their reading ability.

For students who are struggling with literacy in general, our first priority is to make sure that we provide them with plenty of opportunities to read materials that correspond to their developmental levels—more specifically, to their instructional reading levels. Their spelling or word study will also correspond to their developmental level. For example, in Diane Olds' multi-age fourth/fifth/sixth-grade classroom, two students are at the late beginning phase of literacy development. Diane has them working with words that feature simple short vowel patterns as well as consonant digraphs and blends.

For students with a learning disability in the area of literacy, it's important to know that in most cases they follow the same developmental sequence of learning word structure as do other students (Invernizzi & Worthy, 1989). Their *pace* of development, however, will be slower. Occasionally, we find that using concrete manipulatives for word parts is especially reinforcing—for example, LinkLetters® (students construct a word by fitting the separate letter pieces together) and "Vowel Wheels" (see Figure 8.12).

This final stage reflects the broader vocabulary to which students are now exposed in their reading, which includes a considerable number of words from Greek, Latin, and French (see p. 499–506 in the *Teacher's Sourcebook*). Most of this new vocabulary will occur more frequently in print than in spoken language (Chomsky, 1970; Templeton, 1979). During this stage students extend and refine the basic spelling conventions they developed during the previous stage, primarily syllable junctures and the spelling of the unaccented vowel in polysyllabic words—referred to as the "schwa" sound (the sound of *a* in "above").

Word study will focus on exploring derivational relationships or spelling-sound patterns that apply to words related in spelling and meaning. As the students' vocabularies expand during the intermediate years, they will learn words that—although more abstract semantically—are highly regular in terms of the meaning principle. Students will be examining related words such as *compete/competition*, *fatal/fatality*, *clinic/clinician*, and *judicial/adjudicate*.

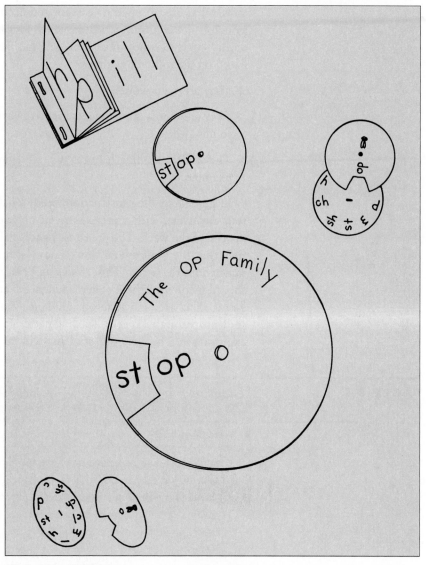

Figure 8.12 **Short Vowel Wheel**

SOURCE: Beau, C., Invernizzi, M., & Templeton, S. (1996). *Words their way: Word study for phonics, vocabulary, and spelling instruction.* Englewood Cliffs, NJ: Prentice Hall.

Guiding Students' Spelling Development

We now understand that, while reading and writing are absolutely critical for spelling development, more systematic exploration of the spelling of words is necessary for most students (Invernizzi, Abouzeid, & Gill, 1994; Zutell, 1994). This exploration, however, need not be as dull or boring as the traditional spelling instruction of the past.

Spelling instruction involves the systematic presentation and study of words that are grouped or categorized according to a common pattern or principle; for example, words in which long *a* is spelled *a*-consonant-*e* or *ai*; words in which the -*dict*- root occurs). These words should be selected based on the following criteria:

◆ They are sight words.

◆ They are words that students use frequently in their writing and are likely to misspell.

◆ They reflect spelling features that students are developmentally ready to examine.

In guided spelling instruction, study of the words occurs in a three- or four-day cycle, with a preassessment on Monday and a postassessment at the end of the week. The preassessment is helpful because students can identify what they know and don't know—therefore focusing their attention throughout the week. This "focusing" can occur in a number of ways but should involve activities where students examine particular elements in the words. This area is where our guidance is so important: we can walk our students through a specific spelling pattern and then engage them in actively exploring it. This way our students will be much more likely to apply the

TABLE 8.2	**Synchronizing the Teaching of Spelling with Children's Developmental Levels of Word Knowledge**

Letter Name

1. Students should be guided to examine and to learn the correct spelling of selected words they are being taught to read.
2. Through activities involving recognition, grouping, substitution, and spelling, beginning consonant elements are examined in the following order: single consonants, common consonant digraphs, and common blends.
3. Short vowel patterns (phonograms) are examined systematically. (A phonogram is the vowel and what follows within a single syllable.)
4. "Continuant" or nasal consonants that precede other types of consonants are examined (wi*n*ter, ca*m*p).
5. The most common long vowel patterns, or phonograms, are examined (m*a*ke, r*i*de).

Within-Word Pattern

1. Additional common long vowel patterns are examined (/ā/ in b*ai*t, w*ei*ght; /ī/ in l*igh*t; /ē/ in m*ea*t, fr*ee*ze).

(Continued)

TABLE 8.2 *(Continued)*

Synchronizing the Teaching of Spelling with Children's Developmental Levels of Word Knowledge

2. *r*- and *l*-influenced vowel patterns are studied (c*ar*d, f*er*n, f*all*, p*ull*).
3. Common diphthongs are introduced (h*ow*, b*oi*l).
4. Compound words are studied.
5. Through the examination of common homophones, students begin to develop an awareness of the meaning principle in spelling.

Syllable Juncture

1. Common and less frequent vowel patterns in stressed syllables continue to be examined.
2. Common inflections and the ways in which they are joined to base words are examined (*-ed, -ing, -ly*).
3. The sound and the meaning of common prefixes and suffixes are analyzed (*un-, re-, -ment, -ness*).
4. The role of stress or accent is introduced in the context of homographs.
5. Unstressed syllables are examined, first in two-syllable words and later in polysyllabic words.
6. More complex prefixes and suffixes are examined.
7. The principle of consonant doubling is examined as it applies to a broader range of vocabulary.

Derivational Patterns: The Spelling-Meaning Connection

1. Silent and sounded consonant patterns are studied (colum*n*/colum*n*ist, resign/resignation).
2. Considerable attention is given to the different vowel alternation patterns, sequenced for study as follows:
   a. Long-to-short (extr*e*me/extr*e*mity, rev*i*se/rev*i*sion)
   b. Long-to-schwa (infl*a*me/infl*a*mmation, def*i*ne-def*i*nition)
   c. Short-to-schwa (exc*e*l/exc*e*llent, leg*a*l/leg*a*lity)
   d. Predictable sound/spelling alternation (con*sume*/con*sump*tion, re*ceive*-re*cep*tion)
3. While the vowel alternation patterns are studied, other accompanying consonant alternation patterns are examined:
   a. Sound change/spelling stable (musi*c*/musi*c*ian, constitu*t*e/constitu*t*ion)
   b. Predictable sound/spelling alternation (explo*d*e/explo*s*ion, absen*t*/absen*c*e, permi*t*/permi*ss*ion)
4. The role of Greek and Latin forms in spelling and in meaning is explored.
5. "Absorbed" or "assimilated" prefixes are examined (*ad* + tract = *at*tract; *in* + luminate = *il*luminate).

knowledge they acquire to their everyday writing. Table 8.2 provides an overview of the sequence of spelling instruction as a function of developmental level.

This is the format for assessing spelling each week:

◆ Usually on Monday a preassessment is administered. Afterwards, students check their own papers.

◆ For any incorrectly spelled words, students look at the correct spelling, write the word correctly on the same line as the misspelled word, check the spelling, then write the word a second time. Students check this second spelling, then turn the paper over and write the word from memory.

◆ During the week students pay particular attention to the words they missed on the preassessment in the context of other meaningful activities with words. A midweek assessment, often administered in a "buddy" system with students working in pairs, can help students monitor their success with misspelled words and focus their study for the Friday assessment.

◆ Periodic *review* of list words is important—usually every six weeks. As a supplement to the teaching of targeted patterns and frequent and wide-ranging reading and writing, this approach will develop and reinforce the approximately 5,000 words that are used most frequently in writing, often referred to as a "core spelling vocabulary."

CLASSROOM EXAMPLE

Minilesson: Guided "Walk-through" of a Word

The following example illustrates how a teacher can model the effective examination or "walk-through" of a problematic word for a group of students:

1. The teacher pronounces the word *wander*, for example, and asks the students how many syllables it has.

2. The students say what letter begins the first syllable [teacher writes it on board], what letter ends the first syllable [teacher writes that on board], what letter begins the second syllable, and what letter ends the second syllable.

3. The teacher asks the students to listen to the first syllable, which is *stressed*, and to say what letter they think spells the vowel sound in the first syllable. The teacher then writes the letter on the board in the appropriate place.

(*Continued*)

4. The teacher next asks the students to listen as she pronounces the unstressed syllable and to offer their best guess of what letter stands for the unstressed vowel sound. For this word, as the teacher has predicted, they will guess the correct letter.

5. The teacher then asks the students if they could be absolutely certain about the spelling of the unstressed vowel if they had not seen the word — is sound, by itself, a clue to the spelling in unstressed syllables? They should answer "no" since this sound can also be spelled, *-or*, *-ir*, and *-ar*.

6. The teacher asks if they were to study the word *wander* to learn its correct spelling, to which part of the word would they pay attention?

Students realize the value of closely examining polysyllabic words such as these. This type of walk-through helps students understand why they should pay attention to accent for purposes of spelling. It shows them

- *what they already know about the spelling* of a polysyllabic word (the vowel pattern in the stressed syllable), and

- what they need to know and therefore pay attention to.

Expand Your Teaching Repertoire

Facilitating Students' Spelling Development

At all levels guided spelling instruction should include examining words in meaningful activities that lead to knowledge that can be *generalized* about spelling patterns. The following are some effective ideas for these activities:

1 **Word sorts** Earlier we discussed *word sorts* with a semantic focus. Here we will examine a particularly critical application of word sorts — sorting according to *spelling features*. In this basic format for sorting words, we will assume that students are well into the letter-name stage (beginning literacy) or just beginning the within-word pattern stage (transitional literacy).

(Continued)

a. Begin with one category. Let's say you're going to focus on the long *i*. Place a card containing a known word with a long *i* (*hike*) at the head of a column. Each student will have a number of word cards that he or she can use in the sort. As the student looks at *and pronounces* each word, he or she will place the words that have the same vowel sound as *hike* underneath that card; words that don't fit the pattern will go in a separate column (the "leftover" or "miscellaneous" column) headed by a blank card.

b. After the sort is complete, ask the students to explain *why* they placed the words as they did. Here is a completed sort:

hike	(*Blank card for* "leftover" *words*)
white	stick
time	sing
smile	fish
light	ship
five	chin
slide	slip
high	give

c. After students are familiar with the single category and the miscellaneous column, initiate two-category sorts. For example, establish a long *i* column, a short *i* column, an "other" *i*-spelling column, and a miscellaneous column as illustrated:

hide	*dig*	*pink*	Miscellaneous (blank card)
time	this	think	first
slide	hiss	ink	been
drive	drip		
night	chin		
light	with		
child	kick		

d. Notice that so far the categories are global—long, short, other. The next step is to set up categories *within* each of these global categories.

For example, with additional words added, the long *i* category can be differentiated into *i*-consonant-*e*, *-igh*, *i*-consonant-consonant (*find*, w*i*ld, ch*i*ld), and consonant-*y* (m*y*, fl*y*).

Other productive sorts involve different vowel letters that follow the same spelling pattern (for example, t*i*me versus g*a*me). Through such sorts students learn the effect of position on sound and discover the logic that underlies some apparent exceptions. By comparing words that end like *grave* and *love*, for example, they will realize that in fact no word in English ends simply in the letter *v*. The reason for this lies in the history of the spelling system—an interesting investigation for some students.

Whenever we believe the students are ready, we can initiate an "open" sort. Of course, it should be clear at first that the categories have to be based on spelling, but later the possibilities can be expanded to include spelling, semantic features, and syntactic categories (see the *Teacher's Sourcebook*).

2 **Word wall** **Word walls** are literally words that have been written on cards and displayed prominently on the wall so that all students can easily see them (Cunningham, 1995). While word walls can be used to illustrate all types of word features, they are particularly effective for words that students use often but frequently misspell. These words can be organized alphabetically so that when students need a particular word, they simply can look at the wall to find it. Eventually, these "frequently misspelled" words automatically become *correctly* spelled.

3 **Word study notebooks** Students should keep **word study notebooks** (see Figure 8.13) that are evidence of their developing understanding of word structure. The notebooks should include words they have studied as well as words they have found during word hunts in particular categories. For example, one page could contain "long *a*" words, another "short *a*" words, and so on. Notably, each category will become further differentiated as children learn more about words. The "long *a*" page will later include words with this sound spelled according to different patterns.

Word study notebooks are excellent companions throughout the grades. As students continue to sort and hunt for words, they can record and collect their sorts and information in their word study notebooks. Figure 8.13 shows a sort for a student at the syllable juncture phase.

(Continued)

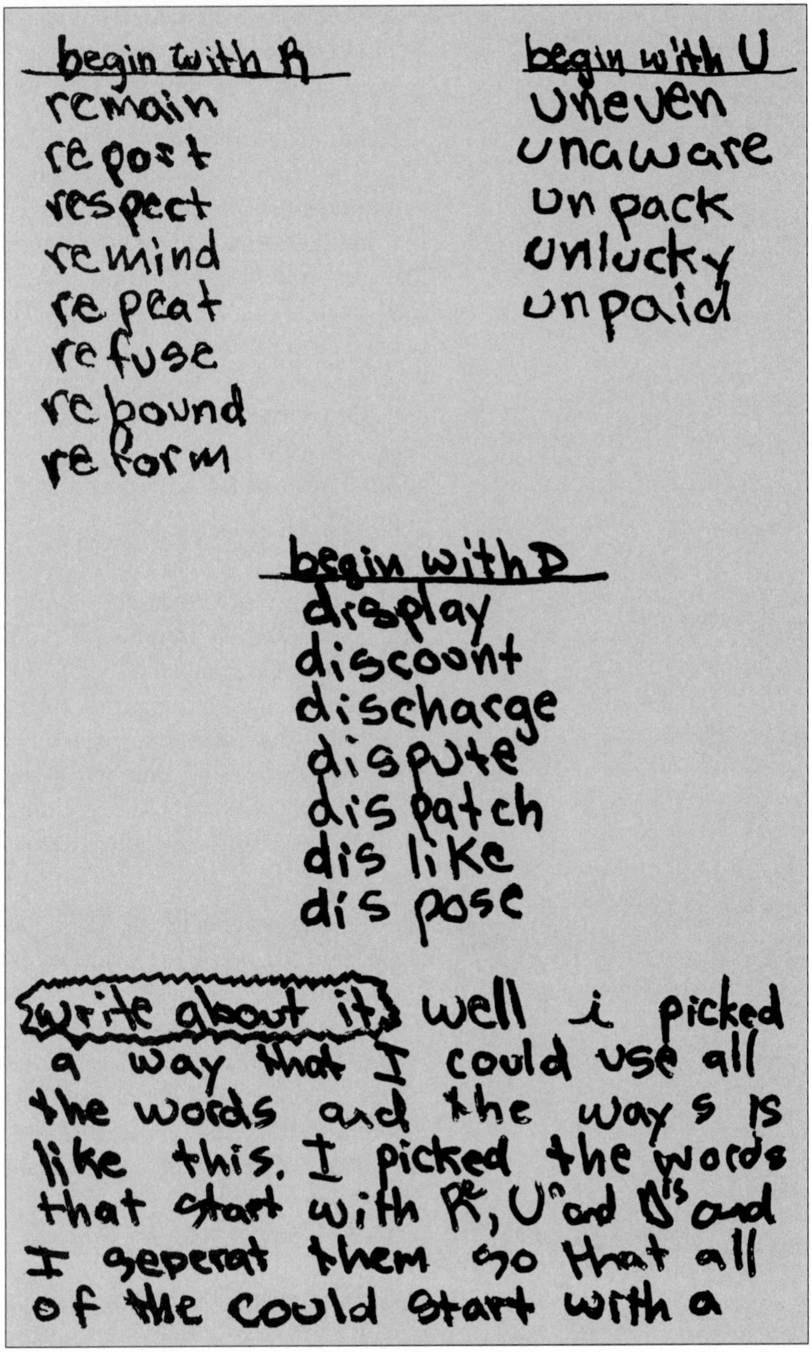

begin with R
remain
repost
respect
remind
repeat
refuse
rebound
reform

begin with U
uneven
unaware
unpack
unlucky
unpaid

begin with D
display
discount
discharge
dispute
dispatch
dislike
dispose

write about it well i picked
a way that I could use all
the words and the ways is
like this. I picked the words
that start with R, U and D's and
I seperat them so that all
of the could start with a

Figure 8.13   Page from Student's Word Study Notebook

(Continued)

4 | **The spelling-meaning connection** In the case of related words, the meaning principle plays its most significant role through the **spelling-meaning connection**. We can state the *spelling-meaning connection* this way:

> Words that are related in meaning are often related in spelling, *despite changes in sound*.

Understanding this phenomenon powerfully aids students in spelling and vocabulary development. This strategy is based on drawing analogies among words. To get a sense of how this connection works, examine the following words that are related in terms of spelling and meaning:

bom*b*	mus*c*le	condem*n*
bom*b*ard	mus*c*ular	condem*n*ation
musi*c*	comple*t*e	
musi*c*ian	comple*t*ion	

Notice how the italicized consonant letter in each word pair changes in pronunciation from the first word to the second. In the first three word pairs, a silent letter becomes sounded. In the last two word pairs, the sound that the italicized letter represents changes. Because the words in each pair are related in meaning, the *spelling* of these changed sounds remains constant.

We can turn students' awareness of the spelling-meaning connection into a strategy based on drawing analogies among words. The following mini-lesson illustrates how we can highlight this connection and teach students a strategy. Figure 8.14 shows how a fifth-grade spelling program handles this presentation.

Greek and Latin Word Roots   Once students understand the spelling-meaning connection—how spelling preserves meaning among related words despite changes in sound—they can then truly benefit from more intensive examination of *word roots*.

CLASSROOM EXAMPLE

Minilesson: The Spelling-Meaning Connection

The teacher writes *inspire* *inspiration* on the board. He asks the students if the two words have a similar meaning. Then he underlines *inspir* in both words.

TEACHER: "Kids, do these letters [pointing to *inspir*] stand for the same sounds in both of these words? Right, they don't! In the word *inspire*, the *i* in the second syllable has a *long* sound, but it changes to a *schwa* sound in the word *inspiration*.

"As we've seen with other types of words we've been examining, these two words are related in meaning *and* in spelling, despite differences in pronunciation. Knowing this can help you spell a word like *inspiration*. Think about it for a minute. The *schwa* sound in the second syllable of *inspiration* gives you no clue to its spelling—unless you think of the related word *inspire*. In the word *inspire*, you can hear the sound in the second syllable: it's a long *i*. The spelling is obvious, and—because words that are related in meaning are often related in spelling—this long *i* is your clue to spelling the *schwa* sound in *inspiration*.

"When you're not sure how to spell a word, try to think of a word that is *related* in spelling and meaning; it should offer you a clue."

Occasionally, the related word that may explain an uncertain spelling may not yet be part of the student's vocabulary. We can turn these words into spelling *and* vocabulary minilessons:

The fifth-grader who spells *condemn* as CONDEM, leaving off the final *n*, may be shown the related word *condemnation*, in which the *n* is clearly heard. By doing this, we reinforce the correct spelling of *condemn* and teach the student a new word—while showing that the meaning of the new word is easily derived from *condemn*.

Spelling-Meaning Strategy

Vowel Changes: Schwa to Short Vowel Sound

Thinking of related words may help you remember how to spell an unclear vowel sound. Read this paragraph.

> The man insisted that what he had done was **legal**. The committee questioned the **legality** of his actions and hired a lawyer.

lega|l
lega|lity

Think
- How are *legal* and *legality* related in meaning?
- What vowel sound does the letter *a* spell in each word?

Here are more related words in which the same letter spells the schwa sound in one word and the short vowel sound in another.

| local | normal | mortal |
| locality | normality | mortality |

Figure 8.14 **Instructional Activities in a Published Spelling Series**

SOURCE: *Houghton Mifflin Spelling and Vocabulary*, Level 6. Copyright © 1990 by Houghton Mifflin Company. Reprinted by permission of Houghton Mifflin Company.

◆ Invariant Greek forms such as *graph* (to write), *therm* (heat), and *photo* (light) should be studied before Latin roots, which—unlike the Greek forms—are often hidden within words and occasionally undergo spelling changes across different words.

◆ Examination of Latin roots should begin with those that occur with greater frequency and which have fairly consistent spellings (Templeton, 1992b). In addition to those mentioned earlier, a few examples are *-pose-* ("to put or place," as in *position*), *-port-* ("to carry," as in *portable*), and *-dict-* ("to speak," as in *diction*). The combination of affixes and roots should be closely examined. The following minilesson illustrates how one teacher discussed this combination in response to a particular spelling error.

The teacher writes the misspelled word *interupt* on the board or on an overhead transparency.

TEACHER: "Kids, I've noticed a particular type of spelling error in many of your papers over the last two weeks, and now is a good time to talk about it. Let's begin by figuring out what's wrong with this word [points to *interupt*]. Alice?"

ALICE: "It's only got one *r*!"

TEACHER: "Right! Why should there be two *r*'s instead of one? After all, we only *hear* one 'r' sound . . ."

The teacher fields the students' responses and then offers the following walk-through: "'Interrupt' is made up of two parts, the prefix *inter*, meaning 'in between,' and the word root *rupt*, which comes from a Latin word meaning 'to break.' When you put *inter* and *rupt* together, you construct a word that means 'to break in between.' If you *interrupt* someone when he or she is talking, you 'break in between' what he or she is saying."

Educational Technology and Word Study

Software manufacturers have for years offered programs for phonics, spelling, and vocabulary development. While we emphasize *contextualizing* so much of students' learning, many "out of context" word study programs can in fact be engaging and *reinforcing* of word features *if* we've already explored these features with our students. Software programs that have students *apply* their word knowledge through a game format can be quite effective. There are programs such as *Word Attack 3* (see Figure 8.15) that combine spelling, vocabulary, and sentence contexts. Often these programs include options for the teacher to add words and definitions.

The vocabulary of the computer and the Internet offers a whole other domain of words and meanings. Students enjoy exploring the definitions and origins of these words. Consider just a few possibilities: web, surf, search engine, browser, gopher, hypertext/hyperstacks/hypercard.

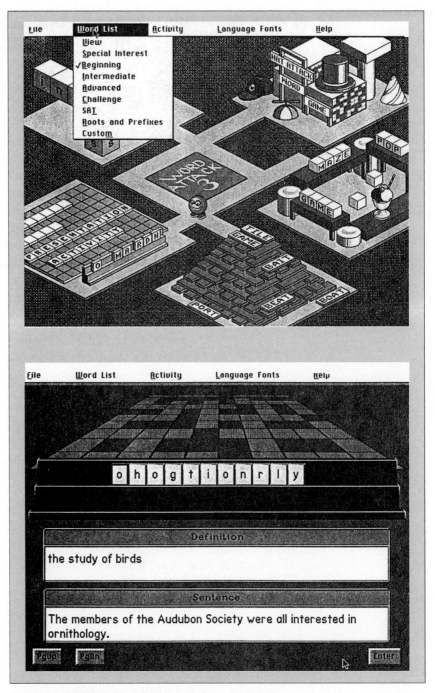

Figure 8.15   Focus on Spelling, Vocabulary, and Sentence Contexts

SOURCE: Willis, J., Stephens, E., & Matthew, K. (1996). *Technology, reading, and language arts.* Boston: Allyn and Bacon.

◆◆◆ **CONCLUDING PERSPECTIVE AND SUMMARY**

Word study and word knowledge are multifaceted. We now know that children do not learn words as discrete, unrelated items. Like the concepts for which they stand, words are understood in relation to each other. Vocabulary development is a process of elaborating and expanding knowledge of these underlying concepts as well as the words that represent them. In contrast to previous thinking, we now realize that spelling and vocabulary development are closely related; knowledge of spelling improves vocabulary skills, and vice versa. Within the context of the integrated language arts, knowledge of vocabulary and spelling supports students' reading and writing proficiency. Conversely, frequent reading and writing will help students at all grade levels increase their vocabularies and recognize and use correct spelling. Discussing words in collaborative class activities also improves students' spelling and vocabulary knowledge.

In this chapter we've addressed the following main points:

◆ Vocabulary study should incorporate students' prior word knowledge and be integrated within other areas of the curriculum.

◆ Wide and frequent reading as well as direct teaching of some new words will increase students' vocabularies.

◆ New words should be introduced in meaning "families" so that students comprehend the semantic and structural relationships among words. Students should also be taught strategies to decipher new words independently.

◆ Primary students' word knowledge increases through frequent discussions and use of new words and the acquisition of sight vocabularies from reading, writing, and participating in word-sort activities.

◆ Word sorts are word-categorizing techniques that focus on semantic and spelling features. They effectively develop word knowledge because they require students to think critically when examining sight vocabulary, corresponding concepts, and word structure.

◆ In the intermediate grades vocabulary development is stimulated by students' awareness and understanding of the morphemic elements that are combined to form English words: affixes and word roots.

◆ Knowing the categories we use to talk about words—synonyms, denotation and connotation, similes and metaphors, antonyms, homonyms, and analogies—can help students develop their vocabularies. Understanding these categories enables students to make more precise distinctions among words and to improve their critical thinking.

◆ We can teach spelling more effectively by understanding the three layers of information in the English spelling system: alphabetic, pattern, and meaning. We can appreciate and thereby explain the logic of this spelling system by examining words that share common spelling features.

◆ Spelling study reinforces word knowledge in general as it is applied in reading and writing. In the intermediate grades spelling and vocabulary become intertwined because students realize that words related in meaning share similar spellings. This visual reminder of meaning becomes the basis for new strategies to test spelling and increase vocabulary knowledge.

Key Terms

alphabet (p. 321)

alphabetic phase (p. 322)

analogies (p. 311)

antonyms (p. 310)

base words (p. 293)

closed word sorts (p. 290)

connotative meaning (p. 311)

degeneration (p. 301)

denotative meaning (p. 311)

derivational patterns stage (p. 325)

elaboration (p. 287)

elevated (p. 301)

expansion (p. 287)

generalization (p. 300)

hands-on experiences (p. 289)

homophones/homographs/ homonyms (p. 310)

meaning (spelling layer) (p. 321)

meaning families (p. 294)

metalinguistically aware (p. 288)

morpheme (p. 293)

morphemic analysis (p. 293)

open word sorts (p. 290)

pattern (spelling layer) (p. 321)

phonemic phase (p. 322)

prefixes (p. 293)

semantic feature analysis (p. 306)

semantic maps (p. 305)

semiphonemic phase (p. 322)

sentence completion (p. 309)

similes and metaphors (p. 311)

specialization (p. 300)

spelling-meaning connection (p. 335)

structural analysis (p. 293)

structured overview (p. 303)

CHAPTER 9

Integrating Oral Communication and the Performance Arts

- ◆ How does the teacher initiate and maintain the types of experiences that fully develop the "communication potential" of each student?

- ◆ Why is oral reading important?

- ◆ How can creative dramatics develop thinking and language in the elementary grades?

- ◆ How will our classroom applications of oral communication provide a foundation for developing the other language arts?

- ◆ How can we help students become perceptive listeners and viewers?

- ◆ What is the value of reading aloud to children? How are interactive "read-alouds" beneficial for students?

INTRODUCTION

The following poem was written by an Apache child in Arizona:

> Have you ever hurt about baskets?
> I have, seeing my grandmother weaving for a long time.
> Have you ever hurt about work?
> I have, because my father works too hard and he tells how he works.
> Have you ever hurt about cattle?
> I have, because my grandfather has been working on the cattle for a long
>   time.
> Have you ever hurt about school?
> I have, because I learned a lot of words from school,
> And they are not my words.
>
> (cited in Cazden, 1988)

Throughout this book we've seen the importance of accommodating the backgrounds and cultures that children bring with them to school. School can be meaningful to children when we respect *their* words as we guide them towards new words and new worlds. In this chapter we'll explore how our oral communication system within the classroom offers a foundation for other modes of expression and learning as well as for extending the classroom language heard, spoken, read, written, acted upon, and reflected upon.

For most individuals oral communication is the primary means of communication. It is also the foundation for acquiring and applying the language arts of reading and writing. Skills developed through listening can be applied directly to reading; those developed through speaking can be applied directly to writing. As we anticipate the speaker, so we will anticipate the writer; as we plan what we will say in light of our listeners, so we will plan what we will write in light of our readers.

We'll begin by examining familiar experiences partly so that children will learn *how* to go about scrutinizing their world closely. As philosophers through the ages have observed, the *examined* experience (or life) is central. By directing children's attention to everyday objects and processes that engage their minds and exercise their language in the everyday world, we can help them develop a better sense of who and where they are. We help the reality and images from everyday life—here and now—become powerful and comprehensible. Egan (1987) has underscored the importance of this examination for young children. He suggests, for example, that children in the primary grades begin with "the close and systematic observation of some particular natural object or process—a tree, rain, a spider's web, a patch of grass" (Egan, p. 467). As teachers, we can use oral language to help children focus these observations so that they can better discuss, reflect on, and organize their thinking about the object or process.

Classroom oral communication is extremely important because it is not only a means of learning but also a means of undertaking other types of learning. Children will learn to apply skills developed in listening and speaking to the other language arts and as a *means of learning* in the other language arts. As discussed in Chapters 6 and 7, reading and writing conferences rely upon effective oral communication among students. So does group work on a particular science project. Moreover, these activities depend upon specific procedures that have themselves been taught through oral communication. If students have not learned how to apply their oral communication skills effectively, their effective learning in reading, writing, and different content areas will suffer.

As teachers we will *model* or demonstrate the range and types of oral communication through our speaking and listening. Our modeling should be clear and straightforward. For example, we should say things like

"This is what I do when I listen to a speaker . . ."

or

"Have you noticed? When I tell a story, the first thing I try to do is create a mood for you. I do this by turning down the lights and putting on my old shawl. Next, I lower my voice slightly to draw you in . . ."

or

"After you have determined what information you're going to give in your oral presentation, you need to think about what props you might need. If you're doing a science experiment, make sure you have containers for your water . . ."

One final important note: as we incorporate a greater diversity of students into our classrooms at a greater rate than ever before in our history, we must also realize that we cannot be experts in all the cultures and languages that they represent. However, we *can* be sensitive to, value, and encourage the diversity we see as we strive to help students adjust to and understand the predominant culture. The environment of our classrooms and the *kinds of language* that are used there will establish the context where this kind of learning can occur.

Listening: From the Simple to the Critical

Listening is probably the language art least addressed—not only in school but probably in our society as well. Because most of us are able to hear fairly well, we assume that what "goes in" is understood just as the speaker intended it to be. We should know better, of course. Like the other language arts, *listening* is not a passive activity. As we pointed out in Chapter 1, meaning does not directly transfer from one individual to another. Meaning travels, with varying degrees of success, over bridges—and in our present situation, oral communication is the bridge. If the listener is attentive, he or she must *construct* the message. Construction is an active process that depends on the context of the situation, and the listener's mood, interest, expectations, and knowledge of the speaker and the topic. Truly active listeners try to approximate as closely as possible the speaker's intended meaning.

"Storytelling" develops imagination, language, literacy—and life.

Depending on the context, this meaning construction may seem almost effortless, or it may be quite challenging, even difficult.

The Range of Instructional Situations in the Integrated Classroom

As we saw in Chapter 2, effective communication depends on

◆ topical knowledge

◆ procedural knowledge (being aware of how to use oral communication well)

◆ self-knowledge (being aware of how successfully one is *applying* procedural knowledge).

"Real-world" listening usually incorporates some or all of the different features and strategies of listening. To be effective listeners, though, students should *explicitly* learn these features and strategies and use them often enough to make them automatic.

A series of instructional formats representing a range of situations is described next. These activities get children thinking about sound *per se* and then build on successive levels of awareness and ability. They should help children actively pay attention and respond to sound in increasingly more complex ways.

Natural Sounds

Direct children's attention to sounds that are naturally occurring around them. If it's possible to hear sounds of the outdoors, so much the better. Begin by having children close their eyes and *listen*; for beginners and young children, one minute is long enough. Then ask them what they heard. At first the class will simply list the sounds; later you can ask children to *describe* the sounds.

Created Sounds

Have students identify some **created sounds**. As with naturally occurring sounds, everyone should close their eyes for a brief period of time while they listen. Nails drummed on a table top, erasers clapped together, paper wadded — these and more exotic sounds can be identified and described. Teachers can model the use of descriptive vocabulary in these situations. For example, use

◆ *scratchy* and *grainy* after playing part of an old 78-rpm recording

◆ *liquid* to describe a particular bird song

◆ *ticklish* to refer to a giggle.

Compare and contrast a single sound or phrase with other sounds:

◆ "This sound is like a jackhammer."

◆ "The air coming through the vents reminds me of when the heater comes on at home and I feel snuggly in my bed."

Voices

After focusing on natural and created environmental sounds, students can focus on the identity and quality of *voices*:

◆ Again, students close their eyes.

◆ The teacher moves about the room, tapping different students.

◆ At each tap a student will respond with a brief phrase or sentence.

◆ The class then tries to guess the child's identity.

As Stewig (1983) noted, this listening exercise allows us to introduce terms related to the "structure" of sound:

pitch—high or low

timbre—harsh, buzzy, mellow

duration—how long the sound or sounds last.

Sequence

This activity is most effective with younger children. We simply ask them to recall a sequence of different sounds, such as tapping, closing a book, and opening a drawer. We ask for the same with events in a story or directions—from two- or three-step directions to sequences that are much longer.

Anticipation

There is a wide assortment of "anticipation" listening activities. They can range from listening to fill in a missing word or phrase in a poem or predictable text (see Chapter 6) to listening for and remembering key events or bits of information.

When students will listen to a speaker, it's important that they first learn something about his or her background and qualifications. In addition, we ask students to keep two questions in mind:

◆ What do you already know about the topic?

◆ What new information do you think you might learn?

Think for a moment about how these activities can help develop students' *writing*. Students' focusing on aspects of sound will help them be more precise and detailed in their own compositions—as, for example, when they listen to and describe a *type* of sound or identify a particular individual's voice.

Critical Listening and Viewing

Our students are capable of listening critically. Our task is to make them aware of this ability so they can apply it appropriately. For example, in many instances students will tell us without hesitation whether a situation on television is "fake" or a commercial realistically portrays a product. Clever programmers can get around this perceptiveness *unless* the children are shown how to apply the insight they already possess to more subtle media presentations. Ask your students: "What technique is being used? How can you tell? What types of information aren't you being given (or how is the information being presented to skew your thinking)?"

These days **critical listening and viewing** often fall within the categories of the "manipulative arts" or "media literacy"; in years past the rather blunt term "propaganda" was used. Regardless of the label, students need to evaluate critically how information is presented to them and comprehend how others may attempt to influence them. This understanding can also be applied to more "objective" presentations of information such as newscasts, documentaries, "docudramas," and informational oral presentations.

The following are the major categories of the manipulative arts:

1. **Glittering generality** This type of statement is obviously true, obviously positive—and far too general! It is worded to influence listeners, but the meanings of the words are usually vague. The politician states that he is in favor of "a free country, without prejudice, with opportunity for all." We may agree with that statement—it's often hard to disagree with glittering generalities—but merely saying that he stands for these goals is hardly the same as telling us how he might *realistically* attain them.

2. **Bandwagon** "You don't want to be left out, do you? Simply *everyone* is buying Skyhigh athletic shoes!" This approach works especially well with both younger and older adolescents. The key is to stress that *everyone* is involved, and *you* don't want to be left behind.

3. **Testimonial** If a well-known and well-respected personality supports something, then—we are urged to conclude—it *must* be good. Support can be verbal, as in a commercial, or subtle, as when a picture of a sports star appears on cereal boxes.

4. **Deck stacking** "Crunchy Munchies cereal is loaded with vitamins." You are not told what the vitamins are, how high the dosage is, or that Crunchy Munchies actually has more sugar than any other cereal on the market! This approach "stacks the deck" with supportive evidence in favor of whatever is being offered and conveniently leaves out the detracting evidence.

5. **Positive association** Something or someone is presented in a situation that has a positive, pleasant, favorable connotation. There is little if any *realistic* association between the two, however. For example, a magazine ad shows an attractive woman in an evening gown standing next to a lawnmower or an attractive man in a tank-top guzzling a soft drink.

6. **Plain folks** Products or people are presented as down-home, "just like us." The subtle message is that highfalutin', often university-educated individuals are somehow not as honest, hard working, and bedrock-values-oriented as the rest of us. In a recent presidential election, for example, both candidates seemed to go out of their way to ignore or downplay the fact that they both graduated from Ivy League universities.

7. **Snob appeal** This is the flip side of the "plain-folks" and "bandwagon" techniques. The attempt is to convince the listener that he or she is special, unique, and somehow more intelligent, perceptive, or attractive than most other people. These are some illustrative slogans: "There aren't many who've worked as hard as you have; you deserve the very best"; "*You* know the meaning of speed and performance—that's why the Super XYZ Sportcoupe takes you out ahead of the crowd . . ."

8. **Name calling** As the term suggests, this technique aims at establishing an association with individuals or ideas that have negative connotations. The association is often unfair because there is no evidence to support the name-calling—for example, referring to someone's beliefs as "neo-Nazi" or to a reporter as a member of the "left-wing liberal media."

Reading Aloud to Children

The setting is a fifth-grade classroom. The teacher is reading Natalie Babbitt's *Tuck Everlasting* (1975) to the students, one chapter per day. It intertwines several themes, perhaps the two most powerful being the whirling emotions and physical turmoil of Winnie, a twelve-year-old girl on the verge of womanhood, and death and its meaning, including the prospect of immortality. The Tuck family is immortal, having discovered and drunk from a spring that could be characterized as a fountain of youth. Winnie, a girl from a nearby village, has discovered the secret of the spring. In the following excerpt the patriarch of this immortal family, Tuck, tries to explain to

The following guided lesson is appropriate for many third-graders and most students from fourth grade and up. It works very well in a whole-class instructional format.

1. Talk about different commercials that students have seen on television. Ask questions such as

   - Is what they present absolutely true?

   - Do you entirely believe them?

   - What is their purpose?

   - How do you think people who make commercials try to influence you—to get you to want what they are selling?

   After discussing these questions with students, explain that they're going to be looking very closely at the techniques people use to influence the opinions and desires of others. Commercials and magazine advertisements are one very widespread format, but there are many other formats and sources.

2. Ask *why* students might think that being aware of these techniques is important. (Here we are highlighting *what* our students are going to learn and *why*.)

3. Using new commercials or advertisements, see what students notice about the language and pictures. Have students work in pairs to go through advertisements, categorizing each one. We can provide feedback where appropriate; often an ad will actually illustrate more than one technique.

   An excellent follow-up to working in pairs is having students share and discuss what they have found with the whole group.

4. Restate the purpose of studying the different techniques of manipulation and discuss how an awareness of them can apply to everyday life, including reading and writing.

5. Students can follow up by making a group book with ads cut from magazines that illustrate different propaganda techniques. They also can catalog various types as viewed in TV commercials or heard on the radio at home. In addition, they can write their own commercials; their scripts could include a description of the setting as well as directions. If possible, follow up with actual videotaping and involve the students in analyzing and identifying the propaganda techniques used.

Winnie why she shouldn't drink from the spring. His explanation is simple, beautiful, and riveting. It should be read in its entirety, of course, but the following excerpt captures a bit of its power:

> Everything's a wheel, turning and turning, never stopping. The frogs is part of it, and the bugs, and the fish, and the wood thrush, too. And people. But never the same ones. Always coming in new, always growing and changing, and always moving on. That's the way it's supposed to be. That's the way it *is* . . . . That's what us Tucks are, Winnie. Stuck so's we can't move on. We ain't part of the wheel no more. Dropped off, Winnie. Left behind. And everywhere around us, things is moving and growing and changing. You, for instance. A child now, but someday a woman. And after that, moving on to make room for the new children . . .
>
> [When Winnie fully realizes for the first time that she *will* die someday:]
>
> She raged against it, helpless and insulted, and blurted at last, "I don't want to die."
>
> "No," said Tuck calmly. "Not now. Your time's not now. But dying's part of the wheel, right there next to being born. You can't pick out the pieces you like and leave the rest . . ."

All the force of language, ideas, and emotions that spring from a story read aloud is clearly evident in the faces of a roomful of fifth-graders transfixed by a tale such as *Tuck Everlasting*.

There is a magic in the air when we read to children of *any* age. There is a rhythm and cadence to the language of books, and for many children, *we* will be the sole source of this language. In a very real way, we will provide the model for the "silent voice" within each child's head, the voice the children will hear when they read for themselves—a factor that is important for older students as well as younger ones. The value and importance of reading stories to young children in particular has been convincingly described by Heath (1982) in her article "What No Bedtime Story Means." Put directly, no bedtime story means that children are not prepared for the types of literacy experiences and expectations that occur in school. Kindergarten experiences, for example, are based on the assumption that children are familiar with stories in the predominant culture.

The following are guidelines for **reading aloud:**

1. Read the book yourself before reading it to the students. This will prevent the occasional embarrassing or awkward instances when you encounter language or situations in the book that really ought not to be shared with a whole class of children.

2. Read a book that *you* enjoy!

3. Have a particular time or a few times each day when you read to the class, and *read every day*. At the primary levels read aloud to the students *several* times a day. If you fall into the habit of skipping days, your commitment and the students' interest will be diluted.

4. At the beginning of reading sessions, allow some time for students to settle down and get back into the story.

5. Sit so that your voice will project out to the whole class. If you are reading a picture book, sit so that when you hold the book for students to see, *all* will be able to do so.

6. This is a time *for listening only*. Although some teachers allow pupils to complete unfinished projects or work on whatever they please during read-aloud time, this practice will at best only approximate your read-aloud objectives. Doodling or drawing, however, is okay — particularly for very active children.

7. Read more slowly rather than faster. Listeners need time to construct pictures "in the mind's eye." This visualization is important not only in listening but in reading as well; a critical aspect of reading comprehension is the ability to visualize as one reads. Reading more slowly also helps establish the rhythm and cadence of the language.

8. Always stop at a suspenseful point. As Trelease (1995) counsels, "Leave the audience hanging; they'll be counting the minutes until the next reading" (p. 59).

9. There should be time for discussion and reaction after the reading. Reaction can take the form of drawing and/or writing, *if the students wish to participate*.

10. *Gradually* ease into longer and more complex stories. For students who are either not in the habit of listening or returning from a long break, begin with shorter, more attention-grabbing selections.

11. Read a variety of books throughout the year.

12. Occasionally read material that will stretch the children intellectually.

Trelease also offers a list of practices that should be avoided. These two are most significant for teachers:

1. Don't continue reading a book that is clearly not working.

2. Don't go into your own ideas about interpretations of the book; too often such explanations become didactic, and the kids adjust their responses accordingly.

Sometimes we will simply read to students without asking any questions. At other times, we can pose questions just as we do in the Guided Reading-Thinking Activity (Chapter 6); at such times, the read-aloud becomes more "interactive":

1. Ask, "What do you think this story might be about?"

2. After reading to a point in the story where the plot and/or action has been raised to a high level of suspense and excitement, ask the students, "*Now* what do we think? We thought that [such and such] would happen. Is that how it has turned out so far?"

3. After discussing predictions the children have made, we can ask, "Now what do you think's going to happen? Why? Why not? — Well, let's listen and find out!"

4. After the read-aloud, we may pose questions: "Would *you* have done the same thing?" "How did you know that . . . ?" "How is this like an experience you have had?" Other questions that facilitate aesthetic responses are "What did you notice in the story? How did the story make you feel? How does the story remind you of your own life?"

CLASSROOM EXAMPLE

"Interactive" Read-Aloud

Let's see how one teacher engaged her first-grade students in a read-aloud early in the year. The teacher is going to read Judith Viorst's *Alexander and the Terrible, Horrible, No Good, Very Bad Day* (1972), a book about everything that goes wrong for the title character from the time he gets up in the morning to bedtime. Everyone has days like this, and Alexander's is a classic!

TEACHER: (showing the book's front cover to the children): "Boys and girls, we're going to listen to a story written by Judith Viorst called 'Alexander and the Terrible, Horrible, No Good, Very Bad Day.' What do you think this story might be about? Jason?"

JASON: "He gonna have a *bad* day!"

TEACHER: "It *does* sound like it, doesn't it? Yes, Annie?"

ANNIE: "He's gonna be sick."

TEACHER: "Okay! What else might happen? Yes, Glen?"

GLEN: "I think he'll have to clean up his room!"

LETISHA: "I think he gonna get blamed for something he didn't do."

TEACHER: "Let's find out! Listen as I read, and we'll see what will happen to Alexander."

The teacher reads the first four pages in which Alexander has

(Continued)

trouble getting ready for the day, does not get a prize in his cereal box (both his brothers get great prizes), and does not get to sit by the window in the car on the way to school. The fourth page ends with a refrain that will recur throughout the book: "I could tell it was going to be a terrible, horrible, no good, very bad day." The teacher stops after the fourth page and says, "*Now* what do we think? We thought that Alexander might get sick, have to clean his room, or get blamed for something he didn't do. Is that how the story has turned out so far?"

GLEN: "Well, we don't know yet, but *I* think he's gonna have trouble at school!"

TEACHER: "How about the rest of us? Do we agree with Glen about not knowing whether something will happen or not?"

CONNIE: "I don't think he's gonna have to clean up his room, 'cause he's not at home anymore."

MONICA: "Yeah, me too!"

MATT: "I still think he's gonna be sick."

TEACHER: "Why do you think so, Matt?"

MATT: "'Cause things will probably just get worse and that's one of the worst things that can happen to you at school."

BONNIE: "I think the car's gonna get a flat tire."

SAM: "Prob'ly not . . . but we don't know for sure yet."

TEACHER: "That's true. How about being blamed for something he didn't do? Might that still happen?" [Several pupils chorus: "Yeah!" "It could. . . ."] "Well, let's listen and find out if the car will have a flat tire, Alexander will have trouble at school, get sick, be blamed for something he didn't do — or maybe something else."

This format continues for the remainder of the reading; some predictions are gradually rejected and others confirmed. With this particular book, the things that *might* happen are almost unlimited, but what the children are able to do fairly well is reject predictions that they realize couldn't happen, given the time frame of the story and the location. *After* the story is finished, you may ask a few questions — just a few — using the guidelines to be discussed. A story such as *Alexander* has great potential not only for tying in with children's own experiences, but also for talking about the perspectives of *other* individuals — in this case, Alexander's parents and his friend at school who shunned him. For example, you could ask, "I wonder . . . Do we sometimes behave toward our friends the way Paul behaved toward Alexander?"

This active listening and responding is critical to all communication, and our read-alouds can lay the foundations for effective interaction with all kinds of texts through the students' own reading, writing, and discussion.

Students: The Role of Oral Reading in the Integrated Language Arts

Oral reading is important. It begins with the *choral reading* (see p. 357) that children do during the beginning literacy phase. In this context oral reading is nonthreatening, enjoyable, and purposeful. In fact, we've already seen that reading out loud is a natural developmental behavior for most young children. As children pass from audible out-loud reading through whispering and on to silent reading, however, the value of oral reading should not diminish. There are three primary purposes for having students read orally: (1) to check comprehension, (2) to enhance appreciation of different genres as well as the nuances of those genres, and (3) to assess and evaluate reading development.

We have already seen how oral reading can be used to check understanding. In the context of a GRTA, for example, a student will locate and read aloud part of the text that supports her answer or opinion. This type of oral reading should be frequent; as is apparent, it can be combined with other important strategies, such as rereading to prove a point and skimming to locate the appropriate passage. Using oral reading in this way, the teacher can check a student's ability in each of the three comprehension categories — not just the minor details.

The second purpose of oral reading — to enhance appreciation of different genres — is implicit in most of the activities we undertake with reading. Much of each genre scheme that students construct depends on the *way* that language is used in different genres — on its sounds, rhythms, and cadence. Used appropriately, oral reading can develop an understanding and appreciation of these various aspects of language. Of course, there is an obvious difference in the language use in poetry and narratives. And *within* each of these genres, language functions in different ways in order to evoke different meanings. When texts are read silently, students often miss these nuances. By reading books or poems orally, students develop a better sense of the uses of language and in turn incorporate this knowledge into their silent reading. For example, the predictability of rhythms and rhymes in poetry delights young children, but for older students this same predictability becomes a parody of poetry — limited to a heavy-handed metrical beat with end-of-line rhymes. These students may benefit from also reading poetry that has more subtle rhythms and that does not end-rhyme.

We'll address our third purpose of oral reading—to assess and evaluate reading development—in Chapter 11.

Inappropriate oral reading tasks, however, can work against students' development as well as diminish their enjoyment and appreciation of reading. It should not be used in a "round-robin" fashion where students take turns reading orally from a basal reader or textbook, going around the reading group circle or the classroom. What usually happens in this situation (you may remember it!) is that instead of listening to the reading or following along in the book, each student spends most of the time looking for the part he or she will read orally to see how "hard" it is and if it contains any unfamiliar words. Of course, the sequence usually is changed along the way and the student winds up having to read a different section!

Why does "round robin" reading happen? At the primary-grade levels teachers want to see how well students are doing and whether they know most of the words. At the intermediate levels teachers realize that students usually do not enjoy reading their textbooks and may, in fact, *not* read them—so by participating in a round-robin class reading, students will have gone through the assigned chapter at least once. As we've seen throughout this text, however, there are far better ways to address these objectives.

Additional Ways to Provide Appropriate Oral Reading Experiences in the Diverse Classroom

Choral Reading

Choral reading is excellent for both small and large groups—and even for a whole class. Readers of less ability and/or students acquiring English as a second language can join in and not "stand out" if they can't remember certain words. Texts for choral readings may be displayed on the wall, projected on the overhead, or photocopied and distributed. At first it's best to use a single text that everyone can see in case you need to point to specific lines or words.

Texts for choral reading will be read and reread, just as Big Books were by beginning readers. Choral readings can simply consist of repeated readings, but they can also be more involved. When we really "get into" a text with students, we can address a number of objectives—really processing the text, and thinking about style, mood, and how the author might have intended the text to sound. Words and phrases that should receive special emphasis can be underlined and rehearsed. Also pace, volume, and pitch can be varied in different places.

Readers Theatre

Closely related to choral reading, **Readers Theatre** is one of the most effective vehicles for developing an appreciation for the sounds of language (Busching, 1981; Stoyer, 1982). In Readers Theatre a number of students read aloud to an audience from a text in their hands. They take turns reading, depending on the type of text. For example, if characters are involved, each student reads a character's part; if the text is a poem, each student may read alternating lines or groups of lines. Usually the only props are stools for students to sit on. Occasionally, minimal props such as masks, backdrops, and simple costumes may be used.

Students rehearse the text before presenting it and convey the action and emotion through their voices rather than acting it out as they would in a play or in creative dramatics. For example, students from third grade on would delight in practicing and presenting Shel Silverstein's "Sarah Sylvia Cynthia Stout Would Not Take the Garbage Out" (1974). In this poem Ms. Stout allows the garbage to accumulate, a process that Silverstein exquisitely describes. It becomes obvious in the poem that she meets an unspeakable fate as the growing mound of garbage takes on monstrous proportions. The reading of this forty-seven-line poem could be divided between two groups of any number of students. The two groups could alternate reading two lines each, or perhaps six. The poem can be partitioned several different ways, but the teacher should make such decisions at first.

Using this poem as an illustration, consider what is being highlighted and reinforced. First, there is delight in the sounds of language through alliteration — such as the /s/ sounds in the name *Sarah Sylvia Cynthia Stout*, which is repeated throughout the poem — and through many captivating internal rhymes, such as the phrase "Rubbery blubbery macaroni." Then there is the visual imagery of a growing mound of garbage and its dire consequences for Sarah.

Another important type of knowledge is developed through Readers Theatre. Because students will reread the same text several times when preparing the presentation, fluency and reading rate develop and new words are reinforced, thus expanding and elaborating students' sight vocabularies.

Author's Chair

In addition to being fostered through choral reading, the confidence to read orally before a group is developed in the "Author's Chair" (Graves & Hansen, 1983). The **Author's Chair** is a privileged place; the students and the teacher will occupy it at different times. The students may read from their own writing or a favorite trade book. In both instances, of course, the children have probably already read the material they will share orally to themselves several times. Questions are usually asked after the piece is read.

If they wrote the piece, students respond as authors; if they read from a trade book, they respond as they believe the author would have.

Plays

Students enjoy presenting *plays*, which also must be read several times before sharing. The Wright Group, for example, has published several selections in a play format for beginning readers. *Radio plays*, which are enjoying a renaissance, also provide excellent models. Older students like these—particularly combining the reading experience with sound effects. The most famous radio play of all time, Orson Welles's adaptation of H. G. Wells's *The War of the Worlds*, is now widely available on tape and record and would be a marvelous introduction to the genre for intermediate-level students.

Sharing, Storytelling, and Oral Presentations in the Integrated Classroom

Sharing

Sharing may be one of the most underappreciated and perhaps underutilized activities in the elementary grades. The skills that students develop through sharing, however, provide the foundation for other, more complex speaking situations such as presenting a report orally and facilitating growth in reading and writing.

In the beginning we should model the ground rules for the activity. This allows us to demonstrate language that helps encourage elaboration and better organization of information to be shared. For both primary and upper-elementary students, the ground rules are simple and straightforward. Drawing on Moffett and Wagner (1993) and Michaels and Foster (1985), the following guidelines are suggested:

1. One person at a time will share.

2. A designated "leader" for the day will decide who gets to share (at first, the "leader" is the teacher).

3. Children must raise their hands if they wish to contribute.

4. If children misbehave, they get one warning from the leader. A second warning sends them back to their seats.

Oral presentations help to develop organization and presentation skills as well as develop confidence.

5. When a student has finished sharing her initial information, listeners may question and contribute.

We can model good *listening* behavior, asking follow-up questions that encourage the sharer to elaborate. These questions can reflect our own natural interest and curiosity. For example, we could ask, " 'When did they give it to you?' 'What happened to the wing there?' 'What's the red button for?' 'What do you do if you want to get the money out again?' 'Where do you keep it?' 'Do you let your brother use it?' " (Moffett & Wagner, 1993, p. 84). Over a period of time, these kinds of requests help children anticipate what others may want to know, thus helping them grow beyond a primarily egocentric perspective.

Our questions can get children to elaborate without changing their focus. As Cazden (1988) reported, teachers must realize *why* children want to share something and not completely change the children's agenda to make it their own. For example: a second-grader brings in his pet kitten. His focus is on his new, cuddly pet; he wants to share information with the class about when it was born, how it behaves, and his love for it. After he shares, the teacher decides that this might be an appropriate time to talk about the difference between domesticated and wild animals. He asks the child if there are cats that are much bigger than the size his kitten will grow up to be, intending to expand the thinking and discussion to lions, tigers, and mountain lions. Even if the child takes the teacher's lead, the talk has gone off on another tack entirely—away from the child's excitement and pride in his new pet and toward an abstraction that is, at least at this particular time, of little concern to the child and may make him somewhat uncomfortable.

If we feel students need help selecting topics for sharing, or if we simply want to change the prevailing focus occasionally, we can ask students to bring something that

◆ has a good story behind it

◆ they made or grew

◆ means a great deal to them

◆ moves or works in a funny or interesting way (Moffett & Wagner, 1993).

Again, these criteria are just as appropriate for older students as for younger ones.

Many of the questions modeled and used during sharing time will also be used in *writing conferences* (Chapter 7). Michaels and Foster (1985) observed that "through discourse activities such as sharing time, teachers help children develop valued language skills and literature discourse strategies that are required in written communication" (p. 156). Developing a sensitivity to one's audience is critical in all facets of the language arts, and this sensitivity is well exercised in sharing groups.

Storytelling in the Integrated Language Arts Classroom

Storytelling is enjoying a renaissance in education because it is a truly entertaining art form and because it powerfully conveys information for young children that will be essential in developing their world and imaginations in general and their literacy in particular. With regard to literacy, storytelling conveys the structure or form of *narratives* and the forms and rhythms of effective language. In addition to motivating children to read, storytelling can introduce them to the values and literary traditions of different cultures. The concept of stories and the roles they play are etched deeply in all civilizations and cultures. Although the conflicts and characters in stories may arise from common psychological roots (Bettelheim, 1976; Jung, 1953; Yolen, 1981), the form and substance that stories or narratives assume are shaped by the particular cultures in which they are shared.

Even very young children can be transfixed by a fairly long story when it is spun by a storyteller. As we all do, they enjoy being "drawn in" to the story, anticipating and chanting refrains along with the storyteller. Remember the billy goats' "trip trap, trip trap" on the bridge? Jay O'Callahan, a master storyteller, tells a delightful story of Herman and Marguerite on video (1986)—the former an earthworm, the latter a caterpillar who later changes into a butterfly. In what is a major creative effort for him, Herman the earthworm manages to write his own song, sung shyly at first, with gusto later on:

> My name is Herman,
> and I like squirmin',
> and I like bein' close to the ground, grum, grum.

This song grows from a silly giggle for children to—believe it or not—an inspiring affirmation of Herman's self and purpose. It comes to be anticipated and, each time it appears, causes delight.

Many teachers are uncomfortable when they first attempt storytelling. Whether we'd rather "debut" in front of peers or children, we should debut nevertheless; we will then probably find ourselves hooked.

The following are guidelines to prepare for storytelling (adapted from Stewig, 1983):

◆ Choose a story *you* enjoy.

◆ Partition the story into "units of action"; that is, identifiable action segments.

◆ Write a brief summary of each unit of action on a card; as you prepare to rehearse the storytelling, you can carry the cards around as aids for remembering.

◆ Do *not* attempt to memorize the story exactly as it is written in a book. Rather, tell it in your own words. There is one exception to this suggestion: important *repeated* words, phrases, or lines—such as "My name is Herman"—*should* be committed to memory.

◆ Many storytellers like to use a prop every time they tell a story—an instant mood-setter to let the students know a story is about to begin. Some examples are a storyteller's shawl, a candle, or a particular hat.

Children's Storytelling

Children will pick up much about the art of storytelling from our attempts and from any other storytellers they may see and hear. Of course, children are in a real sense natural storytellers themselves, so they should have the opportunity to demonstrate their aptitude in class.

To help provide structure for the children's storytelling, encourage them to use props like wordless picture books, flannel boards, and puppets. Children should at first plan to tell short stories. These brief versions may be told to a small group or perhaps to just one other student. Through the process of storytelling, children learn how to abstract and sequence important information. These are important skills for reading and writing as well. Children will quite naturally begin to use language from books read to them and stories they have heard. Using this type of language will in turn promote their comprehension in reading and expression in writing.

Storytelling is an "art" as well, and just like dancing, playing an instrument, and writing creatively, teachers and students can dedicate quality time to it. When storytelling is focused upon this way, it integrates powerfully with the other language arts competencies we are helping students develop. With our guidance applied as needed, here are the steps students can follow (adapted from Hamilton & Weiss, 1990). These can be distributed to students on a handout and discussed.

1. Choose a story *you* enjoy.

2. Read the story aloud several times.

3. Make a *story map* (Chapter 6) to help you visualize the events. Use this to practice telling the story. You should know the plot of your story very well.

4. Tell the story in your own words, but keep a few of the original's interesting expressions or turns of phrase that give the story flavor. To gain confidence, it often helps to memorize the story's first and last lines.

5. If possible, *tape record* your story and listen to it several times to focus on expression and pacing.

6. Really think about your characters so that you have a good image of what they look like and how they speak. This way, *what* you say, *how* you say it, and your *expressions* will enliven your story.

Hamilton and Weiss suggest that we encourage students to practice their stories in the following ways:

◆ Tell the story to an imaginary audience—all the way through, without stopping.

◆ Tell the story as you look into a mirror.

◆ Tell the story whenever you can to anyone who'll listen.

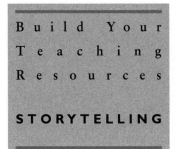

Articles focusing on storytelling appear frequently in journals such as *Reading Teacher*, the *Hornbook*, and the *New Advocate*. The following books are considered classics of storytelling:

Baker, A., & Greene, E. (1987). *Storytelling, art and technique*. New York: R. R. Bowker.

Barton, B. (1986). *Tell me another: Storytelling and reading aloud at home, at school and in the community*. Portsmouth, NH: Heinemann.

Bauer, C. F. (1977). *Handbook for storytellers*. Chicago: American Library Association.

Breneman, L., & Breneman, B. (1983). *Once upon a time: A storytelling handbook*. Chicago: Nelson-Hall.

Hamilton, M., & Weiss, M. (1990). *Children tell stories*. Portsmouth, NH: Heinemann.

Maguire, J. (1985). *Creative storytelling: Choosing, inventing, and sharing tales for children*. New York: McGraw-Hill.

Paley, V. G. (1990). *The boy who would be a helicopter: The uses of storytelling in the classroom*. Cambridge, MA: Harvard University Press.

Ross, R. (1980). *Storyteller*. Columbus, OH: Merrill.

Shedlock, M. L. (1951). *The art of the storyteller*. New York: Dover.

When students learn how to tell a story with this degree of detail and preparation, they should share it as a culminating activity for a thematic unit or at an assembly.

Oral Presentations

The processes of sharing and storytelling help students feel more comfortable and less inhibited when speaking before an audience—even of their peers—and prepare them for presenting an **oral report** before a group. Preparing the content of oral reports is quite similar to preparing written reports (see Chapter 7). We'll focus here on the *delivery* of oral reports.

Presenting oral reports accomplishes several objectives:

◆ Students apply organizing skills when readying material for a clear presentation. This is an important paring-down process that involves identifying what is *most* important—thus requiring students to think critically about their content.

◆ Students learn how to deliver an oral presentation effectively by using oral and body language as well as supporting materials.

◆ Students' confidence is developed.

◆ Oral presentation skills can be very useful throughout the school years and, of course, eventually in the workplace as well. Although each new speaking situation will create a certain amount of anxiety, if students have previous successful experience discussing something before a group, they will have skills to draw upon.

Students should first present their reports before a small audience. Later on, as they gain confidence, they may deliver reports before a larger group. Their initial presentations may, in fact, be one of several oral reports given by a committee that has worked together.

As with sharing, oral reports should involve the use of visuals or props of some type to which children can refer: transparencies on an overhead projector, maps, or materials for a science experiment. These provide important supports for presenters and also help their audience understand the presentation.

When preparing to deliver the report, students should at least audiotape their presentations. This taping allows them to experiment with different speech mannerisms—for example, the speed at which they talk or ways to vary their pitch. If the technology is available, videotaping works best, particularly if students are working together in a group and each member will be giving a report. The students can help each other by constructively evaluating the taped presentations.

Emphasize the following skills of oral presentation:

◆ Speak clearly.

◆ Make eye contact with the audience.

◆ Gesture and move smoothly.

◆ Use space effectively.

◆ Make appropriate and effective use of visual aids.

Variations on oral presentations include "talk-show" and "chatauqua" formats. The *chatauqua* derives from traveling presentations that went by this term in the late nineteenth and early twentieth century. The chatauqua, which has been recently revived, features a famous personality who talks about his or her life and then fields questions from the audience. Intermediate students can study a historical personality—thus becoming an "expert"—and then make a presentation and respond to questions as though they were that personality—as students do with Sara Winnemucca and Sequoia in the Thematic Exploration following this chapter.

Small-Group Discussions in the Integrated Classroom

We have been emphasizing the importance of helping students become independent learners as well as cooperative workers. Both of these objectives will be addressed in the small-group work the students undertake. The collaborative and cooperative learning that such group work allows will underlie most of the learning that occurs in our classrooms. We've already explored many of these small-group activities in Chapters 3, 4, and 6—including the procedures for establishing literature discussion groups and teaching the process of working in small groups. In this section we'll more specifically address how **discussion** can be structured and facilitated within a small group context. Through discussion students will be

◆ identifying issues or problems

◆ defining the parts of these issues or problems

◆ working through a problem-solving process to arrive at a conclusion.

Critical thinking is at work here: one of our major goals is to have students internalize this process so they can apply this reasoning in their independent problem-solving.

Getting Underway

As we saw in Chapter 3 when we discussed *grouping*, small-group work should be phased in gradually. Let's explore the following three guidelines for beginning discussion groups in our classes:

◆ *Start slowly, with one group at a time.*
This approach applies whether we begin with new groups or existing groups. For example, we should "walk through" a group discussion with one group at a time, discussing the procedure and modeling it.

◆ *Start with simple topics.*
We should set students up for success as much as possible by helping them identify discussion topics or selecting them ourselves. Many of these topics will come directly from the literature students are reading and from projects they're exploring as part of a thematic unit. Later on, after students have internalized the discussion process, we can explore more complex and timely issues such as famine or drugs as a school problem—and what we can do about them.

◆ *Focus on the process at first.*
Initially, keep the meeting time fairly brief—fifteen minutes or so. After the first few sessions, we should help students assess how well the discussion group went and how it might be improved the next time around. The content is still important in the beginning, but once students internalize the *process*, subsequent group discussion work can focus exclusively on the task or topics at hand.

Procedural Guidelines

The following are the "basics" for discussion group guidelines (Morris, 1977, cited in Cohen, 1987):

1. Decide what the question to be addressed *means*, then discuss this meaning with the rest of the group.

2. Make sure the group decides on one meaning.

3. Express your own ideas.

4. Listen to others; give everyone a chance to talk.

5. Ask others for their ideas.

6. Give reasons for your ideas and discuss many different ideas.

If all class members have been simultaneously involved in small-group discussions, pull them together afterwards for a wrap-up (Cohen, 1994). This convening also provides an opportunity for one child who has grasped a major concept or idea to "run through" it for the rest of the class. Conclude with feedback on the *process* as well—talk about how well the discussions went.

The Teacher's Role in Small-Group Discussions: Supporting, Questioning, Prompting

Barnes (1976) summed up the teacher's role in discussion well: "The quality of the discussion—and therefore the quality of the learning—is not determined solely by the ability of the [students]. The nature of the task, their familiarity with the subject matter, their confidence in themselves, their sense of what is expected of them, all these affect the quality of the discussion, *and these are all open to influence by the teacher*" (p. 71, emphasis added).

During times when the whole class is engaged in small-group discussions, we should roam about, alert for those opportunities when it is wise—not just convenient—for us to dip into a discussion to "facilitate" through

AT THE TEACHER'S DESK

SMALL-GROUP DISCUSSION IN ACTION

Discussion in small groups can facilitate the solution to significant problems in the classroom, the school, or the community at large. **Brainstorming** is one specific application of small-group discussions that can be an excellent way to address such problems. The objective in brainstorming is for the group to generate a number of ideas or solutions that immediately come to mind.

- Each group should have a "scribe" or recorder who writes down the ideas as fast as they come. There is no comment or evaluation—that will come later.

- After the ideas have been brainstormed, the group goes back and determines how realistic each suggested idea or solution is. Each proposed idea should be considered in terms of whether or not it is immediately feasible, may take a longer period of time, or perhaps is simply unusable.

A more involved extension of brainstorming spreads the problem-solving sessions over five days. Each day a different question is brainstormed:

1. What is the issue, problem, or goal?
2. What has caused this situation or keeps us from accomplishing our goal?
3. What could we do to solve the problem or reach our goal?
4. Is there anything that will prevent us from doing so?
5. What should be our next steps?

questions about the process and the content of the discussion. These questions are aimed at **clarifying, elaborating,** and **qualifying.**

Clarification: Let's say a discussion about poverty in the United States has gotten bogged down. Kneeling next to the group, we excuse ourselves for interrupting and say, "Based on your discussion, I wonder if you're all agreeing on the same definition of *poverty*? Janet, how are you defining *poverty*? Jeremiah, how are *you* defining it?" After thinking about this question, the students—and the group—realize why they were going around in circles. This means of *clarification* should stick in their minds the next time there is a similar problem.

Elaboration: We can consider additional information or possibilities— "Are there any other ways of accomplishing that?" "What else could they do to address the problem?"

Qualification: We can look again at a statement or belief, usually one that is overgeneralized: "Do you think *all* fifth-graders would feel that way?" "Is there a time when this *wouldn't* work as fast?"

Students who have difficulty working with others should be given specific responsibilities within the group. For example, we can ask the chronic interrupter or arguer to be group "scribe" or recorder for a short period of time. This role *requires* that the student listen to what others say and withhold comment. The student will get positive reinforcement from the group at the end of his or her stint as recorder. Students who misbehave to get attention—even negative attention—are more likely to begin to receive some *positive* reinforcement in a small-group situation. The reason is simple: the group is small, so there is more opportunity to get to talk. If these opportunities for talk become egocentric monologues, however, a subtle comment or question from us may be helpful: "Rick, it sounds like you are restating what Karen said . . ." "Gina, are you disagreeing with Mark's statement then?" Such prompts from you are gentle reminders that there *is* a group discussion going on, and perhaps the student ought to pay more attention.

Creative Dramatics in the Integrated Language Arts Classroom

Creative dramatics cover a broad range of activities from informal movement and pantomime through interpretation and improvisation activities (McCaslin, 1990). The key word here is *informal*. Through creative dramatics children become spontaneously aware of themselves, of others, and of a broad range of concepts and emotions, from the noblest of ideas to the function of a part of speech. And very little of it will be "rehearsed."

Creative dramatics begin where the children need to begin. Why? Because at heart creative dramatics are an *extension of play* (Verriour, 1989). They build on what children already know how to do. As Heinig and Stillwell (1974) pointed out, creative dramatics usually aim for "growth and development of the players rather than entertainment of an audience" (p. 5). Creative dramatics can also be used to enact a problematic part of a reading selection; what seems problematic during the reading often becomes clear when it's physically acted out. The following are more literature-based activities.

Because creative dramatics are a fairly direct extension of play, they facilitate children's thoughts about themselves and others. These activities involve *acting* upon the environment in concert with others. In the process experience is transformed into language and related to other knowledge and situations. The adage about "walking a mile in someone else's shoes" before making a judgment about another person is particularly apt; Verriour (1989) has remarked how creative dramatics can allow children to *live* other roles in order to understand these roles better. He has characterized succinctly and effectively the role of drama in the classroom: "Drama has the power to place children in a position to take risks in their learning without fear of penalty, to face and deal with human issues and problems, again

Music and movement sensitize children to pattern, to structure, and strongly support students' development in the language arts.

without penalty, as well as to reflect on the implications of choices and decisions they may have made in the dramatic context" (p. 285). In a review of research investigating the effects of drama on learning, Wagner (1988) observed that "drama has a positive effect on personal attitudes often associated with language growth: self-confidence, self-concept, self-actualization, empathy, helping behavior, and cooperation" (p. 48).

Because creative dramatics tap so many different modes of expression, they reflect the "multiple" intelligences (Gardner, 1991). From the linguistic through the spatial, personal, and kinesthetic, each intelligence is drawn upon and exercised. The following is a sequence of organization and activities that will facilitate realistic, effective, and rewarding creative dramatics in the classroom.

Space and Organization

Most of the time we can use a corner or open area in the classroom that is available for these activities. (See Figure 3.1 on pp. 56–57 in Chapter 3.) To accommodate whole-class activities, we should be able to arrange a space

CLASSROOM EXAMPLE

Creative Dramatics

An entire class of second-graders has been arranged into pairs. The children in each pair are facing each other, apparently moving in the same fashion. It becomes apparent that they are trying to "mirror" each other, but one is the "mover" and the other is the "reflection." Occasionally there is a burst of giggling from one or two pairs, but most are intently moving almost in unison as each "reflection" becomes better attuned to the movements of the other child.

The reflections and movers will switch roles soon, but it is obvious that these seven- and eight-year-olds are becoming quite adept at "reading" another individual—putting all their energies into anticipating what the other will do. This is an important exercise in losing one's egocentricity by trying to make connections—through movement—with another mind.

Now let's walk over two buildings to the upper-elementary wing and observe a group of sixth-graders. In their class they periodically interrupt the reading of *Summer of My German Soldier* (1973) to interpret or improvise, through spontaneous drama, aspects of Betty Greene's novel about the summer of 1943. Today the children are improvising the reactions of the citizens of a small town in Arkansas after they have just discovered that a young Jewish girl has been sheltering an escaped German prisoner of war. The "citizens" are outraged at the girl, but the scene takes a novel and riveting turn when one of the students exclaims, "We're doing exactly what the Nazis are doing—and we're fighting a war with them because of the way *they* are treating people!" Suddenly, fully, the other students realize the impact and understanding of the irony revealed in this insight.

that will allow twenty or more students to move around on their own without restriction.

Materials will be kept in the drama area for small-group work and can be readily available if needed for large-group work. Essential materials for all grade levels include large blocks, both cube- and L-shaped, and fabrics of different colors and textures and different widths and lengths. Essential for younger students is a variety of hats, gloves, and discarded and laundered coats (oversized ones work marvelously). Siks (1983) lists as "useful but not necessary" old bedsheets, towels, and drapery materials. If these are available, we should also have on hand a supply of clothespins to be used for on-the-spot fastening together of fabrics. Not *absolutely* necessary but certainly helpful are a couple of small tables. For younger students collections of empty cereal boxes and safe containers from the supermarket are invaluable; they will be used for creating constructions of different types and in role playing.

A word about *grouping* for these activities: besides whole-class grouping, there are other possibilities for creative dramatics activities. Students can work together in pairs, independently, and in groups of four or five. At times the class will be "half and half," with half involved in an activity and the other half observing.

The "Basics" of Creative Dramatics

Relaxation

Before beginning a creative dramatics activity, we often need to guide the students through some relaxation exercises. Certainly we need to do this at the beginning of the school year; later the students will apply these techniques on their own. These low-risk techniques or "warm-ups" relax and limber up children while getting them in the mood for other types of creative dramatics. They will also help students become more aware of their muscles and sources of control, an awareness they will need as they experience and interpret that experience primarily through their kinesthetic intelligence.

Begin with the following activity, which will help students realize how muscles can be tensed and then relaxed (Siks, 1983):

◆ Have students sit in a circular formation on the floor, with their arms at their sides, their hands on the floor, and their legs and feet straight out in front of them.

◆ Next, have students tilt their heads upward. Tell them to sit up even straighter and lift their heads even higher, while still making sure that their hands are firmly on the floor and their legs are straight out in front of them. Of course, this is going to increase tension in all their muscles, and we may even hear mock groans from some students!

◆ Then tell the students to relax *slowly* by letting the tension go in each body part, one at a time, until they are in a comfortable sitting position with no unnecessary tension.

◆ Our final step is to have the students discuss with a partner the differences between the tense and the relaxed feelings.

Once students consciously understand the contrast between being tense and being relaxed, they will appreciate the value of relaxation activities. The following are some activities that can be used with the whole class which the students can also use on their own (Moffett & Wagner, 1993):

◆ Gently rock your head from side to side.

◆ Pretend to yawn until you *do* yawn.

◆ Scrunch up as much as you can, pretending that you are trying to fit into a tiny space, tightening every muscle; then slowly open up, expanding into as much space as you can.

◆ While lying on the floor, alternately tighten up and relax your muscles, beginning with your toes and working all the way up to your forehead. Then lie still with your eyes closed. When you open your eyes, take a deep breath.

Concentration

In addition to learning how to relax, students also need to develop their ability to concentrate. Children are certainly capable of concentrating. The task in the classroom, of course, is to focus their abilities on the upcoming task at hand. In preparation for creative dramatics activities, we'll provide the information about focus. The following activities (Siks, 1983; Moffett & Wagner, 1993) are excellent for focusing concentration:

◆ We throw an imaginary ball to a student, then he or she throws it to another, and so forth. Everyone "watches" the ball as it is thrown and flies through the air. After awhile tell the students that the ball is getting heavier and heavier; later still, tell them that it is not only getting heavier but *tinier*— "it is like a tiny marble made of lead." The ball can also change to a balloon, a porcupine, or a piece of wood.

◆ Remember the second-graders who were "mirroring" each other? That was a concentration activity. As the students work in pairs, the one who is moving—the "mirror"—must move slowly and with concentration. He or she can move as if carrying out a familiar activity (putting on a shirt or blouse, for example) or move in a free-form fashion. The other student, who is the "reflection," must try to pick up on the movements and move so that an observer would not be able to tell who is the "mover" and who is the "reflection."

◆ Working in pairs, students take turns concentrating on how each one tenses and relaxes his or her body in response to changes we have suggested. For example, we may suggest that students change from an apple to applesauce, uncooked to cooked spaghetti, or a snowman to soft snow.

Trust

Like concentration, trust is something that most children develop naturally. Our overall classroom environment is arranged to establish trust, of course, but now we are going to address it directly.

One of the best ways to develop trust is to have students select a partner for a "walk for the visually impaired." The partner is at first usually a good friend; later partners can be less familiar students. The students will take turns being blindfolded so that one of them cannot see. The seeing partner will guide the blindfolded partner around the room, stopping occasionally to help the latter "see" a particular object by using other senses—touch, smell, and sound. By having to rely so closely on each other, the students become explicitly aware of the concept of trust. This activity can be expanded to include a walk through the school. It also helps sighted children appreciate the world of the visually impaired student.

An activity that should probably be undertaken after students have engaged in the visually impaired walk is one that helps to build *group* trust. In a group of four or five students, one student is blindfolded and then goes "limp." He or she is next held up by the group as members gently push the student around from one to another. Of course, the group encircles the blindfolded student closely enough so that there is no danger of his or her falling!

Simple Movement

When we begin creative dramatics, our whole-class sessions will probably involve *movement* activities. We mainly start with these because students will be much less self-conscious when everyone is moving en masse. Students who are reluctant, inhibited, or who simply want to watch to see how other students perform the activity will not usually stand out in this type of situation. Low-risk movement activities are particularly good for young children and are well worth engaging in two or three times a week.

Music   Music plays an important role in movement activities. If we know how to play an instrument, we're set. We don't have to be a virtuoso and the type of instrument really doesn't matter: piano, autoharp, even a harmonica. Ways to vary the music include alternating between high and low notes, adjusting the length of the notes, and changing the amount of stress placed on the notes. We can also use recorded music. Significantly, as Moffett and Wagner (1993) comment, "learning to discriminate various auditory dynamics will sensitize children to pattern and structure in other media, including literature" (p. 102).

When our students undertake a whole-class activity simultaneously, we should begin with *herd movement*. Arranged in a circle and accompanied by music, students can run, skip, tiptoe, hop, leap, slide-step, or jump, depending on what the music tells them. To encourage *individual invention*, we'll have each student remain in a small area. Again in response to the music, students move different parts of their body while standing or sitting. We can urge them to "try motions that are twirling, angular, smooth, jerking, [or] gliding." Then we ask each student to think about the following questions: "What is happening? Who are you? Where are you?" (Moffett & Wagner, 1993, p. 103).

We should have a starting signal that everyone knows for our activities. For example, we can strum or play a particular chord once to mean "start" and play the same chord twice to indicate "stop" or use one drumbeat to begin the activity and two to end it.

Pantomime

Through **pantomime** feelings, ideas, and stories are portrayed silently by using gestures and actions. Pantomime actively engages students in applying the *kinesthetic* type of intelligence (Gardner, 1991).

I witnessed the power of a simple pantomime and how it could engage young children in my second-grade classroom one year. It was an autumn day, and I was talking with the children about falling leaves. Chris, who was having some difficulty describing how leaves fall, asked if he could *show* us how a falling leaf felt. Pleasantly surprised, I agreed. Chris's facial expression, his arms, and his general motion all coalesced into a strikingly touching portrayal of a leaf—twisted, dry, near death, torn from its home and tossed chaotically, whimsically, and in the end, pathetically by the wind. I was struck by the pathos of Chris's pantomime and by the class reaction; the students were engrossed, moved, and enlightened. What we were only groping at with language Chris had flawlessly captured in movement and expression.

Pantomime helps children turn a conscious lens on past experience in order to analyze it and then form images that they can represent through action. Pantomime activities can be performed in unison, in small groups, or in pairs. They can run the gamut from simple to complex actions, from everyone knowing ahead of time what will be pantomimed to everyone trying to guess the action a particular student is pantomiming. The following sequence is suggested for pantomime activities:

1. The whole class is in unison. While the whole class moves in a circle, actions are suggested by the teacher or by a student. Allow a fair amount of time for each suggested action to be developed before suggesting another. Begin with simple ones and develop them into more imaginative ones. For example, you can tell students:

- You are walking through thick mud.

- You are walking barefoot across a hot parking lot in the summertime.

- You are fighting your way through dense tropical vegetation.

- You are walking on the moon in light gravity.

- You are trudging across the bottom of the ocean when you see a shark, but you cannot swim away. Suddenly, you are whooshed up through the water and are sailing along on a jet stream that whisks you across the country, then you come down on a Ferris wheel at a state fair.

2. Once students are used to pantomiming in unison—like whole-class movement activities, group pantomimes are low-risk and safe—they can pantomime individually. Moffett and Wagner (1993) call these "pretend to be" pantomimes. Simple individual pantomimes include imitating animals (a timeless favorite with younger children). As children develop confidence, they can pretend to be a favorite character from a storybook, a particular type of community helper, or a common household appliance. Your list of possibilities will grow as your students get into this type of activity.

3. "Pretend to do"—a variation on "pretend to be"—involves pantomiming familiar and not-so-familiar actions: washing dishes, tying shoes, combing or brushing hair, wrapping a present, peeling onions, or being a bird listening for a worm. The context for "pretend to be" and "pretend to do" activities can vary; students can try to guess what action someone is pretending to do.

4. The class stands in a circle. We start by saying someone's name as well as the name of an object. As we say the name of the object, we "throw" it into the circle, using the type of movement and expressions that would occur if we were actually throwing the real object. The person whose name we've called catches the "object," again using the movements and expressions that would be appropriate for doing so. That person then calls another name, changes the name of the object, and throws it. The activity continues in this manner. Some examples of "objects" are

an expensive glass vase

a slithery snake

a balloon

a bowling ball

a cockroach

5. "Narrative pantomime" involves students acting out—in pantomime— all or part of a story or poem. A very effective use of narrative pantomime is having students act out problematic or confusing situations they have encountered in their reading. This is an excellent alternative way to reconstruct meaning when the purely verbal track has gotten bogged down.

"Quieting" Activities

Quieting activities are appropriate after whole-class creative dramatics activities. They have two purposes: (1) to calm the students down before they move on to other types of activities; and (2) to allow the experiences, ideas, and emotions that arose during the activities to be absorbed. Heinig and Stillwell (1974) suggest the following:

1. Narrate a very quiet selection, such as a poem, in which the characters are relaxed or tired. The children should close their eyes as they listen, perhaps resting their heads on desks or tables. Excellent poems for this purpose are "Fatigue," by Peggy Bacon; "Lullaby," by Robert Hillyer; "Slowly," by James Reeves; and "Sunning," by James S. Tippett (Heinig & Stillwell, p. 38). To these I would add "Slumber Song," by Louis Ledoux; "The Little Girl Lost," by Barbara Taylor Bradford; and "Shop of Dreams," by Mary Jane Carr.

2. For older students, the teacher can request that [they] pretend to be "floating on a sea of tranquility" (Heinig & Stillwell, 1974, p. 38).

3. The old standby: as children rest their heads, play quiet, calming music.

From Finger Plays to People Plays

When creative dramatics activities take on a story line, however spontaneous or contrived, they move into a wide range of possibilities. **Finger plays** and **puppetry** are small-scale extensions of ourselves, as natural as the movements of an animated child's hands. While surveying a kindergarten classroom one afternoon during rest period, I noticed one boy lying on his back who seemed to be having a "conversation" between his hands. Holding them over his face, he had each hand "talking" in turn. The conversation was growing more animated; each hand seemed to reflect a definite personality. Before long, however, these "hands" had a falling out, and they began "biting" at each other!

B u i l d   Y o u r
T e a c h i n g
R e s o u r c e s

M O V E M E N T,
CONCENTRATION,
W R I T I N G   A N D
R E A D I N G

It's important for us to discuss with students how they can draw upon and use the feelings, emotions, and awareness that arise out of creative dramatics and movement activities. All of the activities we've discussed that focus on movement and creative dramatics provide excellent opportunitites for integration with writing and reading. For example, after reading Strega Nona (De Paola, 1991) students can, through movement, interpret Big Anthony's reactions to the pasta that keeps "growing." After reading *Abiyoyo* by Pete Seeger they can mimic and interpret the monster's walk, and then the monster's dance as the little boy plays his ukelele. After one of the many times the students will want to listen to *Rosie's Walk* by Pat Hutchins, they can take turns pretending to be the hen and the fox who skulks after her.

By concentrating on each other's movements, then discussing which movements were described, students have excellent experiences. They can then focus on the level of detail and description in these experiences that makes writing grow and come alive.

While this lad was certainly amusing himself during the rest period, I was struck by the naturalness with which his hands came alive. They were personalities, certainly, yet still very real extensions of himself. In fact, if he were to put a sock on each hand and continue the exchange, we would then call them "puppets."

Finger Plays

Simple finger plays help young children think directly about language and actions. Finger plays are sequences of finger and arm motions that accompany a short narrative, poem, or song. They work extremely well when you have explicitly planned for them, as well as when they help fill some "down time" in the classroom—while students are waiting for a bus or to go to lunch or when there are a few extra minutes at the school day's end. Here are a couple of classics that lend themselves to finger play or arm motions (Heinig & Stillwell, 1974):

Rhyme	Motions
Hickory dickory dock	One arm swings like a pendulum.
The mouse ran up the clock.	Fingers "run" upwards.
The clock struck one.	Hold up index finger.
The mouse ran down . . .	Fingers "run" downwards.
	Bend over slightly.
I'm a little teapot,	
short and stout.	Place arm on waist.
Here is my handle.	Extend right arm outward from shoulder, bent upward at elbow, with hand extended outward.
Here is my spout . . .	

Puppetry

Puppetry provides an excellent medium through which young children can express themselves creatively. The children can act out moods and emotions without really being personally responsible for them. The charm and effectiveness of puppets is in their link with the child's play. From a young child's point of view, with puppetry no one really knows that he or she is still in control. For those children who may be more reluctant than most to engage in other creative dramatic activities, puppetry provides an excellent transition. The *act* of manipulating a puppet can be liberating, particularly if children have made the puppets themselves.

As already suggested, puppets can be as simple as hands and socks. Although hand puppets—commercial ones or those made with socks—are most common, other popular puppets in the classroom are made from paper plates (attached to rods), paper bags (both sandwich and shopping size), and work gloves (see Figure 9.1). Siks (1983) and others have remarked that puppets have personalities: the paper-plate-attached-to-rod puppets are more dignified while the hand puppets are the "clowns."

For kindergarten and primary-grade children, it is best to begin using puppets in simple play, followed closely by some type of short presentation. When preparing for such a presentation—for example, illustrating a nursery rhyme or simple story—have the children practice how their puppets would move or behave to express different emotions, such as sadness, happiness, exhaustion, or anger, and then talk about these gestures. We can next discuss using voices and have each child try out different voices for their puppets to express various feelings. Hennings (1994) suggests that when young children are ready to put on a puppet show, they should use a tape-recorded sound accompaniment so they can concentrate on their puppet's actions. For older students, the script should be attached to a surface where it can be easily read—on the back of the puppet stage, if one is available, or on the back of a table serving as a stage.

Improvisation

The rudiments of **improvisation** are learned through movement activities and pantomime. As students gain confidence and expertise in these foundational activities, they can branch out into interesting variations that involve true improvisation.

For example, Moffett and Wagner (1993) suggest that students write on separate slips of paper a character, a setting, and a problem. The "character" slips are placed together, as are the setting and problem slips. After the students are divided into small groups, each group draws a setting and a problem, and each student draws a character. Then each group improvises a skit.

Another variation involves giving each small group a line that can be either at the beginning or end of a situation. They could use "They will

Sock Puppet

Paper Plate Puppet

Paper Bag Puppet

Finger Puppet
(Cut-off glove finger)

Figure 9.1   Types of Puppets

never try that around here again" or "You get what you pay for." These lines can be improvised in a skit in different forms—as a drama, a dance, or a comedy.

Improvisation can enfold much larger chunks of the curriculum and available time but do so while addressing curricular objectives. Cecily O'Neill (1989), for example, describes a situation involving kindergarten and first-grade children in which she and the students discussed the fears many children have about beginning school for the first time. O'Neill was the "principal" and the students were the "teachers" who would help allay the anxiety of the new "children"—who were played by real-life parents and teachers. An example at the intermediate level is offered by Erickson (1988), who presents a lively scenario: the teacher greets a fifth-grade class one morning as an aging Irish personality who owns a castle but wishes to sell it. Sensing they are in for an adventure of sorts, the children engage in conversation with this new personality, who is obviously *not* the teacher. The children are drawn further and further into the situation until they find themselves in a full-fledged thematic unit that will involve them in the exploration of medieval castles, ghosts (dead Vikings!), cartography, and legends.

Dorothy Heathcote has described this type of improvisation as involving the "mantle of the expert" and "teacher-in-role," but emphatically *not* teacher-as-entertainer. When children are deemed "experts" in a particular area, they may act as experts and are responded to as such. However, the teacher merely leaves behind his or her usual role and assumes the role of another individual involved in the improvisation.

Drama

As students participate in, reflect on, enjoy, and learn from creative dramatics, the foundation is laid for plays. Students can adapt plays in children's magazines for radio plays or for Readers Theater, as well as for more full-scale productions (see Kohl, 1988). These situations will allow children to reflect on *how* language is expressed and how individuals move to convey meaning. If an entire play is used, take the opportunity to discuss briefly the elements of a play—such as plot (the unifying factor behind characters, theme, and action) and characterization—and how they are developed. This will support our instruction about story elements (see Chapter 6), which, of course, overlap with the elements of a play. *How* the elements are developed in a play, though, is different in important ways from the way they are developed in written narratives, and these differences should be explored with the children. For example, consider questions like "How is *characterization* similar in plays and stories? How is it different? How is *setting* similar or different?"

Technology, Multimedia, and Hypermedia

As we acquire the software for our computers, there will be all sorts of possibilities for students to integrate different media into the construction of all kinds of texts. It is possible to create simple multimedia presentations with existing word processing programs—inserting figures and photographs, for example. Additional possibilities are afforded by programs such as KidPix and HyperCard. KidPix is intended for primary-age students, while HyperCard is for older students and adults. Figure 9.2 shows eight-year-old Lane's creation with KidPix. He imported a clip-art image of a shark with his picture and a recording of his 30-second oral report on the hammerhead shark (cited in Grabe & Grabe, 1996). All the students in Lane's class had similar "cards" with their pictures and reports on them.

These strange looking sharks are easy to recognize. Their hammerlike heads have a thick lobe sticking out on each side. This is where the eyes and the nostrils are found. The eyes are wide apart as much as three feet in a fifteen foot shark.

Figure 9.2   **KidPix Composition**

SOURCE: From Grabe, M., & Grabe, C. (1966). *Integrating technology for meaningful learning.* Boston: Houghton Mifflin.

HyperCard offers almost innumerable possibilities. Like KidPix, a "stack" of cards is created — but compared to KidPix, the possibilities are much more powerful. There are many more options with HyperCard. HyperCard creations offer many options for the viewer as well — reading, listening, and viewing.

◆ ◆ ◆   CONCLUDING PERSPECTIVE AND SUMMARY

Oral communication — listening and speaking — is not only an important tool children use to explore and explain the the world around them. It's also the framework for developing skills that they will internalize and apply in reading, writing, and content area studies.

Creative dramatics, a significant classroom application of oral communication, can stimulate imagination and critical thinking and help students better understand themselves and the nature of human behavior. In our haste to help students comprehend and apply the symbol system of written language, we often lose sight of the value of creative dramatics as both a stimulus and a foundation for learning to use written language.

In this chapter we've addressed the following main points:

◆ Like the other language arts, listening isn't a passive process. Meaning construction actively involves the listener's mood, interest, expectations, and knowledge as well as the context for listening.

◆ We should first sensitize young children to the sounds around them.

◆ We can build on this awareness by alerting children to the nuances of a speaker's delivery as well as his or her words. Doing so helps students develop critical listening and viewing skills.

◆ Teachers should clearly and plainly model the scope and kinds of oral communication when speaking and listening to students, particularly in a diverse classroom.

◆ Reading aloud to children reveals the power of narrative language and prepares them for further classroom literacy experiences.

◆ Sharing helps students hone skills for oral presentations and supports reading and writing growth.

◆ Storytelling develops children's literacy, encourages their reading, and introduces them to the values and literary traditions of different cultures.

◆ Small-group discussions simultaneously promote independent thinking and encourage collaborative and cooperative learning.

Key Terms

Author's Chair (p. 358)

brainstorming (p. 368)

choral reading (p. 357)

clarifying (p. 368)

created sounds (p. 347)

creative dramatics (p. 369)

critical listening and viewing (p. 349)

discussion (p. 366)

elaborating (p. 368)

finger plays (p. 377)

improvisation (p. 379)

oral report (p. 364)

pantomime (p. 375)

puppetry (p. 377)

Readers Theatre (p. 358)

reading aloud (p. 352)

sharing (p. 359)

storytelling (p. 361)

THEMATIC EXPLORATION

"Keepers of the Earth"

Tamara Baren: Intermediate Grades

In this thematic exploration I'd like to "think aloud" and share with you my thought processes as I conceptualize and implement an across-the-curriculum **integrated thematic unit**. Let me first set the stage so you will be better able to see how everything fits together.

First, let's examine our context for learning. This is my fifth year teaching in a multi-age fourth-fifth-sixth-grade classroom. There are several multi-age classrooms in my school, and it's extremely helpful to have other teachers who are philosophically committed to this concept and are invaluable as resources for ideas and planning. Our school is in a working-class neighborhood; half of the students are Anglo and half are African-American, Hispanic-American, Asian-American, or Native American. I have thirty-one students almost evenly distributed across grades four, five, and six. Seven are Hispanic-American; three are African-American, and six are Asian-American. Two children are from the Paiute tribe, and one is from the Washo tribe—tribes with roots that are deep in our part of the country.

I'd like to give you a sense of what's happened in our classroom community up to this point.

Language Arts

In a large, supportive group, all of the students—regardless of ability—have developed schemas for the reading process. Through read-alouds in both picture and chapter books, the students have

◆ listened effectively

◆ developed group-discussion dynamics

◆ examined pictures for information and aesthetic value

◆ collected interesting words

◆ exclaimed over "golden lines"—our term for language in books that really "grabs" us

◆ discussed *feeling* as a foundation for response (Every so often after reading, I'd ask, "How does this story make you *feel*?")

◆ Re-examined texts

THEMATIC EXPLORATION

◆ identified themes by talking about "hot topics"—what really "sticks" with and affects them after they listen to or read a story

◆ written and shared responses as a group.

All the books that I've used in a read-aloud format have been left out on the shelves to encourage rereading during Reading Workshop and Sustained Silent Reading times.

Across the Curriculum

I have an *overall* "theme" for the year focused on *"Our Relationship to the Earth."* We have been exploring this theme in terms of

◆ resources

◆ systems

◆ people and their ideas

My overall goals for the year have been to help students understand

1. that the earth is a series of systems that are interlocking and interdependent

2. that ecosystems are the foundation of life on earth

3. that people live by cultural systems guided by their beliefs about their relationship to others and their environment

4. how Native American cultural systems adapted to their environments

5. how Euro-Americans adapted to the North American environments

6. how people's choices of lifestyle directly impact ecosystems.

Planning for the Integrated Theme

The theme I'd like to share with you here—*"Keepers of the Earth"*—fits within our overall theme for the year. It integrates the language arts with science and social studies most directly; there are also tie-ins with math, art, music, and physical education.

I took the idea for this theme from the title of a wonderful book and teaching resource I discovered several years ago—*Keepers of the Earth: Native American Stories and Environmental Activities for Children* (Ca-

THEMATIC EXPLORATION

puto & Bruchac, 1988). I very much like how this book ties Native American stories together with science as it relates to the environment. I have used this book often during the past few years, but this year I wanted to pull its information and concepts more directly into a theme. I had several reasons for doing this:

I wanted to reflect more directly on the roots of my Native American and Hispanic-American students.

I wanted to focus on the notion of "stewardship"; because the earth gives so much to us, we should care for it in return.

I've wanted for a long time *really* to explore the myths and folktales of Native Americans and to see how they compare to the myths of other cultures such as the Chinese, Greek, and Roman. I know there are similarities, and I'd really like the kids to begin thinking about those as well. Also, "explanatory" myths and folktales are particularly interesting for students at these age levels.

I next brainstorm, using a "web" format with "Keepers of the Earth" in the center. (Often I don't have a "catchy" title for a theme, so I simply write a topic label in the center. As I brainstorm or later read through books, I often find a term or phrase that pops out.) Other topics that I draw around the center of the web are

◆ Web of Life

◆ Native Americans

◆ Protecting the Earth

◆ Myths, Folktales, Legend

Goals

My thinking about the language arts, based on what we've done this year, helps me identify what I'd like the students to be engaged in. They really need to continue to *think* about their reading. I often talk with them about "reading with a picture in your head—getting that movie in your head you can *live* in." So now, in the spring of this school year—given my theme—here are my *Goals for the Language Arts*:

◆ Develop effective reading strategies for longer narratives

◆ Use "imaging" while reading and thinking about the texts we carry around in our heads

THEMATIC EXPLORATION

◆ Continue to develop a vocabulary for our reading strategies and for responding aesthetically to our reading

◆ Develop the foundations for inquiry and research

◆ Work on gathering, organizing, and presenting information effectively in writing.

Drawing on my knowledge of the students and from the curriculum guides for the district, here are my *Content Goals*:

SOCIAL STUDIES

◆ Read and create maps, graphs, and charts

◆ Explore how we know and learn about other peoples

SCIENCE

◆ "Web of Life": Understand concepts of biodiversity, populations, food chains/webs/pyramids

MATH

◆ Explore and apply measurement, scale, and ratio

ART

◆ Study how illustrations in books work with the text to create an aesthetic "whole"

◆ Gain an appreciation of different illustrators' styles and what makes each distinctive

Selecting and Reading the Books

Now it's time to begin gathering texts and other materials. I know I'm going to use the book *Keepers of the Earth* (1988), and there are many good books and resources listed in that. I visit the school media center, talk with the librarian (she'll be pulling some books for me, she reassures me, and she has several good suggestions), and look through several resource anthologies such as *Adventuring with Books* and *The Bookfinder* (see pp. 396–97 for an extensive resource list). These resources give me a brief synopsis of a story, a sense of the difficulty of a text, and its appeal to students. This information is extremely helpful as I think about the range of my students' reading level—from beginning readers through fairly proficient ones. I also

THEMATIC EXPLORATION

do a search on the library computer. Now that the school media center has been "computerized," doing a search is a *lot* easier and quicker than it was just a few years ago. Until quite recently I've also visited the public library to do searches. *This* year, however, the school's computer is linked to the public library system as well as to the state university system, so if there isn't a book immediately accessible, I can place an interlibrary loan request right there "on-line." Also, just this past year I have been delighted with the number of children's literature sites that are appearing on the Web. It's so much easier to access them than it used to be! Simply typing in "children's literature" turned up a number of excellent sites; one of my favorites is the *Children's Literature Web Guide* (http://www.ucalgary.ca/~dkbrown). As you've noticed, I've included its home page just to give you an idea of the different sites where you can go from here. And, of course, each of those sites is linked to many others.

For our first *core text*, I chose *Listening Silence*, a selection which allowed me to develop the reading/thinking strategies we've been learning and to model specific reading and problem-solving skills. It has served a number of my purposes:

◆ Provided a positive role model/female protagonist who survives a wilderness experience

◆ Has detailed yet understandable descriptions of the adaptive life of Native Americans that stimulated interest in the unit topic

◆ Opened the door to discuss belief systems (It focuses on the *healer's* experience rather than that of the "warrior" stereotype.)

◆ Has short chapters with writing interesting enough to engage capable as well as struggling readers—plenty of "golden lines," interesting words, and reasonably drawn characters and settings

◆ Contains a good variation of literary features which can be examined in a group (*Plot* is developed through the use of foreshadowing, flashbacks, cliff hangers, and *implied* as opposed to *explicit* resolution of story problems. *Style* is expressed in part through provocative dialogue.)

◆ Shows enough variety of plot and character development to identify several themes for response and point-of-view writing

◆ Sounded good aloud (Most students were able to follow easily in texts at desks.)

THEMATIC EXPLORATION

Can't display tables? Use this alternate page

W HAT'S N EW ~ S EARCH ~ I NTRODUCTION ~ E MAIL

Children's Literature Web Guide

Internet Resources Related to Books for Children and Young Adults

News: The Newbery and Caldecott Medals were announced on January 22, 1996.		
Movies and Television Based on Children's Books Children's Book Awards Best Books Lists	**Online Children's Stories:** Collections Classics Folklore, Myth and Legend Contemporary Stories	General Children's Literature Resources Children's Literature Journals and Book Reviews Online Internet Discussion Groups
Children's Bestsellers: Resource Links Canadian Bestsellers Publisher's Weekly Children's Bestsellers (U.S.)	Children's Songs and Poetry Readers' Theatre Written by Children	Conferences and Book Events Related Associations on the Internet
Information about Authors and Their Books Children's Book Publishers Children's Booksellers Digging Deeper: Research Guides and Indexes	CANADIAN INTERNET TOP CANADIAN WEB SITE DIRECTORY C Clearinghouse Approved	Resources for Parents Resources for Teachers Resources for Storytellers Resources for Writers and Illustrators
TOP 5% POINT Reviewed By MAGELLAN WIC select GNN EDUCATION FIRST Learning Application		

THEMATIC EXPLORATION

◆ Could be used to develop the Guided Reading-Thinking Activity format in an understandable context

◆ Provided consistent, well-drawn illustrations that developed story

◆ Maintained students' interest: provided bridges from picture-book reading, kept attention, can be used as foundation for art lessons, provided explorations during unit

◆ Short enough to sustain attention (three weeks @ thirty minutes, four days a week)

We will have a read-aloud from *The Listening Silence* every day; every two or three days, we will have a read-aloud from the other, shorter core texts and the short stories in *Keepers of the Earth* (*KOTE*). I chose stories from *KOTE* that, in most instances, came from peoples in the North American West — "closer to home." These tales address other phenomena that represent our relationship to the earth and our world: sun, moon, constellations, water, wind, and so forth.

We read these stories:

"Four Worlds: The Dine Story of Creation"	[Navajo; Southwest]
"How Grandmother Spider Stole the Sun"	[Creek; Oklahoma]
"Gluscabi and the Wind Eagle"	[Abenaki; Northeast]
"How Thunder and Earthquake Made Ocean"	[Yurok; California]
"How Raven Made the Tides"	[Tsimshian; Pacific Northwest]
"How Coyote Was the Moon"	[Kalispel; Idaho]
"How Fisher Went to the Skyland: The Origin of the Big Dipper"	[Anishinabe; Great Lakes]
"Spring Defeats Winter"	[Seneca; Northeast]

For our *extended* and *recreational* texts, we read a series of picture books and folktales that were also related to Native American cultures as well as to the myths, legends, and folktales of other cultures. These texts

◆ extended the independent reading of all students at appropriate levels

◆ allowed students to follow interests and exercise choice (essential for involvement, motivation, and commitment to learning in the unit)

THEMATIC EXPLORATION

◆ developed students' understanding of story sequence through explanatory myths or "how" stories (for example, "How the Stars Fell into the Sky: A Navajo Legend")

◆ introduced elements of explanatory myths

◆ built schema for further North American studies.

As I look over the print-outs of book titles, I realize I've got another topic some or all students could explore within this theme—*author studies*. Paul Goble, Gerald McDermott, and Terri Cohlene have each written and illustrated several books, so the students can compare books from a particular author and then compare and contrast the works of several authors.

Subject Area Objectives Related to the Theme

LANGUAGE ARTS

◆ Reading an extended narrative in a chapter book

◆ Probing a text for ideas

◆ Tracking character development through "webbing"

◆ Responding through a variety of formats such as summary and double entry draft

◆ Identifying and collecting theme "hot topics"

◆ Writing in response to hot topics

◆ Sharing orally and through writing results of investigations into different Native American groups

SCIENCE

◆ As we embark on our study of ecosystems, we'll be investigating a large local pond, noting animals and vegetation and plotting graphs of our observations.

SOCIAL STUDIES

◆ Creating maps, graphs, and charts of information obtained while investigating a particular culture

THEMATIC EXPLORATION

◆ Exploring how we know and learn about other peoples:

Hearsay

Personal stories

Oral traditions/reading legends/myths

Mass media (TV, music, radio)

Artifacts (By focusing on *artifacts*, we can look at people's social roles, lifestyles, and use of resources.)

Historical records

Text reading

Activities/Projects

I use the scheme of **introducing, developing,** and **culminating activities** and projects. To get our unit underway, our first **introductory activity** is a read-aloud of "Four Worlds: The Dine [Navajo] Story of Creation." After the read-aloud, we discuss how this "creation" story made us feel. What part really grabbed us? How is this Navajo creation story like others we have heard? different from others? (Usually someone mentions the flood and how it reminds them of Noah and the great flood. Every now and then a student will point out that everyone in the tale speaks the same language in the beginning—just as people did before the Tower of Babel.) The story provides a context for exploring the notion of "stewardship" of the earth and leads into an understanding of what "ecology" is: "every action we take affects our habitat and those with whom we share it" (Caduto & Bruchac, 1988, p. 35). We next talk about what we're going to be exploring over the next several weeks, and why. I share the types of activities and objectives I have planned, and we "web" related ideas and possibilities for exploration.

Our read-aloud on the second day is "How Grandmother Spider Stole the Sun," an explanatory tale that sets the stage for our discussion of how the Earth and the heavens were conceptualized and how the cycle of night and day affects photosynthesis and energy flow.

Humankind's relationship to the Earth will be explored quite dramatically in *The Listening Silence* as the main character both struggles with the Earth and depends on it for her survival. I begin reading this book aloud on Wednesday of the first week; I've managed to get enough copies for students

THEMATIC EXPLORATION

to share. I pair a stronger reader with one who is not as developmentally advanced. While not all students are able to follow along, a partner usually is, and everyone feels that they are "reading" right along with me. We have journals that accompany *The Listening Silence*; each day students respond to my questions that tap into characterization, theme, conflict, and resolution.

Developing activities include the following:

Guided Reading-Thinking Activities

literature discussion groups

investigating related ecosystems

Some of the projects from which students may choose include

script writing

storytelling

dioramas with writing

simulated television broadcasts (individually, in groups, and in peer or cross-age partnerships)

puppet shows

individual poetry writing and poetry recitation and memorization

a variety of experiences preparing food, making crafts, creating models, and writing plays

While I want to work with students on more "formal" written reports before the year ends, I think it's necessary in this theme exploration to focus on *how* to locate and interpret information. I still require that information collected be well organized and accurate. To accomplish this end, I have students work in cross-age partner pairs. They all undertake an investigation about the culture and environment of a Native American people. They utilize various research materials—standard trade books, encyclopedias, CD-ROMs, and the Internet—to gather and organize their materials. Experienced students show novices the ropes about using time wisely, staying on task, and finding information.

As we go along, we keep a large K-W-L chart on which we list information about native peoples according to our sources. This chart helps students understand how information is gathered, with some emphasis on the stereotyping of one culture by another, especially in reporting on conflicts. I feel it is essential for students to see that there are conflicting sources, primary sources, and differing perspectives from different historical times. Finding actual accounts, diaries, and other firsthand records helps students see how "history" is constructed and whose story is told. This is a subtle and difficult area for both novice and experienced teachers alike to address. It's essential for intermediate students to "see" the history from all angles — for every official "history" there is another untold "history" that deserves consideration. For example, one of my students last year was intrigued by Sarah Winnemucca Hopkins's *Life Among the Paiutes*. She shared the following excerpt with me: "If women could go into your congress, I think justice would soon be done to the Indians."

As I've mentioned, there are opportunities for specific interest group explorations. Several students may choose an author study, others may pursue the "Cinderella"-prototype tales. There are a few Native American tales that reflect this "Cinderella" prototype. I had read a fascinating article in *Reading Teacher* a few years ago about using Cinderella tales (Worthy & Bloodgood, 1993), so as I browsed the "Children's Literature" site, I was delighted to find a link to a separate site dealing exclusively with "Cinderella" tales. I found some titles there that hadn't turned up in my previous searches. Altogether, I gathered the following list:

Cohlene, T. (1990). *Little Firefly: An Algonquin Legend.*
Martin, R., & Shannon, D. (1992). *The rough-face girl*. Putnam.
San Souci, R., & San Souci, D. (1994). *Sootface: An Ojibwa Indian Tale.* Doubleday.
San Souci, R., & San Souci, D. (1978). *The Legend of Scarface: A Blackfoot Indian Tale*. Doubleday.
San Souci, R., & San Souci, D. (1981). *Song of Sedna.*
The Golden Slipper: A Vietnamese Legend, by Darrell Lum. Troll. (1994)
Kao and the Golden Fish: A Folktale from Thailand, retold by Cheryl Hamada, 1993.
Korean Cinderella, Edward B. Adams, 1989.
Lily and the Wooden Bowl, Alan Schroeder, illustrated by Yoriko Ito, 1994. (Japan)
Mufaro's Beautiful Daughters, by John Steptoe, 1987. (Zimbabwe)
Nomi and the Magic Fish: A Story from Africa, by Phumla, 1972. (Zulu)
Princess Furball, by Charlotte Huck, illustrated by Anita Lobel, 1989.
The Talking Eggs: A Folktale from the American South, by Robert San Souci; illustrated by Jerry Pinkney, 1989.

THEMATIC EXPLORATION

Vasilissa the Beautiful, by Elizabeth Winthrop, 1991.
Wishbones: A Folktale from China, by Barbara Ker Wilson; illustrated by Meilo So. Bradbury, 1993.
Yeh-Shen, A Cinderella Tale from China, by Ai-Ling Louie; illustrated by Ed Young. Philomel Books, 1982.

Culminating activities include the final versions of several of the *developing* activities. The following were suggested by students:

pop-up books

posters

oral reports

bulletin boards

"newscasts"

Chatauqua-style presentations: Students assume the role of an individual, learn as much as they can about him or her, then make a brief presentation and answer questions from the audience

Creating a Readers Theatre of a legend or myth

Doing a Venn diagram of myths from different regions, such as North American or European cultures (for example, the Flood story)

Skills Instruction

My *language arts* skills instruction focuses on areas most of my students need to explore:

In *reading*, we need to examine further how to negotiate informational texts—how to use the table of contents and the index, for example. We also really need to discuss and practice our *note-taking* skills.

In *writing*, the students need more involvement in identifying a topic and asking questions of it. These are the "hot topics" to which I have referred. If necessary, how do we narrow questions down?

How do we then move from this "hard data" to *conveying* the information? All along the way, I keep asking the students, "What's the problem? Where do we need to go?" As we work with our writing, I will be doing minilessons on sorting out the main idea and the details and on writing leads.

Our word study is two pronged. First, we have our ongoing word study

THEMATIC EXPLORATION

in which students explore spelling patterns that are developmentally appropriate. The reading we are doing provides many possibilities for word searches. Second, all the students are interested in the unique features of Native American words, so we talk about differences in the sound and "feel" of the words. Our reading of Greek and Roman myths and legends provides a rich context for learning about the sources of so many of our everyday and scientific words: *cereal* from the goddess Ceres; *flora*, *fauna*, and *chlorophyll* all from Greek and Latin names. These terms also fit into our exploration of ecology and the environment. I can use these words to teach general processes of word creation and meaning as well as add a few of them as important vocabulary terms for our unit.

Sequence and Schedule

By this time of the year, my students are used to working collaboratively. We still need to "fine-tune" from time to time, but usually things go along well. This allows both the students and me to be more flexible in our sequencing and scheduling. I do maintain a definite sequence for our guided reading, however, and there is a planned sequence to my skills instruction. After the beginning of our thematic exploration, I also am able to involve the students to a considerably greater degree in the planning.

CORE TEXTS

Caduto, M., & Bruchac, J. (1988). *Keepers of the earth: Native American stories and environmental activities for children.* Golden CO: Fulcrum.

Baylor, B. (1987). *And it is still that way.* Trails West Publishing.

Baylor, B. (1987). *The desert is theirs.* New York: Aladdin Books.

Bierhorst, J. (1994). *The way of the earth: Native America and the environment.* New York: Morrow.

Highwater, J. (1977). *Anpao: An American Indian odyssey.* Philadelphia: Lippincott.

Root, Phyllis (1992). *The listening silence.* New York: HarperCollins. [Illustrated by D. McDermott.]

Rucki, A. (1992). *Turkey's gift to the people.* Flagstaff, AZ: Northland.

EXTENDED AND RECREATIONAL TEXTS

Cohlene, T. (1990). *Clamshell Boy.* Mahwah, NJ: Watermill Press.

Cohlene, T. (1990). *Ka-ha-si and the loon.* Mahwah, NJ: Watermill Press.

Cohlene, T. (1990). *Quillworker.* Mahwah, NJ: Watermill Press.

Cohlene, T. (1990). *Turquoise Boy.* Mahwah, NJ: Watermill Press. [Navajo legend]

THEMATIC EXPLORATION

Cohlene, T. (1990). *Dancing drum*. Mahwah, NJ: Watermill Press.

Cohlene, T. (1991). *Native American legends illustrated by Charles Reason*. Wonderstorms.

dePaola, T. (1983). *The legend of the bluebonnet*. New York: Putnam.

dePaola, T. (1988). *The legend of the Indian paintbrush*. New York: Putnam.

Dearmond, D. (1988). *The seal oil lamp*. San Francisco: Sierra Club.

Goble, P. *Buffalo Woman*. New York: Bradbury.

Goble, P. *The great race of the birds and animals*. New York: Bradbury.

Goble, P. (1991). *Iktomi and the buffalo skull: A Plains Indian story*. New York: Orchard.

Goble, P. (1992). *Love flute*. New York: Bradbury.

Goble, P. (1986). *The gift of the sacred dog*. New York: Simon & Schuster.

Lacapa, M. (1990). *The flute player: An Apache folktale*. Flagstaff, AZ: Northland.

Martin, R., & Shannon, D. (1993). *The boy who lived with the seals*. New York: Putnam.

McDermott, G. (1977). *Arrow to the sun: A Pueblo Indian tale*. New York: Penguin.

Steptoe, J. (1984). *The Story of Jumping Mouse*. New York: Lothrop.

Bilingual

Rohmer, H. (1987). *Mother Scorpion Country: La tierra de la madre escorpion*. Children's Book Press. (Spanish/English)

Rohmer, H., & Wilson, D. (1987). *Scorpion country: A legend from the Miskito Indians of Nicaragua/La tierra de la Madre Escorpion: Una leyenda de los indios miskitos de Nicaragua*. (Spanish/English)

Additional "How" Stories

Johnston, T. (1994). *The tale of Rabbit and Coyote*. Illus. T. dePaola. New York: Putnam.

Oughton, J., & Desimini, L. (1992). *How the stars fell into the sky: A Navajo legend*. Boston: Houghton Mifflin.

Additional Resources

Anderson, V. (1994). *Native Americans in fiction: A guide to 765 books for librarians and teachers, K–9*.

Pellowskiu, A., & Sweat, L. (1990). *Hidden stories in plants: Unusual and easy-to-tell stories from around the world, together with creative things to do while telling them*. New York: Macmillan.

Slapin, B. (1992). *Through Indian eyes: The native experience in books for children*.

Worthy, M., & Bloodgood, J. (1993). Enhancing reading instruction through Cinderella tales. *Reading Teacher, 46,* 290–301.

CHAPTER 10

Pulling It All Together: Integration, Inquiry, and Theme Exploration

- How does thematic exploration stimulate students' critical thinking, problem-solving abilities, and other levels of inquiry? What learning tools do they apply in these processes?

- How can theme study help students comprehend connections among the language arts and across the elementary curriculum?

- How can we select themes that will accommodate the needs of *all* of our students—particularly diverse learners?

- How can we determine the appropriate breadth and scope of a theme study? What is the role of student input?

- How should we choose texts and plan the sequence of activities for our thematic exploration? What goals should we keep in mind?

◆ ◆ ◆ ## INTRODUCTION

We began this text with the "big picture": looking at a classroom where the language arts are meaningfully integrated within the elementary curriculum. The text has also been referring you at many points to the two thematic explorations. Now that we've focused on specific important aspects in each of the preceding chapters, it's time to look again—this time in some depth—at how to pull together the contexts, literature, strategies, and activities presented throughout this book and to integrate them all comfortably and effectively. I hope the thematic explorations have given you a good feel for this, so this chapter's main purposes are

◆ to look carefully at the processes involved in developing thematically organized units

◆ to provide plenty of examples of integrating across the language arts.

We will build on the basics established in Chapter 3 when we considered classroom organization and management. It should help to keep in mind the principles laid out there—managing time, organization, goal-setting, and grouping students for different purposes—as we explore thematic instruction.

Inquiry and Theme Exploration

Throughout this book thematic instruction or theme explorations have been emphasized as a powerful and effective means of organizing our instruction and our students' learning. At a fundamental level themes engage students in critical thinking, problem-solving, and *inquiry* (Pappas, Kiefer, & Levstik, 1995; Short, Harste, & Burke, 1996). Through thematic instruction our students become aware of the relationships across the language arts and the connections among other areas of the elementary curriculum such as science, social studies, and math. Through thematic instruction students also explore ideas more deeply and learn how to apply the tools of learning—how to sustain *inquiry* about a question or topic. In addition, theme explorations more effectively accommodate the diverse learners in our classrooms.

Thematic units allow us to involve students in **reading and writing** both **intensively** and **extensively** in the context of meaningful, engaging explorations (Harste, Short, & Burke, 1989). That is, some texts students read, analyze, grapple with, and discuss at length — *intensively*. Other texts — more in number — they will read *extensively*, just to enjoy them. Both types of engagements with literature can be personally gratifying and enlightening and can help build a life span's appreciation for literature that meaningfully explores the nature of humankind. Much of students' *writing* will be intensive as well as they explore a topic and develop a "published" composition. So much of their other writing will be *extensive* — less focused on eventual product but helpful in their reflections, note-taking, and so forth. Both modes of reading and writing — intensive and extensive — can develop through the types of activities we will be arranging in our classrooms.

We first looked at thematic units in Chapter 3, and I've referred throughout the book to the inserts (the thematic explorations) which illustrate the development and structure of two thematic units; the first is an example of a **literature-based theme** and the second of an **across-the-curriculum integrated theme**. In Chapter 3, the unit based on Peter Spier's book *People* (1980) is an example of a unit that connects with different areas of the curriculum. In this chapter we will discuss how to construct and conduct both types of thematic units, using illustrative units for the primary and intermediate levels. Both types of thematic unit will involve the strategies we have been teaching: discussion, guided reading, process writing, word study, and so forth. Discussion will include response groups as well as individual and group conferences with the teacher. While there is still often overlap between these two categories, they do represent a difference in degree of focus for a thematic unit and a progression for becoming a thematic teacher.

How Much Integration?

As we think about organizing our instruction and students' learning thematically, it will help if we think about the various *degrees* of integration within thematic instruction.

◆ *All* of the content we need to teach at a particular time is incorporated within a unifying theme; there is no real division among the different subject matter areas, and there are seldom any separate time blocks labeled "science" or "social studies."

◆ *Some* subjects are integrated; social studies and/or science are integrated with literature, while the other subjects such as math are taught separately at other times of the day.

◆ Subjects are taught separately but tied together thematically — for example, reading historical fiction that is set in Japan during Reading Workshop, studying about Japan during the social studies time block, or studying the geology of volcanoes and earthquakes during science.

◆ A *single* area is explored thematically, as in a genre study in literature or the theme of "neighborhoods" in social studies.

Types of Themes

There are several different **types of themes**, and a particular theme may be categorized more than one way (Walmsley, 1993; Weaver, Chaston, & Peterson, 1993). It's helpful, though, to think about these different types or categories because they are an excellent way for *us* to make decisions about how we're going to approach the concepts we need to address during a particular year. As we brainstorm about possibilities, we'll see whether a particular theme will lend itself quite easily to "total" integration or be more effectively explored with a narrower curricular focus. Themes can be based on

◆ subject matter areas

◆ the calendar

◆ biographies: important historical figures, people in community, author/illustrators

◆ current events

◆ form:

genre (mysteries, folktales, poetry)

elements of narrative (characterization, plot/conflict)

motifs (journeys, the number "three," the role of the fool or the trickster).

Now, having shown you some common types of themes, I'll throw out the challenge for thematic teaching. Many authorities suggest we should approach our themes *conceptually* rather than *topically* (Pappas, Kiefer, & Levstik, 1995; Weaver, Chaston, & Peterson, 1993). *Topics* are easy to come up with—such as "frogs," "Westward Movement," or "plants." However, there is a risk that students' learning will be superficial, centered primarily on learning facts rather than ideas, on memorizing as opposed to really *thinking*. Some also suggest we try to avoid thinking in terms of how other subject matter areas such as "science," "social studies," and "math" will be incorporated; the concern is that students and teachers will be too limited by our notions of what these subject areas are and thus not as likely to discover new ideas and directions. Instead, we should think *outward* from our theme and subthemes and see where our thinking and planning goes.

These concerns are important and legitimate, but if we remain aware of the pitfalls, we should be fine as we begin thematic instruction. I *do* encourage you, however, to think broadly—"outwardly"—to ensure that students will still be challenged and involved in critical thinking and learning. You will find, in fact, that "subthemes" may also emerge as you work outward from a single theme. These are related categories that inevitably wind up reaching into subject matter areas such as science, social studies, and math anyway. In addition, these subthemes often overlap; while it *sounds* messy, in reality it's a blessing! As we'll soon see, a single activity may address different subject areas as well as different subthemes.

To illustrate: think back to Sandy Madura's "Cynthia Rylant" author theme. A major focus for this theme is the awareness that writers' ideas come from their own lives. Sandy facilitates her students' experiences and activities so that their awareness of the role a writer's life plays is always close to the surface. There are "subthemes" such as *friendship*, *city/country*, *senior citizens*, and *types of illustrations*, yet they are woven into the fabric of the major theme.

Steps in Constructing Thematic Units

We can follow eight general steps in constructing both literature-based and integrated thematic units. In practice, there is overlapping among these steps and back-and-forth movement among them. Still, it is important to have this road map in mind as we plan. These steps are "webbed" in Figure 10.1.

Selecting a Theme and Brainstorming Connections

When selecting a theme, it's important to keep in mind our students' developmental levels. Younger children can grasp concrete themes easily—either themes that are directly "hands-on" or which bring an abstract concept down to a concrete level: "friendship," "brothers and sisters," "city and country." However, older students have the potential to work explicitly with more abstract concepts. At both primary and intermediate levels, there can be a "tension" to the theme, as there is with "brothers and sisters" and "differing points of view" (Walmsley & Walp, 1990). Children could approach a unit focused on "fire," for instance, by comparing its beneficial and detrimental effects—"Fire: Friend or Enemy?" Themes such as these allow children to stretch their thinking and come to a fuller understanding of abstract ideas. Older students can begin to understand the universal "themes" of history, for example: the "struggle for freedom against tyranny,

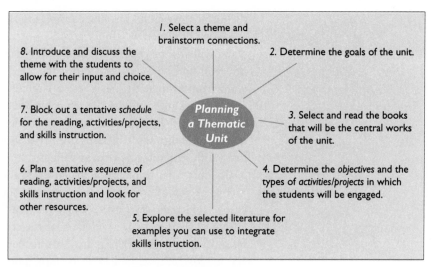

Figure 10.1   **Steps in Constructing Thematic Units**

for peace against violence, for knowledge against ignorance, for power against powerlessness" (Egan, 1987, p. 467). The following is just a sampling of the possible themes we can focus on. As a quick glance indicates, most of these can be addressed in some fashion at *all* elementary-grade levels:

authors and/or illustrators	journeys
fantasy versus reality	growing things
"spaces"	relationships
genre: compare/contrast	change: in humans, in seasons
most common folktale motifs— journey, confrontation, rescue, trick	pets: more than "just an animal"?
"Let's eat"	stories in which *heroine* is problem-solver
friendship	stereotypes
roots: family, language, cultures	courage
"It's important to be different"	symbolism
"Exploration affects explorers *and* explored"	dialects

The "brainstorming connections" aspect of constructing an integrated thematic unit is exciting; some teachers prefer to do this alone, but most find that working with at least one other teacher is preferable. Work on a large sheet of paper; "webbing" seems to work best for most people, but lists are fine, too. What other themes, topics, or ideas occur to you as you think about your theme? Remember Tamara's and Sandy's initial brainstorming? There will always be more than you can explore, but it's better to start large and whittle down. As you brainstorm, you will probably see certain goals and objectives emerging; write these down as you go. When you're finished, you will look again at your web and think directly about goals and objectives.

Determining the Unit Goals

What are the major understandings, generalizations, and concepts we want our students to learn? When we've identified these, we've identified our **goals**. We will have goals for the language arts, and—if appropriate—the other content areas. In determining goals we look on one hand at the web we've just brainstormed, and on the other we consider (1) our knowledge of our students—their ages, interests, and social and emotional development and abilities; (2) our knowledge of the required language arts concepts and

Thematic units provide opportunities for meaningful inquiry through the language arts and throughout the curriculum.

skills; and (3) our knowledge of the concepts and skills in the other subject matter areas that are required in the curriculum for the school district. Our goals then guide our selection of books and our planning of activities and projects.

Selecting the Books

While all sorts of resources are used, *trade books* are at the heart of thematic units. The following are general **guidelines for selecting appropriate books** (Templeton, 1995):

◆ Use different types of books and literature: narratives, informational books, picture books, and so forth.

◆ Different cultures should be represented.

◆ The books should be at different levels of readability or difficulty.

◆ Students' interests should be represented as much as possible — particular topics within an overall theme and favorite authors/illustrators.

Let's look more closely at book selection and organization within the context of a theme. Given the diversity within our classrooms and the wider society that our students will be a part of, it's important to attend to the **cultural authenticity** of the books we select. We wish to represent different cultures and to do so appropriately. The following guidelines will help ensure cultural authenticity:

◆ Avoid stereotypes in both texts and illustrations; individuals from different cultures should be portrayed in various roles and living environments.

◆ Whenever possible, include biographies of men and women who are respected in their own cultures.

◆ Provide additional versions of events and movements from other cultural perspectives: how the tribes under Chief Powhatan perceived the English who settled Jamestown; the experiences of the Chinese who came to California in the late nineteenth century to work; Mexican workers and their families who enter the United States — legally and illegally — to work.

Once we have selected our books, we can read them and consider how they will best "fit" in our unit. Given our goals, objectives, and the nature of the books themselves, which books should be experienced by everyone, which may be read by smaller groups of students, and which should be available for individual, independent reading by the students? These three categories into which we place our books are termed **core, extended,** and **recreational reading.**

◆ *Core selections* are books that all students in the class experience, usually in a read-aloud format. Students discuss these books *intensively*. The books are presented in a sequence, building upon each other. Occasionally, a core selection may consist of a single book with a whole unit built around it.

◆ *Extended selections*, books that are related to the theme, are read and discussed in smaller groups.

◆ *Recreational* or "motivational" texts, related in some way to the theme, are often read during Sustained Silent Reading or Reading Workshop.

We can draw upon a number of resources in order to locate appropriate books. Librarians or media specialists and fellow teachers can be invaluable. In addition, some of the best print and other media resources are listed in the *Build Your Teaching Resources* feature on page 408. We should keep our major goals and objectives in mind as we look for books—though it's important to remember that when we use a range of books in a unit, the odds are that we'll have many opportunities to address those goals and objectives.

Determining the Objectives and Types of Activities and Projects

Based on our goals and the texts we've collected, we should next brainstorm objectives and instructional ideas for our unit. **Objectives** are what students will be learning and are "measurable"—that is, what the students will be doing will provide us with evidence that they are, in fact, learning and attaining the goals we have set for our unit. This is why I suggest you generate your objectives *as* you plan your activities and projects; they usually offer the most appropriate contexts for "measuring." Based on the *extended* selections, for example, we often pose specific questions for discussion and response in the students' literature circles and journals. We will read through these selections with this purpose in mind—facilitating students' reflection on *characterization*, *theme*, *dialogue*, and so forth. An example of a "measurable" activity for assessing students' grasp of the concept of "theme" in narratives would include responding in journals and through discussion to questions such as

1. Why do you think the author wrote this story?

2. What do you feel is the most important word, phrase, sentence, passage, or paragraph in this story? Why?

Build Your Teaching Resources

RESOURCES FOR ASSEMBLING MATERIALS FOR THEMATIC UNITS

Blackburn, G. M. (1994). *Index to poetry for children and young people, 1988–1992.* Bronx, NY: H. W. Wilson. [Several previous editions have been published, going back to 1942.]

Breen, K. (1988). *Index to collective biographies for young readers.* New York: R. R. Bowker. [Previous edition: Silverman, J. (1979). *Index to collective biographies for young readers.* New York: R. R. Bowker.]

Children's books in print [updated annually]. New York: R. R. Bowker. [This bibliography is divided into subject and author.]

Commire, A. (1985). *Something about the author.* Detroit, MI: Gale Research.

Dreyer, S. (1989). *The bookfinder* (Vol. 4). Circle Pines, MN: American Guidance Service.

The elementary school library collection. New Brunswick, NJ: Bro-Dart Foundation. [Published annually; includes films, filmstrips, and other media as well]

Flowers, A. A. (Ed.). (1990). *The Horn Book guide to children's and young adult books.* Boston: The Horn Book.

Jensen, J., & Roser, N. (1993). *Adventuring with books: A booklist for pre-K–grade 6.* Urbana, IL: National Council of Teachers of English. [Previous edition: Jett-Simpson, M., and the Committee on the Elementary School Booklist (Eds.). (1989). *Adventuring with books: A booklist for pre-K–grade 6.* Urbana, IL: National Council of Teachers of English.]

Kingman, L., Hogarth, G., & Quimby, H. (Eds.). (1978). *Illustrators of children's books, 1967–1976.* Boston: The Horn Book. [Three previous volumes covering earlier illustrators have also been published.]

Kobrin, B. (1995). *Eyeopeners II!* New York: Scholastic. [Earlier publication: *Eyeopeners!: How to choose and use children's books about real people, places and things.* (1988). New York: Viking Penguin.]

Lima, C., & Lima, J. (1989). *A to zoo: Subject access to children's picture books* (3rd ed.). New York: R. R. Bowker.

Notable books in language arts, *Language Arts.* Urbana, IL: National Council of Teachers of English. [Published yearly in November issue]

Pillar, A. M. (1992). Resources to identify children's books. In B. E. Cullinan (Ed.), *Invitation to read: More children's literature in the reading progam* (pp. 150–165). Newark, DE: International Reading Association.

Reading Teacher. Newark, DE: International Reading Association. [Each year "Teachers' Choices" and "Children's Choices" are published. The International Reading Association also periodically publishes under separate cover "Children's Choices," a list which covers several years.]

Science and children. Washington, DC: National Science Teachers Association. [In March issue outstanding trade books in science are listed.]

Social Education. Arlington, VA: The National Council for Social Studies. [Annual list of "notable children's trade books in the field of social studies" published in April/May issue]

Subject guide to children's books in print. New York: R. R. Bowker. [Published annually]

(Continued)

What *strategies* should we teach or reinforce with our students that will support their involvement with the activities—for example, Guided Reading-Thinking Activities, getting writing going, and keeping it going? These, too, represent objectives we will set out in the unit.

Tamara Baren, the teacher in the Thematic Exploration following Chapter 9, asks herself the following questions as she brainstorms possible activities and objectives:

◆ How is this activity related to the theme?

◆ Is critical thinking embedded in the activity?

◆ Does this activity help meet curriculum goals?

◆ Can this activity be adapted to a cooperative format that builds community and involvement and extends understanding?

◆ How will I tie this new learning to past experiences?

◆ What will *I* need to do in terms of direct teaching, discussion, or lecturing to tie this learning experience together so that students have a more coherent overview?

◆ How will I assess student learning? How will the students keep track of that learning so that, through review of their materials, their learning deepens? (We'll address this matter in depth in Chapter 11.)

◆ What other audiences for our work could be developed?

◆ Can this activity meet *several* objectives—combining reading and writing skills, math and science, mapping, and so forth? For example:

Writing letters (personal and business)

What mathematics- and science-based experiences can be incorporated?

What estimating, graphing, or probability opportunities will be possible?

Exploring the Selected Literature for Examples to Integrate Skills Instruction

What specific *skills* should we teach? We'll use whatever texts — literature, newspapers, advertisements, or the World Wide Web — for sources of our examples. We will then be able to model the application of the skills. For example, if we're exploring *figurative language*, we can look through the literature that a group or the whole class will be reading and find examples of idioms, similes, or metaphors. These can be the basis for our minilessons as well as for the students' application — and in this case, collection — of examples.

Planning a Tentative Sequence and Looking for Other Resources

When we think about appropriate activities for a thematic unit, it helps to think in terms of those for **introducing, developing,** and **culminating** the unit (refer to the Thematic Explorations). *Introductory* activities should really engage our students — for example, an intriguing science experiment, a read-aloud of a truly absorbing book, the posing of and response to a perplexing problem or question, or an art experience. From that point on, *introductory* activities may involve browsing through texts we have on hand as extended texts, locating places on a map, or beginning a K-W-L chart. *Developing* activities are the heart of the unit — projects, writing, creating — with most of them moving students toward the *culmination* of the unit — publishing, sharing, and celebrating new awareness and understanding.

Blocking Out a Tentative Schedule

Overall, how long do you estimate the unit will last? Back in Chapter 3, we saw the example in Figure 3.4 where the teacher has planned for monthly themes. These can vary, of course, but she has a road map at the beginning of the year. Usually, the length of your unit depends on how broad it is and how much you hope to accomplish. You don't want the students to "burn out" on the theme, of course, but neither do you want to treat the content superficially.

Realistically, aim for a certain number of weeks, then block out the unit week by week. Again, I emphasize that this schedule is tentative; your students' input may change this time line, or you may realize that you need to change the initial schedule as you move through the unit.

Introducing and Discussing the Theme with Students for Their Input and Choice

After we have introduced the unit and engaged the students' interest, we should talk about what they are interested in pursuing within the context of the unit and the types of projects and/or activities we will undertake. How much choice we believe is appropriate for students depends on their familiarity with the kinds of activities with which we'll be occupied; we may want to allow more choices as we move further into the year. Just about always, though, students should have choice in selecting books. When we involve students in a larger role in planning, it's helpful to have a class discussion and make a "web" together.

Thematic Units in Action

Every day you will read orally to the students from the core selections. The format may be similar to a GLTA in which students make predictions orally and/or in their response journals. We may have the students respond freely as well as to questions that we have provided and/or passages in the reading; again, responses may be both oral and written.

Students read the extended selections independently and talk about them in smaller groups, often meeting with us for the discussions. Activities can occur during the Readers' and Writers' Workshop in the morning, and as appropriate, during the afternoon — particularly with across-the-curriculum integrated units. We will be meeting with individuals and groups to assess how projects are coming along and to provide feedback and help as needed.

The following thematic unit webs illustrate the result of putting these guidelines to work. As you look over each, note how most activities can address more than one objective and how one objective can address more than one goal. Teachers have established a coherent organization among goals, objectives, and activities/projects.

Goals
- Understand story structure and how each part of a story relates to the others: beginnings, middles, endings
- Beginning understanding of more complex stories—the "story within a story"
- Understand roles of main character and supporting characters
- *Inferencing* based on the text and the illustrations
- Understand the role of *meaning* in the spelling of homophones

Language Arts Objectives
- Identify features of the different parts of a story during reading and discussion
- Apply knowledge of the different parts of a story through composition of an original cat tale
- Students internalize process of predicting, checking, and confirming through Guided Listening-Thinking Activities and Guided Reading-Thinking Activities
- Demonstrate understanding of how *homophones* work through word study activities and conventional spelling during writing (Note: This activity does not apply to all students.)

Cats: Reality and Fantasy*

Activities/Projects
Compare/contrast charts for *Nobody's Cat* and *Puss in Boots*
Locate riddles and poems about cats; favorites are copied and illustrated by students
Collage modeled on Keats's *Hi, Cat!*
Illustrate homophones (*tale/tail; hair/hare; son/sun*)
Venn diagrams or comparison/contrast charts:
  one core text and one extended or recreational text
As culminating activity, compose original cat tales:
  Use chart to plan and modify story:
  setting, beginning, problem/solutions, ending
Bookmaking: students create covers and bind their stories

Activities generated by the students:
Investigate history of cats and how different civilizations have thought about them
Poems modeled on "cat poems" that have been located
Students write stories about their *own* pet cats; illustrate with drawings and/or snapshots

Literature-based Thematic Unit: Second Grade

*Adapted from J. Moss (1991). *Focus on literature: A context for literacy learning.* Katonah, NY: Richard C. Owen.

Core Texts

Nobody's Cat
Guided Listening-Thinking Activity
Discussion: Interpreting pictures—How do cats communicate with humans?
Story structure: chart beginning, middle ("What happened?"), ending

Puss in Boots
GLTA: How do we know what type of book this is?
Follow-up questions focus on inference, recurring motif
Story structure: add "setting" to chart

"Do Not Open" ("story within a story")
GLTA
Make parallel charts of two *smaller* stories; see how they are linked

The Witch Who Lost Her Shadow
GLTA—Follow-up questions focus on double-meaning of
"shadow" (Cat's name, cat is black, literal and figurative "shadow");
ending of story; who is the "real" *main* character?

Extended Texts (Guided Small-Group Reading) and Recreational Texts

Easy/Average

Averill, E. (1960). *The fire cat.* Harper & Row.
Carle, E. (1988). *Have you seen my cat?* Putnam.
Ehlert, L. (1990). *Feathers for lunch.* Harcourt.
Flack, M. (1989). *Angus the cat.* Doubleday.
Foreman, M. (1985). *Cat and canary.* Dial.
Gag, W. (1928). *Millions of cats.* Coward.
Goss, L., & Goss, C. (1989). *The baby leopard: An African folktale.* Bantam. [Illustrated by S. Bailey-Jones and M. Jones.]
Keats, E. (1970). *Hi, Cat!* Collier Books.
Krause, R. (1971). *Leo the late bloomer.* Windmill Books. [Illustrated by J. Aruego.]
Marzollo, J. (1990). *Pretend you're a cat.* Trumpet Club. [Illustrated by J. Pinkney.]
Robinson, T. (1938). *Buttons.* Viking. [Illustrated by P. Bacon.]
Rylant, C. (1990). *Henry & Mudge and the happy cat.* Trumpet Club. [Illustrated by S. Stevenson.]
Rylant, C. (1994). *Mr. Putter & Tabby walk the dog.* [Illustrated by A. Howard.] Scholastic.
Seuss, D. (1957). *The cat in the hat.* Houghton Mifflin.
Seuss, D. (1958). *The cat in the hat comes back.* Houghton Mifflin.
Smith, L. (1991). *The big pets.* Scholastic.

Average/Challenging

Bunting, E. (1994). *Smoky night.* Harcourt. [Illustrated by D. Diaz.]
Cleary, B. (1973). *Socks.* Dell.
Fatio, L. (1954). *The happy lion.* Scholastic. [Illustrated by R. Duvoisin.]
Herriot, J. (1977). *Oscar, cat-about-town.* St. Martin's Press. [Illustrated by R. Brown.]
Kent, J. (1971). *The fat cat.* Parent's Magazine Press.
Larrick, N. (Ed.) (1988). *Cats are cats.* Philomel. [Illustrated by E. Young.]
Livingston, M. (1987). *Cat poems.* Holiday House.
Ness, E. (1966). *Sam, Bangs, and Moonshine.* Trumpet Club.
Polacco, P. (1992). *Mrs. Katz and Tush.* Dell.
Polacco, P. (1994). *Tikvah means hope.* Doubleday.
Purdy, C. (1994). *Mrs. Merriwether's musical cat.* Putnam.
Robertus, P. (1988). *The dog who had kittens.* Trumpet Club. [Illustrated by J. Stevens.]
Viorst, J. (1971). *The tenth good thing about Barney.* Aladdin Books. [Illustrated by E. Blegvad.]
Wild, M. (1989). *The very best of friends.* Harcourt. [Illustrated by J. Vivas.]
Zaum, M. (1985). *Catlore: Tales from around the world.* Atheneum.

Language Arts Goals

Learn structure and type of content in informational texts

Use biographical and informational materials
  in the process of discussion and writing

Language Arts Objectives

Identify, interpret, and apply important information in both
  biography and informational texts

Represent information in alternative formats

Human Body: Moving, Breathing, Living

Content Goals

Understand the roles of three of the major systems in the body:
  musculoskeletal, circulatory, and respiratory

Understand and appreciate the role of three scientists whose work
  discovered and explored these systems

Content Objectives

Social Studies		Science
William Harvey and his times	← →	Explore and explain circulation of blood
Ellie Metchnikoff and her times (won Nobel Prize)	← →	Explain the purpose of why blood flows to and gathers at a wound
Karl Landsteiner (won Nobel Prize)	← →	Types of blood
Charles Drew	← →	Explain challenges in storing blood
		How smoking affects breathing
		Artificial limbs/parts of the body
		How bones grow and heal

Core Texts

Balestrino, P. (1990). *The skeleton inside you.* Scholastic.

Banard, C. (1983). *Junior body machine.* Crown.

Facklam, M., & Facklam, H. (1987). *Spare parts for people.* Harcourt.

McGowen, T. (1988). *The circulatory system: From Harvey to the artificial heart.*
Franklin Watts.

Weart, E. (1964). *The story of your respiratory system.* Coward, McCann.

Integrated Thematic Unit: Third Grade

*Adapted from P. Brambaugh (1993). Human body: A third grade theme. In S. Walmsley, *Children exploring their world: Theme teaching in elementary school.* Portsmouth, NH: Heinemann.

Extended Texts:

Easy/Average

Bertol, R. (1970). *Charles Drew*. Thomas Crowell.

Branley, F. (1967). *Oxygen keeps you alive.* Thomas Crowell.

Broekel, R. (1974). *Your skeleton and skin.* Children's Press.

Marr, J. (1971). *A breath of fresh air and a breath of smoke.* M. Evans.

Weart, E. (1966). *The story of your bones.* Coward, McCann, & Geoghegan.

Average/Challenging

Asimov, I. (1986). *How did we find out about blood?* Walker.

Avraham, R. (1989). *The circulatory system.* Chelsea House.

Bornancin, B. (1983). *Know your own body.*

Caselli, G. (1987). *The human body and how it works.* Grosset & Dunlap.

Cole, J. (1987). *The magic school bus: Inside the human body.* Scholastic.

Goldsmith, I. (1975). *Anatomy for children.* Sterling.

Recreational Texts:

Easy/Average

Allen, G., & Denslow, J. (1970). *Bones.* Franklin Watts.

Bertol, R. (1970). *Charles Drew.* Thomas Crowell.

Burstein, J. (1977). *Slim Goodbody: The inside story.* McGraw-Hill.

Drew, D. (1992). *Body facts.* Rigby.

Education Reading Service, (1971). *My super book of the human body.*

Lauber, P. (1962). *Your body and how it works.* Random House.

MacLeod, S., Skelton, M., & Stringer, J. (1993a). *Body business.* Rigby.

MacLeod, S., Skelton, M., & Stringer, J. (1993b). *The body machine.* Rigby.

Turner, E., & Fenton, C. (1961). *Inside you and me.* John Day.

Average/Challenging

Cole, J. (1987). *The human body: How we evolved.* Morrow.

Dunbar, R. (1984). *The heart and circulatory system.* Franklin Watts.

Grey, V. (1982). *The chemist who lost his head.* Coward, McCann.

Grolier Society (1963). *The book of popular science.*

Nolen, W. (1971). *Spare parts for the human body.* Random House.

Parker, S. (1982). *The lungs and breathing.* Franklin Watts

Activities/Projects

GRTA with biographical and informational texts

Draw and color code these different body systems

Draw and label four different animals;
    explain each of their breathing processes
    (these will be combined into a class book)

Create graph of the number of bones different animals have

Write or dramatize an episode in Harvey's, Metchnikoff's, or Landsteiner's life

Field trip: X-ray department

Descriptive writing: how smoking affects breathing—and the rest of one's life

Red Cross worker discusses blood collection and storage

Learning log: measure respiration and pulse, exercise, measure, rest, measure

Language Arts Goals
Work cooperatively to
* solve problems
* compose through writing and drawing
Use *learning logs* on a regular basis
Apply descriptive/persuasive composition skills
Develop locational skills in texts and on the Internet
Learn purpose and format of business letter
Compare/contrast different modes of presentation
Read, respond to, and apply understanding of *biography* and *informational* texts

Language Arts Objectives
Use textbooks appropriately as *resources*
Learn how to navigate on the Web: narrowing and expanding searches
Compose informational text applying *description* and *persuasion*
Write effective informational letter

"Necessity Is the Mother of Invention"

Content Goals

Science
* Learn about and apply *scientific method*
* Understand basic principles of
  Air Pressure
  Buoyancy
  Friction
  Magnetism
* Understand workings of simple machines
* Solve real-life problems through application of scientific principles

Social Studies
* Identify and predict *positive* and *negative* effects of inventions
* Familiarize students with inventors and their inventions
* Support position with fact rather than opinion

Math
* Estimation
* Averaging
* Measuring
* Simple Ratios
* Weighing

Art and Music
* Drawing objects to scale
* Understand how *sound* is created through *vibration*

Integrated Thematic Unit: Fifth/Sixth Grade

*Adapted from a unit developed by Stephanie White, University of Nevada, Reno.

Core Texts
Fleming, I. (1964). *Chitty chitty bang bang*. Random House.
Stevens, B. (1983). *Ben Franklin's glass armonica*. Carolrhoda.

Extended Texts
du Bois, W.P. (1947). *The 21 balloons*. Viking.
Duffy, B. (1991). *The gadget war*. Penguin.
Fritz, J. (1976). *What's the big idea, Ben Franklin?* Coward McCann.
McCloskey, R. (1943). *Homer Price*. Viking.

Recreational Texts
Aaseng, N. (1986). *More with less: The future world of Buckminster Fuller*. Lerner.
Aaseng, N. (1990). *Better mousetraps*. Lerner.
Aaseng, N. (1991). *Twentieth-century inventors*. Facts on File.
Asimov, I. (1981). *Wild inventions*. Raintree.
Blashfield, J. (1995). *Women inventors. (Vols. I–IV)*. Capstone.
Burch, J. (1991). *Fine print: A story about Johann Gutenberg*. Carolrhoda.
Caney, S. (1985). *The invention book*. Workman.
Cooper, C. (1984). *How everyday things work*. Orbis.
Egan, L. (1987). *Thomas Edison, the great American inventor*. Eisan, Durwood.
Feldman, E. (1990). *Benjamin Franklin, scientist and inventor*. Franklin Watts.
Freedman, R. (1991). *The Wright Brothers: How they invented the airplane*. Holiday House.
Jones, C. (1991). *Mistakes that worked*. Doubleday.
McKissack, P., & McKissack, F. (1994). *African American inventors*. Millbrook.
Macaulay, D. (1988). *The way things work*. Houghton Mifflin.
Mahy, M. (1987). *The terrible topsy-turvy, tissy-tossy tangle*. Children's Press International.
Mitchell, B. (1986). *We'll race you, Henry: A story about Henry Ford*. Carolrhoda.
Murphy, J. (1986). *Guess again: More weird and wacky inventions*. Bradbury Press.
Nye, B. (1995). *Bill Nye the science guy's consider the following*. Disney Press.
West, D. (1992). *53 1/2 things that changed the world*. Millbrook.
Wulffson, D. (1981). *The invention of ordinary things*. Lothrop, Lee and Shepard.
Yount, L. (1991). *Black scientists*. Facts on File.

Activities/Projects
Read-aloud: *Chitty Chitty Bang Bang* and view movie version—create comparison/contrast chart
Write letter to U.S. Patent Office applying for a patent for the team-created "invention"
As students are working on inventions and constructions, they will keep detailed records in their learning logs
Based on Macaulay's *The Way Things Work*, read about and discuss some simple machines
Experiments—Activities in *Bill Nye the Science Guy's Consider the Following* to learn about
air pressure/buoyancy/friction/magnetism

Team
(1) Create "invention" that will solve real-life problem posed by teacher;
   write descriptive and persuasive composition that will explain how *best*
   the problem will be solved by this invention, and *why* this is the best way
(2) Prepare detailed blueprint/drawing for the "invention"

Partners
(1) Design paper airplane and fly several times: *measure* each flight, determine *average* for all flights,
   and *graph* results on computer for all partner groups
(2) Based on these results, design *new* plan: *estimate* distance it will fly, conduct flights, then compare to estimates
   Report all observations, estimations, and results in learning logs

Activities That Integrate Reading, Discussion, and Writing

The following ideas, activities, and projects help elementary students "read like writers" and "write like readers" as they explore in both literature-based and integrated thematic units:

"Deep" Reading of Texts

In the context of a literature discussion group, students read or listen to a selection at least twice. Present a series of questions that require a "deep" reading of the material—in other words, questions for which there will likely be no single correct answer (Plecha, 1992; Templeton, 1995). Questions can cover any facet of the story's elements as well as probe ethical issues—the "rightness or wrongness" of behavior given the specific situation in the story. Ask questions that tap central ideas, conflicts, and issues. Here are two examples.

Based on the book *A Bridge to Terabithia*, by Katherine Paterson (1996), one teacher handed out the following directions and questions:

Decide whether each of the following statements is true or false. Be prepared to support your answers with evidence from the story. Each group should try to reach agreement.

1. Young people react to terrible events differently than adults do.
2. Most boys of Jesse's age wouldn't become involved in either the real or make-believe world of Terabithia.
3. The relationship between Jesse and his younger sister is better than the relationship most brothers and sisters have.

You can qualitatively increase the challenge of your questions, as the following activity based on *Tuck Everlasting*, by Natalie Babbitt (1975), illustrates:

Give students a dilemma:

Should Winnie have helped Mrs. Tuck escape from prison?

Present some complicating factors:

What if *everyone* believed they were justified in breaking the law? After all, Mrs. Tuck murdered a man (or did she?). Could Mrs. Tuck have been justified in killing "the man in the yellow suit"? (Is there ever a time when we can justify killing another human being?)

Shouldn't Winnie first attempt to explain to everyone that if Mrs. Tuck is hanged, she will not die?

As students discuss these types of questions, we can sit in with the group, facilitating the process if necessary:

◆ *As* they are sharing, we can take notes, getting down the gist of their responses.

◆ After each student has responded, we can ask questions to help them clarify their answers and compare and contrast their responses with each other.

◆ We can then summarize the students' responses while noting where most students agreed and where there were areas of disagreement.

Working in pairs, students first read a poem silently. Then one student describes to the other what the poem means to her. Next, both read the poem a second time, and then the other student explains what it means to him. If they wish, the students can read the poem a third time and discuss it again. Then the students write in their response journals about what the poem means to them. This activity underscores the value of discussing and gradually coming to understand the potential of a poem—the different ideas it can evoke—and doing so in a social context.

Understanding Commonalities among Texts and Narratives

Comparing and Contrasting Versions of Folktales and Fairy Tales

For example, variants of the "Little Red Riding Hood" tale are *Lon Po Po* (1989) and Emberley's *Ruby* (1990). Students can work on a chart in which they compare the different versions according to setting, characters, problem, magic, events, ending, titles, similarities, differences, and conclusions. They can also construct Venn diagrams, as the eight-year-old did in Figure 10.2 on page 421. (Note also the different versions of the "Cinderella" tale in the Thematic Exploration following Chapter 9.) An effective follow-up activity is to have the students write their *own* versions of the folktale.

Storyboards are motivating and very instructive devices for grasping narrative structure in reading and for applying that knowledge in writing (see the Thematic Exploration following Chapter 9). They help students of all ages understand the structure of a story—beginning, sequence, problem/resolution, and ending—as well as character development. *Storyboards* are created by students and eventually used to plan their *writing* of stories. Tamara Baren begins with a storyboard that consists of six segments:

Teacher and students participate in a discussion about the beginning and the ending of the story—then the "middle" is filled in. The middle, of course, is the "meat" of the story and includes what happens as characters attempt to solve problems. During this discussion, we can help students identify the most important events or occurrences in the story and decide which comes first, second, third, and fourth. As we talk about the different segments in the storyboard, we encourage the students to describe *in their own words* what is going on. Just as with language-experience dictations, we can then write in the smaller "caption" box what the students say—helping them summarize as concisely as they can.

At first, we may go through a whole story this way. Soon, however, we can divide the students into groups or partners. When assigning partners, it's an excellent idea to pair students who are second-language learners with native speakers or to pair students with special needs with other students. Students then work together to create an illustration in the larger box that goes along with that particular part of the story and/or *in their own words* create the text in the caption box. Groups or partners then come together when they have finished to assemble their separate segments as part of the "whole."

Both primary and intermediate students can benefit from working with storyboards. Whole bulletin boards and walls can eventually be covered with one or more storyboards, representing different works from a single author or those within the same genre written by different authors.

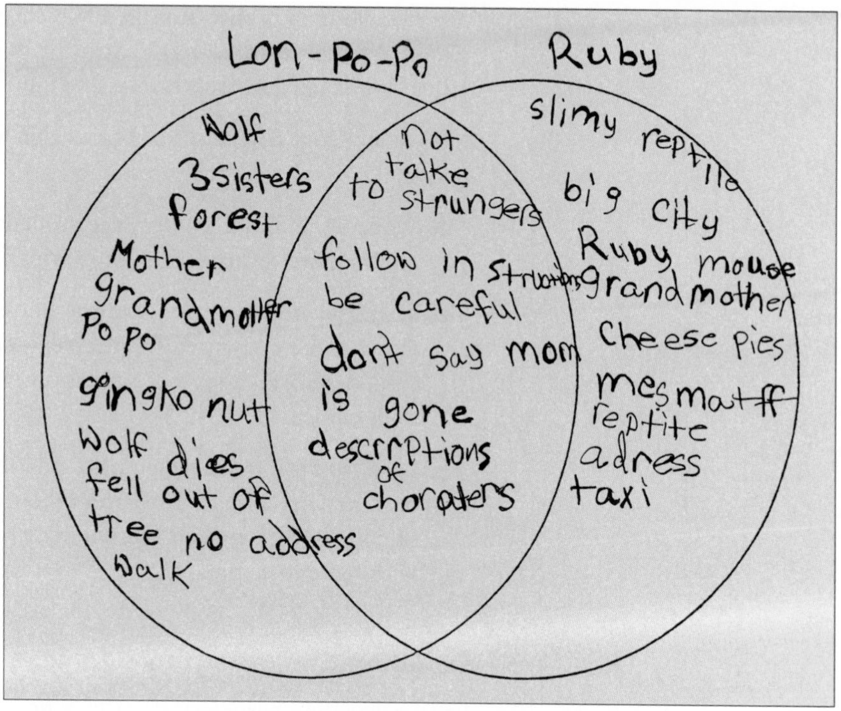

A hand-drawn Venn diagram comparing **Lon-Po-Po** and **Ruby**.

Left circle (Lon-Po-Po): Wolf, 3 sisters, forest, Mother, grandmother, Po Po, gingko nut, Wolf dies, fell out of tree, no address, walk

Center (overlap): not talke to strangers, follow instructions, be careful, don't say mom is gone, descriptions of choraters

Right circle (Ruby): slimy reptile, big city, Ruby, mouse, grandmother, cheese pies, mesmouff, reptile, adress, taxi

Figure 10.2   Lon Po-Po and Ruby Venn Diagram

Students can also use storyboards to plan the composition of their own stories. The format of the storyboard provides a concrete means for moving frames around and trying out different sequences of events.

In addition, storyboards help students understand the thinking and planning that *artists* engage in when they make decisions about what and how to illustrate a story. The illustration is not just a representation of exactly what is said in the text. It can fill in gaps, interpret, and provide transitions between events—conveying the story on an equal basis with the written text.

After students conceptually grasp how a storyboard works, they can use it to *generate* a story—moving frames around and deciding how much of the story they wish to convey through illustration and how much through writing. And as students explore picture books and the various types, media, and formats of different authors and author/illustrators, they come to understand how text and illustration work *together* to create the story experience.

◆ *Compare and contrast books in different genres.* Students can sort a group of books according to categories. *They* may establish the categories; your only direction is, "Which of these books do you think belong together in some way?" Students will probably come to understand that books may, in fact, be classified in more than one way.

◆ Have students read a set of books that won the Newbery Award (given annually for the best children's fiction).

1. Working in small groups, the students then derive what they believe are the criteria for determining which book receives the award.

2. Then the students may read the books nominated for the award during the current year and decide which one should win and which should receive honorable mention. They should discuss and defend their choices.

3. After you tell them which titles have actually won, let them try to determine why a book other than their own choice was selected (unless, of course, they picked the winner, too!). Furthermore, do they agree with the choice or not?

Exploring Character Development

Writers develop characterization in a number of ways. To explore this development, students may do the following:

◆ Working in pairs, students can examine a story or chapter for the different ways that a particular character is developed—through conversation, description, letters, and so forth. In Patricia MacLachlan's *Sarah Plain and Tall* (1985), for example (appropriate for third grade and up), we learn much about Sarah through her letters before she appears in person.

◆ When students are each reading different books, have them meet in small groups to introduce the main character in their respective books, describing or impersonating the character and telling about the particular problems he or she faced. Other students may then ask questions of the "character." Each character may discuss whether his or her own problems are worse than those of other characters. A variation of this activity is to have characters respond as though they were being interviewed on a television talk show.

◆ Students can rate story characters on several traits along a continuum (good/bad, large/small, brave/cowardly, hot/cold, honest/dishonest). They should be prepared to defend their ratings orally or in writing (Johnson & Louis, 1987). Figure 10.3, from Johnson and Louis, illustrates a rating scale for Bilbo Baggins in J.R.R. Tolkien's *The Hobbit* (1938/1990).

BILBO BAGGINS	very	quite	neither, both, don't know	quite	very	
good	x					bad
large				x		small
brave	x					cowardly
hot		x				cold
honest			x			dishonest

Figure 10.3

A Student Rating Scale of a Character in *The Hobbit* According to Different Traits

SOURCE: Used by permission of Thomas Nelson Australia from T. D. Johnson and D. Lewis, *Literacy Through Literature* (Portsmouth, NH: Heinemann Educational Books, Inc., 1987).

◆ Johnson and Louis (1987) develop the application of rating scales further; Figure 10.4 is their profile of "excitement" plotted against time in the story "The Three Little Pigs" (p. 108). (Note, by the way, how this activity also teaches *graphing*.)

Becoming a Character

Through both discussion and response journals, students can take the perspective of different characters. For example:

◆ Students may take a perspective that differs quite markedly from their own usual perspective, an exercise which leads to an excellent writing activity. First, share an example of "the other point of view." A good prod for primary students is the book *Clyde Monster*, by Robert Crowe (1976), in which Clyde, a young monster, is afraid of the dark because *people* might be lurking about to "get him" when he's asleep. His monster parents explain that people really don't do things like that, and gradually his fear subsides. All students—but particularly intermediate students—enjoy Jon Sciezska's *The True Story of the Three Little Pigs* (1989), in which the wolf tells the story in the first person. After such

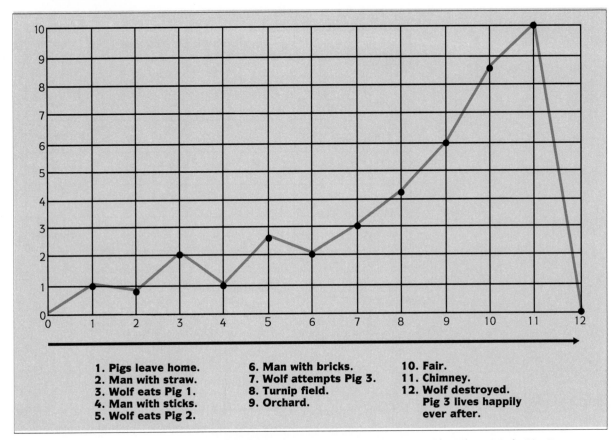

Figure 10.4   A Profile of "Excitement" versus Time in "The Three Little Pigs"

SOURCE: Used by permission of Thomas Nelson Australia from T. D. Johnson and D. Lewis, *Literacy Through Literature* (Portsmouth, NH: Heinemann Educational Books, Inc., 1987).

reading experiences, students can write stories, poems, or reflections from these "alternative" perspectives.

◆ How does the giant in "Jack and the Beanstalk" view the intrusion of Jack?

◆ What does the witch think about the appearance of Hansel and Gretel?

◆ How does the maid in *Summer of My German Soldier* (1973) respond after her first conversation with the German prisoner of war? (Betty Greene, the author, gives us some insight during the conversation; how does the maid's perspective change after this point?)

◆ An interesting twist is to have students write entries in their response journals that a character might have written had he or she kept a journal.

Response Journals

While we encourage students' genuine responses to their reading, often it is helpful if we provide some prompts they may use if they wish—usually questions that help them reflect on characters, plot, setting, what *they* would do if they were in the book, or connections to their lives. For example, Bianca's journal response in Figure 10.5 is based on lines from *Nettie's Trip South* by Anne Turner (1987); Nettie is a ten-year-old who travels to Virginia just prior to the start of the Civil War. Bianca's teacher provided three different excerpts from which students could choose. The one Bianca chose—"What are they missing?"—reflects Nettie's confusion about the Constitution's stating that slaves are three-fifths of a person.

After reading *Gila Monsters Meet You at the Airport* (1980), by Marjorie Sharmat, Yazmin and Pedro responded in their journals to the teacher's question, "What were your favorite parts?" Note how Yazmin and Pedro responded differently (Figure 10.6).

Terriesita's response in Figure 10.7 was written after she read Gary Soto's short story "The Marble Champ" (1990).

It is important to discuss different types of responses and model how to respond—"thinking aloud" as we do so. Once students form the habit of reacting to their reading in response journals, they may use their journal observations as jumping-off points for discussions with each other. You may also ask them to use their written responses as part of a more structured response activity.

Have students write a synopsis or summary of what they've read. Second, ask them to jot down any personal associations they have made during the reading and to indicate what they believe is the most important part of the text and why. Third, have them meet in small groups to discuss this last point, being prepared to support their judgment (Bleich, 1975). This process can be used for both narrative and expository texts. A particularly effective follow-up activity is to publish a synopsis of a book together with the students' final responses. Other students can then compare and contrast their own reactions with those in this publication.

Two other effective applications of response journals are (1) a basic **dialogue journal** format, in which the teacher responds to the student's observations, and (2) a **Double Entry Draft** (DED) format, also involving teacher response.

Dialogue Journals   In "dialogue" journals students write to their teacher or to another student about anything that interests them; the teacher or student then responds (Fulwiler, 1987; Barone, 1992). This format allows teachers to have an ongoing conversation with each student. Among her

Netties trip south

by Ann Turner

"What are they missing"?
    Nettie thinks the slaves
are missing a shoulder, arm, Leg, feet,
eyes, mouth, er, a nose, but she
does   not Know that they are missing
freedom. Nettie says that she
is Lucky to be white, because
She said to her Sister "we would be
a slave only if we were difrent"
color. Nettie got so sick when she
wached   the guy in a white suite
sole the slaves.

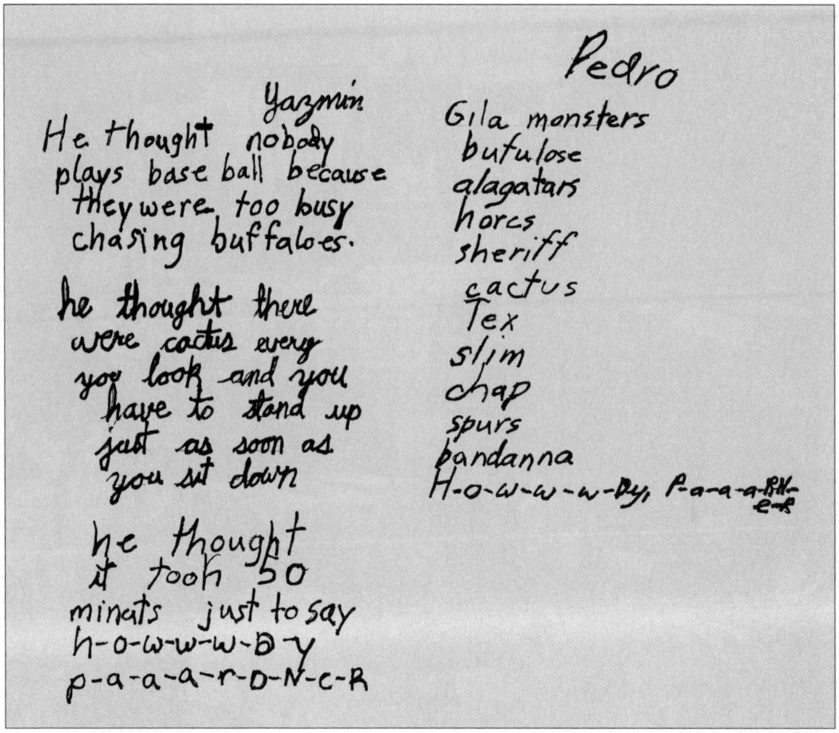

Yazmin

He thought nobody
plays base ball because
they were too busy
chasing buffaloes.

he thought there
were cactus every
you look and you
have to stand up
just as soon as
you sit down

he thought
it took 50
minuts just to say
h-o-w-w-w-d-y
p-a-a-a-r-o-N-c-R

Pedro

Gila monsters
butulose
alagatars
horcs
sheriff
cactus
Tex
slim
chap
spurs
bandanna
H-o-w-w-w-dy, P-a-a-ftk-
e-r

Figure 10.6   Yazmin and Pedro's Responses

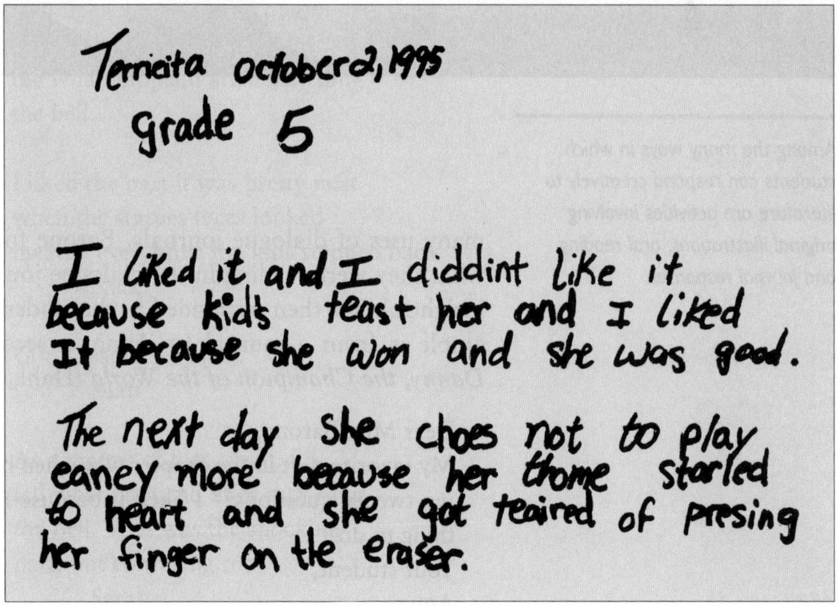

Terriesita october 2, 1995
grade 5

I liked it and I diddint like it
because kid's teast her and I liked
It because she won and she was good.

The next day she choes not to play
eaney more because her thome starled
to heart and she got teaired of presing
her finger on the eraser.

Figure 10.7   Terriesita's Response

Double Entry Draft (DED) On the left side of their journal pages, students write down a sentence or phrase that particularly engages, puzzles, or delights them. On the right-hand side of the page they write their response, and then the teacher writes her response below. The following is an example of a "DED" from Allan, a third-grader who was reading *Mr. Popper's Pen-*

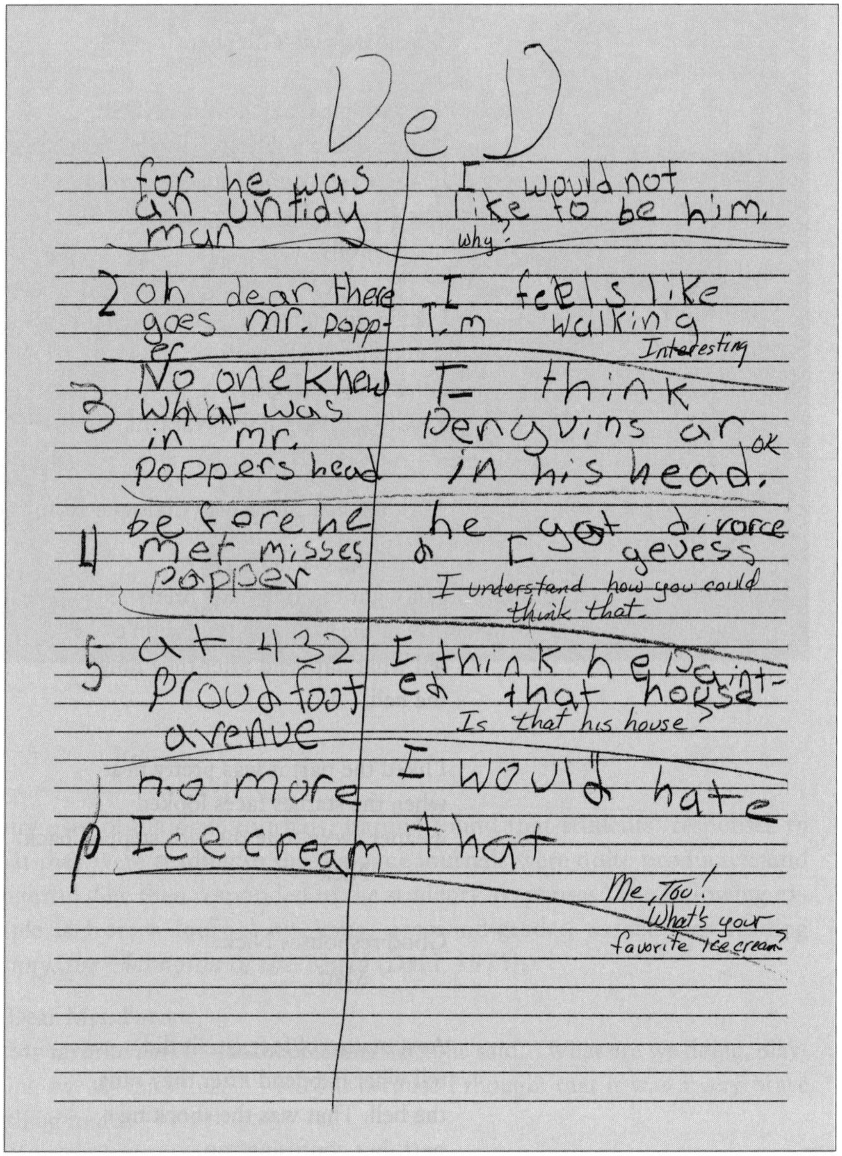

Figure 10.8   Allan's "Double Entry Draft"

guins (1993); notice how his responses show how he is moving beyond the literal and is inferring and interpreting based on the text.

Including Charts and Diagrams in Reading Reponse Logs   In addition to their writing and illustrations, students can include charts and diagrams generated by a small group or the whole class, as well as their own "originals" in their reading response logs. All of these modes represent different ways of thinking about and reflecting on the reading. In addition, it's helpful for students to chart the characters and plot in more involved chapter books.

"Writer's Notebook"   Throughout this text I've emphasized the importance of encouraging students to observe, explore, examine, and reflect; journals can help them do these things. We can also think of journals in terms of a **Writer's Notebook** (Calkins, 1991, 1994) — notebooks in which students are encouraged to enter their observations, recollections, quotes they really like, whatever ideas occur to them, or quick sketches. Then they periodically read through their notebooks for ideas to explore through writing — for example, ideas for a story, short descriptive piece, poem, or song. The very act of writing down whatever occurs to them generates reflection and connection with other thoughts and ideas and can be an important part of how they are better able to reflect on their world and make sense of it.

Other Classroom Reading and Writing Activities

Here are some other classroom activities involving reading and writing:

◆ Writing letters to authors is an excellent activity. If the students pose questions, these should arise from genuine interest. Quite often, questions that arise in response group sessions are ones that only the author can answer. Students should do their best when writing, revising, and copying the final drafts of their letters. If the students are in first or second grade, and if the teacher allows invented spellings to remain, the teacher should write a cover letter explaining why there are still misspellings (although authors may identify quite well with children, they may not be privy to the newer perspective on how children learn about the writing system!). Self-addressed, stamped return envelopes should be included as well.

◆ Arrange for a favorite author to visit the school for a day. If possible, this visit can follow a whole-school focus on a particular author or theme. Authors may be contacted by writing to their publishers; most, if not all, of the initial and follow-up correspondence can be handled by the students themselves.

◆ Have a "Character Day" when students dress up as characters from books that they have been reading.

◆ In an excellent variation of the traditional book report, have students prepare a short selection from a favorite story to read to the class. Tell them that their selections should motivate other students to read the story or book. They may practice their oral reading by taping themselves on a cassette recorder. Then have them listen to themselves as they follow along in the text. They may continue practicing until the reading sounds natural and fluent. Next, they should share the reading with the class.

◆ A book review, either written or shared orally, can add variety to book sharing or "booktalk" time. Bring in a book review clipped from the newspaper and explain that this is how many of us get our information about books. Often only using this information, we decide whether we wish to buy a book or check it out of the library (you can explain that *any* book should be available through a special system called the "inter-library loan system"). Discuss how the writer has organized the review and has attempted to attract the reader's interest. Point out how the reviewer has described the book's "negatives" (if any) and what he or she has focused on when recommending the book.

◆ *Students* can conduct GRTAs (Bear & Invernizzi, 1987). They should meet with you beforehand to review their plans and follow-up questions they have prepared and afterward to evaluate how it all went.

◆ The following approach to folktales would tie in nicely with social studies and learning about different cultures: Have a wide range of folktales on hand and tell students that these tales are the only means they have to find out about the countries of their origin. Mention to students that clues may be found in the beliefs, food, music, climate, and animals depicted in the tales.

Learning Logs We encourage students to use **learning logs** which become ongoing records of their learning. In these logs, students summarize, list, or describe in their own words what they have gained as the result of a particular learning experience—citing information as well as reflections on the *process* of learning (Fulwiler, 1987; Tchudi & Tchudi, 1983). There are many and varied formats for entering information and observations in the learning log that we should model and remind students about. The following are just a few possibilities:

◆ Observations of experiments (measuring plant growth and describing appearance)

- Class and/or individual K-W-L charts
- Clusters
- Explaining the solutions to math problems
- Original word problems

We can help students reflect on the *process* of their learning by offering these questions (Short, Harste, & Burke, 1996):

- What "sticks out" about what I learned in class today?
- What didn't I understand?
- What am I able to do better today than yesterday?
- What am I wondering about?

When we first introduce these questions to students, we should set aside a time at the end of the day when they can respond to them in writing for several minutes and then share afterward. As time goes on, sharing will be on an occasional basis. Notably, students can reflect on these questions with longer periods of time in mind—a week, a month, or longer—as part of their portfolio self-assessment (see Chapter 11).

Figure 10.9 shows Richard's first effort at reflecting on his experience

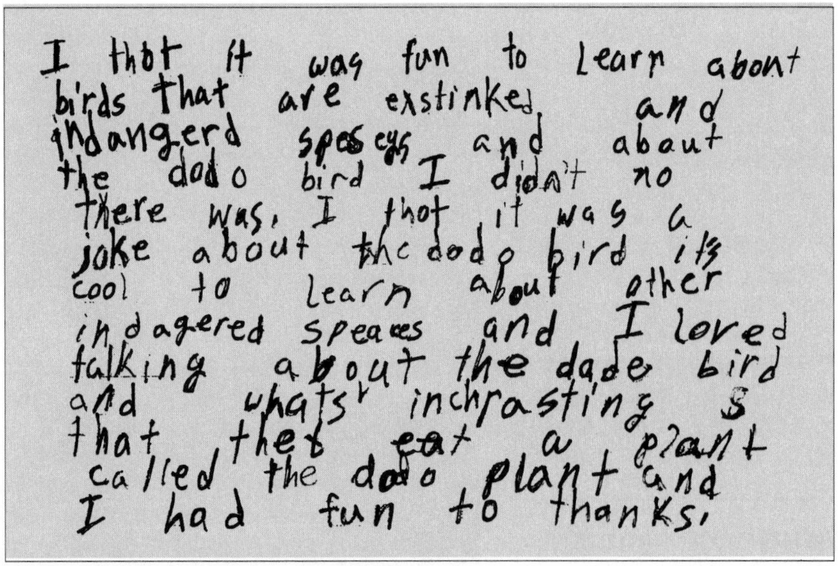
I thot it was fun to Learn about
birds that are exstinked and
indangerd spesegs and about
the dodo bird I didn't no
there was, I thot it was a
joke about the dodo bird it's
cool to learn about other
indagered speaces and I loved
talking about the dade bird
and whats inchrasting is
that they eat a plant
called the dodo plant and
I had fun to thanks,

Figure 10.9 **A Fifth-Grader's Learning Log "Reflection"**

with an exploration of different informational texts that dealt with extinct animals.

Responding and Exploring Through Art in the Integrated Classroom

◆ Have students create an *art project* in response to their reading; dioramas, paintings, drawings, murals (individual or group), and models can all be used to represent important characters, events, settings, or significant concepts.

◆ Students' response journals can also be **sketchbooks** in which their drawings can be an effective response at any point as they experience a story or book. For example, if you are reading *James and the Giant Peach*, by Roald Dahl (1961), to the students, you can stop before James enters the peach and have students draw what they think the inside will look like — and what James will find there (even if they've seen the movie — encourage them to stretch their *own* imaginations). At other times, sketching

Art provides a powerful means of extending and transforming literary experiences.

can involve a student in more thoughtful response to what she is reading, leading to insights that might not come solely through discussion or writing.

◆ From a number of texts, select passages that can easily be illustrated. Type each passage on a sheet of paper and distribute the sheets. The students then "assume the role of illustrator." Have on hand several types of art media, including "magazines, wallpaper samples, old greeting cards, and yarn" (Romatowski, 1987, p. 38). This activity can also be an excellent prelude to storyboards.

◆ Have students discuss *how* artists decide ways to illustrate books. Talking about the role and composition of illustrations can highlight many of the aspects of critical thinking you have been developing through other response activities. Moreover, these discussions can provide the groundwork for introducing a unit on a particular artist or comparing and contrasting two or three artists (Kiefer, 1994; Madura, 1995). You can focus on any book with illustrations. Some effective guiding questions are

- "What's the first thing you notice when you look at these illustrations? How do they make you feel? Why?" (Madura, 1995, p. 115)

- What medium has the artist used? For example, if it is obvious that the artist has used watercolor, oils, pencil, or collage, you can discuss *why* the artist may have selected a particular medium. If different media are used throughout the book, why might this be?

- How do the illustrations work with the text?

- How and where is the art placed on each page?

- How does an artist decide which scenes or events to illustrate?

- Do artists always try to show us exactly what is there, or do they interpret what they find in the book? (You may wish to elaborate on this discussion by sharing various versions of the same story and comparing and contrasting the work of the different illustrators.)

- What reasons do the students believe the artist had for illustrating one scene or event more elaborately than another? (Sometimes the more elaborate illustration represents a more important event, for example.)

- How do the colors—or the absence of color—reflect the elements of the text?

◆ ◆ ◆ **CONCLUDING PERSPECTIVE AND SUMMARY**

Using thematic units—a powerful and effective means of organizing instruction—encourages students' critical thinking, problem-solving abilities, and other means of inquiry. The framework outlined in this chapter provides guidance for constructing and teaching thematic units. It should help refine our abilities and bolster our confidence as we plan ways to involve students of all levels in this creative learning environment.

In this chapter we've addressed the following main points:

◆ Thematic unit instruction makes students aware of the relationships across the language arts and among the components of the elementary curriculum.

◆ By employing literature-based and integrated themes, we can engage students in both *intensive* and *extensive* reading and writing.

◆ Ideas for themes can come from just about anywhere—literature, curricular areas, current events, fascinating and/or important individuals, or the students' own interests.

◆ When choosing and planning how to teach a theme, consider the students' various developmental levels and select texts and other materials accordingly.

◆ While all sorts of texts and resources can and should be used, *trade books* are the heart of thematic units. All of these materials should authentically represent a variety of cultures and viewpoints.

◆ To accommodate individual as well as group reading, and required as well as extracurricular reading, arrange texts in *core*, *extended*, and *recreational* categories.

◆ We should organize classroom activities in categories for introducing, developing, and culminating the theme study.

Key Terms

across-the-curriculum integrated theme (p. 401)

core texts/reading (p. 407)

culminating activities (p. 410)

cultural authenticity in texts (p. 406)

dialogue journal (p. 425)

developing activities (p. 410)

Double Entry Draft (DED) (p. 425)

extended texts/reading (p. 407)

extensive reading and writing (p. 400)

goals (p. 405)

guidelines for selecting
appropriate books (p. 406)

intensive reading and writing
(p. 400)

introducing activities (p. 410)

learning logs (p. 432)

literature-based theme (p. 401)

objectives (p. 407)

recreational texts/reading (p. 407)

sketchbook (p. 434)

types of themes (p. 402)

Writer's Notebook (p. 431)

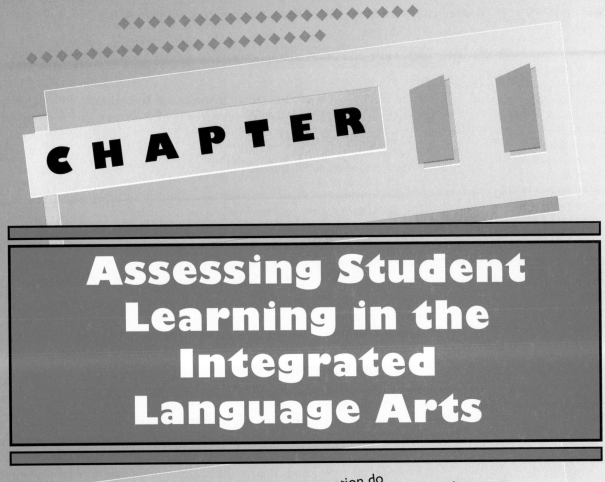

CHAPTER 11

Assessing Student Learning in the Integrated Language Arts

◆ What are *portfolios*? What types of information do they include? Why are they the most effective basis for assessing student development?

◆ Why do we group students for guided instruction in the language arts?

◆ How do we evaluate oral language skills in classroom situations?

◆ How do we determine students' developmental levels in literacy?

◆ What does assessment of spelling knowledge tell us about students' word knowledge in reading and writing?

◆ How is formal assessment of reading and writing changing?

◆ ◆ ◆ INTRODUCTION

Up to now we've been addressing the "what" of language arts instruction. Now it's time to address these questions in depth:

How do we know *where* to begin with students?

How do we know *what* to teach?

What information should we collect to document our students' growth in the language arts, and how should we organize it?

Perspectives and Definitions

Informal classroom assessment strategies provide the most relevant and valuable insight into our students' growth. Based on the ongoing reading, writing, and discussion in which they're engaged, these strategies include both planned and unplanned observations. In general, our assessment process includes analyzing and then synthesizing the information we gather in order to make decisions about individuals or groups.

There are two aspects of our informal classroom assessment: *initial* assessment and day-to-day *ongoing* assessment. Initial assessment determines the developmental levels of our students; using this information, we generally know the types of instructional activities appropriate for them. Once we know our students' general developmental levels, *ongoing* day-to-day information tells us what specific skills and strategies we should address more directly.

Formal assessment, the type of evaluation most familiar to the lay public, involves administering and interpreting standardized or *norm-referenced* tests to see how well large *groups* of students are performing. Whether at the national, regional, state or provincial, or local level, these standardized assessments are far less precise and informative with respect to *individual* students.

Informal Classroom Assessment in the Integrated Language Arts

We use informal assessment for two purposes:

◆ As an early measure of identifying a particular student's developmental level, skills, and knowledge

◆ As an ongoing measure for determining how well individual students and the class as a whole are responding to and learning from specific instructional situations and lessons.

As we've seen throughout this book, whenever we interact with students individually or in groups, we pick up information about how well they are developing, understanding, and applying knowledge about reading, writing, speaking, and listening. We are what Yetta Goodman calls a **"kid-watcher"** (Goodman & Goodman, 1989). That is, through authentic reading, writing, and discussion activities, we gain truer insight into our students' developing learning. The mistakes or **miscues** we observe them making in reading, writing, or spelling "often show their underlying competence, the strengths they are developing" (K. Goodman, 1987, p. 41). From time to time we will also "set the stage" a bit by presenting students with specific tasks and then observing their responses—how they discuss a piece of literature in terms of theme and setting, for example, or how they sort words. We may also prepare specific tasks to check their understanding—a list of questions, for example, to which each student in a group will respond.

We can record and organize our ongoing information in several ways. The following are the two teachers most often use:

◆ Carry a clipboard with one-inch gummed labels on it. Write your observations about a particular student on one label, date it, and put it in the child's writing folder on the "Assessment" page at the end of the day.

◆ Using tabs, partition a spiral notebook into sections for each of the students; enter observations and date them.

This information can then be periodically reviewed—preferably with the student—and then transferred to the *portfolio*.

Ultimately, every teacher has to discover a method he or she is most comfortable using to record and organize his or her assessment of students. The various examples in this chapter are good for beginners (stay with them if they prove workable and comfortable), but we should not feel that there is only one "right" or "true" way to undertake classroom assessment.

Portfolios: True Representations of What Students Know and Can Do

Portfolios are a popular concept in assessment, and rightly so (Hill & Ruptic, 1994; Tierney, Carter, & Desai, 1991). They can be used to document all types of student learning. Just as artists develop portfolios to represent a range of their best work, so too will each student have a portfolio or file that contains samples of his or her learning efforts (Valencia, 1990). The portfolio provides an extremely helpful basis for students' self-assessment as well as for our assessment of them. Common portfolio information includes

◆ samples of work selected by the student and the teacher — for example, published compositions, reading response entries, learning logs, **reading logs,** samples from the word study notebook, or artwork

◆ teacher observations — "ongoing" observations and conference notes, checklists, and **running records**

◆ the student's self-assessments

As an example, Figure 11.1 shows nine-year-old Tessa's self-assessment as a learner in math.

Ideally, portfolios should be maintained throughout the year and from year to year. Examples of each student's reading and writing will, of course, be represented in most of the material selected. For example:

◆ To reflect their growth as *writers*, students may select compositions that they believe best represent their work in a particular genre

◆ To reflect their development as *readers*, they may select the reading response journal or journal entries they kept as they read a particular book.

This selection process involves self-assessment as students reflect on *why* particular pieces are most representative of what they have learned. As part of this process, it's helpful for students to ask themselves the following questions and to discuss them with us (Graves, cited in Cordeiro, 1992):

◆ What can you do now that you couldn't do before?

◆ What are you good at?

◆ What do you need to learn next? How will you learn it?

Usually, portfolios are large file folders, loose-leaf notebooks, or artwork portfolio packets. As we incorporate technology more in our classrooms, our students can use multimedia software such as KidPix and HyperCard to organize and present their portfolios. When they do this, they will not only showcase their work but discuss it as well.

Introducing the Concept of "Portfolios" in the Integrated Classroom

We can introduce the concept of portfolios by bringing in a bag of objects that are important to us and sharing the reasons for their significance with our students. We can talk about the origin of portfolios — the world of art — and can also invite older students in to discuss their portfolios with the class.

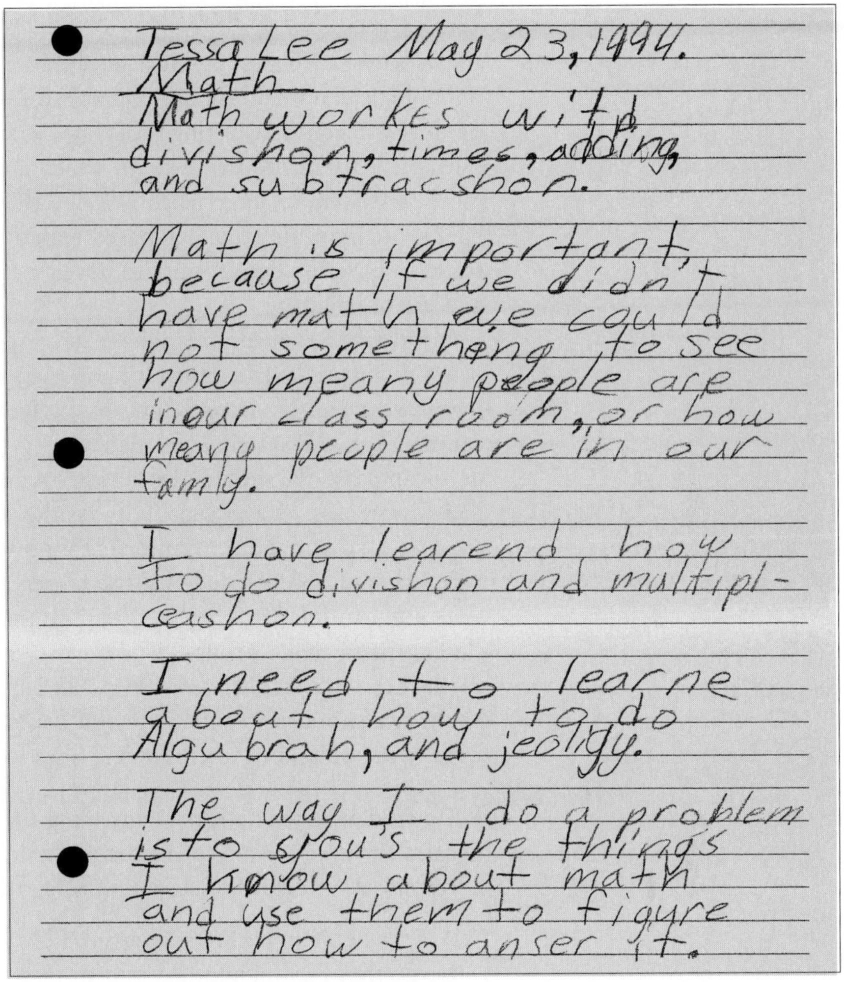

> ● Tessa Lee May 23, 1994.
> Math
> Math workes with
> divishon, times, adding,
> and subtracshon.
>
> Math is important,
> because, if we didn't
> have math eve could
> not something to see
> how meany people are
> inour class room, or how
> ● meany people are in our
> famliy.
>
> I have learend how
> to do divishon and multipl-
> ceashon.
>
> I need to learne
> about how to do
> Algubrah, and jeoligy.
>
> The way I do a problem
> ● isto sfou's the things
> I know about math
> and use them to figure
> out how to anser it.

Figure 11.1   Self-Assessment as a Learner in Math

If we choose to include some or all of *our* notes and checklists in the students' portfolios, we should discuss this component with the students and explain that we will *all* be using the same criteria for materials selection. We will have already conferenced with them, so they should have a feel for the kinds of questions we will ask about their work and how we can help them assess it. We can brainstorm with them: what kinds of things could illustrate their best thinking and efforts in reading and writing? awareness of how to go about reading and writing? the different purposes to which they apply their reading and writing abilities? (Templeton, 1995) We'll be looking at specific aspects of **portfolio assessment** for reading and writing ability later in this chapter.

Oral Language in the Integrated Language Arts Classroom

As we saw in Chapter 2, most of children's basic syntactic structures and phonological systems are developed before formal schooling begins. Development will continue during the school years—but with a major difference: "what is learned and the order in which it is learned becomes progressively more dependent on experience" (Wells, 1986, p. 32). This is where *we* come in. Through all the language-based experiences in which we involve them, students have the opportunity to develop further the structure, vocabulary, and use of language.

Informal assessment of language development provides the best means of determining students' competence and language use at the beginning of the school year and on a continuing basis. We should attend to each student's command of the systems of language—syntax, phonology, and semantics or vocabulary. We should also observe students' *pragmatic* development— their awareness of and sensitivity to the different contexts in which language is used and the conventions that govern language appropriateness.

We should observe students' use of oral language in different social contexts and for different purposes: at play and during learning activities—including pairs, small groups, whole class, and one-to-one conferences with us (Barr et al., 1988; Raines, 1995). On our clipboards or in our spiral notebooks, we should enter the date and context for each notation. As we observe, we should keep the following questions in mind:

◆ Do students speak clearly, expressing themselves through syntax and vocabulary appropriate to the task? Or do they rely on stock phrases and responses, reluctant to elaborate when their meaning is unclear?

◆ Are they able to rephrase appropriately when their meaning is not clear? Or do they rely on another student or students to explain for them?

◆ Do they usually understand others, or do they appear often confused? Do they consider the feelings and ideas of others? If they do appear confused, do they really *listen* to others, or do they seem distracted when others are speaking?

◆ In the context of discussion groups, do they contribute freely? Do they attend to what others are saying? Do they respect the guidelines according to which the group operates?

◆ Do they try out language structures and vocabulary that come from their reading and/or read-alouds?

Sometimes teachers of younger children are concerned when their students have not developed all the significant phonemes in the language. It is not unusual for a few sounds not to have developed, but if this situation persists, it should be investigated by a speech therapist. Usually the child has not further differentiated the rules governing the articulation of the sound. For example, common phonemes that are still incorrectly used at these early levels are /w/ instead of /r/ ("vewwy" instead of "very") and /th/ instead of /s/ ("thaw" instead of "saw").

Of course, if students are learning English as a second language, we should note their developing acquisition of the syntax, grammatical structure, and vocabulary of English. However, we should remember that it's as important for us to keep assessment records for second-language learners as it is for native speakers.

Reading in the Integrated Classroom

Initial Assessment of Students

How do we assess our students' reading knowledge so we can provide appropriate guided and independent experiences with texts?

◆ First, we should determine our students' *developmental levels*. Refer to Table 5.2 on pp. 159–160, where we listed the developmental phases and the major characteristics of each. Chapter 3 discussed how to determine some of these levels, and we'll be looking at additional ways in this chapter.

◆ Second, we'll need to "fine-tune" this developmental picture for *reading* in order to assess our students' specific strengths and areas for growth; doing so will enable us to bring them together for appropriate guided instruction.

For students who may be at the *late emergent* or *beginning literacy* phases, we can check their *concept of word in print* individually or in small groups (see Chapter 5, p. 165), working with a predictable text or language-experience dictations.

For students at the *transitional* literacy phase and above, we can watch the following as they readjust to the classroom setting during the first school weeks:

◆ Observe their book choices during Sustained Silent Reading, noticing how they handle information.

◆ Spot-check individually: for example, ask a student to read a paragraph aloud.

After this readjustment, we can bring together several students who we believe are of similar ability. We'll go through a Guided Reading-Thinking Activity with them, observing the following:

◆ each student's willingness to make predictions

◆ accuracy in prediction

◆ ability to support a position by referring to and/or locating relevant information in the text

◆ responses to our questioning

◆ reading rate.

In the intermediate grades we should conduct both narrative and content GRTAs early in the year. During these small-group guided reading sessions, we will usually find a few students who need to be involved in guided reading at a different level. We can point out that we'll be doing a lot of group work this year and that these reading groups are part of this work—a system that will allow us to work more closely with smaller groups of students.

We may still feel we need additional information about a few students. If the students are beyond the beginning reading phase, then an **Informal Reading Inventory (IRI)** can be quite helpful. An Informal Reading Inventory includes a series of graded passages that students read and respond to. Conducted one-to-one with a student, the IRI yields three major types of information about a student's reading:

◆ comprehension in oral and in silent reading

◆ oral reading fluency

◆ word knowledge in context and outside of context.

However, informal reading inventories do have limitations. They are not as "natural" or authentic a reading task, and they do not sample across larger segments of texts or several different types of reading. On the other hand, if there is good rapport between the teacher who is administering the IRI and the student, then the results do provide a good indication of a student's reading "power."

An important part of the information yielded by IRIs is the type of oral reading **miscues** or errors that a student makes. We will discuss how to code these miscues when we discuss running records.

Organizing Ongoing Portfolio Assessment in Reading

Throughout the year we'll be collecting information through our continuing observations of students as they go about reading tasks, through their written responses to reading, and through their oral responses in our group and

Build Your Teaching Resources

INFORMAL READING INVENTORIES (IRIs)

To get a "feel" for administering IRIs, as well as to gain valuable insights into the reading process, it's helpful to select one of the following inventories and administer it to a student, preferably one in the intermediate grades who is having difficulty reading:

Burns, P. C., & Roe, B. D. (1995). *Informal reading inventory*. Boston: Houghton Mifflin.

Ekwall, E., & Shanker, J. (1992). *Ekwall-Shanker reading inventory*. Needham Heights, MA: Allyn & Bacon.

Flynt, E. S., & Cooter, R. B. (1995). *Reading inventory for the classroom (2nd ed.)*. Scottsdale, AZ: Gorsuch Scarisbrick.

Leslie, L., & Caldwell, J. (1995). *Qualitative reading inventory–II*. New York: HarperCollins.

Swearingen, R., & Allen, D. (1997). Classroom assessment of reading processes. Boston: Houghton Mifflin.

Woods, M. L., & Moe, A. J. (1995). *Analytical reading inventory (5th ed.)*. Columbus, OH: Merrill.

individual conferences (Lipson, 1996). Table 11.1 provides a framework for assessing our students' reading on an ongoing basis. There are four general areas we can assess; the developmental and grade levels of students determine how many of the characteristics of each area are assessed. We can summarize the understandings, skills, and strategies we've been teaching by including a checklist in each portfolio.

As we work with our students to help them become better able to think about their own reading, what they're good at, and what they need to work on, we can ask questions such as

◆ What have you liked to read in the past?

◆ What are you good at as a reader?

◆ What do you find difficult or challenging when you read?

◆ What did you enjoy or remember most about this piece?

◆ What in the piece affected you most?

◆ How is this piece similar to or different from other pieces that you have read?

◆ Why did you choose one journal entry response to this piece over another entry?

◆ What did you learn from this reading selection?

Portfolio assessment provides opportunities for reflection and making decisions about learning.

There are three major contexts in which *we* can gather and organize information about students' reading:

◆ Meeting with groups and individual student conferences

◆ Students' written responses to their reading

◆ Students' engagement in reading activities.

Meeting with Groups and Individual Student Conferences   Through the students' retellings and our own judicious probing, we can note their use of strategies for approaching different texts and setting reading purposes. Watch carefully for these strategies and attend to any comments about them in discussions; write these down. Table 11.2 presents a checklist for observations during guided and/or strategic reading, with questions that we can ask a student if he or she needs help at any point during the reading.

To help monitor students' use of procedural and self-knowledge strategies, we often ask the following three questions in conferences:

What did you learn about reading today?

How do you do it (apply the strategy or information you learned)?

When should you use it for reading, and why?

TABLE 11.1   **Framework for Assessing Reading**

Constructing Meaning

	Seldom	Occasionally	Always	Comments
Makes/Revises Predictions				
Recall and Use of Detail				
Ability to Infer Meaning				
Ability to Recognize or Infer Sequence and Cause/Effect				
Understands Differences Between Narrative and Expository Text				
Identifies and Understands Elements of Informational Text: • Main Ideas/Supporting Details • Fact vs. Opinion				
Appropriately Relates Text to Personal Experiences				

Knowledge
Text Knowledge

	Seldom	Occasionally	Always	Comments
Conventions of Punctuation				
Identifies and Understands Elements of Story: • Characterization • Setting • Plot • Theme				

Expository Text Structure
• Table of Contents
• Index
• Headings/Subheadings
• Text Patterns
   Cause/Effect
   Problems/Solution
   Comparison/Contrast				

Strategies • Before, During, and After				

Knowledge
Word Knowledge

	Seldom	Occasionally	Always	Comments
Applies Knowledge of Contextual Cues • Pictures • Sentence • Beyond the Sentence (Paragraph, Overall)				
Applies Knowledge of Phonic Cues • Beginning Consonants • Short Vowel Patterns • Consonant Blends • Consonant Digraphs • Long Vowel Patterns • Combines Phonic Knowledge with Context				
Applies Knowledge of Structural Analysis Cues • Prefixes • Base Words • Suffixes • Word Roots				
Understands Figurative Use of Words • Connotation • Idioms • Simile and Metaphor				

Attitudes and Ownership

	Seldom	Occasionally	Always	Comments
Motivation to Read				
Persistence in Reading (Sticking with the Task)				
Takes on Challenging Readings Tasks				
Has Developed Preferences in Reading				
Able to Monitor Own Progress and Achievements				

Informal, impromptu writing conferences offer an excellent opportunity to observe and evaluate an individual student's development in writing.

Running Record A *running record* (Clay, 1993) is kept throughout the school year and details 1) a student's development of word recognition and word-analysis abilities in authentic reading contexts and 2) reading fluency and expression. The procedure for gathering and recording information is similar to that for an Informal Reading Inventory.

◆ We first have a student orally read one passage at his or her independent level and one passage at the instructional level.

◆ Following along in our own copy of the passage being read, we record the "miscues" that the student makes.

◆ Later, we can determine what sources of information the student is or is not applying when encountering difficulty—usually an unfamiliar word.

TABLE 11.2   **Framework and Summary for Guiding the Think-Aloud and Profiling the Student**

Name _____   Date _____

Passage _____

Think-Aloud Checklist

Prompts	STOP 1	STOP 2	STOP 3	STOP 4
PAUSE AND REFLECT				
1. Does this part make sense?				
2. Do the words and sentences in section make sense together?				
HYPOTHESIZE				
3. What do you think will be presented next? (OR, what will the next part talk about?)				
4. What do you think this story is going to be about?				
MONITOR				
5. Is there any part you didn't understand?				
6. Did this part talk about what you predicted (expected)?				
7. Did you change your mind about anything?				
INTEGRATE				
8. Does the information in this part fit with what you knew before reading?				
9. Does the information in this part fit with the information presented earlier in the text?				
10. What's the most important thing(s) in this part? (OR, what is the main ideas of this part?)				
11. Did you get any pictures in your head about this part?				
CLARIFY				
12. Did you ask yourself questions about this part?				
13. Do you need to go back in the text to clarify anything? (OR, do you need to REREAD anything?)				
14. What did you do when you didn't understand a word, a sentence, or a part of a sentence?				

Summary of Strategy Use: *Does the student . . .*

❑ Stop and think?

❑ Make predictions?

❑ Self-monitor?

❑ Make connections (integrate)?

  • With prior knowledge

  • Within the text

  • With other texts

❑ Regulate and self-correct?

Summary of Comprehension: *Does the student respond with . . .*

❑ Accurate/inaccurate recollection of content?

❑ Comprehensive/partial recollection of content?

❑ Personal elaboration of content?

❑ Personal response to reading?

Is the student primarily relying on visual and/or phonic cues, syntactic cues, semantic cues, or some combination of these?

◆ We then place a copy of the passages the student has read, with our markings, in the assessment portfolio and attach a summary sheet indicating the number and type of errors or miscues for each passage. This is valuable information for our planning of instruction as well as an excellent means of noting development. In our ongoing day-to-day work, we may add to this summary page as we notice a student's particular miscues and self-correction strategies. This information will also be useful in our individual reading conferences.

TABLE 11.3

Types of Reading Miscues

Omissions are any word, part of a word, or phrase that is left out. The omission is circled.

(My) mother works as a waitress.

Insertions are words or parts of words that are *added* to what is on the page.

I put half of ‸my money into the jar.
    all

Substitutions are words that are read in place of words that appear on the page; they may be meaningful substitutions or mispronunciations that do not make sense. For example, a meaningful substitution would be reading the word *house* instead of *home* in the following sentence: "Bonnie was glad to return to her home." A nonmeaningful substitution would be the word *happy* instead of *home*.

                            house
Bonnie was glad to return to her ~~home~~.

Repetitions are words and phrases that are repeated.

Sometimes my mama is laughing when she comes home from work.

Self-corrections are miscues that the student goes back to correct. Often repetitions and corrections occur together, since in correcting a miscue the student rereads the phrase in which it occurred. A check mark is used to indicate self-corrections.

                        looking ✔
Sometimes my mama is ~~laughing~~ when she comes home from work.

Excellent descriptions of running records may be found in Clay (1993) and in Lipson and Wixson (1991). With experience and a little practice, we can make some fairly accurate judgments about how a student is applying word knowledge during reading. Table 11.3 lists a categorization of miscues and shows how to mark them quickly as the student reads.

By examining each miscue, we can usually identify a trend or pattern. This is important information that helps us identify possible *strategies* the student is using. This knowledge in turn helps us make more informed

TABLE 11.3 (*Continued*)

Types of Reading Miscues

Assistance is given by the teacher for a word the student is unable to figure out. After the student has either tried to identify the word for several seconds or simply has stopped reading and is staring silently, we can go ahead and say the word for him or her. We should put parentheses around the word.

Sometimes my mama is (laughing) when she comes home from work.

If we've made a copy of the text the student is reading, or if we're using an Informal Reading Inventory, we can mark miscues in the passage itself—as in the above examples. If we don't have a copy, we can indicate miscues on a separate piece of paper, as in the following example. For each word the student correctly reads, we make a check.

Henry made Mudge sit while	✔ ✔ ✔ ✔ ✔
Annie went into the house.	✔ wanted in ✔ ✔
Mudge wagged his tail and drooled	✔ wags ✔ ✔ ✔ (drooled)
on the porch as she walked by.	✔ ✔ ✔ ✔ ✔ ✔ ✔
Then he followed Henry inside.	✔ ✔ follows ✔ ✔
Annie was on the couch.	✔ ✔ ✔ ✔ (couch)
Before Henry could say no,	✔ ✔ ✔ ✔ ✔
Mudge went over and kissed Annie	✔ goes ✔ ✔ kisses ✔
on the face.	✔ ✔ ✔
Annie turned pink.	✔ turns ✔

[From *Henry and Mudge and the Careful Cousin* (1994) by Cynthia Rylant—"Annie Turns Pink"]

instructional decisions. When we examine the miscues, we can ask the following questions (Lipson & Wixson, 1991):

◆ Is the meaning of the sentence changed by the miscue?

◆ Does the miscue make sense in the context of the whole passage that is being read?

◆ Did the student correct his or her miscue?

◆ Is the miscue similar in sound and spelling to the word in the text?

We can gain important insights into students' understanding during their reading by asking them to *retell* what they've read. During their retelling, we can note the degree to which they address the following aspects:

◆ Characters and descriptions of the characters

◆ Setting

◆ Plot—what happens and the sequence in which it happens

◆ Summary, theme, or main idea.

Students' Written Responses to Their Reading   Observe the type and nature of students' reading responses in their *response journals*. Figures 11.2 and 11.3 are examples of responses from Eldon's journal. Eldon, a second-grader, wrote each response during his reading of a chapter book. The teacher included these in his portfolio because they illustrate his development in writing, spelling, and reasoning in relation to his reading. Figure 11.2 (September 24) is Eldon's response shortly after beginning Beverly Cleary's *Dear Mr. Henshaw* (1983). Figure 11.3 (March 3) is his response toward the end of reading Roald Dahl's *Danny, the Champion of the World* (1975). Although the second response strikes us initially as somewhat disjointed, remember that this is an unedited, first-impression response. Comparing the nature of the two responses, we can see that the second is qualitatively richer. Rather than giving a straightforward description of things, as does the first response, the second response shows that Eldon has "stepped outside" his own reading and enjoyment of the book to reflect on a broader phenomenon that characterizes many books, not just *Danny, the Champion of the World*—the wording of *titles*, what they mean, and when the reader finally constructs a meaning that works for him or her. As Eldon points out, a lot of children may indeed "give up" on their reading if they are merely wondering why a book has a particular title.

Two other examples illustrate children's reflections on their responses. In Figure 11.4, Tessa put a Post-it note on one of her journal response pages

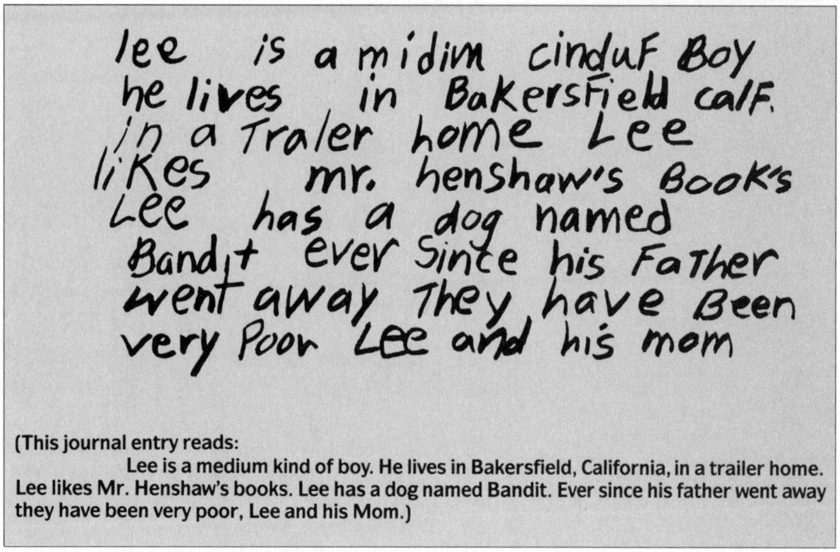
lee is a midim cinduf Boy
he lives in BakersField calf.
in a Traler home Lee
likes mr. henshaw's Book's
Lee has a dog named
Band,t ever Since his Father
went away They have Been
very Poor Lee and his mom

(This journal entry reads:
Lee is a medium kind of boy. He lives in Bakersfield, California, in a trailer home. Lee likes Mr. Henshaw's books. Lee has a dog named Bandit. Ever since his father went away they have been very poor, Lee and his Mom.)

Figure 11.2 Second-grader's Journal Response to a Chapter Book, Included in His Assessment Portfolio (September)

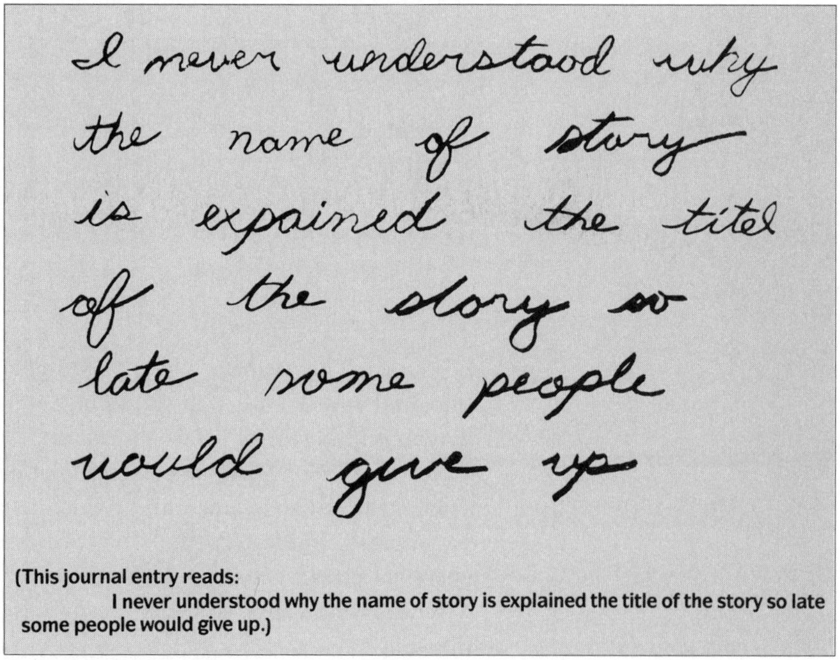
I never understood why
the name of story
is expained the titel
of the story so
late some people
would give up

(This journal entry reads:
I never understood why the name of story is explained the title of the story so late some people would give up.)

Figure 11.3 Second-grader's Response to a Chapter Book, Included in His Assessment Portfolio (March)

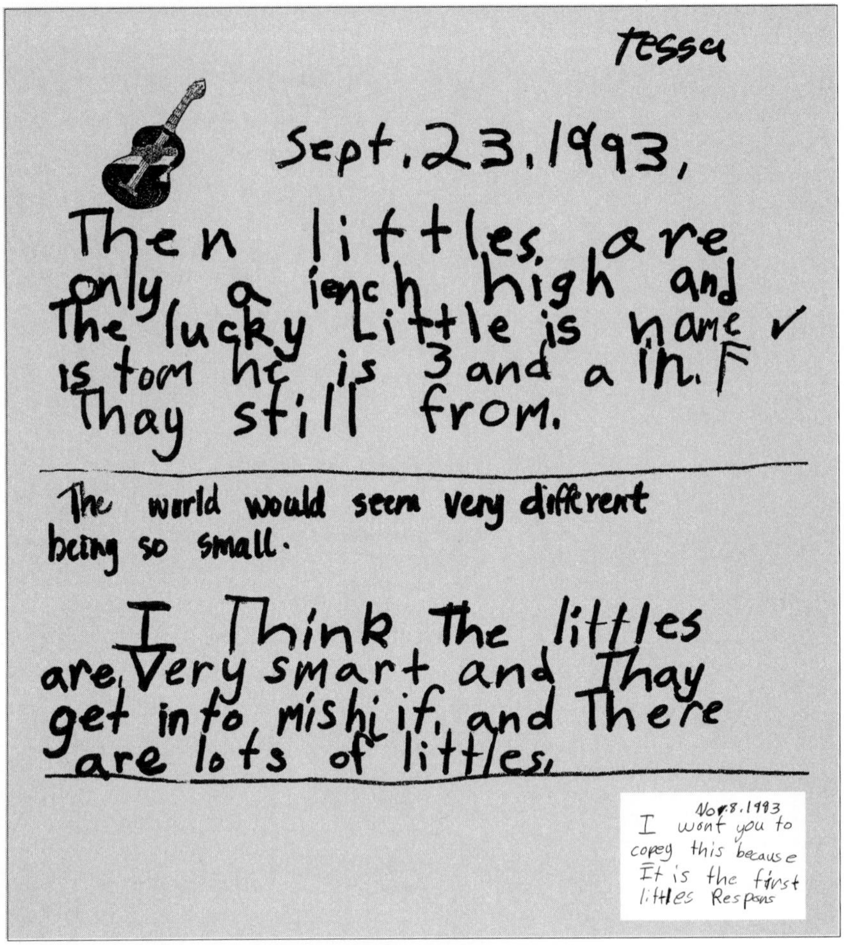

Tessa

Sept. 23, 1993,

Then littles are only a iench high and the lucky Little is name ✓ is tom he is 3 and a in. F Thay still from.

The world would seem very different being so small.

I Think the littles are Very smart and Thay get into mishiif, and There are lots of littles.

Nov 8. 1993
I wont you to copey this because It is the first littles Respons

Figure 11.4   Tessa's Response to John Peterson's *The Littles* (1970)

indicating to her teacher which page she wanted photocopied for her portfolio, and why. Figure 11.5 shows one of Matt's choices—a response to his own book! In Figure 11.6 we see Natalie's response to Judi Barrett's *Cloudy With a Chance of Meatballs* (1978). Natalie, a third-grader, had written an article in the school newspaper which summarized *Cloudy* in a way that would create interest in the book. She also posted her work on the Web, where her class has its own home page.

When we discuss students' responses with them, we should do the following:

◆ Encourage them to measure their growth in reading knowledge by comparing their earlier and more recent responses to literature

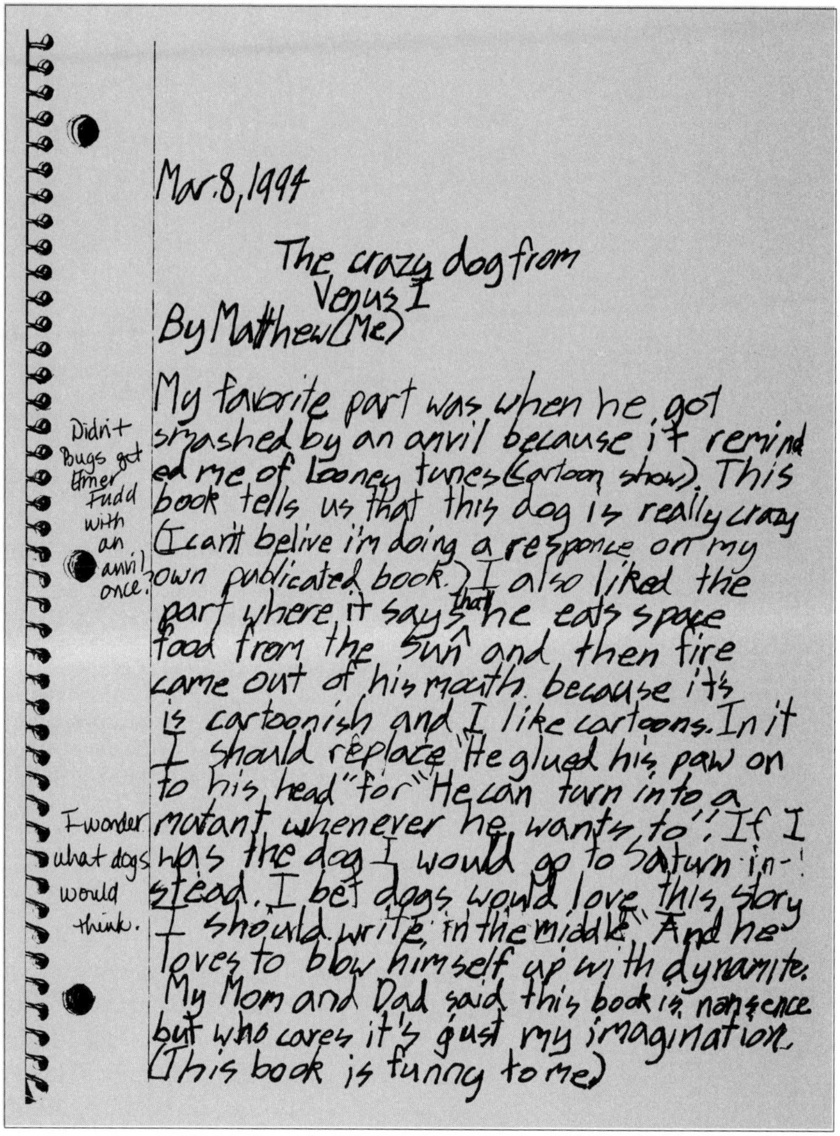

Mar. 8, 1994

The crazy dog from
Venus I
By Matthew (Me)

My favorite part was when he, got
smashed by an anvil because it remind
ed me of Looney tunes (cartoon show). This
book tells us that this dog is really crazy
(I can't belive i'm doing a responce on my
own pudicated book.) I also liked the
part where, it says that he eats space
food from the sun and then fire
came out of his mouth. because it's
is cartoonish and I like cartoons. In it
I should replace "He glued his paw on
to his head" for "He can turn into a
mutant whenever he, wants to." If I
was the dog I would go to Saturn instead. I bet dogs would love this story
I should write in the middle. And he
loves to blow himself up with dynamite.
My Mom and Dad said this book is nonsence
but who cares it's just my imagination.
(This book is funny to me)

Marginal notes:
Didn't Bugs got Elmer Fudd with an anvil once.

I wonder what dogs would think.

Figure 11.5 Matt's Response to *The Crazy Dog from Venus*

◆ Use their responses to discuss explicitly what we will be focusing on in upcoming instruction.

Students' Engagement in Reading Activities We're able to keep track of how students feel about reading and their motivation to read through our conferences with them and by having them keep a *reading log* in their response journal that we will check periodically. The reading log is simply a

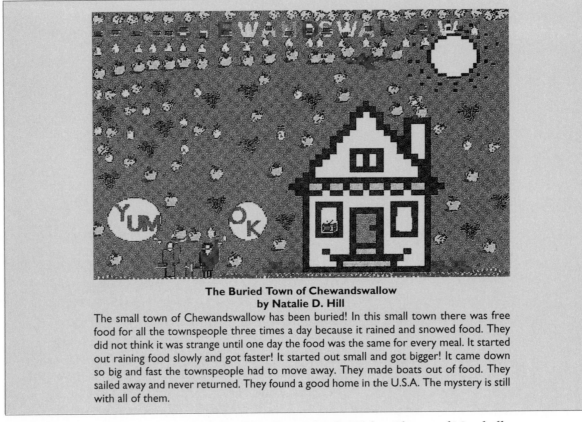

The Buried Town of Chewandswallow
by Natalie D. Hill
The small town of Chewandswallow has been buried! In this small town there was free food for all the townspeople three times a day because it rained and snowed food. They did not think it was strange until one day the food was the same for every meal. It started out raining food slowly and got faster! It started out small and got bigger! It came down so big and fast the townspeople had to move away. They made boats out of food. They sailed away and never returned. They found a good home in the U.S.A. The mystery is still with all of them.

Figure 11.6　　　　　　　　Natalie's Response to *Cloudy With a Chance of Meatballs*

sheet that is stapled in each student's response journal where they record the title, author, and date(s) for each book they read. From time to time, we should look over these reading logs to summarize and assess students' voluntary reading; this information will help us plan individual conferences to discuss the types of genres and/or authors they prefer. Au, Scheu, Kawakami, and Herman (1990) suggest we include the following in our notes for each student:

◆ number of books read

◆ reading levels of the books (independent, instructional, frustration)

◆ types of genre read

◆ favorite book

◆ favorite author

AT THE TEACHER'S DESK

**A WORD ABOUT
REPORT CARDS**

Let's face the issue novice teachers grapple with. In most school systems teachers have to assign grades. We first broached this issue in Chapter 3. If the students know why they are being involved in certain activities and projects, then they know what we're focusing on for grading. Be frank and discuss these matters at the beginning of the year. We are grading *process*, which they will also keep tabs on themselves, as well as *product*. We can reassure students that they will know what they will be graded on because we'll be discussing the grading together. In the context of openly discussing evaluation, we will be able to help our students learn how to set challenges for themselves, as well as meet challenges that we encourage them to attempt. At grading time we can discuss the degree to which they — and we — believe they have met those challenges. Significantly, they should come to see their grades as reflecting what *they* accomplish.

◆ observations about a student's voluntary reading — for example, "Reads every day" or "Often selects books on higher reading level but seems to get information and enjoyment from them."

Assigning Grades in Reading

When it's time to assign grades at report-card time, Table 11.1 (p. 449) will also be very useful. Because it provides a framework for assessing our students' reading on an *ongoing* basis, the chart helps guide our thinking as we look over 1) each student's work and 2) our continuing anecdotal and conference notes. Often it's a good idea to include a copy of this matrix along with the regular report card that is sent home.

Writing in the Integrated Classroom

Organizing Ongoing Portfolio Assessment in Writing

Just as with reading, throughout the year we'll be collecting information through our continuing observations of students as they go about their writing as well as through individual conferences. We will be including the following information:

◆ attitudes and understandings about writing

◆ the nature of the students' written productions.

We'll ask questions such as

◆ Why did you choose to include this particular piece?

◆ Why did you choose one story instead of another that you've written?

◆ How is this piece similar to or different from other pieces that you have written?

◆ What types of writing do you like most to do? Least? Why?

◆ What are you good at as a writer?

Figure 11.7 shows two of Tessa's choices for her writing portfolio. While she included the final published version of *The Lion and Her Cub*, she also

Figure 11.7 Tessa's "Published" Title Page: *The Lion and Her Cub*

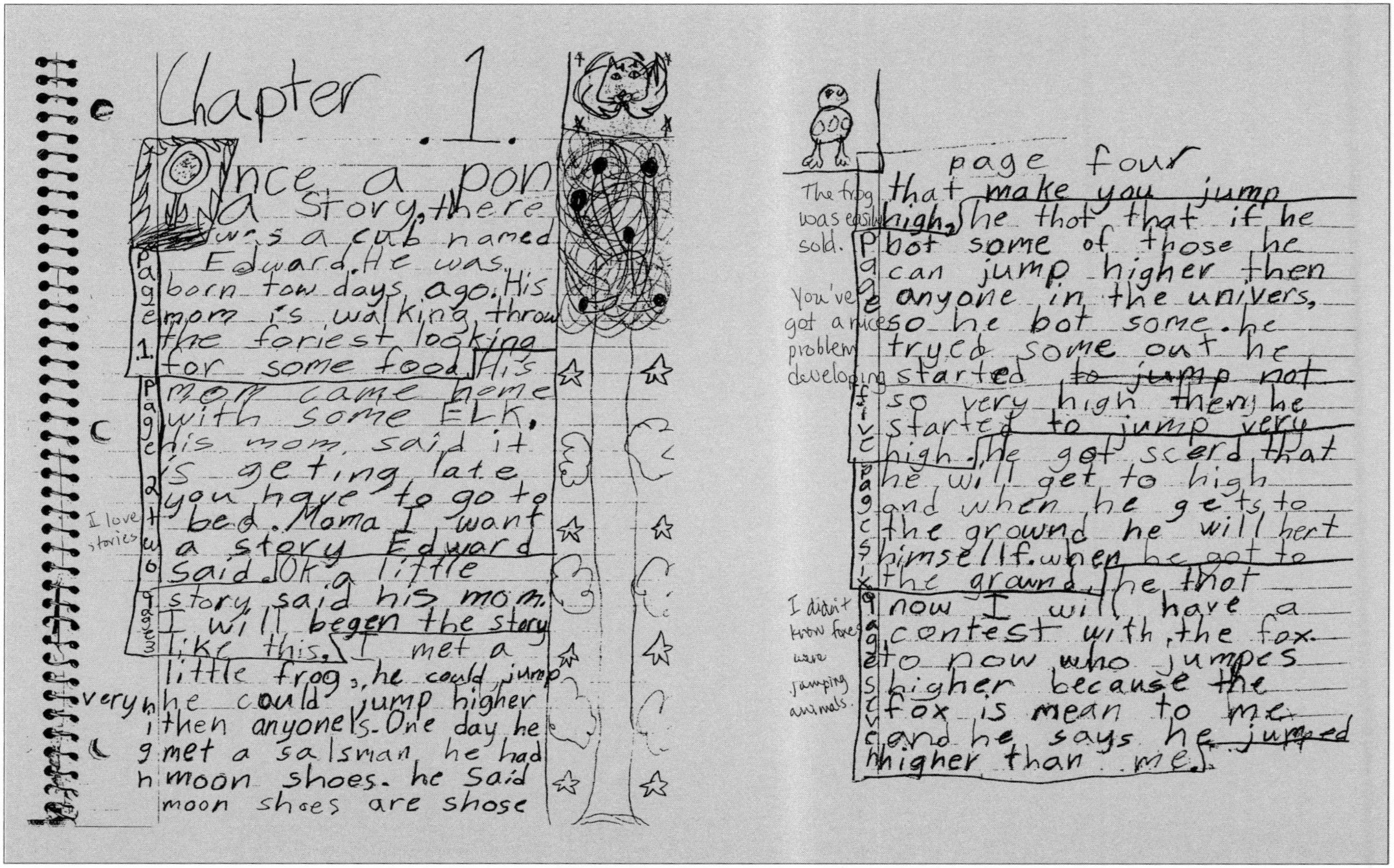

Figure 11.7 (*Continued*)   Tessa's First Draft with Planned Page Breaks: *The Lion and Her Cub*

TABLE II.4	**Assessing Writing: Process and Product**

	Beginning Writers (Grades 1, 2)	Transitional Writers: Early (Grades 1, 2, 3)
Writing Process	Writes during writing time Uses appropriate strategies for getting his or her writing going Participates when writing is shared (e.g., during Author's Chair activities) Invents spelling of most words	Writes during writing time Uses appropriate strategies for getting his or her writing going Is serious about teacher/student and student/student conferences Listens to other students' drafts and offers helpful feedback Considers feedback from other students and from the teacher Understands difference between revising and editing Participates when writing is shared
Grammar, Usage, Mechanics		Adequate space between words Handwriting is legible First word in each sentence begins with a capital letter, and each sentence ends with a punctuation mark Balance between invented and conventionally-spelled words Uses complete sentences
	Transitional Writers: Later (Grades 2, 3, 4, 5)	**Intermediate Writers (Grades 3, 4, 5, 6)**
Writing Process	Writes during writing time Uses appropriate strategies for getting his or her writing going Is serious about teacher/student and student/student conferences Listens to other students' drafts and offers helpful feedback	All of the aspects of *process* and *product* for the previous levels apply here. In addition: Writes effectively in different forms Uses vivid and precise language Initiates own revision Easily uses proofreading marks

wanted to include samples of her drafting phase. She was particularly pleased with her ability to plan the amount of text per page; her lines and labeling indicate her decisions.

From a developmental perspective, Table 11.4 presents what we should assess in students' writing at the beginning, transitional, and intermediate

TABLE 11.4 *(Continued)*   **Assessing Writing: Process and Product**

	Transitional Writers: Later (Grades 2, 3, 4, 5)	Intermediate Writers (Grades 3, 4, 5, 6)
Writing Process	Considers feedback from other students and from the teacher	
	Understands difference between revising and editing	
	Participates when writing is shared	
	Different forms of writing used appropriately	
	Uses other sources of information available in the classroom: checklists and guidelines, informational materials, dictionaries	
	Uses simple proofreading marks	
Grammar, Usage, Mechanics	Adequate space between words	
	Handwriting is legible	*In addition to previous skills:*
	First word in each sentence begins with a capital letter, and each sentence ends with a punctuation mark	Uses quotation marks correctly
		Uses appropriate capitalization (proper nouns, titles of books)
	Uses commas appropriately	Uses pronouns appropriately
	Uses words appropriately and effectively	Consistently uses correct verb tense
	Uses complete sentences	
	Subject and verb agree	
	Breaks composition appropriately into paragraphs	
	Most words spelled conventionally	
	Uses resources to check spelling	

levels. These criteria reflect what the students are working on in their writing, so they are useful in our conferences with students, in students' self-assessments, and as the basis for assigning grades. By examining our students' writing with the above criteria in mind, we will know which students—if developmentally ready—we should schedule for specific mini-lessons. Not all students, of course, need to have all aspects of writing taught explicitly, but some students may need more attention in specific areas.

Assigning Grades in Writing

We can use the criteria in Table 11.4 as a guide to our assessment for a grading period. For many students in the transitional phase and most in the intermediate phase, we can base a good portion of the grade on compositions that *they* wish to submit for grading—pieces they've likely chosen for their portfolios. These compositions will most often be published pieces. The students will be keeping drafts and completed pieces in a writing folder, so by leafing through these folders, they will be able to make selections for their portfolios fairly easily.

Depending on the level of our students' development, we will assess **process** and **product**. As we've seen, product may be assessed in terms of content and mechanics. We should be sure that students understand the criteria for each area because these criteria will vary, depending on the type of writing being evaluated. We may use a point system, provide comments, or do both. Much of our assessment will be *holistic*, based on consideration of the overall composition in terms of content and mechanics. We may also provide some *focused* evaluation, considering one or two specific elements in content and/or mechanics. Figure 11.8 shows a sample evaluation form for fifth grade that uses a point system. Note that we can use whatever numbers we wish to fill in the rating scale because we will want to assign a greater number of points for some criteria than for others. For example, we may decide to rate correct spelling on a scale of 1–5, and clear paragraph sequencing on a scale of 2–10. In Figure 11.8, the first score is for content and organization, and the second is for mechanics.

Spelling in the Integrated Language Arts

Recall from Chapter 8 that spelling, far from being mere memorization of letter sequences, reflects a wide range of word knowledge. Assessing spelling knowledge, therefore, gives us considerable insight into our students' overall word knowledge in reading and in writing.

Initial Assessment of Spelling

Our initial assessment will provide valuable information about students' spelling or word knowledge. Just as there will be different levels of reading proficiency in our classrooms, there will be different levels of spelling or word knowledge, thus students should be grouped accordingly for their guided instruction and word study.

Table 11.5 presents an initial assessment for spelling, the **Qualitative Spelling Inventory** and instructions for its use (Bear, Invernizzi, & Templeton, 1996). This initial assessment helps us determine our students' levels of spelling knowledge (see Chapter 8, pages 321–326).

◆ Administer the inventory in small groups. Begin by telling the students that you are going to ask them to write some words but this work will

NAME *Keith*   DATE *4/28*

TYPE OF WRITING *Persuasive letter*

Skills Checked	Rating Scale
Reasons clearly stated	2 4 6 ⑧ 10
Reasons in order (strongest to weakest/ weakest to strongest)	1 2 ③ 4 5
Each reason supported	2 4 ⑥ 8 10
	Total 17/25
spelling	1 2 3 4 ⑤
punctuation	1 2 3 4 ⑤
sentence structure	1 2 3 ④ 5
correct letter format	2 4 6 ⑧ 10

Comments: *Good thinking, Keith. Good improvement on spelling & punctuation. Should add more support for your reasons.*   Total   22/25

Figure 11.8   Completed Evaluation Form Using a Point System

not be graded. If they are uncertain about the spelling of any word, they should do the best they can. It's useful information for us to see how they try to spell a word they aren't sure is correct.

◆ Look over all the students' papers. For each student note particular misspellings and locate them in the common misspellings in Table 11.6. If a particular misspelling is not there, it helps to write in on the form close to the misspelling it most closely corresponds to. (If this table is photocopied, there can then be a separate sheet for each student—this helps with assessing each student.) Circle each misspelling; the level where most of the misspellings cluster probably corresponds to that student's level of spelling knowledge.

TABLE 11.5	**Elementary Qualitative Spelling Inventory**

Elementary Qualitative Spelling Inventory
Spelling-By-Stage Assessment

This is a short spelling inventory to help you learn about your students' orthographic knowledge. The results of the spelling inventories will have implications for reading, writing, vocabulary, and spelling instruction.

Instructions: Let the students know that you are administering this inventory to learn about how they spell. Let them know that this is not a test, but that they will be helping you be a better teacher by doing their best:

Possible script: "I am going to ask you to spell some words. Try to spell them the best you can. Some of the words will be easy to spell; some will be more difficult. When you do not know how to spell a word, spell it the best you can; write down all the sounds you feel and hear."

Say the word once, read the sentence and then say the word again. Work with groups of five words. You may want to stop testing when students miss three out of five words. See the text for further instructions on administration and interpretation. Have students check their papers for their names and the date.

Set One	1. bed	I hopped out of *bed* this morning. *bed*
	2. ship	The *ship* sailed around the island. *ship*
	3. drive	I learned to *drive* a car. *drive*
	4. bump	That is quite a *bump* you have on your head. *bump*
	5. when	*When* will you come back? *when*
Set Two	6. train	I rode the *train* to the next town. *train*
	7. closet	I put the clothes in the *closet*. *closet*
	8. chase	We can play run and *chase* with the cats. *chase*
	9. float	I can *float* on the water with my new raft. *float*
	10. beaches	The sandy *beaches* are crowded in the summer. *beaches*
Set Three	11. preparing	I am *preparing* for the big game. *preparing*
	12. popping	We are *popping* popcorn to eat at the movies. *popping*
	13. cattle	The cowboy rounded up the *cattle*. *cattle*
	14. caught	I *caught* the ball. *caught*
	15. inspection	The soldiers polished their shoes for *inspection*. *inspection*
Set Four	16. puncture	I had a *puncture* in my bicycle tire. *puncture*
	17. cellar	I went down to the *cellar* for the can of paint. *cellar*
	18. pleasure	It was a *pleasure* to listen to the choir sing. *pleasure*
	19. squirrel	We found the tree where the *squirrel* lives. *squirrel*
	20. fortunate	It was *fortunate* that the driver had snow tires during the snowstorm. *fortunate*
Set Five	21. confident	I am *confident* that we can win the game. *confident*
	22. civilize	They had the idea that they could *civilize* the forest people. *civilize*
	23. flexible	She was so *flexible* that she could cross her legs behind her head. *flexible*
	24. opposition	The coach said the *opposition* would give us a tough game. *opposition*
	25. emphasize	In conclusion, I want to *emphasize* the most important points. *emphasize*

TABLE 11.6   Elementary Inventory Error Guide

Stages	Early Letter Name	Letter Name	Within-Word Pattern	Syllable Juncture	Derivational Constancy
1. bed	b bd	bad	bed		
2. ship	s sp shp	sep shep	sip ship		
3. drive	jrv drv	griv driv	drieve draive drive		
4. bump	b bp bmp	bop bomp bup	bump		
5. when	w yn wn	wan whan	wen when		
6. train	j t trn	jran chran tan tran	teran traen trane train		
7. closet	k cs kt clst	clast clost clozt	clozit closit		
8. chase	j jass cs	tas cas chas chass	case chais chase		
9. float	f vt ft flt	fot flot flott	flowr floaut flote float		
10. beaches	b bs bcs	bechs becis behis	bechise beches beeches beaches		

Stages			Within-Word Pattern	Syllable Juncture	Derivational Constancy
11. preparing			preparng preypering	praparing prepairing preparing	
12. popping			popin poping	poping popping	
13. cattle			catl cadol	catel cattle cattel cattle	
14. caught			cot cote cout cought caught		
15. inspection			inspshn inspechin	inspecshum inspecsion inspection	
16. puncture			pucshr pungchr puncker	punksher puncture puncture	
17. cellar			salr selr celr seler	seller sellar celler cellar	
18. pleasure			plasr plager plejer pleser plesher	plesour plesure	pleasure
19. squirrel			scrl skwel skwerl	scqoril sqrarel squirle squirrel	
20. fortunate			forhnat frehnit foohinit	forchenut fochininte fortunet	fortunate

Stages			Within-Word Pattern	Syllable Juncture	Derivational Constancy
21. confident				confedint confedent confident conphident confiadent confedent confendent confedent confedent confident	
22. civilize				sivils sevelies sivilicse cifillazas sivilize sivalize civalise civilise civiliz	
23. flexible				flecksibl flexobil fleckuble fleckible flexeble flexibel flaxable flexibal flexible	flexible
24. opposition			opasion opasishan opozcison opishien opasitian	opasion oppasishion oppisition	oposision oposition opposition
25. emphasize				infaside infacize emfesize emfsize imfasize ephascise empasize emphasise	emphsize emphasize

Adapted from Bear & Barone (1989).

Formal or "Standardized" Assessment

The usual purpose of formal assessment is to provide comparative information about *groups* of students. This is information that, of necessity, can only be gained through tests administered to whole groups in a single sitting. Most formal testing provides very little data about *individual* students—the type of information teachers need to facilitate appropriate instruction.

There are reasons, though, why formal or **norm-referenced testing** is still a significant part of our educational world. Our society relies on "numbers" in many ways; quantitative information will always at least give the illusion of precision. So, when the nation—or a local school board—wants to know how well students are doing, they want to see the bottom line expressed in numbers. Significant efforts are under way, however, to change both the nature of large-scale assessments and the public's perception of educational testing; these efforts should begin to have some effect in the next few years. The newer, large-scale assessments should yield much more helpful, insightful, and valid information than the current norm-referenced tests.

Standardized refers to the procedure for administering the test. The person giving the test, usually the teacher, follows the directions in the test administration manual exactly, right down to the wording of the directions and the moment when the test booklet is opened. There's a reason for this strict procedure. Any variation in presentation—say, for example, in explaining a point further—could affect the test performance of some students by giving them an edge that other students wouldn't have. It would then become extremely difficult to make comparisons among the groups.

Norm-referenced means that the scores obtained on the standardized test are "referenced" or based on the *normal curve*. The normal curve is often referred to as the bell-shaped curve because that is the shape the distribution of a large number of students' scores will take when they are plotted. Usually a very large number of students take the test before it is published; the scores of all students who later take the test are then based on this distribution of scores—on this bell curve.

What are some of these scores? *Standardized* or *normal-curve equivalent* scores tell us where on the normal curve a student has scored—how far above or below the mean (the average). These scores in turn can be expressed as **stanines** (another way of indicating where the student scored on the curve) and **percentiles** (how many students scored above and below a particular student).

We are often in the position of explaining to parents the purpose and re-

AT THE TEACHER'S DESK

"TRADITIONAL" AND
"NEW GENERATION"
STANDARDIZED TESTS

Reading: "Traditional" standardized reading tests usually have subtests labeled "comprehension," "word analysis," "vocabulary," and so forth. More extensive achievement tests such as the *Stanford Achievement Test*, the *Iowa Test of Basic Skills*, and the *Comprehensive Test of Basic Skills* have several additional subtests in listening, spelling, and language. Whereas real, authentic reading usually involves larger chunks of text, formal standardized tests usually have shorter segments, often only one paragraph long, which do not allow students to "get their teeth into" a selection. In addition, standardized group tests attempt to "control for" background information by including passages that may be of little interest or concern to elementary students; therefore, we do not see how well the students are able to apply their background knowledge.

Recently many reading and language arts educators in several states and at the national level (National Assessment of Educational Progress) have begun constructing standardized group tests in reading that do not have many of the shortcomings of the traditional norm-referenced tests. Assuming that standardized group tests will always be an educational fact of life, these educators believe that the challenge is not to attempt to eliminate these tests but to make group testing as realistic and valid as possible. The tests they are formulating represent recent thinking about the reading process: the reader, the text, and the context must all be considered.

The most recent National Assessment of Educational Progress, a "new generation" in large-scale reading assessment, taps different types of engagements with texts: *initial understanding*, *interpretation*, *personal response*, and *critical stance* (Valencia, Hiebert, & Kapinus, 1992). Reading passages are longer, and students are allowed more time to respond.

Writing: Large-scale formal assessment of writing has been more realistic in recent years than similar reading assessment has been. Both **holistic** and **primary trait assessments** are used. There are important similarities between large-scale holistic assessment and our own classroom assessment. In large-scale writing assessments, the *product* is evaluated in terms of features a particular type of writing should evidence — and students should clearly understand these features because they have been emphasized in our teaching. In addition, however, we will assess the students' writing *process*.

In holistic assessment compositions are read for their overall organization and effect. The criteria for rating are determined by a group of evaluators after they have read a small sample of compositions from the larger batch to be evaluated. The ratings are expressed numerically (for example, 0 to 4, with 4 being "best" and 0 being "poorest"). In total holistic scoring the rater considers all aspects of the composition and makes an overall rating of the piece. The National Assessment of Educational Progress has used this format in the past, and most statewide writing assessments are usually conducted this way.

sults of formal norm-referenced reading and language arts tests. It's important that we are familiar with these tests and know what the various types of scores mean. However, we should also explain that these tests are not the be-all and end-all of their child's ability and that we do not make important instructional decisions solely on the basis of these scores. Such information can only be obtained from our individual, informal classroom assessment.

◆ ◆ ◆ ## CONCLUDING PERSPECTIVE AND SUMMARY

Meaningful assessment in the language arts is an ongoing process, so we should make good use of planned and unplanned classroom observations and interactions with students. This chapter presented a brief overview of informal and formal assessment in significant areas of the language arts. We can use informal assessment with our whole class as well as with individuals to identify strengths and weaknesses and to group students. This kind of assessment and evaluation yields our most important information. On the other hand, we should know the purpose and limitations of formal assessments so we can effectively discuss aspects of their children's performance with parents.

Large-scale, formal, standardized reading assessments can be useful if meant to provide a general picture of large-group performance. Traditional standardized tests, however, do not assess reading as validly as do more recently developed tests, such as several state-level tests and the National Assessment of Educational Progress.

In this chapter we've addressed the following main points:

◆ *Formal assessment* involves administering and interpreting standardized or *norm-referenced* tests to compare and contrast *groups* of students. Such testing will always be part of education, but teachers should help parents and the community understand its limitations.

◆ *Informal classroom assessment* provides initial and ongoing information about individual students.

◆ Portfolios provide the basis for both our assessment of students and their own self-assessment.

◆ *Oral language* in all its aspects is best assessed in ongoing classroom situations.

◆ The initial assessment of students' *reading* determines their developmental levels and specific strengths and weaknesses.

◆ *Informal reading inventories* can be helpful tools for initially assessing particular students.

◆ We gather and organize information about students' reading in three major contexts: group and individual conferences, students' involvement in reading activities, and their written responses to their reading.

◆ Ongoing *writing* assessment involves both *attitudes and understandings* about writing and the *nature* of students' writing.

◆ Assessing spelling knowledge provides insight into students' word knowledge in reading and writing.

◆ Both teachers and students should clearly understand the criteria for assigning grades in reading and writing.

Key Terms

formal/"standardized" assessment (p. 440)

holistic assessment (p. 469)

informal classroom assessment (p. 440)

Informal Reading Inventory (IRI) (p. 446)

"kid-watcher" (p. 441)

miscues (p. 441)

norm-referenced testing (p. 468)

percentile (p. 468)

portfolio assessment (p. 443)

portfolios (p. 441)

primary trait assessment (p. 469)

process (p. 464)

product (p. 464)

Qualitative Spelling Inventory (p. 464)

reading log (p. 442)

running record (p. 442)

standardized test (p. 468)

stanines (p. 468)

TEACHER'S SOURCEBOOK

The purpose of this Teacher's Sourcebook is to be a quick-reference resource for you as well as a guide for additional teaching ideas and strategies. The Sourcebook is divided into eight sections:

The first part provides A Knowledge Base for Professional Classroom Development and includes:

◆ Overview of language history: The development of writing

◆ Overview of the English language and of American English

The rest of the Sourcebook provides a wide variety of teaching and learning resources including:

◆ Discussion of the categories of children's literature along with recommended titles

◆ Multimedia resources—audiovisual as well as technological

◆ A resource for word study:

Word lists from which you can pull developmentally appropriate spelling patterns

List of frequently occurring Greek and Latin word elements

A brief discussion of etymology and how it can support intermediate students' developing word knowledge

◆ Grammar—The first part of this section addresses those basic concepts that are appropriate for elementary students to acquire: parts of speech, sentences, and matters of usage.

The second part of this section provides *teaching strategies and activities.*

The third part is a *quick-reference resource guide* for students and teachers; it presents examples that you can use with elementary students and also serves as a quick check for teachers.

◆ Study skills—How to teach the "basics" of study skills to intermediate students

◆ Handwriting—In an age of word processors, handwriting is still important, both as a skill for recording information quickly and for following the "etiquette" of corresponding by letter. There are many times when writing by hand is by far the more appropriate vehicle than is the message run off on a printer.

An important feature of this Sourcebook is the "prototype" minilessons you'll find throughout—how to teach sentence structure, for example, in a meaningful context. These minilessons are meant to be frameworks for teaching and modeling how to use all kinds of information about language, its structure, and its use.

Contents

A KNOWLEDGE BASE FOR PROFESSIONAL CLASSROOM DEVELOPMENT

I. The Development of Written Language: A Brief History

Some familiarity with the origins and historical development of language in general and of the English language in particular can be an important and enjoyable part of your knowledge foundation. While we do not explore these aspects extensively in the elementary grades, it is reassuring to be able to field some of the questions students will raise about why words are the way they are — why they mean what they do and are spelled as they are. This knowledge base can be very helpful in our teaching of spelling and vocabulary.

In the Beginning: The Indo-European Language

Beginning in the eighteenth century, language scholars found marked similarities in form and meaning among many languages; these similarities were so numerous that scholars concluded they could not be based merely on chance but rather on a source common to all of the languages — a single language that existed at a much earlier point in time. Similarities were noted among languages from "Iceland and Ireland in the west to India in the east, and from Scandinavia in the north to Italy and Greece in the south" (Watkins, 1985, p. xiv). This earlier language came to be called Proto Indo-European, or simply Indo-European, and today it is acknowledged as the parent language of the Indo-European family of languages.

There are two primary reasons why Indo-European is of interest to educators. First, the languages in this family comprise those of half of the Earth's population; second, more than half of the basic roots found in Indo-European exist in some form in present-day English. By understanding something about how Indo-European works, we can help our students comprehend the origins and vocabulary of a large number of words in English.

To get an idea of the effects of the Indo-European language (IE), notice the similarity among "cognates" from several different modern languages: For example, *mother* was *mater* in IE; it is *madre* in Italian, *mère* in French. *Three* was *trei* in IE; it is *tres* in Spanish, *trois* in French.

Over time, the groups that spoke Indo-European moved beyond their original location — the area from the Balkans in eastern Europe to the Russian steppes north of the Black Sea — to settle in other areas. Without contact with the original culture, the language spoken by these groups began to change. Eventually, these languages became quite different from the original Indo-European. Further change occurred when members of this newer culture in turn moved on, and their language inevitably changed as well. Given enough time, peoples who spoke these new languages spread far and wide, and their languages were in turn influenced by the languages of people they met in the areas where they settled. Over the past 7,000 years, this process has resulted in many different branches of languages, nine of which still exist today. One of these, Germanic, includes the English language.

The Development of Written Language

By the age of seven, most children acquire understandings about written language that took humankind approximately 30,000 years to accomplish. Looking at the historical development of written language helps us appreciate this accomplishment. As we take this historical look, keep an eye open for any parallels with how language appears to develop in children.

The development of writing can be discussed in terms of the following stages:

◆ pictographic

◆ logographic (sometimes referred to as ideographic)

◆ syllabic

◆ alphabetic

It's important to remember that the shift from one type of representation to the next is usually a gradual one, with characteristics of each type overlapping at any one time.

Pictographic representation is not really written language, but it is an important predecessor. Cave drawings and paintings attest to humankind's desire to represent experience and control the environment. As early as 30,000 years ago, cave dwellers may have used notches on tools and weapons to signify or symbolize important aspects of their world. For example, crescent notches on a tool may have represented a primitive moon calendar, a means of keeping track of time over the passing of a year.

Writing has its beginning in these prehistoric efforts. The symbolic representation of the real world in cave drawings also served important purposes. At first, the drawings or pictographs simply represented events — for example, a particular hunt or fishing expedition. The following pictograph stands for "Man catches fish":

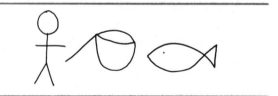

Gradually, pictographs became more "stylized." They ceased being strictly pictographic and came to stand for one word or idea in a particular language; they became *logographic* systems:

This now means "Man catches cow." The net has become a *logograph*, still meaning "catches" but not specifically limited to the catching of fish. Its meaning has become extended to the more general sense of "catching things." In the next stage, the graphs have lost any obvious pictorial reference, though they still mean "Man catches cow":

In a logographic system the intended meaning of a sign depended on the context — the meaning — of the particular text being read. The sign for the sun, for example, could also mean "bright," "white," or "day." This posed a problem — eventually, therefore, logographs came to represent sounds that were independent of their meanings. This process probably began with the need to indicate the personal names of individuals. Gelb (1963, p. 67), offered an example of how the name "Neilson" might be written in such a system. The sign for *kneel* would be combined with the sign for *sun*; together, the signs would phonetically render "Neilson." The signs, though, would no longer represent their original logographic meaning — they no longer represent *ideas* but rather represent *sound*.

Once begun, this process spread quickly. It provided the spark that led to a writing system based on *syllables*, the next significant development in the history of writing. Spurred by trade and commerce, syllabic writing in turn spread rapidly, from Sumeria to Egypt and to the east, quite possibly stimulating the development of Chinese writing. One drawback to the Sumerian syllabic system was the *number* of signs — more than 600 were necessary to represent the language's syllables. In addition to this number of signs, as with logographic systems, the reader had to rely heavily on context — knowledge of what the text probably was about.

Another syllabic system that was used by the Phoenicians was eventually borrowed by the Greeks. The Phoenician system, however, did not work well when applied to the Greek language. How could a syllabic-based alphabet intended for a language with a simpler syllabic structure be applied to a language that was quite complex syllabically? The Greeks answered this question, and in doing so accomplished what some have referred to as the most significant technological advance in the last 2,500 years — they developed a true alphabet.

The Greeks separated consonants from vowels and gave separate symbols to each. This system allowed them to write whatever they wished clearly and unambiguously, making the task of reading much easier. In contrast to users of most syllabic-based systems, speakers of Greek who had never before seen a particular text in Greek but who understood the sound equivalents for each of the symbols or letters in the alphabet could easily decode the message.

Eric Havelock (1982), a scholar who has studied the development of the Greek alphabet, suggested that the Greeks "did not just invent an alphabet; they invented literacy and the literate basis of modern thought" (p. 82). The long-range consequences of this "were new inventible ways of speaking about human life, and therefore of thinking about it, which became preservable and extendable in the alphabetic literatures of Europe" (Havelock, 1982, p. 88).

II. The English Language and American English: A Brief History

Since Shakespeare's time the English language has grown from being the native language of approximately five million people to one that is spoken as a first language by 350 million and as a second language by 400 million. In many respects, English is unique as languages go because its history and sources are more diverse than those of most of the other 2,700 languages spoken in the world today. As is the case with a knowledge of the history of language in general, some knowledge of the development of English will be a valuable resource when we explore vocabulary and spelling with our students.

Old English

Over the centuries English has been shaped by Latin and Greek and by early German, Danish, and French. After the Romans left Britain after a four-hundred-year occupation around A.D. 410, Britain was left vulnerable to the invasions of the Germanic tribes — the Angles, Jutes, and Saxons. These tribes spoke the language that was to become English, and the Angles became the namesake of the land (Angleland) and the language.

While Old English seems like a foreign language to us today, the core vocabulary in Modern English comes directly from Old English: All of the one hundred most frequently used words are from Old English, and of the second hundred, eighty-three are from Old English. It is virtually impossible to utter a sentence without using some of this vocabulary. For example, simple words like *the*, *is*, *on*, *we*, and *in* are all Old English. Some of the earliest words reflect the agricultural orientation of the Anglo-Saxon society: *sheep*, *earth*, *wood*, *work*, *dirt*, *tree*, and the verb *rake*. Around A.D. 600, due in large part to the establishment of monasteries, Latin began to influence Old English. Some words contributed by Latin during this time include *psalm*, *angel*, *talent*, and *temple*. In the late eighth century, the Vikings invaded, but their conquests were eventually halted by Alfred the Great. Eventually, the Viking culture and vocabulary mingled with the Old English. The Danish vocabulary added considerably to Old English.

By the end of the ninth century, English was the language of intellectuals throughout medieval Europe. Then, after A.D. 1066, written English virtually disappeared for some two hundred years.

Middle English

The Norman French king William the Conqueror defeated the English at the Battle of Hastings in 1066, and the rule of England passed into French hands. Norman French became the language spoken by the rulers. It was used in the royal court, in parliament, and in legal matters. Written correspondence was usually in French except writing regarding religion and scholarly matters; for these, Latin was used. The long-range consequence of the Norman invasion was the injection of a large segment of French vocabulary into the English language. Approximately 40 percent of modern-day English has French origins.

In the latter part of the fourteenth century, Middle

English received its finest expression in the writing of Geoffrey Chaucer. Best known for *The Canterbury Tales*, Chaucer used the language in such a way that today readers can still be moved and delighted.

Surnames emerged around the time of Chaucer in the 1300s. Their origin was usually based on four factors:

1. "Son of" someone; for example—*Johnson, Thomson*.

2. Where someone lived; for example—*Brooks, Rivers*.

3. Occupation; for example—*Butcher, Hunter, Miller, Mason*.

4. Continental names; for example—*French, Fleming, Holland*.

During the fourteenth century, the wealth of the merchant class increased, and paper was introduced on a widespread basis. These two developments led to an increased demand for books. The monasteries, where books had been produced by scribes for centuries, could not fill the demand, and book production passed to the "scriveners"—professional scribes who were not monks or members of the clergy. With the coming of the printing press in the next century, printers would even better meet the need for books. The continuing demand for books led William Caxton to set up a printing press in London in 1476. He realized the advantage he would have over professional scriveners. Despite the inferior quality of his product, it *was* less expensive than the books of the scriveners, and inevitably their days—and their products—became numbered.

The printing press indisputably affected the growth and structure of the English language, but toward the end of the fifteenth century another phenomenon was to have a tremendous influence—the Renaissance, which literally means "re-birth." Throughout Europe, the Renaissance was actually a time for rediscovery of the legacy of classical Greece and Rome. This legacy encompassed the arts, literature, and language. The Latin language was admired for its precision and structure, and many English scholars believed it was vastly superior to their own language.

Both Latin and Greek lent themselves well to the formation of new words, and language scholars and scribes began to change the spelling of a great many English words to reflect what they believed were the original classical roots of the English words. For example:

ver*dit* changed to ver*dict*, from the Latin *dicere*;

dette changed to *debt*, from the Latin *debitum*;

doute changed to *doubt*, from the Latin *dubitare*;

egal changed to *equal*, from the Latin *aequalis*;

bankrout changed to *bankrupt*, from the Latin *ruptus* ("to break");

sisourses changed to *scissors*, from the Latin root *cid-* ("to cut").

By the end of the fifteenth century, the English language had changed tremendously when compared to Old English. In writing and in speech, it very closely resembles the English spoken today. For this reason, the year A.D. 1500 is often cited as the break between Middle and Modern English.

Modern English

Modern English is often broken down into two periods: Early Modern (1500–1700) and Late Modern (1700 to the present).

The forces and events that were at work during the latter part of the Middle English period continued to influence English after 1500. Apart from the Renaissance, the astounding advances in science and world exploration were to have a profound effect on the development of English. As we have seen, the Renaissance brought a renewed interest in Greek and Latin. In addition to having an effect on the spelling of English, Latin—together with Greek—provided the building blocks for creating new words to describe the new discoveries in science and exploration.

Science provided new phenomena to name and explain. The voyages of discovery by many European explorers revealed new lands, new plants and animals, and new human societies and cultures. In response, hundreds of new words were created by combining Latin and Greek word parts or by adding certain prefixes and suffixes to these parts—for example, *atmosphere*, *thermometer*, and *gravity*. In addition, many old words came to be used in new ways. William Shakespeare (1564–1616) single-handedly contributed a significant share to the growth of English at this time. During a period when the language was evolving at a rate that even astounded people of the time, Shakespeare used the language in ways and to serve purposes that may never again be realized by a single writer. He stretched words to create new connotations and coined phrases that have since formed the bedrock of Modern English. In addition, because of his love of words and his habit of using them in new ways, Shakespeare was able to speak to a variety of audiences—which partly explains his popularity during his lifetime.

In those days people spelled pretty much as they pleased, and it was not uncommon for someone to spell the same word several different ways in the same document. Around the time of Shakespeare, *spelling books* appeared, helping to establish the concept of correct versus incorrect spelling.

By 1700, the stabilization of English spelling was just about complete; some fine-tuning of the language remained to be done, though, and this task was magnificently accomplished by Samuel Johnson. In 1745, Johnson began writing his *Dictionary of the English Language*; ten years later his project was completed and published. Although other dictionaries had been published earlier, none approached the comprehensiveness of Johnson's, and none was as elegantly written.

Another dictionary to which scholars refer along with Johnson's was published in 1828, seventy-three years after Johnson's. It was published by Noah Webster, and it also exerted a significant influence on the language. There is an important difference between the two dictionaries, however: whereas Johnson's was a dictionary of the English language, Webster's was a dictionary of *American* English.

American English

Throughout the 1500s, the English as well as the Spanish, Dutch, and French explored the New World first accidentally encountered by Columbus in 1492. Because several European peoples eventually established settlements in the New World, all of their languages would come to influence English. England began establishing settlements in earnest in the early 1600s, and from that time on, the English language was in turn influenced by the languages of the Native Americans.

The English adopted many of the Native American names for the new animals and plant life they encountered. Some of these words remained intact: *hickory*, *hominy*, *totem*, *moccasin*, *igloo*. Others became changed over time: *raccoon* from *raughroughouns*, *skunk* from *segankn*, *squash* from *isquontersquash*.

In the late 1700s and early 1800s, there was a strong sense of nationalism and patriotic pride in the United States, and these feelings extended to the language as well. The individual who did more than anyone else to advance this pride in the language was Noah Webster.

In particular, Webster wanted to reform many English spellings. In his *American Dictionary of the English Language*, he made some spelling changes that to this day distinguish British from American spellings. A few examples follow (the first spelling is British; the second is American): *honour* versus *honor* and *colour* versus *color*; *theatre* versus *theater*; *defence* versus *defense*; *benefitted* versus *benefited*; *axe* versus *ax*; *phantasy* versus *fantasy*; *publick* versus *public* (in the latter two examples the British spelling would later change to the American!).

As the new nation grew in territory and in outlook throughout the nineteenth century, Spanish and Native American vocabularies increasingly were incorporated into the language. In fact, of all the languages, Spanish has exerted the most influence on English over the past century.

Of course, the growth of the new nation was not without some wrenching soul-searching and conflict. The American Civil War and the related issue of slavery are the two most critical examples of this. The "peculiar institution" of black slavery, however, nonetheless left an indelible linguistic mark on the English language.

Originally, the languages of West Africa blended with the English spoken in the American colonies. According to J. L. Dillard (1972), the first step in this process was the development of a *pidgin* English — a variety of English that allowed Africans who spoke different languages to communicate. Pidgin English was a form of simplified English in which features of the language that were least important for minimal mutual understanding were omitted; for example, verbs like *is* and the present-tense inflectional endings. These are features that in fact still characterize the dialect of American English referred to as Black English. As with other dialects and languages that have contributed to Modern English, Black English dialect and the literary and artistic culture it represents have profoundly influenced the development of American English, and in general, American society.

As in earlier centuries, immigration was an important phenomenon. Throughout the nineteenth century and the early part of the twentieth, millions of immigrants came to begin new lives in the United States: Irish, Chinese, Germans, Scandinavians, and Central Europeans. All of these groups brought their native languages, and as they learned English, their native languages in turn influenced American English.

For a multitude of reasons, new immigrants were rarely welcomed with open arms, and the history of the accommodation of these groups into American society is often an unpleasant one. Nonetheless, with time the animosity lessened, and the nation as a whole benefited immeasurably from the knowledge, culture, and language brought by each group of immigrants.

The trend of immigration continues. The new immigrants from Central and South America, Mexico, and the Pacific Rim bring still more linguistic and cultural perspectives to a continually evolving American society, language, and culture.

TEACHING RESOURCES

III. Children's Literature Resource Guide

This resource provides brief descriptions of the major categories of children's literature. For each category you'll find several titles listed. While emphasizing recent titles, I've also included books that have been enjoyed and admired for years.

Start Your Own Bookfile

Now is an excellent time to begin your own "bookfile." This will be a 3x5 file box or a file you keep on a computer. Follow this procedure for every children's book you read:

◆ Fill out a 3x5 card or type in information listing the author, title, publisher, date of publication, and the type of book.

◆ In addition, write a brief summary of the book, *your* reaction to the book, and the age range and type of children for whom you believe the book would be particularly enjoyable and beneficial. Eventually, you

---

O'Dell, Scott. Sing Down the Moon. Houghton Mifflin, 1970. Historical fiction.

Summary: Through the eyes of a Navajo girl, Bright Morning, we witness the forced removal of a band of Navajo from their homeland to Fort Sumner in 1864. O'Dell's prose really captures the physical and spiritual defeat of the Navajos. The book also demonstrates the power of the individual spirit and will, as Bright Morning persuades the disillusioned brave she has married to escape with her and return to their homeland. There they will raise their young son. The book ends with an uplifting sense of renewal.

The book is powerfully written and will be a real eye-opener for most students. We also get a realistic and identifiable portrayal of Bright Morning, who has the same feelings most girls experience, regardless of time and place. Upper elementary.

Figure R.1   Example of a Book File

will be classifying the books in different sections of your file when the numbers become too great for alphabetizing.

◆ You might also note the type of thematic unit for which the book would be appropriate. Then, when the time comes to organize a unit, a quick search through the file will yield a number of titles.

Why keep your own bookfile when you can consult the many resources that already provide information and reviews? Quite simply, you can still use your own file more quickly. Besides, you will soon have read so many books that you will forget certain titles and authors. If you have taken the time to write in your bookfile, this information will remain in your long-term memory much more efficiently.

I strongly recommend that you store your file on a computer or floppy disc. Not only will your file be more efficient and easier to access, but you will also be able to do a number of things with it. For example, your search for appropriate titles for a unit can be swift because you simply will use the "search" function on your word processor. Once you type in the important terms ("historical fiction," "biography," "siblings," "detectives," and so forth), *everything* in your file will be searched, including your comments about the books. A list of books that have been identified may be dumped into a separate file and then printed when you're finished. You now have your list of titles to choose from. From time to time, you will also wish to print information from your file for your students; this task can be performed easily and efficiently.

Over time, invite your students to contribute to your file. Their comments can be coded differently in your file, so that only their comments and not yours will appear when you print lists for other students.

Booklists

To assist you in locating books for particular interest levels and representing various cultural backgrounds, a coding system is used. For most categories of literature in this list, the *interest levels* of books are coded as follows:

P = Primary (K–2)

I = Intermediate (3–6)

A = All levels

Most books are coded according to the culture they reflect:

AA   African/African-American

AAP   Asian-/Asian-Pacific American

C   Canadian

EA   European-American

HA   Hispanic-American/Latino and Caribbean

J   Jewish

NA   Native American

ALPHABET BOOKS

Alphabet books may teach "the basics"—that is, *print awareness* as well as the *shapes*, *names*, and *sounds* of the letters—but many of them work on several levels. Authors and illustrators often suggest visual metaphors and symbols that engage the older reader as well. You will find that most of these books are an enchanting visual feast, and for young children they will constitute powerful and warm visual images that will reinforce learning these building blocks of written language. Here are just a few of many excellent alphabet books.

Selected Alphabet Books

Anno, M. (1976). *Anno's alphabet: An adventure in imagination.* Crowell/Farrar.

Baskin, H., Baskin, T., & Baskin, L. (1972). *Hosie's alphabet.* Viking.

Bayer, J. (1984). *A, my name is Alice.* Dial.

Brown, R. (1991). *Alphabet times four: An international ABC.* Dutton.

Bruna, D. (1967). *B is for bear.* Macmillan.

Drucker, M. (1992). *A Jewish holiday ABC.* Harcourt Brace.

Ehlert, L. (1989). *Eating the alphabet: fruits and vegetables from A to Z.* Harcourt Brace.

Feelings, M. (1974). *Jambo means hello: Swahili alphabet book.* Dial.

Gordon, R. (1990). *A Canadian ABC: An alphabet book for kids.* University of Toronto Press/Penumbra. [Illustrated by T. MacDonald.]

Greenaway, K. (1993). *A apple pie.* Derrydale.

Hague, K. (1984). *Alphabears: An ABC book.* Holt, Rinehart, & Winston.

Hoban, T. (1982). *A, B, see!* Greenwillow Books.

Hoban, T. (1987). *26 letters and 99 cents.* Greenwillow Books.

Hubbard, W. (1990). *C is for curious: An ABC of feelings.* Chronicle Books.

Ipear, D. (1964). *I love an anteater with an A.* Knopf.

Isadora, R. (1983). *City seen from A to Z.* Greenwillow Books.

Kellogg, S. (1987). *Aster Aardvark's alphabet adventures.* William Morrow.

Kitchen, B. (1984). *Animal alphabet.* Dial.

Lobel, A., & Lobel, A. (1981). *On Market Street.* Greenwillow Books.

Lyon, G. E. (1989). *ABCedar: An alphabet of trees.* Orchard Books.

Magee, D., & Newman, R. (1990). *All aboard ABC.* Cobblehill.

McNab, N. (1989). *A–Z of Australian wildlife.* Lamont.

McPhail, D. (1989). *David McPhail's animals A to Z.* Scholastic.

Musgrove, M. (1976). *Ashanti to Zulu: African traditions.* [Illustrated by L. & D. Dillon.]

Pallotta, J. (1986). *The icky bug alphabet book.* Charlesbridge.

Provensen, A., & Provensen, M. (1978). *A peaceable kingdom: The Shaker abecedarius.* Viking.

Rice, J. (1990). *Cowboy alphabet.* Pelican.

Sendak, M. (1990). *Alligators all around: An alphabet.* Harper Trophy.

Van Allsburg, C. (1987). *The Z was zapped.* Houghton Mifflin.

Wildsmith, B. (1963). *Brian Wildsmith's ABC.* Franklin Watts.

Zabar, A. (1990). *Alphabet soup.* Stewart, Tabor & Chang.

PICTURE BOOKS

Do the pictures tell most or all of the story in a book? If they do, the book will usually be classified as a picture book — even if it has accompanying text. As we've seen in this book, pictures and illustrations can provide excellent stimuli for critical thinking. Picture books can encompass the topics and themes of the other categories of children's literature; they also comprise most of the predictable literature for primary students and some of the predictable themed literature for intermediate students. The following are some suggested titles.

Selected Picture Books

Aardema, V. (1977). *Who's in the rabbit's house?* Dial. [Illustrated by L. & D. Dillon.] (P/AA)

Barrett, M. (1994). *Sing to the stars.* Little, Brown. [Illustrated by S. Speidel.] (A/AA)

Bemelmans, L. (1962). *Madeline.* Viking. (P/E)

Bruchac, J. (1993). *The first strawberries: A Cherokee story.* Dial. [Illustrated by A. Vojtech.] (A/NA)

Bruchac, J., & London, J. (1992). *Thirteen months on Turtle's back: A Native American year of moons.* Philomel Books. [Illustrated by T. Locker.] (A/NA)

Burton, V. L. (1939). *Mike Mulligan and his steam shovel.* Houghton Mifflin. (P)

Carrick, D. (1976). *The deer in the pasture.* Greenwillow Books. (P)

Carrick, D. (1982). *Harald and the giant knight.* Clarion. (A)

Choi, S. (1993). *Halmoni and the picnic.* Houghton Mifflin. [Illustrated by K. Dugan.] (P/AAP)

dePaola, T. (1975). *Strega Nona.* Prentice Hall. (A/EA)

Ehlert, L. (1990). *Feathers for lunch.* Harcourt Brace. (P)

Emberly, B. (1967). *Drummer Hoff fired it off.* Prentice Hall. (P)

Garza, C. (1990). *Family pictures/Cuadros de familia.* Children's Book Press. (I/HA)

Gibbons, G. (1986). *Up goes the skyscraper!* Four Winds Press. (P)

Greenfield, E. (1988). *Grandpa's face.* Philomel Books. [Illustrated by F. Cooper.] (P/AA)

Haggerty, M. (1993). *A crack in the wall.* Lee & Low. [Illustrated by R. DeAnda.] (P/HA)

Hall, N., & Syverson-Stork, J. (1994). *Los pollitos dicen/The baby chicks sing.* Little, Brown. [Illustrated by K. Chorao.] (P/HA)

Han, O., & Plunkett, S. (1993). *Sir Whong and the golden pig.* Dial. [Illustrated by O. Han.] (P/AAP)

Hansen, J. (1994). *The captive.* Scholastic. (I/AA)

Hoban, R. (1964). *Bread and jam for Frances.* Harper and Row. (P)

Hoban, T. (1973). *Over, under and through and other spatial concepts.* Macmillan. (P)

Hodges, M. (1984). *St. George and the dragon.* Little, Brown. [Illustrated by T. Hyman.] (I/EA)

Hoffman, M. (1991). *Amazing Grace.* Dial. [Illustrated by C. Binch.] (P/AA)

Hutchins, P. (1968). *Rosie's walk.* Macmillan. (P)

Johnson, A. (1989). *Tell me a story, mama.* Orchard Books. [Illustrated by D. Soman.] (P/AA)

Johnson, A. (1990). *Do like Kyla.* Orchard/Richard Jackson. [Illustrated by J. Ransome.] (P/AA)

Keats, E. J. (1962). *Snowy day.* Viking. (P/AA)

Leaf, M. (1987). *Eyes of the dragon.* Lothrop, Lee & Shepard. [Illustrated by E. Young.] (P/AAP)

Lister, R. (1990). *The legend of King Arthur.* Doubleday. [Illustrated by A. Baker.] (I/EA)

McCloskey, R. (1941). *Make way for ducklings.* Viking. (P/AM)

Noble, T. (1980). *The day Jimmy's boa ate the wash.* Dial/Puffin Books. [Illustrated by S. Kellogg.] (P/AM)

Ringgold, F. (1991). *Tar Beach.* Crown. (A/HA)

Rockwell, A., & Rockwell, H. (1972). *Toad.* Doubleday. (P)

Rylant, C. (1985). *The relatives came.* Bradbury Press. (A/AM)

Shelby, A. (1990). *We keep a store.* Orchard Books. [Illustrated by J. Ward.] (P/AA)

Van Allsburg, C. (1984). *The mysteries of Harris Burdick.* Houghton Mifflin. (A)

Vander Els, B. (1985). *The bombers moon.* Farrar, Straus & Giroux. (I/AAP)

Waber, B. (1972). *Ira sleeps over.* Houghton Mifflin. (P)

Weisman, J. (1993). *The storyteller.* Rizzoli. [Illustrated by D. Bradley.] (P/NA)

Wild, M. (1991). *Let the celebrations begin.* Orchard Books. [Illustrated by J. Vivas.] (P/J)

Williams, K. (1991). *When Africa was home.* Orchard Books. [Illustrated by F. Cooper.] (P/AA)

TRADITIONAL LITERATURE

The traditional literature category embraces a large number of genres: nursery rhymes, fables, folktales and fairy tales, myths, legends, and Biblical stories. Many of these genres can be introduced through storytelling (see Chapter 5). *Fables* and *folktales* reflect standards of behavior and belief. Often the moral is explicitly stated. In fables the main characters are usually animals; in folktales humans predominate. These stories are basically optimistic in tone.

Myths and *legends* usually represent a people's attempt to come to grips with more grandiose themes: creation, life, and death. Myths have attempted to account for the tremendous variety of natural phenomena that early peoples observed: the seasons; the sun, moon, and stars; storms, floods, and earthquakes. The basic narrative format in all forms of traditional literature developed and flourished as a response to the psychological and emotional needs of the listeners—and later, of readers.

Selected Traditional Literature

Aardema, V. (1975). *Why mosquitos buzz in people's ears.* Dial. (A/AA)

Aesop's fables. (1981). Viking Penguin. [Illustrated by H. Holder.] (A/EA)

Argueta, M. (1990). *Elly Simmons magic dogs of the volcanoes/Los perros magicos de los volcanes.* Children's Book Press. (A/HA)

Bang, M. (1985). *The paper crane.* Greenwillow Books. (P/AAP)

Bierhorst, J. (1986). *The monkey's haircut and other stories told by the Maya.* William Morrow. [Illustrated by R. Parker.] (I/HA)

Bierhorst, J. (1990). *Mythology of Mexico and Central America.* William Morrow. (I/HA)

Birdseye, T. (1990). *A song of stars.* Holiday House. [Illustrated by J. Chen.] (I/AAP)

Brett, J. (1989). *Beauty and the beast.* Clarion. (A/EA)

Brown, M. (1947). *Stone soup.* Scribner's. (A/EA)

Bruchac, J. (1991). *Native American stories.* Fulcrum. [Illustrated by J. Fadden.] (I/NA)

Bruchac, J. (1994). *The great ball game: a Muskogee story.* Dial. [Illustrated by S. Roth.] (P/NA)

Bushnaq, I. (1986). *Arab folktales.* Pantheon. (A)

Chaikin, M. (1987). *Exodus.* Holiday House. (A/J)

Climo, S. (1993). *The Korean Cinderella.* HarperCollins. [Illustrated by R. Heller.] (P/AAP)

D'Aulaire, I., & D'Aulaire, E. (1962). *D'Aulaire's book of Greek myths.* Doubleday. (I)

Demi. (1980). *Liang and the magic paint brush.* Holt. (P/AAP)

Dorris, M. (1994). *Guests.* Hyperion. (I/NA)

Dyer, V. (1982). *The brocade slipper and other Vietnamese tales.* Addison-Wesley. (A/AAP)

Ginsburg, M. (1988). *The Chinese mirror.* Harcourt Brace. [Illustrated by M. Zemach.] (P/AAP)

Goble, P. (1989). *Iktomi and the berries.* Orchard Books. (A/NA)

Goble, P. (1992). *Crow chief: A Plains Indians story.* Orchard Books. (A/NA)

Goble, P., & Goble, D. (1978). *The girl who loved wild horses.* Bradbury Press. (A/NA)

Greenfield, E. (1977). *Africa dream.* Crowell. (A)

Haley, G. (1970). *A story, a story.* Atheneum. (A/AA)

Hamilton, V. (1988). *The people could fly.* Knopf. (A/AA)

Hastings, S. (1985). *Sir Gawain and the loathly lady.* Lothrop, Lee, and Shepard. (I/EA)

Hogrogian, N. (1988). *The cat who loves to sing.* Knopf. (P/EA)

Johnston, T. (1994). *The tale of Rabbit and Coyote.* Putnam. [Illustrated by T. dePaola.] (P/HA)

Kellogg, S. (1984). *Paul Bunyan* [Retold]. William Morrow. (A)

Lattimore, D. (1989). *Why there is no arguing in Heaven.* HarperCollins. (A/HA)

McDermott, G. (1972). *Anansi the spider: A tale from the Ashanti.* Holt, Rinehart, and Winston. (A/AA)

McDermott, G. (1974). *Arrow to the sun.* Viking. (A/NA).

McKissack, P. (1988). *Mirandy and Brother Wind.* Knopf. [Illustrated by J. Pinkney.] (P/AA)

Ober, H. (1994). *How music came into the world: An ancient Mexican myth.* Houghton Mifflin. [Illustrated by C. Ober.] (P)

Perrault, C. (1976). *The sleeping beauty.* Crowell. (A/EA)

Polacco, P. (1988). *Rechenka's eggs.* Philomel Books. (P/EA)

Ross, G. (1994). *How Rabbit tricked Otter: And other Cherokee trickster stories.* HarperCollins. [Illustrated by M. Jacob.] (I/NA)

Seeger, P. (1986). *Abiyoyo.* Macmillan. [Illustrated by M. Hays.] (P/AA)

Serwer, B. L. (1970). *Let's steal the moon.* Little, Brown. (A/J)

Sherman, J. (1988). *Vassilisa the Wise: A tale of medieval Russia.* Harcourt Brace. (A/EA)

Zemach, M. (1976). *It could always be worse.* Farrar, Straus, and Giroux. (P/J)

POETRY

A poet once said that we should first listen to poetry with our hearts rather than with our ears. He was expressing the belief that we should not try to figure out "what it means" when we hear a poem but simply allow it to wash over us. The effect we will then feel will be the true effect of poetry. Somewhat later, we can analyze *how* and *why* we experienced this effect and respond to what Sebesta (1984) aptly described: "The printed poem, with its unique arrangement on the page, and accompanying illustrations, may have a visual impact that, in itself, has power to arouse the reader" (p. 68).

Selected Poetry Books

Adoff, A. (1968). *I am the darker brother.* Macmillan. (A/AA)

Adoff, A. (Ed.). (1974). *My black me: A beginning book of black poetry.* Dutton. (P/AA)

Bierhorst, J. (Ed.). (1971). *In the trail of the wind: American Indian poems and ritual orations.* Farrar, Straus and Giroux. (I/NA)

Blake, Q. (1983). *Quentin Blake's nursery rhyme book.* Harper and Row. (P)

Bodecker, N. M. (1976). *Hurry, hurry, Mary dear! and other nonsense poems.* Scribner's (A)

Brewton, S., et al. (Compilers). (1973). *My tang's tungled and other ridiculous situations.* Crowell. (A)

Ciardi, J. (1961). *The man who sang the sillies.* Lippincott. (A)

Cole, W. (1964). *Beastly boys and ghastly girls.* Collins World. (A)

de Gerez, T. (Trans.). (1984). *My song is a piece of Jade: Poems of ancient Mexico in English and Spanish.* Little, Brown. (A/HA)

de la Mare, W. (1979). *Collected poems.* Faber and Faber. (I)

Gardner, J. (1977). *A child's bestiary.* Knopf. (A)

Greenfield, E. (1988). *Nathaniel talking.* Writers & Readers. [Illustrated by J. S. Gilchrist.] (A/AA)

Hoberman, M. A. (1978). *A house is a house for me.* Viking. (P)

Hopkins, L. B. (Ed.). (1970). *City talk.* Knopf. (A)

Hopkins, L. B. (1982). *Rainbows are made.* Harcourt Brace. (A)

Hughes, L. (1993). *The dreamkeeper and other poems.* Knopf. [Illustrated by B. Pinkney.] (I/AA)

Hughes, L. (1994). *The sweet and sour animal book.* Oxford. [Illustrated by students from the Harlem School of the Arts.] (P/AA)

Johnson, J. (1993). *The creation: A poem.* Little, Brown. [Illustrated by C. Glolembe.] (P/AA)

Lear, E. (1951). *The complete nonsense of Edward Lear.* (H. Jackson, Ed.). Dover. (A)

Lee, D. (1974). *Alligator pie.* Houghton Mifflin. (P)

Livingston, M. C. (1972). *Listen, children, listen.* Harcourt Brace. (A)

Livingston, M. C. (1982). *Circle of seasons.* Holiday House. (A)

Lobel, A. (1974). *The man who took the indoors out.* Harper and Row. (A)

Marzollo, J. (1986). *The rebus treasury.* Dial. (A)

McCord, D. (1977). *One at a time.* Little, Brown. (A)

Merriam, E. (1962). *There is no rhyme for silver.* Atheneum. (A)

Prelutsky, J. (1984). *The new kid on the block.* Greenwillow Books. (A)

Prelutsky, J. (1986). *Ride a purple pelican.* Greenwillow Books. (A)

Silverstein, S. (1974). *Where the sidewalk ends.* Harper and Row. (A)

Spier, P. (1969). *And so my garden grows.* Doubleday. (A)

Yolen, J. (1990). *Dinosaur dances.* Putnam. (A/I)

Zim, J. (1975). *Shalom my peace.* Tel Aviv: Sabra Books. (A/J)

HISTORICAL FICTION

Works in the genre of historical fiction are set in definite historical periods and are based on actual historical events. Historical figures may play a role in a work, though it is usually minor. The main character is fictional, as are the supporting characters in most cases.

The range of historical fiction is wide: works reflecting the distant past through the Vietnam War, for example, are classified in this genre. This is a powerful genre because readers not only gain a strong feel for the historical period, but they are also able to identify with the main character, who is usually close to their own age. This character is therefore dealing with the same universal questions, anxieties, and hopes that the reader is. These two aspects combine to leave young readers with a more visceral impression of the reality of the past; although period clothing may seem humorous and physical settings peculiar, such impressions fade and are overridden by a new awareness of those commonalities of human existence that really do transcend the ages.

Selected Historical Fiction

Armstrong, J. (1992). *Steal away.* Orchard Books. (I/AA)

Armstrong, W. (1969). *Sounder.* Harper and Row. (I/AA)

Berry, J. (1992). *Ajeemah and his son.* HarperCollins. (I/AA)

Brenner, B. (1978). *Wagon wheels.* Harper and Row. (P/EA)

Bunting, E. (1988). *How many days to America? A Thanksgiving story.* Clarion. (A/HA)

Clapp, P. (1977). *I'm Deborah Sampson: A soldier in the War of the Revolution.* Lothrop, Lee, and Shepard. (I/EA)

Clifford, M. (1993). *When the great canoes came.* Pelican. [Illustrated by J. Haynes.] (I/NA)

Collier, J., & Collier, C. (1974). *My brother Sam is dead.* Macmillan/Four Winds Press. (I/EA)

Dalgliesh, A. (1954). *The courage of Sarah Noble.* Scribner's. (I/EA)

Fleischman, P. (1990). *Saturnalia.* HarperCollins. (I/NA)

Forbes, E. (1943). *Johnny Tremain.* Houghton Mifflin/ Dell. [Illustrated by L. Ward.] (I/EA)

Fox, P. (1973). *Slave dancer.* Bradley. (I/EA & AA)

Greene, J. (1988). *Out of many waters.* Walker. (I/J)

Haley, G. (1973). *Jack Jouett's ride.* Viking. (A/EA)

Hamilton, V. (1968). *House of Dies Drear.* Macmillan. (I/AA)

Hamilton, V. (1985). *Junius over far.* HarperCollins. (I/HA)

Hopkins, D. (1993). *Sweet Clara and the freedom quilt.* Knopf. [Illustrated by J. Ransome.] (P/AA)

Hurmence, B. (1982). *A girl called boy.* Houghton Mifflin. (I/AA)

Johnson, D. (1993). *Now let me fly: The story of a slave family.* Macmillan. (A/AA)

Johnson, J. (1994). *The princess and the painter.* Farrar. (I/HA)

Lord, B. B. (1984). *In the year of the boar and Jackie Robinson.* Harper and Row. (I/AAP)

MacLachlan, P. (1985). *Sarah, plain and tall.* Harper. (I/EA)

O'Dell, S. (1960). *Island of the blue dolphins.* Houghton Mifflin. (I/NA)

O'Dell, S. (1970). *Sing down the moon.* Houghton Mifflin. (I/NA)

O'Dell, S. (1981). *The feathered serpent.* Houghton Mifflin. (I/HA)

O'Dell, S. (1989). *My name is not Angelica.* Houghton Mifflin. (I/HA)

Sperry, A. (1940). *Call it courage.* Macmillan.

Taylor, M. (1976). *Roll of thunder, hear my cry.* Dial. (I/AA)

Taylor, M. (1981). *Let the circle be unbroken.* Dial. (I/AA)

Taylor, T. (1962). *The Maldonado miracle.* Harcourt Brace. (I/HA)

Uchida, Y. (1971). *Journey to Topaz.* Scribner's (I/AAP)

Uchida, Y. (1985). *A jar of dreams.* Aladdin Books. (A/AAP)

Wilder, L. I. (1932). *Little house in the big woods.* Harper and Row. (A/EA)

Yep, L. (1975). *Dragonwings.* Harper. (I/AAP)

CONTEMPORARY REALISM

As the label suggests, the genre of contemporary realism addresses the reality of contemporary life. Such "reality," however, is multifaceted, and this genre has matured markedly over the past twenty years or so to reflect this aspect. Everything that concerns adults — and which is therefore addressed in books *for* adults — is now addressed in children's books as well. Books that we classify as contemporary realism deal with the many different "realities" of contemporary life that children experience: humor, tragedy, the drama of simply growing up, and — more specifically — physical and mental handicaps, psychological and physical abuse, drug or alcohol addiction, alternative lifestyles, and racism and bigotry.

Through these books elementary students can alternately escape from their concerns or deal with them. Again, by identifying with a main character, they can realize both that having concerns or problems is quite normal and that these problems can often be worked out. They also come to understand that they may have to accept and adjust to situations with no clear-cut resolution.

Selected Contemporary Realism

Blume, J. (1981). *The one in the middle is the green kangaroo.* Bradbury Press. (I)

Boyd, C. (1987). *Charlie Pippin.* Macmillan. (I/AAP)

Burch, R. (1966). *Queenie Peavy.* Viking. (I)

Byars, B. (1970). *The summer of the swans.* Viking. (I/EA)

Cleary, B. (1983). *Dear Mr. Henshaw.* William Morrow. (I/EA)

Corcoran, B. (1974). *A dance to still music.* Atheneum. [The protagonist becomes deaf.] (I)

Dorros, A. (1993). *Radio man.* HarperCollins. (P/AAP)

Estes, E. (1944). *The hundred dresses.* Harcourt Brace. (I)

Fitzhugh, L. (1964). *Harriet the spy.* Harper and Row. (I)

Flournoy, V. (1985). *The patchwork quilt.* Dial. [Illustrated by J. Pinkney.] (P/AA)

Greene, B. (1974). *Philip Hall likes me, I reckon maybe.* Dial. (I/AA)

Heide, F. P. (1970). *Sound of sunshine, sound of rain.* Parents Magazine Press. [The protagonist is blind.] (A)

Hurwitz, J. (1990). *Class president.* William Morrow. [Illustrated by S. Hamanaka.] (I/HA)

Klein, N. (1973). *It's not what you expect.* Pantheon. [Divorce and remarriage] (I)

Konigsburg, E. L. (1967). *From the mixed-up files of Mrs. Basil E. Frankweiler.* Atheneum. (I/EA)

Korman, G. (1988). *The zucchini warriors.* Scholastic. (I/C)

Miles, M. (1971). *Annie and the old one.* Little, Brown. (A)

Myers, W. D. (1988). *Me, Mop and the Moondance Kid.* Delacorte. (I/AA)

Naylor, P. (1991). *Shiloh.* Atheneum/Dell. (I/EA)

Ness, E. (1966). *Sam, Bangs and Moonshine.* Holt, Rinehart, and Winston. (I)

Paterson, K. (1977). *A bridge to Terabithia.* Crowell. (I/EA)

Rattigan, J. (1993). *Dumpling soup.* Little, Brown. [Illustrated by L. Hsu-Flanders.] (P/AAP)

Rawls, W. (1961). *Where the red fern grows.* Doubleday. (I/EA)

Sachs, M. (1971). *The bear's house.* Doubleday. (I/EA)

Soto, G. (1990). *Baseball in April.* Harcourt Brace. (I/HA)

Spinelli, J. (1990). *Maniac Magee.* Little, Brown/Trophy. (I)

Tate, E. (1987). *The secret of the gumbo grove.* Watts. (I/AA)

Yashima, T. (1955). *Crow boy.* Viking. (A/AAP)

Yep, L. (1977). *Child of the owl.* Harper and Row. (I/AAP)

MODERN FANTASY

The genre of modern fantasy combines fantasy and reality but does so with logic and consistency. Consider, for example, the worlds created and developed in J.R.R. Tolkien's *The Hobbit* (1938) and in C. S. Lewis's "Narnia" books (the most famous being *The Lion, the Witch, and the Wardrobe*). Stewig (1988) expressed in part the challenge to authors of modern fantasy: "If, in the universe the author has imagined, the frogs can speak English, there had better be a good reason why the horses cannot. Or if the goats are wearing trousers, why are the pigs' bottoms exposed to the air?" (p. 509). As with much of traditional literature, modern fantasy is a literary playground on which pri-mal themes are played out. The now classic "Narnia" tales, for example, address a powerful range of themes and issues: good versus evil, the existence of God, a messiah, growing up, and interpersonal relationships among children on the verge of adolescence.

Literary folktales are a subgenre of modern fantasy, reflecting certain forms of traditional literature such as legends and fairy tales. Examples are Rudyard Kipling's *Just So Stories* (1996) and the works of Hans Christian Andersen. In contrast to traditional folktales that have been handed down through the oral tradition and that probably do not have a single author, literary folktales have been written by known authors, though they share the same form and features as traditional folk-tales.

Modern fantasy also includes stories about animals with special abilities, as in Beverly Cleary's *The Mouse and the Motorcycle*, Robert O'Brien's *Mrs. Frisby and the Rats of NIMH*, E. B. White's *Charlotte's Web*, and Kenneth Grahame's *The Wind in the Willows*. Trips through time and space are another aspect of this category, as in Madeline L'Engle's *A Wrinkle in Time* and, to a degree, Natalie Babbitt's *Tuck Everlasting*.

Selected Works of Modern Fantasy

Alexander, L. (1977). *The town cats and other tales.* Dut-ton. (I)

Alexander, L. (1978). *The first two lives of Lukas-Kasha.* Dutton. (I)

Azimov, J., & Azimov, I. (1990). *Norby and the oldest dragon.* Walker. (I)

Bang, M. (1977). *The buried moon and other stories.* Scribner's. (I)

Bellairs, J. (1973). *The house with a clock in its walls.* Dial. (I)

Bond, M. (1960). *A bear called Paddington.* Houghton Mifflin. (A)

Boston, L. (1961). *A stranger at Green Knowe.* Harcourt Brace. (I)

Carroll, L. (1983). *Alice's adventures in Wonderland.* (Rev. ed.). Knopf. [Illustrated by S. M. Wiggins.] (A)

Cooper, S. (1965). *Over sea, under stone.* Harcourt Brace. (I/EA)

Cooper, S. (1973). *The dark is rising.* Atheneum. (I/EA)

Dorros, A. (1991). *Abuela.* Dutton. (P/HA)

Henkes, K. (1993). *Owen.* Greenwillow Books. (P)

L'Engle, M. (1978). *A swiftly tilting planet.* Farrar. (I)

LeGuin, U. (1968). *A wizard of Earthsea.* Parnassus. (I)

LeGuin, U. (1988). *Catwings.* Watts. (A)

Lewis, C. S. (1951–1956). The "Chronicles of Narnia" series. Macmillian. (I)

McKinley, R. (1982). *The blue sword.* Greenwillow Books. (I)

Milne, A. A. (1926). *Winnie-the-Pooh.* Dutton. (P)

Rodgers, M. (1972). *Freaky Friday.* Harper and Row. (I)

Sendak, M. (1963). *Where the wild things are.* Harper and Row. (P)

Yolen, J. (1989). *The faery flags: Stories and poems of fantasy and the supernatural.* Orchard Books. (I)

Williams, M. (1983). *The velveteen rabbit.* Knopf. (A)

INFORMATIONAL BOOKS

The number of informational or nonfiction books for children has increased tremendously over the past few decades. Moreover, the content and quality of these books have improved. While textbooks often repre-sent the terrain to be covered in a content area, infor-mational books will usually be the resource that breathes life into that content. The following is just a sampling of hundreds of excellent titles.

Selected Informational Books

Aaseng, N. (1992). *Navajo code talkers*. Walker. (I/NA)

Ada, A. (1991). *The gold coin*. Atheneum. [Illustrated by N. Waldman.] (A/HA)

Aliki. (1976). *Corn is maize: The gift of the Indians*. Crowell. (A/NA)

Andronik, C. (1989). *Search for a king: Searching for the real King Arthur*. Atheneum. (I/EA)

Ashabranner, B. (1986). *Children of the Maya: A Guatemalan Indian odyssey*. Putnam. (I/NA)

Baylor, B. (1978). *The way to start a day*. Scribner's (A/NA)

Branley, F. (1973). *Experiments in the principles of space travel*. Crowell. (I) [One in a series of excellent scientific books for elementary students by the same author]

Charlip, R., Ancona, M. B., & Ancona, G. (1974). *Handtalk: An ABC of finger spelling and sign language*. Parents Magazine Press. (A)

Cheripko, J. (1994). *Adventures on the Delaware*. Boyds Mills. (I)

Cole, J. (1976). *A chick hatches*. William Morrow. (I)

dePaola, T. (1977). *The quicksand book*. Holiday House. (A)

Ehlert, L. (1992). *Moon rope/Un lazo a la luna*. Harcourt Brace. (A/HA)

Farley, C. (1991). *Korea: Land of the morning calm*. Dillon. (I/AAP)

Fisher, L. (1986). *The Great Wall of China*. Macmillan. (I/AAP)

Fisher, L. (1989). *The Wailing Wall*. Macmillan. (I/J)

Greenfield, H. (1979). *Rosh Hashanah and Yom Kippur*. Holt. [One in a series of books on Jewish holidays by the same author] (A/J)

Hurd, E. T. (1973). *The mother whale*. Little, Brown. (A)

Kamien, J. (1979). *What if you couldn't . . . ?* Scribner's. (A)

Kohl, H., & Kohl, J. (1977). *The view from the oak*. Sierra Club Books/Scribner's. (A)

Kuskin, K. (1982). *The philharmonic gets dressed*. Harper and Row. (A)

LaPierre, Y. (1994). *Rock art: Messages from the past*. Thomasson-Grant. [Illustrated by L. Sloan.] (I/NA)

Leon, G. (1989). *Explorers of the Americas before Columbus*. Watts. (I)

Macaulay, D. (1975). *Pyramid*. Houghton Mifflin. (A)

Marrin, A. (1986). *Aztecs and Spaniards*. Atheneum. (I/HA)

Meltzer, M. (1976). *Never to forget: The Jews of the Holocaust*. Harper and Row. (I/J)

Meltzer, M. (1980). *All times, all peoples: A world history of slavery*. (I)

Meltzer, M. (1982). *The Hispanic Americans*. Crowell. (I/HA)

Morrison, M. (1989). *Central America*. Silver Burdett. (I)

Pringle, L. (1977). *The hidden world: Life under a rock*. Macmillan. (A)

Scarry, H. (1985). *Looking into the Middle Ages*. HarperCollins. (A/EA)

Spier, P. (1980). *People*. Doubleday. (A)

BIOGRAPHY

Books in the genre of biography tell the life stories of individuals, living or deceased. Elementary students can read biography for a number of purposes. Just as they can identify with fictional characters in contemporary realism, for example, so too can children identify with historical individuals and the conflicts they faced.

As with informational books, the number and quality of biographies written for young people have increased significantly. These include compelling new versions of the lives of individuals who you would have thought had been overwhelmingly "biographied" by now, as well as *collective biographies* that present several shorter biographies within one volume. Recently biographies of noted minority figures have proliferated, and there are also new books that present the "victory over adversity" theme.

A list of recommended biographies and collective biographies follows.

Selected Biographies

Averill, E. (1993). *King Phillip, the Indian chief.* Shoe String/Linnet. [Illustrated by V. Belsky.] (I/NA)

Burchard, P. (1995). *Charlotte Forten: A black teacher in the Civil War.* Crown. (I/AA)

Cooper, F. (1994). *Coming home: From the life of Langston Hughes.* Philomel Books. (A/AA)

Frank, A. (1967). *Anne Frank: The diary of a young girl.* [Autobiography] (I/J)

Freedman, R. (1987). *Lincoln: A photobiography.* Houghton Mifflin. (I/EA)

Fritz, J. (1983). *The double life of Pocahontas.* Putnam. (I/NA)

Gherman, B. (1986). *Georgia O'Keeffe.* Atheneum. (I)

Giblin, J. (1994). *Thomas Jefferson: A picture book biography.* Scholastic. [Illustrated by M. Dooling.] (I)

Hamilton, V. (1972). *W. E. B. DuBois: A biography.* HarperCollins. (I/AA)

Hamilton, V. (1992). *Paul Robeson: The life and times of a free black man.* HarperCollins. (I/AA)

Haskins, J. (1977). *The life and death of Martin Luther King, Jr.* Lothrop, Lee, and Shepard. (I/AA)

Lee, B. (1979). *Charles Eastman: The story of an American Indian.* Dillon. (I/NA)

McKissack, P. (1984). *Paul Laurence Dunbar: A poet to remember.* Children's Press. (I/AA)

Merriam, E. (1973). *Growing up female in America.* Dell. (I/EA, AA, J, NA)

Myers, W. D. (1993). *Malcolm X: By any means necessary.* Scholastic. (I/AA)

Pinkney, A. (1993). *Alvin Ailey.* Hyperion. [Illustrated by B. Pinkney.] (P/AA)

Nelson, M. C. (1972). *Maria Martinez.* Dillon. (I/HA)

Newlon, C. (1972). *Famous Mexican Americans.* Dodd, Mead. (I)

Stevenson, A. (1983). *Benjamin Franklin, young printer.* Bobbs-Merrill.

Tobias, T. (1970). *Maria Tallchief.* Crowell. (I/NA)

IV. Multimedia Resources

This section is intended to serve as a resource primarily for teachers, but much that is here—especially the web sites—would also be appropriate for students.

The following companies are some of the most prominent publishers of films, videocassettes, audiocassettes, and laserdiscs:

Adventure Productions
3404 Terry Lake Road
Ft. Collins, CO 80524

AIMS Media
9710 DeSoto Avenue
Chatsworth, CA 91311-4409
800–367–2467

Audio Bookshelf
RR #1, Box 706
Belfast, ME 04915
800–234–1713

Audio Editions
Box 6930
Auburn, CA 95604–6930
800–231–4261

Churchill Films
12210 Nebraska Ave.
Los Angeles, CA 90025
800–334–7830

Creative Video Concepts
5758 SW Calusa Loop
Tualatin, OR 97062

Encounter Video
2550 NW Usshur
Portland, OR 97210
800–677–7607

Films for Humanities and Science
P.O. Box 2053
Princeton, NJ 08543
609–275–1400

HarperAudio
10 East 53rd Street
New York, NY 10022
212–207–6901

Kidviz
618 Centre Street
Newton, MA 02158
617–965–3345

Listening Library
One Park Avenue
Old Greenwich, CT 06970
800–243–4504

Live Oak Media
P.O. Box 652
White Plains, NY 12567
518–398–1010

Media Basics
Lighthouse Square
705 Boston Post Road
Guilford, CT 06437
800–542–2505

Milestone Film and Video
275 W. 96th Street
Suite 28C
New York, NY 10025

National Geographic
Educational Services
Washington, DC 20036
800–548–9797

The Nature Company
P.O. Box 188
Florence, KY 41022
800–227–1114

Rabbit Ears
131 Rowayton Avenue
Rowayton, CT 06853
800–800–3277

Rainbow Educational Media
170 Keyland Court
Bohemia, NY 11716
800–331–4047

Random House Media
400 Hahn Road
Westminster, MD 21157
800−733−3000

Recorded Books
270 Skipjack Road
Prince Frederick, MD 20678
800−638−1304

SelectVideo
7200 E. Dry Creek Road
Englewood, CO 80112
800−742−1455

Spoken Arts
10100 SBF Drive
Pinellas Park, FL 34666
800−126−8090

Time-Life Education
P.O. Box 85026
Richmond, VA 23285−5026
800−449−2010

Multimedia SourceSite

This section is intended to serve as a resource for both teachers *and* students. The number of very good web sites is increasing daily; the best have links to other sites. So, whether you're exploring for a particular topic or merely "surfing," you'll quickly find your own favorite sites. The following list will provide an incredible amount of information for you as well as get you launched into the vast resources available on the World Wide Web.

◆ **The Schoolhouse**
   http://www.nwrel.org/school_house
   Provides comprehensive educational resources, projects, discussions, interactions, collaborations, lessons, curricula, and standards for grades K−12.

◆ **Berit's Best Sites for Children**
   http://www.cochran.com/theosite/
   Ksites_part2.html#fun
   This site is a very good clearinghouse and list of links. For example, it provides information about several key pals sites, both national and international, which can be accessed easily and are listed by age range, location, and interests. Students can easily add themselves to the list.

◆ **SuperKids: Educational Software Review**
   http://www.superkids.com/aweb/pages/
   contents.html
   Provides fairly objective evaluations from teachers, parents, and students.

◆ **Children's Publishing**
   http://www.ucalgary.ca/~dkbrown/writings.html
   Links to on-line magazines, encyclopedias written by students, getting students' art on the Web, puppetry activities and scripts, students' poetry, and much more.

◆ **KidPub**
   http://en-garde.com/kidpub/intro.html
   Another site listing lots of publication opportunities for students.

◆ **ERIC Clearinghouse on Reading, English, and Communication**
   http://www.indiana.edu/~eric_rec/
   A rich resource for teachers, including for example: educational materials, lesson plans, READPRO (a listserv for educators interested in all aspects of learning and teaching reading), bibliographies (many provide links to related websites), and summaries of current research in reading and the language arts.

◆ **Internet Public Library: IPL Youth Division**
   http://ipl.sils.umich.edu/youth/HomePage2.html
   An excellent site that focuses on motivating, interesting, and exciting reading for students. Features include "Ask the Author," in which authors and illustrators respond to students' questions; "Story Hour," in which particular books are engagingly shared; "The World of Reading," where students share information about good books — in all possible genre/categories; and "Dr. Internet" for exploring math and science.

◆ **Online Songs and Poetry for Children**
http://www.ucalgary.ca/~dkbrown/storsong.html
This site is an engaging complement to the contemporary poets mentioned in this book. More "traditional" poets who have written for and about the young are included: Edward Lear, Wordsworth, Robert Louis Stevenson, Walter de la Mare.

◆ **Folklore, Myth, and Legend**
http://www.ucalgary.ca/~dkbrown/storfolk.html
Aimed at elementary and middle students, this site is an excellent resource. In addition to "traditional" tales, myths, and legends, creation tales of various indigenous cultures are also included.

◆ **Reader's Theater Editions**
By Aaron Shepard
http://www.ucalgary.ca/~dkbrown/readers.html

Scripts adapted from published stories by Aaron Shepard and others. Scripts include information about genre, culture of origin or setting, theme, appropriate grade level (for readers—as Shepard notes, these scripts may be read to younger audiences), suggested number of roles as well as how long the script usually takes, and approximate reading time.

◆ **True Stories—Many Truths (True Stories for American Indians)**
http://indy4.fdl.cc.mn.us/~isk/stories/stories.html
This is an incredibly rich resource that addresses grades K–12. Traditional and contemporary stories, historical and biographical information, links to other resources (including Native American literature resources).

V. Words: Their Structure, Origins, and Spelling

This section can be a resource for words you can use for word sorts, word games, and lessons on word structure.

◆ Once you have administered the Qualitative Inventory of Spelling Knowledge (see Chapter 11) and determined the developmental phases of your students, you can present appropriate spelling patterns pulled from these lists.

◆ The Table of Frequently Occurring Greek and Latin Word Elements will provide examples of elements and words you can use to teach about these structural elements—for example, through root webs, word sorts, and games. This list will also be a handy reference when you want to check the meaning of a particular element.

◆ The brief discussion of etymology—word origins—will help set the stage for your modeling of how to use the information in a dictionary about word origins.

"Starter" Lists: Words That Represent Different Spelling Features and Patterns

Refer to the spelling "sequence of instruction" chart on p. 465 in Chapter 11. The following "starter" lists are based on the developmental sequence of spelling patterns and features presented in that chart.

PHONEMIC OR "ALPHABETIC" PHASE

Short Vowel Patterns

bat	big	job	rug	pet
mat	dig	not	mud	wet
sat	pig	hot	tub	net
man	tip	got	rub	get
fan	rip	hop	nut	leg
pan	rig	nod	run	peg
bad	fig	fog	sun	bed
bag	dip	dot	gun	red
tag	sip	dog	bug	beg

Consonant Digraphs

she	chin	that
shop	chop	than
ship	chick	this
fish	church	with
shot	chat	bath

Consonant Blends

stop	spot	small	frog	glad	trip	blue	club	drop
store	spin	smile	fry	glow	trick	black	clap	drip
step	spill	smell	flag	play	train	blimp	clip	drive
stone	spank	smash	flip	plug	truck	blubber		

"Continuant" Consonants before Another Consonant

went	jump
dump	wink
lamp	drink
sink	damp
tank	stamp
long	

WITHIN-WORD PATTERN PHASE
Long Vowel Patterns

make	day	train
lake	play	mail
	may	sail
	stay	rain

bike	
kite	
keep	clean
green	mean
wheel	please
boat	slow
coat	show
cold	
old	

l-influenced Vowels

ball	still
call	chill
small	mall
fall	grill

r-influenced Vowels

car	store
yard	for
farm	morning
part	corn

Other Vowel Patterns

food	look	town	house
moon	book	brown	mouse
room	good	down	found
soon	took		

Homophones

plane/plain	tale/tail	meet/meat
rode/road	deer/dear	cheep/cheap
whole/hole	pale/pail	heal/heel

Other Vowel Spellings

night	flew	fruit
high	blew	cruise
find	stew	bruise
kind		

Compound Words

bedtime	bedroom	baseball
cookbook	sunshine	campfire
breakfast	football	someday
cannot	daylight	grandmother

Compound Words (*continued*)

somebody	birthday	grandfather

anything

Common Contractions

I'll

you're

isn't

I've

hasn't

SYLLABLE JUNCTURE PHASE
Simple Inflectional Endings

VC + -ed/-ing	VCe + -ed/-ing
batted	liked
stopped	hoping
shopping	named
clapped	riding
sitting	chased
hugging	closed

Common and Less-frequent Vowel Patterns in Single-Syllable and Polysyllabic Words

neighbor	though
weigh	head
straight	spread
sew	friend

Two-Syllable Words Are Examined

"VCCV" Pattern	versus	"VCV" Pattern
tender		baby
sister		chosen

"VCCV" Pattern	versus	"VCV" Pattern
member		raking
dinner		pilot
canvas		robot
kitten		prefer
happy		bacon

/er/ Endings

sailor	enter	sugar
harbor	ladder	beggar
favor	shower	collar
doctor	bitter	
motor	feather	

Simple Prefixes + Base Word

redo	uneven
rebuild	unsure
refill	unload
rewind	unpack

Simple Suffixes + Base Word

endless	illness	painful
restless	kindness	fearful
hopeless	darkness	beautiful

Three-Syllable Words

deliver	hospital
another	department
carpenter	victory
together	tomorrow

DERIVATIONAL PATTERN PHASE:
SPELLING-MEANING CONNECTION

Consonant Alternation Patterns:

Silent-Sounded	Sound Changes	Predictable Change
sign/signal	connect/connection	different/difference
muscle/muscular	locate/location	evident/evidence
column/columnist	confuse/confusion	silent/silence
	music/musician	patient/patience
	critic/criticize	
		persuade/persuasion
		collide/collision
		comprehend/comprehension
		include/inclusion
		erode/erosion

Vowel Alternation Patterns:

Long-to-Short	Long-to-Schwa	Short-to-Schwa
televise/television	compete/competition	normality/normal
nature/natural	oppose/opposition	locality/local
serene/serenity	regulate/regulatory	legality/legal
grave/gravity	propose/proposition	formality/formal
inquire/inquisitive		

Etymology

In terms of vocabulary development, *etymology*—the study of word origins and histories—can prove to be a fascinating and beneficial pursuit. Most of the time, the structure of words represents not only their meaning but their origins and history as well. In this section we will examine some aspects of etymology that can be explored with intermediate students. (Note: An asterisk indicates the element occurs frequently.)

FREQUENTLY OCCURRING GREEK AND LATIN WORD ELEMENTS

Prefixes			Examples
Number			
amphi	(Gr.)	both	amphibian, amphitheater
mono*	(Gr.)	one	monorail, monarch

Prefixes   *Examples*

uni*	(Gr.)	one	uniform, unicycle
bi*	(L.)	two, twice	bicycle, bimonthly
di	(G.)	two	dioxide, diphthong
tri*	(L.)	three	triangle, tripod
quad	(L.)	four	quadruped, quarter
quin	(L.)	five	quintet, quintuplets
penta	(L.)	five	pentagon, pentangle
sex	(L.)	six	sextet, sextant
hexa	(L.)	six	hexagon
sept	(L.)	seven	September
octa	(L.)	eight	octopus, October
nov	(L.)	nine	November
non	(L.)		nonagon
dec	(L.)	ten	decade, December
poly	(L.)	many	polygon, polysyllabic
semi*	(L.)	half	semicircle, semiannual
milli	(L.)	1/1000	millisecond, millimeter
multi*	(L.)	many	multicolored, multiply

Opposite

dis*	(L.)	opposite	disconnect, discomfort
im*	(L.)	not	immovable, impartial
in*			incorrect, inactive
il			illegible, illiterate
ir			irregular, irreplaceable
ob	(L.)	against	obstruct, objection
un*	(L.)	not	undone, unsure

Place in Time or Space

ante	(L.)	before	antedate, antecedent
com*	(L.)	together, with	compose

Prefixes			Examples
col*			collaborate
cor*			correspond
e*	(L.)	out	eject, erupt
ex*			extract, excerpt
exo			exoskeleton, exoderm
extra	(L.)	outside, beyond	extraordinary, extracurricular
inter*	(L.)	between, among	international, interrupt
intra	(L.)	within	intrastate, intramural
intro	(L.)		introspect, introvert
mid*	(L.)	middle	midway, midwestern
para*	(G.)	beside	paragraph, parasite
per*	(L.)	through	permanent, perpetual
peri*	(G.)	around, near	perimeter, periscope
post	(L.)	after	postgame, postscript
pre*	(L.)	before	prewar, predict
pro*	(L.)	in front	program, prologue
sub*	(L.)	under, below	submarine, subtract
super*	(L.)	over, above	supernatural, supersede
syn	(G.)	together, with	synonym, synchrony
syl			syllable, syllabus
sym			symphony, sympathy
trans*	(L.)	across, over	transcontinental, transfer
Size			
macro	(G.)	large	macroscopic, macrocosm
micro*	(G.)	small	microscope, microphone
Other			
de	(L.)	down, away	depopulate, detract
dis*	(L.)	apart from	dismiss, dislocate
hyper*	(G.)	over, beyond	hyperactive, hypersensitive

Prefixes			*Examples*
hypo*	(G.)	under, too little	hypodermic, hypoactive
im*	(L.)	in, into	immigrate, implant
in*			intake, incision
il*			illuminate, illustrate
mal	(L.)	bad	malpractice, malady
mis*	(OE)	bad	misbehave, mistake
pro*	(L.)	in favor of	pro-American, proslavery, pro-civil rights
pro*		forward	progress, project
proto	(G.)	first	prototype
pseudo	(G.)	false	pseudonym, pseudoscience
re*	(L.)	again	reread, readmit
re*		back	retract, refund
retro	(L.)	back	retrorocket, retrospection

*Suffixes**		*Examples*
able, ible	can be done, inclined to	workable, credible, peaceable, terrible
ance, ence	state of	tolerance, confidence
ation	process, action, state of, result of	consideration, decoration, occupation
en	made of, to make	soften, wooden
er, or, ar	one who	runner, creator, vicar
ful	full, full of	hopeful, forgetful
hood	state, quality	falsehood
ic	of the nature of, characterized by	angelic, volcanic
ion	act, process, state of, characterized by	construction, revolution, ambition, suspicion
ish	having the qualities of	childish
ist	person who	geologist, pianist
less	without	hopeless, childless
ly	like	happily, forgetfully
ment	action or process, state of	development, government, puzzlement, amazement

*Suffixes**			*Examples*
ness	condition		kindness
ship	skill, condition		friendship
ward	towards		forward, leeward
y	full of		sandy

Roots			*Examples*
aqua	(L.)	water	aqueduct, aquarium
aud*	(L.)	hear	auditory, auditorium
bene	(L.)	good	benefit, benevolent
bio*	(G.)	life	biology, biography
cap	(L.)	head	capital, decapitate
cav	(L.)	hollow	cavern, excavate
ced	(L.)	go, yield	precede, concede
cess	(L.)	go, yield	process, incessant
chron(o)	(G.)	time	chronicle, chronometer
cide*	(L.)	kill	insecticide, homicide
circ*	(L.)	ring	circle, circular
cis*	(L.)	cut	incision, scissors
civ	(L.)	citizen	civic, civilization
cogn	(L.)	know	cognitive, recognize
crat	(G.)	rule	democrat, autocrat
cred*	(G.)	believe	incredible, discredit
demos	(G.)	people	democracy, epidemic
dent	(L.)	tooth	dentist, trident
dict*	(L.)	say	dictate, contradict
div	(L.)	separate	division, divorce
duce*	(L.)	lead	introduce, induce
duct*	(L.)		aqueduct, reduction
equ*	(L.)	equal	equality, equator

Roots			Examples
fac*	(L.)	to do, make	factory, facility
fect*	(L.)	to do, make	perfect, defect
flect	(L.)	bend	deflect, reflect
flex		bend	flexible, reflex
fract*	(L.)	break	fracture, infraction
fuse*	(L.)	pour	transfusion, diffuse
gene*	(L.)	birth	generation, progeny
gen	(L.)	of the same class	gentry, gentlemen
geo*	(G.)	earth	geometry, geology
gno	(G.)	know	diagnose, agnostic
gram	(G.)	written	grammar, telegram
graph*	(G.)	write	telegraph, autograph
gress*	(L.)	move	progress, aggression
hom	(G.)	man	homage, homicide
hydr	(G.)	water	dehydrate, hydrant
ject*	(L.)	throw	reject, projectile
junct	(L.)	join	conjunction, juncture
kilo	(G.)	one thousand	kilometer, kilowatt
lect*	(L.)	gather	collect, select
leg*	(L.)	law	legal, legislate
leg*	(L.)	read	legible, legend
liber	(L.)	free	liberate, liberty
liter	(L.)	letter	literature, literate
loc*	(L.)	place	locate, local
log	(L.)	speech	dialogue, prologue
lum	(L.)	light	illuminate, luminous
luna	(L.)	moon	lunar, lunatic
magni	(L.)	great	magnify, magnificent
mare	(L.)	sea	marine, maritime

Roots			*Examples*
mater	(L.)	mother	maternal, maternity
math	(L.)	learning	mathematics, polymath
matur	(L.)	ripe	maturity, immature
mis*	(L.)	send	mission, missile
mit	(L.)	send, allow	transmit, permit
medi*	(L.)	heal	medicine, remedial
mode*	(L.)	manner, measure	model, moderate, mode
mort	(L.)	death	mortal, mortuary
nat	(L.)	born	natural, native
neo	(G.)	new, modern	neoclassic, neophyte
opt	(G.)	sight	optical, optometrist
pater	(L.)	father	paternal, patriarch
ped*	(L.)	foot	pedal, pedestrian
pend*	(L.)	hang	pendulum, suspend
phon*	(G.)	sound	telephone, phonics
photo*	(G.)	light	photograph, photosynthesis
port*	(L.)	carry	transport, portable
polis	(G.)	city	metropolis, police
pos*	(L.)	place	position, preposition
press*	(L.)	force	pressure, oppression
rect*	(L.)	straight, right	correct, rectangle
sacr	(L.)	devote	sacrament, sacred
scope*	(G.)	watch	periscope, telescope
scrib*	(L.)	write	inscribe, describe
script*			scripture, manuscript
sist*	(L.)	stand	insist, persist
spect*	(L.)	look	inspector, spectacle
spire*	(L.)	breathe	respiration, expire
struc*	(L.)	build	construct, instruct

Roots			Examples
tain, ten*		hold	retain, contain, detention, tenacious
tele	(G.)	distant	telescope, television
terra	(L.)	earth	terrestrial, terrace
tract*	(L.)	pull	tractor, abstract
ven*	(L.)	come	tractor, abstract
vent	(L.)	wind	vent, ventilation
vert*	(L.)	turn	convert, invert
vid, vis*	(L.)	see	video, evidence, vision, visible
voc	(L.)	call	vocal, evocative
vol	(L.)	will	voluntary, volition

A very large number of English words came from Greek and Latin. Learning about those that came from the mythology of those cultures can be quite interesting and can introduce students to some important myths. The following are just a few of the mythological allusions underlying some of our contemporary vocabulary; many more can be explored through the references listed in Chapter 8, p. 302.

Arachnid: Arachnids are a class that includes spiders, a nice tie-in with science study. Arachne was a young woman who was a very skillful weaver. She was challenged by the goddess Athena to a weaving contest. As usually happened when mortals and immortals competed, Arachne lost the contest. In humiliation Arachne hanged herself, but Athena spared her life by turning her into a spider (arachnid), in which form her descendants to this day continue to weave.

Flora, fauna: Flora was the Roman goddess of flowers. Today we can use *flora* to stand for all vegetation, and we also use *flora* more specifically in the word *floral*. In Greek mythology her name was *Chloris*, the root of the Greek form for "green"; she lives on today in the derivations of the *chlor* stem, as in *chlorophyll*.

Faunus: Faunus was the Roman equivalent of Pan, patron of shepherds and their flocks — thus the guardian of *all* animals. The *fauns*, derived from *faunus*, were woodland creatures, half man and half goat. The Greek Pan could also be unpredictable and sometimes downright mean; it's no coincidence that our words *panic* and *pandemonium* are derived from *Pan*. He could also be vengeful. In one version of a popular myth, he was so enraged with a nymph who spurned his advances that he sent a group of shepherds into a *panic*. They tore the nymph to pieces until nothing remained but her voice — her name was *Echo*. (See Isaac Asimov's *Words from the Myths* (1961) for other engaging word stories.)

The Role of the Dictionary in Exploring Word History

Dictionaries are the primary and most readily available source of etymological information. Increasingly, publishers print dictionaries for the intermediate grades that include etymological information, usually in a simplified format. Such a format clearly presents the basics of a word's history but does not include the various forms the word has taken — including Indo-European, Greek, and Latin origins. Usually only derivations for selected words are given. Still, elementary dictionaries provide a lot of historical information that was until recently excluded in dictionaries intended for this level. Many also present an engaging, informative essay on language in general and English in particular in the front matter.

Nevertheless, intermediate students should also be shown how and encouraged to use "adult" dictionaries. The major publishers' "collegiate" editions are excellent, but if you can provide an unabridged dictionary, you will really encourage word exploration. For most entries these dictionaries will include information about etymology and pronunciation and, whenever applicable, give a word's Indo-European root.

When your intermediate students are ready, present a lesson on how to interpret etymological information. Begin by "walking through" a few entries, talking about the information you are deriving. Choose interesting words for starters and prime the students with a question like "Did you know that left-handed people were once considered unlucky, even *sinister*?" Follow this up with the etymological information written on the board or prepared on a transparency.

For example, the *American Heritage Dictionary* (Third College Edition) gives the following for *sinister*:

> [ME *sinistre*, unfavorable, < OFr. < Lat. *sinister*, on the left, unlucky]

While pointing to the appropriate symbol or word, talk through the entry in this fashion: "This informs us that—in Middle English—the word *sinister* was *sinistre*, which was what the word was in Old French as well. This word in Old French came from the original word in Latin, which was *sinister*." After such a holistic presentation, you can then explain the specific abbreviations, such as those for the different languages, and what the "<" symbol means.

VI. Grammar: Our Vocabulary for Thinking and Talking about Language

Grammar refers to the study or analysis of the structure of a language—of how the words and phrases work and are organized into sentences. Grammar and its vocabulary provide the *tools* for talking and thinking about language. Grammatical knowledge helps students when they think about the *pragmatics* of language—when they use a particular type of speech or writing, and why.

Parts of speech, how they work in sentences, and simple sentence structure are the main types of grammatical concepts that are addressed in the elementary grades. Because we are involving students in much reading and writing, there will be many opportunities for them to see examples of these concepts in real texts—texts that they read as well as ones that they write. In addition, we can pull from resources such as published programs if there are good examples there. In this section we'll look at how to introduce these concepts and at some activities for developing them.

Parts of Speech

The logical progression for introducing *parts of speech* usually follows a concrete-to-abstract continuum. The general sequence is

(1) proper nouns
(2) common nouns
(3) verbs
(4) adjectives
(5) pronouns
(6) articles or determiners
(7) adverbs
(8) prepositions
(9) conjunctions

The labels for parts of speech provide "handles" that make it easier to talk about words that writers use. When we first introduce parts of speech, we may want to use other more familiar labels, such as "naming words" for nouns, "action words" for verbs, and "describing" or "exact" words for adjectives. This way the conceptual domain is developed first, and then the terms that represent concepts are added.

Sentences

By paying attention to the parts of sentences and how they expand and combine, students learn important labels that they can use when responding to the styles of authors in their reading and to each other as they discuss their writing. The wide reading that students do provides the best models of varied sentence constructions. This is true both of the students' own reading as well as our read-alouds. Read-alouds "feed in" language and structure just beyond the point where the children are in their own natural development. The following is the developmental sequence for examining sentence structure:

◆ *Concept of a sentence* We can assess whether students have acquired a *concept of a sentence* by determining if students write according to basic convention and read a sentence with natural intonation. Not surprisingly, much of this understanding is tacit, but there is strong support for this underlying concept (deBeaugrande, 1985; Perfetti, 1985).

"Sentence boundaries often function as conceptual boundaries as well" (deBeaugrande, 1985, p. 67).

◆ Students consciously attend to the *order of words* in sentences.

◆ The basic *subject-predicate* (subject/verb) division: Students recognize specific *subjects* and *predicates* in simple sentences. The *subject-predicate* is, in fact, a "topic/comment" distinction—the subject is a "topic," and the predicate is a "comment" about that topic. In a sentence we highlight something (the subject) and say something about it (the predicate).

◆ Students expand specific *subjects* and *predicates* in simple sentences.

◆ Students create more complex sentences by means of their increasingly sophisticated language facility. They observe how words and phrases get attached to or embedded in simple sentences and eventually learn how to link sentences together with logical connectives. It is also during this period—in fifth and sixth grade, for most children—that the complexity of students' written sentences can exceed the complexity of their spoken sentences.

Matters of Usage

Usage refers to word choice, sentence structure, and appropriateness—what is preferred in the standard dialect of the language and/or is appropriate in a particular context (see Chapter 4). As students learn the "vocabulary" of grammar, they usually find matters of usage easier to discuss.

For example, if we are talking about when to use *bad* versus *badly*, it is much easier for us and for the students if we can illustrate our point using the terms *adjective* and *adverb*. Put simply, *bad* is an adjective that refers to the subject of the sentence: "Sherry feels *bad*" (meaning *Sherry* is "not well"). On the other hand, *badly* is an adverb that refers to the verb: "Sherry swims *badly*" (meaning Sherry's *swimming* is "not very

good"). By using the terms *adjective* and *adverb*, we can save a lot of time and confusion discussing usage because students will now think in terms of grammatical categories rather than trying to memorize specific examples or instances where *bad* and *badly* are used. In order to strengthen their understanding, we can have the students analyze what a particular sentence means when we use an adverb instead of an adjective, and vice versa: "I feel badly," for example, describes the way the subject "I" goes about feeling things!

All writers must refer to a usage guide at some point, usually to settle a question about how to best arrange language or select particular words according to common standards. It is important for students to realize that, although some usage elements are quite convenient to know automatically, others are considerably less vital. Consulting a usage guide is the best strategy for attending to infrequent usage questions. We should have several on hand in the classroom—to use, for example, when a student needs to check the correct use of *he/she* in a sentence he or she is writing.

Elements of usage that students need guidance in learning should be presented directly through minilessons and reinforced in the contexts of revising and editing their writing.

Teaching Strategies and Activities: Grammar

PARTS OF SPEECH

The following is a lesson for introducing and teaching a specific part of speech—*adverbs*—to a class of fourth-graders. The basic format and style of this lesson would work for many different grammar/usage lessons.

MINILESSON
Teaching Parts of Speech

Meeting with a small group, the teacher writes the words *quickly*, *yesterday*, and *someplace* on the board. He next asks the students to use each word in a sentence and then writes their sentences on the board. The students' sentences are

Tonya ate her lunch *quickly*.

I forgot my homework *yesterday*.

My homework is *someplace* at home in my messy room.

TEACHER: "Let's think about each of the words as they function in your sentences. Take *quickly*: it tells how something happened—in this case, how Tonya ate her lunch. *Yesterday* tells us when something happened—when the homework was forgotten. *Someplace* tells us where something happened—in this sentence, at home.

"Each of our underlined words, then, tells us something about the action in the sentence. What type of word or part of speech expresses *action*? [Students respond, "Verbs."] Good. So these underlined words tell us something about the verb—the action.

"Here's the main idea, then, kids: words that tell how, when, or where the action occurs are called *adverbs*. They 'go with' the verb, even though they may be separated from the verb by other words. They are still adverbs because they answer the question how, when, or where.

"Now, let's say you're working in a response group, and you're giving feedback to your partner. You notice that a couple of sentences are kind of flat—they've got good verbs, but something else is not quite right. Here are a couple of examples. [Puts a transparency of part of a composition on the overhead projector. Two sentences are in brackets, and the teacher directs the students' attention to the first of these.]

"Okay, let's check out this sentence: 'My stomach twisted hard at the sight of the climber dangling from the cliff.' Now, we'd probably all agree that this sentence is on its way to being quite a strong sentence—it's going to affect the reader. Think about the action now—the verb—and the word that tells you *how*, *when*, or *where* about the action. First, which word is the adverb here? [Students respond.] Good! 'Hard' tells us about the action. Does it tell us how the stom-

ach twisted, where it twisted, or when it twisted? [Students respond.] Sure, it tells us *how* it twisted. Is 'hard' the most powerful word here—or is there another adverb the writer could use? Tracey?"

TRACEY: "Well, maybe *violently* would work here?"

TEACHER: "Good! Are there any others? Mike?"

MIKE: "How about *squeamishly*?"

TEACHER: "Group? What do you think? Do you think *squeamishly* would work? Okay! I think you've gotten the idea." [Proceeds with next sentence in the same fashion]

TEACHER: "Okay, kids, we've got a term we can use to talk about words in our reading and writing that tell us about the verb or action—that tell us how, when, and where the action occurred. If we need feedback about descriptions in our writing or need to *give* feedback, we can use the term 'adverb' instead of having to say the long way, 'the words that talk about the action'—or 'the words that give you a better picture of what's going on.' Do you see how much easier it is just to use the term 'adverb'? The same goes when we're impressed by an author's description of the action in our reading—we'll have a label to place on the words that we think describe the verb well."

If necessary, we can follow up with other examples of adverbs and then ask the students to look over a group of additional sentences, identify the adverb in each, and justify their decisions. Then they could search for examples of effective adverbs in trade books as well as in their own compositions. Students later get back together to share and discuss their adverbs and the sentences where they were located.

Using transparencies of students' compositions (as always, with their permission), discuss more "exciting" or "specific" adverbs. Not all adverbs should be replaced, of course; in fact, strong, well-used adverbs should be acknowledged and discussed at the outset.

Grammatical Games: Parts of Speech

We can reinforce awareness of and knowledge about *parts of speech* through a number of activities.

"SILLY SYNTAX"

In this activity, appropriate for intermediate students, sentences are constructed based on randomly selected words (Kohl, 1981; Moffett & Wagner, 1983). The activity also helps students elaborate their "sentence sense," an understanding of the potential of the sentence as language frame.

◆ Set up five piles of blank 3x5 cards. Each pile is marked by a card with one of the following labels on it:

article   adjective   noun   verb   adverb

◆ In the first pile, under the "article" card, place just two cards: *the* and *a*. Fill in the remaining piles by having students write down any adjectives, nouns, verbs, and so on that they can think of. There should be about twelve cards in each pile. (If there are four players, then each player would think up three adjectives, three nouns, and three verbs.) Students should not let others see what words they have written.

◆ Shuffle the cards and place them face down. Each student then takes a turn successively drawing a card from each pile and reading the resulting sentence. Kohl (1981) commented that "the interest is in the created sentence, not in some final outcome of the game" (p. 56). Students may be amused by the sentences that result and may wish to keep track of them.

◆ After students are familiar with the format, we can add an additional pile of conjunctions or *linking words* (*meanwhile*, *nevertheless*, *then*, and so forth), and the sentences can be linked together with delightful results. Kohl (1981) offers this example of such a sentence:

> The boring dictator spoke curiously,
>
> nevertheless, the slug attacked inconsiderately,
>
> while the energetic politician retreated warmly. (p. 56)

COMPOUND WORDS

Once students understand the concept of compound words (see Chapter 8), we may strengthen this understanding and reinforce the labels for parts of speech in an activity that *generates* compound words — some real, some nonsense, and some "possible" words that do not presently exist. This activity helps us teach parts of speech "through the back door."

◆ Label four columns with the following parts of speech: *pronouns* and *nouns*, *adjectives*, *adverbs* (and if appropriate, *prepositions*), and *verbs*. Brainstorm with the students to come up with words that fit each category. Here is a sample:

Pronouns/ Nouns	Adjectives	Adverbs/ Prepositions	Verbs
cat	hard	happily	swim
him	soft	quickly	run
goose	fluffy	in	yell
foot	pretty	softly	slip
fence	green	out	look

◆ Have students examine the columns to determine whether any existing compound words could be constructed from these lists. They will find that, based only on their brainstorming, some real words will usually result — for example, *lookout* and *run-in*.

◆ Ask the students to look for words that are close to existing compounds or that could be new compound words in their own right. These combinations will become exciting, instructive, and a bit crazy! Consider the following compounds generated by a group of fifth-graders: *hardfence*, *slip-in*, *greencat*, *yell-quickly*, *run-out*, *soft-swim*, *gooselook*, *catyell*, *catlook*, *catslip*, *footswim* — their list went on and on.

◆ A definition could be written for each word. Students may assemble a *Dictionary of Words that Almost Exist* — including each word's part of speech, and if appropriate, an illustration.

WORD SORTS

This is an excellent follow-up to word-building activities in which students combine word roots with affixes to make existing words and create new words (see page 297, Chapter 8).

Students sort words according to base word and type of suffix:

respect			respectable
reject	rejection		
contract	contraction	contractor	
import			importable
subtract	subtraction		
transgress		transgressor	
predict	prediction	predictor	predictable
retract	retraction	retractor	retractable

Discuss the *function* that each of the words in a particular column serves. For example, guide students to see that all of the words in the first column have to do with an *action* of some type. Ask, "What label or term do we give to words that show *action?*"

In the second column we can point out that all of the words have to do with the *result* of that action; when these words are placed in sentences, their function will be that of *nouns.*

In the third column each of the words has to do with the person or thing that performs the action: a *transgressor* is one who transgresses; a *retractor* is someone or something that retracts. These, too, are nouns. Discuss the few remaining words in the same way—in terms of their function—and then determine which parts of speech they are.

The final step in this type of word sort is to have the students come up with a generalization about the part of speech in each column based on the suffixes. For example, "If you have a base that ends with the suffix *-ion* (or *-or*, or *-able*), what part of speech is the word likely to be?"

GRAMMATICAL TERMS: WHAT'S IN A NAME?

Through this activity, students come to understand better the *meanings* of the terms for parts of speech. Analyzing the grammatical terms themselves can effectively overlap with our students' exploration of structural analysis. This activity is appropriate for intermediate students after they have been exploring affixes and word roots:

◆ *Pronoun* comprises a prefix, *pro*, plus the base, *noun*. Together they mean "standing in for (*pro*) the *noun*."

◆ *Adjective* is made up of *ad-* ("to" or "toward") plus the stem *-ject-* ("thrown"). An adjective is a word that is "thrown toward" (that "goes with") another word—specifically, a noun.

◆ *Adverb*, just like *adjective*, is a word that goes "to or toward" (that is, "goes with") the verb.

◆ A *preposition* is "positioned" *pre-* ("before") the phrase that it usually introduces.

◆ An *interjection* is "thrown" (*-ject*) "between" (*inter*) sentences.

Teaching about Sentences

SENTENCE EXPANSION

Sentence expansion is an excellent way to help primary children develop a basic concept of a sentence and become consciously aware of the potential of sentences. The object of this activity is to show students how to construct sentences by adding on ideas. After introducing the format with a small group, have the students work in pairs. They can start with a simple sentence and take turns adding on words. For example:

Susan likes okra.

In the summer Susan likes okra.

In the afternoon in the summer Susan likes okra with her family.

In the afternoon in the summer Susan likes okra and cornbread with her family and her friends.

UNDERSTANDING THE SUBJECT (NOUN PHRASE) AND PREDICATE (VERB PHRASE)

Developing the understanding of the complete subject involves simply talking about *how well* the complete subject is described. For example, instead of just saying "my dog," students may think about providing more information about the dog: What color is he? How big? Is he friendly? In a rich literature environment, such questions in response groups will eventually lead to expanded subjects such as "My big, brown dog" and "My friendly brown dog."

The expansion of complete predicates or verb phrases is similarly accomplished: Did your dog run quickly? Where did he run? Why? Many of your students may begin to expand both complete subjects and complete predicates at roughly the same time. This is great.

MANIPULATING PHRASES

Holding large pieces of tagboard with phrases written on them, students shift their phrases around in front of the class or a smaller group. The students can literally see how many ways the phrases can be combined; this exercise can develop a good sense of the *moveability* of phrases in English.

Start with no more than three phrases on separate pieces of tagboard, such as

through the gate   Brian rode   on his bike

In a subsequent exercise, supply more than three phrases, such as

behind the garage   before daylight   five cats

because they weren't friends   had a fight

Of course, there will be many possible combinations. Discuss them with students, focusing on why some are quite good, others not good at all, and still others somewhere in between. Discuss the different sense or meaning that different arrangements convey.

SENTENCE COMBINING

We can introduce sentence combining with short, simple sentences. We can choose them from the stu-

dents' writing or from fiction and informational texts, or construct them ourselves. If we do the latter, it's a good idea to use the students' names — this is always a powerful motivator.

In the following classroom example, the teacher discusses an author's descriptive language and works in a focus on sentence combining.

MINILESSON

Working with Sentences

A group of sixth-grade students has been reading Susan Cooper's fantasy, *Over Sea, Under Stone,* the first in a series of five fantasies centered in England and Wales. The fantasies become more believable and chilling because they arise out of everyday life in which evil is seen to lurk in ordinary places and people.

On this particular day, the follow-up questions the teacher has given the group for discussion focus on how Cooper manages to draw the reader or listener into the world of the book and feel the terror of true evil. Cooper is masterful at this, and the teacher's objective is to lead the students toward an awareness and appreciation of how Cooper uses language to describe sinister and evil entities and situations.

The students are asked to share the examples they have found; the teacher intends to question them further. The following are two passages from *Over Sea, Under Stone:*

And then, like the sudden snapping of a bow, the noise came.

Into the air over their heads, a dog howled: a long weird note so unexpected and anguished that for a moment they all stopped dead. It echoed slow through the harbour, a freezing inhuman wail that had in it all the warning and terror that ever was in the world. (p. 196)

The tall dark figure stopped abruptly, completely still, with its back still turned. For a moment there was absolute silence in the room. It was as if Barney had pressed a switch that would any moment bring an avalanche thundering down. He sat motionless and almost breathless in his chair.

Then very slowly the figure turned. Barney gulped, and felt a prickling at the roots of his hair. Mr. Hastings was at the darker end of the room, near the door, and his face was hidden in shadow. But he seemed to loom taller and more threatening than he had ever done before, and when he spoke there was a different throb in the deep voice that paralysed Barney with fright. "You will find, Barnabas Drew," it said softly, "that the dark will always come, and always win."

Barney said nothing. He felt as if he had forgotten how to speak, and his voice had died forever with his last words. (pp. 192–193)

The group next discusses Cooper's choice of particular words or expressions to achieve her effect, such as "freezing inhuman wail," "prickling at the roots of his hair," "throb in the deep voice," and "the dark will always come, and always win." The teacher observes that Cooper seems to "pack a lot" into her descriptions without going on and on.

TEACHER: "How does she manage to do that, Angela? Any ideas?"

ANGELA: "I think by the words she chooses, probably, just like we've been talking."

TEACHER: "Is it just the words themselves, do you think, or how she *combines* the words?"

ANGELA: "Hmm . . . they seem to fit together well . . ."

TEACHER: "How 'bout the rest of you guys? Let's think about her *sentences* . . . In these passages are they short, staccato-like, or longer?"

CLASS: "Longer!"

TEACHER: "Yeah . . . Let's look at the *ideas* she's expressing and see how she has combined them in these sentences. For example, let's take the sentence 'It echoed slow through the harbour, a freezing inhuman wail that had in it all the warning and terror that ever was in the world.' She really grabs you with that one, doesn't she? But there are a number of ways she could have expressed the idea, and she chose this way for maximum effect.

"First, think about her ideas: she's got this sound echoing through the harbor, it's echoing slowly, she

says it's freezing, it's inhuman, it is a wail, it has warning in it, terror in it, and that this warning and terror is as much as was ever in the world. Wow! Let's see . . . that's at least eight separate ideas. She *could* have written separate sentences like 'The sound was freezing. The sound was inhuman. It was a wail. It had all the warning and terror that was ever in the world.' Hmmm . . . is that as effective as the original? No? Why not?"

JUSTIN: "It kind of rolls along, the way she's got it . . . you kind of get this feeling all in one piece."

TEACHER: "That's a fascinating way to put it, Justin. I see by the other nodding heads we agree. She's *combined* or wrapped up some very effective words and phrases within *one* sentence that really grabs us.

"You know, when we think about having this kind of effect in our writing, we experiment with different *ways* of organizing the ideas. That's what we're getting at here—once we've selected the words that we want to represent our ideas, we still need to think about how to combine them to best express what we mean.

"We don't have to figure all this out all at once, of course. In our first draft we just get it down, and later we can play with fine-tuning our word choice and setting up our sentences. I'd be surprised if Susan Cooper wrote these passages just this way the first time!"

Because everyone is an "author" in the classroom, we can capitalize on particularly effective sentences that the students craft themselves by examining and discussing them. We can also take particular sentences from the reading students are doing and discuss their structure. This can include breaking the sentences down into their simpler parts, an exercise which can impress students with the number of ideas that can be expressed in a single sentence.

Mechanics: Punctuation and Capitalization

As with parts of sentences and parts of speech, introducing the elements of capitalization and punctuation follows a concrete-to-abstract sequence. The following minilesson and follow-up illustrate this sequence. In it, a *comma* is successfully introduced in the familiar context of a *letter* where the function of the comma for separating items in a series can be explored.

MINILESSON
Aspects of Punctuation

◆ The teacher introduces the "friendly letter" form, which includes the return address at the top, the greeting, body, and closing. Because most of the students in the class are reading *Sarah, Plain and Tall*, by Patricia MacLachlan (1985), as a part of a thematic unit on the Westward Movement, the teacher takes advantage of the many examples of the friendly letter form in Sarah's letters to the different members of the Witting family. The teacher points out the role of the comma after the greeting and after the closing (before the signature).

◆ After the minilesson, the students write their first drafts of a letter to their grandparents, asking about what it was like when they were children.

◆ In discussions of the first drafts, the teacher notes that many children need to use the comma to separate a series of items — a common instructional objective in third grade. She selects a draft from a student who has used the comma correctly this way, makes a transparency of it, and discusses the use of the comma in a whole-class format. She then pairs up students to work on this matter; one member has the concept; the other doesn't. The teacher will rely on this "peer-teaching" context to teach the concept. (Of course, if the teacher feels the whole-class presentation isn't absolutely necessary, it may be skipped.)

◆ A general strategy for helping students notice and then use simple punctuation is to read sentences orally the way a student has or has not punctuated them (a long sentence without commas becomes a humorous run-on that ends with a gasping teacher . . .). We follow this lesson up, though, by walking through the composition again, punctuating it as we go. For example, when we get to a point where a comma is required, we pause in our reading, write the comma, and continue. This procedure is so natural that, over time, it is relatively easy for the students to internalize it as a strategy.

Quick-Reference Guide
for Teachers and Students

Capitalization and Punctuation Guide

ABBREVIATIONS

Abbreviations are shortened forms of words. Most abbreviations begin with a capital letter and end with a period.

Titles

Mr. (*Mister*) Mr. Juan Albano
Mrs. (*Mistress*) Mrs. Frances Wong
Ms. Susan Clark

Sr. (*Senior*) John Helt, Sr.
Jr. (*Junior*) John Helt, Jr.
Dr. (*Doctor*) Dr. Janice Dodd

Note: *Miss* is not an abbreviation and does not end with a period.

Words Used in Addresses

St. (*Street*)
Rd. (*Road*)
Ave. (*Avenue*)

Dr. (*Drive*)
Rte. (*Route*)
Apt. (*Apartment*)

Pkwy. (*Parkway*)
Mt. (*Mount* or *Mountain*)
Expy. (*Expressway*)

Words Used in Business

Co. (*Company*)

Corp. (*Corporation*)

Inc. (*Incorporated*)

Other Abbreviations

Some abbreviations are written in all capital letters, with a letter standing for each important word.

P.D. (*Police Department*)
J.P. (*Justice of the Peace*)

P.O. (*Post Office*)
R.N. (*Registered Nurse*)

Some abbreviations do not have capital letters or periods.

mph (*miles per hour*)   hp (*horsepower*)   km (*kilometer*)

Abbreviations of government agencies or national organizations usually do not have periods.

NPR (*National Public Radio*)
FBI (*Federal Bureau of Investigation*)

(Continued)   **Capitalization and Punctuation Guide**

Other Abbreviations   The United States Postal Service uses two capital letters and no period in each of its state abbreviations.

AL (*Alabama*)	LA (*Louisiana*)	OH (*Ohio*)
AK (*Alaska*)	ME (*Maine*)	OK (*Oklahoma*)
AZ (*Arizona*)	MD (*Maryland*)	OR (*Oregon*)
AR (*Arkansas*)	MA (*Massachusetts*)	PA (*Pennsylvania*)
CA (*California*)	MI (*Michigan*)	RI (*Rhode Island*)
CO (*Colorado*)	MN (*Minnesota*)	SC (*South Carolina*)
CT (*Connecticut*)	MS (*Mississippi*)	SD (*South Dakota*)
DE (*Delaware*)	MO (*Missouri*)	TN (*Tennessee*)
FL (*Florida*)	MT (*Montana*)	TX (*Texas*)
GA (*Georgia*)	NE (*Nebraska*)	UT (*Utah*)
HI (*Hawaii*)	NV (*Nevada*)	VT (*Vermont*)
ID (*Idaho*)	NH (*New Hampshire*)	VA (*Virginia*)
IL (*Illinois*)	NJ (*New Jersey*)	WA (*Washington*)
IN (*Indiana*)	NM (*New Mexico*)	WV (*West Virginia*)
IA (*Iowa*)	NY (*New York*)	WI (*Wisconsin*)
KS (*Kansas*)	NC (*North Carolina*)	WY (*Wyoming*)
KY (*Kentucky*)	ND (*North Dakota*)	

TITLES

Underlining   Titles of books, magazines, newspapers, and movies are underlined.

<u>Oliver Twist</u> (*book*)   <u>Springfield Herald</u> (*newspaper*)
<u>Cricket</u> (*magazine*)   <u>The Black Stallion</u> (*movie*)

Quotation Marks   Titles of short stories, articles, songs, book chapters, and most poems are enclosed in quotation marks.

"The Necklace" (*short story*)   "Home on the Range" (*song*)
"Three Days in the Sahara" (*article*)   "Wind Song" (*poem*)

QUOTATIONS

Quotation Marks with Commas and Periods

Quotation marks are used to set off a speaker's exact words. The first word of a quotation begins with a capital letter. Punctuation belongs *inside* the closing quotation marks. Commas separate a quotation from the rest of the sentence.

"Where," asked the visitor, "is the post office?"
"Please put away your books now," said Mr. Emory.
Mary said, "Let's eat lunch."

(Continued)	**Capitalization and Punctuation Guide**

CAPITALIZATION

Rules for Capitalization	Capitalize the first word of every sentence.

What an unusual color the roses are!

Capitalize the pronoun *I*.

What should I do next?

Capitalize every important word in the names of particular people, places, or things (proper nouns).

Emily G. Hesse	District of Columbia	Lincoln Memorial

Capitalize titles or abbreviations used with a person's name.

Governor Bradford	Senator Smith	Dr. Lin

Capitalize proper adjectives.

We ate at a Chinese restaurant.   She is French.

Capitalize the names of months and days.

My birthday is on the last Monday in March.

Capitalize the names of buildings and companies.

The Empire State Building   The Bell Company

Capitalize the names of holidays.

Flag Day	Thanksgiving	Fourth of July

Capitalize the first and last words and all important words in the titles of books, newspapers, movies, and songs.

From Earth to the Moon
The New York Times
"The Rainbow Connection"
"Growing Up in the South"

Capitalize the first word in the greeting and the closing of a letter.

Dear Marcia,   Yours truly,

Capitalize the first word of each main topic and subtopic in an outline.

I. Types of libraries
  A. Large public library
  B. Bookmobile

(Continued)	**Capitalization and Punctuation Guide**

PUNCTUATION

End Marks

There are three end marks. A *period (.)* ends a declarative or imperative sentence. A *question mark (?)* follows an interrogative sentence. An *exclamation point (!)* follows an exclamatory sentence.

The scissors are on my desk. (*declarative*)
Look up the spelling of that word. (*imperative*)
How is the word spelled? (*interrogative*)
This is your best poem so far! (*exclamatory*)

Apostrophe

To form the possessive of a singular noun, add an apostrophe and *s*.

sister's	family's	Tess's	Jim Dodge's

For a plural noun that ends in *s*, add an apostrophe only.

sisters'	families'	Smiths'	Evanses'

For a plural noun that does not end in *s*, add an apostrophe and *s*.

women's	mice's	children's

Use an apostrophe in contractions in place of the dropped letters.

isn't (*is not*)	wasn't (*was not*)	I'm (*I am*)
can't (*cannot*)	we're (*we are*)	they've (*they have*)
won't (*will not*)	it's (*it is*)	they'll (*they will*)

Colon

Use a colon after the greeting in a business letter.

Dear Mrs. Trimby: Dear Realty Homes:

Comma

A comma tells the reader to pause between words. Use commas to separate words in a series. Use a comma before the conjunction that connects the items.

We bought apples, peaches, and grapes.

Use a comma to separate the simple sentences in a compound sentence.

Some students were at lunch, but others were studying.

Use commas to set off an appositive in most cases.

Vermont, the Green Mountain State, has lovely scenery.

Use commas after introductory words such as *yes, no, oh,* and *well*.

Well, it's just too cold out.   No, it isn't six yet.

(Continued)	**Capitalization and Punctuation Guide**

Use a comma to set off a noun in direct address.

Jean, help me fix this tire.   How was your trip, Grandpa?

Use a comma to separate the month and day from the year. Use a comma to separate the year from the rest of the sentence.

My sister was born on April 9, 1980, in Detroit.
July 4, 1776, is the birthday of our nation.

Use a comma between the names of a city and a state.

Chicago, Illinois   Miami, Florida

Use a comma after the greeting in a friendly letter.

Dear Deena,   Dear Uncle Rudolph,

Use a comma after the closing in a letter.

Your nephew,   Sincerely yours,

Use a comma after an interjection that begins a sentence.

Hey, I got the tickets.

Exclamation Point	Use an exclamation point after an interjection that stands alone.
	Wow! Did you see that?

ADJECTIVE AND ADVERB USAGE

Adjective or Adverb?	Use adjectives to describe nouns or pronouns. Use adverbs to describe verbs.
	Lena is a quick runner. *(adjective)* Lena runs quickly. *(adverb)*
Comparing	To compare two things or actions, add *-er* to adjectives and adverbs or use the word *more*.
	This plant is taller than the other one. It grew more quickly.
	To compare three or more things or actions, add *-est* or use the word *most*.
	This plant is the tallest of the three. It grew most quickly.
	Use *more* or *most* with an adjective or adverb that has two or more syllables, such as *careful* or *politely*. Do not add *-er* or *-est* to long adjectives or adverbs.
	agreeable — more agreeable — most agreeable slowly — more slowly — most slowly

(Continued)	**Capitalization and Punctuation Guide**
good, bad	The adjectives *good* and *bad* have special forms for making comparisons.

good — better — best   bad — worse — worst

NEGATIVES

A negative is a word that means "no" or "not." Do not use double negatives in a sentence.

INCORRECT: We didn't go nowhere.
  CORRECT: We didn't go anywhere.

PRONOUN USAGE

Agreement

A pronoun must agree with the noun to which it refers.

Kee bought a newspaper. Mary read it.
Jeff and Cindy came to dinner. They enjoyed the meal.

Double Subjects

Do not use a double subject — a noun and a pronoun — to name the same person, place, or thing.

INCORRECT: The food it was delicious.
  CORRECT: The food was delicious.

I, me

Use *I* as the subject of a sentence and after forms of be. Use *me* after action verbs or prepositions like *to*, *in*, and *for*. (See *Subject and object pronouns*.)

Jan and I are going to the show.
She is taking me.
Will you hold my ticket for me?

When using *I* or *me* with nouns or other pronouns, always name yourself last.

Beth and I will leave. Give the papers to Ron and me.

Possessive Pronouns

A possessive pronoun shows ownership. Use *my*, *your*, *his*, *its*, *our*, and *their* before nouns.
My report was about our trip to the zoo.

Use *mine*, *yours*, *his*, *hers*, *its*, *ours*, and *theirs* to replace nouns in a sentence.

Hers was about a visit to the museum.

Subject and Object Pronouns

Use subject pronouns as subjects and after forms of the verb *be*.

He composed many works for the piano.

(Continued)	**Capitalization and Punctuation Guide**
	I am <u>she</u>. The most talented singers are <u>we</u>. **Use object pronouns after action verbs and prepositions like *to* and *for*.** Clyde collected old coins and sold <u>them</u>. (*direct object*) Let's share these bananas with <u>her</u>. (*object of preposition*)
Compound Subjects, Compound Objects	To decide which pronoun to use in a compound subject or a compound object, leave out the other part of the compound. Say the sentence with the pronoun alone. Lu and _____ ride the bus. (*we, us*) <u>We</u> ride the bus. Lu and <u>we</u> ride the bus. I saw Dad and _____. (*he, him*) I saw <u>him</u>. I saw Dad and <u>him</u>. Mom sang to Amy and _____. (*she, her*) Mom sang to <u>her</u>. Mom sang to Amy and <u>her</u>.

We and Us with Nouns	**Use we with a noun that is a subject or that follows a linking verb.**
	
	INCORRECT: Us girls are the stagehands.
	   CORRECT: <u>We</u> girls are the stagehands.
	INCORRECT: The ushers are us boys.
	   CORRECT: The ushers are <u>we</u> boys.
	
	Use *us* with a noun that follows an action verb or that follows a preposition such as *to*, *for*, *with*, or *at*.
	
	INCORRECT: Dr. Lin helped we players.
	   CORRECT: Dr. Lin helped <u>us</u> players.
	INCORRECT: She talked to we beginners.
	   CORRECT: She talked to <u>us</u> beginners.

VERB USAGE	
Agreement: Subject-Verb	A present tense verb and its subject must agree in number. Add *s* or *es* to the verb if the subject is singular. Do not add *s* or *es* to the verb if the subject is plural or if the subject is *I*.

(Continued)	**Capitalization and Punctuation Guide**

The road bends to the right.

Mr. Langelier teaches fifth graders.

These books seem heavy.

I like camping.

Change the forms of *be* and *have* to make them agree with their subjects.

He is taking the bus today. Have you seen Jimmy?

They are going swimming. Mary has a large garden.

Agreement:
Compound Subjects

A compound subject with *and* takes a plural verb.

Jason, Kelly, and Wanda have new dictionaries.

Could Have, Should Have

Use *could have, would have, should have, might have, must have*. Avoid using *of* with *could, would, should, might,* or *must*.

She could have (*not* could of) spoken louder.

Juan would have (*not* would of) liked this movie.

We should have (*not* should of) turned left.

I might have (*not* might of) left my wallet on my desk.

It must have (*not* must of) rained last night.

Irregular Verbs

Irregular verbs do not add *-ed* or *-d* to form the past tense. Because irregular verbs do not follow a regular pattern, you must memorize their spellings. Use *has, have,* or *had* as a helping verb with the past tense.

Verb	Past	Past with Helping Verb
be	was	been
begin	began	begun
blow	blew	blown
break	broke	broken
bring	brought	brought
choose	chose	chosen
come	came	come
fly	flew	flown
freeze	froze	frozen
go	went	gone
grow	grew	grown
have	had	had
know	knew	known
make	made	made

Capitalization and Punctuation Guide

ring	rang	rung
run	ran	run
say	said	said
sing	sang	sung
speak	spoke	spoken
steal	stole	stolen
swim	swam	swum
take	took	taken
tear	tore	torn
think	thought	thought
wear	wore	worn
write	wrote	written

VII. Learning and Teaching Study Skills

There are a few basic study skills we should provide for our intermediate students. These will not only support their inquiry at the intermediate level but will also give them a solid foundation of inquiry skills for the middle grades and beyond.

Notetaking

The following steps help students develop an understanding of the why's and how's of notetaking (Templeton, 1995):

1. Read aloud a chapter from an informational trade book. Afterward, ask the class what they remember from the text and make a list of their responses.

2. Over the next few days, read another chapter from the book. Then have the students write those facts that they recall in their journals. Students may also write questions they have about the topic—what are they curious about? These daily entries will lead to other reading and discussion topics.

3. Students later take notes from their own independent reading. They choose an informational book that they believe will provide information about the topic they want to investigate. Based on the title and cover illustration, they list questions they think the book might answer. They then read for several minutes. Afterward, without looking at the book, they can write any answers they've found. It usually takes several such sessions for students to become confident in their ability to write important information

in their own words. This procedure helps students avoid falling into the "copying" mode.

NOTETAKING BASED ON INDEPENDENT READING

When students understand the structure of informational texts and the relationship between main ideas and subordinate ideas, we can model this process:

From a well-structured textbook or informational trade book, copy the first page of a chapter on the left-hand side of a transparency and leave the right-hand side blank. At an overhead projector, "think aloud" while reading the passage out loud, underlining important information and phrases. On the blank right-hand side of the transparency, make notes based on that information.

Outlining

Outlining can be a valuable study technique if introduced and used as one of several options for study reading. The following are the purposes of outlining:

1. Reinforces students' learning of expository text structure.

2. Helps students organize and understand the relationship among information in expository texts.

3. Helps in studying and retaining important information.

4. Helps establish good notetaking skills for lectures, a mode of information presentation used sparingly in

the upper-elementary grades but extensively beginning in the middle grades. All too often, middle-grade teachers assume students know how to outline while listening to a lecture—thus, outlining winds up seldom being taught appropriately at *any* level.

When and how should we teach outlining? Some fourth-grade students and most fifth- and sixth-graders are definitely ready for outlining—after they have been reading expository material for quite some time and after they are comfortable using the Guided Reading-Thinking Activity (GRTA). By this time they should be familiar with graphic aids to reading and writing, such as webs or clusters, and with graphic post-organizers.

MINILESSON
Outlining during Reading and while Listening

◆ Show students a visual schematic that clearly represents the levels and relationships among the main ideas. Figure R.2 shows such a visual schematic for a chapter in a fifth-grade science text. This schematic would be displayed on a transparency. Where and why each level occurs where it does is explained: "Life Forms of Earth," at the top, is the main idea, with other important supporting ideas or concepts one level down. Specific examples of each

subdivision are at the next level, and so forth. This schematic shows relationships among the topic, supporting main ideas, and other elements, rather than simply presently a collection of facts arranged one after another.

◆ Walk students through the chapter, constructing the outline as you proceed. Explain how the outline represents the main ideas, supporting ideas, and details within each level. Main ideas are the section headings and are designated by Roman numerals; supporting ideas and details are represented by capital letters and arabic numerals, respectively. Next, expand students' understanding of the hierarchical concept of main idea/supporting ideas/details.

An excellent extension of outlining is to use it as a notetaking strategy while listening to a lecture—a particularly important point in sixth grade, given that students are soon to enter the middle grades:

◆ Begin by listing your major points, in Roman numerals, on the chalkboard. Then deliver a brief lecture, following these points as you talk, and have the students fill in the rest of the information at each point of the outline. Afterward, students can compare and discuss their outlines with a partner or a small group. You can conclude by showing the students *your* outline on a transparency so that they can see how closely they approximated it as they listened.

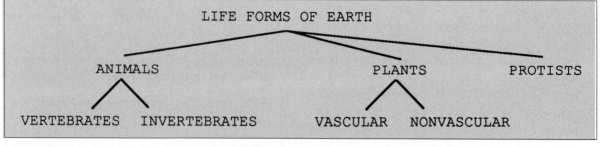

 Figure R.2   Visual Schematic for a Chapter in a Science Text

VIII. Learning and Teaching Handwriting

The need for writing in a legible script is no less important in an age of word processors. We still need to ensure that children will learn to write legibly and comfortably by hand. Although it is important to teach handwriting directly to most students, it is not necessary to spend a lot of time on it; we should spend more time allowing students opportunities to *apply* what they are learning about handwriting. We now are more realistic than teachers of the past since we aim primarily for a consistent, legible style.

At all levels we can follow these same general guidelines for teaching handwriting:

◆ Be consistent.

◆ Be good models when using our own handwriting. If not confident of our own ability, we can practice the forms presented here or go through exercises in a handwriting book.

◆ Clearly display the model of the style we are teaching. Most teachers put these models above the chalkboard or at least at about that height in the classroom. An additional aid for primary students is to have a model taped to their desk or table.

◆ Emphasize *real* writing tasks.

Students save their best handwriting for the final copying of a composition for publication. This does not mean, however, that messy and illegible handwriting during drafting is acceptable. Others will have difficulty reading the draft, so they'll also have difficulty responding to the content of what the student has written. If legible handwriting is "automated," then it can be hurried during the drafting phase and still be read by others. Legibility is always the objective, but in final editing and copying tasks, students should do their very best.

Students first learn *manuscript* writing—more commonly referred to as "printing"—and then they learn *cursive*.

Handwriting Styles

There are a number of handwriting styles, some of which are illustrated in Figure R.3 and Figure R.4. As is apparent, most of the variation among styles is within cursive script.

It makes good sense to teach manuscript before cursive. First of all, manuscript letters look more like letters in books. Second, the letters are easier to write given the children's small-muscle dexterity; cursive is more demanding. Third, when children learn about the shape and composition of manuscript letters in handwriting instruction, this knowledge should strongly support word knowledge through the bonding of print to sound and meaning.

Teaching Manuscript and Cursive Writing

For most children, instruction in manuscript writing begins in first grade. The following are guidelines for

Figure R.3

The D'Nealian Model of Handwriting

SOURCE: Scott, Foresman and Company, Glenview, IL. Reproduced by permission.

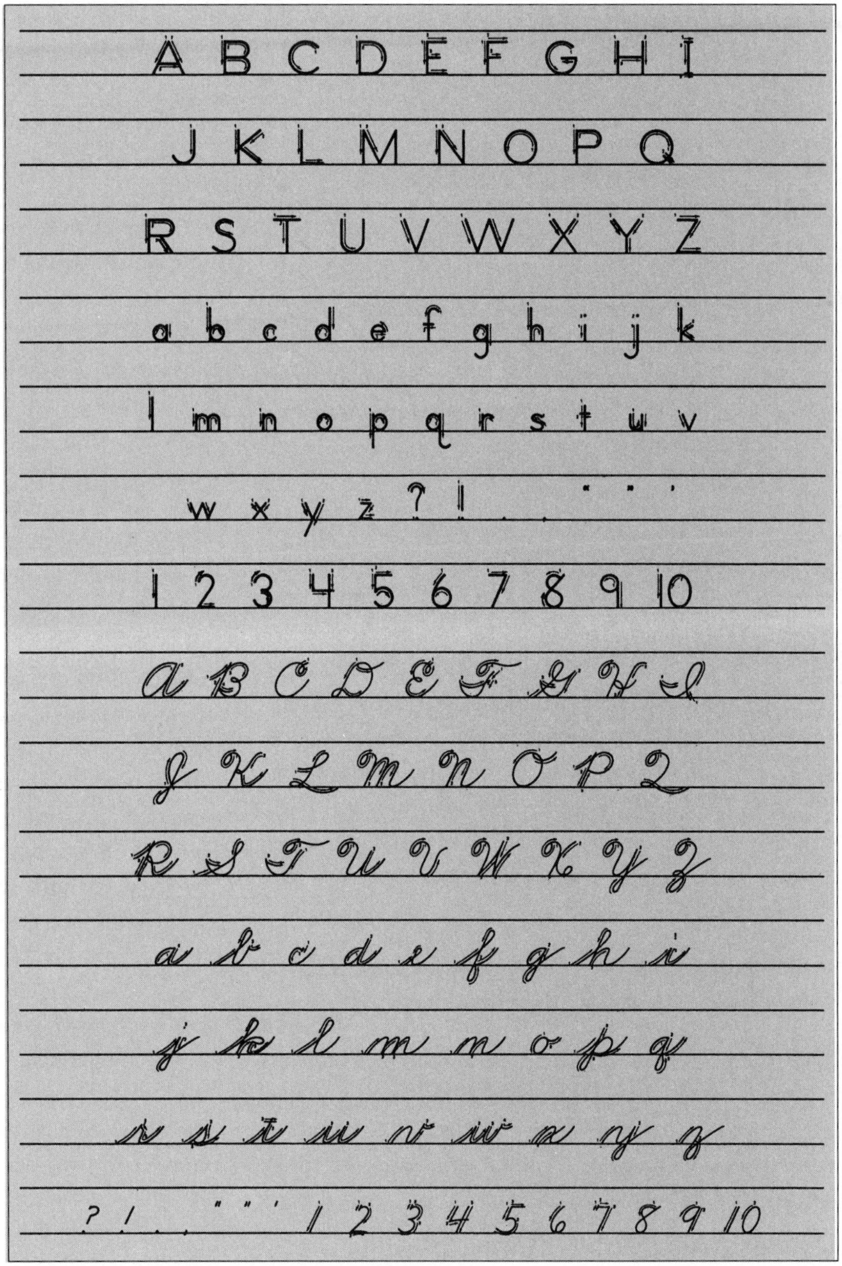

Figure R.4

The Zaner-Bloser Model of Handwriting

SOURCE: Used by permission of the publisher, Zaner-Bloser, Inc., 1459 King Ave., Columbus, OH 43212.

determining when we can teach handwriting more directly to young children:

◆ *"Play writing" must be clearly developed.*

This criterion is the single best indicator that a child is ready to benefit from direct teaching in handwriting (Nathan, Temple, Juntunen, and Temple, 1989). We'll be able to determine this early in the school year through observations of the children's writing and drawing. Are identifiable letters recombined and arranged in a linear fashion across an unlined sheet of paper? If so, the child is ready for some direct teaching.

◆ *Hand dominance must be established.*

By first grade most children have clearly established a preference for their right or left hand. A very few children are still as likely to use one hand as the other. We can offer these children objects so that they are likely to grasp them with their right hands (it is, after all, a right-handed world, and if they can learn to use their right hand more often, matters will be easier in the long run). On the other hand, one should never attempt to change a left-hander; although they will have to learn to cope with the right-handed world, they will be able to do so with fewer problems than if we try to change them.

◆ *Children must be able to use crayons, brushes, scissors, and pencils in a number of different tasks.*

These implements all require small-muscle dexterity, and a good way to see how well these small muscles can operate is to observe a child using these implements for several tasks. If the child is awkward, then we hold off on formal instruction, although we should continue to involve him or her in a wide range of small- and large-muscle tasks. These may include activities that are letter-oriented, such as drawing on the chalkboard and making different shapes with clay, in sand, or in shaving cream. As with all skill development, cognitive as well as motor, the more experience a child has with implements such as paintbrushes, scissors, and crayons, the less he or she will need to attend directly to the task, trying to think about several things at once. Once they have automated these composite movements, the children can benefit from our direct teaching.

◆ *Children should be able to copy simple shapes.*

This, of course, is a more challenging task than generating shapes of one's own. If children seem to have a fair amount of difficulty copying, then certainly hold off on the handwriting instruction. This ability will develop more readily and less painfully if students are given few copying tasks and more opportunity to develop the small muscles further.

When children are ready according to these criteria, we can usually move directly to systematic teaching of handwriting. Furthermore, we do not need to use the large "primary pencils" so popular in first grade. Most children can use good old Number 2 pencils, just like the rest of us—just as long as we do not sharpen them to a fine point.

For both manuscript and cursive handwriting, the pencil or pen should be held in a way that is comfortable. Encourage both right- and left-handers from the beginning to hold the pencil between the forefinger and index finger, supported by the thumb, which rests naturally and firmly against the pencil. For many children this position will be quite different from their usual grip, in which all but the little finger are pressed against the pencil. Although this position gives the "feel" of firmness, it can cause fatigue.

Figure R.5 illustrates how the paper should be positioned for right-handers and for left-handers. Note that these positions prevent the writer's hand from covering the line during the writing. Left-handers, by the way, will likely constitute from five to ten percent of our classrooms. If you are right-handed, invite a left-hander to model letter formation for your students; this could be another teacher or, more often, an older student. If the left-hander's paper is positioned as in Figure R.5 and if the end of the pencil or pen is aimed

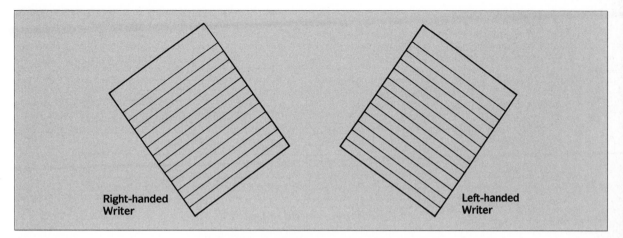

Figure R.5   Positioning the Paper for Right- and Left-handed Children

at the student's left shoulder, then the writing will be comfortable, and neither the line on which the child is writing nor any previous line will be obscured.

Prior to instruction, draw lines on the board or on a transparency that resemble the lines on the children's paper. For a manuscript, the 8½ × 11-inch paper with the line design shown in Figure R.6 is appropriate. For cursive writing, the same design, though smaller, will be fine. Here is the suggested sequence for directly teaching handwriting:

1. *Modeling and guided observation* Draw the letter you are introducing and talk about how and what you are doing so your students will know what to try. Refer to where you begin, where you stop, the number of strokes involved, and how large you are making each line, circle, or semicircle.

2. *Application and verbalization* The students follow your guide, talking through the process of forming the letter, just as you did in the first step.

3. *Comparison with the model* After students complete the letter, they should compare what they did with your model. As necessary, repeat the first step.

For *manuscript* writing, organize the sequence of let-

ters to introduce according to shared features: for example, "circle letters," "straight-line letters (*l*)," "point letters (*v, w*)," "tail letters (*j, g, y*)," and "hump letters (*m, n*)." (Most handwriting programs are organized this way.) Similarly, for *cursive* writing, group letters that share similar features: *m* and *n*, *y* and *g*, *a* and *c*, and so on.

Make the rationale for spending time with handwriting explicit to the students. In addition to the more obvious purpose of helping others read what we've written, we will need to know how to write effectively by hand. In the intermediate grades and beyond, the students will be taking notes during presentations and as they read. Also, there will be times when a handwritten note or letter is more fitting than a word-processed one, and when a letter is more appropriate than a quick phone call. Students who insist that a word processor is all they need should be reminded of these other writing situations.

Just as you do with other aspects of revision and editing, put compositions on transparencies so that you can discuss features of the handwriting with the whole class. If you want to examine poorer handwriting, choose your examples from writing by students in previous years — not by current students.

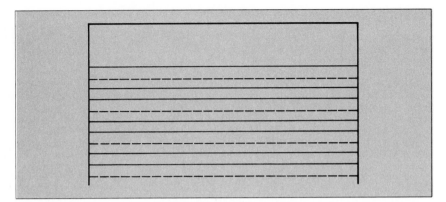

Figure R.6   Lined Paper for Handwriting Lessons

Assessing Handwriting

In teaching and assessing handwriting, Barbe and others (1984) suggest that you focus on the following "six elements of legibility":

Letter formation How the letters are formed. Definite strokes are made in a certain order, and the direction and order of the strokes reflects the easiest, least awkward manner of letter formation. In cursive writing the connecting strokes between letters are also highlighted.

Size and proportion When children first begin to write manuscript, the size of their letters is comparatively large, and upper-case letters are twice as large as lower-case. When the transition to cursive occurs, this proportion remains the same. With time, though, the lower-case letters will become even smaller and the proportion between upper- and lower-case letters will be three to one.

Spacing refers to both the spaces between letters (in manuscript) and those between words. In manuscript there should be approximately one letter space between words and two between sentences. The spacing within words in cursive should obviously not be too "stretched" or "bunched"; the criterion is consistent spacing.

Slant should be consistent as well — vertical for manuscript and slanted to the right for cursive. Ideally,

both right- and left-handed students' cursive writing should slant slightly to the right.

Alignment simply means that the letters should sit on the line and that all upper-case letters are the same size and all lower-case letters are also the same size.

Line quality is the consistent quality of the thickness, darkness, and direction of the lines. Students should move their pencils or pens in a manner that results in even, fluid, and uniform strokes.

When students assess their *own* handwriting, however, they should attend to the following elements:

1. Correct formation of letters

2. Letters neatly sitting on the baseline and touching either the midline or topline

3. Even spacing between letters and words

4. Correct slant of letters (or up-and-down for manuscript)

For students whose handwriting is consistently below acceptable standards, continue direct teaching but always bear in mind Shaughnessy's (1977) wise recommendation: "[the] answer to this is practice — writing and more writing, preferably in modes that encourage a flow of words (journals, free writing, notations or observations), until the pen seems a natural extension of the hand, and the hand of the mind itself" (p. 16).

References

Adams, M. (1990). *Beginning to read: Thinking and learning about print*. Cambridge, MA: MIT Press.

Anders, P., & Bos, C. (1986). Semantic feature analysis: An interactive strategy for vocabulary development and text comprehension. *Journal of Reading, 29,* 610–616.

Anderson, R., Hiebert, E., Scott, J., & Wilkinson, I. (1985). *Becoming a nation of readers*. Washington, DC: U.S. Department of Education.

Anderson, R., Osborn, J., & Wilson, P. (Eds.). (1984). *Reading education: Foundations for a literate America*. New York: Free Press.

Anglin, J. (1977). *Word, object, and conceptual development*. New York: Norton.

Armbruster, B., Anderson, T., & Ostertag, J. (1989). Teaching text structure to improve reading and writing. *Reading Teacher, 43,* 130–137.

Atwell, N. (1987). *In the middle*. Portsmouth, NH: Heinemann/Boynton-Cook.

Au, K. (1980). Participation structures in a reading lesson with Hawaiian children: Analysis of a culturally appropriate instructional event. *Anthropology and Education, 11,* 91–115.

Au, K. (1993). *Literacy instruction in multicultural settings*. Fort Worth, TX: Harcourt Brace.

Au, K., & Kawakami, A. (1985). Research currents: Talk story and learning to read. *Language Arts, 62,* 406–411.

Au, K., Scheu, J., Kawakami, A., & Herman, P. (1990). Assessment and accountability in a whole literacy curriculum. *Reading Teacher, 43,* 574–578.

Banks, J. (1993). *Multiethnic education: Theory and practice*. Needham Heights, MA: Allyn & Bacon.

Barnes, D. (1992). *From communication to curriculum* (2nd ed.). Portsmouth, NH: Boynton/Cook.

Barnitz, J. (1986). *Reading development of nonnative speakers of English*. Englewood Cliffs, N.J.: Prentice Hall.

Barone, D. (1992). "That reminds me of": Using dialogue journals with young students. In C. Temple & P. Collins (Eds.), *Stories and readers: New perspectives on literature in the elementary school*. Norwood, MA: Christopher-Gordon.

Barr, M., Ellis, S., Hester, H., & Thomas, A. (1988). *The primary language record*. Portsmouth, NH: Heinemann.

Baumann, J. F., & Kameenui, E. J. (1991). Research on vocabulary instruction: Ode to Voltaire. In J. Flood, J. M. Jensen, D. Lapp, & J. R. Squire (Eds.), *Handbook of research on teaching the English language arts* (pp. 604–632). New York: Macmillan.

Bear, D., & Invernizzi, M. (1987). Student-directed reading groups. *Journal of Reading, 28,* 248–252.

Bear, D., Invernizzi, M., & Templeton, S. (1996). *Words their way: Word study for phonics, vocabulary, and spelling instruction.* Englewood Cliffs, NJ: Prentice Hall.

Beck, I. (1984). Developing comprehension: The impact of the directed reading lesson. In R. C. Anderson, J. Osborn, & R. Tierney (Eds.), *Learning to read in American schools: Basal readers and content texts.* Hillsdale, NJ: Lawrence Erlbaum Associates.

Beck, I., & McKeown, M. G. (1991). Conditions of vocabulary acquisition. In R. Barr, M. L. Kamil, P. Mosenthal, & P. D. Pearson (Eds.), *Handbook of reading research* (Vol. 2, pp. 789–814). White Plains, NY: Longman.

Benedict, S., & Carlisle, L. (Eds.). (1992). *Beyond words: Picture books for older readers and writers.* Portsmouth, NH: Heinemann.

Bird, L. (1989). *Becoming a whole language school: The Fair Oaks story.* Katonah, NY: Richard C. Owen.

Bishop, R. (1994). *Kaleidoscope: A multicultural booklist for grades K–8.* Urbana, IL: National Council of Teachers of English.

Bleich, D. (1975). *Readings and feelings.* Urbana, IL: National Council of Teachers of English.

Bloomfield, L. (1933). *Language.* New York: Henry Holt.

Bos, C. S., & Vaughn, S. (1993). *Strategies for teaching students with learning and behavior problems* (3rd ed.). Needham Heights, MA: Allyn & Bacon.

Boyer, E. (1987). Early schooling and the nation's future. *Educational Leadership, 44*(6), 4–6.

Boyle, O., & Peregoy, S. (1990). Literacy scaffolds: Strategies for first and second-language readers and writers. *Reading Teacher, 44,* 194–200.

Bradley, L., & Bryant, P. (1985). *Rhyme and reason in reading and spelling.* Ann Arbor: University of Michigan Press.

Brown, R. (1973). *A first language.* Cambridge, MA: Harvard University Press.

Brown, R. (1977). Introduction. In C. Snow & C. Ferguson (Eds.), *Talking to children: Language input and acquisition.* New York: Cambridge University Press.

Bruer, J. (1994). *Schools for thought.* Cambridge, MA: MIT Press.

Brumbaugh, P. (1993). Human body: A third grade theme. In S. Walmsley, *Children exploring their world: Theme teaching in elementary school.* Portsmouth, NH: Heinemann.

Bruner, J. (1975). The ontogenesis of speech acts. *Journal of Child Language, 2,* 1–19.

Bruner, J. (1983). *Child's talk: Learning to use language.* New York: Norton.

Bruner, J. (1988). Life as narrative. *Social Research, 54,* 11–32.

Burrows, A., Ferebee, J., Jackson, D., & Saunders, D. (1939/1952). *They all want to write.* New York: Prentice Hall.

Busching, B. (1981). Readers theatre: An education for language and life. *Language Arts, 58,* 330–338.

Bussis, A., Chittenden, E., Amarel, M., & Klausner, E. (1985). *Inquiry into meaning: An investigation of learning to read*. Hillsdale, NJ: Lawrence Erlbaum Associates.

Calkins, L. (1983). *Lessons from a child*. Portsmouth, NH: Heinemann.

Calkins, L. (1991). *Between the lines*. Portsmouth, NH: Heinemann.

Calkins, L. (1994). *The art of teaching writing* (2nd ed.). Portsmouth, NH: Heinemann.

California State Department of Education. (1987). *English-Language arts framework*. Sacramento: Author.

Cambourne, B. (1984). Language, learning and literacy. In A. Butler & J. Turbill (Eds.). *Towards a reading-writing classroom* (pp. 5–10). Portsmouth, NH: Heinemann.

Cambourne, B. (1988). *The whole story: Natural learning and the acquisition of literacy in the classroom*. New York: Ashton-Scholastic.

Campbell, R., Kapinus, B., & Beatty, A. (1995). *Interviewing children about their literacy experiences*. Washington, DC: National Center for Education Statistics.

Campione, J. C., Gordon, A., Brown, A., Rutherford, M., & Walker, J. (1994). Now I'm a *real* boy: Zones of proximal development for those at risk. In N. Jordan & J. Goldsmith-Phillips (Eds.), *Learning disabilities: New directions for assessment and intervention* (pp. 245–274). Boston: Allyn & Bacon.

Carey, S. (1985). *Conceptual change in childhood*. Cambridge, MA: MIT Press.

Carlsen, J. (1985). Between the deaf child and reading: The language connection. *Reading Teacher, 38*(5), 424–426.

Cazden, C. (1988). *Classroom discourse: The language of teaching and learning*. Portsmouth, NH: Heinemann.

Chomsky, C. (1970). Reading, writing, and phonology. *Harvard Educational Review, 40*, 287–309.

Chomsky, C. (1972). Stages in language development and reading exposure. *Harvard Educational Review, 42*, 1–33.

Chomsky, N. (1965). *Aspects of the theory of syntax*. Cambridge, MA: MIT Press.

Chukovsky, K. (1971). *From two to five* (M. Morton, Ed. and Trans.). Berkeley: University of California Press. (Original work published 1925)

Clark, E. (1993). *The lexicon in acquisition*. New York: Cambridge University Press.

Clay, M. (1991). *Becoming literate: The construction of inner control*. Portsmouth, NH: Heinemann.

Clay, M. (1993). *An observation survey of early literacy achievement*. Portsmouth, NH: Heinemann.

Cohen, E. (1994). *Designing groupwork: The language of teaching and learning* (2nd ed.). New York: Teachers College Press.

Coles, R. (1989). *The call of stories*. Boston: Houghton Mifflin.

Collier, V. (1992). A synthesis of studies examining long-term language minority student data on academic achievement. *Bilingual Research Journal, 16*, 187–212.

Comer, J. (1987). New Haven's school community connection. *Educational Leadership, 44*, 13–16.

Cooper, J. D. (1997). *Literacy: Helping children construct meaning* (3rd ed.). Boston: Houghton Mifflin.

Corcoran, B. (Ed.). (1987). *Readers, texts, teachers.* Portsmouth, NH: Boynton/Cook.

Cordeiro, P. (1992). *Whole learning: Whole language and content in the upper elementary grades.* Katonah, NY: Richard C. Owen.

Cullinan, B. (1981). *Literature and the child.* Orlando, FL: Harcourt Brace.

Cunningham, P. (1995). *Phonics they use* (2nd ed.). New York: HarperCollins.

Dale, E., O'Rourke, J., & Bamman, H. (1971). *Techniques of teaching vocabulary.* Palo Alto, CA: Field Educational Enterprises.

Day, F. (1994). *Multicultural voices in contemporary literature: A resource for teachers.* Portsmouth, NH: Heinemann.

Delpit, L. (1988). The silent dialogue: Power and pedagogy in educating other people's children. *Harvard Educational Review, 58,* 280–298.

Dixon, C., & Nessel, D. (1983). *Language experience approach to reading (and writing).* Hayward, CA: Alemany Press.

Dyson, A. (1989a). *Multiple worlds of child writers: Friends learning to write.* New York: Teachers College Press.

Dyson, A. (1989b). Research currents: The space/time travels of story writers. *Language Arts, 66,* 330–340.

Dyson, A. (1991). The word and the world: Reconceptualizing written language. *Research in the Teaching of English, 25,* 97–123.

Dyson, A. (1993). *Social worlds of children learning to write in an urban primary school.* New York: Teachers College Press.

Edelsky, C. (1986). *Writing in a bilingual program: Habia una vez.* Norwood, NJ: Ablex.

Eeds, M., & Wells, D. (1989). Grand conversations: An exploration of meaning construction in literature study groups. *Research in the Teaching of English, 23*(1), 4–29.

Egan, K. (1987a). *Imagination and education.* New York: Teachers College Press.

Egan, K. (1987b). Literacy and the oral foundations of education. *Harvard Educational Review, 57,* 445–472.

Ehri, L. (1993). How English orthography influences phonological knowledge as children learn to read and spell. In R. Scholes (Ed.), *Literacy and language analysis* (pp. 21–43). Hillsdale, NJ: Lawrence Erlbaum Associates.

Ehri, L., & Wilce, L. (1987). Does learning to spell help beginners learn to read words? *Reading Research Quarterly, 22,* 47–65.

Eisner, E. (1991). *The enlightened eye: Qualitative inquiry and the enhancement of educational practice.* New York: Macmillan.

Elbow, P. (1981). *Writing with power.* New York: Oxford University Press.

Englert, C., Rozendal, M., & Mariage, M. (1994). Fostering the search for understanding: A teacher's strategies for leading cognitive development in "zones of proximal development." *Learning Disability Quarterly, 17,* 187–204.

Enright, S. (1986). Use everything you have to teach English: Providing useful input to young language learners. In P. Rigg & S. Enright (Eds.), *Children and ESL: In-*

tegrating perspectives (pp. 115–162). Washington, DC: Teachers of English to Speakers of Other Languages.

Enright, S., & McCloskey, M. (1988). *Integrating English*. Reading, MA: Addison-Wesley.

Erickson, K. (1988). Building castles in the classroom. *Language Arts, 65*(1), 14–19.

Ferreiro, E., & Teberosky, A. (1985). *Literacy before schooling*. Portsmouth, NH: Heinemann.

Fish, S. (1980). *Is there a text in this class? The authority of interpretive communities*. Cambridge, MA: Harvard University Press.

Ford, A., Schnorr, R., Meyer, L., Davern, L., Black, J., & Dempsey, P. (Eds.). (1989). The Syracuse community-referenced curriculum guide for students with moderate and severe disabilities. Baltimore: Paul H. Brookes.

Fromkin, V., & Rodman, R. (1993). *An introduction to language* (5th ed.). Fort Worth, TX: Harcourt Brace.

Fulwiler, T. (1987). *The journal book*. Portsmouth, NH: Boynton/Cook.

Galda, L. (1984). The relations between reading and writing in young children. In R. Beach & L. S. Bridwell (Eds.), *New directions in composition research*. New York: Guilford Press.

Gamberg, R., Kwak, W., Hutchings, R., & Altheim, J. (1988). *Learning and loving it*. Portsmouth, NH: Heinemann.

Garcia, E. (1994). *Understanding and meeting the challenge of student cultural diversity*. Boston: Houghton Mifflin.

Gardner, H. (1983). *Frames of mind: The theory of multiple intelligences*. New York: Basic Books.

Gardner, H. (1991). *The unschooled mind*. New York: Basic Books.

Gardner, H., & Wolf, D. (1983). Waves and streams of symbolization. In D. Rogers & J. Sloboda (Eds.), *The acquisition of symbolic skills*. London: Plenum Press.

Gee, J. (1985). The narrativization of experience in the oral style. *Journal of Education, 167,* 9–35.

Gee, J. (1987). *What is literacy?* Paper presented at the Literacy Assistance Center, New York.

Gee, J. (1991). Memory and myth: A perspective on narrative. In A. McCabe & C. Peterson (Eds.), *Developing narrative structure* (pp. 1–25). Hillsdale, NJ: Lawrence Erlbaum Associates.

Geller, L. (1985). *Wordplay and language learning for children*. Urbana, IL: National Council of Teachers of English.

Gibbons, P. (1993). *Learning to learn in a second language*. Portsmouth, NH: Heinemann.

Gibson, M. (1983). *Home-school-community linkages: A study of educational equity for Punjabi youths*. Washington, DC: National Institute of Education.

Gleitman, L., & Newport, E. (1995). The invention of language by children: Environmental and biological influences on the acquisition of language. In L. Gleitman & M. Liberman (Eds.), *Language* (pp. 1–24). Cambridge, MA: MIT Press.

Goldenberg, C. (1990). Research directions: Beginning literacy instruction for Spanish-speaking children. *Language Arts, 67,* 590–598.

Goodman, K. (1986). *What's whole in whole language?* Portsmouth, NH: Heinemann.

Goodman, K., & Goodman, Y. (Eds.). (1989). *The whole language evaluation book*. Portsmouth, NH: Heinemann.

Goswami, U., & Bryant, P. (1992). Rhyme, analogy, and children's reading. In P. Gough, L. Ehri, & R. Treiman (Eds.), *Reading acquisition* (pp. 48–63). Hillsdale, NJ: Lawrence Erlbaum Associates.

Grabe, M., & Grabe, C. (1996). *Integrating technology for meaningful learning*. Boston: Houghton Mifflin.

Graves, D. (1983). *Writing: Teachers and children at work*. Portsmouth, NH: Heinemann.

Graves, D., & Hansen, J. (1983). The author's chair. *Language Arts, 60*(2), 176–183.

Guthrie, J., Schafer, W., Yin Wang, Y., & Afflerbach, P. (1995). Relationships of instruction to amount of reading: An exploration of social, cognitive, and instructional connections. *Reading Research Quarterly, 30*, 8–25.

Haggard, M. (1988). Developing critical thinking with the Directed Reading-Thinking Activity. *Reading Teacher, 41*, 526–533.

Hakuta, K., & Gould, L. (1987). Synthesis of research on bilingual education. *Educational Leadership, 44*(6), 38–46.

Hall, M. (1981). *Teaching reading as a language experience*. Columbus, OH: Merrill.

Halliday, M. (1975). *Learning how to mean*. London: Edward Arnold.

Halliday, M. A. K., & Hasan, R. (1976). *Cohesion in English*. London: Longman.

Hamilton, M., & Weiss, M. (1990). *Children tell stories: A teaching guide*. Katonah, NY: Richard C. Owen.

Hancock, J., & Hill, S. (Eds.). (1987). *Literature-based reading programs at work*. Portsmouth, NH: Heinemann.

Harris, V. (1993). *Teaching multicultural literature in grades K–8*. Norwood, MA: Christopher-Gordon.

Harste, J., Short, K., & Burke, C. (1989). *Creating classrooms for authors: The reading/writing connection*. Portsmouth, NH: Heinemann.

Harste, J., Woodward, V., & Burke, C. (1984). *Language stories and literacy lessons*. Portsmouth, NH: Heinemann.

Havelock, E. (1982). *The literate revolution in Greece and its cultural consequences*. Princeton, NJ: Princeton University Press.

Hayes, C., & Bayruth, R. (1985). Querer es poder. In J. Hansen, T. Newkirk, & D. Graves (Eds.), *Breaking ground: Teachers relate reading and writing in the elementary school* (pp. 97–110). Portsmouth, NH: Heinemann.

Heald-Taylor, G. (1987). How to use predictable books for K–2 language arts instruction. *Reading Teacher, 40*, 656–661.

Heard, G. (1989). *For the good of the earth and sun: Teaching poetry*. Portsmouth, NH: Heinemann.

Heath, S. (1978). Teacher talk: Language in the classroom. *Language in education 9: Theory and practice*. Arlington, VA: Center for Applied Linguistics.

Heath, S. (1982). What no bedtime story means: Narrative skills at home and school. *Language in Society*, *11*(2), 49–76.

Heath, S. (1983). *Ways with words: Language, life, and work in communities and classrooms*. New York: Cambridge University Press.

Heath, S. (1986). Sociocultural contexts of language development. In *Beyond language: Social and cultural factors in schooling language minority students* (pp. 143–186). Los Angeles: Evaluation, Dissemination and Assessment Center.

Heathcote, D. (1990). *Collected writings on education and drama*. Cheltenham, U. K.: Stanley Thorms.

Heimlich, J., & Pittelman, S. (1986). *Semantic mapping: Classroom applications*. Newark, DE: International Reading Association.

Heinig, R., & Stillwell, L. (1974). *Creative dramatics for the classroom teacher*. Englewood Cliffs, NJ: Prentice Hall.

Henderson, E. (1990). *Teaching spelling* (2nd ed.). Boston: Houghton Mifflin.

Henderson, E., & Beers, J. (Eds.). (1980). *Cognitive and developmental aspects of learning to spell English*. Newark, DE: International Reading Association.

Hennings, D. G. (1994). *Communication in action: Teaching the language arts* (5th ed.). Boston: Houghton Mifflin.

Hiebert, E., & Taylor, B. (1994). *Getting reading right from the start*. Boston: Allyn & Bacon.

Hirsh, E. (1987). *Cultural literacy*. Boston: Houghton Mifflin.

Hornsby, D., Sukarna, D., Parry, J. (1986). *Read on: A conference approach to reading*. Portsmouth, NH: Heinemann.

Hubbard, R. (1986). Structure encourages independence in reading and writing. *Reading Teacher*, *40*, 180–185.

Hummel, J., & Balcom, F. (1984). Microcomputers: Not just a place for practice. *Journal of Learning Disabilities*, *17*, 432–434.

Hunt, N., & Marshall, K. (1994). *Exceptional children and youth: An introduction to special education*. Boston: Houghton Mifflin.

Invernizzi, M., Abouzeid, M., Gill, J. (1994). Using students' invented spellings as a guide for spelling instruction that emphasizes word study. *Elementary School Journal*, *95*, 155–167.

Invernizzi, M., & Worthy, M. J. (1989). An orthographic-specific comparison of the spelling errors of learning disabled and normal children across four grade levels of spelling achievement. *Reading Psychology*, *10*, 173–188.

Irwin, J. (1991). *Teaching reading comprehension processes* (2nd ed.). Englewood Cliffs, NJ: Prentice Hall.

Iser, W. (1976). *The act of reading*. Baltimore: Johns Hopkins University Press.

Johnson, D., & Johnson, R. (1975). *Learning together and alone: Cooperation, competition, and individualization*. Englewood Cliffs, NJ: Prentice Hall.

Johnson, D., & Pearson, P. D. (1984). *Teaching vocabulary* (2nd ed.). New York: Holt, Rinehart, & Winston.

Johnson, T., & Louis, D. (1987). *Literacy through literature*. Portsmouth, NH: Heinemann.

Jordan, N., & Goldsmith-Phillips, J. (Eds.). (1994). *Learning disabilities: New directions for assessment and intervention.* Boston: Allyn & Bacon.

Juel, C. (1991). Beginning reading. In R. Barr, M. Kamil, P. Mosenthal, & P. D. Pearson (Eds.), *Handbook of reading research: Vol. 2* (pp. 759–788). New York: Longman.

Karmiloff-Smith, A. (1992). *Beyond modularity: A developmental perspective on cognitive science.* Cambridge, MA: MIT Press.

Katz, L., & Chard, S. (1989). *Engaging children's minds: The project approach.* Norwood, NJ: Ablex.

Kiefer, B. (1994). *The potential of picture books: From visual literacy to aesthetic understanding.* New York: Macmillan.

Kirk, S., & Gallagher, J. (1989). *Educating exceptional children.* Boston: Houghton Mifflin.

Koch, K. (1970). *Wishes, lies, and dreams: Teaching children to write poetry.* New York: Harper and Row.

Kohl, H. (1989). *Growing minds: On becoming a teacher.* New York: HarperCollins.

Krashen, S. (1982). *Principles and practices in second language acquisition.* London: Pergamon Press.

Krashen, S., & Terrell, C. (1982). *Child-adult differences in second language acquisition.* Rowley, MA: Newbury House.

Langer, J. (1981). From theory to practice: A prereading plan. *Journal of Reading, 25,* 152–156.

Langer, J. (1986). *Children reading and writing.* Norwood, NJ: Ablex.

Lasnik, D. (1995). The study of cognition. In L. Gleitman & M. Liberman (Eds.), *Language* (pp. xi–xvii). Cambridge, MA: MIT Press.

Lindfors, J. (1987). *Children's language and learning* (2d ed.). Englewood Cliffs, NJ: Prentice Hall.

Lipson, M. (1996). Conversations with children and other classroom-based assessment strategies. In L. Putnam (Ed.), *How to become a better reading teacher: Strategies for assessment and intervention* (pp. 167–179). Englewood Cliffs, NJ: Merrill/Prentice Hall.

Lipson, M., & Wixson, K. (1991). *Assessment and instruction of reading disabilities.* New York: HarperCollins.

Lipson, M., & Wixson, K. (1993). Integration and thematic teaching. *Language Arts, 70,* 252–263.

Loban, W. (1976). *Language development: Kindergarten through grade twelve.* (Research Monograph No. 18). Urbana, IL: National Council of Teachers of English.

Lopate, P. (1975). *Being with children.* Garden City, NY: Doubleday.

Madura, S. (1995). The line and texture of aesthetic response: Primary children study authors and illustrators. *Reading Teacher, 49,* 110–118.

Martinez, M., & Roser, N. (1985). Read it again: The value of repeated readings during storytime. *Reading Teacher, 38,* 782–786.

Marzano, R., & Marzano, J. (1988). *A cluster approach to elementary vocabulary instruction.* Newark, DE: International Reading Association.

McCabe, A., & Peterson, C. (Eds.). (1991). *Developing narrative structure*. Hillsdale, NJ: Lawrence Erlbaum Associates.

McCaslin, N. (1990). *Creative drama in the classroom* (5th ed.). New York: Longman.

McGee, L. (1995). Talking about books with young children. In N. Roser & M. Martinez (Eds.), *Book talk and beyond: Children and teachers respond to literature* (pp. 105–115). Newark, DE: International Reading Association.

Michaels, S. (1986). Narrative presentations: An oral preparation for literacy. In J. Cook-Gumperz (Ed.), *The social construction of literacy* (pp. 94–116). New York: Cambridge University Press.

Michaels, S., & Foster, M. (1985). Peer-peer learning: Evidence from a student-run sharing time. In A. Jaggar & M. T. Smith-Burke (Eds.), *Observing the language learner*. Newark, DE: International Reading Association, and Urbana, IL: National Council of Teachers of English.

Moffett, J., & Wagner, B. (1993). *Student-centered language arts and reading, K–13: A handbook for teachers*. Boston: Houghton Mifflin.

Morris, D. (1992). Concept of word: A pivotal understanding in the learning to read process. In S. Templeton & D. Bear (Eds.), *Development of orthographic knowledge and the foundations of literacy: A memorial Festschrift for Edmund H. Henderson*. Hillsdale, NJ: Lawrence Erlbaum Associates.

Morris, D. (1993). The relationship between children's concept of word in text and phoneme awareness in learning to read: A longitudinal study. *Research in the Teaching of English, 27*, 133–154.

Morris, R. (1977). *A normative intervention to equalize participation in task-oriented groups*. Unpublished doctoral dissertation, Stanford University, Palo Alto, CA. Cited in E. Cohen (1987), *Designing Groupwork*. New York: Teachers College Press.

Morrow, L. (1987). Promoting inner-city children's recreational reading. *Reading Teacher, 41*, 266–275.

Morrow, L. (Ed.). (1995). *Family literacy: Connections in schools and communities*. Newark, DE: International Reading Association.

Moskowitz, B. (1978). The acquisition of language. *Scientific American, 236*, 92–110.

Moss, J. (1984). *Focus units in literature*. Urbana, IL: National Council of Teachers of English.

Moss, J. (1990). *Focus on literature: A context for literacy learning*. Katonah, NY: Richard C. Owen.

Murray, D. (1982). *Learning by teaching*. Montclair, NJ: Boynton/Cook.

Nagy, W. (1988). *Teaching vocabulary to improve reading comprehension*. Urbana, IL: National Council of Teachers of English, and Newark, DE: International Reading Association.

Nathan, R., Temple, F., Juntunen, K., & Temple, C. (1989). *Classroom strategies that work: An elementary teacher's guide to process writing*. Portsmouth, NH: Heinemann.

Nathenson-Majia, S. (1989). Writing in a second language: Negotiating meaning through invented spelling. *Language Arts, 66*, 516–526.

Nelson, K. (1986). *Event knowledge: Structure and function in development.* Hillsdale, NJ: Lawrence Erlbaum Associates.

Nelson-Herber, J. (1986). Expanding and refining vocabulary in the content areas. *Journal of Reading, 29,* 626–633.

O'Callahan, J. (1986). *Herman and Marguerite* [Video]. West Tisbury, MA: Vineyard Video Productions.

Ogle, D. (1986). K-W-L: A teaching model that develops active reading of expository text. *Reading Teacher, 39,* 564–570.

Olsen, R. (1989). A survey of limited English proficient student enrollments and identification criteria. *TESOL Quarterly, 23,* 469–488.

Olson, D. (1977). From utterance to text: The bias of language in speech and writing. *Harvard Educational Review, 17,* 257–281.

O'Neill, C. (1989). Dialogue and drama: The transformation of events, ideas, and teachers. *Language Arts, 66,* 147–159.

Orelove, F., & Sobsey, D. (1991). *Educating children with multiple disabilities* (2nd ed.). Baltimore: Paul H. Brookes.

Orlich, D., Harder, R., & Callahan, R. (1994). *Teaching strategies.* Lexington, MA: D. C. Heath.

Palincsar, A., & Brown, A. (1989, March). *Discourse as a mechanism for acquiring process and knowledge.* Paper presented at the American Educational Research Association, San Francisco.

Pappas, C., Kiefer, B., & Levstik, L. (1995). *An integrated language perspective in the elementary school* (2nd ed.). White Plains, NY: Longman.

Pearson, P. D., & Johnson, D. (1978). *Teaching comprehension.* New York: Holt, Rinehart, and Winston.

Peregoy, S., & Boyle, O. (1993). *Reading, writing, and learning in ESL: A resource book for K–8 teachers.* New York: Longman.

Perfetti, C. (1985). *Reading ability.* New York: Oxford University Press.

Phillips, S. (1983). *The invisible culture: Communication in classroom and community on the Warm Springs Indian Reservation.* New York: Longman.

Piaget, J. (1985). *Equilibration of cognitive structures.* Chicago: University of Chicago Press.

Pikulski, J. (1994). Preventing reading failure: A review of five effective programs. *Reading Teacher, 48,* 30–39.

Pinker, S. (1994). *The language instinct.* New York: William Morrow.

Pinnell, G., Fried, M., & Estice, R. (1990). Reading recovery: Learning how to make a difference. *Reading Teacher, 43,* 282–295.

Pinnell, G., & Matlin, M. (1989). *Teachers and research: Language learning in the classroom.* Newark, DE: International Reading Association.

Plecha, J. (1992). The Great Books method of interpretive reading and discussion. In C. Temple & P. Collins (Eds.), *Stories and readers: New perspectives on literature in the elementary classroom* (pp. 103–114). Norwood, MA: Christopher-Gordon.

Purves, A. (1990). *The scribal society: An essay on literacy and schooling in the information age.* White Plains, NY: Longman.

Raines, S. (Ed.). (1995). *Whole language across the curriculum: Grades 1, 2, 3*. New York: Teachers College Press.

Ramsey, P. (1987). *Teaching and learning in a diverse world*. New York: Teachers College Press.

Raphael, T. (1986). Question-answer relationships, revisited. *Reading Teacher, 39*, 516–522.

Raphael, T., Goatley, V., McMahon, S., Woodman, D. (1995). Promoting meaningful conversations in student book clubs. In N. Roser & M. Martínez (Eds.), *Book talk and beyond* (pp. 66–79). Newark, DE: International Reading Association.

Raphael, T., McMahon, S., Goatley, V., Bentley, I., Boyd, F., Pardo, L., & Woodman, D. (1992). Research directions: Literature and discussion in the reading program. *Language Arts, 69*, 54–61.

Rayner, K., & Pollatsek, A. (1994). *The psychology of reading* (2nd ed.). Hillsdale, NJ: Lawrence Erlbaum Associates.

Read, C. (1975). *Children's categorization of speech sounds in English*. Urbana, IL: National Council of Teachers of English.

Read, C., & Hodges, R. (1982). Spelling. In H. Mitzel (Ed.), *Encyclopedia of Educational Research* (5th ed.). New York: Macmillan.

Reyes, M. de la Luz. (1992). Challenging venerable assumptions: Literacy instruction for linguistically different students. *Harvard Educational Review, 62*(4), 427–446.

Rhodes, L., & Dudley-Marling, C. (1988). *Readers and writers with a difference: A holistic approach to teaching learning disabled and remedial students*. Portsmouth, NH: Heinemann.

Richgels, D., McGee, L., Lomax, R., & Sheard, C. (1987). Awareness of four text structures: Effects on recall of expository text. *Reading Research Quarterly, 22*, 177–196.

Rico, G. (1983). *Writing the natural way*. Los Angeles: J. P. Tarcher.

Ridley, L. (1990). Enacting change in elementary school programs: Implementing a whole language perspective. *Reading Teacher, 43*, 640–646.

Romatowski, J. (1987). Author! author! In D. Watson (Ed.), *Ideas and insights*. Newark, DE: International Reading Association.

Rosenblatt, L. (1978). *The reader, the text, the poem: Transactional theory of literary work*. Carbondale: Southern Illinois University Press.

Roser, N., & Martinez, B. (Eds.). (1995). *Book talk and beyond: Children and teachers respond to literature*. Newark, DE: International Reading Association.

Rouse, J. (1983). On children writing poetry. *Language Arts, 60*, 711–716.

Routman, R. (1991). *Invitations: Changing as teachers and learners, K–12*. Portsmouth, NH: Heinemann.

Scardamalia, M. (1981). How children cope with the cognitive demands of writing. In C. Frederiksen & J. Dominic (Eds.), *Writing: The nature, development, and teaching of written communication*. Hillsdale, NJ: Lawrence Erlbaum Associates.

Sebesta, S. (1989). Literature across the curriculum. In J. Stewig & S. Sebesta (Eds.), *Using literature in the elementary classroom*. Urbana, IL: National Council of Teachers of English.

Shannon, P., & Goodman, K. (Eds.). (1994). *Basal readers: A second look*. Katonah, NY: Richard C. Owen.

Short, K., Harste, J., & Burke, C. (1996). *Creating classrooms for authors and inquirers* (2nd ed.). Portsmouth, NH: Heinemann.

Siks, G. (1983). *Drama with children*. New York: Harper and Row.

Skinner, B. F. (1957). *Verbal behavior*. New York: Appleton-Century.

Skrtic, T. (1991). *Behind special education: A critical analysis of professional culture and school organization*. Denver, CO: Love.

Slaughter, J. (1993). *Beyond storybooks: Young children and the shared-book experience*. Newark, DE: International Reading Association.

Slavin, R. (1986). Learning together. *American Educator, 10*, 6–13.

Sleeter, C., & Grant, C. (1994). *Making choices for multicultural education: Five approaches to race, class, and gender* (2nd ed.). New York: Merrill.

Sloan, G. (1991). *The child as critic: Teaching literature in elementary and middle schools* (3rd ed.). New York: Teachers College Press.

Smith, C. (1989). Prompting critical thinking. *Reading Teacher, 42*, 424.

Smith, E. (1995). Concepts and categorization. In E. Smith & D. Osherson (Eds.), *Thinking: An invitation to cognitive science* (Vol. 3, pp. 3–33). Cambridge, MA: MIT Press.

Smith, F. (1983). *Essays into literacy*. Portsmouth, NH: Heinemann.

Snell, M. E. (1987). *Systematic instruction of persons with severe handicaps*. Columbus, OH: Merrill.

Spangenberg-Urschat, K., & Pritchard, R. (Eds.). (1994). *Kids come in all languages: Reading instruction for ESL students*. Newark, DE: International Reading Association.

Spivey, N. (1987). Constructing constructivism: Reading research in the United States. *Poetics, 16*, 169–192.

Stahl, S. (1986). Three principles of effective vocabulary instruction. *Journal of Reading, 29*, 662–668.

Stanovich, K. (1992). Are we overselling literacy? In C. Temple & P. Collins (Eds.), *Stories and readers: New perspectives on literature in the elementary classroom* (pp. 209–231). Norwood, MA: Christopher-Gordon.

Staton, J. (1988). ERIC/RCS report: Dialogue journals. *Language Arts, 65*, 198–201.

Stauffer, R. (1969). *Directing reading maturity as a cognitive process*. New York: Harper and Row.

Stauffer, R. (1970). *The language experience approach to the teaching of reading*. New York: Harper and Row.

Stauffer, R. (1975). *Directing the reading-thinking process*. New York: Harper and Row.

Stevens, R. (1994). Cooperative learning and literacy instruction. In N. Ellsworth, C. Hedley, & A. Baratta (Eds.), *Literacy: A redefinition*. Hillsdale, NJ: Lawrence Erlbaum Associates.

Stewig, J. (1983). *Exploring language arts in the elementary classroom*. New York: Holt, Rinehart, and Winston.

Stoll, D. (1994). *Magazines for kids and teens*. Newark, DE: International Reading Association.

Stoyer, S. (1982). *Readers Theatre: Story dramatization in the classroom*. Urbana, IL: National Council of Teachers of English.

Strickland, D., & Morrow, L. (1989). *Emerging literacy: Young children learn to read and write*. Newark, DE: International Reading Association.

Sulzby, E., & Teale, W. (1991). Emergent literacy. In R. Barr, M. Kamil, P. Mosenthal, & P. D. Pearson (Eds.), *Handbook of reading research* (Vol. 2, pp. 727–757). New York: Longman.

Sutton, C. (1989). Helping the nonnative English speaker with reading. *Reading Teacher, 42*, 684–688.

Takaki, R. (1993). *A different mirror: A history of multicultural America*. New York: Little, Brown.

Taylor, B., Frye, B., & Maruyama, G. (1990). Time spent reading and reading growth. *American Educational Research Journal, 27*, 351–362.

Taylor, D., & Dorsey-Gaines, C. (1988). *Growing up literate: Learning from inner-city families*. Portsmouth, NH: Heinemann.

Tchudi, S., & Tchudi, S. (1983). *Teaching writing in the content areas: Elementary school*. Washington, DC: National Education Association.

Templeton, S. (1979). Spelling first, sound later: The relationship between orthography and higher order phonological knowledge in older students. *Research in the Teaching of English, 13*, 255–264.

Templeton, S. (1991). Teaching and learning the English spelling system: Reconceptualizing method and purpose. *Elementary School Journal, 92*, 185–201.

Templeton, S. (1992a). New trends in a historical perspective: Old story, new resolution—sound and meaning in spelling. *Language Arts, 69*, 454–463.

Templeton, S. (1992b). Theory, nature, and pedagogy of orthographic development in older students. In S. Templeton & D. Bear (Eds.), *Development of orthographic knowledge and the foundations of literacy: A memorial Festschrift for Edmund H. Henderson*. Hillsdale, NJ: Lawrence Erlbaum Associates.

Templeton, S. (1995). *Children's literacy: Contexts for meaningful learning*. Boston: Houghton Mifflin.

Templeton, S., & Bear, D. (Eds.). (1992). *Development of orthographic knowledge and the foundations of literacy: A memorial Festschrift for Edmund H. Henderson*. Hillsdale, NJ: Lawrence Erlbaum Associates.

Tierney, R., Carter, M., & Desai, L. (1991). *Portfolio assessment in the reading-writing classroom*. Norwood, MA: Christopher-Gordon.

Tirosh, D. (Ed.). (1992). *Implicit and explicit knowledge: An educational approach*. Norwood, NJ: Ablex.

Tompkins, G. (1995). *Teaching writing: Balancing process and product* (2nd ed.). Englewood Cliffs, NJ: Merrill/Prentice Hall.

Tompkins, G., & Yaden, D., Jr. (1986). *Answering students' questions about words*. Urbana, IL: National Council of Teachers of English.

Topping, K. (1989). Peer tutoring and paired reading: Combining two powerful techniques. *Reading Teacher, 42*, 488–494.

Trelease, J. (1995). *The read-aloud handbook*. New York: Viking Penguin.

Tunnell, M., & Jacobs, J. (1989). Using "real" books: Research findings on literature-based reading instruction. *Reading Teacher, 42,* 470–477.

U.S. Office of Special Education and Rehabilitative Services. (1992). *Fourteenth annual report to Congress on the implementation of the Individuals with Disabilities Education Act.* Washington, DC: U.S. Government Printing Office.

Valencia, S. (1990). A portfolio approach to classroom reading assessment: The whys, whats, and hows. *Reading Teacher, 43,* 338–340.

Valencia, S., Hiebert, E., & Kapinus, B. (1992). National assessment of educational progress: What do we know and what lies ahead? *Reading Teacher, 45,* 730–734.

Verriour, P. (1989). Creating worlds of dramatic discourse. *Language Arts, 63,* 253–263.

Viadero, D. (1989). Side by side. *Teacher Magazine, 1,* 40–46.

Vygotsky, L. (1934/1986). Thought and language. Cambridge, MA: MIT Press.

Wagner, B. (1988). Research currents: Does classroom drama affect the arts of language? *Language Arts, 65,* 46–55.

Walmsley, S. (1994). *Children exploring their world: Theme teaching in elementary school.* Portsmouth, NH: Heinemann.

Walmsley, S., & Walp, T. (1990). Integrating literature and composing into the language arts curriculum: Philosophy and practice. *Elementary School Journal, 90,* 251–274.

Wanner, E., & Gleitman, L. (Eds.). (1982). *Language acquisition: The state of the art.* New York: Cambridge University Press.

Warner, M. (1994). Special education bureaucracy and the dilemma of modernism. *Holistic Education Review, 7,* 51–61.

Weaver, C., Chaston, J., & Peterson, S. (1993). *Theme exploration: A voyage of discovery.* Portsmouth, NH: Heinemann.

Wells, G. (1981). *Learning through interaction: The study of language development.* Cambridge, England: Cambridge University Press.

Wells, G. (1986). *The meaning makers.* Portsmouth, NH: Heinemann.

Wells, G., & Chang-Wells, G. L. (1992). *Constructing knowledge together: Classrooms as centers of inquiry and literacy.* Portsmouth, NH: Heinemann.

Willis, J., Stephens, E., & Matthew, K. (1996). *Technology, reading, and language arts.* Boston: Allyn & Bacon.

Winner, E. (1988). *The point of words: Children's developmental understanding of metaphor.* Cambridge, MA: Harvard University Press.

Winograd, P., Wixson, K., & Lipson, M. (Eds.). (1989). *Improving basal reading instruction.* New York: Teachers College Press.

Wong, S. (1993). Promises, pitfalls, and principles of text selection in curriculum diversification: The Asian-American case. In T. Perry & J. Fraser (Eds.), *Freedom's plow: Teaching in the multicultural classroom* (pp. 109–120). New York: Routledge Kegan-Paul.

Wong-Fillmore, L. (1982). Language minority students and school participation: What kind of English is needed? *Journal of Education, 16,* 143–156.

Yaden, D., Jr. (1988a, December). *A classification scheme for categorizing the types of questions that children ask during storybook read-alouds: Theoretical and em-*

pirical proofs. Paper presented at the thirty-eighth annual meeting of the National Reading Conference, Tucson, AZ.

Yaden, D., Jr. (1988b). Understanding stories through repeated read-alouds: How many does it take? *Reading Teacher, 41,* 188–214.

Yaden, D., Jr., Smolkin, L., & Conlon, A. (1989). Preschooler's questions about pictures, print convention, and story text during reading aloud at home. *Reading Research Quarterly, 24,* 188–214.

Yolen, J. (1981). *Touch magic.* New York: Philomel Books.

Ysseldyke, J., & Algozzine, B. (1994). *Introduction to special education.* Boston: Houghton Mifflin.

Zinsser, W. (1985). *On writing well.* New York: Harper and Row.

Zutell, J. (1994). Spelling instruction. In A. Purves, L. Papa, & S. Jordan (Eds.), *Encyclopedia of English studies and language arts* (Vol. 2, pp. 1098–1100). New York: Scholastic.

Children's Literature Cited

Armstrong, W. (1969). *Sounder.* New York: HarperCollins.

Babbitt, N. (1975). *Tuck everlasting.* New York: Farrar, Straus, and Giroux.

Cleary, B. (1968). *Ramona the pest.* New York: Dell.

Cleary, B. (1977). *Ramona and her father.* New York: Dell.

Cleary, B. (1984). *Dear Mr. Henshaw.* New York: Dell.

Coutant, H. (1974). *The first snow.* New York: Knopf.

Cowley, J. (1980). *Hairy Bear.* San Diego: The Wright Group.

Cowley, J. (1983). *The Jigaree.* San Diego: The Wright Group.

Crowe, R. (1976). *Clyde Monster.* New York: Dutton.

Dahl, R. (1961). *James and the giant peach.* New York: Knopf.

Dahl, R. (1964). *Charlie and the chocolate factory.* New York: Knopf.

Dahl, R. (1975). *Danny, the champion of the world.* New York: Knopf.

dePaola, T. (1973). *Nana upstairs and nana downstairs.* New York: Putnam.

dePaola, T. (1981). *The hunter and the animals.* New York: Holiday House.

dePaola, T. (1991). *Strega Nona.* New York: Scholastic.

DuBois, W. (1947). *The twenty-one balloons.* New York: Scott, Foresman.

Emberley, M. (1990). *Ruby.* Boston: Little, Brown.

Freedman, R. (1995). *Eleanor Roosevelt: A life of discovery.* Boston: Houghton Mifflin.

Greene, B. (1973). *Summer of my German soldier.* New York: Dial Books for Young Readers.

Greenfield, E. (1980). *Grandmama's joy.* New York: Philomel Books.

Gwynne, F. (1979). *The king who rained.* New York: Simon & Schuster.

Hazen, B. (1979). *Tight times.* New York: Penguin.

Hoffman, M. (1991). *Amazing Grace.* New York: Dial Books for Young Readers.

Hutchins, P. (1968). *Rosie's walk.* New York: Macmillan.

Hutchins, P. (1971). *The doorbell rang*. Boston: Houston Mifflin.

Johnson, A. 1992). *Tell me a story, Mama*. New York: Orchard Books.

Juster, N. (1961). *The phantom tollbooth*. New York: Harper and Row.

Keller, H. (1903). *The story of my life*. New York: Doubleday.

Kellogg, S. (1984). *Paul Bunyan*. New York: William Morrow.

Konigsberg, E. (1967). *Jennifer, Hecate, Macbeth, William McKinley, and me, Elizabeth*. New York: Simon & Schuster.

Lewis, C. S. (1969). *The magician's nephew*. New York: Simon & Schuster.

Lord, B. B. (1984). *In the year of the boar and Jackie Robinson*. New York: HarperCollins.

Macaulay, D. (1988). *The way things work*. Boston: Houghton Mifflin.

MacLachlan, P. (1985). *Sarah plain and tall*. New York: HarperCollins.

Marshall, J. (1973–1981). *George and Martha* series. Boston: Houghton Mifflin.

Martin, B. (1983). *Brown Bear, Brown Bear*. New York: Henry Holt. [Illustrated by E. Carle.]

Martin, B. (1989). *White Dynamite and Curly Kidd*. New York: Henry Holt.

Mathis, S. (1978). *The hundred penny box*. New York: Viking.

McMillan, B. (1995). *Puffins climb, penguins rhyme*. Orlando, FL: Harcourt Brace.

Meltzer, M. (1984). *The black Americans: A history in their own words*. New York: HarperCollins.

Meltzer, M. (1987). *Mary McLeod Bethune: Voice of black hope*. New York: Puffin Books.

Merriam, E. (1993). *Quiet, please*. New York: Simon & Schuster.

Miles, M. (1971). *Annie and the old one*. Boston: Little, Brown.

Paterson, K. (1977). *A Bridge to Terabithia*. New York: HarperCollins.

Polacco, P. (1992). *Mrs. Katz and Tush*. New York: Bantam.

Root, P. (1992). *The listening silence*. New York: HarperCollins.

Rylant, C. (1983). *Miss Maggie*. New York: Dutton.

Rylant, C. (1992). *An angel for Solomon Singer*. New York: Orchard Books.

Salisbury, G. (1994). *Under the blood-red sun*. New York: Bantam.

Sciezska, J. (1989). *The true story of the three little pigs*. New York: Viking.

Seeger, P. (1994). *Abiyoyo*. New York: Macmillan.

Sharmat, M. (1980). *Gila monsters meet you at the airport*. New York: Simon & Schuster.

Silverstein, S. (1974). *Where the sidewalk ends*. New York: HarperCollins.

Soto, G. (1990). The marble champ. In *Baseball in April*. Orlando, FL: Harcourt Brace.

Speare, E. (1958). *The witch of Blackbird Pond*. Boston: Houghton Mifflin.

Spier, P. (1980). *People*. New York: Doubleday.

Strand, M. (1987). *Rembrandt takes a walk*. New York: Crown.

Taylor, M. (1991a). *Let the circle be unbroken*. New York: Puffin Books.

Taylor, M. (1991b). *Roll of thunder, hear my cry*. New York: Puffin Books.

Taylor, M. (1992). *The road to Memphis*. New York: Puffin Books.

Tolkien, J. R. R. (1938/1990). *The Hobbit: Or there and back again.* New York: Ballantine.

Turner, A. (1987). *Nettie's trip south.* New York: Simon & Schuster.

Viorst, J. (1972). *Alexander and the terrible, horrible, no good, very bad day.* New York: Atheneum.

Wagner, J. (1976). *The bus ride.* Glenview, IL: Scott, Foresman.

Yee, W. H. (1993). *Big black bear.* New York: Bantam.

Young, E. (1989). *Lon Po Po.* New York: Putnam.

Name Index

Subject Index